Usable Social Science

Usable Social Science

Neil J. Smelser and John S. Reed

UNIVERSITY OF CALIFORNIA PRESS

Berkeley   Los Angeles   London

University of California Press, one of the most distinguished university presses in the United States, enriches lives around the world by advancing scholarship in the humanities, social sciences, and natural sciences. Its activities are supported by the UC Press Foundation and by philanthropic contributions from individuals and institutions. For more information, visit www.ucpress.edu.

University of California Press
Berkeley and Los Angeles, California

University of California Press, Ltd.
London, England

Library of Congress Cataloging-in-Publication Data

Smelser, Neil J.
Usable social science / Neil J. Smelser and John S. Reed.
    p. cm.
Includes bibliographical references and index.
ISBN 978-0-520-27356-6 (cloth : alk. paper)
1. Social sciences—Research. I. Reed, John S. (John Shepard), 1939–
II. Title.
H62.S545   2012
300.72—dc23   2012025107

Manufactured in the United States of America

21   20   19   18   17   16   15   14   13   12
10   9   8   7   6   5   4   3   2   1

In keeping with a commitment to support environmentally responsible and sustainable printing practices, UC Press has printed this book on Rolland Enviro100, a 100% post-consumer fiber paper that is FSC certified, deinked, processed chlorine-free, and manufactured with renewable biogas energy. It is acid-free and EcoLogo certified.

CONTENTS

Preface   *vii*

Introduction: The Problem and Our Take on It   *1*

PART ONE. ARENAS OF USABILITY

1. Space and Time: Constraints and Opportunities   *15*

2. Some Dynamics of Cognition, Judgment, and Bias   *53*

3. Sanctions in Organizational and Social Life   *90*

4. Groups, Teams, Networks, Trust, and Social Capital   *121*

5. How Decisions Are Made   *151*

6. Organizations and Organizational Change   *185*

7. Economic Development and Social Change   *229*

8. Methods of Research and Their Usability   *254*

PART TWO. THE BIG PICTURE OF USABILITY

9. Social Change, Social Problems, and Demands for Knowledge *293*

10. The Production of Knowledge in the Social Sciences   *315*

References   *355*
Index   *411*

Bankers and sociologists seldom work together. Nor do they overlap very much in their social circles. Most of them do not seem to mind this void; some probably like it that way. As coauthors of this book, we are an exception to this principle of noncontact. In this preface, we explain both this anomaly and the circumstances of our collaboration.

Reed had been in banking not only for his entire career before retirement, but also with the same organization. After earning a BS in economics at the Massachusetts Institute of Technology in 1961, he joined Citibank as a trainee. Over the years, he moved upward in responsibility, and was appointed chairman in 1984, a position that he held until his retirement in 2000. Unlike most with such a career, however, he developed an interest in, appreciation of, and commitment to the social sciences in general. He has always read extensively in relevant subjects, and over the years he has sat on the boards of trustees of many social-science organizations: the Russell Sage Foundation, the Center for Advanced Study in the Behavioral Sciences, Spencer Foundation, the National Bureau of Economic Research, and MDRC. Through these organizations, and by residing in New York, Princeton, and the Boston area, he has accumulated many social-science academics as friends.

Smelser has been an academic sociologist his whole career, and almost all of it with the same organization, too—the University of California, Berkeley—serving on its faculty from 1958 to 1994 and as professor emeritus since 2001. Yet the tower in which he has lived is not made entirely of ivory. Over the years, he served in many administrative and advisory positions at UC and was active organizationally and politically in its Academic Senate. Outside the university, he maintained involvements with many foundations, government agencies, and professional groups (for example, he spent almost twenty years in an advisory capacity with the American Board of Internal Medicine). For seven years (1994–2001), he was a minor "CEO" as director of the Center for Advanced Study in the Behavioral Sciences at Stanford.

We met through our common membership on boards of trustees, overlapping for many years on the Russell Sage and Stanford center boards. Reed was on the board of trustees during Smelser's entire term as director of the latter. We not only survived that last relationship but over the years developed a strong and increasing respect and friendship, and we and our families are close friends, even though we reside at different ends of the country.

The idea of a synthetic project on the usability of social- and behavioral-science knowledge germinated in Reed's mind many years ago, but it was not until 2005 (as we remember) that he approached Smelser with the suggestion that he (Smelser) take a leadership role in such an enterprise. After a season of stewing, Smelser agreed. As a first step, we decided to assemble a small group of leading social scientists to evaluate the idea and to brainstorm about topical areas to be covered. We met at Citibank in New York on September 14, 2007. Besides ourselves, the group included Susan Fiske (psychology, Princeton University), Robert Jervis (political science, Columbia University), Alan Krueger (economics, Princeton University), James Peacock (anthropology, University of North Carolina, Chapel Hill), Richard Scott (sociology, Stanford University), and Stephen Stigler (statistics, University of Chicago). The meeting was extremely productive, and though we did not designate an exact format or table of contents, the topics designated by the chapter titles of this book were front and center in our discussions. We would like to thank these colleagues for their role in the enterprise.

At that moment we faced a crucial decision as to how to proceed. We knew we wanted a book as the outcome of our efforts, but should it be an edited collection of contributions from experts, or should it be the product of one or two authors writing collaboratively? We debated for some time over the advantages and disadvantages of each model. In the end, one factor turned out to be decisive in our minds: on the basis of extensive experience, we—especially Smelser, with a long history of editing collected contributions—had concluded that, despite all advance coaching of the contributors and no matter how heavy-handed the editors, all such collections always fall short of coherence, both intellectual and stylistic. After a time, Smelser agreed to take the lead in the huge enterprise of exploring, selecting, reading, and digesting research in the various social sciences and to take responsibility for writing up the results. This commitment meant a dedication, almost full time, for three years to this project.

At all stages, Reed was closely involved as coauthor. We met for sustained periods when convenient to do our own brainstorming. Reed read every page of all drafts several times as they appeared, identifying mistakes and mistaken emphases, topics neglected, and new directions—all of which led to rewriting and new work. In addition, Reed agreed to reconstruct a number of important decision-making moments and situations in his executive career. These appear as the boxed inserts throughout the volume. Smelser reworked these and attempted to identify points of linkage with social-science principles and knowledge for each of the vignettes.

We would like to thank the Russell Sage Foundation for administering the funds necessary for the project, especially its president, Eric Wanner, as well as Caroline Carr and Kelly Westphalen, who efficiently disbursed funds and maintained financial records. We also thank Claude Fischer, Michael Hout, Ed Lawler, and Jonathan Turner for critical readings of selected chapters. Smelser profited from the services of several research assistants at the University of California, Berkeley—Olga Antonenko, Jackie Bass, Ziza Delgado, and Mary Katherine Stimmler. Their searching, digesting, and draft preparing in crucial topical areas was of the highest quality and essential for the project.

Introduction

The Problem and Our Take on It

GENERAL ORIENTATION

The starting point of our thinking about usable social science is that all purposeful human action—whether the behavior of individuals, organizational action, or activities by collectivities such as social movement groups—is informed by some kind of definition of the situation in which the action takes place. Put another way, any action is always accompanied and given direction by an explicit or implicit "theory" about one's own motivations and intentions, what kinds of effects the action is likely to have, how others might react, how the world operates in general, and, often, notions about the larger social or moral meaning of the action one is undertaking.

The origins of such informing perspectives are rooted in the life histories of actors, and are often codified in distinctive, somewhat consistent assumptions and a typified style. Any actor's orientations are variable with respect to accuracy and adequacy in any given situation. They invariably contain some well-founded facts, an accurate grasp of the meaning of those facts, partially articulated and partially correct assessments, and, inevitably, a reservoir of ignorance, error, guesses, and misjudgments.

Another core assumption that informs our enterprise is that the accumulated efforts of social scientists have yielded knowledge that, when properly grasped, interpreted, and applied, improves the level of information and the assumptions underlying purposeful actions—and, by that route, improves their quality. Some of this social-science knowledge is consistent with what is thought to be common sense; some of it improves on common sense; some of it runs counter to common sense; and some of it will become future common sense. The aim of this book is to identify and assess a sample of areas of relevant social-science knowledge.

SOME SIMPLE VERSIONS OF APPLIED KNOWLEDGE

Social scientists and others have envisioned clear schemata for applying scientific knowledge, many modeled explicitly or implicitly on the "hard" sciences. We believe that these are worth recording, but acknowledge in advance that all have proved inadequate because they underestimate the contingency of things and, for that reason, do not match actual situations in which decisions are formed, made, and executed. Here are some examples:

1. Utilitarian and social-engineering models. Engineering in areas such as construction, sanitation, and civil projects involves identifying a problem to be solved and the goals that must be reached to solve it. It also involves assembling relevant principles of mathematics, physics, geology, and other relevant sciences. It combines those principles—along with estimates of risks and necessary precautions—in an operational plan to produce practical, durable solutions in constructing dams, bridges, office buildings, stadia, and drainage systems.

   Various social analogies to engineering have appeared, the most fanciful of which was the vision of technocracy in the first half of the twentieth century. This movement, in its strong version, imagined the application of technical principles to the organization of whole societies (Akin, 1977). A more modest adaptation of engineering principles to social issues and problems is found in a major report commissioned by the administration of President Herbert Hoover (himself an engineer in training and outlook). The work of a national committee of social scientists, the report is called *Recent Social Trends in the United States* (President's Research Committee on Social Trends, 1933) and presents a coherent statement of a social-engineering approach to solving social problems. William F. Ogburn, perhaps the leading spokesman for positivistic social science of the time, headed the committee and formulated its approach.

   According to Ogburn, social problems are real things in society—contrary to our social-process view in chapter 9—that arise because institutional changes lag behind technological changes. For example, the automobile, a material-technological advance, generated an outward drift of the population into suburban areas; one consequence was that the central districts were "left to the weaker economic elements and sometimes to criminal groups with resultant unsatisfactory social conditions" (xiii). Ogburn's envisioned solution for social problems was a series of scientifically based steps: to document the problems by the most objective, scientific, and quantitative means available; to come up with some sort of social invention (for example, a law or a new form of social organization such as a regulative body); and then, by deliberate application, to ameliorate that social problem and achieve some measure of social betterment. The role of social scientists in this process was to provide objective facts, presented with scrupulous attention to their own neutrality. This utilitarian model was criticized even at the time as too empiricist, too quantitative, and too mechanical, but has nevertheless persisted in modified forms of applied social science and manifested in specific disciplines in ideas such as normative economics and applied anthropology.

2. The medical model. Rooted in the historical development of medicine, this model typically involves identifying a specific disease that manifests identifiable causes, symptoms, course of development, and outcome. Part of the model is the idea of a "cure" that requires an intervention to ameliorate or erase the affliction. Models of prevention stress an attack on causes rather than on symptoms. Such a model was taken over in nineteenth-century psychiatry, and figured significantly in Freud's early psychoanalytic writings. In sociology, Durkheim located a prototypical pathology in advanced society, which he called anomie, and for which he attempted to devise a remedy in the form of occupation-based groups that would re-infuse a new kind of solidarity into the afflicted societies (Durkheim, 1997 [1893]). This model later made its way into the concepts of social pathology and social disorganization, both derivatives from Durkheim. It also made an unusual appearance in the 1980s in a brief social movement—mainly in California—called the self-esteem movement, in which it was argued that a deficit in individuals' self-esteem was a major source of social problems. The main political proponent of this movement, Assemblyman John Vasconcellos, argued that raising the self-esteem of the state's citizens would constitute a "social vaccine" against school dropouts, alcoholism, drugs, teenage pregnancy, and chronic welfare dependency (Vasconcellos, 1989). Such formulations also invited criticisms for naïvete and for projecting the state into the private lives of citizens.

3. More specific examples of scientific and rational models appear in writings by managerial and organizational leaders as well as social scientists:

   · Taylorism, created by Frederick Winslow Taylor at the end of the nineteenth century. This system of scientific management stressed efficiency through division of labor, measuring the time and motion of all operations, and strict supervision and control (Taylor, 1912). This extreme example of engineering left human beings almost entirely out of the organizational equation. Taylor's school was a negative model for the human relations school that developed in the mid-twentieth century.

- Fordism, the system of mass production and the assembly line employed in the production of inexpensive automobiles. This was, in effect, a system of engineering, wherein the movement of the line and the requirements of specific assembly tasks at each stage dictated the time and motion of workers.
- The principles of *organization of bureaucracy* of Max Weber (1967), while stressing social-organizational factors of impersonal authority, functional specialization, hierarchy, written records, formal accounting, and systematic control, constitute a rational formula for creating efficient organizations. This model was criticized in subsequent decades as being overly rational, in that it ignores dysfunctions, inefficiencies, and informal relations. A more systematic version of scientific organization is found in operations research, a creation of the mid-twentieth century (Churchman, Ackoff, and Ackoff, 1957) that retained some vitality thereafter (Hiller and Lieberman, 2005). This approach envisions specialized departments with specific assignments, each carried out in accord with scientific principles. It rests on the stages of formulating a problem, constructing a mathematical model, deriving a solution, testing that solution, and applying rules for changing course in midstream.
- Rational-choice models have been a staple in economists' analyses of the decisions of producers, workers, buyers, and sellers. These have been exported to the study of voting, legislators' behavior, crime, race relations, and marriage choices (Downs, 1957; Becker, 1978). We review the status, limitations, and reformulations of such models in different contexts.
- Game theory is a species of rational-choice theory—in that maximizing gains and minimizing losses are fundamental assumptions—in situations involving conflict between actors, and has been elaborated in envisioning policies and strategies in international relations and other areas. Nuclear deterrence theory is a special version of game theory, positing rational responses of actors when the stakes of the conflict are such that each side in a conflict can obliterate the other (see chapter 3).
- A more diffused version of rational-choice thinking is found in ideas of cost effectiveness, applied widely in economics, in budget analysis, in business, and in the assessment of social policies and programs. This approach incorporates the "rationality" of balancing costs into formulating and executing lines of action with gains (expressed in terms of effectiveness). The main problems that arise in using this method

include identifying all the relevant costs (financial resources, political support, reputation and good will, loss of future cooperation) and all the ingredients that constitute effectiveness, as well as distortions that arise in attempting to quantify both costs and effects in a common, comparable measure such as money.

We return to these kinds of models periodically in this book, approaching them from different angles. Our general orientation toward them is mixed. On the one hand, they define decision problems precisely and help enormously in developing scenarios for decision and action—for example, applying economic reasoning to issues such as the impacts of minimum wage, tax levels, and fringe benefits on hiring and spending behavior. At the same time, we regard all such formulas as "unreal" in the sense that in the empirical world, all decisions involve taking many uncertainties and contingencies into account. Almost never are all other things "given" or "equal" or even known. Making those decisions, moreover, often involves uninformed simplifications and mental shortcuts. Only in rare circumstances can a fully rational model be the sole basis for decision-making and assessing consequences. As a result, all such models are best regarded as idealized or normative statements, to be consulted as sensitizers for decision-makers, but not as full scenarios or directives for action.

THE KINDS OF KNOWLEDGE ASSEMBLED IN THIS VOLUME

More than three decades ago, a National Research Council panel commissioned to assess the "value, significance, and utility" of behavioral and social-science research (Adams, Smelser, and Treiman, 1981) came up with three levels of application of knowledge:

1. Ways to generate knowledge, such as the sample survey, standardized testing, and the assembly of economic data. These are not types of knowledge as such, but rather *methods* to generate knowledge. It is appropriate to ask about the kind of knowledge generated by these techniques, and to itemize the value as well as the pitfalls involved in gathering and representing that knowledge.
2. Discrete principles and facts applied to purposeful action. Ready examples are the use of different kinds of pedagogies in the classroom; psychiatric and learning theory in psychotherapy; knowledge derived from market analysis and applied to marketing decisions; knowledge of resource availability and workers' preferences in locating centers of production and distribution; and the use of evaluation research to assess policies and programs. These principles and facts vary in completeness and quality.

3. The general ways we look at things. This is the most general application of all and refers to cognitive orientations that inform a whole range of behaviors and policies. Later we cite, as examples, the profound importance of changing views of thinking about race and unemployment (see chapter 10). While changes in these general ways of thinking do not translate automatically into specific policies and practices, they orient practitioners and policy-makers to different *classes* of policies and to different understandings about the impacts of those policies.

In chapter 10, we expand this classification of knowledge, reaching, we hope, a way to identify the articulations between the social-science enterprise and the "world of action."

AUDIENCES

In its simplest rendition, this book is about the kinds of knowledge that social and behavioral scientists[1] can offer those responsible for making decisions in organizational contexts; attacking social problems both formally and informally; and designing, establishing, and executing social policies.

We have four primary audiences in mind. The first is actual and potential users of knowledge. These include the following:

- Corporate, business, and commercial leaders and managers, who daily make organizational decisions in market and social environments that they are well advised to know about, because their success or failure—and even continued existence—often depends on the outcomes of those decisions.
- Government officials, including politicians, judges, military leaders, and bureaucrats (civil servants, city managers, city planners), who rely on knowledge and are also typically accountable for their decisions, though in political and public rather than market contexts.
- Professionals, whose responsibilities are the application of knowledge in their areas of expertise; these include physicians, lawyers, journalists, engineers, teachers and academic leaders, consultants, and others; by definition, having a *profession* means that one possesses and uses specialized knowledge and techniques not fully available to the recipients of professional services or the public at large (Abbott, 1988). Professionals, too, are held accountable for their decisions in the market, in their public roles, or by their professional associations.
- Leaders in voluntary associations and social movements, who are forever making decisions that affect others in their search for strategies and tactics and in directing their organizations; they base these decisions on knowledge emanating from their beliefs, their political assessments, and their informa-

tion about allies, opponents, and leaders of competitive movements. Their accountability lies in the organizational dynamics of accession, effectiveness and ineffectiveness, succession, and demise.

· Less obviously, individuals in their capacity as spouses and parents, citizens, voters, and neighbors; these agents make decisions and base those decisions in part on knowledge, but typically the scope and impact of these decisions are less than those of persons in formal power, and their accountability is highly variable.

The second audience is students in training programs that typically lead to the assumption of decision-making roles—mainly students in business, law, public policy, and other professional schools and in undergraduate programs that typically feed into these applied fields.

The third audience is interested social scientists, the generators and suppliers of some kinds of knowledge relevant for users. This is also a varied group with respect to what they do and produce. Some fancy themselves as applied social scientists; some know what they do is broadly relevant but do not concern themselves directly with that relevance; some believe they are not doing anything useful and take pride in that purity. Yet because of their subject matter, they produce social knowledge that is potentially usable, whether or not they admit or like that fact.

The fourth audience is that residual and lesser-known population called the intelligent lay community, nonexpert in either the generation or application of knowledge, but having curiosity and concern about how and how well the social world works. This group is an important part of public opinion in society.

It makes sense to distinguish between suppliers and users of knowledge, but we acknowledge the distinction to be imperfect. Many social scientists occupy decision-making positions, and others in such positions have had some training or are knowledgeable in those sciences. Furthermore, as we will discover, people in positions of decision-making continuously improvise social-science-like knowledge on their own, and are thus amateur knowledge-makers. More generally, everyone in the world is his or her own psychologist, economist, sociologist, even historian and anthropologist, in that they carry around theories about the world—a mélange of their predilections, personal experiences, prejudices, current situations, and discrete items of knowledge. These qualifications made, we still employ the distinction between users and suppliers as if it were a neat one.

TERMINOLOGICAL NOTES

Because we have used the words *decision* and *decision-making* several times in these introductory remarks, it is advisable to venture a preliminary definition. A decision is a commitment of resources—usually some combination of monetary, political, interpersonal, and personal ones—to a line of action that is binding, in that it devotes those resources to that line of action and not another. Decisions differ in the degree to which knowledge informs them—impulse purchases at one end of the continuum and high-court judicial decisions at the other. Decisions also vary in their finality or revocability. They vary, finally, in the degree to which and in what ways the decision-makers are held responsible for them. With respect to the other frequently occurring word—*knowledge*—much of the exposition in this volume is devoted to identifying and characterizing its many facets and dimensions.

The core proposition that informs this book is that the social sciences, which generate knowledge about individuals and their behavior, social relations, groups, institutions, societies, and culture, provide materials that are usable in varying ways by those who make decisions. We note that such decisions may be correct, incorrect, or mixed. We also note that knowledge may be utilized for instrumental purposes other than oriented decision-making—for example, as political ammunition, as an excuse to delay or divert action, to discredit others, to shut off discussion, or to claim prestige by being associated with prestigious knowledge (see Weiss, 1997). We note these kinds of usability from time to time, but focus more on the situation of the decision-maker. We acknowledge, finally, that some uses may be made for good (for example, to promote the democratic participation of citizens) and some for evil (for example, the subjugation, torture, and killing of subjects in totalitarian societies). As a general rule, however, we regard the goodness or evil of decisions to lie in the purposes of those who make them, and believe that most knowledge on which decisions are based is morally neutral, in that it can be turned in either benign or mischievous directions.

We decided on the term *usable* after much deliberation. The term has appeared in the literatures on theory, decision-making, social problems, and social policy (see Lindblom and Cohen, 1979; Rueschemeyer, 2009), though not very often. More common terms are *useful* or *applied*. (The purpose of the American Philosophical Society, the child of the utilitarian Benjamin Franklin, is for "promoting useful knowledge"; the terms *applied social science, positive economics, applied sociology,* and *applied anthropology* imply using knowledge for practical goals). Both of these words have utilitarian overtones we do not intend. *Useful* seems to promise that using knowledge will be positive in its outcomes; *applied* suggests a mechanical, perhaps formulaic, meaning that we regard as misleading. The term *usable* is more open-ended, conveys both potential and actual use, complexity rather than simplicity, and a lack of certainty and finality, all consistent with our orientation.

A simple model of knowledge and decision-making that emanates from these preliminary remarks is that of an abstracted decision-maker who possesses knowledge, some of it coming from or consistent with the behavioral and social sciences, and who executes decisions based in part on this knowledge. We rely on such a model of act-in-situation in later chapters on discrete topics. But such a model does not tell the whole story. The problem we have decided to address is embedded in so many social, political, and cultural contexts that we must grasp these larger contexts to grasp the problem of decision-making itself and to come up with reasonable solutions to it.

WHAT THIS BOOK IS NOT

This book contains selected discussions of many ideas that populate the social-science literature. A few of these are relative deprivation, path dependency, attribution, memory dynamics, rational decision-making, primary groups, deterrence theory, large-scale social changes, and unanticipated consequences of intended actions.

Such subject matter overlaps with many other kinds of publications in the social sciences, but we should take care to distinguish our enterprise from these related others. Accordingly:

- The book is not an encyclopedia, because we do not attempt to be exhaustive (encyclopedic). We stress potentially applicable knowledge, not knowledge in general.
- By the same token, it is not a handbook, which usually organizes knowledge by discipline, subdiscipline, or topic (for example, economic sociology, organization theory, or family and socialization).
- It includes some of what a dictionary of the social sciences might include, but it is not a dictionary because it goes far beyond definitions.
- It is not an attempt to identify the "leading edges" or "most promising" areas of research or the advancement of knowledge, as an article in an annual review might do; much of the knowledge assembled is not necessarily new; the criterion for inclusion is its potential usefulness.
- It is not a simple catalogue of discoveries or findings or regularities; it includes some of all of these, but, once again, selectively.

To attempt a volume that is none of these, but a presentation based on our judgments about usability, imposed a further set of requirements on us, requirements mainly having to do with *selectivity*. Given our purposes, we cannot hope to exhaust any topic or any research tradition. The sheer volume of research available dictates this. Every time we selected a theme or topic for investigation and presentation, we searched for a relevant stream of literature. In every case, we found not a stream, but a torrent. Furthermore, that torrent was not a simple stream of principles and laws, but was filled with findings, criticisms, qualifications, hedging, and reformulations. We simply cannot (and should not) trace all these complexities and contingencies. Our choices, then, rest on necessities and are subject to criticism for inaccuracies and misinterpretations, but not for incompleteness.

THE PLAN OF THE VOLUME

The book is divided into two parts. Part I is more immediate, focused on substantive social-science knowledge and methods and their relations to decision-making, problem-solving, and policy. From among many possible candidates for inclusion, we have chosen the following emphases:

- The constraints and opportunities of space and time; space and time coordinates of activity (chapter 1)
- Dynamics of cognition, judgment, and bias (chapter 2)
- Sanctions in personal and social life (chapter 3)
- Groups, teams, networks, trust, and social capital (chapter 4)
- How decisions are made (chapter 5)
- Organizations and organizational change (chapter 6)
- Economic development and social change (chapter 7)

Then comes a transitional chapter (chapter 8) focusing on the usability of different social-science research methods (experimental, statistical, comparative, etc.) as these might be applied to less controlled natural settings.

Part II moves in a more general direction. We ask first (chapter 9) why there is or should be a demand for usable social-scientific knowledge in the larger society, and mobilize a series of cultural and social-structural arguments to throw light on that question. We pay special heed to the notion of social problems. Next we turn to the social sciences themselves as potential suppliers of usable knowledge (chapter 10). We examine these sciences as quasi-autonomous systems of scientific activity with their own logics and dynamics. Some social-scientific activities look in applied directions, but others are oriented to different ends and hence are indifferent or irrelevant to practical affairs.

AN INITIAL, IMPORTANT CONFESSION ON OUR PART

From the articulated beginnings of the history of social science to the present, its champions have articulated high hopes for a world based on scientific knowledge and have generated special intellectual designs via which actions could be rational, policies could be correct, and the world could be made better as a result. From time to time we identify some of these devices, schemata, and promises as we make our way through the volume. Corresponding to this optimism have been contrary expressions of antagonism and skepticism—charges that social scientists are out of touch with reality, that their knowledge and schemata have little to do with how things really get done, that practical experience (for example, meeting a payroll) is a better guide than theory. These contrary sentiments emanate mainly from those in the practical world, but to some degree also come from social-science practitioners who see themselves as generating knowledge for other than practical purposes or who acknowledge the simplicity and limited usefulness of their own creations. It affords some psychological comfort to place oneself at either the optimistic or the pessimistic extreme of this spectrum of usability, because both extremes offer a neatness and certitude of outlook. Furthermore, those at either simplified extreme tend to be impatient with qualified middle positions.

Our confession is that both of us, coming from contrasting life experiences, have independently arrived at the middle. Reed has spent his lifetime in the "practical" corporate world, and has always believed in the complexity and contingency of things, but he has developed an appreciation and faith in relevant knowledge generated by proper execution of social-science research. Smelser has spent his lifetime as an academic sociologist with an interdisciplinary affliction, and has always been concerned with the potential usefulness of the world of knowledge that he inhabits. Coming from these different directions, each of us has arrived at a similar, intermediate position: we believe that social-science knowledge is an enormous resource for anyone or any organization engaged in purposeful and decision-making activity, but that the only certainty that neat formulae, surefire schemata, and universal solutions yields is that they will fall short and even misguide us in a complex world. We realize that this stance may be regarded as a weak expression of faith, and that readers in both optimistic and pessimistic directions from our position may be inclined, respectively, to ask for more specificity or to suspect we are claiming too little or too much. We acknowledge this vulnerability of the middle, but hold to this position because of our belief that in a complex and contingent world the proper stance is one of informed sensibility, standing somewhere between the extremes of assurance arising from a sense of certitude and despair arising from a sense of chaos. Psychologists have called such a middle position "tolerance of ambiguity," which we regard as a human virtue.

NOTE

1. *Behavioral and social sciences* is an inclusive term referring to the disciplines of psychology, anthropology, economics, political science, and sociology, as well as other fields (psychiatry, law, and education, for example) that overlap with and make use of these disciplines. Throughout this volume, we use the term *social sciences* as inclusive shorthand, simply to avoid wordiness.

PART I

Arenas of Usability

Space and Time

Constraints and Opportunities

We focus first on two omnipresent dimensions of human life: space and time. Their very pervasiveness, however, sometimes renders their precise influence elusive. It is not common to find them as chapter headings in books such as this one. Therefore, our gathering of knowledge under these headings as organizing principles for usable knowledge is unorthodox and sometimes speculative, but also, we hope, novel at times.

PECULIAR FEATURES OF SPACE AND TIME

We notice initially an apparent paradox. Time and space can be regarded as both universal and unyielding but at the same time manipulable by humans and therefore culturally and socially variable. They are universal in that both have to be confronted as existential conditions of life. All actions occur in space, and space is forever an obstacle to complete freedom of movement. The same can be said of time. Furthermore, the rhythms of nature (diurnal, seasonal, annual) and body processes (e.g., menstruation, reproduction, generations, life-cycle regularities, and death) impose themselves (Silverman, 2001). Yet there is enormous personal, social, and cultural variation in representing both space and time, as anthropologists and others have demonstrated (Levinson, 2001; Gell, 1992). Both are also objects of endless symbolization, as revealed in expressions such as *social time, political time, ritual time, geographic space, social space, personal space,* and *symbolic space*. It is essential to keep this double aspect of universality and variability in mind.

Space and time are represented differently in the social-science disciplines.

Geography is most explicit in its incorporation of space; place arrangements, distribution of populations, and movement in and constraints of space have been at the center of that discipline (e.g., Pred, 1973). Urban studies, planning, architecture, and design deal explicitly with spatial arrangements, as does social ecology. Even though much of neoclassical equilibrium theory is presented as "timeless" (Vickers, 1994), economists explicitly refer to time in discussing topics such as interest, investment, inventory cycles, business cycles, and economic growth, and consider space in the analysis of markets and location theory. Sociologists acknowledge a sociology of time, and a few write about it (Sorokin, 1943; Gurvitch, 1964; Zerubavel, 1981). Anthropologists have analyzed the centrality of time in political contestation and the exercise of power (Rutz, 1992), as well as the apparently universal relationship between space and a sense of belonging (Lovell, 1998). Psychologists write on how individuals organize their own sense of space (Eliot, 1987), on neuropsychological mechanisms involved in temporal processing (Pastor and Artieda, 1996), and on ways of experiencing time over the life cycle (Levin and Zakay, 1989). Demographers take time and space into consideration in analyzing trends, generational and cohort effects, migration patterns, and the aging of populations. At the same time, these two variables have limited visibility in these disciplines. If one examines the list of "sections" of their professional associations, there are no subdisciplines or sections with the names "psychology of time," "sociology of time," or "anthropology of time" among their dozens of subspecializations, and there is a similar lack of explicit reference to space as a category.

Despite this semihidden status, social scientists have recognized the power of these fundamental dimensions of human existence, incorporated them directly into their research, and produced relevant and usable research findings. In this chapter, we draw together a sample of their results.

TWO CLASSICAL STUDIES ON THE SPACE-TIME AXIS
Friendships in a Housing Project

More than six decades ago, three psychologists, all later to become very distinguished, published a study (Festinger, Schachter, and Back, 1950) of social dynamics in a housing project for married veteran graduate students at the Massachusetts Institute of Technology. They focused on small friendship groups and cliques, norms, conformity, and deviance. They employed a method (sociometric analysis) favored at the time and since reborn and employed under different names in network analysis (see chapter 4, pp. 130–39). Using that method, the investigators simply asked respondents about whom they saw socially and whom they liked and disliked. Then they proceeded to construct sociometric maps of friends, "stars," and isolates.

Earlier Stouffer (1940) had written about the importance of space in social life in general: "Whether one is seeking to explain 'why' persons go to a particular place to get jobs, 'why' they go to trade at a particular store, 'why' they go to a particular neighborhood to commit a crime, or 'why' they marry the particular spouse they choose, the factor of spatial distance is of obvious significance" (845). The authors of the MIT study were especially interested in the principle, well established in the literature, of residential propinquity in marriage—an inverse relationship between the residential distance between potential marriage partners and frequency of marriages. In a word, space appears to play a central role in the opportunity structures people face. Some economists and economic geographers incorporate spatial barriers into notions of transaction costs—e.g., how much does it cost to move people and commodities from point A to B?

Each building of the housing project was spatially arranged as a number of apartments on two floors, with exits from the second floor available only by stairwells leading to the first floor at each end of the building. These arrangements alone dictated in large part the "passive contacts" among residents: that is, meetings that occurred in the daily rounds of coming and going. The investigators assumed further that frequency of passive contacts would facilitate speaking relationships, acquaintances, and friendships.

The findings were striking. Mere physical distance between apartments proved to be a predictor of friendships. Those living in the same building had more friendships with one another than with those living in different buildings. Those living on the same floor had more social relationships with one another than with those living on different floors. Those on the first floor who exited onto the courtyard frequently ran into others while entering and leaving their residences, and friendships clustered among them as well. Those who lived at the ends of houses with exits directly facing the street were involved in fewer friendships than those who faced an open courtyard. Those living in apartments on the first floor at the base of the stairwells had more friends among those from the second floor (who passed by their apartments going to and fro) than did those who were isolated from the stairwells. While other factors, such as personal compatibility and not having or having children of the same ages, were also determinants, spatial contiguity retained a central role. Festinger and his colleagues also traced the evolution of friendship patterns into enduring cliques—along with their features of conformity, social pressure, and deviance. These, too, followed the spatial contours of the housing project.

The principles demonstrated in this research are evidently generalizable to other settings: housing in college dormitories, placement of recruits' bunks in basic training, cell assignments of inmates in prisons, classroom seating arrangements, closeness of workers to one another on assembly lines, and nearness of desks to one another in offices. Summarizing research on physical proximity in workplaces, Sundstrom (1986) noted that "people in factories and offices choose to converse with their closest neighbors and make friends with them" (262). He also noted the social (as well as practical) drawing power of "activity nodes," such as corridors, water fountains, bulletin boards, coffeepots, computer terminals, and vending machines (ibid.: 263–78). More generally, when one moves from one neighborhood to another, one begins to shop in different places, take different walks, bank at a different branch, and, over time, visit with nearby new friends more than now-distant old ones. With respect to the encouragement of informal associations, we should also mention the social wisdom built into university commons rooms and lounges, common residences such as fraternities and sororities, the clustering of lockers in the halls of high schools, neighborhood parks, the placement of coffee machines and water dispensers in offices, and even the location of employees' mailboxes. Recent studies (e.g., Hipp and Perrin, 2009) have reaffirmed the impact of different kinds of distance on network ties: the greater the physical distance, the weaker the ties; the greater the social distance (as measured by wealth), the weaker the ties.

A few different, though related, observations: Throwing people together in spatially isolated settings—ocean voyages and rafting trips, for example—magnifies the development of intense, short friendships, most of which dissolve as these groups disperse. The spatial ecology of cities, hinterlands, and rural areas dictates in part the loci of market exchange and travel patterns. Residential segregation by race and class produces spatially based slums, ghettoes, suburbs, exurbs, and pockets of gentrification—and transitional zones among them—all of which contribute to differing exposure to personal danger, environmental contamination, quality of medical care, and educational opportunities, as well as endogamous acquaintance, friendship, and marriage patterns (Massey and Denton, 1993).

A further, negative example confirms this centrality of space and time. In the late 1980s, Smelser was asked to evaluate the sociology department at Sonoma State University in Cotati, California. In visits with the chair, he learned that she had been concerned for some time about anomie among students in the department. Some of them complained of impersonality, inaccessibility to faculty and other students, and lacking a sense of belonging. Some years earlier, in an enlightened moment, she had managed to beg resources from the university administration to set aside space for a conveniently located commons room complete with easy chairs, a small library, coffee, and open doors. The experiment was a failure. Almost nobody came. The reasons for the failure, moreover, were *other* space-and-time considerations affecting the students. Since this was not a residential college, many of them commuted from a distance, many worked part-time or full-time, and many were married with children. Most simply drove to the campus for classes or meetings with faculty, then departed to run errands or go home. So while the students might have continued to feel isolated and alienated, their own, more important space-and-time exigencies defeated the space-time experiment designed to make them feel more at home.

One further point about the pervasiveness of space. We mentioned the anthropological work linking space and a sense of belonging. Even in a presumably neutral living place such as the MIT housing project, the residents had a definite sense of residing in a spatial unit and expressed varying degrees of satisfaction about living there (Festinger, Schachter, and Back, 1950: 30–40). More generally, space is a fundamental defining element of people's expanding circles of belonging and identity—their rooms, their homes, their gathering and loitering spots (Whyte, 1943; Liebow, 1967), their neighborhoods, their communities, their cities, their athletic teams (often identified with and named after spatial entities), their regions, their nations, and, in a weaker way, their world or planet. The nation-state is above all a spatial entity with borders.

With space comes territoriality, a trait shared with nonhuman species and one of the most fundamental driving forces in human life. Territoriality involves identification of boundaries, defense against intruders, aggression against outsiders, and sometimes expansion into others' territories (as in gang wars, regional competition, colonialism, aggressive wars, and academic imperialism). Like space in general, territoriality is capable of symbolic representation, as the phrases "personal space," "social space," and "living space" (Lebensraum) reveal. As we will observe in chapter 10, academic life is fraught not only with competition over physical space in the form of the size and location of offices and laboratories, but also with symbolic jurisdiction and defense of subdisciplines, schools of thought, and theories.

While these illustrations establish the omnipresence of space and time in social relations, we should remind ourselves that these variables alone do not solely determine and perpetuate relationships. Kinship and friendship bonds motivate people to transcend spatial and temporal barriers in order to keep contact with distant others. Technological innovations such as the telegraph, telephone, and computer—to say nothing of the ease, convenience, and cost of travel—compress both space and time and permit continued contact at relatively low cost. Furthermore, as people's financial resources increase, they are more willing to spend those resources in traveling longer distances to visit loved and liked ones. Despite all this, the dimensions of space and time continue to matter. Later we will show how these ramify in many symbolic directions, including the symbolization of importance, status, and authority, and in that way constitute bases for individuals' satisfaction and dissatisfaction, as well as group conflict.

An Experimental Study of the Structure of Communication

About the same time that Festinger and his colleagues were conducting their research, Bavelas published an essay on patterns of collaboration in task-oriented teams (1950). A year later Leavitt (1951) constructed a laboratory situation in

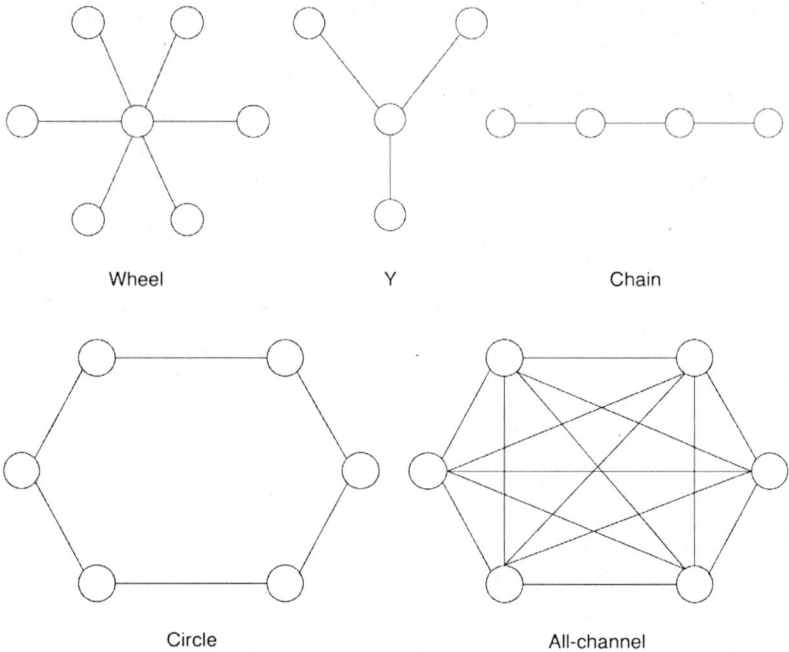

FIGURE 1. Patterns of communication.

which five different kinds of task-oriented groups were instructed to limit their communication among themselves to one of five types: the wheel, the "Y," the "chain," the "circle," and the "all-channel," represented graphically in figure 1.

In the wheel, the central member could communicate with everyone else in the group, but the others could communicate only with the central member. The wheel and the Y are centralized, and the chain, circle, and all-channel are decentralized. In the experiments, communication was controlled by having the subjects pass notes to one another through slots between cubicles. Participants in the wheel and Y patterns reached solutions faster; in the circle and other groups, people sent more messages and made more errors.

Over the next several decades many variations of this simple experiment were repeated, and as of 1981, Shaw could report the following consistent findings:

- Centralized networks perform more efficiently (faster and with fewer errors) than decentralized ones.
- Decentralized networks send more messages than centralized ones.
- Centrally located members in centralized groups emerge as leaders, whereas no leadership patterns emerge in decentralized networks.

- Decision-making in decentralized groups are arrived at by slow consensus-building, whereas in centralized ones messages are passed to the leader and decisions announced.
- Members in decentralized groups express more satisfaction with the experiments than those in centralized ones, though centrally located members in the latter express high satisfaction. These differences can be traced to the degree of participation and responsibility experienced in decision-making processes.

(The last point is perhaps culturally specific insofar as it reveals a positive association between individual participation and level of satisfaction. We might expect this association in cultures with a high premium on individualistic and democratic values, but it might not be found in cultures with collectivist or hierarchical traditions.)

This early experimentation captured the two dimensions that have dominated small-group and to some degree organizational studies—group performance and member satisfaction. In addition, the power of small networks to influence group process, decision-making, and in some measure satisfaction has persisted, even though technology has altered the space-time axes. Consider the following illustrations:

1. The telephone conference call, in which both space and time are radically compressed. Often designed as task-oriented committee work, a conference call has a structure of communication that combines the all-channel and the wheel principles. All participants have access to one another, but there is typically a "chair" for the call, which places him/her in a central position. The participants are usually not anonymous. Because they are not visible to one another and their voices cannot always be recognized, however, special means of identification are sometimes called for, such as speaking one's name at the beginning of an intervention. Also because of the lack of eye contact, gestures, and other face-to-face communication, special conversational rules develop for initiating, turn taking, interrupting, and finishing, sometimes evolving unconsciously and sometimes engineered by the chair of the call. Emotional expression is limited to verbal forms, and for that reason is not as rich as in face-to-face meetings. Finally, in conference calls it is easier for participants to engage freely in other activities, such as reading mail or simply zoning out if bored or unengaged in the business of the call. We know of no systematic research on the relative performance level, efficiency, and satisfaction levels of conference calls, but we suspect that they complete their work faster and are affectively more neutral than face-to-face committee meetings, even dull ones.
2. Videoconferencing. This form of communication is more varied than the typical conference call. Sometimes it is similar in structure, with space and

time compressed, but because vision is possible, it can be placed somewhere between invisible and face to face. Often, however, a videoconference is a meeting between two groups at different physical locations, thereby calling for a more complex communication structure. Some leaders or central persons in the system of communication are called forward to monitor interventions, move the meeting along, offer summary suggestions, call for or indicate consensus on specific items, and suggest when the meeting is approaching the end of its work.

3. E-committees. Later in the chapter we will take up the general topic of electronic communication, which an extreme compression of time and space dimensions. At this moment we mention only one type: committee work by computer.

We offer two impressions based on our own experience. In various e-committees on which we have sat, we have developed the impression that the chair of the committee probably has a degree of power greater than he or she would in standard face-to-face committees. While in principle all members can communicate with all or some others at any time, in practice they do not bother to do so. The chair initiates communications, receives input, digests it, informs members of tentative or final conclusions, and typically deals with individual members on refinements or wording of the committee's conclusions. This dynamic resembles the classic circle or Y patterns even when chairs are committed to including everyone in the proceedings. This centralization appears to derive in large part from the medium.

We should also mention a peculiar type of e-group, an all-channel decision-making structure without any leadership. An example serves best. When Smelser was director of the Center for Advanced Study in the Behavioral Sciences at Stanford in the late 1990s, it was the custom for each class of forty to fifty fellows to decide on a collective gift for the center in appreciation of their year of scholarly freedom. Normally a small gift committee chosen by fellows processed the decision and produced a recommendation, usually acceptable to and welcomed by the center. The director did not intervene in the committee's deliberations except occasionally to veto an outrageous suggestion (such as an espresso machine, which was anathema to the kitchen staff, who would have had to clean up around it several times a day). One year the gift committee decided to go fully democratic and ask everybody to make suggestions and to circulate every suggestion to all forty-five other fellows by using email's "reply all" option. Within less than a day this process fell into chaos. Many fellows responded to others' suggestions by pointing out that they were good, not suitable, or outright stupid, and sometimes offered countersuggestions, always sending the message to "all." The result was a muddled flurry of suggestions, all ventured in a mass way, without any machinery for deliberating or reaching consensus, that produced some flaming, counterflaming, insulting, and wounded feelings. At a certain moment the director had to intervene with a message to "all," announcing that matters had gotten out of hand and that the gift committee should reconstitute itself and proceed along more conventional consultative lines. The lesson: It is difficult to reach a structured decision without a structure, and it is easy to lose control in a free-for-all communication setting.

SPACE-TIME AND SYMBOLIC ELABORATION

One lesson deriving from many lines of social-science work is that the human being is a symbolizing animal. The extent of symbolization is without apparent limit; almost anything can be a symbol for something else. Once a symbol is created and fixed, furthermore, it can become the object of personal affection and identity, as well as a source of symbolic wounds, often as real in their consequences as physical wounds. We refer to this general principle from time to time, but limit ourselves to a few observations on space and time symbolization in this section.

Consider territoriality in the world of work. A large private office for an executive or administrator obviously offers a larger place to work, but it also connotes privacy and control over information as well as freedom from surveillance. It is also a major symbol of status and authority. As such, holders of large private offices are motivated to defend their occupancy of them. Transfer to a smaller office, while perhaps justifiable from a practical or cost point of view, is more often than not a personal threat (suggesting that one is now smaller in others' regard) that leaves the transferee wondering where he or she stands *in general*. Office accouterments also become a matter of status and personal entitlement: desk placement, distance of desk from door, composition of desk (plastic, metal, wood, type of wood), type of desk lamp, wooden chairs or armchairs, convenience to phone, type of computer, windows or none, view or none, type of view (Sundstrom, 1986: 228). All these are matters to notice, covet, and fight over. Such jurisdictional preoccupations become all the more salient when an office or company migrates from one location to another. These moves are typically accompanied by extended seasons of jockeying and struggling for the desirable spatial accouterments of the new home. Academics are not immune from territorial symbolization. All of the above matter to them. More abstractly, they claim ownership and compete over intellectual territory as well, appropriating theories and approaches as their own and not others', and defending them against attack. It has been remarked that college and university faculties (like inhabitants of monasteries) fight more or less exclusively over symbols, not only because they live in the world of ideas, but also because so little *real* power resides in these kinds of organizations.

MOVING

Moving an organization inevitably has profound consequences. It always involves economic costs, which may or may not be outweighed by short-term and long-term benefits. To move stirs up enthusiasms and resistances, and usually a mixture of both, among managers and employees alike. It invites comparison, sometimes invidious, between the old and the new locations. It creates conflict over space and placement in the new location, along with all the status and political concerns that location symbolizes (see p. 23). No matter how smooth, moving creates problems of personal adaptation and adjustment. These problems are multiplied in our era of two-career families, and often raise troublesome questions—even if unspoken—about what the move means for children, whose interests and convenience (always difficult to bring into the open) are always relevant, and about whether spousal commuting is preferable to a family move and, if so, who will do the commuting. Dual careers augment problems of staff turnover, ever-present when changing locations.

I review three moves I engineered in my own career, each with a different rationale and each with a different mix of excitement and headaches.

Our New York Headquarters

The first move was a "non-move," in that we never abandoned our home base in New York City. But I have to include it because I fussed over the possibility of moving many times in my career. Why was it worth thinking about? I had two main motivations. First, while it is true that New York was always a center for important branches of our business, over time we developed major centers of activity in other parts of the world (London, Singapore, Hong Kong, São Paulo, and elsewhere), and there seemed to be value in moving our headquarters and its functions away from any single business center. I personally saw great value in such a move. The second motive was less explicit, but in the end more important. It had to do with a certain kind of groupthink (see pp. 182–84). I was concerned about provincialism—that we would miss something important if we remained in a place that had a kind of industry consensus. If we were to move geographically, we would perforce break away from that consensus and consequently be better able to free up our thinking.

I had experienced that kind of groupthink directly in New York. The financial industry and its most important regulator, the New York Federal Reserve Bank, are both concentrated in that metropolis. We interacted in both formal and informal ways all the time (see pp. 188–90). We talked, we agreed, and we ignored, sanctioned, or banished outliers. Sometimes this "groupish" mentality produced common outlooks that proved counterproductive. I mention three:

- In the late 1970s, when Paul Volcker took over the Fed with a mandate to kill inflation, our group came to the informal consensus that he would not follow through on this. We were wrong, and as a result took losses on our

bond portfolios (at that time a practice of holding bonds for liquidity reasons), and the beginning of the Latin American debt crisis was upon us.

- When that debt crisis hit, I noticed that every bank in the world—with the
exception of the Hongkong and Shanghai Banking Corporation (HSBC)—
had developed a common group view of sovereign lending; as a result, we
were all exposed when the defaults began.
- I observed that these group effects, which resulted in constricted cultures
and rigidities, were widespread. The United States automobile industry,
concentrated in Detroit, was especially victimized—I should say self-
victimized—by these kinds of processes.

These observations kept stirring up my interest in moving, which I saw as a
counterforce to groupthink. The obstacles to moving the bank were many and
strong. Our origin was in 1812 in New York City—bad timing, coinciding with
the British Embargo that year! Origins and their stories always make for deep
community roots (see pp. 195–96). Despite the fact that we needed an international ambiance because of the global makeup of our senior staff, there were
obstacles to moving to a single place. And as always, some families would not
move, so we would lose talent and experience if we moved or even indicated we
might move. And, as a pervasive principle, engulfment in day to day bank business consumed our energies and interests, and made it difficult to dwell on long-
term projects, especially those that were likely to be disruptive.

South Dakota

The motive for some relocations are internal, as in the case of the impetus to
disperse from the New York area, which never happened. Other moves are dictated by outside forces. This applied to our move to South Dakota. While initially not a move that we chose, it turned out to be a fortuitous one.

The trigger was Paul Volcker's monetary policy. To slow the economy and
combat inflation, the Federal Reserve raised interest rates to unprecedented
levels. As a result, funding costs for banks reached the low teens in interest percentage rates. It was also the case that forty-five states, including New York, had
usury laws that capped interest rates at 10 to 12 percent on consumer loans, creating an impossible squeeze on lenders. We had just begun a major nationwide
bank card business and found ourselves losing money even before accounting
for our operating and credit costs. We tried to convince the state of New York to
address this issue legislatively, but it was an election year and politicians balked.

I dispatched a senior colleague to go to those few states without such usury
laws to see if we could re-create a local bank and move there. Among those
states was South Dakota. It welcomed us and the prospect of local jobs. We
moved 2,500 jobs to Sioux Falls, South Dakota, from Long Island, creating a de
novo processing facility that proved to be very efficient, and we found an exceptional labor force. We offered our New York staff the opportunity to move, and

this created two groups. A number of employees simply could not or would not leave the city. A second group did, and most were amazed how much they liked their lives in this new setting and expressed no interest in returning. This successful move set a pattern. We took advantage of what we had learned and subsequently moved facilities (and about the same numbers of staff) to Hagerstown, Maryland; Las Vegas, Nevada; San Antonio, Texas; and Tampa, Florida. We had learned how to move, and each move produced the same kinds of positive results.

Geography and Our Emerging Market Banking Business

Until the 1980s, banking in New York was geographically restricted and compartmentalized. We could not even do business in Westchester or Long Island before that time. Partly as a result of these constrictions, we focused our energies internationally and built up a banking business around the world. We ran that business from New York City, and usually staffed the offices with expatriates. Up until the era of easy international phoning and air travel (about the 1960s), communication with these local offices was difficult. Overseas posts were autonomous and trips to the head office were rare. We permitted vacations to the United States every third year.

With the easing of communication and travel, things changed radically. It became increasingly unnecessary to employ people who knew overseas markets to talk to customers. The customers themselves traveled. The New York point of view became less relevant to overseas visitors, so gradually we moved regional operations to the regions themselves. This was movement by accretion. Eventually we located the leadership of our global efforts in London, because it was in a more convenient time zone internationally than New York and because, given London's banking history, it had an even stronger global ambiance and perspective than New York.

The moral: Staying almost always seems easier than moving, given the high levels of habituation, uneasiness with change, and preferences and prejudices of those who may be moved. It is often more convenient to yield to these inertial obstacles even when it might seem rational to make a move. However, especially with careful planning, consultation, and giving as much choice as possible to the parties involved, these geography-based factors turn out to be variables rather than fixed obstacles.

—*John S. Reed*

Those who control a given space in a workplace also make symbolic use of it. Who travels to whose office for a meeting typically symbolizes the superior power or status of the one who hosts. If the superior goes to the subordinate's office, this may communicate a symbolic message of equality or friendship. An office person attempting to influence a client may move from behind his or her desk and sit next to the client, symbolizing equality and friendliness; he or she may also use the desk to symbolize authority and distance from subordinates by sitting behind it. In committee and board meetings, who sits to the right or left of—and how far from—the boss typically corresponds to the rank, authority, and status of the members attending. Alternatively, if leaders are interested in promoting equality or a participatory culture, they may strive to symbolize that equality in spatial ways such as identically sized cubicles for all or randomized circular seating in meetings. Finally, those in workplaces turn space into extensions of personal identity through adornment with their own special coffee mugs, photographs of family, and other memorabilia. That these, too, are important is revealed in the resistance that often develops when superiors initiate neatness and "clean desktop" campaigns.

It is a saying among real estate brokers is that the key to selling houses is "location, location, location." Some of this preoccupation may be practical— access to shopping, transportation, schools, and services. Another part is more symbolic and raises issues of location in the world of status. What *kinds* of shops and schools are nearby? What *kinds* of people live nearby and ride the buses? Is the neighborhood regarded as high, acceptable, marginal, transitional, or low in status?

Time is also an important symbol of status. Low-status employees have to punch clocks; others do not. Some are expected to stick by their desks; others are not. When and how many breaks (and of what length) one may take from work, when one may arrive at or leave from work, and how one is paid (hourly, weekly, monthly) are also temporal manifestations of status. And just as coming from a distance for a meeting is a symbolization of status in space, so having to sit and wait for an appointment is a temporal symbolization of status. It is said, no doubt as an unfriendly cultural jibe, that professors in Japanese universities are obliged to delay a requisite amount of time before admitting a waiting student into the office, or else risk losing status. More generally, the symbols of both space and time attributes evolve into normative realities. They are subject to expectations and control, and breaking these often excites alarm, opposition, blame, and efforts to restore the status quo.

FURTHER DEMONSTRATIONS OF THE POWER OF SPATIO-TEMPORAL ARRANGEMENTS
The Power of Seasons, Events, and Scheduling

Versions of the annual calendar are a typical feature of civilizations. They express astronomical, solar, lunar, climatic, agricultural/fertility, and religious ingredients. The division of the dominant Judaic-Christian calendar into weeks, for example, is derived from the days of the Lord's work as described in Genesis, and sets boundaries for work and rest; days of travel and nontravel to work; times of opening and closing offices and commercial establishments; leisure; and travel (two weeks or a month of vacation per annum)—all basic dimensions of life. Such scheduling shapes patterns of shopping and commercial activities, and produces and aggravates certain types of problems, such as traffic congestion, overcrowding, noise, and periodic cluttering and environmental spoiling of specific locations.

The annual calendar is a powerful, time-based influence on human affairs. In western experience, it is originally derived mainly from religious sources (seasons such as Christmas and Lent, often influenced by the timing of pagan fertility and celebratory rites), saints' days, and other observances. The rise of the nation-state superimposed new calendric moments. The enthusiasts of the French Revolution rewrote the annual calendar in a wholesale (though, as it turned out, temporary) way, with a new, more rational decimal monthly system and an entirely new set of secular celebrations of the revolution (Zerubavel, 1981). Derived from the new nation-state are national holidays celebrating historical events such as Bastille Day, the signing of the Declaration of Independence, Armistice Day, and the admission of states to the Union. Still other holidays are determined by historically political forces or events (Labor Day, Martin Luther King Day), and some special annual days are remembered and noted widely but are not official national holidays (December 7, September 11).

The individual life cycle, imposed in the first instance by the biological clock, is also organized by temporal scheduling. The most important is the day of birth, typically celebrated on a regular annual basis. The assumption of memberships, rights, and duties—religious confirmation, voting, service in the military, sexual consent, and license to drive—is scheduled by age. Less distinct and more variable—but also time-bound—are the seasons of life such as youth, adolescence, early adulthood, adulthood, midlife, and the senior years (see Furstenberg, 2002). Marriage anniversaries and remembering deaths of loved ones are also counted by years. Even the personal experience and social expression of feelings such as joy, nostalgia, sadness, and grief are tied to these temporal rhythms of life.

Nowhere is annual scheduling more constraining than in the world of athletics. The year is divided into "seasons" according to when certain types of sports are played (football, soccer, basketball, track, baseball, and others). Superevents such as the World Cup and the Olympic Games are quadrennial but also regular in schedule. During any given year, fans prepare for and participate as mass spectators in specifically annual climaxes such as the Super Bowl, March Madness, the National Basketball Association playoffs, the All-Star Game, the World Series, traditional rivalries such as the Army-Navy, Harvard-Yale, and USC-UCLA games, the traditional New Year's Day and other bowl games, and then the Super Bowl again. Time and sequencing also determine the structure of individual athletic events. Baseball games have nine innings, each of which must proceed in order. The sequence of football kickoffs, runbacks, snaps of the ball, kicking extra points, and penalties all must be ordered in time; otherwise the game would make no sense. Major athletic events also determine patterns of commercial activity (ticket buying, travel to the site of the event, advertising, and hawking) and aggravate social problems such as traffic jams, overcrowding, overloaded sewage systems (during commercial breaks), pickpocketing, threats to physical safety, and, recently, threats from terrorists. They perhaps reduce other social problems; the day of the Super Bowl regularly produces the lowest number of thefts among all other days of the year, presumably because so many viewers are watching the events in their homes (thus discouraging intrusion) and because many potential criminals are viewing instead of working.

The Political Calendar

One of the central institutions of representative democracy is the conduct of elections, the main mechanism—supplemented by other forces—for expressing the voice of the people and influencing those in power. In some democracies, elections are not precisely scheduled but are held on the occasion of a parliamentary defeat or called by a party in power; even though not scheduled, they are nevertheless expected to be held periodically. The American constitution and political tradition call for a more rigid temporal scheduling (with variations such as recall elections, initiatives and referenda, and special elections) on specific dates of specific years. Elections constitute a formal use of time as a means of political control—an opportunity for the electorate to speak, an opportunity for different individuals and parties to assume power, and an opportunity for others to lose it. Scheduled elections are supplemented by other temporally based arrangements, for example term limits, an institutional device to limit the concentration of power by means of curtailing the duration of office holding. Impeachment is still another potential limitation on power, though not scheduled.

Scheduling national, state, and local elections profoundly influences politics and policies. Scheduling mandates that politicians must, among other things, cast their eyes on the next election from the moment they are elected, if they are good politicians. Under these circumstances, the building of political credit and the avoidance of political liability necessarily become important imperatives for political survival. Politicians and parties out of power are aware of the same temporal exigencies, and schedule their discrediting and damaging efforts according to the same clock. To many, such a system overemphasizes political opportunism, strategic-tactical considerations, and public relations, and underemphasizes political statesmanship. Certainly it generates an outlook of political short-termism that induces political leaders to concentrate on immediate (e.g., pocketbook) issues and to downgrade (if in power) or exaggerate (if not in power) emotional or dramatic issues (e.g., religious anxieties, political scandals). Perhaps most consequential, short-termism leads politicians away from issues that may be grave in their long-term consequences, such as the impact of budget deficits on future generations, long-term survival of social-security systems, and environmental planning, because these issues are not experienced as pressing within the time-scope of the next election or two. In a word, election arrangements involve governing officials and government itself in a temporal trap. We observe, finally, that electoral and other time constraints on the political process are extremely difficult to alter because they are embedded in the national constitution, generally regarded as sacred and legally protected from change by the cumbersomeness of the procedures required to amend it.

The Agenda as Calendar

At a more microscopic level, the agenda is an example of the political manipulation of time. It is a device employed in boards of trustees and standing committees as well as in temporary instrumental forms such as task forces, commissions, committees, and working groups. An agenda is a simple device, determining (by a list of topics) what will be talked about and in what order, and what kinds of decisions are expected. As a rule an agenda is adhered to, though there is some latitude in the time given to each item and in skipping or postponing items.

Who writes the agenda exercises power, largely because he or she determines what is on it and, perhaps more important, what is not. The leader or administrator who writes a committee's "charge" tells it what to attend to, and can call it to account if, in its deliberations and report, it fails to address items in the charge. The committee chair also has discretion in emphasizing or downplaying specific items in the charge, and, more important, in scheduling specific meetings and writing more detailed agendas for them. The mechanism of overruling the chair limits this discretion to a degree. Two other players also carry some discretionary power: first, the secretary or notetaker, though the general understanding is that this person is mainly a recorder and, furthermore, the mechanism of approving and correcting minutes limits that power. Second, and more important, the person (most often the chair) or subcommittee responsible for drafting the report of the committee's deliberations presumably expresses the group's will and consensus but can exercise power through omission, selective emphasis, and use of rhetorical devices.

The order of items on the agenda is consequential. The first item is likely to take time and possibly to generate heat, because consideration of it is mingled with requisite processes of airing general concerns, establishing philosophical points, and engaging in rituals of status-claiming and status-cementing on the part of members (the "baboon" phase of meetings). Taking these into account, a skilled chair may place less important items at the beginning of the agenda to permit the opening phases of meetings to occur without contaminating important work. Placing items near the scheduled end of a meeting is also an important exercise of power. A skilled chair may put the most critical and most controversial items at the end, when resistance is likely to be reduced on account of members' exhaustion, their eagerness to get away, or even the actual attrition of attendance. It has been observed that a strategy of communist groups in labor union or political meetings was to introduce crucial issues late in meetings and argue for them passionately and at great length to take advantage of this exhaustion factor.

Getting onto the agenda of political agencies (legislatures, executive officers) is also a matter of consequence. The media play a role in this agenda-setting process by selecting which news to report when and polling citizens about which issues are most on their minds (Weaver, Graber, McCombs, and Eyal, 1981). Other important mechanisms are the noisiness of lobbyists, influence brokers, special interest groups, and social movements, as well as the occurrence of scandals, natural disasters, or crimes (Kingdom, 1984). Numerous case studies of establishing an agenda—for example, on child abuse (Nelson, 1984)—in the public and political mind have been carried out, as have studies on denying the importance of keeping issues *off* the political agenda (Cobb and Ross, 1997). It goes without saying that knowledge of the temporal dynamics of agenda setting constitutes directly usable knowledge for all parties involved in the struggles of political life; these dynamics themselves may become the focus of open struggles.

Some Time-Space Considerations in Economic Life

As noted, economists sometimes build an assumption of timelessness and spacelessness into their analyses: for example, the instant availability of full market information and complete mobility of resources in classical models of the perfectly competitive market. Transaction-cost analyses have demonstrated the practical unrealism of such assumptions, as the acquisition of information and resources is never complete and requires time, the overcoming of obstacles, resistance to movement, and, in consequence, costs.

Time enters into the analysis of economic and social processes in myriad other ways, and the knowledge of the consequences of this constitutes usable economic knowledge.

1. The division of the business year into quarters—a temporal factor—has come to have profound effects. Many businesses *must* report on their diverse lines of activity to themselves, their directors, and regulatory agencies such as the Securities and Exchange Commission. In some cases they are required or forbidden to undertake certain activities for a specified time after a report has been issued. When aggregated, quarterly reports become an important economic signal for investors and government agencies alike. The schedul-

ing of meetings of boards of directors and trustees also imposes a lunar or quarterly cycle of activity on an organization, a cycle that structures a great deal of its reporting behavior and sometimes imparts a cyclical pattern to the level of anxiety experienced in the organization.

2. Just in time systems. These are a part of the "total quality control" approach invented by Japanese firms, which involves compression in time as a means of rationalizing production and distribution systems by the systematic manipulation of time. Inventories, for example, involve the storage of goods in space in anticipation of their sale. The primary costs are rent and maintenance of the space. One principle underlying the "just in time inventory" is reduction of those costs by rapid, last-minute distribution of products to markets. The process compresses storage time and shipment time (Hirano and Furuya, 2006).

3. The *tragedy of the commons* means long-term negative externalities for the collectivity that result from individuals' short-term rational behavior in using resources. Time is clearly built in as an assumption, even though duration is not precisely specified in abstract models. The logic is most clearly applicable to issues of environmental degradation and exhaustion.

4. Path dependency and related processes. Path dependency is a widely applied formulation in economics and elsewhere. More than forty years ago, Shackle wrote about the principle of "no going back" to a previous, prechoice state of affairs after an economic decision is made (1969). The concept refers in the first instance to investment or commitment of resources. The "path" created is the difficulty of reversing or changing that commitment without substantial costs. Three commonplace economic examples are (1) the QWERTY lettering of the typewriter, which, once it became internalized in the skill sets of millions and millions of clerks and typists, could be unlearned (and another learned) only at tremendous cost, even though it was demonstrated that alternative lettering systems are more efficient. That lettering system created a path that carried over to computer keyboards. (2) The internal combustion engine, the foundation of so much economic activity, persists not only because it is economical, but also because it is embedded in so many facets of transportation and leisure and because so much of the economy has become implicated in its perpetuation. (3) At the social-structural level, the adoption of an employer-based health insurance system in the United States set up vast, ongoing machinery that, among other things, now constitutes an obstacle to taking other paths.

The notion of path dependency extends widely as a social principle and, as such, has accumulated many meanings. Carroll and Hannan (2000) have given it the name of environmental imprinting, a term broader than path dependency. The history of organizations, they argue, is greatly influenced by the structural characteristics embedded at the moment of the founding of an organization; these characteristics impart enduring definitions of how attachment to the organization is defined, how employees are selected, and how internal control is exercised and justified (for example, by rules, professional commitment, voluntary cooperation, or some combination of these factors). The literature on organizational culture has also stressed the enduring impact of the "myth of the founder" of the organization, in whose name different values, practices, and modes of internal control are referred and legitimized. At the same time, these imprinted patterns become sources of organizational inertia. In fact, the age of an organization has been identified as a kind of master clock that yields an organizational life cycle of the vigor (plus uncertainty) of newness, the dynamism (plus vulnerability) of adolescence, and the maturity (plus brittleness) of older organizations (Carroll and Hannan, 2000).

Another variant of path dependency is "sunk costs." One simple meaning of this term is an unwise past investment that is scrapped and written off. A second meaning refers to an initial commitment of economic and organizational resources to a line of action, which often exerts pressure to continue along that line because those costs have already been made, or sunk. The logic is that if these costs are discontinued, the organization will experience a loss. Daily life experience and some experimental literature on heuristics (Arkes and Blumer, 1985) indicate that people often distort the importance of sunk costs (when compared with "rational" gain-loss figures), biasing judgments in the direction of sticking with them because they do not want to "waste" what has already been committed. A less appreciated dimension of sunk costs is its connection to political conflict: such costs often create conflicts between those who advocated sinking the costs in the first place (and want to continue the course) and those who want to bail out because they consider that the initial investment launched the organization on a losing course. This political dimension supplements the straightforward economic assessment of path dependency.

To move to another area, the enactment of laws constitutes an example of deliberately created path dependency. A national constitution is a society's program for the future, against which the legitimacy of legal and political arrangements is measured. In addition, the message of a new law is, by definition, that "this is the way that things are to be done from now on." The enactment of laws is a continuous process of setting society's gyroscope, and it retains this significance even though laws themselves change when their limitations or irrelevance (for example, requiring hitching posts for horses) or the need for new ones are discovered. Despite their revocability, however, the general expectation associated with laws is that they bind society into an indefinite future. The same can be said for many organizational decisions, in that they commit resources to a given line of action and not others, and lay down directions for organizing resources and actions in the future.

An extension of path dependency is found in the concept of punctuated equilibrium (Gould, 2002) as a principle of social change. The logic of this: At a given moment of discovered need, social imbalance, or even social crisis, those responsible for decisions in society establish laws, rules, or other arrangements to set things right. An example is enactment of a law that provides health insurance for a part of the population heretofore not covered. Under such a law, new implementing administrative machinery is established, and as the law is implemented, the system of health care continues with a new, altered gyroscope to guide it. Suppose, further, that over a period of years these arrangements appear to yield an unacceptable increase in costs for the health care system that alarms the economy-minded, who agitate to remedy that trend. After a season of political debate, the government then enacts new, corrective rules, and these set the course of health expenditures on another trajectory that extends into the future until *its* tendencies produce the need for additional adjustments. The general principle is that newly established equilibria establish their own—sometimes unsuspected—tendencies for imbalances and perhaps crises in the future. This is what "punctuates" processes and gives them an episodic character. It is a more dynamic formulation than simple path dependency, which implies a more rigid determinative path into the future. Punctuated equilibrium implies continuously interrupted and changing patterns of path dependency.

5. Capitalism and short-termism. A central feature of capitalism is that entrepreneurs' and businesspeople's level of self-generated capital is typically not sufficient for economic innovation and new enterprises. More capital must be generated from third parties such as friends and relatives, investors, banks, and governments through the mechanisms of investment, loans, and credit. The prices of capital are scheduled interest payments, scheduled loan reduction, and scheduled dividends to stockholders, all presumably derived from the productivity, market success, and profits of the enterprises. These payments for capital, even long-term loans, are mandatory if the enterprise is to survive. The advancers of capital thus become a class of constituents in the sense that they expect the obligations of enterprises to be met. On some occasions, such as the rise and consolidation of the shareholder interest culture in the last third of the twentieth century, the demands for short-term performance by enterprises is accentuated, and, as a result, short-termism as a business outlook and as a spur to profit-making rises in salience.

In light of these arrangements, short-termism is understandable as a recurring feature of capitalist economic activity. It is also a feature that builds in incentives for excessive and harmful business practices: the motivation to ignore damaging externalities such as environmental degradation because these costs detract from earnings and profits; cutting corners; sometimes engaging in damaging labor- and human-relations practices or unethical and criminal practices; and irrational exuberance and reckless investments that promise short-term gains but often result in economic overreaching. These failures, moreover, initiate periodic seasons of demands for reform, social justice, and regulation. In sum, if we combine the political short-termism fostered by our system of democracy and the economic short-termism fostered by our system of capitalist organization, we discover a recipe for dynamism and responsiveness in the short run, but neglect its consequences in the long run.

ECONOMIC DEVELOPMENT AS TRANSFORMATION OF TIME AND SPACE

Economic development is most often described in terms of increases of wealth, technology, motive power and productivity, changes in composition of the labor force, transformation of organizations, expansion of markets and trade, urbanization, and, in some quarters, human betterment or human suffering (see chapter 7). Economic geographers see these as radical transformations of space and time and as central features of development. By way of illustration:

·   The putting-out system, which predated the rise of the factory system in British textile production in the late eighteenth century, involved distributing yarn to weavers scattered over the countryside, then collecting the woven goods at a later time. By comparison with what was to come, this system was cumbersome from the standpoint of management of time (weavers worked at their own pace, and mechanisms for ensuring work discipline were minimal) and involved time-consuming fetching and hauling of materials over long distances.
·   The onset of the factory system in its various forms radically altered such rhythms by bringing workers to central places (first to water-powered country mills, then to steam-powered factories in urban communities). This concentration of workers permitted on-the-spot supervision and discipline that were, however, often difficult to impose because of inherited understandings about the pace of work. Work time was also radically altered by the consolidation of the factory-associated workday, with a beginning, an end, and machine-imposed rhythms.
·   The rationalization and control of both time and space in factory and office settings reached new heights with the "time-and-motion" principle of Taylor's engineering approach and with the mass-production methods of Fordism, in which the movement of the assembly line dictated in detail where work-

ers were located and how they spent their time. The rise of automation as a productive process in the mid-twentieth century extended and consolidated this process.

- In many ways, later developments in the twentieth century undid much of the extreme discipline of Taylorism and Fordism with respect to the control of time and space. The list of changes, some noted elsewhere in this and other chapters, includes the movement toward flexible specialization of work (Piore and Sabel, 1984), downsizing and outsourcing, reliance on teams and networks, increases in part-time and short-term employment, work-at-home, and the "virtualization" of many aspects of work. These have in common a deemphasis on time in favor of an emphasis on results, a deemphasis on onsite authority and discipline in favor of cooperation and coordination, and temporal and spatial dispersion of work activities made possible by information technology.

- In another arena, the imposition of instrumental rationality and discipline has given rise to principles and movements that assert that the "human" sides of work and organization are short-changed by the rational organization of time and space, as well as by the systematic control of work. Among these reactions are the human relations movement in industry in the mid-twentieth century; ongoing literature on deskilling (Braverman, 1974) and alienation (Blauner, 1964); the *Bürolandschaft,* or open office-space, movement in the 1950s (Boje, 1971); and the more recent strand of literature that stresses the human costs involved in corporate restructuring (Pucik and Evans, 2003). In fact, the history of organizational and labor studies can be regarded as a process of punctuated reassertion—if not a full dialectic cycle—of two dominant emphases, the rational-technical and the human.

RESHUFFLES

From time to time, it appears useful to make small changes in structure and process in an organization. True, these may seem large to those involved at the time; they may be resisted; they may misfire. At the same time, they can liberate the organization from accumulated shackles and improve its performance. I relate two episodes of reshuffling, unrelated to each other but with some common elements.

Space

At the time I took over the leadership of Citicorp, I decided to restructure our executive space. This was not a high priority, and I did not spend much time on it, but it reflected that I at some level wanted to work with our senior staff in a different way. My predecessor, Walt Wriston, who had been CEO for seventeen years, had understandably evolved and settled into his own style. I was forty-five years old when I became CEO and had every reason to believe I would be living for a while with any changes I made, so my thinking was very far from anything like "change and run." (By contrast, when I was later in an interim position at the New York Stock Exchange [see pp. 160–65], I made no structural changes at all.) Mr. Wriston's system had worked well, but I had the sense that being with a critical group of senior executives in relatively open spaces would make for better informal contacts and create a different feel. I suppose I was thinking about connections between space and organizational culture (see pp. 23, 26–27), but I certainly didn't word it that way.

Our headquarters were at 399 Park Avenue. Even moving there was signifi-cant, because we were the first bank to leave Wall Street for Midtown. The bot-tom seven floors were large (86,000 square feet), the next five sizeable (46,000 square feet). A smaller tower (16,000 square feet) rose above these levels. From the time I joined the company, the CEO and the president, vice-chairman, and corporate secretary occupied the fifteenth floor of the tower. (Space and author-ity were thus symbolically fused at the top.) The individual offices were comfort-able, each with a shower and a bathroom, which made changing for the innu-merable formal dinners easier.

My vision was a different one, but I cannot articulate why that was so. Cer-tainly I was of a younger generation and less committed to hierarchy than were my senior associates. I also had a more pragmatic, direct, and no-nonsense view of work. In any event, I moved to the second floor, previously used for storage and miscellaneous office functions. It was an easy move, physically and finan-cially. Also, before I became CEO, I had run the consumer business for Citicorp, and I felt comfortable being a part of the hustle and bustle of the city, better in many ways than being up at the top, contemplating its skyline. On the second floor, you could walk up the stairs to the office rather than being whisked there on an elevator.

We put a corridor around the perimeter of the second floor, thereby elimi-nating any outside offices with windows. All of the offices were internal, but with glass fronts to permit more light, to convey a sense of openness, and to see people working (or not working). We substituted a central set of showers and lockers for the private bathrooms. With such a large space on that floor, we were able to locate all senior management and staff on the same level and have a common dining room as well. It was easy for everyone to see one another, to meet formally or informally, and to sense that they were part of the senior team. The boardroom was on the same floor, so at board meetings the members felt more a "part of us"; so did the individual customers who came to meals in the dining room.

I became convinced that the new floor arrangements worked superbly, par-ticularly during crises when a common presence was needed. This was notably true during the early 1990s, when we had to deal expeditiously with a situation of diminished capital and the real estate crisis. That "emergency" lasted more than two years and required intense, continual interaction among people who would otherwise have been scattered throughout the building. We did well during that period, and I assign some credit to the physical working arrangements; they made teamwork easier. There were some costs, however, mainly created by separating the senior team from those who reported to them. We tried to counter this by opening internal stairwells to the third and fourth floors in order to create an "open psychology" for staff visitors and maximize movement between floors. These arrangements contrast with those of many banks, with executive floors staffed by unwelcoming guards and receptionists, closed doors, and meetings held elsewhere. Our arrangements were much less exclusive.

Five to G-12

As indicated, we faced a serious crisis in the early 1990s. The world's economies were reacting to excess growth by raising interest rates, and real estate values were dropping (both typical in economic slowdowns). We simply did not have enough capital to support the anticipated write-offs on our $25 billion portfolio of real estate. We had responded rapidly by raising new capital and setting up a plan to be implemented over two years to increase the difference between our revenues and expenses (the monies available to cover losses, dividends, and retained earnings, if any) from the existing $4.3 billion to $8.2 billion. Much of this was to come from cost cutting, but we did not expect to lose revenues. That plan turned out to be a good one. It was not popular with many Wall Street people, who preferred the "surer" route of selling assets to cover losses. I had rejected this strategy, however, on the grounds that it would compromise our long-term prospects, and, in any event, we could still go that route if my approach failed. So we announced our plans and began to execute them.

In those years, our senior organizational structure was a traditional one. I was CEO, and there was a president who had five executive vice presidents, each reporting to him on their principal line of responsibility. Both the president and a number of senior staffpeople reported to me. During the first two quarters of the crisis, these arrangements seemed to suffice; we made good progress. During the first part of the third quarter, however, the president expressed his belief to me that we were not going to stay on track for the third quarter and beyond. I immediately called a meeting with the president and his executive vice presidents to review their plans and forecasts. We worked into the night, and I emerged from these sessions with the clear sense that we would not make it if we continued along our current path.

The following morning, I began to reach out for different ways of thinking and alternative strategies. I will not review that whole process, but in the end we decided to reshuffle the senior staff structure and modify our review processes.

I myself communicated these changes to each person, told them what we were doing, and laid out what I expected of them. What we created was a flatter structure. It consisted of approximately twelve seniors, each with responsibility for a specific line of business, and one person running our global real estate portfolio (the crisis had started in Australia, then migrated to Canada and the United States, and then to the United Kingdom and continental Europe). We also created revenue and expense task forces. We reviewed matters at monthly meetings, each held on a weekend at a suburban hotel, with seniors flying in from as far away as Buenos Aires, Tokyo, and Singapore. At each meeting we reviewed the past month's performance, starting with real estate losses, and sought ways to cover them, then developed estimates for the following month. With this intensified process, we did get back on track, achieved our eight-quarter plan objectives, and put the company on a sustained path of improved performance.

The interesting thing about these adjustments was that we made them without changing our original plan and without changing the membership of the team of senior people. However, in the earlier configuration of responsibilities, we seemed not to make it, but with the second one we overcame our problems. This leads me to a final reflection. The first and simplest level of change can be described as literal changes in location, defined roles, and responsibilities, and new lines of reporting. These often do not seem very important or dramatic in themselves, and one is therefore surprised if better results follow. The second level is more symbolic and more elusive, but, in my opinion, is probably more significant. It has to do with the *meanings* assigned to the reshuffling—perhaps a sense of urgency, perhaps the message that the organization is not simply floating but that leadership is taking initiative. Based on that, perhaps leadership inspires new confidence and a boost in team morale. These less tangible effects frequently more than compensate for the resistance to change and the individual ego bruises that invariably accompany restructuring and redefining responsibility.

—*John S. Reed*

A second, massive reorganization of the spatial and temporal dimensions of life is urbanization, also closely linked to economic development. This process is above all spatial: it brings together large numbers of people into a central space, mainly for purposes of work in and residing near factories and offices. The movements toward suburbanization, exurbanization, and industrial dispersion are partial reversals of this centralizing tendency, but nonetheless involve spatial reorganization and patterns of temporal movement. Among the benefits of urbanization have been its economic efficiency, its concentration of culture (urbanity), and the increased availability of that culture.

Urbanization has also produced many real and perceived social problems (Lincoln Steffens wrote of "the shame of the cities"). Early industrial cities suffered from lack of sanitation, spread of disease, and inadequate disposal of accumulated waste—all subsequently ameliorated by reforms. Other effects are the development of urban slums and the concentration of poverty; residential segregation by class and concentration of class conflict; ghettos; property crime; urban gangs; and some new adverse social and psychological effects of crowding (Nagar, 1998; for general effects and "noneffects," see Fischer, 1984). The history of urbanization has also been a history of social movements, inventions, and institutions meant to alleviate these real and perceived problems. These include the development of urban police forces, mass transportation systems, public health measures, slum clearance, and attempts to revitalize neighborhood life. Many other adaptations have been less formal: new patterns of visiting; the social use of the telephone; and the consolidation of racial, ethnic, and friendship communities in urban settings (Fischer, 1992). The history of urbanization also reveals a pervasive tension between commercial/economic emphases and reforms meant to ease or eradicate the presumed human costs of urban life, especially depersonalization and anomie. Urban planning, in particular, reveals a contrapuntal pulsation similar to that observed in the world of work: between rational-technical and engineering principles on the one hand and the humane, communal, and aesthetic dimensions of urban life on the other. Recurrent sequences of action-reaction between these first principles also constitute part of ongoing academic and political dialogues.

THE INFORMATION REVOLUTION
SPACE AND TIME

Among the major transformative revolutions in history (see chapter 9), the information revolution ramifies throughout economic, social, cultural, and political life. Here we consider its features as they relate to space and time. Research on this massive topic is of mixed quality, largely because researchers are feeling their way on a new topic and because it, like many new topics, it is the subject of ongoing and not easily resolvable debates, such as the merits and demerits of face-to-face versus "lean" computer communication (Sadowski-Raskers, Duysters, and Sadowski, 2006). Nevertheless, some revealing findings have emerged.

Generic Features of Computer-Mediated Communication

The defining core of computerized communication is both spatial and temporal. Unlike the movement of published information (personal letters, newspapers, and pamphlets), it does not face the obstacles associated with spatial movement that consume time. It is written (and now photographic) communication that can be delivered instantaneously (in no time) and to anywhere in the world that is online. It can be one on one (like most telephone calls); it can be among a few (as with telephone conference calls); or it can be from one to a potentially unlimited number of receivers (not possible by telephone). At the same time, it is communication without voice or physical presence, though this feature is being overcome in large part by transmitted aural and visual images. Considering e-mail as a special form, these features make for great speed; uninterruptibility while a communication is being composed or sent (unlike personal or telephonic conversation); and flexibility in responding (one may or may not respond and, if responding, can choose his/her time to do so). Yet at the same time e-communication remains a lean form of communication, as contrasted with face-to face contact. The main features of leanness are as follows:

- Spontaneous interactive discussion is somewhat inhibited because of the structured message-response requirement of e-mails.
- Communicators often have little real-time knowledge about one another because of the lack of immediate social presence; even frequent communicators lack this knowledge unless it has been explicitly communicated or inferred from cues in past messages.
- Social-context cues, such as gender, age, physical attractiveness, and race, are unavailable unless a sender makes them available. It has been remarked that, because of this feature, the Internet makes for equal status among users and greater freedom of expression (McKenna, 2008).
- Communication tends to bend to the formal, explicit side in comparison with face-to-face conversation.
- Communication lacks many ongoing corrective devices, such as turn taking, interruption, discourse markers, and conversational repair, stressed by conversation analysts (Heritage, 2001).
- Feelings of liking, friendship, and sexual attraction may develop, but in the absence of many of the usual cues that have proved to be powerful determinants of these feelings (Yamauchi, Yokozawa, Shinoihara, and Ishida, 2000; McKenna and Green, 2002).

These principles of leanness must be qualified by the fact that they apply best to situations in which those who communicate are strangers. If such communication is among people who already know one another (as many e-mail and other virtual communications are), then otherwise unavailable cues and contextual features are filled in from background knowledge about those in communication.

More generally, electronic communication presents some peculiar features that call for adaptations. Consider the following:

1. With respect to the leanness of meaning and emotional poverty of computer communication, one adaptation is that communicators invent or have access

to symbols for smiling and frowning—e.g., :) and : (—and have devised hundreds of abbreviations (e.g., *lol* for "laughing out loud" [not "little old lady"]; 2G2BT for "too good to be true") to communicate in shorthand some meaning or emotion that is not otherwise readily expressible in the medium (thus the name emoticons). A compilation of abbreviations (available on the Web) yielded a list of thirty-four single-spaced pages (and growing, no doubt) of chat acronyms, a minilanguage in itself. Many of these are understood by only a few (e.g., "FGDAI" for "Fuhgedaboudit" or "Forget about It"; AFAHMASP for "A Fool and His Money Are Soon Parted"), and some are ways to disguise profanity or sexual references. In general, these codes and emoticons save time, vividly express ideas and emotions, and perhaps generate a certain intimacy—the sense that the communicators are part of a group that understands this invented language.

2. With respect to time, three aspects stand out: (1) the initiator of or responder to a communication has time to postpone, think through, and prepare the message, which is not as true in face-to-face or telephone conversation, with its norms for immediate feedback; this operates to improve the quality of communication in an otherwise lean medium. (2) Not needing to respond immediately or at all, the responder to a message can delay responding and think before he or she writes, or may not respond at all, thus making the process leaner than it already is and making possible irresponsibility or deviance through nonresponding. Both of these are countertendencies to the highly advertised characteristics of efficiency and speed of Internet technology. (3) Those who work collaboratively on the Internet have explicated rules of thumb and practical guidelines designed to minimize problems associated with these features by making ideas explicit, describing the context of communications fully, soliciting feedback, expressing appreciation, and apologizing for mistakes (Knoll and Jarvenpaa, 1998).

3. Cross-cultural misunderstandings are a generic problem, not restricted to the electronic mode. They arise whenever people with different backgrounds and outlooks communicate with one another, and are more important when people from different cultures do so. Electronic communications simply aggravate the problem because of the absence of contextual cues about other persons, the inability to recognize from others' reactions if one has been insensitive or insulting, and the lessened ability to do face-to-face repair work once a gaffe has been committed.

4. In terms of personality variables, some research (Phillips, 2006) indicates that otherwise introverted people tend to be more at ease when communicating on the computer because they do not have to deal immediately and directly with many of the cues and anxieties that face-to-face interaction

creates for them. Enhanced freedom of expression and initiative-taking afforded by the impersonality of the medium also makes for greater satisfaction among inhibited users (McKenna, 2008). Other research shows that having too few extroverts on a team may diminish performance, but too many extroverts may cause the group to lose focus on task completion (McCrae and John, 1992).

5. As communication on the Internet exploded, some voiced apprehensions that the medium would become addictive (Greenfield, 1999), with terms such as *Internet addiction, Internet abuse, Internet dependency, compulsive use,* and *problematic Internet behavior* appearing in the literature. Special foci of interest are searching for pornographic materials, abuse in interactive games, and, more recently, gambling on Internet poker (Morahan-Martin, 2008). Views of the Internet as a seductive monster have softened as research has shown that those addicted generally bring preexisting clinical disorders, such as depression, bipolar disorders, delinquent behavior, and sexual problems, to the medium (Phillips, 2006). A small field of "cybertherapy" has also emerged, with doctrinal subdivisions as to the most effective type (Suler, 2008).

6. Deviance and pathologies constitute another problem. Carayan, Kraemer, and Bioer (2005) mention hacking, sending viruses, theft of proprietary information and identity, political abuse, spying and terrorism, and personal aggression. Of special interest is *flaming,* a term that refers to uncivil, insulting, or generally aggressive behavior made possible by lowered inhibition on the part of computer users and encouraged by the impersonality of the medium and the unavailability of immediate censure and other corrective feedbacks. To this range of intentional violations, we should add those sometimes massive and damaging consequences arising in large part from "innocent" human error—"wrong-button" disasters such as erasing databases and disseminating secured information.

Other peculiarities and adaptations will appear when we consider virtual teams and other forms of cooperation on the computer (see below, pp. 46–47). But already we may conclude that the mass adoption of e-communication has set up a demand for understanding its special social psychology. Certain dynamics such as cue processing, categorization, and stereotyping continue to be applicable. But many features of conversational analysis (interrupting, feedback, repair) either are not relevant or must be recast. Modification of attribution theory (see below, pp. 63–65) is probably called for as well, as is reconsideration of the determinants of affiliation, friendship, and love on the Internet—for example, the relative decline of physical attractiveness and spatial proximity as factors (A. J. Baker, 2005).

Telework

Another offshoot of computer technology is the modification of work roles and organizations through the rise of work performed full-time or part-time in the home, with primarily virtual communication between the organization center and widespread dispersion of domestic workplaces. This is commonly called telework. It has been defined formally as "a work arrangement in which organizational employees regularly work at home, or at a remote site, one or more complete workdays a week, in lieu of working in the office" (Duxbury, Higgins, and Neufeld, 1998: 221). It has been hailed as "the return of cottage industry," a reversal of the spatial separation of workplace and home, and a core feature of factory and office development. Its growth involves a convergence of factors during the past several decades on both the supply and demand sides: (1) general increases in the service sector (many aspects of which involve the generation and supply of information and not the production and movement of physical products); (2) the development of virtual communication technologies that reduce or erase the exigencies of space; (3) general trends toward decentralization, outsourcing, and downsizing in spatially based organizations; and (4) the interest of workers, especially married women workers, in flexible scheduling of work in order better to meet family obligations (Owen, Heck, and Rowe, 1995). Tax advantages (e.g., deductions for home workspace and child care) are also motives. As indicated, most home-based workers are in the service sector (e.g., editing, marketing, consulting). They are also better educated than workers in general, live in larger-than-average households, and express stronger-than-average attachments to those households (ibid.).

Home-based work removes or eases a number of the features of central-place work: spatial mismatch (people can do telework at any distance from the center), direct visual supervision, and the cost and inconvenience of commuting to and from work. Many issues of space allocation in the same building—as well as the myriad complications associated with status symbolization—more or less disappear. Telework also radically alters the temporal pace of work (typically giving more flexibility) and the nature of the workday (results of work tend to replace time spent in accomplishing it as the main criterion). By the same token, supervision is less continuous and more indirect, and for some managers less effective. The principle that workers do not appropriate capital is also compromised by the ownership of home computers, printers, and copying machines by some employees, as well as the use of private automobiles for work purposes. At the same time, the dispersion of the workforce into homes dissipates the large critical masses of workers concentrated in workplaces, neighborhoods, and urban centers, and for that reason directly weakens the capacity of workers to organize. As a consequence, work at home has emerged as an object of concern and antagonism on the part of labor organizations and feminist groups who fear that decentralized work arrangements "can lead to exploitation . . . can undermine labor standards such as: health and safety regulations, minimum wage laws, maximum hours, child labor laws" (Donaldson and Weiss, 1997: 34).

The keenest areas of research interest in home-based work are the level of worker satisfaction and the tensions between work and family. The majority of surveys show high levels of satisfaction with telework on the part of both men and women workers; the reasons cited are flexibility of work schedule, increased control over work, saving time, avoiding hassles (Heck, Owen, and Rowe, 1995), easing some of the conflicts between work and family obligations, and ease in combining a career with parenting (Hill, Hawkins, and Miller, 1996; Duxbury, Higgins, and Neufeld, 1998). On the negative side are reports of intrusiveness of work on family and leisure time in the form of clients coming into the home; sacrificing home space to business space; telephone calls at all hours of the day, night, weekends, and holidays; and difficulty in setting limits on amount of time worked (Rowe and Hick, 1995; Zadeck and Mosler, 1990). As with most institutional innovations, the costs and benefits of the new cottage industry show a mixed picture, but in this instance the positive aspects appear to outweigh the negative, especially for workers in the home.

Virtual Teams

The last quarter of the twentieth century witnessed the flowering of the idea of teams as instruments in the workplace (see below, pp. 128–30). The idea was inspired and given impetus in the 1970s by the apparent success of semiautonomous teams in manufacturing units such as Volvo, the "quality of worklife" movement in the United States, and the "quality circles" movement in Japan and elsewhere (Levi, 2001). Teams occupy a central place in some current managerial theories and ideologies. The growth of the approach was consistent with larger movements affecting organizations in general: flexibility in organizing and executing work and organizational flattening as alternatives to hierarchy and authority.

With the spread of computer technology, it was a short step to imagining and implementing virtual teams. The movement took off in the 1990s. The term came to refer to project groups, standing groups, and sometimes entire organizations. A virtual team can be defined simply as an instrumental group that does not interact on a face-to-face basis but relies on electronic communication (Jones, Oyung, and Pace, 2005). In practice it also covers groups that supplement e-interaction with occasional face-to-face meetings and/or telephone calls. Virtual-team development was also timely in that it combined the efficiencies of Internet communication with master trends toward cost reduction through downsizing, restructuring, outsourcing, and "crossing silo lines" in differentiated organizations. Teams, including e-teams, are typically egalitarian in structure, though this shades into informal coordinative and leadership roles. Early reactions to virtual teams as either magical formulas or misdirected fads have given way to a more realistic assessment of their strengths and weaknesses, and to the realization that "virtual teams . . . are not appropriate for all jobs, all employees, or all managers" (Cascio, 2000: 81).

Interaction in electronic teams reveals all the generic peculiarities of electronic communication, plus a few more specific to itself. Because its assigned work is instrumental and it involves a cooperating long-distance group, several exigencies stand out:

· A virtual team has to deal with what has been called team opacity (Cuevas, Fiore, Salas, and Bowers, 2004), which refers to an atmosphere of ambiguity; decreased awareness of team members' actions; a process loss of hand gestures, nonverbal ingredients, and paralinguistic cues; and a lack of shared mental models. Some correctives to this can be addressed in training and in feedback mechanisms, but these are more limited than in face-to-face groups. When misunderstandings, unproductive emotional reactions, and hurt feelings appear in such opaque settings, moreover, fewer and less effective corrective mechanisms are available.

· The establishment of a team culture is important. This includes early clarification of goals; a need to be familiar with the rules and procedures to be followed; a period of deliberate socialization before beginning work of those who join the team midway; inclusion of all members of the team at all times; and developing tele-rituals such as joking, small talk, and revealing personal information from time to time (Connaughton and Daly, 2004).

· Because direct leadership is often minimized in favor of cooperation, the leadership that does exist often evolves and is exercised informally. This fact, combined with the paucity of other mechanisms to generate conformity and cooperation, leads to a premium on *mutual trust* in the virtual team. Almost all analysts stress this element, using phrases such as "trust is the single most important driver for the success of virtual teams" and the "virtual handshake" (Jones, Oyung, and Pace, 2005: 27–28). This illustrates a more encompassing axiom: In the absence of unambiguous information, direction, and structured controls, more personalized attitudes (trust, charisma, and suspension of critical judgment) rise to greater salience in execution and coordination (see chapter 4).

· One suggestive finding is that virtual teams appear to be superior in efficiency when the assigned task is a divergent one (less structured brainstorming), whereas face-to-face groups do better when the task is convergent (calling for coming to a consensus) (Rutte, 2006). If reliable, this finding makes sense in light of the fact that virtual interaction is limited in enforcing influence and conformity, to say nothing of imposing groupthink (see chapter 5); such freedom may yield a marginal advantage for deliberating in virtual groups.

· Certain forms of deviance are particularly disruptive in virtual work groups. Expressions of aggression (flaming) and scapegoating threaten mutual trust and are difficult to bring under control. The other is "cyberloafing": putting forth minimal effort for the team, not answering communications, not submitting work on time, and generally being regarded as not pulling one's oar—all damaging to the culture of cooperation.

· When e-groups are international or multicultural, two additional problems rise in salience: differences in cultural outlook and nuance, which can be erosive of trust via the avenues of misinterpretation, insult, and distrust; and the almost ineradicable limitations of different time zones, which can lead to delays in response to communications, chaotic work schedules, irregular sleep, and impatience. Those who have participated in international e-teams find that contending with zonal time differences is invariably burdensome. This is an extension of the long-experienced difficulties in telephone communication between the coasts of the United States and between the United States and other countries.

Virtual Organizations

Also linked to Internet communication, this term refers not to a single entity, but to a variety of networking arrangements, including temporary consortia of networking among partner organizations to pursue a marketing task; more enduring networks among organizations acting as one organization and interacting mainly through virtual means; and a dispersed firm carrying out much of its business through telecommunication. Other names for the phenomena are virtual enterprise, lean enterprise, extended enterprise, and agile manufacturing (Camarinha-Matos and Afsarmanesh, 2005). They extend the ideas of reducing transaction costs and outsourcing, and incorporate economies based on information sharing, time saving, risk spreading, market accessing, synergy creating, and operating on cooperative rather than formal-legal linkages (Kürümlüoglu, Nøstel, and Karvonen, 2005). Viewed another way, virtual organizations are an expanded system of principal-agent relations, knit together mainly but not exclusively by electronic communication. As such, they place a high premium on mutual trust and a cooperative culture. In addition, a number of new security arrangements specific to information control have been regarded as necessary (Magiera and Powlak, 2005). Some notable commercial successes, such as GANT and IKEA, have been identified, and certain countries (e.g., Sweden) and regions (the European Community) have been leaders in virtual organizing (Hedberg, Dahlgren, Hansson, and Olve, 1997). The future of virtual organizations seems assured, but it also seems certain to raise new issues of legal status and regulation at both national and global levels.

GLOBALIZATION
A SPATIAL AND TEMPORAL REVOLUTION?
A WHOLE NEW WORLD?

If a single topic has dominated the macrosocial sciences in the past three decades, it is globalization. This emphasis is not entirely new, having been foreshadowed by earlier preoccupations with colonialism, cultural diffusion, imperialism, modernization, dependency theory, and world-systems theory (see chapter 7); but none has reached the magnitude of the multifaceted and often elusive subject of globalization.

Globalization is many things, but in the first instance it involves dramatic reorientations of economic and other activities in space and time: a vast increase in world trade, capital flows, and financial institutions; the transformation of production into world phenomena (largely through multinational corporations); increased movement of peoples via internal and international migration and tourism; and an accelerated international flow of information. Via these changes, globalization has thus produced a paradox: On many counts it has expanded world horizons through its incorporation of the globe; with respect to the information revolution, however—almost always included in discussions of globalization—the world has shrunk by virtue of its instant reachability.

Globalization has altered the time contours of the factors of production, but differentially so:

- Capital. Information, knowledge, and ideas (intellectual capital) can be spread to anywhere in the world in an instant. So can financial capital. Embedding capital into the physical means of production, however, consumes time and occupies space.
- Labor. The movement of labor is more fluid than ever before, but both internal and external migration (e.g., to sites of multinational manufacturing firms) generates serious problems of adaptation on the part of migrants. International migration is not a simple flow, but meets resistance from receiving populations and restrictions by many governments. If international migration includes adaptation and assimilation in addition to the physical movement of persons, then the process takes years, perhaps generations, to run its course. Shifting personnel (e.g., managers) from one international assignment to another also involves time-consuming processes of accommodation. Adaptation of traditional women's roles to wage labor in the market poses special issues of change and conflict.

- Organization. Manufacturing firms and service organizations can be transferred from place to place, or even dispersed to many places, but their implantation into new geographical and cultural settings often occasions adaptations to different conditions and subsequent structural modifications.
- Land. Considered in its narrow sense, land is the most spatially immobile of all the factors of production. The other factors must be brought to it and assembled. Furthermore, location in a specific place involves both initial commitment and a form of path dependency in that movement to another site involves costs, even though it may be economical in the long run.

The net effects of increased international flows of resources and globalization of production, trade, and finance have been an unprecedented porosity of national boundaries, increased dependency of nations and societies on one another, and myriad other ramifications. Conspicuous among these are the following:

1. The nation-state as a formally sovereign entity remains the world's dominant form of political organization. This form is the product of the political evolution of the West over the centuries; states were the operative units that initiated, executed, and solidified the colonization of the world; they were the model—national independence—to which movements in those colonies aspired; and they were the institutional form that was adopted as colony after colony broke from western domination. The nation-state is the membership category in the United Nations (see chapter 7). In ideal-typical form, the state is the spatially bounded locus of political organization (as the principal war-fighting unit, controller of borders, and monopolist of the use of legitimate force within them); the ultimate regulator of economic life (the national economy); a common language and perhaps a common religion; citizenship; and the solidarity of peoples (Marsh, 1967).

   Many forces have conspired to erode this ideal state form, including (1) the "unnatural" inclusion of religiously and ethnically/racially/tribally diverse populations in colonially imposed divisions of domination; (2) the continuation of that inclusion in postcolonial states (Iraq is a prime example) and the granting or imposing of statehood when the peoples affected were not culturally prepared for it (Libya is a prime example); (3) migration, which has generated expatriate, diaspora, religious, linguistic, and ethnic/racial subcommunities within nations; (4) an explosion of world tourism, simultaneously generating increased cosmopolitization of those who travel and cultural diversification of areas that host tourists; and (5) partly as a result of the porosity of borders and border regions arising from (3) and (4), many identity issues have arisen for subpopulations living on or near the borders between nations. Globalization has accelerated all these effects, plus one that is even more profound: it renders more problematic the political sovereignty of nations.

International turbulences of trade, inflation, and currency rates are sometimes beyond the powers of governments (especially small, weak, and poor ones) to resist them and their impact on the economic lives of their peoples. Multinational corporations constitute a new political entity within the nations they inhabit. Intergovernmental and international organizations such as the United Nations, the European Union, the International Monetary Fund, and the World Bank, international environmental agencies, and other international nongovernmental organizations (NGOs)—numbering in the thousands and growing annually—all partially limit the sovereignty of states. One observer concludes that *"the operation of states in an ever more complex international system both limits their autonomy (in some spheres radically) and impinges increasingly upon their sovereignty"* (Held, 1995: 135, italics original).

Such a flat conclusion must be qualified in two ways: (1) While their sovereignty is thus threatened, states still retain *formal* political responsibility and (depending on their level of democracy) political accountability for their fortunes, and often find themselves beleaguered in the sense that they come under political attack for affairs over which they have little or no control; for example, they may promise to rein in inflation, but fundamentally they cannot. (2) The very fact of the increasing political impotence of states and state leaders creates a motive for them to strive to become more activist in order to overcome that impotence. This sets up a paradox—a process of simultaneous *decline* and *increasing salience* of the nation-state, and weakened states struggling to maintain, recover, or enhance their strength.

2. The cultural ramifications of economic and political globalization have been profound. We mentioned cultural diversification and multiculturalism generated by migration and tourism. Several other cultural complications may be mentioned. (1) Exposure to alternative cultural values and beliefs are magnified through international communication, especially the mass media, particularly television. This acceleration is made possible by the condensation of time and the irrelevance of space permitted by technological advances in communication. Among the most important messages that are imparted—mainly in communications emanating from the advanced countries—are the cultures of materialism and consumerism, democracy (especially democratic participation and responsibility), human rights, and secularism. All these cultures communicate new *standards of expectation and evaluation* that typically contrast with traditional values of the receiving cultures, and are often presented as desirable and enviable. Widespread effects on the receiving peoples include a sense of relative deprivation (traditional cultures fall short materially, politically, and culturally); feelings of dispossession; yearning for liberation from the burdens of traditional values;

generational conflict; and movements for gender liberation and equality. (2) The penetration of new cultural standards invariably incites their opposites—antagonism to foreign or western values as material, profane, godless, and corrupting—thus creating multiple internal conflicts expressing the oppositions between modernism and traditionalism/fundamentalism. (3) A principal manifestation of traditional reactions is social movements reasserting localist principles along regional, religious, and linguistic lines. (4) The longer-term effect of the international diffusion of values is neither the cultural homogenization of the world nor the successful reassertion and continuity of traditional values. Nor is it some massive "clash of civilizations." It is, rather, a continuous process of modification, syncretism, and compromise among competing cultural models (Hannerz, 1990). (5) Alongside these effects are the growth of global cultures that crosscut those based on regional and national differences—among international civil servants, among those sharing common NGO membership, a "World Bank culture," a "UN culture," a diffuse "culture of globality" (Robertson, 1992), and many others. (6) The ultimate effects of cultural globalization, then, are a multiplicity of processes: increased international understanding, increased international misunderstanding, cultural diversification, cultural ambivalence, cultural conflict, and cultural syncretism and synthesis.

The lessons to be learned from this review of economic, political, and cultural globalization, then, are the same the lessons learned about other phenomena of change. As global forces intrude, being relatively unfamiliar, they excite immediate and somewhat polarized reactions along the spectrum extending from Panglossian to Cassandrian views—a brave new world and a road to positive revolutionary changes, or an avenue leading to ruination and disaster. Both views persist despite the reality of all social change, which is always partial, always checkered, always a mixture of the new and the old, always a dynamic force superimposed on habits, vested interests, resistances, path dependencies, and traditionalism that conspire to moderate change, to defeat revolutionary potential, and to disappoint both Panglossian and Cassandrian seers.

CONCLUSION

This is the first of a half-dozen chapters to deal directly with *substantive* knowledge that might be usable to people in positions of decision-making, problem-solving, and policy-making. We decided to begin by tracing the ramifications of space and time in the organization of social life. Social scientists have contributed a great deal of knowledge to these topics, but have not bundled them into discrete, tightly disciplined lines of inquiry. For that reason we built this

.chapter from many topics that are seldom related to one another. Highlighting space-time dimensions, however, sets up continuities among otherwise scattered phenomena.

With respect to usability, many ingredients in this chapter constitute potentially useful orienting knowledge. Consistent with our belief that usability is of many types (chapter 10), we move from the generally orienting to the more specifically applicable:

- By focusing on time and space, we identified a number of dimensions that help us in understanding the way the social world is constituted, and that are ever-present in assessing decisions and policies.
- More specifically, we have identified a number of specific *ways of conceptualizing* space and time in different settings.
- By stressing space-time dimensions (for example, the infusion of time and space into expressions of social status), we hope to persuade actors to pay more attention to them, and to recognize them as ingredients in decisions that affect the organization and conduct of life.
- We have identified a number of implications of space and time for power (e.g., agenda setting), status (e.g., standing in organization), and performance (e.g., the limitations of virtual communication), all of which are tied closely to dimensions of morale, satisfaction, and interpersonal conflict. They can be taken directly into account in designing and managing workplaces.
- We have identified a few pitfalls in *not* thinking about time and space; examples are the failure to explicitly recognize the power of sunk costs and other path dependencies, and failures in designing office space and the symbolic placement of people and things.

Despite their tangibility, all these potential points of usability are in the nature of informing reminders and cautionary tales rather than fixed formulae. We do not regard this as a shortcoming, however, because throughout our analysis we treat social-science knowledge mainly as orienting and informing, not as direct or complete devices for solutions.

In the next few chapters, we move closer to discipline-based lines of knowledge, bringing many psychological and organizational variables to bear on the quality of deliberation, decision-making, and policy.

2

Some Dynamics of Cognition, Judgment, and Bias

In this chapter we present a view of the mind as embedded in its personal history and its contemporary—including its social—situation. Our account yields a special perspective on human nature. Not all its ingredients are new; many echo ancient philosophical traditions that still inform our worldviews. The view we represent derives primarily from systematic, often experimental, scientific traditions in many disciplines, all from their recent histories. We describe our depiction of human behavior as neither *rational* (as in some philosophies and some social-science accounts in economics, political science, and law) nor *irrational* (as in some philosophical works [Nietzsche], some psychological traditions [Freudian psychology], and in some social-science traditions ["Italian irrationalism" in political theory]). What emerges is a human being who is largely *nonrational* but *purposeful* in orientation, that is, perceiving, thinking, and behaving *outside* the principles and strictures implied in both rational and irrational approaches. This means that individuals sometimes act rationally and sometimes irrationally, but most often nonirrationally—a term that permits or implies *purpose* and *adaptation,* but is independent of and not captured by the logics of true-false, right-wrong, pessimistic-optimistic, or rational-irrational. We hope to avoid both the passion for neatness that characterizes rationalist approaches and the passion for chaos that frequently characterizes irrationalist ones. We regard this nonrational view as the most realistic, and certainly the most viable, with respect to the use of knowledge in decision-making, problem-solving, and policy-making.

INTELLECTUAL DYNAMICS AND
THE QUALITY OF KNOWLEDGE

Running through this chapter—and elaborated in chapter 10—are two instructive themes in the accumulation of knowledge. One theme is negative polemicism: A certain scholar, group of scholars, or nascent school is typically driven in part by the discovery or the assertion that other, "received" knowledge is oversimplified, limited, or wrong. Such observations are the foil against which some new line of scientific endeavor is carried out and often justified. Sometimes the negative polemic stereotypes the received position under attack, highlighting its most vulnerable aspects. Moreover, negative polemics gain notice and electricity because they are directed *against* a scientific position that some group of "established" scientists defend; this often imparts a personal- or group-conflict dimension to the polemic. Here is a sample of received views that have been reacted *against* during the past century in psychology:

- Perception is a mirror or photograph of objective reality.
- Memory is an accurate reproduction and preservation of experience.
- Learning occurs by acquiring knowledge through repeated exposure (conditioning) in the experience of individuals.
- The actor in a social context is knowledgeable, intelligent, rational, and basically free from error and from nonrational or irrational impulses. The two most conspicuous arenas in which this principle held sway were (1) classical economic analysis, portraying actors as rational choosers in a market context; and (2) some strands of democratic thought, portraying the political actor as informed, enlightened, attentive to political issues, deliberative, aware of his/her political interests, and not swayed by irrational appeals.
- Thinking processes of individuals are inferentially and logically sound.
- Emotions and reason are opposed. The former are private, perhaps bodily based experiences, foreign to and disruptive of rational thought. Emotion is a source of error, superstition, and mischief; reason is the source of truth, proper action, and moral virtue. Scientists of all types, long having identified themselves as among the rational classes in society, have been partially responsible for perpetuating this view, partly, no doubt, in the interest of enhancing themselves and their pursuits.

To acknowledge that all these views have been challenged, reformulated, and rejected and that new ways of thinking have triumphed is *not* to say that they have disappeared. In fact, the tensions, disagreements, and disputes between the presumably discredited and the presumably more accurate and adequate formulations are the bases for ongoing and recurrent controversies over the nature of the world and the best ways to describe, interpret, and act in it.

As a result of these repeated cycles of criticism of received knowledge → reformulation → new bursts of theory and research → refinement → new criticism (see chapter 10), views of the world become both more realistic and more complicated. Simplistic worldviews become more qualified and contingent. More emphasis is placed on *connections* between previously isolated processes—fusions between the psychological and social aspects of emotions; fusions between affect and cognition in perception and learning; fusions among perception, affect, and experience in memory; and fusions between the rational and nonrational. In this process, sharp lines between traditional academic disciplines blur, and new perspectives and knowledge alter existing lines of research.

A further dynamic flows from this one. In cognitive and social psychology (and probably in all other fields), research themes continuously wax and wane. Master themes such as learning through conditioning, cognitive dissonance, attribution theory, and the effect of motivation on perception swell and recede but never disappear. (In chapter 10 we enunciate a preference for this view of knowledge-creation over the view of additive accumulation.) Jones (1998) lays out the main determinants of the rise and consolidation of research themes in social psychology: the rise of new cultural worldviews in the larger society (for example, the "cultural turn" in thinking toward the end of the twentieth century); the personal concerns of innovating researchers and their followers; the theoretical and practical promise and power of new lines of thinking and research; methodological innovations that permit new lines of analysis; the prestige of intellectual innovators and their institutions; funding priorities of agencies outside the academy that stimulate specific lines of research; and the sense of excitement and freedom generated by asking questions at the frontiers of a field.

What contributes to the waning of once-dominant research themes? Jones mentions the problem that arises when an intellectual puzzle is solved: research reaches a dead end; methodological flaws undermine the viability of findings and applications; and new ethical standards countermand previously accepted research practices on human subjects (for example, misleading, punishing, or otherwise damaging people in research situations) (11–14). We might add a generational effect: neophilia, or the rejection of masters' work by their students who are struggling for novelty and recognition.

These processes pose difficulties and dilemmas for those interested in the usability of knowledge in practical situations. Their legitimate desire is for findings and principles that will inform and direct their decisions, policy preferences, and solutions with maximum certainty. What they find in academic fields, however—by virtue of the dynamics identified above—is contingency, uncertainty, tentativeness, qualification, and controversy, all of which render that knowledge less available and accessible to the practitioner who may be intelligent but not expert in evaluating technically based knowledge nested in tedious qualifications. The service we hope to provide in this and other chapters is to dip selectively into these cauldrons of knowledge and identify approaches, perspectives, and findings that, negatively, describe traps and pitfalls, and, positively, frame and inform practitioners' problems and dilemmas.

THE UNIVERSALITY OF PSYCHOLOGICAL CATEGORIZATION AND ITS EXTENSIONS

Categorization, the tendency to simplify reality by sorting experience into types, classes, and encompassing terms, is a fundamental and universal cognitive process. It is the drawing of boundaries—"understanding what some thing is by knowing what other things it is equivalent to and what other things it is different from" (McCartney, 1999: 1). Categorization involves confronting an undifferentiated, complex, and confusing flow of experience and sorting it into mental creations that are meaningful and adaptive. The process helps determine what is important, unimportant, and irrelevant in the world. It is partly an automatic and unconscious process. Many categories remain latent and unconsulted bases for behavior. Derivatively, categorization is an experiential precondition for identifying what is to be noticed or not noticed, embraced or avoided, and loved or hated.

Social scientists of all types have noticed the centrality of categorization. Cognitive psychologists (for example, Fiske and Taylor, 2008) have demonstrated that categorization is omnipresent in perception and development—essential as an adaptive device in reducing the uncertainty, ambiguity, and complexity of raw experience. One tradition of research has shown that people's perceptions of others' social status categories (based on factors such as education, social class membership, skin color, accent, pattern of speech) strongly influence the level of influence, respect, and deference shown in interaction (Berger, Fisek, Norman, and Zelditch, 1977). Categorization has been described as an efficient sorting device that reduces repetitive searching in novel situations and constitutes an economical navigational guide to adaptive behavior (the categorizer as "cognitive miser"). More recent developments in social identity theory emphasize motivational and self-esteem components of categorization: individuals make distinctions in the interest of self-enhancement by sorting others into preferred or nonpreferred social categories. This becomes the basis of prejudice, which we treat as an extension of categorization. The essential point is that categorization is universal; not one of us escapes it; we all participate in its adaptive virtues and distorting vices.

Other traditions of social science stress that categorization is more than individual adaptation. Most important categories of experience are not invented by individuals. They are handed to them as parts of the cultural and social milieux in which they are socialized and which they internalize. A central feature of anthropologists' concept of culture is its *selectivity* of certain values, norms, beliefs, categories, and priorities from the panoply of possibilities, thus creating a simplified and not entirely coherent view of the world that is a basis for organizing and conducting social life. The ideas of categorization and classification are standard ingredients for scholars who study culture, and they are the centerpieces of a tradition of French sociology and anthropology found in the works of Émile Durkheim (1965 [1912]), his student Marcel Mauss (Durkheim and Mauss, 1963 [1903]), and more recently Claude Lévi-Strauss (1965). Some sociological traditions highlight categorization as well. For example, labeling theory treats the essence of deviance not as individual motivation, but rather as descriptions of others in terms of categories (criminal, insane, deformed, handicapped) that become the basis for their degradation (Becker, 1963). Other sociologists (for example, Berger and Luckman, 1967) treat the need for simplification and routinization in human interaction as the origin of social structure and institutional life, which become the basis of objectification and reification of the categorized versions of reality into which individuals are socialized and which in large part govern their life. In a word, most of the categories learned by individuals are supplied by socialization and social experience. These categories are not completely uniform or regimented because society and culture themselves are always heterogeneous and imperfectly integrated, but nonetheless they remain as the major source of social categorization.

Categorization moves to center stage when strangers meet, when people confront an interpersonal situation in which knowledge of the other is minimal. An initial and necessary feature of such confrontations is the formation of first impressions, a process of mobilizing categories into a simplified but coherent view of the stranger.

What guides this process are *preexisting categories* in the mind of the perceiver, who notices or applies them to what is perceived—familiar categories such as physical size, posture, age, race, complexion, acceptable decorum, and one's pet peeves. The various categorical inferences that are drawn about the perceived are combined into a composite known as a first impression. The author of the very popular book *Blink* (Gladwell, 2005) advances the argument that first impressions are frequently uncannily accurate. Yet they are also sometimes erroneous. In all events, first impressions endure, and are not always corrected by future interaction and new knowledge about the "target." Finally, we might speculate, with others (e.g., Todorov, Mandisodza, Goren, and Hall, 2005), that with the long-term increase in the importance of the media in political campaigns, with the appearance of mechanisms such as e-interviews, and with the astronomical growth of visual-impressionistic innovations such as Facebook, action and outcomes based on first impressions may become even more salient in making important social judgments about others in the future.

Even though they are not based on the assessment of sufficient or full evidence, categorical reactions—like much of heuristic thinking—are an adaptive, even necessary component of the cognitive process. A darker side, however, appears when we consider two terms derived from categorization—*stereotype* and *prejudice*—subjects of lasting interest in social psychology and other social sciences. Investigators have argued that categorization is a precondition for both of these (Taylor, Fiske, Ercoff, and Ruderman, 1978). The word *stereotyping,* which might be described in shorthand as categorization + rigidification, is derived from the process of setting newspaper type into lead plates, by which the type becomes fixed. Cognitively, stereotypes are views and opinions, usually of social groups, that attribute characteristics to other groups that are assumed to be given by nature or derivative from membership in those groups. Like categories in general, stereotypes derive both from individual psychological processes and from "givens" in the lore of societies and cultures, which include dozens of received beliefs and ideas (in varying degrees of crystallization) about groups and subgroups within and outside themselves. These are acquired through socialization, social learning, and social reinforcement.

Prejudice, by extension, is categorization + rigidification + affect, that is, when stereotyped groups come to be regarded negatively (as inferior, lazy, disgusting, dirty, stupid, greedy, scheming) or positively (superior, likeable, honest, trustworthy). Many psychological explanations of prejudice have been advanced over time, including projecting (externalizing) the negative side of one's own unresolved conflicts onto other groups—this has been posited as a strategy of "authoritarian personalities" (Adorno, Sanford, Frankel-Brunswik, and Levinson, 1950). Currently the most influential approach is that of social identity, originated by Tajfel (1982). The concept of self plays a central role. The primary differentiation is between self and others, with the notion that both are embedded in a nesting of relevant and emotionally laden groups, either in-groups or out-groups or somewhere between those extremes. Prejudiced thinking also entails depersonalization of both out-group and in-group members, in that their individual characteristics are subordinated to group-stereotyped categories. With dozens of reinforcing mechanisms available, the dynamics of categorization, self-enhancement, and derogation of others form the psychological substrate of prejudice and group conflict. When organized into belief systems, these combinations of stereotypes, prejudice, and their group reinforcement yield cultural views about "the stranger" and "the foreign," as well as systems of racism, ethnocentrism, and xenophobia. Such beliefs also form the ideological substrate for tragic episodes of ethnic cleansing and genocide.

Interestingly, this rise of self and identity in the social psychology of attitudes in the last part of the twentieth century coincided with the "discovery" of the role of self-enhancement in cognitive heuristics, identity politics (in contrast to interest politics) in political science, identity movements in sociology, and the appearance of the self-esteem movement as an approach to social problems—all of these were part of a general cultural turn from material interest and structural determinants toward group beliefs and commitments. This is a striking example of Jones's observation that general changes in worldview influence academic disciplines and determine in part their vicissitudes in emphasis.

Stereotypes are pervasive and resistant to change, even though some methods, such as involving different groups in cooperative projects, educational programs, and efforts to decategorize, result in some decrease in prejudiced attitudes. Other research shows that category-based prejudices affect perceptions and judgments even when individuals deny having such prejudices. Even instructing experimental subjects *not* to think about negative categories appears to stimulate them to think more about them (Wegner, 1994). Noticing these and other facts, psychologists have refined the idea of prejudice by inventing and investigating concepts such as symbolic racism, ambivalent racism, aversive racism, subtle racism, and modern racism (Hogg and Abrams, 2003). The logic behind these terms is that human tendencies to categorize and denigrate groups continue as major psychological and social forces, but many counterforces promoting tolerance are also at work. Examples of these counterforces in recent decades are the civil rights movement, social legislation against discrimination, educational and awareness movements, and even humor (for example, poking fun in the media at the blatant biases of an Archie Bunker). A common adaptation to this tension is to deny—perhaps honestly deny—racist and other prejudicial attitudes publicly or when asked (for example, in a public opinion survey), but to retain them at implicit or unconscious levels, and to manifest them in subtler forms such as polite avoidance, use of euphemisms, or feigned or condescending attitudes. A subtle chasing game develops: As "new" forms of prejudice are uncovered, people adapt by camouflaging them further—remaining guilty, as it were, but continuously making it more difficult to be proven guilty.

A further step in the categorization process is *discrimination,* which can be described as categorization + rigidification + affect + deliberate action. This description covers overt, intended exclusionary behavior, such as not hiring, not admitting, not insuring, and not selling property to others on the basis of their group characteristics. Despite negative campaigns, social legislation, affirmative action programs, and evident progress in some areas, intentional discrimination remains a force. Moreover, it is hard to locate or even estimate its occurrence because it is difficult to establish deliberate intent and because forces other than personal discrimination may be producing group inequalities (for example, differences in socialization and educational deficiencies). However, in areas such as selling and renting residences, field experiments in which people from different racial and ethnic groups apply for housing have yielded evidence of intentional discrimination by sellers and landlords.

In recent decades, social scientists have extended the idea of discrimination by referring to indirect, institutional, derived, or systemic discrimination. An example is the imposition of minimum height standards in the recruitment of police officers, which results in higher rejection rates for people from ethnicities who are generally short in stature. Another example is insurance companies' practice of using high school grade-point averages in determining insurance rates for young drivers, which operates indirectly to exclude individuals on both racial-ethnic and class grounds. Still other examples are social programs designed to differentially benefit target populations. For example, the GI Bill, which enabled World War II veterans to attend college on federal scholarships, has been generally regarded as a legitimate privilege for those who gave service to their country. Indirectly, however, that program had discriminatory effects on women (who were greatly underrepresented in the military) and racial minorities (more of whom had not completed high school, and were therefore not eligible for college admission). Perhaps the most important area of systemic discrimination is in housing segregation, whereby concentration in ghettos of categorical groups yields a cumulative list of disadvantages in income, education, family stability, social support, exposure to danger and disease, and social attitudes, all of which create and sustain the current and future disadvantages of their residents (Massey and Denton, 1993).

The relative importance of intentional and systemic discrimination, to say nothing of the interactions between them, is difficult to unscramble. The distinction, however, suggests that a mixed pattern of strategies and reforms should be in the repertoire of mechanisms to alter them. Educational and motivational programs (e.g., "consciousness-raising") and targeted legislative efforts seem more appropriate to affect deliberate discrimination, whereas more comprehensive social reforms such as antipoverty programs, taxation strategies, and housing policies are required to initiate changes in the institutional bases of systemic discrimination. Scholars have noticed a split between the two bases of discrimination over the past decades. On the one hand, surveys have shown decreases in prejudicial attitudes, for example the decline in self-reported biases in public surveys and the increased tolerance with respect to willingness to live in the same neighborhood or even intermarry with other groups. The increased willingness to vote for a black presidential candidate is perhaps the most dramatic change. At the same time, only minimal changes have been observed in actual institutional arrangements. Occupational and income inequalities, housing segregation, de facto educational segregation, neighborhood mixing, and intermarriage have changed much less. And racial signs, such as skin color, evidently retain their strength as judgmental categories (Hunter, 2005). Such anomalies underlie scholars' preoccupation with subtle and evasive racism, and have led them to seek new sociological formulations, such as "racism without racists" and "colorblind racism" (Bonilla-Silva, 2003), which recognize but do not solve the mysteries of continuing discrimination-based inequalities.

In this account of the social-psychological dynamics of categorization, stereotyping, prejudice, and discrimination, we have followed the lead of scholars in that we emphasize class, educational, racial, and ethnic groupings. This emphasis is understandable, given the multiple social problems and injustices based on group categorization, and given the generally liberal and reformist orientations of academic researchers. We must stress, however, that the fundamental dynamics involved also apply to other—indeed all—categories. We should expect these simplifying and distorting processes to be found in minorities' attitudes toward majority groups (reverse racism), in nonsmokers' and antismokers' attitudes toward smokers, in employees' attitudes toward management (and vice versa), and, indeed, in liberals' attitudes toward bigots. In the game of oversimplification and its consequences, all parties are guilty.

A final research focus in the categorization process is the *effects* on those subjected to prejudice and discrimination on the basis of assigned group characteristics. Most obviously, they are materially and socially disadvantaged according to the type of discrimination involved—housing, medical treatment, education, income, status, and so forth. Other research teases out distinctive psychological consequences. Those on the receiving end of the stereotyping, prejudice, and discrimination are often regarded as having a taint—signifying a lack of moral worth—a characteristic that social scientists have designated by the term *stigma* (Jones, Scott, and Markus, 1984; Goffman, 1963). Categories of people who have a history of stigmatization are the diseased (lepers, mental patients, victims of AIDS); the addicted; the handicapped (the blind, the deaf, the lame); the aged; the ugly; the obese; criminals; prostitutes; the unemployed; and those dependent on welfare, to say nothing of the standard minority categories based on race, ethnicity, gender, and sexual preference. Typically, negatively charged slur words are the currency used to describe individuals in these categories. When those offended by these terms attempt to substitute more benign and dignified ones— "visually challenged," "seniors," "sex workers," children with "special educational needs"—these efforts often fail because the negative affect follows the new words, yielding a kind of chasing game between benign description and contaminating affect (Matza, 1966).

Those subjected to stigmatization in society typically know, with varying awareness and articulation, that they carry the stigmata imposed upon them. They develop different postures toward that fact, ranging from resentment and rejection at one extreme to the belief that the stigmata are correct and deserved at the other. The latter adaptation is the tragic one, typically leading to a range of negative consequences, including self-defeating behavior on the part of the stigmatized. Examples of these kinds of consequences are as follows:

- Affective and behavioral consequences such as lowered self-esteem, depression, self-hatred, and psychiatric symptoms (for example, Swim and Cohen, 1989). An early and extreme characterization was that of Bettelheim (1943), who used the psychoanalytically based phrase 'identification with the aggressor" to depict the positive attachment of some inmates to guards in Nazi concentration camps.
- Diminished performance. Steele (1988) and others have demonstrated that when open attention is drawn to stigmatized status characteristics (such as race and gender) in the instructions to subjects in experimental settings, those having those characteristics perform less well than in testing situations that are described more neutrally or positively.
- Hiding from social notice, including disidentification; "passing"; concealing the stigmatized attribute (e.g., sexual preference) or avoiding situations in which it might be an issue; or acknowledging the stigma and requesting special treatment on account of it. Often these adaptations involve strategies of impression management (Goffman, 1959).

Many of these adaptations are instances of a more generic phenomenon, the self-fulfilling prophecy, which refers to a situation in which "a . . . social belief leads to its own fulfillment" (Jussim, 2001: 13830). A simple example is the belief expressed by spokespersons for the homeless in New York City in 1989 that authorities would undercount them in the upcoming census. On the basis of that belief, they urged the homeless not to cooperate with the census, thereby guaranteeing the undercount! With respect to self-defeating behavior of the stigmatized, the self-fulfilling prophecy is that the stigmatized manifest, even reinforce, some of the very conditions assigned to them by stigmatizers.

More active and often constructive responses on the part of the stigmatized include protesting the degradation, advocating reforms in media portrayal, turning a negatively charged attribute into a positively charged one—for example, "black is beautiful"—and advocating legislation mandating improved treatment for the historically disadvantaged (for example, ramps and elevators for the handicapped, equal pay, affirmative action).

To conclude this section, we raise an issue that has recently assumed salience: diversity in organizational settings. This has become a focus of interest for scholars, politicians, educators, labor unions, and others as it has become a more widespread social fact. The complicated historical unfolding of the civil rights movement, the women's movement, affirmative action, the gay rights movement, agitation by and on behalf of groups such as the aged and handicapped, and the intellectual movement of multiculturalism has yielded a gradual diversification of many organizational settings, though resistances remain.

The issue of diversity and its consequences has also invaded many lines of social-science inquiry. Major research concerns have to do with whether diversity of teams and organizations makes for greater or less productivity and satisfaction, and how this relationship changes over time; and whether stereotyping decreases as more information about others is communicated in daily interaction (Cvetkovich, 1978; Macrae and Bodenhausen, 2001). Results are mixed: One line of research suggests that greater homogenization makes for greater trust, commitment, satisfaction, and effectiveness on the job (Schneider, 1987), and another that greater diversification produces more absenteeism and turnover (Tsui, Egan, and O'Reilly, 1991). Another, more optimistic line finds that diversity enhances problem-solving (Jackson, Brett, Sessa, Cooper, et al., 1991); another finds that homogenous groups perform better than heterogeneous ones initially, but that these differences reverse after a few months (Watson, Kumar, and Michelson, 1993).

One set of observers describes the literature on diversity and its effects as "large, sprawling and essentially unruly" (Kulik and Bainbridge, 2006: 25), mainly because the literature itself reflects the substantive conflicts that divide students of organizations on this topic. One approach to diversity is instrumental, treating it as something to be managed as a way of "leveraging human difference toward organizational effectiveness and productive business goals" (Plummer, 2003: 13). Other approaches concentrate on the human relations aspects of interaction in diverse contexts. More critical approaches, such as feminism, postcolonialism, critical theory, and cultural studies, stress continuing legacies of domination, inequality, and injustice (Konrad, Prasad, and Pringle, 2006). Despite this somewhat chaotic—though expected—diversity of approaches to diversity, the relevance of categorization, its derivatives, and its dynamics will prove central to understanding and coping with its origins, nature, and consequences.

OTHER FUNDAMENTAL COGNITIVE-EMOTIONAL PROCESSES

Attribution

In ways that we will note, this process has several continuities with categorization and its derivatives, though it is usually discussed separately in the literature. The idea was originally crystallized by Heider (1958). The basic process is this: When an individual is attempting to account for another's behavior, especially in a novel or uncertain situation, the first individual may refer to situational factors (e.g., explaining another's lapse of memory by referring to his or her weariness) or to some generic dispositional *attribute* (explaining the lapse of memory by referring to the other's stupidity) (Jones, Kanouse, Kelley, Nisbett, et al., 1972). For several generations this idea has had influence in psychology, though, like most influential concepts, it has undergone many extensions, additions, refinements, and criticisms.

One influential refinement of attribution is termed the fundamental attribution error. This refers to the process of—presumably erroneously—assigning cause to dispositional rather than situational characteristics. This results in a reduction of contingency in explaining others' behavior. It also results in stereotyping, i.e., condemning the observed individual as agent (or victim) of general, perhaps unchangeable traits or motives. (This is where attribution and categorization converge.) When the dispositional features are seen as typical of some in-group or out-group and an emotional valence is attached to that group, we arrive at prejudice via the route of attribution. Pettigrew (1979) extended this line of thinking in his reference to an "ultimate attribution error," which is an elaborate pattern of rationalization whereby seemingly positive aspects of a disliked out-group are written off as aberrations or as being determined by accidental circumstances, but seemingly negative aspects of liked in-groups are explained as accidents or exceptions. Both processes maintain the consistency and strength of stereotypes.

Among the extensions of attribution theory are the locus of control and self-efficacy theories, in which individual adaptation and achievement are explained according to whether one assigns the origins and outcomes of one's behavior to one's own actions under one's own control, or takes a more passive route by assigning outcomes to unchangeable personal traits or external circumstances. Reliance on the latter may produce a responses known as learned helplessness, which is conducive to a passive coping style and perhaps low self-esteem and depression. Other, more practical lines of research on attribution stress, e.g., the pathologies in parents' describing children's behavior (to the children) as the product of negative dispositions (stubbornness, stupidity, laziness, undesirable traits inherited from grandparents, aunts, uncles, etc.) (Dix and Grusec, 1985). Similarly, educational psychologists have identified damages to pupils' sense of self-esteem and self-efficacy when they are labeled as "immature," "slow," or "uncooperative." Such attribution processes produce a kind of stigmatization. Finally, one dimension of leadership has been traced to attribution processes, i.e., the qualities imputed to a leader that bolster that leader independent of his or her intrinsic qualities of leadership (Calder, 1977). Mechanisms such as these lead to exaggerated perceptions of the power of leaders (for example, the president of the United States, athletic coaches), the infallibility of experts (especially medical ones), and, more generally, the overpersonalization of reality. In extreme cases, these mechanisms might extend to paranoid interpretations of political and social life.

Psychologists have extended their analyses of cognitive structures by noting combinations of categorizations, attributions, assumptions, and inferences from experience into complex forms referred to as schemata, mental models, or cognitive maps (e.g., Fauconnier, 1997). These constitute people's everyday working theories, which they carry around as resources to help themselves know what to expect of others, how to interpret familiar and unfamiliar situations, how to frame choices, and how to cope with different situations. Schemata and mental models contain comprehensive accounts of how the world goes round. They identify the good, the bad, and the neutral people, and they signal whom and what should be trusted or mistrusted. They are important ingredients in adapting to the parade of real-life situations and demands. These generalized dispositions are of special interest because they constitute important ingredients of framing, adaptation, and decision-making in practical settings. They constitute individuals' and groups' psychological representations of reality. Moreover, insofar as these mental models come to incorporate insights, findings, and points of view derived from social-science knowledge, they are psychological avenues through which that knowledge becomes usable.

Two reflections are in order. First, despite their different names and paths of development, the attribution and the categorization traditions bear many similarities. The main difference is that attribution is narrower in scope, focusing on how people assign *cause* to the behavior of others; categorization is a more general process, referring to how people pigeonhole others according to classificatory concepts. Yet both are perceptive and cognitive shortcuts that people employ seemingly universally. Also, assigning dispositional motives to others is a way to categorize them—as highly motivated, indolent, clownish, arrogant, laid-back, or whatever. Finally, sorting people into categories seems to set in motion extensions that end up as simplified stereotypes, group distinctions, group preferences, group antagonisms, and, ultimately, patterns of prejudice and discrimination.

Second, both attribution and categorization and its derivatives have incorporated multiple dimensions of human experience—perception, cognition, affect, and group membership—under a single heading, and are the richer for that reason. Both begin with first impressions, broadly conceived, and both have moved beyond these to trace the implications of these relatively primitive mental formations in more inclusive contexts. At the end of this chapter, we put together our best thoughts on how these various psychological themes of research, considered both separately and together, enlighten our master issue of the usability of social-science knowledge.

Cognitive Dissonance and Balance Theory

One of the most influential theories of the second half of the twentieth century originally went by the name of cognitive dissonance theory. The notion was formulated by Festinger (1957) as an explicit critique of stimulus-response theories. The concept refers to situations in which an experience occurs that is inconsistent (dissonant) with or even contradicts a person's attitudes. As examples: "I told someone I really liked that movie, when in fact I didn't like it at all," or "I bought that bicycle after reading an ad about it, but I dislike advertising because it is false and manipulative." Further, dissonance generates discomfort and produces an emotion called aversive tension. (The formulation of dissonance theory thus involved a synthesis of cognitive and emotional elements—Harmon-Jones [2001].) A typical response to dissonance is for a person to alter an attitude, consciously or unconsciously, to make it more consistent with his or her behavior. This adaptation resembles rationalization as a defense mechanism, as elaborated in psychoanalytic thinking. Behavior might change as well; for example, people typically listen to political candidates or television news channels with viewpoints and focuses similar to their own, also in the interests of consistency. The theory of cognitive dissonance is one of a larger family, and may be regarded as a subtype of balance theory, articulated by Heider (1958), which assigns motivational significance to the internal consistency of perceptions and cognitions.

About the time that cognitive dissonance rose in salience, two related formulations appeared in other social sciences. The first is the notion of cross-pressures in political science (for example, Sperlich, 1971). This refers to situations in which individuals or groups are exposed to messages or pressures that pull them in different directions—for example, their political party comes out for legalizing abortion while their church argues against it. Political scientists attempted to link cross-pressures (a form of inconsistency) with political outcomes such as political indifference and failure to vote. In sociology, the same logic appeared in the concepts of status crystallization, status inconsistency, and status disequilibrium (for example, Lenski, 1954). This refers to the degree to which an individual's or group's position is consistent or inconsistent with respect to various status markers (wealth, power, prestige, group membership). Examples of such roles would be a union leader (high on power, low on prestige) and a black doctor (high on prestige, low on group category membership). Such discrepancies were posited to be sources of discomfort (because they were inconsistent) and to influence people's decisions and behaviors: for example, attracting them to extremist movements with ideologies that offer simplified views of the world.

Social Comparison Theory and Relative Deprivation

Festinger (1954) realized that a major component of the process of striving for consistency between attitudes and behavior is individuals' continuous comparisons of themselves with their own and other groups and standards. As a rule, people feel comfortable comparing themselves "upward," sharing characteristics with groups of higher status. However, upward comparisons may also generate feelings of inferiority, envy, and hostility. When people think of their own negative traits, they might compare themselves "downward," comforting themselves by thinking how much better off they are in relation to less fortunate or inferior others (Wills, 1981). We will return to the principles of self-enhancement and self-serving when we consider heuristics and biases.

The idea of social comparison is pervasive in the social sciences. We point to the following diverse illustrations:

· A finding arising from research on the United States Army in World War II (Stouffer, Suchman, DeVinney, Starr, et al., 1949) was that satisfaction among soldiers in different military branches varied according to the groups with which they compared themselves. For example, satisfaction among military police—a low-status group—was higher than in some other branches because, in comparing themselves to others, they did not *expect* much social recognition.

· The findings from the same work *(The American Soldier)* were consolidated and extended theoretically by Merton and Rossi (1968) under the heading of reference group behavior, which includes relative deprivation as a component. This essay carried the analysis to many other topics, such as social mobility, and found echoes of reference group theory in earlier theories, such as Sumner's (1906) formulation of in-group–out-group relations and early American social psychologists' views of the self (including the "looking-glass self" generated by referring to others' views of oneself).

· Both the cross-pressure concept in political science and the status crystallization concept in sociology are rooted in individuals' comparisons with meaningful social groups and standards of judgment emanating from them.

· Though methodological individualism—the principle of independence of actors from one another—is at the core of most economic analyses, reference groups play a role in many of them. Veblen's theory of conspicuous consumption (1934) stresses emulative and emulated behavior of social classes; *conspicuous* means, above all, directed toward audiences. To the "Veblen effect," Leibenstein (1950) added the "bandwagon" (join the group) and "snob" (separate oneself from the group) effects—both obviously involving comparisons—in spending behavior. Keynes's theory of the "stickiness of money wages" (1936)—i.e., the reluctance of workers to work for reduced wages—may involve feelings of falling behind others. In collective bargaining, standards of what other categories of workers are earning are always present, if not explicit. Duesenberry's (1954) early but lasting theory of consumer behavior is based on the assumption that consumers continuously make comparisons with others and consider whether their income has risen or fallen from some previous level. Many economic notions, such as comparable worth, equity, and a fair wage, are rooted in social comparisons, as are concerns with social justice (Runciman, 1966) and a fair world (Lerner and Lerner, 1981).

- Relative deprivation has been incorporated into thinking about social dissatisfaction and political revolution. Relying on insights generated in Tocqueville's study of the French Revolution and Durkheim's discussions of *anomie,* some (Davies, 1962; Gurr, 1970) have argued that a major determinant of revolutionary activity is relative improvement on the part of groups followed by an abrupt reversal in their fortunes—processes that generate feelings of dissatisfaction and injustice. The same logic has been extended to the origin of social and religious movements (Suls and Wills, 1991).
- Some modes of heuristic thinking, as we will see, involve social references. In particular, one of the most important, called anchoring and adjustment, explicitly does so. The mechanism involved is that a subject is given an initial bit of information (the "anchor"), which might be social-comparative in character, e.g., a range of payments an average worker might earn for a given type of job. Then the subject is asked what he or she deserves to be paid for the same job. The anchor typically serves as a reference point, and subjects "adjust" their responses around it because it has framed the situation for them.
- A telling illustration of relative deprivation is found in the study of Olympic medalists by Medvec, Madey, and Gilovich (1995). Gold, silver, and bronze medalists were interviewed after the games were held. Gold medalists were obviously satisfied with their performance and the outcome. Interestingly, however, bronze medalists showed higher satisfaction than silvers. "Silver medalists seem to be focused on the gold medal they almost won, whereas bronze medalists seem content with the thought that 'At least I did this well'" (607). The key to satisfaction is the comparison group, not the absolute rank.
- A few homier, familiar illustrations of social comparisons include "keeping up with the Joneses" in homeownership and other spending (phenomena documented empirically by, e.g., Furstenburg and Hughes, 1997); the spread of business practices via competitive copy-catting among firms; invidious status distinctions between employees in factories and firms (see above, pp. 23, 26–27); faculty members' sensitivity to the salaries and teaching loads of others at their level of rank and longevity; politicians' envy of other politicians' perks and their scrambles to equalize or exceed them; justifications of petty crime and rule-breaking on grounds that "everybody does it"; and sibling rivalries in families. Social comparisons are at the heart of all.

In a word, the widespread significance of relative deprivation establishes it as a key to understanding group, organizational, and larger societal processes, and as a device for interpreting otherwise unexpected and anomalous social outcomes. Yet it is also important to recognize a limitation of the concept: It is a perspective, or at best a principle, not a full explanatory theory. Individuals and groups carry around dozens of comparative standards that may be mobilized from occasion to occasion, and "the theory fails to predict which of many possible comparison standards the citizen will use; citizens do not invariably choose the source that provides the most invidious comparisons" (MacCoun, 2001: 8643). As such, relative deprivation is a stronger tool for generating ex post facto explanations than for predicting behavior. Nevertheless, its pervasiveness as a principle is striking.

DYNAMICS OF MEMORY

A massive change in the psychological understanding of memory is found in Freudian psychoanalysis. Decisive human memories are not those that are neutrally recorded, but those that are embedded because they have been associated with a childhood trauma (usually sexual) or conflict associated with unwanted impulses. Because they are threatening, these memories are *repressed* (with partial effectiveness)—that is, driven into an *unconscious* state. When they threaten to break through into consciousness, the individual *defends* against them by, for example, projecting impulses associated with them onto other people or distorting them through denial or rationalization. In the psychoanalytic view, memories are embedded representations of human experience, to be sure, but they are infused with affect, distorted, volatile, and often not available to the rememberer. More generally, the recovery of mental representations is not a matter of calling up "stored things"; rather, "representations are better regarded as active and interactive processes, flexibly constructed moment by moment in a manner that is intrinsically influenced by the context and content of other knowledge, rather than being statically 'stored,' 'searched for,' and 'retrieved' unchanged" (Smith, 1998, vol. 1: 434).

While recent developments in psychology have revised much of classical psychoanalysis, the notion of memory as an unreliable representation of reality has persisted. In this section, we review research that have demonstrated, illustrated, extended, and qualified the frailty of this mental facility.

Incompleteness

The most general principle is that memory is not a full account of the history of individuals who remember. Much, probably most, of memory is simply lost. How many memories can one recover, for example, from earlier than the ages of three or four? Sometimes none, sometimes few, and those few are fleeting and truncated traces, blended with memories of what parents, siblings, or others have told us what we *do* or *ought to* remember from those years. In order to survive, even in distorted form, memories probably have to be nested in associations with other memories, affects, and meanings. Moreover, they are not completely available for recall, often appearing in consciousness only when some contemporary situation stimulates them, or when some special circumstance, such as free-association during therapy, brings them up in full, partial, or distorted form.

The Emergence of the False Eyewitness

The western legal tradition regards direct eyewitness reports as a major source of evidence in trial proceedings; they are often considered more decisive than circumstantial evidence. To give credence to this evidence means to regard it as reliable, accurate, and trustworthy. Of course, it is possible for attorneys to challenge eyewitness testimony as questionable, inaccurate, or biased, but to do this is part of the ongoing legal procedure, not based on first assumptions about witness perception.

Research has challenged these long-standing legal assumptions. Pioneered by Loftus (1979), this research brought together masses of experimental and other research that demonstrated, convincingly, unsystematic and systematic errors in recalling described or visualized accounts of accidents, violence, and other relevant situations. Even the language used in describing such events affects recall. Participants in an experiment viewed a film of two cars colliding. Some were asked simply to estimate the speed at which the cars were moving when they hit. For other participants, the word *hit* was replaced by other words, such as the more neutral *contacted* and the more dramatic *smashed*. Striking differences were produced: those describing the "contact" situation estimated 31.8 miles per hour; those describing the "hit" estimated 34 miles per hour; and those describing the "smash" situation estimated 40.8 miles per hour (Loftus and Palmer, 1974).

Needless to say, the repercussion of such findings and the interpretations stemming from them were a bombshell in legal circles, evoking both demands for evaluating, revising, or even scrapping "unjust" evidential procedures and vigorous defense of these procedures by legal conservatives.

About the same time, a similar controversy arose in psychiatric and psychoanalytic circles. The starting point was Freud's idea, "discovered" in his own self-analysis and those of patients, that "remembered" childhood traumas (especially incest and other sexual abuse) were not remembered at all, but were "false" in the sense that they were produced in patients' defensive strategies in dealing with their own infantile wishes. In publications by Masson (1984) and others (e.g., Crews, Blum, Cavell, Eagle, et al., 1995), Freud's view was challenged. There were accusations that he advanced the sexual fantasy theory out of a motivation to protect his reputation by covering up actual cases of incest among his respectable Viennese patients. This attack developed into a widespread and emotional controversy over "false memories" in the literature (see Praeger, 1998; Loftus and Ketcham, 1996) and in public discourse. Numerous lawsuits were brought against parents by patients who claimed that their memories of abuse were real, not false.

A small and defensive counterassociation of parents wronged by "false accusations" formed. The issue of false reports and memories also infused debates about sexual harassment in the workplace and allegations of child abuse in general, as well as subsequent revelations of sexual abuse by Roman Catholic clergymen.

Interpersonal and Social Dimensions of Memory

Shortly after World War II, Allport and Postman (1947) published a now-classic volume on rumor. As part of their studies, they conducted a simple experiment among Harvard undergraduates. First they asked an undergraduate to view a picture of a scene on a bus, in which one man (evidently white) was holding a knife and facing another man (evidently black), with a number of people seated in the background. They asked the initial viewer to pass a description on to another student who had not seen the picture, then that student to pass the description on to another student, and so on. The result was the production of a rumor. In the process, the "memory" of the picture accumulated distortions: for example, the knife typically "moved" from the hand of the white to that of the black man; some details of the picture were sharpened; most of the other details dropped out; and, perhaps most important, the story became assimilated to racial stereotypes. The same patterns of sharpening, leveling, and assimilation were found in scores of wartime rumors that the researchers gathered; they also were observed in studies of rumors and stories in urban race riots (for example, Lee and Humphrey, 1943). These principles of distortion have stood the test of time in studies of rumor, urban legends, and urban disturbances (Fine, Campion-Vincent, and Heath, 2005).

The study of collective memory is a more historically oriented line of research that illustrates the dynamics of remembering historical persons, events, and eras over generations and longer spans. Most official stories of these historical phenomena do not include the notion of flux; the lore of peoples, nations, and cultures is generally regarded as fixed in history, as inherited and often sacred legends that give meaning to the past and present of those who hold them in memory. Yet studies of the paths of historical remembering of wars and battles (for example, the Crusades and the American Revolution) (Macleod, 2008; Mithander, Sundholm, and Troy, 2007) and studies of the memories of past monarchs, presidents, and generals show a picture of selection and forgetting; changes in emphases that reflect current preoccupations (rewriting history); contestations over historical meanings and how to commemorate them; and political struggles over who owns the right to give meaning to history. New regimes' practices of tearing down statues and other memorials and the denaming and renaming of streets and other markers are vivid examples of these struggles. They are deliberate but not always successful efforts to rewrite sociocultural memory.

COMMUNICATING WITH THE MEDIA

During the course of my business career, I evolved a practical working philoso-phy about the media and how to deal with them. I report this philosophy here for several reasons: first, I was driven into accepting it by personal and organi-zational reasons; second, my view is atypical, even idiosyncratic; and third, it served me well.

It was during the presidency of Lyndon Johnson that I first began assuming positions of responsibility in Citibank. As a literate, media-consuming citizen, I noticed and was impressed, in a negative way, by how he felt he had to respond to virtually all press comments. (This approach was not his alone; each of our three most recent presidents has enunciated, in his own way, a political position of "let no item go unanswered" as part of his overall political strategy.) I noticed that by responding to everything in the media, one becomes the slave of the media, which in effect own the agenda. I had seen similar dispositions among businessmen. Since I was—or should have been—knowledgeable about my own company, I wondered why I should get embroiled in secondary interpretations of what was going on within it. I concluded I would not read or otherwise pay attention to media coverage of the bank. In retrospect, this decision was the right one for me, even though it meant renouncing two human temptations: to enjoy the egotism excited by flattery and to enjoy the righteous outrage excited by others' errors and insults.

I observed one exception to my general rule. I knew that what others read might be important, so I commissioned one of my senior executives to keep an ear to the ground with respect to the media and tell me what he believed I should know. With regard to nonbank news, I was and am an avid reader of the press; however, I am a skeptical reader, assuming always that there is a gap between what I read and what a full account of things would be. (Incidentally, these effects have been only exaggerated by the growth of e-mail and other Internet sources. People can write anything in them. Because this informa-tion is essentially free and uncontrollable, it surprises me that people accept so much of it as accurate and responsible, even though there are many reasons to believe otherwise.)

There was one unanticipated side effect of my policy of avoidance. Those reporters who had criticized the bank or me were impressed that I did not react negatively to them. It was easy for me not to react, because in most cases I had not read what they had written.

Over the decades, I have noticed another trend. As a rule, the media pay attention to the large, the prestigious, and the powerful because they make bet-ter news than the small and less visible. As a result, large organizations and their members are greatly impacted by media reports. As a further result, they have taken to using the media to communicate with the world. This pushes the management of enterprises, always tough and demanding in any case, in the direction of becoming a spectator sport. It has produced the cult of the CEO (CEO used to be only an acronym found in company by-laws), parallel to the cult of personality in the electoral and political worlds. This has led many business leaders to develop a public presence, to curry public favor, and to respond to real and imagined criticisms by real and imagined publics. Even silence is sometimes interpreted as some disposition on the part of "the public." Inevitable as all these effects might be in both business and politics, they are, as often as not, a distraction for those whose job it is to get something done for organizations.

I should not push these points too far. There are times when you are prominently in the news and must talk with the media or else be seriously threatened or damaged by media reports. In such cases, I have always found it important to establish and use alternative channels for communication. For example, during our real estate crisis of 1991–92, I began the practice of writing frank and detailed letters to the board each month. We also designated a small number of board members with whom I kept in daily contact. Also within our organizational purview, I communicated monthly in two-day weekend meetings with our senior team and issued quarterly tapes to all the staff around the world. I also wrote quarterly letters to about fifteen hundred of our key customers.

As for other constituencies, we scheduled monthly meetings with the senior regulators (the Federal Deposit Insurance Corporation, the Comptroller of the Currency, and the Federal Reserve) to keep them up to date. I kept in touch with other important constituencies as well, for example, the chairman of the Morgan bank in New York, the Swiss Banking Corporation in Zurich, the Bank of Tokyo, and the Governor of the Bank of England. All these were important correctives to press accounts as well as rumors that might be circulating about our bank. I also sought out "nonpress" outside views. I arranged special meetings with one of our bankers, Morgan Stanley, which managed various capital issues. I met quarterly with three of its top people for a day of talk followed by dinner. In these meetings, they informed me about what the market was thinking and worrying about, and I responded with information about what we were doing; we tried to hammer out an agreement on how we should both go forward. It was important to regard these contacts as more than simple correctives to misinformation; I tried always to give other parties both the good and the bad news and, as much as possible, to receive both kinds as well.

In the end, in spite of my personal philosophy about reading in the media, and despite all the efforts I made to develop and use other kinds of communications, I admit that I could never beat the media. The typical Citibanker, no matter what his or her position, virtually always formed his or her sense of reality from newspaper, Internet, or TV accounts of a particular event and, by extension, based much of his or her sense of reality on them.

Two final, general points relating to the social science of information: First, as we notice in many places in this volume, social scientists have often treated decision-makers either as possessing full, accurate, and correct knowledge (the rationality model) or as facing situations of deficit where information is wrong, incomplete, or uncertain. As the information revolution in all its facets has evolved, both representations seem to be limited. The current situation that often faces decision-makers, citizens, and consumers alike is not lack of knowledge, but too much knowledge of unknown quality and reliability. The corresponding challenges are deciding what is relevant, searching selectively to find it, and eliminating that which is clutter.

Second, and related, it seems important to extract one insight from those social scientists who insist that knowledge is socially constructed by groups in line with their respective circumstances and interests. We do not have in mind the negative implications that such representations of reality are arbitrary or wrong; and we do not accept the radical extensions of this perspective toward relativistic and even nihilistic rejections of truth, reality, and science. What is true is that the increasing complexity of social structure, the increasing diversity of social groups, and the ability to make information available have produced an array of bewildering and competing claims about what is real, important, and relevant. The problem, then, is *not* the availability of knowledge and its informing perspectives, but rather how to make discriminations in the face of overavailability of and competition among these and other versions of reality. These new circumstances reduce the transaction costs of securing knowledge, but multiply the processing costs of selecting and evaluating it.

—*John S. Reed*

Among the most dramatic historical memories are cultural traumas—those shocking and tragic historical events that remain as scars on the historical tissue of societies that are compelled to remember them. Dramatic examples are the Reign of Terror in the French Revolution, the American Civil War, the Holocaust in Nazi Germany, many other massacres and episodes of ethnic cleansing and genocide, and September 11, 2001. Over time these historical memories manifest all the dynamics just mentioned, plus a special compulsion expressing both the impulses to *celebrate* and commemorate them as historic ("Remember Pearl Harbor"; "Remember the Alamo") and to *forget* them (both processes are generated, perhaps, by collective shame or guilt). Erecting monuments and celebrating anniversaries are important parts of the process; in more extreme cases, political leaders attempt actively to manipulate memory by destroying monuments and replacing them with new ones (as was done with public memorials to Stalin in post-Soviet Russia). In general, the memories of cultural traumas *and* cultural glories work their way into cultural legends, and are important ingredients of collective identities (Alexander, Eyerman, Giesen, Smelser, et al., 2004). Battles over the ownership and control of the meaning of cultural traumas show a special intensity and bitterness, as demonstrated by the struggles between regretters (mainly pacifist groups) and celebrators (mainly veterans' groups) of the *Enola Gay* and the dropping of the first atomic bomb on Hiroshima.

At all levels, then, memory and remembering turn out to be a process rather than an identifiable thing. They are rooted in the cognitive, emotional, interpersonal, and social dynamics that pervade personality and society. The cumulative impact of research on these subjects has been to instill a sense of contingency and skepticism in our thinking about memory as photographic or accurate mental reproduction. While generating humility, however, these insights also instill a sense of realism about the powers and limitations of memory, and increase our capacity *not* to err in evaluating memory as an ingredient in people's adaptive repertoire.

THE HEURISTICS-AND-BIAS REVOLUTION

Many processes already discussed—categorization, stereotypes, attributions, evoking memories—can be described as *heuristics,* broadly defined: simplified mental shortcuts that provide rules of thumb for recognizing meaningful aspects of the environment and offering formulae for coping with and mastering them. In recent decades, a more targeted line of research has given more special meaning to the term. We refer to research often identified with the publication of a seminal work by Tversky and Kahneman (1974) called "Judgment under Uncertainty: Heuristics and Biases" and later consolidated in a book with the same title (Kahneman, Slovic, and Tversky, 1982). This work has continued in the fields of behavioral economics and social psychology; it has also virtually commandeered the term *heuristics* for itself, despite the wider reference of the term. It has been sufficiently revolutionary to earn a Nobel Prize in Economics for Kahneman (Tversky had died before the award was made, or it surely would have been awarded jointly). The major characteristics of this research are as follows:

- Knowledge about heuristics is based mainly, but not exclusively, on experimentation.
- It focuses on the knowledge (rules of thumb) mobilized for problem-solving and decision-making.
- The emphasis on cognitive representations as directly influencing behavior is consistent with other developments in cognitive psychology, especially categorizing and stereotyping, and with the insights of bounded rationality and "satisficing" (Simon, 1947) in administrative science, with its stress on

the "mind as computer with limited capacity" (Gilovich and Griffin, 2002; see below, pp. 157–58).

- It gives a special place to uncertainty and risk (threat of loss) as reasons to rely on heuristic thinking.
- It has been driven by both a positive and a negative polemic. The first is a scientific desire to discover and establish patterns of thinking that inform decisions; the second is a desire to dispute the results expected from traditions of rational thinking and decision-making (namely, rational choice theory, game theory, probabilistic statistics, and other rationality-dominated approaches).
- As the decisive addition, "and bias," connotes, most research findings suggest that the rules of thumb observed constitute erroneous deviations from the results expected from rationality traditions, and thus constitute biases away from solutions expected from them. The debate over the validity of the "and bias" assumption and the efficiency and effectiveness of heuristic thinking has appeared in the heuristics literature itself, as in, for example, Gigerenzer and Todd's (1999) emphasis on "fast and frugal" heuristics that "make us smart" (see also Gigerenzer, Dzerlinski, and Martignon, 2002).

An ironic point arises from the last observation. One of the original three heuristics identified by Tversky and Kahneman—and one of the most enduring—is "anchoring and adjustment," already mentioned in connection with social comparisons and relative deprivation. Its essence is that setting an initial standard, even a nonsensical or random one, is a powerful framing device, and establishes the terms for estimates that experimenters ask subjects to make about when an event occurred, the value of an object or commodity, or imagined outcomes of events. Anchoring and adjustment has been widely observed empirically. Secondary school teachers follow students' past experience as anchors that guide them in subsequent grading (Caverni and Péris, 1990). Jurors in mock juries award plaintiffs higher compensation based on how much the plaintiffs originally ask for, even though plaintiffs can demand any amount they wish (Chapman and Bornstein, 1996). Both real estate agents and naïve amateurs base their estimates of house value on sellers' initial asking prices, even when they are told that those prices should not be taken into account because homeowners are free to set any price they want (Northcraft and Neale, 1987). Retailers routinely play anchoring-and-adjustment tricks in announcing, "Was $5.99, now $3.99—one-third off!" A recent instance is observable in the rapid fluctuation of gasoline prices at the pump. Before prices rose precipitously to more than four dollars per gallon in 2008, three dollars per gallon was regarded as outrageous. After the high peak, however, when prices eased back to around three dollars, that price seemed less objectionable. The standard of four dollars per gallon provided the anchor for this reaction.

The irony is that the entire enterprise of heuristics-and-bias research can be regarded as an illustration of the anchoring-and-adjustment principle. That is to say, the objects of negative polemic—normative rationality and statistical theory—have been the anchor points to which behavioral research is oriented. Furthermore, if the results were *not* held to these standards but, rather, were examined by themselves, it would more be difficult to label them as biased. It is in relation to these standards that bias is defined and gives the phrase "and bias" most of its force. Without such a target, the results might be more simply defined as cognitive shortcuts, like many other phenomena identified in psychological research.

This observation raises a more general one, elaborated in chapter 10, on the dynamics of research. Much research that generates excitement inside and outside the academy emanates both light and heat. Much of the light derives from the fact that discoveries are new and therefore "enlightening." That is a principal aim of science, to discover new knowledge and establish it according to methodological standards. Much of the heat is generated by its negative agenda—its "giant-killing" significance—namely, displacing or criticizing received knowledge that many academics value and in which they have invested themselves. Behavioral economists in particular have consistently identified the "giant" as rational thinking, which they are bringing down. Gilovich and Savitsky (1996) make the following assessment: "The negative agenda [of heuristics-and-bias research] appears to have garnered more attention and motivated more subsequent research—both hostile and congenial to Kahneman and Tversky's original ideas—than the positive. This may be because accusations of irrationality raise the ire of some scholars and challenge the theoretical foundations of much work in the social sciences" (35).

We do not fully understand why this negative aspect should be such a source of fascination, passion, and preoccupation, but it is itself a salient, nonrational principle in the dynamics of knowledge creation and knowledge displacement. To observe this irony is not, however, to dismiss the importance of heuristics theory and its contribution to both cognitive psychology and the study of economic behavior.

The other two initially identified heuristics are the availability heuristic and the representativeness heuristic. The former is relatively simple: When people are asked to estimate the likelihood of a certain event, their judgment is influenced by how readily it comes to mind or how easy it is to recall. In one experiment, people were asked if words beginning with the letter *K* were more common than words with *K* as their third letter. They voted in favor of the former (even though there are really twice as many words with *K* as the third letter), simply because it is easier to think of words with *K* as the beginning letter (Tversky and Kahneman, 1973). A less trivial example is the tendency of people to overrate plane crashes as a cause of fatalities because accounts of these are dramatic and easier to recall than other causes of death (Kahneman and Tversky, 1986). When people are asked to list companies in the Fortune 500, popular consumer names (Pepsi, General Mills, and Google) are overrepresented in their estimates. The frequency of multiple divorces among Hollywood movie stars is also typically overestimated. Availability arises because certain things are more familiar to us than others, because they may have made a striking impression, or because it is too much trouble to seek beyond the familiar. Reporting in the media and gossiping also contribute to availability. Whatever the causes, the availability heuristic distorts true probabilities of events and situations.

The heuristic of representativeness also appears to be central to everyday thinking. When a person is asked to assign an object or person to a category, he or she does so on the basis of its similarity to other instances that resemble the object or person in question. For this reason, this heuristic is also called the similarity principle. Such judgments are convenient, but are also at odds with formal statistical bases for assigning probability. In a now-classic experiment (ibid.), subjects were presented with an imaginary person named Linda, described as age thirty-one, single, outspoken, and very bright, with a degree in philosophy and with deep concerns about issues of social justice and discrimination. Then they were asked to assign her to one of several listed categories. Among these were "bank teller" and "bank teller and is active in the feminist movement." In responding, more than 85 percent thought that it was more likely that Linda was a bank teller and a feminist than that she was simply a bank teller, even though "feminist bank tellers" is a subset of bank tellers in general. Kahneman and Tversky concluded that people seem to assign others to groups based on what they know about a group rather than the actual number in the group.

The early work on heuristics and bias created an immediate stir and set off a cascade of research in the following decades. Without attempting to include all the results, we list a number of additional heuristics:

- One line of work is prospect theory, which says that people are more willing to take risks in situations with the prospect of gain than in those with the prospect of loss, even when the probabilities in each case are the same. The factor of risk aversion leads people away from making decisions on the basis of probability—another example of bias away from rationally based decisions. A related discovery is the endowment effect. If an individual acquires a certain object (a souvenir, a bottle of fine wine, a gift from a loved one) and that object takes on sentimental value, he or she endows it with more value than it has in the market and becomes reluctant to part with it.
- Empirical research has also uncovered a heuristic referred to as "stopping rules," or rules of thumb that people adopt to set limits on searching. An

example is "I will look for this dress in five different shops, and if I don't find it by then, I'll quit looking." This is similar to a principle of transaction costs in the new institutional economics—when searching and locating reach a point where the cost of searching is greater than the prospective gain, people quit searching. The difference is that transaction cost analysis lends itself to rational, even mathematical representations, whereas the idea of stopping rules stresses the arbitrary (nonrational) character of the rules (Moon and Martin, 1990).

- An example already mentioned (chapter 1) is sunk costs, by virtue of which sums already invested in a project come to be overestimated (in relation to the results of the logic of optimization). The heuristic can be stated as "I'm already in this far; I may as well go all the way" or "In for a penny, in for a pound" (Arkes and Blumer, 1985), even though the loss incurred by sticking with sunk funds may be greater than that of scrapping the earlier commitment.
- Other heuristics are self-serving and self-congratulatory. Among these are the hindsight bias—"I knew it would come out that way"—and the overconfidence bias in one's own judgments and predictions, both of which resist correction by "de-biasing" techniques (Fischoff, 2002). Another is the planning fallacy, or believing that one can meet set deadlines despite past evidence to the contrary (Buehler, Griffin, and Ross, 2002).
- Other heuristics have been grouped under the heading of the affect heuristic (Slovic, Finucane, Peters, and MacGregor, 2002). This means basing decisions and actions on feelings alone (Zajonc, 1980). Some have describe a related phenomenon of "risk as feelings," i.e., a tendency to base reactions to risk on feelings of dread, worry, or anxiety rather than on any cognitive evaluations (Loewenstein, Weber, Hsee, and Welch, 2001). That people are frequently led astray by acting on their emotions is what justifies the "bias" judgment, though such feelings are sometimes ennobled as producing better solutions than cool and dispassionate reflections do—"I felt it in my guts."
- Behavioral economists have also uncovered empirical situations that deviate from standard economic expectations—for example, taxi drivers who do not maximize fares but quit work after they have earned a daily amount that is regarded as enough (Camerer, Babcock, Loewenstein, and Thaler, 2004). They have also analyzed overreactions and other deviations from expected utility analysis (Werner, De Bondt, and Thaler, 2002), and have joined others, including those of a psychoanalytic stripe (Tuckett, 2011), who have described unconscious fantasies (e.g., dreams of omnipotence) that operate irrationally in stock markets.
- A generic feature of many heuristics is "framing," or producing different estimation and decision results according to wording that loads a situation

and affects judgments (see Kahneman and Tversky, 1986). This was observed in the differences between *gain* and *risk* wordings, which affect choosing different options. Another illustration, given above, shows the power of the words *contact, hit,* and *smash* to influence estimates of the speed of cars involved in accidents. Finally, a long tradition of assessing the impact of different wordings of survey questions in eliciting agreement or disagreement also demonstrates the role of framing in judgment.

These are some examples of the heuristics that have accumulated in the work of behavioral economists and social psychologists. The movement has made heuristic- and-bias hunting something of an enthusiastic game. Critics argue that heuristics researchers choose trivial problems ("parlor games"); that heuristics research often involves circular reasoning (producing a finding and naming it a bias); and that many of its findings, resting on "artificial" experimental results, cannot be applied in nonexperimental situations.

In the end, however, heuristics research has produced a wealth of findings that constitutes a revolutionary intellectual movement. Many of its contributions are negative in the sense that they chip away at the rational foundations of behavior, but some insights from behavioral economics have also been advocated as sensible solutions to issues such as demands based on seniority and the effect of incentives (Frank and Hutchens, 2004; Gneezy and Rustichini, 2004). Some findings from behavioral economics have been developed into formal mathematical models (Rabin, 2004). A culmination has been an explicit formulation of a schema of "two systems of reasoning" (Sloman, 2002). On one side is rule-based reasoning, based on deliberation, explanation, formal analysis, and the rules of rationality; on the other there is associative reasoning, based on fantasy, creative imagination, visual representations, and mental shortcuts. The distinction revives long-standing philosophical distinctions between reason and intuition, and echoes the psychoanalytic distinction between primary and secondary mental processes.

What does all this imply for economic analysis, especially the postulates of maximization and rational choice? For decades these foundations have been attacked by economic anthropologists, economic sociologists, and political scientists. The former have assailed them as ethnocentric western inventions that do not apply to cultures in which economic behavior is embedded in kinship, clanship, and stratification; in fact, they do not even apply well to the western market societies in which they were invented. Economic sociologists have questioned the individualistic-atomistic assumptions of economics (that actors do not influence one another) and have demonstrated that economic behavior is embedded in institutional settings and interpersonal influences (Granovetter, 1974). In the mid-1990s, Green and Shapiro (1994) issued a trumpet blast on the "pathologies of rational choice analysis" as an approach to political behavior. A year later, a major symposium mobilized a panoply of favorable and unfavorable assessments of rational choice analysis in political science (Friedman, 1995). More popular, often savage critiques have also appeared (Ariely, 2008). None of these, however, has decisively undermined the psychological assumptions of formal economics. Critiques from behavioral economics and cognitive psychology attack the psychological underpinnings of rational calculation; behavioral economics also claims superiority because it is empirical ("behavioral"), in contrast to the deductive and normative emphases of rational choice theory. Yet behavioral economics has been more readily assimilated into economic analysis and into the discipline's infrastructure (many behavioral economists are appointed in departments of economics and business schools). Critiques from economic anthropology, economic sociology, and political science, by contrast, remain more remote in their influence.

The net effect of all these lines of inquiry has been to discredit the postulate of rationality in both its *psychological* assumptions regarding the fixity of tastes, assumptions of maximization of utility, consistency of preferences, and the absence of impulsivity, error, incomplete information and knowledge, and in its *social* assumptions regarding the independence of actors from one another and the "givenness" of institutions and culture. Recognition of this prompted Hastie to ask: "Will the field [of economics] ever escape the oppressive yoke of normative 'rational' models?" (1991: 138). (In a similar vein, we might ask why rational choice analysis has been extended into political science, law ["law and economics"], and management science, and to a lesser degree into sociology and anthropology.)

We cannot answer Hastie's question fully, but we venture the following lines of thinking:

- Economics has proved adaptive in encompassing heterodoxy, for example, imperfect competition and situations of less than complete knowledge, uncertainty, and risk. The appearance of new approaches such as agency theory, institutional economics, and behavioral economics itself also illustrates this adaptability. In fact, the nibblers-away and the heterodox are well represented in the ranks of Nobel Prize winners in economics (e.g., Kenneth Arrow, Herbert Simon, Daniel Kahneman, George Akerlof, Douglass North, and Oliver Williamson). Such developments have diminished the theoretical unity of economics and moved it toward the other social sciences with respect to paradigmatic diversity. At the same time, a parade of counterassertions continues—arguments that economics is more nearly a science than the other fields, that it has more theoretical unity, that rational choice is still viable, and that competitive market models are the most efficient guides to policy. This complex adaptive strategy resembles religious traditions that continuously adapt to worldly changes but simultaneously assert a continuity of faith (Smelser, 1995).

- Economists retain a strong representation in the worlds of economic policy and advice (e.g., the Council of Economic Advisors), and economists occupy a more central place in the political establishment than any other field except law. Their knowledge and expertise, even when wrong, are the most used and considered most usable in policy arenas. And while economists differ frequently on policies, a consistent general message is the advocacy of market solutions (based on individual choice) to policy problems—for example, in the areas of regulation/deregulation and energy conservation—which are promoted as being more efficient than administrative or political solutions (see below, pp. 213–14).
- Traditional assumptions of free, rational choice still resonate with long-standing American cultural traditions of individualism, freedom, and mastery of the world (see below, pp. 150–53), not to mention the ideology of capitalism as an economic system. All these constitute abiding sources of legitimacy for the discipline of economics and the messages it conveys.

THE IDEA OF MULTIPLE RATIONALITIES

Among the many critiques of economic analysis that have appeared over the decades, we now recall one made in the early 1940s by Talcott Parsons, a theoretical giant of midcentury sociology (Parsons 1954a [1939], 1954b [1940]). He criticized traditional economic theory for representing rationality and self-interest as a *psychology,* as a driving force in *individuals.* Instead, he treated capitalist markets and economic motivation as embedded in an *institutional system.* In a word, Parsons posited a "sociology of selfishness," a combination of permissiveness and constraints on individual self-seeking. This means that self-interest is part of a system of rules and expectations that mandate depersonalization, calculation, and self-interest in business roles. Included among these is the idea that if a businessman does not live up to them, he risks experiencing negative sanctions such as diminished profit or even bankruptcy. Parsons contrasted the business role with that of the professions (such as medicine, law, and academia), which resemble the business role in many respects (for example, achievement orientation), but in which other norms of service and fiduciary obligation (Parsons called them collectivity-oriented norms) limit the play of self-interest. From the standpoint of individual psychology, professionals can be every bit as selfish as businessmen, but they are embedded in an institutionalized nexus that restricts self-interest. We might also observe that these professional roles have their own institutionalized rationalities, which overlap with business roles but also differ with respect to socially embedded norms.

Parsons's critique resonated with arguments made by economic anthropologists about the social embeddedness of economic action (Polanyi, Arensberg, and Pearson, 1957), but it had little impact on the status of rationality in economic theory. It is worth remarking, however, that more than fifty years later, behavioral economists, coming from a different critical direction, activate the same idea—*normative* models—to characterize rational economic action. They argue that such models are idealized standards for economic behavior and institutions, but do not describe the actual *behavior* of economic actors, which embody different—mainly heuristic—psychological processes than calculation and maximization.

Parsons's insights also echo a distinction made by Weber (1968) between formal rationality and communal (also called substantive) rationality, two of Weber's "ideal types." Formal rationality resembles economic rationality in that it stresses the autonomy of the enterprise, calculability on the basis of utility, and freedom from noneconomic considerations. The rationality of markets is based on market freedom and minimizing kinship, status privileges, military needs, and community welfare in determining the distribution of resources and products (vol. 1: 73).

Social organizations based on communal rationality operate under contrasting normative constraints. Communal memberships rest on "various types of affectual, emotional, or traditional bases" (vol. 1: 41), as in families, religious brotherhoods, erotic relationships, or relations among friends. Members in communal units have mutual responsibility for one another's welfare. Membership is usually compulsory; for example, an individual cannot freely choose his or her parents. The principle for distributing resources is substantive rationality, or the principle of common welfare among members. This principle "may consider the 'purely formal' rationality of calculation in money terms as of quite secondary importance or even as fundamentally inimical to their respective ultimate ends" (vol. 1: 86). To choose a homey example of nonmixability, it would scarcely do for a man courting a woman to point out that he has recently invested $150 in taking her out to two dinners, and to ask what sexual value he deserves in return. To mix the logics of economic calculation and love is unacceptable in this instance. Tetlock (2002) has discussed the idea of taboos on tradeoffs between the sacred and the profane; they do not mix. The Durkheimian tradition (Durkheim, 1965 [1912]) holds that these two worlds are mutually exclusive.

Extending the insights of Parsons and Weber, we might argue that a differentiated society is made up of a *multiplicity* of institutions (economic, military, political, medical, communal), and a corresponding multiplicity of concerns (public safety, social justice, environmental protection) as they are embedded in legislation, institutions, and social movements. Each of these nodes of differentiation develops a distinctive "rationality"—value preferences, normative rules, desired modes of behavior, desired policies, desired outcomes—and this guides and justifies behavior in these partially separated spheres. Sometimes the dictates of one rationality are consonant with others; more often they point in different directions and act as restraints. They are the source of efforts in societies to contain conflicts, seek resolutions, and choose among alternatives. Concrete policies and solutions are best characterized not as *maximizing* any one of these rationalities, but rather as fashioning *compromises* among several of them. Most economically relevant decisions—and the behavior that flows from them—in contemporary society are not the product of a single type of calculation; they are complicated compromises that incorporate criteria arising from the exigencies of economic rationality, social justice, environmental protection, political pressures from relevant interest groups, and other considerations. It is possible to represent some of the competing criteria—for example, environmental protection—simply as economic "costs." More generally, however, they constitute fundamental and often conflicting forces and should be incorporated systematically into models of economic and social processes. At the level of the individual actor, including the decision-maker and policy-maker, the actor is best regarded not as a *maximizer* of any single rationality, but rather as one who is continually engaged in a *balancing act* among many of them, struggling to arrive at satisfactory decisions and lines of action that, when considered according to the standards of a single rationality, are always inadequate. This formulation is more far-reaching than Simon's idea of "satisficing," which is mainly a motivational/cognitive reformulation of the idea of maximizing (see below, pp. 157–58).

EMOTION, COGNITION, AND BEHAVIOR

The study of emotions has experienced a surge in the past several decades, though it is not as heralded as developments in cognitive psychology. That surge has diminished the inherited equation of emotions with passions and appetites, and above all the assumption that they disrupt deliberative, rational thought. Emotional reactions have come to be regarded as intertwined with, not as separate from, cognitive and judgmental processes. We present several lines of research to supplement these general points.

Before doing so, we enter a methodological caution. Many of the results reported below are from experimental studies in which emotions are aroused by playing happy or sad music, by telling happy or sad stories, or by otherwise stimulating experimental subjects. To stimulate emotions in experimental settings is a methodologically ticklish operation. It is difficult to know whether such techniques really stimulate emotions and, if so, whether the emotions stimulated are the intended ones. Furthermore, subjects are likely to experience these emotions in a more tepid form than in real life. Despite all that is done to counteract the unreality or artificiality of experiments, that feeling persists and affects subjects' experience. To make this point is to remind ourselves of the issue of external validity (see chapter 8) in the experimental study of emotions.

Emotions are generally regarded as being experienced quickly (though the idea of moods as emotions suggests longer duration), prior to higher-order cognitive assessments, and often unconsciously; they manifest themselves in facial and bodily expressions and by physiological markers (e.g., trembling); they are linked with specific action tendencies (fear with flight; anger with fight). Yet they are also closely linked with other mental and behavioral processes. Above all, experiencing affects provides information (Clore, Casper, and Garvin, 2001) about the personal relevance of the stimuli that evoke the affects. Furthermore, an integral part of experiencing emotions is appraising them—what they mean to the individual, whether they are harmful or beneficial, and what kinds of coping they call for (Lazarus, 1991). In a word, affects are embedded in the whole adaptation-in-environment process, not foreign to it. As noted above, emotional reactions can be treated as an adaptive heuristic along with other, primarily cognitive mechanisms.

More particularly, emotions have been discovered to play a determinative role in many mental and social processes. Some illustrations:

- Experiencing positive moods apparently is associated with relying on stereotypes in thinking, whereas negative moods are associated with the use of analytic thinking and more systematic evaluation of information (Fiedler, 2001), on the general principle that when we experience difficulties, we are driven to think more than when we are content.
- Experiencing emotions directs us to perceptions of objects and events that are relevant to those feelings (Niedenthal and Setterlund, 1994).
- Emotional arousal affects attention. Experiencing fear apparently heightens vigilance to potentially threatening cues (Anderson and Phelps, 2001).
- Emotional arousal facilitates memory. We tend to remember events that are more salient emotionally, and to remember shocking events better than mild ones (Berntsen, 2002). These findings apparently are counter to psychoanalytic theories of repressing unpleasant materials. We are better at remembering events that match our current mood (Erk, Kiefer, Grothe, Wunderlich, et al., 2003). Free association in the psychoanalytic setting often follows affect in the sense that otherwise incomparable thoughts are linked by common emotional reactions to them.
- Experiencing emotions affects decision behavior. People who experience fear and anticipated regret gamble less. More generally, positive moods are associated with people's willingness to take risks (Kuvaas and Kaufmann, 2004). When disgust is stimulated, this reduces what people are willing to pay for a commodity (possibly out of fear of contamination), whereas people in whom sadness is induced are willing to pay more (possibly out of a desire to cheer themselves up) (Lerner, Small, and Loewenstein, 2004).

- Emotions are the currency of social interaction, especially in attachment to others (love and friendship), in social distancing, in power relations involving subordination to authority, and in situations in which feelings of relative deprivation are generated. In fact, emotions can be regarded as both a language and a currency through which people communicate with one another. They signal goals and meanings, which in turn excite emotional responses in others. The significance of emotions in economic behavior and interactions is gaining greater appreciation (Rick and Loewenstein, 2008; Berezin, 2005).
- The social dimension is important in another sense. Emotional expression is potentially disruptive and productive of conflict. As a result, emotional expressions are typically regulated by norms that indicate if and how emotions are to be expressed or suppressed in different situations, which emotions are to be expressed, and how reactions to others' emotional expression are to be manifested. The normative structure of "good manners" is largely a set of rules regarding the whens, wheres, and hows of emotional expression and inhibition. Students of impression management and conversation analysts track how interaction is repaired when it goes or threatens to go off track; a significant part of this repair involves the monitoring of emotional expressions. All these concerns are part of the subfield of the sociology of emotion, a small but growing enterprise.
- A subfield of the sociology of emotion is "emotions in organizations." As the name implies, investigators focus on the dynamics of emotional expression in organizations and trace and assess their impact. Relevant aspects are the interplay of group emotions in the workplace; nostalgia for a past golden age of an organization; play, teasing, flirtation, and harassment; sentimental storytelling; the dynamics of narcissism and narcissistic wounds; and the organizational consequences of group loyalties and antagonisms (for a sample of work, see Ashkanasy, Zerbe, and Härtel, 2005).
- Emotions play a salient role in the development of trust (itself a complex emotional disposition) and the role of trust in negotiating situations. Stereotypes of different kinds of negotiators—poker face, happy face, and rant 'n' rave—imply that the manipulation of emotions is a part of negotiating behavior (Thompson, Medvec, Seiden, and Kopelman, 2001). More generally, if negotiators experience positive affects, this apparently increases trust and the willingness to make concessions; experiencing negative affects generates the opposite. Trust, once established, diminishes negotiators' rigidity and increases the probability of positive outcomes. Third parties—for example, tough-minded attorneys who are present in a negotiating process—can increase distrust between constituencies whom negotiators represent. Negotiators sometimes form a common culture and may trust one another

across the table but cannot afford to do so openly because of pressures from militant constituencies (Kramer and Carnevale, 2001).

Such are some of the ways that emotions enter the fabric of social life. Like the other recent traditions of research reviewed, this line underscores the seamlessness and continuous interaction among the ingredients of psychological and social life. We will turn explicitly to interpersonal influence and group processes in the chapters on personal and group ties (chapter 4) and decision-making (chapter 5).

CONCLUSION
SOME REFLECTIONS ON USABILITY

We conclude by noting that most messages about usability deriving from this chapter are general and indirect. As a result, we warn—as we do in the book as a whole—that we cannot and do not wish to generate a user's manual with directly applicable principles and techniques, fail-safe approaches, specific tips, or silver bullets. It is an axiom that decision-making, problem-solving, and policy-making involve synthesizing many kinds and levels of knowledge of varying value and usefulness. The rationale for any decision or organizational action is never complete, and all decisions leave a residue of uncertainty, contingency, and second thoughts in their wake. In a word, in a chapter in which heuristics and other mental shortcuts assume a large role, we are not in the position to offer any fast and frugal—to say nothing of foolproof—heuristics as guides to action.

That being said, we may make a few more positive points. At the beginning we observed that the cumulative result of recent theoretical and empirical thinking in the behavioral and social sciences is to delineate a view of human actors as fundamentally *nonrational*—that is to say, simultaneously struggling for adaptive mastery of the world and coping to the best of one's ability, but proceeding with limited roadmaps and compasses. Purposeful activity usually produces neither blacks nor whites, only grays. Solutions seldom produce final results, and almost inevitably produce new problems to be confronted, also imperfectly. Yet this global insight is valuable for decision-makers, who in their struggles with uncertain environments and imperfect tools are forever tempted toward either undue optimism (resolving uncertainty by means of neat solutions based on certain knowledge) or undue pessimism (believing that one is the passive victim of fates that cannot be avoided or controlled). The message that emerges is that tolerance of ambiguity is an asset for decision-makers, problem-solvers, and policy-makers.

From the diversity of lines of inquiry traced in this chapter, we can be more specific on certain points:

- Of all the heuristics discussed, one set is especially significant for decision-makers and demands special vigilance: the self-congratulatory, self-enhancing, and self-promoting heuristics. Among these are hindsight bias, the overconfidence bias, the planning bias, and the "bias" that one is superior or preferable because of membership in a special group. The reasons we mention these are that they do indeed distort; they are among the more intractable sources of bias; they resist criticism from others; when the holders of such biases are criticized, this generates irritation, defensiveness, and perhaps revenge; and they motivate the holders of those biases unduly to seek approval of themselves and their opinions—motivations that are mainly self-referential and not attuned to the realities of the decision-making environment.

- Decisions made and actions taken under conditions of extreme uncertainty, urgency, or crisis are a special point of vulnerability. Under these conditions, hurried decisions based on automatic and heuristic-burdened responses are frequently made. We make this point in full knowledge that many decisions must be made under dire circumstances, and we dedicate a section of the chapter on decision-making to the special topic of naturalistic decision-making under extreme conditions (see chapter 5). At this point, however, we observe that it is valuable for organizations to put in place mechanisms that activate flashing amber lights—for example, institutionalizing informal groups dedicated to identifying tripwires and pitfalls; anticipating potential surprises, conflicts, and crises that might be on the horizon; and scheduling meetings of trusted groups when crises arise, in order to give at least a brief critical review of the reasons for urgency and to raise questions about whether alternative lines of action are available.

- Some insights relating to categorization, prejudice, and discrimination provide guidance in understanding and dealing with group conflict in organizations. We noted that diversification of workplaces and in other organizations has by now become a reality; the future will bring more of the same. We also noted that much discourse about diversity is laden with oversimplifications, naïve hopes, conflict, and polarization. The lesson to be learned is that prejudices, conscious and unconscious discriminatory behavior, exclusion, and overt and covert bullying are constant features of the organizational landscape, and do not lend themselves to full solutions. They are ever-present processes subject to lulls and spurts, but they never disappear; categorical issues such as racial tension or harassment may seem to become latent only to reappear in unexpected and sometimes more subtle ways as the fortunes of organizations change. To appreciate the recurring and sometimes intractable features of group attitudes and group conflict both heightens consciousness about them and permits more realistic approaches to them.

· More generally, the insights regarding categorization, distortions of information in transmission (such as rumor), and the consolidation and evolution of collective memory are especially valuable in understanding and defusing conflict in the workplace and in bargaining situations. Brittleness and polarization of attitudes are most likely to arise in situations of conflict. It is also in these situations that active intervention and communication is most needed to minimize such effects.

We conclude that familiarity with the principles of perception, cognition, and bias is a key ingredient of the virtues of calmness, humility, sensibility, and deliberation in the heat of organizational battle.

3

Sanctions in Organizational and Social Life

The play of sanctions—devices to influence behavior by rewarding or punishing—is pervasive in social life. We praise, cajole, withhold love, and sometimes coerce when rewarding and punishing our children. Sanctions are the cement of informal social relationships, as we see in the flow of influence and power in families, friendships, and small groups. They are the lubricants of organizations, as evidenced in the interplay among financial rewards and punishments, the exercise of authority, and informal processes of influence and resistance. Monetary sanctions are the lifeblood of markets and finance, and political sanctions are among the mechanisms for sustaining social institutions and maintaining social control. Legal systems live by sanctions, their engines for enforcement. As more or less socialized individuals, we experience the effects of external pressures as well as internal shame, embarrassment, and guilt—residues derived from past learning of rights and wrongs. We react against sanctions by ignoring or defying them. The power of sanctions is acknowledged in adages: "Money talks," "Honor among thieves," and "It's who you know, not what you know, that counts."

The working of sanctions is thus essential to understanding all social life, and knowledge of how they work is clearly usable for decision-makers, policy-makers, and those addressing social problems. Pervasiveness, however, does not mean simplicity, and one of our goals is to tease out some subtleties in the interplay of sanctions. Furthermore, sanctions, while widely noticed and incorporated into many social-science disciplines, do not themselves constitute a distinguishable subfield. Hence our illustrations will range widely in subject matter and scope.

Initially, we remind ourselves that sanctions typically are *not* isolated or autonomous forces, but always are nested in and justified by larger contexts. For example, different sanctions are not completely interchangeable with one another. It is almost universally regarded as illegitimate to gain sexual favors through physical coercion. Except for the sometimes illegal, sometimes institutionalized practice of prostitution, it is also generally regarded as unacceptable to offer money to gain such favors. To do so through persuasion and charm, however, is more acceptable. As family norms have changed, physical coercion has become less acceptable as a way to discipline children. Under the influence of the Reformation, it became a wrong to offer money to the church to gain indulgence or salvation. When corruption comes to be regarded as criminal or immoral, it becomes unacceptable to offer money for political favors, and vice versa.

To characterize this wider context more formally, we ask: What makes the exercise of sanctions legitimate or illegitimate? A first answer is that they are so judged by referring formal or informal *norms*. We justify punishing criminals because they have broken the law, itself a system of norms. We may also oppose the use of sanctions if a law is regarded as unjust. We punish the use of force, theft, and fraud in markets, in part because they violate the norms of peaceful exchange. We condemn disorderly or rude public conduct—legal and illegal—because it violates norms of civility. We frown upon misplaced silverware on the table according to manners articulated in finishing schools and Emily Post manuals.

As a next step, we ask: What makes those norms legitimate or illegitimate? We answer this by referring to a cultural *value,* a principle that specifies what is desirable in social life. Electoral rules and procedures, holding of office, rejection from office, and exercise of authority are legitimized by the values of representative democracy. Punishment of adultery is not simply a matter of invoking rules against it; these rules are rooted in values of monogamous marriage, themselves embedded in religious traditions. Alternative values—such as that of open marriage—erase the legitimizing basis for that punishment by rejecting traditional family values and invoking other, libertarian ones.

Finally, we ask: What makes such values legitimate or illegitimate? They are typically judged to be so by some encompassing cultural *worldview* (religion, cosmology, ideology) that describes the ultimate nature of things and justifies things as desirable or undesirable, right or wrong. Historically, most such worldviews are found in religious systems, but secular versions, such as society as social contract, society as secular utopia (as in the communist world vision), and other first principles, also serve as ultimately legitimizing points of reference.

The interplay of sanctions, then, must be viewed not as something on its own, but as embodied in hierarchies of cultural ingredients. This principle is a corrective to views of social control as the exercise of raw power or solely material incentives. These cultural ingredients vary from society to society and from tradition to tradition. They are also subject to constant examination, interpretation, contestation, and change. In all events, cultural embeddedness must be a reference point for understanding the dynamics of sanctions.

AN OLDER BUT USEFUL CLASSIFICATION OF SANCTIONS

Half a century ago, Parsons (1963) advanced a classification of sanctions that induce people to behave in one way or another. He derived his scheme from his general theory of action, but we do not have to enter its thickets to appreciate the scheme's usefulness for understanding the give-and-take and the complexity of these social forces.

Parsons's most general category is sanctions. These are either positive (rewarding) or negative (punishing). Even this initial division demands a few clarifications:

- The term *sanction* is ambiguous because it can have both meanings. It can mean something positive, as in "I sanction your decision to go to college." More often, it means something negative, as in speaking of rewards versus sanctions, or in applying international sanctions against a misbehaving nation-state. Other variations can be found. In American English, the phrase "violators will be cited" means that lawbreakers will be charged; in British English, it suggests that rapists will be rewarded! We stay with the inclusive connotation that *sanctions* refer to both positive and negative forces.
- Specific sanctions can have both positive and negative effects. For example, giving a bonus to an executive for superior performance is clearly positive; if, however, the bonus is smaller than expected, it can be experienced as a punishing act. The same principle applies in giving or withholding love.
- The second distinction Parsons made was whether an agent, in exercising a sanction, (1) appeals to the *intentions* of the person he/she wants to influence or (2) manipulates the *situation* of that person. Trying to persuade a friend to go to a movie is an example of the former; offering to pay for the friend's ticket is an example of the latter, in that it is an offer to change the individual's circumstances if he/she goes along.

Using those distinctions, Parsons produced a fourfold classification (see table 1).

Persuasion is an appeal to another to go along with a line of action. That appeal in turn is based on some common membership—for example, in a family, a group of friends, an organization, a voluntary association, a nation. Employers who appeal to company loyalty rely on persuasion based on common member-

TABLE 1 Types of Sanction

Sanction	Intentional	Situational
Positive	Persuasion	Inducement
Negative	Activation of commitments	Deterrence

ship. Advertisers peddling their products appeal to common membership in age-based cliques (positioning a product as an "in" symbol for adolescents, for example) or a vaguely delineated sense of membership in a social class or identity group (for example, "the pick-up truck and rifle" niche of consumers). To persuade is neither to buy nor to force. It is to appeal on the basis of some real or imagined social cohesion.

Inducement is commonly identified with the power of monetary incentives to influence people to take employment, to reward those who work effectively (bonuses), or to join in a contractual arrangement ("for consideration"), but we should also remember the negative connotations of withholding or manipulating monetary rewards.

Deterrence is perhaps not the best word to connote the exercise of political or power-based sanctions, because that term is associated with a historically specific set of sanctions in crime control and international relations (see below, pp. 95–96). Considered more broadly, this type of sanction is a political one. The use of force (physical coercion) to gain compliance lies at one extreme, though the category includes weaker forms such as the threat to use force, as well as less radical forms of power-based influence by legitimate authorities over willing subordinates.

Finally, activation to commitment is an appeal to a (presumably commonly held) value, especially a sacred one, to influence behavior. The appeal to religious or ideological commitments is the most obvious example, but one should also mention appeals to values of decency, humanity, fairness, and justice as ways to influence others to behave consistently with those values.

FOUR SANCTION-BASED THEORIES AND THEIR FORTUNES

We now review four influential theoretical approaches based on the place of sanctions in people's lives: behaviorism (mainly in psychology, with echoes in sociology and political science); deterrence theory (mainly in political science, law, and game theory); rational choice theory (mainly in economics, but exported to other disciplines); and role and deviance theory (mainly in psychology, sociology, and anthropology).

Behaviorism

This approach was dominant in psychology for much of the twentieth century but has been largely dethroned by cognitive approaches (Amsel, 1989) that we consider elsewhere in this book. To our knowledge, behaviorism has not been often characterized as a theory based on sanctions, but we interpret it as such.

As its name suggests, behaviorism is focused on objective *behavior,* in contrast to internal states of mind. Its proponents were motivated toward this emphasis to gain scientific precision by studying hard, objective and measurable *facts,* in contrast to more elusive mental states. Behaviorism was also committed to discovering and verifying scientific *laws* by rigorous experimental methods. Much of the experimental work was carried out on animals (monkeys, pigeons, and rats), earning behaviorism the unfriendly label "rat psychology" from critics.

Behaviorism's central tenet is that behavior can be best explained by understanding the stimuli to which an organism is exposed. Its main principles are associations between stimuli and responses and the process of conditioning, whereby new, associated stimuli gain the power to elicit behavior. Also central is the notion of operant conditioning, associated with the work of B. F. Skinner, which involves the reinforcement of behavior by rewarding, not rewarding, or punishing. This is where sanctions come in. Some behaviorists distinguished between positive reinforcement (a rewarding response to behavior) and negative reinforcement (a punitive response or aversive stimulus). Through these mechanisms, behavior is established. The logic of behaviorism was also extended to the excitation of affects, to a theory of learning, and to a form of psychotherapy known as behavior modification.

The definition of a positive reinforcer is one that an organism will approach; correspondingly, it will try to reduce or avoid negative reinforcers. These are referred to as the *incentive functions* of stimuli (Reynolds, 1975). The notions of "positive" and "aversive" necessarily say something about the *disposition* of the organism to react to the two types of stimuli. The idea of reinforcement, then, refers to a *relation* between the character of the stimulus and the organism's experience of that stimulus as punishing or rewarding, which is sometimes called expectancy (Walker, 1968). Thus, reference to internal states—readiness to recognize and respond to pleasure and pain—did find its way indirectly into the antimental outlook of the behaviorists.

Late in the twentieth century, behaviorism fell out of favor in the face of longstanding criticisms of its extreme emphasis on the external environment and its generalizing from animals to humans, and because of the discovery that the meanings (cognitions) assigned to stimuli intervene decisively between stimulus and behavior. Versions of "neobehaviorism" survive, but a lesson learned from its history is that to establish mechanical and universal relations between sanctions (stimuli) and behavior is to pursue a phantom.

Deterrence

In its general definition, *deterrence* refers to the application of any negative sanction to prevent the occurrence of undesired behavior. Its practical use is as old as punishment itself, but efforts to investigate it systematically are relatively new. A coherent theoretical explanation is found in the utilitarian concept of disutility, which makes the pain of a certain line of behavior greater than the pleasure it might yield. (Diminishing positive sanctions—for example, keeping only a small amount of money in the cash register of a gas station—can also deter.) Deterrence is also one way to deal with deviance, along with other instruments such as rehabilitation, reform, and retribution.

Deterrence theory and practice have focused on crime. The principal theoretical justification is a form of rational choice theory: those inclined to crime will find it less attractive if they are more likely to be apprehended, quicker to be punished, and punished more severely. Most criminal laws and some civil laws are based on this premise. In practice, however, research findings on the effectiveness of targeted deterrence efforts are mixed. Some research suggests that people's estimates of whether they will be apprehended and punishment have a stronger deterrent effect than estimates of the severity of the punishment (Paternoster and Simpson, 1996). Other evidence suggests that police crackdowns on crimes such as drug sales, disorderly behavior, and drunk driving have at least a short-term deterrent effect (Nagin, 2001). In other cases, such as prostitution, deterrence efforts may not work, but may cause a migration of perpetrators to other neighborhoods. Opinions are heated and evidence is mixed on the deterrent effects of the death penalty, with few social scientists believing that it has distinct and discernable effects (Sarat, 2001). More generally, the scientific study of criminal deterrence is hobbled by methodological difficulties in measuring crime rates, arrest records, and the level of awareness of deterrence measures in the population.

Another application of deterrence theory appeared during the Cold War, specifically in dealing with the prospect of nuclear attack and annihilation. The magnitude of that threat alone was no doubt a sufficient cause to generate concern. By the 1960s, a significant literature on nuclear deterrence had solidified (Kaufmann, 1956; Kahn, 1961; Schelling, 1966). Most of it derived from special adaptations of game theory. In many cases, the "solutions" generated in hypothetical confrontational games were given precise mathematical formulation. Over time, research on deterrence bifurcated into highly theoretical expressions on the one hand, and, on the other, historical case studies of incidents such as the Berlin Airlift and the Cuban Missile Crisis that revealed a mix of uncertainty, stumbling, midstream revisions, and luck, and provided an unknown level of support for formal deterrence theory. The theoretical approaches were more rigorous but suffered from unreality—they included tight, questionable assumptions about credibility of opponents' threats, correct assessments, good communication, common values, and unitary goals. The historical-descriptive accounts were more realistic but suffered from indeterminacy about the respective roles of deterrence and other strategies.

The ultimate success of deterrence theory and practice during the Cold War is not known. On the one hand, it can be claimed to have worked, in the final sense that nuclear war did not occur; yet that claim, as a counterfactual, is as frail as claims that the absence of successful terrorist attacks against the United States since 9/11 proves the effectiveness of our efforts to defend against them. On the other hand, deterrence threats—or anything else—did not prevent the massive mutual buildup of nuclear stockpiles by the superpowers, and it had unknown effects in minor wars and other conflicts between the contending powers.

The romance with deterrence theory and policy has waned recently, largely because the immediacy of nuclear destruction has receded (though long-term threats of proliferation have not). In addition, its generalizability to the contemporary scene, where international terrorism is the threat of the day, is questionable, partly because its assumptions of credibility, common understandings, and adequate communication among adversaries are even more remote than they were in the Cold War (Smelser and Mitchell, 2002). More generally, deterrence theory, like behaviorism, has settled into the status of a relevant and widely employed principle, but it is scarcely a general theory of sanctions.

Rational Choice

We treat the tradition of rational choice at different places in this book, according to its different contexts and types of usability. Here we look at it as a theory of sanctions—a term not often used to describe rational choice, but an accurate term once the theory is dissected.

As refined in neoclassical economics, rational choice is built on the following simplifying assumptions:

- Individual actors are motivated to maximize their well-being (utility).
- Individual actors are not influenced by others; they are unconstrained by norms (Coleman, 1990).
- Actors possess complete information about their tastes, their resources, and the availability, quality, and prices of products, job opportunities, and other market conditions.

- Actors calculate and behave rationally—they do not make errors; they do not forget what they know; they do not act on impulse or otherwise irrationally—or, if they do any of these things, the effects cancel out in the aggregate.
- Tastes are "given"—that is, they are stable and not to be explained; they are the starting point and not the object of analysis.
- Institutions are given—in particular, a legal framework guarantees a stable monetary system and assures that that market exchange will be peaceful and that coercion and fraud will be ruled out.
- The interaction between two actors, the buyer and the seller, produces an equilibrium point at which exchange occurs, and at this point supply and demand and utility and cost converge.

By virtue of all of these assumptions, the actor is hemmed in by postulates and conditions to such a degree that the theory, as applied, becomes a theory of responses to sanctions (offers, prices, and other market conditions). So binding are the assumptions that they guarantee "rational" outcomes. Ironically, then, in explanations based on rational choice, both formulaic words lose their meaning. Explained behavior is not rational in the classical philosophical sense of the term (that is, it need not involve reflection or reasoning). It need not be consciously calculated. This is so because behavior conceived of as the product of rational choice is, in the end, determined by a number of objective factors (e.g., price and quantity). Furthermore, even though alternatives are available, the explanatory power of preferences and conditions is (or should be) complete, and thus there need not be choice in the decision situation; the givens and the external sanctions determine the outcome. Though the idea of rational choice resonates with many philosophical traditions and with cultural values of individualism, neither reason nor choice is necessary for what passes as rational choice.

As we have mentioned, the neoclassical assumptions of givens have been relaxed or reformulated on the basis of research by economists themselves, behavioral economists, game theorists, cognitive psychologists, economic sociologists, and economic anthropologists. Economists now analyze situations with incomplete information, inflexibility of demand, risk and uncertainty, unstable preferences, power differentials (influence) among actors, satisficing rather than maximizing, and so on. In addition, rational choice has been extended to behavior other than the strictly economic, such as voting, marriage, criminal behavior, participation in social movements, and addiction. All these developments have meant *both* relaxation of original rational choice assumptions to extend and refine the model *and* academic imperialism. Above all, these developments in rational choice analysis involve a conceptual stretching of the idea of the rational and threaten a theoretical degeneration: everything becomes rational if you push hard enough, and *rational* becomes more or less synonymous with *reasonable* or *adaptive*.

Despite relaxations and extensions, rational choice analysis retains a certain theoretical continuity. Even if conditions of risk, uncertainty, lack of knowledge, third parties, and other variations are incorporated, the rational choice analyst's frequent strategy is to convert them into parameters and ask, "Given those different parameters, how will individuals behave rationally?" This is answered by building a model of rational behavior under newly hypothesized conditions, frequently expressed mathematically and sometimes related to empirical data.

Norms, Conformity, Obedience, and Deviance

A pioneering experiment on the formation of norms and their influence on judgment was described in an article by Sherif (1936). A group of subjects were asked to judge how much a small dot of light fifteen feet away moved. In actuality, the light did not move at all, but only appeared to move as a result of the visual phenomenon known as the autokinetic effect. While initial estimates of movement varied among subjects, over time judgments converged toward a common estimate, and subjects came to agree on that figure. On the basis of this and other experiments, Sherif posited a group tendency toward conformity, a tendency that strengthened when subjects were motivated by the experimenter to get a right answer. The group-set standard even carried over into subsequent experiments when the subjects did tasks alone. Practical applications of the conformity principle are evident in the dynamics of fads and fashions.

Further demonstration of the conformity principle was provided by Asch (1955), who presented subjects with a number of lines of different lengths and asked them to say which was the same length as a standard line. However, Asch introduced a confederate into the experimental groups, and asked that subject to give a wrong answer in twelve of eighteen experimental trials. This brought many of the experimental subjects into line with the wrong opinion. Refinements on this research demonstrated that in many cases a vociferous, argumentative minority can change the beliefs and behavior of the majority (Muscovici and Nemeth, 1974). The term *bad apple* refers to a situation in which a minority influence is negative from the standpoint of producing conflict or diminishing performance.

A dramatic extension of the conformity experiments was initiated in 1961 by Milgram (1974), in which recruited subjects were assigned the role of "teacher" and instructed to inflict physical harm on a "learner" (a confederate in the experiment) on the instructions of an experimenter, in order to induce learning. No shocks were given, but the confederate feigned being shocked. Very few subjects refused to administer the shocks, and there was an unexpectedly high degree of obedience in the experiments. The results created immediate excitement and debate, in part because of the general belief that people could not be induced to be so cruel, in part because the notion of "the authoritarian personality" had posited that such personalities would submit blindly to leaders (Adorno, Sanford, Frankel-Brunswik, and Levinson, 1950), and in part because the experiments were conducted during the trials of Adolf Eichmann for crimes against Jews. One line of defense was that Eichmann was not culpable because he was merely following the orders of superiors. As expected, the experiments were followed by a season of replications and variations (some crossnationally), conflicting interpretations of what psychological mechanisms might be involved in producing such results, and criticisms based on the idea that the experimental subjects, being in an experiment, did not really believe they were punishing others. The findings fed into the heated discussions of depersonalized killing in the Vietnam War. They also stimulated ethical debates about experimental manipulation and deception, and served as a reference point for imposing limits on the use of human subjects.

With respect to the psychological mechanisms involved in obedience to morally reprehensible commands, Milgram posited an "agentic state" wherein the inflictor of pain came to regard himself as an instrument carrying out another person's wishes, and therefore was not responsible for his actions. Another interpretation was that the subjects experienced learned helplessness. In a summary of the psychological literature, Kelman (1973) suggested that three mechanisms were in operation: authorization (Milgram's interpretation), routinization (believing the extraordinary to be ordinary), and dehumanization (coming to believe that the victims were less than human and not deserving of humane treatment). As also might be expected in the wake of such controversial research, subsequent experimentation challenged the results and sought conditions that produce defiance rather than obedience (Modigliani and Rochat, 1995). In our context, the Milgram experiments stand out as an extreme example of the power of sanctions.

Anthropology and sociology have also produced theories and explanations based on sanctions, but they have dealt more with sanctions' pervasiveness in routine personal interaction, institutional behavior, and social control. We choose as an example role theory and deviance, a body of thinking that gained prominence in midcentury in the "functionalist" writings of Parsons (Parsons and Shils, 1951) and Merton (1968b), among others.

The starting point is the notion of *role*—for example, that of husband, student, or church member. Any given individual has multiple roles, and all of these involve relations with other actors. The key ingredient of a role is the *expectation* that the actor will meet his or her obligations by performing in certain ways. Perhaps the clearest examples of expectations are found in legal codes and contracts, which are explicit about prohibitions and obligations. Contracts, for example, spell out when and where deliveries of goods and payments for goods are to be made. Other normative expectations are more informal, such as those found in codes of ethics and the norms of civility expected when meeting strangers. Norms vary according to whether they are explicit or vague, whether conformity is required or optional, and whether behavior is required or prohibited. Sanctions are instruments by which people attempt to secure compliance with role expectations. These may be formal and explicit, such as the requirement to pay a person for working or to physically restrain people if they threaten to commit a crime; they may also be informal and subtle, for example, a chilly silence that conveys to another that he or she is out of place.

Roles and their expectations may create strains. They can be overburdening; they can be ambiguous in their expectations; and they can create role conflicts that call for contradictory behaviors—for example, a student is motivated by his or her teachers to excel in studies and motivated by peer groups not to be a "grind" or "nerd." Role incumbents have ways to minimize these conflicts, for example, by isolating or keeping behaviors secret or separated from one another, or by rationalizing discrepancies to make them less inconsistent with one another. One particular adaptation, however—*deviance*—received special attention in role theory. Deviance takes multiple forms, such as withdrawing from role responsibilities, conforming to the letter but not the spirit of expectations, and rebelling. When deviance occurs, moreover, it excites mechanisms of *social control*—usually sanctions designed to bring deviants back into line and restore conformity.

Role and deviance theory came in for vigorous criticism in subsequent decades. It was criticized for portraying the individual role incumbent as passive or "oversocialized" (Wrong, 1961); as overemphasizing stability and underemphasizing conflict and change; and as ignoring the political dimension of deviance, which others (Becker, 1963) treated as the ability of powerful individuals (doctors, judges, law enforcement officials) to label people as the source of deviance, rather than treating it as the motivated behavior of "deviants" themselves.

All four of the sanction-based theories reviewed—behaviorism, deterrence theory, rational choice, and role deviance theory—displayed similar patterns. Each generated theoretical excitement and enjoyed a day in the sun; each also ran aground in the face of convincing criticisms; each has diminished in theoretical influence as a result; none has died, but each has been transfigured and lost its hegemony. Together they constitute a constant and "usable" reminder that almost all human behavior transpires in the context of individual motivation, orientation, and striving on the one hand and external social constraints on that behavior on the other.

AN EXPLOSIVE SITUATION OF
POLITICAL CONFLICT

In early January 1965, Martin Meyerson, the new acting chancellor of the University of California, Berkeley, called me into his office and asked me to be his special assistant for student political activity. Meyerson himself had been appointed only a few days earlier. He had, moreover, inherited a situation that was not to be envied.

As of the beginning of 1965, the Berkeley campus was in an institutional shambles. In September 1964, the Berkeley administration had invoked a rule prohibiting political advertising and soliciting on a thin strip of land at Telegraph and Bancroft Avenues. Students had enjoyed informal use of this strip for years. The action occurred in the context of a history of extensive political activism during the preceding years (Heirich and Kaplan, 1965) and in the context of the heated 1964 presidential election campaign. The revocation triggered the months of the Free Speech Movement, which involved massive rule violations, demonstrations, vacillating and ultimately unsuccessful efforts to discipline students, a giant rally and sit-in in Sproul Hall on December 2, and a decisive faculty resolution on December 8 that rebuked Chancellor Edward Strong and called for granting some of the students' demands. (A detailed history is given in Heirich [1971].) The protesters and many others regarded December 8 as a decisive and heroic victory. Discredited, Strong was excused from office on January 2 and Meyerson was named acting chancellor for an indefinite period.

At the moment he took office, Meyerson faced a situation in which campus authority was more or less nonexistent; the protesting students were exuberant and hopeful, though without a unified program; the faculty was divided and confused; and nobody really knew what to do. That was the situation that Meyerson faced in early January, and the situation into which he brought me.

The situation we faced, moreover, was so disorganized that we were not aware of what kind of knowledge was necessary for us to carry out the job. We were aware of the general goals called for by the situation: to restore a measure of authority, to keep the goodwill and support, or at least acquiescence, especially of faculty but also of other interested groups such as alumni, regents, and representatives of the state government of California, all of whom had been perplexed at best and horrified at worst at the seemingly total breakdown of the university and its capitulation to a group of dissident students. We also became acquainted with the prospective students' aims as of their postvictory situation a month ago during our early meetings with them in January 1965. The students did not speak with one voice, though several messages came through: they were glad to be rid of Strong; they were flush with victory and did not want the new administration to roll back any of their gains; they wanted full freedom to do what they wanted by way of political activity on campus; and they exuded hope that the Meyerson administration would be receptive to furthering the objectives of the student movement, though these objectives were not very well artic-ulated. We also knew about the dispositions of angry insiders, namely a small group of very conservative faculty, a few remaining staff members in the chancellor's office who were sympathetic with ex-Chancellor Strong, some conservative regents, and some political figures in Sacramento. We knew about the political events of the past several months and the university administration's bungling, but this was selective and imperfect knowledge.

Knowledge of these facts helped orient us, but they were only that—facts—and did not constitute guidelines as to how we were to behave in the face of the multiple and contradictory demands that were constantly bombarding the chancellor's office. There were many kinds of facts we did *not* have at hand. We had no intelligence machinery to speak of except for a small and unprepared campus police force, and as a result we had virtually no access to knowledge about the activists' strategies and tactics, hammered out in meetings unavailable to us and kept secret from a campus administration regarded mainly as an enemy.

As for myself, I didn't even know what my role was at the beginning—it was only special assistant. My duties and assignments evolved with the situation on the campus. I came to meet with representatives of the Free Speech Movement and other student groups; I became the administration's contact person with deans responsible for discipline and with the campus police; I met with the leadership of the Academic Senate and other faculty groups; I fielded and responded to (mainly hostile) communications from parents of activist students, alumni individuals and groups concerned about the fate of the campus they remembered, regents, past administrators, and state officials; and, of course, I spoke often and continuously with Meyerson and other staff in the chancellor's office on all political matters facing the campus. These assignments helped define my situation, but they didn't offer me any guidelines about how to react or take the initiative in dealing with concrete situations.

Quite by accident, I had recently acquired some general knowledge that was clearly social-scientific in nature. In my early years as a faculty member in the sociology department at Berkeley, I had conducted very ambitious comparative research on collective behavior (panics, crazes, riots) and social movements, both reform and revolutionary. I published the results of this research in a general treatise called *Theory of Collective Behavior* (Smelser, 1962). In announcing my appointment to the chancellor's office, the local press made much of my work. The headline on the article reporting my appointment in the *San Francisco Examiner* on January 13 was "Meyerson Picks Expert on Mobs." The other news accounts all stressed this background item. The two evident implications of such publicity were that the chancellor's office was mainly interested in "handling" and "controlling" the dissidents, and that I was brought in to apply my expert knowledge. Both implications made good news for the press in the context of the times, but both were misleading. Neither Meyerson nor I—nor nobody else in the chancellor's office at the time—had an articulated philosophy of manipulating the movement or the dissidents; we were living day by day, without much time to reflect or plan, and were most often forced by events to be reactive. I frequently joked that our lead time for decision-making was five minutes.

By the same token, it could not be imagined that what we were doing or would do was "applied social science." To imply anything like that was to endow us with a rationality we did not have. On the other hand, there were several conclusions that I had reached in my comparative study of collective behavior and social movements (Smelser, 1962) that informed my thinking in a general way and served me well: (1) I had asked what happens after social movements score a dramatic success and had concluded that success generally creates a psychological letdown, generates internal divisions about what to do next, and leaves the movement floundering and seeking new agendas and justifications. This conclusion was consistent with what I saw happening with the Free Speech Movement that spring. (2) I had concluded that among the most incendiary influences on a social movement is authorities' vacillation between punitiveness and weakness, which serves simultaneously to victimize and embolden the movement. I had also seen this principle in action during the late months of 1964 on the Berkeley campus. (3) A closely related conclusion was that the authorities' most legitimate policy was not to engage in direct, partisan ways with activists and antagonists, but to stick, as steadfastly as possible, to a posture of neutrality. In retrospect, these lessons seemed to inform my outlook and supply me with usable knowledge, but they were useful only as general orientations and never as fixed principles to be trotted out as specific rules to be applied.

As time went by, I learned other useful things, mainly through direct dealings with student activists and my colleagues.

First, it seemed important to invent ways not to provoke the activists or to overreact to their provocations. Unnecessary provocation through the sudden imposition of strict discipline, I had learned, was one of the principal failings of the previous administration. So we stumbled through the policy of permissiveness for political activities as long as they adhered to minimal "time-place-manner" rules that were enacted in early January. We frequently let tiny provocations (token rule-breaking) pass without action. For more serious breaches, we tried to avoid sending police in to break up rallies, shut down amplification equipment, or break heads. When such an incident occurred, we asked deans to take down names of violators and submit those names to the appropriate disciplinary committees for later action.

Second, I learned something about group dynamics that develop when two groups (in this case, administration and student activists) regard each other as enemies and are adamantly polarized. Each side develops a kind of collective paranoia about the other. Each exaggerates the intelligence and plotting capacity of the other, sees a purpose in everything, and spends a great deal of time trying to figure out what the other side is up to. In reality, as I observed, both sides were muddling through, not really knowing what they were doing much of the time, and not knowing the consequences of what they were doing. The consequence of this is that both sides made errors of misjudgment in dealing with each other because they operated with an inflated view of the purposefulness of the "enemy."

Third, I discovered another related tendency. That is, when some incident occurred that might appear to be damaging to the university or its image, some members of the chancellor's staff would opine that something had to be done immediately and publicly to counter the incident and would "set things straight" by issuing an official statement or preparing a press release. Contrary to this impulse, I gradually developed a sense of how short the public memory of such incidents is, and learned that reacting to everything is likely to create a sense of weakness—defensiveness, if not panic—on the part of the administration. Such reactions also tend to keep the memory of the original incident alive. I thought that "coolness," except in the case of very serious and very damaging incidents, should be the normal policy.

Throughout the spring and to some extent the summer of 1965, the administration, in consultation with and usually with the support of major faculty groups, stumbled along, confronting little and big potential and real crises emanating from both within and outside the campus, trying to hold everything at bay and trying to work gradually toward a situation closer to campus "normality." This pattern of coping was not systematic; we handled each situation anew, and without a grand strategy. We regarded ourselves as neither succeeding nor failing, but only as struggling. In retrospect, the brief administration of Martin Meyerson has been regarded as a success because it held in check, more or less, explosive demonstrations and attacks on the university and avoided major institutional breakdowns on the campus. We did not permanently restore peace to the campus, because the antiwar movement kept the campus in turmoil for several years thereafter. I regarded the "success" of those months mainly as holding the line.

A final word is necessary on the kinds of knowledge I referred to above in our contending with this very unstable campus situation. Some it was in the form of general orienting principles, which I had indeed extracted from my own research on collective behavior and social movements, and some took the form of evolving rules of thumb based on our collective experience as time went on. But this knowledge was not in the form of hard facts or definite formulas to be applied. It served as general background knowledge, often not consciously in mind, and never systematized as a corpus of usable knowledge. Taken as a whole, however, that knowledge provided the basis for carrying out a general policy of institutional calmness and sanity in the face of campus chaos. That does not sound very much like applied knowledge. It did not feel like that, either, but it served as the basis for an institutional posture that succeeded— again, not consciously—in not aggravating things and in permitting a volatile protest movement to splinter and ultimately to move toward its own demise.

—*Neil J. Smelser*

THE INDECISIVE STATUS OF
MONETARY COMPENSATION

Monetary compensation for human services is an arena involving the inter-play of sanctions and behavior; by definition it involves rewards for behaving according to rules. Monetary compensation is as old as wage labor and money systems themselves, though monetary wages and salaries have become more salient as mechanisms as capitalism and markets have conquered the world and as alternative systems such as slavery have been replaced. Some nonmarket or partial-market residues, such as conscription into military service, prison labor, and administered economies, still survive, though they are generally regarded as special or exceptional. In some of these, such as volunteer or mercenary armies, however, market inducements are conspicuous.

The most consistent theory of monetary compensation is found in neoclassi-cal versions of labor economics. Labor, along with land and capital, is one of the classic factors of production. When labor is offered, its market should behave like other markets. That is to say, labor is offered at an equilibrium price that expresses an intersection between an employer's willingness to pay and a laborer's willing-ness to perform. Like other markets, the market for labor services is governed by assumptions of scarcity and rational choice on both sides of the exchange. The aggregation of transactions yields a market structure, expressing wage levels and inequalities. A textbook definition of labor economics itself is that it is "primarily concerned with the behavior of employers and employees in response to the general incentives of wages, prices, profits, and nonpecuniary aspects of the employment relationships, such as working conditions" (Ehrenberg and Smith, 2009: 2–3). Labor economists are the first to acknowledge the role of nonmonetary aspects in labor markets, and most analysis has to be qualified by the understanding that, realistically, analysis of pecuniary factors always carries an implicit footnote: "*insofar* as pecuniary factors, among others, produce an effect."

This economic logic is powerful in generating both explanations and policy recommendations. One empirical regularity is that increases in the price of labor (wages, income taxes, health insurance and other benefits) induce firms to use fewer workers and lengthen work weeks (Hamermesh, 2001). Another example is that employers choose higher wages in order to reduce turnover (which is often costlier than the higher wages), and that, in response, laborers lower quit rates as wages are raised. Still another is the observation that a higher minimum wage raises unemployment rates because employers choose to employ nobody rather than a worker for more than they are willing to pay; this principle informs debates about differential minimum wage rates and their consequences for unemployment rates. The other side of the debate is whether higher minimum wages are justified on grounds of welfare or equity, thus bringing nonmarket considerations to bear on the question of wage levels.

In fact, research in labor economics, as well as that in sociology, anthropology, psychology, and management science, has uncovered noneconomic factors at work and incorporated them into labor market analyses. This has led one observer to conclude that "labor markets are . . . the least [economically] self-regulating among all markets" (Carré, 2001: 12980). In this section we focus on the interplay among pecuniary and nonpecuniary aspects. A particular point of emphasis is the ways in which monetary sanctions are or become *symbols* of other things of value.

We divide this section into two parts: (1) the intrusion of noneconomic factors into labor markets and their interplay with economic ones, and (2) executive and managerial compensation, a topic of study and debate in the past several decades.

The Fusion of Pecuniary and Nonpecuniary Factors in Employer-Employee Relationships

A number of factors supplement or contaminate—depending on one's point of view—the role of wages and other pecuniary factors in employer-employee relations.

Political Factors   Laborers have seldom constituted a completely atomized and fragmented class of agents who simply come to agreed-upon contracts expressing wage rates and a willingness to work as directed. Some collective interest typically comes into play. This impulse predates the rise of unionism. Peasant revolts against economic conditions, as well as Luddism and other expressions of antagonism to technological change, are early examples. Even bread riots, widely interpreted as consumer protests, expressed a relationship between bread prices and consumers' ability to pay (wage levels). The Marxist economic tradition represented capitalists' use of labor as a constant political struggle. The human relations tradition described ways in which individuals and groups of workers modify the conditions of labor. One contemporary approach to organizational "deviance" treats it as an expression of workplace and class protest (see below, pp. 200–202).

The history of labor unions reveals the most conspicuous intrusion of collective political action into labor markets. In one respect, unions are imperfections in ideal labor markets; in another, they represent a larger political movement to protect labor against unregulated capitalism. Labor economists and others have studied ways in which they influence wage levels; employers' decisions about whom to employ and fire; productivity; the balance between wages and benefits in the employment package; and the recent weakening of unionism. In all events, unions have "skewed" wages, as envisioned in neoclassical economics, *away* from being a product of the working out of market forces *toward* a system of wages as a product of political conflict and negotiation. In the tradition of business union-ism—the dominant American pattern—unions attend more to wages and the conditions of labor, though they have also become powerful players in elections and lobbying. In the tradition of political unionism and other, more militant forms in Europe and elsewhere, unions make more use of direct political action through public protests, disruptions, and even periodic general strikes.

Other political influences on market-determined labor solutions come from outside the economy, mainly from the state in its efforts to counter the negative externalities and other effects of unregulated capitalism. These are the effects of taxation policy, including loopholes, on both wages and capital; regulation of the labor of children, women, and the aged; retirement and pension policies; regulation of conditions of labor, especially health and safety; and antimonopoly provisions and other forms of price regulation, to say nothing of fiscal and monetary management of the economy. Sometimes state interventions are themselves responses to political pressure on the part of unions, pressure groups, and social movements (for example, women's groups pressing for equal pay, civil rights groups working against discrimination and for affirmative action). In sum, no realistic account of wage levels, inequalities, and changes can be made without incorporating political factors.

Complications of Utility One tradition of social psychology has been built around two different forms of motivating rewards: (1) external incentives, such as monetary rewards, power, praise and support, and the benefits of group membership; and (2) intrinsic forces, or internally generated or internalized (through socialization) interests and motivations that persist somewhat independently of external rewards; these include personal "drive," love of one's work, and vocational interests. Psychologists and others often regard the latter as steadier and surer sources of effective performance (for example, Deci and Ryan, 1985). In addition, while many occupations are institutionalized as jobs that build pay-for-performance into contracts, others include nonmonetary understandings. Some traditional crafts, as well as religious, scientific, and academic roles, retain elements of the idea of a "calling," and while incumbents are paid, it is openly or tacitly assumed that love of work and prestige are salient (see Smelser and Content, 1980). Accordingly, universities with high prestige can sometimes offer lower salaries to recruit talent than lower-rung institutions. In other cases, prestige and income are positively related. At least one historical understanding about public service is that rendering it generates some psychic income and need not be highly paid. This principle is honored in the breach as much as the observance, however, in the political arena, which has a conspicuous history of self-serving and personal gain among politicians.

Social Comparisons and Relative Deprivation   The main theory of wages emanating from economics is expectancy theory, via which compensation levels are
determined by the intersection of expected utility schedules on the part of employers and workers. Alongside this has grown a second tradition, equity theory,
according to which individuals and groups strive for "balance *relative* to the . . .
perceived contributions and inducement as applying to a referent" (Thierry, 2001:
11133; italics original). Points of reference for equity are unending: an abstract
notion of a "just" wage; the income of groups perceived as above, equal to, or
below a self-reference group; what income has been in the immediate past; income
relative to an expected standard of consumption, also perceived in relation to
other groups; government wage guidelines; benefits packages of other classes of
workers; discrepancies between women's and men's pay; and discrepancies traceable to racial-ethnic discrimination. Equity theory necessarily introduces a collective dimension to complement the individualistic assumptions of classical theory. At the very least, an executive or administrator should be aware of the social
environment—social movements, network attachments among employees, past
practices with respect to pay differentials—that defines the bases of social comparisons. This principle also plays a central role in executive and management
compensation, to which we now turn.

Executive and Management Compensation

We address this issue because of the high priority given to top-level executive
responsibility in corporate, governmental, and other administrative positions;
because changes in this compensation have been conspicuous in recent decades;
and because the issue is fraught with ambiguities and controversies.

In principle, executive and management compensation should be soluble by
standard economic and pragmatic formulae: executives and managers, like all
labor, should be paid according to the marginal value they contribute (Pavlik
and Belkaoui, 1991: 7). As one handbook puts it, "There is universal consensus
that the majority of executive pay should be based upon 'performance'" (Lipman
and Hall, 2008: 13). An additional intent of compensation is to motivate better
performance in the future. In practice, however, this principle is so bedeviled by
measurement problems and other forces that it seems fruitless to hope that any
simple, definitive formula can be derived from it.

Over recent decades, other principles of remuneration for executives and
managers have evolved, each aimed at rewarding performance, and each generating unintended side effects. The main components of compensation packages,
distilled from texts and manuals on executive compensation, are the following:

- Base salary. Usually determined by a negotiation-decision process at the time
  of assuming a position, this system long constituted the basic form of remu-

neration for executives and managers. It reflects the perceived level of an executive's skill and competence, presuppositions and expectations on the part of compensation committees and boards of directors, and the essentially political process of negotiation between firm and prospective executive. Annual salary is a somewhat blunt motivating instrument, however, largely because it is infrequently altered (usually annually), and its reward-for-performance aspects are often contaminated by understandings based on customary career trajectory and seniority considerations. In the past few decades, the salary components of executive compensation have declined as a proportion of total compensation (Balsam, 2007), largely as a result of the emergence of other forms.

- Bonuses. Beginning in the 1970s, annual bonuses came to be established as rewards above and beyond base salaries for employees. In some cases, annual bonuses exceed base salaries. In principle, bonuses appear to be a more sensitive motivating instrument than salaries because they can be awarded with direct attention to special performance. They are also preferred because of their flexibility; they are one-shot, nonrepeated rewards that do not reverberate into the future as part of the base salary, and they carry no fringe benefits. In practice, however, annual bonuses drift toward being incorporated into lifestyles and thus toward becoming annually expected increments (achievement gives way to ascription). When this occurs, the intent of bonuses moves *away* from motivating future performances and *toward* judging them in the light of past bonuses (a bonus only slightly higher than last year's can thus be regarded as a negative) or in the light of bonuses granted to comparable others (Wilson, 2003).

- Bonuses in the form of stock options and other equity-related programs, designed to enhance loyalty and commitment to the company through ownership. These are popular during periods of expansion and growth of stock values, but recipients often find themselves losing wealth when company fortunes are reversed.

- Variable pay plans such as profit-sharing, team performance, gain-sharing plans, and project-based incentive plans, as well as special awards, such as "employee-of-the month," which usually combine public recognition with some kind of monetary prize. Contests and competitions are also mechanisms, though these are often criticized as childish "gold star" games and "summer camp" activities (ibid.)

- Increases in nonsalary benefits (especially retirement and health). These are another means to increase compensation, but they tend to be regarded as general benefits of executive employment in an organization rather than specifically performance-motivating devices.

- Perks (larger offices, paid memberships in societies and clubs, free cars and drivers, executive planes, meetings in posh settings, and the like). These are often appreciated and have status-empowering value. They are also often a special point of sensitivity on the part of compensation committees and boards of trustees, however, because apparent excesses excite such critical attention by the media and negative public reactions.

Three general points can be made about all of these forms of remuneration. First, chronic problems in measuring individual performance hinder the translation of these measures into meaningful compensation. An example is tying bonuses for individual executives to company performance and increased share values, when these increases may result from market effects or accidents having little or nothing to do with executive performance. Individual performance reviews are more direct efforts to measure, but can be regarded as imprecise and unfair. Second, many forms of executive and management compensation practices have a "fishbowl" aspect and are thus partially determined by forces external to the organization. Federal and state regulatory agencies exercise direct control over compensation in some areas; significant increases or decreases in taxation rates also have an effect. Actual or supposed public opinion, thought to translate into good or bad will for the organization, is also a constant point of sensitivity. Of special significance are "fat cat salaries" (Tysun, 2005), "bonuses for failure" (Norris, 2005), and excessive perks—all regarded as fuel for corporate criticism and class antagonism. Third, most forms of executive and management compensation, while originally conceived under the preferred reward-for-pay logic, evolve toward taking on unanticipated symbolic meanings or separate lives of their own, and move in the direction of emphasizing inequities and entitlements, both of which divert from the original logic. (One manual titles a chapter "Transform Rewards from Entitlement to Achievement" [Wilson, 2003].)

Most manuals on executive compensation offer guidelines for compensation policies. Examples include "maintain the proper balance of intrinsic and extrinsic rewards" (McCoy, 1992: 20); customize the plan; align plans with overall business strategies; trust your employees; use noncash as well as cash awards; tell people how they are doing all the time; make use of role modeling; and "create a smorgasbord of plans" (Parker, McAdams, and Zielinksi, 2000). While one hesitates to dismiss these as bromides—many seem generally sensible—such formulae remain indeterminate as to how to translate them into specific policies to be applied in specific settings, and many appear to have more cheerleading than practical value.

A KEY PRINCIPLE IN UNDERSTANDING SANCTIONS

Distilling from discussions in this chapter, we enunciate a principle of progression affecting rewards in social life. It is a widespread principle, though we would not necessarily claim universality. We capture it as follows: reward → privilege → entitlement. Smelser noticed this principle during the time he was director of the Center for Advanced Study in the Behavioral Sciences at Stanford. Each year some four dozen fellows spend an academic year there. Usually they bring with them sabbatical pay of half or two-thirds of a year's academic salary; some have funds from research grants as well. The center supplements these funds in order to bring the annual salary up to its full level at each fellow's home institution; the amount is set in advance of his or her arrival.

Selection to the center has long been regarded as a kind of career gift, bestowed for past scholarly accomplishment and future promise. Most fellows regard it as such, are grateful to receive the gift, and subsequently report it as a prize or honor—something like a Guggenheim Fellowship—on their curriculum vitae. Yet for some fellows, a subtle change comes about. Once the stipend is fixed for the year, feelings about it begin to evolve toward considering it not so much a gift as a privilege, something they deserve for being there, and as something of a fixed base from which they might demand other privileges—time away from the center during their year, additional funds for research expenses incurred, perhaps a housing allowance, special demands on the center's library service, or special dietary attention in the center's cafeteria. The financial stipend becomes a kind of fixed expectation on which to build—in a word, a privilege. From here, it is a short step toward treating it as an entitlement, something fully deserved and built upon, and a source of resentment if tinkered with.

The principle applies more generally. Keynes enunciated it in his "stickiness of money wages" concept, by virtue of which wage cuts are severely resisted. Once raises are granted, however, they are considered to be permanent, not to be whittled down except under severe conditions when the company is faced with potential market failure. Differential merit increases manifest the same principle; another example from the center illustrates it. Each year the board of trustees authorizes an average salary increase for staff employees (3 or 4 percent, usually), often following guidelines set by Stanford University policies. However, the director is instructed to allocate this differentially among employees, according to evaluation of performance. Each year the director faces outrage from those on the staff who receives anything less than the norm approved by the board, and treats the news as a wound. Consider also employee and management bonuses. If granted for a series of years and then reduced, the act is usually regarded as punitive, as though the employee is not getting what is deserved. The same principles apply with respect to certain social welfare measures: Social Security premiums, child support allowances, food stamps, and medical coverage. Once established, these measures move toward regularization, if not full entitlement. The principle is established institutionally in the budgets of state and federal governments when they designate legislation as an "entitlement," namely with the requirement that its budgetary allocation will be carried over into the following year and possibly increased, but not decreased.

To seek a mechanism for this progression, we return to our discussion of the heuristic of anchoring and adjustment, as well as social comparison theory and relative deprivation (see chapter 2, pp. 66–69). The mechanism is that establishing or increasing a level of reward *continuously creates new anchor points;* recipients' expectations are reset accordingly, and if subsequent changes are forthcoming, *they are continuously assessed according to the new anchor point,* and become the basis for new definitions and experiences of relative deprivation. If a reference group is involved in relation to these anchor-adjustment changes, the perceived situations of that reference group is also activated. This mechanism also instructs us that preferences and tastes are not stable, that expectations usually have a history, and that maximizing advantage in relation to stable expectations cannot be a general principle.

Sometimes the pressure for entitlement—as contrasted with periodic systematic adjustment of rewards—becomes institutionalized. All forms of job security are protection of income in the face of vicissitudes, and are seen as a kind of entitlement. These are expressed in an extreme way in tenure systems in academic institutions, whereby faculty positions have evolved into a kind of lifetime job security, often with periodic advancements and pay increases over time built in, subject to satisfactory performance and accelerated if performance is superior. Similar, though not as extreme, arrangements are found in military and civil-service organizations. While extremely rewarding to incumbents, occupational-security principles frequently build rigidities into budgets, and help account for the fact that budgets in these organizations are difficult to alter because such a large proportion of items are carried over from year to year. In democratic systems, pressures on the part of political groups—the aged, civil servants, law enforcement officials—often result in formal or informal agreements that a certain *percentage* of the government's budget will be dedicated to one line of expenditure or another—prisons, healthcare, primary education. It is the dream of all political groups to attain such official entitlement status, and at the same time it is one of the chronic sources of the tendency in democratic societies to accumulate spending deficits.

SANCTION SYSTEMS THAT BRIDGE MARKETS AND THE POLITY

We turn now to an important arena for the interplay of sanctions, but one that is not routinely considered under that heading. After venturing a few general points, we consider first the informal economy and then corruption in its many forms.

In taking up organizational dynamics, we call attention to the longstanding distinction—made in different guises—between formal and informal organization. On the one side, we find visible and explicit positions and roles, relations expressed in organizational charts and lines of authority as well as in explicit rules and expectations. On the other, we find less distinct roles, such as expressive leaders, the loyal, and the troublemaker; friendships and cliques; implicit understandings; and patterns of influence different from those exercised in the formal structure. Sometimes the relations between the formal and informal are friendly and complementary; they grease the wheels of the organization and get things done faster and better than by formal means. Sometimes these relations are antagonistic and act as sand in the wheels. In all events, decision-makers cannot proceed intelligibly without understanding and appreciating the dynamics of the informal side.

The formal-informal distinction is a subtype of a more generic feature of social life. A feature of any institution (law, medicine, business, education) is that it specifies roles with definite relations with others, expectations for performance, and different sanctions (payment of salary or wages, authority in the form of rights to give orders and to expect responsible behavior on the part of those to whom authority is delegated). However, and apparently paradoxically, establishing any kind of institution and its procedures creates a number of alternative possibilities:

- Rules may be ignored, defied, or broken. Criminality is the obvious case, but so are the irresponsible spouse, the lazy worker, the wayward or corrupt manager, and the venal public official. The implication of these examples (and deviance in general) is that *there must be a rule in order for there to be deviance.* Poaching as deviance is possible only within the context of property rights and privileges. When an unpopular law (such as prohibition of manufacturing and selling alcohol) is taken off the books, previously banned behaviors are moved from the realm of the deviant into the realm of the tolerated, even though they may be regulated through the imposition of taxes and limits on sales. Many social reforms mean simply that that which was once considered legal, even desirable (e.g., child labor), is now prohibited or subject to regulation—that is, made deviant.
- Rules may be negotiated. Children are forever bargaining with their parents about television-watching rules or how late they may stay up or out at night. Students attempt to negotiate deadlines for submitting term papers, to say nothing of grades. A fully institutionalized negotiation system is found in the practice of plea bargaining, in which the severity of punishment is bargained downward if the criminal is willing to confess or to implicate others.
- An alternative system of expectations and activities for achieving the same or different ends as fully institutionalized forms may be invented or evolve

without plan. Informal organization provides the prime examples. Such supplementary systems may involve both deviance and negotiation. In all events, these alternative systems can be considered separately from deviance or negotiation. A prime example of an alternative system is the informal economy, to which we now turn.

The Informal Economy

While unnoticed or unregulated economic activities are as old as economic activity itself, "the informal economy" came to be recognized as a type by economists, sociologists, anthropologists, and governments only once formal economic institutions (primarily markets, but also administered systems) developed as the favored means of economic production, distribution, and consumption. While economists frequently call formal markets "free," they are always constrained by property and contractual systems, laws and customs preventing coercion, fraud and violence, and state taxation and regulation.

In one sense, the informal economy is a mirror opposite of the formal one. It operates outside the formal economy for the most part. Its specific forms may involve bartering, running errands, street and bazaar hawking, casual hiring for cash, self-employment, cottage industry production, and black markets, as well as making and distributing contraband articles, smuggling, and other criminal activities. Some forms are illegal, some are not, and many lie somewhere between. Above all, informal economic activity is likely to be unreported, unrecorded, and less noticed than formal activity. As such—like many marginal activities—it poses special problems of measurement and estimation, and, as a consequence of being unmeasured or poorly measured, it leads to underestimations of a society's total economic activity. Like many social phenomena, moreover, it has proved difficult to define and has spawned many definitions. One consensus definition reads as follows: "[The informal economy] is unregulated by the institutions of society, in legal and social environments in which similar activities are regulated" (Castells and Portes, 1989: 12). Thus, informal economies may be "freer," in the economists' sense, than formal markets because they are more removed from extra-economic (mainly state) influences on market activity. At the same time, informal economic activity is regulated in other ways. It is fused with family, tribal, ethnic, and other associational ties that lubricate and coordinate its production and distribution activities.

Until recently, economists and other social scientists considered informal economic activity to be a trademark of less-developed societies, in part because formally organized production and marketing were less in evidence there. More recently, it has been recognized as present in all societies, even those with the most developed economies. It has been estimated—keeping measurement difficulties in mind—that in Latin American countries between 30 and 50 percent of economic activity is informal; the level is almost 10 percent in the United States (Economic Commission for Latin America and the Caribbean, 2000; United States Bureau of the Census, 2000). Commonly recognized informal forms in the United States include babysitting, hiring domestic workers and gardeners, employing college students to help in moving to a new residence, street selling, and sweatshop contracting and manufacturing. Immigrants, especially undocumented ones, populate the informal sector because their labor is cheap and because they are motivated to keep their economic activities clandestine. Most informal activity is illegal because it involves tax evasion; some aspiring politicians and judges in this country have had their careers derailed when it has come to light that they have hired illegal immigrants as domestics and failed to pay Social Security taxes.

What are the origins of the informal economy? Accounts in the literature reveal several sources: (1) as a means to avoid high-paid union labor by hiring unorganized, lower-paid workers, usually immigrants; (2) as a reactions against high costs of regulation, both monetary and administrative (hassling), by state systems; (3) recently, as a response to heightened competitive pressure resulting from cheaper manufacturing in the global economy; and (4) as a result of increasing levels of economic inequality domestically and worldwide, which produces armies of poor people willing to work at low wages (Castells and Portes, 1989). Economists might thus describe informality as the creation of new markets in the face of different kinds of market failures. The formal economy out of which informality grows need not be a capitalist one. The burdensomely overregulated economy of the Soviet Union combined with a tradition of political corruption to produce systems of informal economic activity, partly to avoid regulations and partly to meet requirements in ways that formal conformity could not (Grossman, 1989). That informality, including a great deal of criminal activity, has continued in post-Soviet Russia.

Informality thus produces a dualism between official and unofficial. The informal economy supplements the formal by filling in economic spaces that the latter does not reach. In some extreme cases, such as Bolivia, informal and illegal drug traffic activities are massive and produce distortions of the entire economy (Jiménez, 1989). Significant informal activities also reinforce or extend the inequalities that contribute to their rise. They also may reinforce structural divisions between immigrants and nonimmigrants and among ethnic groups. In these ways the informal economy creates greater heterogeneity in the labor force and reverses predictions of the homogeneous proletarianization of workers. Its overall effects are not uniform; as Castells and Portes (1989) describe it, the informal economy "simultaneously encompasses flexibility and exploitation, productivity and abuse, aggressive entrepreneurs and defenseless workers, libertarianism and greediness" (11).

The state and the informal economy stand in an ambivalent relation. On the one hand, the informal economy is welcomed as a valued part of the commitment of states to increase their economic activity and growth. It also is a mechanism that may convert what would otherwise be a starving and desperately poor population into a minimally surviving and near-desperate one and thus lessen the impulse to extreme expressions of social unrest. On the other hand, the existence of informal and illegal activities fly in the face of the state's regulatory apparatus and in some cases significantly reduce revenues from taxation. The most common resolution of this ambivalence is a kind of tolerant, live-and-let-live attitude toward informal economic activities on the part of the state, which, however, retains and sometimes exercises the power to crack down on them when, for example, they flagrantly cross the line from semilegality to open illegality or when external criticisms mount. In extreme cases—massive drug activities are the best example—the state becomes economically dependent on the informal sector and incapable of taking political, including military, action against it.

The informal economy can be expressed in the language of sanctions. In one sense, it avoids many of the sanctions imposed on other economic activities by virtue of its unregulated status. At the same time it is uneasily regulated by the *threat* of sanctions by the state apparatus or international firms and agencies. It also generates and operates through a pricing and distribution system of its own and is further regulated by the sanctioning force of particularistic bonds and loyalties. Above all, the informal economy is inventive with respect to stabilizing its activities through the play of alternative sanction systems. It reminds us again of the power of human ingenuity, expressed in its ability to capitalize on new opportunities when existing ones do not suffice, and to devise institutional governance for formally ungoverned activities.

Corruption and Its Cousins

Corruption is in an important part of the informal economy in that it supplements formal market systems with subterranean exchanges that exist alongside formal markets, taxation, and regulatory machinery, often working at cross-purposes with these systems. Corruption has proved notoriously difficult to define and measure, inclusive and heterogeneous in its manifestations, variable in the degree to which it is considered a problem, and elusive of explanations. We consider these features in order.

Many definitions of corruption have been ventured, and as a result it is a contested concept in meaning and connotation. Nye put forth a definition that has been widely accepted: "behavior which deviates from the formal duties of a public role because of private-regarding (personal, close, family, private clique) pecuniary or status gains, or violates rules against the exercise of private-regarding influence" (1967: 419). The inclusion of the terms "formal duties" and "public" already reveals a difficulty. It presupposes some separation between public and private; this further suggests a level of differentiation of a polity as a distinct sphere of public organization; and it certainly implies some standards that define items of behavior as corrupt. Where such a separation does not exist (in many less-developed countries) or is imperfectly realized (for example, in some postsocialist societies, in which corruption is "emblematic" [Grekova, 2001]), most behaviors commonly defined as corrupt—gift giving, tax evasion, informal exchanges, doing favors for family, friends, or fellow-tribesmen—are not so regarded, and are sometimes treated as matters of obligation. New forms of corruption appear in unexpected places; for example, some companies have tried to recapture frequent-flyer miles from employees traveling on company business; they considered it a form of corruption if employees reaped private benefits from official business (most efforts to recapture failed on account of employee antagonism and resistance). All these considerations not only make corruption difficult to define and operationalize, but also complicate positive or negative value judgments about it. Furthermore, changes in framing make the same item of behavior unacceptable or acceptable. For many decades the University of California and other institutions had regulations against nepotism and prohibited the hiring of kin and relatives in the same academic unit. Subsequently, under pressure from feminist groups that regarded this rule as discriminatory, these rules were removed from the books and such hiring policies were no longer regarded as corrupt.

A clear definition of corruption is not helped, moreover, by the large and changing family of behaviors that are included under the heading. Most commonly, it involves purchasing political favors or exemptions with money—or, in the language of this chapter, a crossover of economic and political sanctions. But many things that have been included under its umbrella do not fit or overlap with that connotation—treason; kleptocracy (including larceny and stealing); forgery and embezzlement; padding of accounts; skimming; undeserved pardons; deceit and fraud; perversion of justice; cronyism and parasitism; bribery and graft; gerrymandering and tampering with elections; trading sexual favors for political favors; kickbacks; blackmail; swindling; tax evasion; nepotism; acceptance of improper gifts as corruptions of the democratic process; black markets; organized crime; excessive perquisites; and conflicts of interest (Caiden, 2001: 17). Corruption overlaps but is not identical to cousins such as aggressive lobbying and gift giving to politicians, patronage, and scandal ("Scandal is corruption revealed" [Lowi, 1988: vii]). Nor does it help that new forms of corruption are continuously being added as circumstances change—international bribery and money laundering, for example, which emerged vividly as expressions of globalization and international finance.

Ambiguity of definition and heterogeneity of inclusion render measurement difficult. Should each subtype, even if agreed upon as an instance of corruption, require a different measure? If so, how should they be measured and aggregated? Should "perception of corruption" measures (such as Transparency International's Corruption Perception Index) be used, or are "harder" behavioral measures preferred? Are measures reliable over time? To these standard methodological problems, add two more specific sources of distortion: Most behavior regarded as corrupt is, like crime, kept deliberately secret by those who engage in it; and if discovered, that discovery is often contested on grounds that no wrongdoing was committed. Furthermore, because corruption is often a hot political subject, groups making claims about its extent are likely to distort it upward or downward because those groups have an interest in downplaying or exaggerating it. Even when information is scarce or unavailable, social scientists often approximate availability by creating "rates" from hopelessly inadequate information bases. That is part of their trade, however, and part of the impulse to make information "useful" for those want to explain, police, or shepherd it.

It is commonly agreed that, despite conceptual and measurement difficulties, some corruption can be found in all political systems, and it is probably impossible to eradicate it completely (Caiden, 2001). It is also true that public and scholarly attitudes and evaluations vary over time and region. As values of democracy and economic liberalization spread, so do sensitivity to and preoccupation with corruption. Also, corrupt behavior becomes a subject of condemnation and concern during movements for civil-service reform. In the United States, the spoils system and municipal machines in the nineteenth century were regarded variably as corrupt, tolerable, or inevitable (Freedman, 1994). The Progressive Era of the late nineteenth century singled out political municipal activity as venal and initiated multiple reform movements against it. The social-scientific regard of corruption at that time was also more or less uniformly negative. In the mid-twentieth century, however, a season of "functionalist apologies" (Klitgaard, 1988: ix) appeared, in which positive features of corruption were identified—as a way to involve or integrate marginal (often ethnic) groups into the polity, as a positive antidote to bureaucratic paralysis, and as a way to facilitate economic development (Wraith and Simpkins, 1963; Leff, 1964). More recently, the pendulum has swung back in the negative direction (Kahn, 2006), with corruption being regarded as nonproductive rent-seeking (Lambsdorff, 2007), as the source of increasing inequality (R. Baker, 2005; Uslaner, 2008), as antipathetic to economic growth (Lambsdorff, 2007), and as destructive of the quality of government (Menes, 2006).

What are the causes of corrupt behavior? As on all aspects of corruption, there is little consensus on this score, but the following factors can be identified as components of an explanation:

- Personal immorality and greed. Appeal to these causes of corruption is a repetitive theme, almost a constant. The power of motives of private gain has been formalized in one pessimistic version of principal-agent theory in the concept that no agent will behave altruistically, but will always be motivated—by both legitimate and corrupt means—to maximize private gain (Szanto, 1999). Greed has to be one factor, but as a variable it has little explanatory value, largely because it reveals little about national-cultural and historical variations in corruption.

- Economic need. It can be argued that most of the petty corruption in the world stems from woefully inadequate salaries for civil servants and functionaries, particularly in developing countries. It is perhaps best regarded as a means to supplement salaries, a strategy that lies in that no-man's-land between legitimacy and illegitimacy (Quah, 2010).

- Red tape. This refers to the potential of inefficient rules and procedures and balking bureaucrats to generate illegitimate ways to get around them through bribery and influence. The logic is simple: If you cannot get the service via normal channels and if you value the service, you will seek other channels. Paying to secure visas or passports, securing an "unavailable" bed-sleeper on a train from a conductor, straightening out tax snarls, and avoiding months of waiting for a license are examples. They grease both the machinery and the palms of enforcers and administrators; they are corrupt, to be sure, but often they are regarded as the only way to get things done under the circumstances.

- Opportunity structure. Scholars have observed that in recent decades there has been a worldwide increase in corruption as well as in concern with its negative consequences and control by both national governments and international bodies such as the United Nations (R. Baker, 2005; Bishop and Hydoski, 2009). We believe this assertion is true, and that the main reason for it is the increased availability of opportunities associated with the acceleration of globalism, computer technologies, and the internationalization of finance. These have made a number of practices easier and less detectable: money laundering, tax-sheltered offshore accounts, easy transfer of funds, and secret transactions.

- Weak states. This is also largely an opportunity factor. They make corruption easier in several ways: weak institutionalization of meritocracy and commitment to office; inability to monitor corrupt transactions; inability to discipline their own officials and thereby secure enforcement; susceptibility to corruption on the part of government officials themselves; and the consequent spread of a culture of corruption among the citizenry. This variable—the capacity to prevent, contain, and punish corruption by the state—is among the most important ones in explaining crossnational differences in corruption, insofar as these can be measured adequately. A corresponding factor at the level of international corruption is that international laws, regulation, and enforcement have lagged behind the efforts of discrete nation-states to control corruption.

It is generally agreed that corruption, being inevitable and universal in the nature of social life, cannot be eradicated entirely, but only reduced and managed. Recommendations for reform include better means of detection through surveillance (including computer technologies); institutionalizing countervalues such as civic responsibility; a culture of integrity in office and meritocratic and universalistic values (important but difficult to superimpose formally); reduction of motivation by making legitimate behavior more attractive (e.g., adequate salaries for civil servants and police); and streamlining administrative procedures; punishing corruption in an impartial, noncorruptible way, thus discouraging the powerful corrupt from escaping the consequences of their corrupt behavior. However, such are the power of sanctions (rewards) that sustain corruption, and such are the limitations of sanctions that discourage it, that corruption must be regarded as a kind of granite rock. It can be clawed at, but only limited traction can be gained by clawing.

A CONCLUDING NOTE

In reflecting on this chapter, we notice that the discussion of the topic of sanctions is somewhat scattered and not conceptually unified. One reason for this is that while scholars in every social science recognize the play of sanctions in their own ways, the subject is seldom treated consistently and never uniformly. Even self-conscious attempts to include them—for example, in the sociological topic of "social control," thought by many to be central to the field—has had a tradition of conceptual sprawl. We do record one clarifying conclusion (and this is perhaps another reason for that sprawl): wherever we turn, the play of sanctions is always somewhat elusive. They work imperfectly; they are forever backfiring or producing unanticipated consequences; those sanctioning and being sanctioned are most inventive in altering them or inventing alternatives. These insights are useful in their own way: if we as social actors recognize both the ubiquity and the imperfections of sanctions and sanctioning systems, it encourages us not to build artificial and unrealistic systems of social control, and it renders us more intelligent both in exercising sanctions and in reacting to them.

4

Groups, Teams, Networks, Trust, and Social Capital

In perusing the social-science literature, we often find that a research topic—for example, individual stress—is claimed to be *both* important in itself *and* more important in social life than ever before. Reasons for this are then given. It is also sometimes claimed that the phenomenon is being studied more than ever before. Another variant is that, while the phenomenon is important, it is understudied in relation to its importance (is any topic ever proclaimed to be "overstudied"?). Such assertions are usually not well documented, and one suspects that they are rhetorical, if not self-serving for the authors who pen them. After all, to say that one's topic is more important or important but neglected is to proclaim the importance of one's taking it seriously. In these ways, the assertions may say more about the author than about the topic.

Nevertheless, such assertions may reveal something real. It is notable, for instance, that every topic listed in the chapter title has received similar advertisements:

- Groups: "Group frenzy . . . an age of groupism . . . In recent years, the emphasis on groups and teams has gone beyond any rational assessment of their practical usefulness" (Locke, 2001: 501–02).
- Teams: "Teams are everywhere in business and industry, in government, in schools, hospitals, professional associations—indeed almost anywhere people gather to get things done" (LaFasto and Larson, 2001: xi). "Empowerment and teams have taken the world by storm" (Klein, 2000: xxi). "'Virtual teams' is one of the many hot topics in business these days" (Pauleen, 2004: viii).
- Networks: "Networks have become a buzzword among academics and policymakers alike. Scholarship on networks has multiplied as fast as . . .

networks [themselves]" (Martinez-Diaz and Woods, 2009: 1). "Inter-organizational relations and networks are in vogue" (Knoben, 2008: 2).

- Trust: "For more than a decade now, the topic of trust has been at the center of scholarly research on organizations" (Kramer and Cook, 2004: 1). "Social scientists have become obsessed with trust . . . lamented the lack of it, given it credit for any number of positive social outcomes" (Cleary and Stokes, 2008: 308).
- Social capital: "Social capital has become a buzzword among political and academic elites" (Halpern, 2005: 1).

Though skeptical, we cannot ignore such statements altogether. Their agreement is striking enough that we should ask *why* they agree. Part of the reason for the uniformity of assessment is, we will discover, that all of the concepts are part of a family—interrelated, overlapping, and perhaps addressing a broader movement. In this chapter, we unscramble the claims, identify the essence of each topic, pinpoint trends, and comment from time to time on usability.

We proceed by the following steps: (1) noting a historical trend to downplay group relations in the history of the social sciences; (2) identifying some repeated "discoveries" of the group in the twentieth century; (3) selectively summarizing some accumulated knowledge about groups in social psychology; and (4) analyzing late-twentieth-century surges of interest in and research on teams, networks, trust, social capital, and their applications. At the end of the chapter, we reflect on why these surges occurred in these areas and offer a brief commentary on our times.

THE FATE OF *GEMEINSCHAFT* IN SOCIAL THEORY

A major theme in nineteenth-century social science was the triumph of the impersonal over the personal side of life. Ferdinand Toennies (1964 [1887]) asserted the victory of the principle of society *(Gesellschaft)* over the principle of community *(Gemeinschaft);* Weber (1968), the victory of the rational and legal over the traditional; Durkheim (1997 [1893]), the victory of organic solidarity (contractual) over mechanical solidarity (communal); Redfield (1941), the victory of the urban over the folk; the Chicago school of sociology, the victory of secondary over primary relations in urban life (Reiss, 1964); and, in early developmental studies, the victory of the developed over the underdeveloped (Lerner, 1958). Economists neglected the personal with their assumptions of the depersonalized market and the atomized, unattached, rational, and unsentimental economic actor. Firms were internally undifferentiated actors that behaved like individuals. Political scientists were preoccupied with the larger principles and institutions of democracy. Anthropologists did concentrate on the small societies dominated by principles of kin, clan, and tribe, but these were far away from the contemporary West and in any event were headed toward extinction in the evolutionary march of civilization. Verdicts on these grand transformations were mixed. The dominant response was to hail them as progress. Romantics, sentimentalists, and traditionalists (see White, 1962) and some revolutionaries (see Engels, 1952 [1887]) rued the transition and idealized the rural and the village as worlds we had lost.

REDISCOVERIES OF THE PERSONAL AND INFORMAL

Against this dominance of the formal, the rational, and the structural, any demonstration of the salience of the informal had to be regarded as a "discovery" because it exposed what had historically been pushed toward invisibility. We mention several of the dozens of studies on the topic in the twentieth century, all of which played the same melody:

· Work. Among other discoveries, the Hawthorne Studies (Roethlisberger and Dickson, 1934) identified group recognition as a factor in worker productivity (the Hawthorne effect), and, contrariwise, demonstrated the negative effects of worker cliques in defying management and setting their own terms of productivity. These studies spawned the human relations school in industrial sociology (see chapter 6, pp. 189–90).
· Military life. One lesson learned from the monumental studies of the American soldier in World War II was the centrality of social solidarity at the small-group level. A dramatic extension was the demonstration of the importance of tight-knit primary groups ("buddies") in generating morale, in contrast to nationalistic and ideological beliefs (Shils and Janowitz, 1948). Subsequent work (Moskos, 1970) demonstrated the same principle in reverse in the Vietnam War. Service was based on one-year rotations (in contrast with service "for the duration"), which appeared to weaken group continuity and fostered more privatized beliefs about the war.
· Consumer and political behavior. Work emanating from the Columbia group on communication (Katz and Lazarsfeld, 1955) uncovered the importance of personal ties, community leadership, and influence in areas previously conceived of mainly as sites of individual decision-making, such as purchasing decisions, moviegoing, and voting. While subsequently criticized, extended, and modified, these discoveries foreshadowed the later preoccupation with networks.
· Economic and political life. Extended studies of interlocking directorates, business elites, the informal economy (see chapter 3), and the centrality of particularistic ties and group loyalty in "the ethnic economy" (Light, 2005)

all reveal the penetration of personal ties in the economic and political scenes.

- Disaster studies. Traditionally the imagery of responses to disaster or its threat emphasized individual reactions, especially irrational ones driven by extreme fear. Research based on tornado-stricken communities (Killian, 1951) showed a more complicated picture of role conflict. Policemen, firemen, and public-utility workers faced the question of whether to carry out essential leadership roles in meeting the crisis or to return to their families and friends. Others in less central roles faced a choice between fleeing or joining loved ones and rescuing and giving relief to distressed others. In most cases, the question was resolved in favor of family or friendship groups. Since then, the emphasis on personal ties has become a staple of disaster research. Such knowledge appears to be directly usable as well, for example, in understanding and predicting population movements in cases of disaster and terrorist attacks. For example, if a disaster precipitates a mass evacuation of an urban area during school hours, much of the population would not rush directly to evacuate but would clog city streets in an effort to collect their children before leaving.

We could cite other examples (see chapter 1, pp. 39–40, for reference to the impersonality of urban life), but we would gain little by doing so. All point in the same direction: the salience of personal and interpersonal considerations. We speculate here, but suggest that these cumulative rediscoveries may have been of some comfort to social scientists and consumers of social science alike, for they seemed to say that *Gemeinschaft,* while less immediately visible, is alive and well, and its world is certainly not lost in the march of *Gesellschaft.*

THE TRADITION OF GROUP RESEARCH
IN SOCIAL PSYCHOLOGY

Our observations about the history of the social sciences certainly do not apply to social psychology and small-group research in sociology. For decades, the study of groups has held a solid place in research and curricula, even though it has had its ups and downs in emphasis; for example, it experienced a "down" period during the ascendance of the cognitive revolution, which drove psychology more into the mind. Both theory and research have produced recognizable knowledge, and group psychology texts are predictably organized around standard topics. We review this knowledge now—necessarily superficially—because it appears to be usable in the sense that it identifies principles and processes from which anyone involved in organizational contexts can gain, and, if they ignore them, they do so at their own peril.

Definition of a Group

Because groups are so omnipresent in human life, one would hope for a stable definition. Such is not the case. Minimal characteristics are that a group is a collectivity with a sense of membership and an awareness of boundaries between members and nonmembers, with correspondingly different rates and kinds of interaction between members and nonmembers (Furnham, 2005). Other definitions sprawl, however, with identifying conditions expanded to include similar beliefs among members, self-categorization by group membership, group identity, group perceptions, common interests, and cohesion (Stangor, 2004). Furthermore, the idea of a group fuses with that of social aggregates (people standing in a queue are a categorical aggregate but may become a transient group if they begin to talk and complain to one another) and with networks (normally considered linkages rather than groups, but they may be groups on occasion), social movements, and formal organizations (which generally include many groups but which may develop a group sense). We therefore must live with some vagueness of denotation.

Functions of Groups

Most writing concentrates on positive functions, including groups' role in socialization; social support; empowerment (and derivatively, group psychotherapy, which is socializing, supportive, and, if successful, empowering); camaraderie; information; defining reality for members; contribution to task completion; social control; and decision-making (Sampson and Marthas, 1990). Negative consequences have also been identified, including excessive demands for conformity (which, at its extreme, becomes brainwashing); the excesses of obedience; depersonalization (including the "bystander effect" of not taking responsibility in dangerous or extreme situations); and adverse effects on performance and decision-making (for example, social loafing and groupthink).

Group Structure

One structural dimension is the simple size of groups. Concerns have included the apparent fall-off in both performance and individual satisfaction as size increases, as well as a decrease in cohesion and an increased incidence of social loafing. The literature also indicates that groups with odd numbers of members (five or seven) have advantages over even-numbered ones (four, six, or eight) in avoiding ties and deadlocks; and that groups of more than three people are more likely to avoid the isolated or scapegoated minority member.

While a group is generally less internally differentiated than other collectivities, various roles have been noted. "Task roles" include initiator-contributor, information seeker, opinion seeker, information giver, elaborator, coordinator, orienter, evaluator-critic, energizer, procedural technician, and recorder. Among group-building and maintenance roles, we note the encourager, harmonizer, compromiser, gatekeeper and expediter, group observer, and follower. Among individual roles, we find the aggressor, blocker, recognition-seeker, self-confessor, playboy, dominator, help seeker, special-interest pleader, joker, and silent member (Ellis and Fisher, 1994). Intragroup differentiations include friendships, cliques, blocs, and caucuses. A most important structural characteristic is group cohesion. Among all these lines of differentiation, the emergence of individual roles and the formation of subgroups seem to be most problematic, because both are more difficult to anticipate and control, and both play a crucial role in fostering both group solidarity and group conflict.

Group Processes

This is an enormous area, and we select a few typical ones, postponing the discussion of decision-making to chapter 5:

- Group formation, especially the incorporation and socialization of new members.
- Phases of group process—for example, information seeking, information assessment, suggestions, evaluation, and decision-making in problem-solving groups.
- Group response to deviance, with an initial increase of communication toward the deviant (to bring him or her back into line), often followed by ignoring, rejection, and isolation.
- Group influence, imposition of conformity, and obedience (see chapter 3, pp. 98–100). A countertrend is found in the influence of a minority member or minorities, effective when their investment is high, when they appear to be consistent and fair in their arguments, and when majority opinions are not firm (Muscovici, 1976).
- One consistent line of findings falls under the heading "expectation states" (Berger, Fisek, Norman, and Zelditch, 1977). The kernel is that in group processes, a disproportionate level of influence, respect, and deference is enjoyed by people who have high status outside the group—for example, highly educated people, professionals, and leaders in organizations—largely because of the sense of competence and worth ascribed to those group members. As a result, high-status members tend to speak more, to be listened to more carefully, and to exercise more power in groups. Status-expectation variables are, as a result, among the most important forces in generating power inequalities. The literature yields consistent findings not only in experimental but also in applied settings such as jury deliberation.

Power in Groups

This includes the exercise of leadership (see chapter 6, pp. 190–93) as well as group conflict and its resolution, domination, social control, and negotiation. Of special importance is group justice, rooted in the tradition of relative deprivation. This breaks down into (1) concern with distributive justice, which refers to the satisfaction, dissatisfaction, and conflict allocation of rewards in relation to expectations of justice, equity and fairness; and (2) procedural justice, which brings into question the rules and practices that are evoked in sharing and rewards. Conflicts over procedural justice are often more fundamental to group functioning and survival than tensions over distributive justice because they raise questions about the basic rules of the game and the legitimacy of the entire group enterprise (Hegtvedt, 1994).

Group Performance

This is another huge field, and we note a few areas of research and application:

- Social facilitation. An early emphasis in social psychology, this principle refers to the positive effect of audiences and competitors on individual performance. For a long time, this was held to be a general principle, but subsequent research qualified it by pointing out aspects of groups that diminish performance—evaluation anxiety and accompanying distraction, for example (Brown, 2000).
- Groups appear to be superior in performance if (1) they agree on the group's values and procedures; (2) group members are heterogeneous in talents, experiences, and education; (3) commitment is high; (4) team members mesh with one another in technical skills and personal traits; and (5) the group is oriented toward high standards (Frey and Brodbeck, 2001). Motivational complications of working in groups include social loafing (slacking off) and free riding; these are encouraged when the tasks assigned to groups are unattractive, when it is difficult to evaluate individual contributions, and when one's contribution to the collective work seems insignificant. A derivative of social loafing is the "sucker effect," when a normally productive worker suspects that others are loafing and refuses to be made a sucker by doing more and more work (Stangor, 2004).
- Brainstorming. This involves the search for ideas and suggestions by instructing groups to engage in interactive, free-for-all discussion. At one time this appeared to be a favored idea because it is a way to flex a group's imagination and come up with a wide range of ideas. Subsequently this process was also seen to produce social loafing, anxiety, and paralysis over evaluation; to block

productivity through diversions of discussion; and to encourage the development of illusions of group effectiveness. The anonymity of electronic brainstorming appears to reduce some of these effects (ibid.).

· Intergroup relations. Group psychology deals in part with the processes of categorization, attribution, group identity, prejudice, and discrimination as well as practical measures available to reduce inequities and conflicts among groups (see chapter 2, pp. 56–63).

Such are some of the standard preoccupations of social psychologists and some sociologists. Their findings are in many cases strong and consistent. As in many other areas of social-science research, however, the literature shows a high level of refinement, qualification, and controversy over how general such group tendencies are, and under what conditions they do or do not hold true. For example, status-expectation influences seem to be most evident when groups are small enough to permit face-to-face acquaintance and interaction, when group goals are agreed upon, when standards for success are shared, and when groups have a collective orientation (Balkwell, 1994).

The cumulative result of these traditions of research is that the principles enunciated are in the nature of tendencies rather than laws (see chapter 7, p. 240)—connections to be found widely but not universally. They do not provide formulaic guides, but rather points of sensitivity. This observation also tells us about their usability. These kinds of findings and relationships are usable in the sense that they appear frequently in the daily routines of organizational life and, furthermore, are important variables in determining the group's effectiveness, ineffectiveness, cooperation, conflict, satisfaction, and morale.

TEAMS

Conventionally, the team has been regarded as an instrumental type of group, connoting the need for coordination among members. It has also been associated with groups involved in competitive athletic games, connoting intense pressure to win, "teamwork," "team spirit," and pressures (ambivalent ones, as we will see) to subordinate individual performance to team effort (as seen in the saying "There is no 'I' in 'team'"; and the use of the derogatory term *hot dog* to refer to the team member who flaunts his virtuosity). We include a short section on teams because they, like the other topics in this chapter, have enjoyed a boom in the business, managerial, and organizational literatures in recent decades.

The driving forces in the increasing salience of teams as productive units appear to be two. First, there was an assault on traditional business organization and performance in the late twentieth century. Elsewhere (see chapter 6), we note the trends covered by the ideas of flexible specialization, transient and project-based work, the erosion of work-as-career, organizational flattening and leveling, quality management, the decline of hierarchy, and the decline of organizational continuity through outsourcing and corporate restructuring. Teams as an idea—cooperation-based, self-managing, flexible, adaptive, efficient, innovative, and democratic—appeared to be the engine of improved productivity under these new circumstances (Jackson, 1999). One enthusiastic author asserted that traditional hierarchies were simply becoming less competitive (Fisher, 2000). Another characterized teams as "people with different views and perspective coming together, putting aside their narrow self-interests, and discussing issues openly and supportively in an attempt to solve a larger problem or achieve a broader goal" (LaFasto and Larson, 2001: xxvii). Second, new information technologies that break down spatial and temporal barriers to communication make for greater efficiency in information processing, increase the capacity to cooperate in groups that are not face to face, and reduce the need for organizational-geographical proximity (see chapter 1, pp. 40–43). The two forces combined yield the notion of the virtual team, a special target of enthusiasm.

In chapter 1, we treated electronic teams in terms of their time-space logic and identified a range of promises, contingencies, and obstacles (see pp. 45–47). We need not repeat that analysis here. We underscore a few special points, however, dealing with the themes of this chapter.

Virtual teams are based *both* on a high level of cooperation and on a diminished potential for supervision. The fact that they are autonomous entails loss of traditional, direct control by authorities and a potential increase in loafing, defiance, and deviance. Those who write on virtual teams emphasize self-motivation and commitment on the part of workers; these serve to counter the potential loss of control. Analysts have identified partially new mechanisms that can be used to reinstill control, including what is called clan control, or extensive socialization of team members and ceremonials (Picherit-Duthler, Long, and Kohut, 2004).

Another prominent theme is *trust*. One set of authors asserts simply that "trust is the single most important driver for the success of virtual teams" (Jones, Oyung, and Pace, 2005: 27). It is cultivated by management as part of team culture (Bradley and Vozikis, 2004). The apparent benefits of trust are that it facilitates communication and cooperation and helps to reduce uncertainty, promote common understanding, and resolve conflicts, and thereby reduce transaction costs. The same analyst who stresses these virtues adds, however, that virtuality increases the potential for distrust and vicious circles of mistrust in teams; as a result, working in teams involves walking along the trust-mistrust tightrope (Fernández, 2004). We stress this emphasis on trust in the virtual-team literature because it also appears in parallel ways, as we will see, in the work on networks, social capital, and trust as mechanisms for reestablishing control and predictability.

Another issue is how to reward teams for performance. It is part of the general preoccupation of boards and managers with compensation (see chapter 3, pp. 108–10). As we saw, most of the compensation literature concentrates on salaries, bonuses, stock options, and so forth for *individuals*. Yet insofar as teams, as collective sources of productivity and innovation, play up group responsibility and thereby deemphasize individual heroics, a new issue of compensation is raised: how to reward the group collectively? One guidebook on the subject (Parker, McAdams, and Zielinksi, 2000) does include chapters on "project team incentives" and "organizational unit (group) incentives," but most of the examples describe rewards to groups in much the same way as those as for individuals: compensation and other recognition for reaching or exceeding targets.

In such formulae we note a dilemma. Here is our take on it: American culture remains predominantly individualistic, competitive, and achievement-oriented (see chapter 5, pp. 151–53), and downgrading these emphases creates discomfort. If we look at grading in schools, colleges, and universities, for example, it is almost exclusively focused on individuals and individual accomplishments. Uneasiness prevails about giving the same grade to two or more individuals who write up a collective research effort into a single paper (we want to know who contributed what); this is foreign to most assumptions about talent, accomplishment, and rewards. Consider also the suspicion among school athletic leaders about "expressive" views of sports—good in themselves for participants, with the implication that excessive competition is damaging to those who are average or who are losers. This view is typically countered by assertions that winning is everything, that individual accomplishment builds character and leadership, that losers learn by losing, that competition prepares the young for the adult world, and that the presumed benefits of the "experience" of playing itself are a frail excuse for competitive softness. And in collegiate and professional sports, while the team is often proclaimed to be the thing by coaches and athletes alike, their preoccupation with the all-star player and the most valuable player remains as salient. It is not surprising that this dilemma carries forward into adult occupational and organizational worlds. It reflects the simultaneous love-hate affair that Americans have with groups, collectivism, and collective responsibility, given their dominant cultural traditions.

NETWORKS

The rest of the chapter discusses the interlocking concepts of networks, trust, and social capital. These have received major shifts of attention in many social sciences and related fields such as administrative and management science. These developments, however, are not without their paradoxes and puzzles, and unscrambling them is a formidable task.

A Few Historical Notes

An initial paradox, seen often in the history of the social sciences, is that what is broadcast as a new direction is in large part a revitalization of concepts that have been visible for a long time in different language and garb. This applies in part to network analysis. The nineteenth-century formulations of *Gemeinschaft* and its kindred categories certainly stressed the density and intensity of social relations in rural and village settings, though these were regarded as fading in significance. Durkheim elevated the concepts of cohesion, integration, and solidarity to a central place in his analysis. His study of the density of social interaction and its protection against suicide (1951 [1897]) was network analysis under another name. This research foresaw a major emphasis in network analysis a century later: the apparently positive effects of social ties on mortality, morbidity and health generally (see below, pp. 134–35). Simmel's work (Wolff, 1950) on webs of affiliation and social circles dealt explicitly with social networks. These emphases were carried forth in the "social disorganization" and "anomie" lines of thought in American sociology in the first half of the twentieth century. Social integration was also central in functionalist sociology, which dominated the field in the mid-twentieth century (Parsons, 1951); role and institutional analysis stressed structured interaction patterns. It seems a small step to observe that the logic of networks is in many ways the same as that of many earlier emphases on social cohesion and solidarity, but this observation is overwhelmed by proclamations of the new.

More explicit forebears of network analysis appeared in the twentieth century. The noted rediscoveries of the primary group qualify, even though they focused on primary groups with face-to-face interaction rather than extended linkages. The sociometry of Moreno and his followers (1945) on affiliative ties was straightforward network analysis. Another stream was the research of the Manchester school of anthropology, whose work concentrated on kinship and other affiliative ties in urban settings (Mitchell, 1969; Bott, 1957). The importance of interpersonal ties in communities was also a central theme of the American community studies in Yankee City, Elmtown, Jonesville, and elsewhere, which were informed by British anthropology.

Despite this significant history, network analysis by that name was vitalized in the 1970s, and is now established as a multidisciplinary field spreading into sociology, anthropology, mathematics, economics, political science, epidemiology, physics, organizational behavior, and management studies. A frequently cited innovator is Harrison White (1970), who brought in methodological advances from mathematics and physics and aggressively pressed network analysis. Other significant leaders were Peter Blau, James A. Davis, and Edward Laumann. The pioneering work of James S. Coleman on social capital—which focused mainly on social linkages—fed directly into the excitement. As research and enthusiasm spread and as network scholars began to populate major academic departments, the approach crystallized with the formation of networks of network scholars, a professional association, conferences, annual meetings, publications, and text-books (Freeman, 2004).

To which other areas has network analysis spread? The simplest answer to that question is "everywhere." At the turn of the century, Freeman (ibid.) listed the following: "The study of occupational mobility, the impact of urbanization on individuals, the world political and economic system, community decision-making, social support, group problem-solving, sociology of science, corporate inter-locking, belief systems, social cognition, markets, sociology of science, exchange and power, consensus and social influence, and coalition formation . . . primate studies, computer-mediated communication, intra- and inter-organizational studies, marketing, health and illness, particularly AIDS" (350–51).

From this partial list—partial because it deals only with social networks in the social sciences—we select a few for more detailed illustration:

- Economic life. A very influential study of networks was Granovetter's (1973) study of personal relationships ("weak ties") in finding jobs and recruiting labor, a supplement to other studies stressing kinship ties (Smelser, 1959; Hareven, 1982). Market success relies in part on establishing personal ties (above and beyond advertising). This principle is part of the story of phar-maceutical representatives' gift-giving and entertainment of medical staffs as well as publishers' efforts to cultivate personal relations with potential authors and purchasers of texts (see below, p. 178). More recently, the literature on globalization has stressed regional network linkages (Belussi and Sammarra, 2010) and globally dispersed production networks associ-ated with commodity value chains (Lane and Probert, 2009). Connections through information technology apparently have been so notable that "the network society" has been advanced as a new theory (Castells, 2010). Net-work logic has also been applied to interlocking directorships, the flow of ideas and influence among boards of directors, and, at a more general level, patterns of consolidating and exerting political power among corporate busi-ness elites (Mills, 1956; Domhoff, 1967). The role of personal ties in bolstering economic life among immigrant minorities is well understood, as is their role in informal economies, social insurance, and banking, especially in less developed economies (see chapter 7, pp. 249–51).

Two themes stand out in the literature on economic networks. First, emphasis is placed on networks as sources of information and therefore as centrally relevant in reducing transaction costs. One simple definition of networks is "regular patterns of person-to-person contact that are typically characterized by the exchange of information among humans" (Monge, 1987: 39). As we will see, however, much more than information is involved in the life of networks. Second, these economic/political applications—especially when linked with trust and social capital—emphasize the positive conse- quences of relying on networks with respect to performance and productiv- ity. We will also qualify this emphasis later by pointing to some paradoxes connected with the positive emphases and by noting the darker side of networks.

- Organizations. This focus overlaps with but is distinguishable from market analyses. It deals with how leaders conceive of and develop informal ties, how they exercise influence through them, and how they treat them as a means to achieve goals and coordinate action (Kilduff and Krackhardt, 2008). One important variable is the use of ties to others with high reputa- tions in the exercise of influence and power; "the performance reputations of people with prominent friends will tend to benefit from the public perception that they are linked to those friends" (39). (More generally, this insight exposes a major motive for name-dropping, as well as an explanation of why name-dropping can backfire if it is used blatantly or to excess or is discovered to lack foundation.) At the worker level, it has been demonstrated that workers in informal networks are more productive and have higher satisfaction levels than those who lack them (Rath, 2006), and that workers who have been hired via personal contacts have better performance records and remain longer in organizations than those who were hired through less personal avenues (Castilla, 2005). Schools and universities appear to run primarily on network influence, perhaps because authority is less systemati- cally built into those organizations than it is in more hierarchical ones (the military, for example, and some corporations) (Deal, Purinton, and Waetjen, 2009). Finally, informal networks and peer influence among adolescents in school settings are notoriously strong, because normative standards and personal identities are so much in flux at this stage of life that the search for standards and emulation becomes intense (Cotterel, 1996).

- Governance. This is a more problematic area, but insofar as networks are avenues for exercising power and influence, their connection with governing organizations becomes clear. At the international level, some analysts have argued that, with the overshadowing of state sovereignty that globalization has occasioned, networks have stepped in with respect to agenda setting, consensus building, and policy coordination. The basic hypothesis is that "networks emerge as a reaction to real and perceived failings of formal institutions, and of international organizations" (Martinez-Diaz and Woods, 2009: 16). Case studies have documented the network-dominated activities of central banks, specialized nongovernmental organizations, and regional

groups of finance ministers, all of which operate to clarify international problems, set international standards, and mobilize for policy changes (ibid.).
The mechanisms are sociability and influence, not the exercise of sovereign
power, but many of the outcomes are the same (Grewal, 2008).

· Technology. One consequence of high-level information technology has been
to facilitate informal networks among anonymous and semianonymous
people. This is demonstrated by the enormous popularity of interactive blogs
and Facebook. It has also facilitated commercial and practical work, as evidenced by the growth of telework, virtual organizations, and international
networking among organizations. The Web was also claimed to be, and
apparently was, an important instrument in mobilizing political support
and financing during Barack Obama's presidential campaign of 2008, and
is regarded as a major political instrument in popular uprisings (strongly in
evidence in the Arab Spring in the Middle East).

· Health. The largest area of study of networks has been their role in affecting
different facets of health (Albrecht and Adelman, 1987). In this area, networks
are usually treated as "who knows whom or who talks to whom in a community or organization" (Valente, 2010: 4). The ties encompass kin and friends
as well as less personal contacts; more recently, the potential to expand them
has been increased via telecommunication technologies. Networks play a role
in epidemiological processes, for example, the spread of infectious diseases,
including the AIDS epidemic (Laumann, Gagnon, Michael, and Michaels,
1994). A major factor in the diffusion of medical innovations is personal
interaction among physicians in their own communities (Coleman, Menzel,
and Katz, 1956). Other applications of network analysis include dissemina-
tion of information about community health projects, collaboration among
medical organizations, and spreading information to improve health-care
performance (Valente, 2010).

Most work in the health area has concerned the role of social support
from networks kin, friends, and neighbors in reducing mortality and morbidity as well as mitigating the negative effects of specific disorders. Early
studies linked low social support to high blood pressure, tuberculosis, low
birth weight, and arthritis (Cobb and Ross, 1997). One notable effort was a
nine-year longitudinal study of four thousand people in Oakland, California.
Holding other causes constant—socioeconomic status, obesity, physical
exercise, smoking, and alcohol use—these authors demonstrated a long-term
positive relationship between social support measures and rates of death
(Berkman and Syme, 1979). Social support groups have also been shown to
protect against the onset of psychological stress, to increase the capacity
of individuals to cope with stress, and to enhance the treatment of stress
in group psychotherapeutic and rehabilitation contexts (Young and Blake,

1999). Replication studies point in the same direction; this led the authors of an extensive review of the literature to claim that the causal link between social support and health is as strong as the positive link between smoking and cancer (House, Landis, and Umberson, 1988).

While these associations are remarkable, the *mechanisms* linking network support and better health outcomes are less well defined. The following are plausible: (1) kin, friends, and contacts offer material aid in seeking diagnoses and paying for treatment; (2) they offer advice in understanding disorders and finding the right places to go for treatment; and (3) they offer information about the disorders themselves, their symptoms, their causes, and their course of development (such advice and information, especially when combined with information available on the Web, has eroded physicians' monopoly of knowledge and control of the doctor-patient relationship); (4) they offer emotional support in times of distress and informal counseling in the form of "talk therapy"; and (5), less tangibly, group support may result in improved self-esteem, itself important in physical and mental well-being.

- Personal coping. Network affiliations appear to have effects on domestic coping and childrearing. Among the reference groups to which families turn are other families, who serve as sources of advice, emotional support, and role models. Such influence extends to fathers as well as mothers (Riley, 1990). Contacts are especially important for one-parent homes and for families with absentee spouses (Cochran, 1990). Sharing information and advice among friends and acquaintances in the pregnancy and childrearing years is also evident, qualifying the once strongly held opinion that commercial childrearing manuals were replacing folk wisdom (the Spock effect). As is true of almost all other social resources, however, lower social classes and disadvantaged ethnic groups suffer from a relative deficit of such support (Cross, 1990; Fischer, 1982). On a more subterranean level, personal contacts and networks were shown to play a significant role in locating an abortionist at the time when the procedure was illegal (Lee, 1969).
- Illicit purposes. One aspect of the darker side of networks, to which we will return, is that they are a resource in facilitating undesirable outcomes. Crime is perhaps the best example (Sampson and Laub, 1993). Much of the effectiveness of the Mafia and related organizations rests on the strength of personal ties, loyalties, and influence (Gambetta, 1993). The spread of international crime as part of globalization is also sustained by personal networks. The study of terrorism has revealed that an essential principle of mobilization is to recruit terrorists through family, local, and sometimes religious ties; the resulting horizontal "hubs" or organizational networks of terrorists, moreover, are less likely than hierarchical organizations to be destroyed by decapitation of leaders (Sageman, 2004). Another case is the

power of informal ties in the communist Soviet Union and postcommunist economies. In both instances, they emerged as forms of deviance from—and sometimes ways of improving—cumbersome and inefficient administrative bureaucracy. Such networks are also core features of widespread corruption. These illustrations underscore the truth that precise social mechanisms and strategies are not in themselves good or evil; those qualities arise from the purposes for which they are employed.

All these illustrations concern *social* networks, our major area of interest. Network analysis has also taken off in technological applications (for example, power grids), biological networks, computer modeling, and epidemiology. Network theory has also moved toward mathematical expression, employing random graphs, network models, computer algorithms, and diffusion models (see Newman, 2010). As a result, the field of networks has bifurcated into technical-formal and empirical-substantive directions.

These developments have implications for usability. There has been a growth of interest in the potential offered by new techniques of social network analysis. However, this potential has been seen as unachievable for many, who have found it difficult to come to terms with the technical and mathematical language. Those wanting to take advantages of the techniques of social network analysis have been practical researchers with substantive interests as well as organizational leaders and policy-makers. However, texts and other sources on these techniques have been produced by highly numerate specialists with mathematical backgrounds (Scott, 2000: 1). The same tension appears in econometrics, applications of game theory, and some lines of demographic analysis. On the one hand, formal and mathematical expression achieves greater precision and—less often acknowledged explicitly—endows the authors of this expression with an aura of science and its accompanying claims to prestige. At the same time, this expression decreases accessibility on the part of nonnumerate audiences and generates impatience on the part of those who deal daily with complex and messy, not formally neat, situations.

The Analytic Status of Networks

A comprehensive definition of the significance of social networks is "relationships among social entities and on the patterns and implications of these relationships" (Galaskiewicz and Wasserman, 1994: xii). This is clear enough, yet it is too broad to distinguish networks from other relational systems studied by social scientists—especially groups and institutional structures, with which networks overlap. We now attempt to sort out these distinctions. First, we indicate the kinds of variables commonly used in network analysis:

- Two levels of analysis are most commonly employed in depicting networks: the standpoint of the *individual actor* in networks—his or her perceptions, assessments, roles, and behavior in networks—on the one hand, and *relations* among actors in a system of ties on the other. Most network analysts insist on the reality and importance of the second level, and that leads them to insist that networks are *structures* of relationships that display distinctive properties and processes at that level.

- A core distinction is between strong and weak ties. Kin relations and neighborhood friendships are strong; widely dispersed information networks about job opportunities are weak. Strong ties are characterized by feelings of intimacy and specialness, a desire for companionship, frequent interaction in multiple contacts, and a sense of mutuality (Walker, Walker, and Wellman, 1994). Weak ties are less personalized, are more instrumental, and involve less frequent interaction.

- Among the key factors that have contributed to understanding how networks function are (1) homophily, the principle that recruitment to networks is based on similarities in attitudes, behavior (for example, smoking and drinking), ethnic and racial group membership and identity, and "friends of friends" (Lazarsfeld and Merton, 1954); (2) density of interaction; (3) centrality, referring to the strategic place that discrete members have in networks, which is closely related to leadership; and (4) the idea of "structural holes," or gaps in communication, in networks. One line of entrepreneurial activity is to move into these holes, establish new contacts, and capitalize on them (Burt, 1992).

Networks as a Distinct Type of Collectivity

We now turn to some ambiguities concerning networks as collectivities. Every point we make has to do with the quality of "in-betweenness" of networks in relation to other grouplike categories.

- A common distinction in the social sciences is between micro- and macro-levels of analysis (Alexander, Giesen, Münch, and Smelser, 1987). It appears in economics as microeconomics and macroeconomics; in sociology as the macroscopic and macroscopic; and in political science as political behavior and political institutions. On the micro side are individual behavior, interpersonal interaction (e.g., friendship), and primary groups; on the macro side are aggregates, institutions, and whole economies, polities, and societies. In one sense, networks link the two levels. Some analysts have noted the quality of *embeddedness* of large social networks; by that they mean that they often include and overlap with more intimate social ties within kinship, friendship, and ethnic groupings (Kilduff and Krackhardt, 2008).

The functioning of networks is often facilitated by these closer ties. They make otherwise weak ties stronger. At the same time, network processes are mechanisms in the macroscopic relations *between* large organizations and *among* polities and societies.

· An important distinction in the "new institutional economics" is that between hierarchies and markets (Williamson, 1985). The first refers to vertical relations in organizations such as business corporations, where action is directed by authority and managerial coordination. The second deals with the exchange of goods and services in the economy and involves price payments for goods and services, extension of credit, and so on. Economists and others have asked about the relative efficiency of these two modes, especially in relation to transaction costs and principal-agent relations. The logic of organizational outsourcing and restructuring is based on the idea that economies can be gained by replacing authority with markets.

Networks are mechanisms that stand *between* hierarchies and markets, supplementing the activities of both and connecting them in many ways. Networks are primarily nonhierarchical in that they are usually based on lateral ties among parties—most often "equal" partners who cooperate but do not give orders to one another. Though some networks (between producers and consumers) do involve selling and buying, they are more commonly identified as mechanisms facilitating market processes—lubricating, smoothing, and strengthening them by exchanges of information and influence. This interstitial quality is what gives meaning to the assertion that networks are "neither market nor hierarchy" (Powell, 1990).

· Some networks, especially those based on kin, friendship, and identification, have many defining characteristics of groups—a sense of commonality, belonging, membership, and loyalty. Weaker ties do not manifest these features, being mainly instrumental in their exchanges. "Membership [in networks] is less precise, less categorical, and more fluid [than in groups], which makes it sometimes hard to determine the nature of links between people" (Cotterel, 1996: 47). In those senses, networks stand analytically *between* groups and aggregates, and serve as independent bases for understanding social interaction separate from both the group and the aggregate perspectives.

· Network analysts usually emphasize that their level of analysis is "structural" and that networks are "structures." As we noticed, this insistence stems in part from the effort to move away from focusing on the individual actor. Yet to identify network analysis in this way generates ambiguity about the idea of the structure. One tradition in the social sciences, especially in sociology and anthropology, uses "structure" in a strong sense, as contained in the concepts of institutional structure (law, medicine, kinship, military, or social structure in general). What makes this use strong is that it contains identifiable roles with identifiable expectations and norms, values legitimizing those norms, an array of sanctions and other mechanisms (sometimes laws) to ensure conformity, and mechanisms to bring deviants back into line (see chapter 3, pp. 98–100). Analysts of networks sometimes include such elements, but more often than not network "structure" tends to connote repeated interaction, understanding, and some sanctioning, but without the elaborate framework of controls connoted by the stronger use of the term. In this case, networks stand *between* loose social aggregations and structure in the strong sense. Heydebrand (2001) captures the essential differences: "Social networks . . . are generic social structures. Networks differ from organizations and institutions in that they are informal, private, self-organizing, noncontractual, unaccountable, nontransparent, and typically of limited focus, size, and duration. Networks are the least structured social forms that can be said to possess any structure at all, yet whose structural configurations affect the behavior of their members" (15231).

These observations on the interstitial nature of networks demonstrate that they have an analytical function independent and different from the standard repertoire of the concepts of group, formal organization, market, and social aggregate. This function, moreover, offers one clue to the explanation of the takeoff of network analysis and its applications in the past several decades. In a word, network analysis accomplishes analytically something that the related battery of concepts does not. While the existence of networks is age-old, and while other traditional concepts of cohesion and integration capture some of the their essence, their framing is novel, as is its exposure of the social realities of interaction. Toward the end of the chapter, we assemble a few other reasons for its rise in salience, and we turn now to the rise of its cousins, trust and social capital.

TRUST

Background

In his classic on the division of labor, Durkheim (1997 [1893]) posited that as society becomes more specialized, new forms of integration are demanded. The common memberships of small, undifferentiated communities will no longer do. To demonstrate, he turned to law in modern societies, especially contract and restitutive law, in which different and conflicting interests could be resolved. He called the resulting form of integration "organic solidarity." (Weber also linked the growth of formal administrative law to the development of modern society.) Yet Durkheim also realized that formal contracts were not enough. He coined the phrase "the noncontractual elements of contract" to capture the agreements and understandings, the unspoken rules, and the handshakes that invariably accompany legal agreements. Though he did not phrase it so, Durkheim's reasoning evoked the idea of trust.

To extend this reasoning to the theme of this chapter, we note that groups typically generate a level of trust through their sense of membership. Common membership is, after all, a source of commonality; groups thus are not only in part a product of homophily (sameness), but also breed that sense. One trusts group members more than nonmembers; social psychological research typically yields this result (Foddy and Yamagishi, 2009). Though this group loyalty and mutual trust are often unspoken, they come with the idea of a group. Networks, however, as we have noted, are usually something less than groups. They are often more ad hoc and instrumental; they are often dispersed over long distances; and they often involve relationships with near-strangers. Without the base of group membership, trust thus becomes more problematical in networks and is driven toward explicitness. Just as the rediscovery of group life earlier in the twentieth century reasserted the personal, the emphasis on trust reasserted the same impulse in a different way in the late twentieth century. The rise of interest in networks and in trust coincided. That is because they expressed the same general reaction to perceived changes in the world.

Like the idea of networks, the idea of trust has a long history, though it has not always gone by that name. Understandings about civility among strangers stretch back through ancient times. It is seen in the interaction among vehicle drivers and between drivers and pedestrians (in most cases strangers), who live by a moment-by-moment trust that drivers will not speed excessively, swerve suddenly, or deliberately drive their vehicles into one another. The same observation applies to behavior in queues, subject to expectations and anticipations about crowding in line, appropriate topics of conversation, and common civility—showing, however, cultural variation and degrees of adherence. Among the "givens" that classical economists assumed about markets were that transactions transpired without violence, coercion, or fraud. The absence of fraud is an affirmation of trust among exchanging partners. The idea of normative expectations in sociological role theory implies that interacting partners normally trust one another to conform. The theory of democratic representation in political science is based on assumptions of trust between voters and representatives. That trust is often broken in all these contexts and that it requires supplementary referees and enforcers do not make it less real.

A more explicit concern with trust appeared in theoretical statements on the topic by Barber (1983) and Luhmann (1979), both heavily influenced by the work of Parsons. The theoretical work of Gambetta (1988), Coleman (1990), Giddens (1990), Fukuyama (1995), and Sztompka (1999) all have trust at the center of their analyses, and most of these regarded it as a new and pressing exigency derived from increasing social complexity. The works of Putnam (1994; 2000) embed trust in both democratic and communitarian traditions. Two of his central assertions are that trust is essential for a functioning democracy, and, of more consequence, that trust in contemporary American society is eroding with the demise of voluntary associations and related social forms. In the 1990s, the Russell Sage Foundation established a major research program on trust, and that enterprise has produced a steady flow of publications on its different kinds, aspects, and dynamics.

Definition, Types, and Further Connections

A minimal psychological definition of *trust* is "an expectation of beneficent reciprocity from others in risky situations" (Foddy and Yamagishi, 2009: 17). This is not inaccurate, but it is inadequate. Even at the psychological level, trust reveals degrees of intensity. Sztompka (2001) distinguishes among three levels of strength: (1) minimum expectations of regularity, reasonableness, and efficiency; (2) morally responsible and honorable conduct, fairness, and justice; and (3) altruism, disinterestedness, benevolence, and generosity—corresponding, evidently, to different strengths of ties. Scholars have also distinguished among different analytic levels of trust. The simple definition above is psychological, but if expanded would include aspects that are cognitive (expecting consistent behavior), affective (low levels of anxiety and hostility), and behavioral (an openness that follows from these dispositions). If such traits are general, we speak of a "trusting person," a notion closely related to the idea of *generalized trust,* which refers to beliefs that most others have benign intentions, as well as trust in the larger system in which one lives. Trust can also be viewed *intersubjectively,* that is, as a relation between actors that is negotiated, interpreted, corrected, and repaired. We may also note a distinctively social type, *institutionalized* trust, or formally enforced norms (including laws), sanctions, and enforcement agents such as police and courts. These are not psychological in the first instance; in fact, they are societal creations that acknowledge the limits of psychological trust, and provide controls to assure that people will be trustworthy. The distinctions demonstrate that trust is both individual and systemic.

In an effort to distill the essence of trust, Heimer (2001) isolates two key elements: uncertainty and vulnerability. Each has objective and subjective aspects. Uncertainty and vulnerability may be objective; faith and confidence are psychological strategies to mute both. Trusting individuals subjectively minimize both uncertainty and vulnerability; distrusting individuals maximize both. The idea of risk ties uncertainty and vulnerability into a single bundle. Network ties both demand greater trust and make trust more problematic. We suggest further that it is not surprising that the social-science literature on risk exploded in the same period that the literature on networks and trust did. They are parts of the same complex (see below, pp. 202–4).

Areas of Research and Application

The expansion of a general interest in trust is paralleled by more studies on specific relationships. We review some these here to move closer to the ground and to the usability of knowledge about trust.

· The physician-patient relationship. This arena is a natural for the study of trust because it scores so high on both uncertainty and vulnerability. From the patient's point of view, disease and injury can strike at any time, and these range from trivial to life-threatening. Moreover, despite scientific advances in medical technology, a great residue of uncertainty about treatment remains. The factor of uncertainty appeared as a core variable in both sociological analyses of the doctor-patient relationship (Parsons, 1951) and deviations of the market for medical services from classical economic models (Arrow, 1963). Vulnerability is self-evident, because many health issues are life-and-death matters, and because patients remain relatively helpless because of their lack of medical knowledge. Medical associations' publications on professionalism stress physicians' scientific qualifications and their commitment to service, altruism, and respect for patients—all appearing, among other things, to allay anxiety and increase trust on these scores.

Factors contributing to patient trust of physicians include evidence of caring and empathy; eye contact; body language; attentive or active listening; providing and explaining information; patient participation in decision-making; perceived competence of the physician; physician availability; and physician time spent with the patient. Factors contributing to distrust are suspicious nonverbal behavior; perceptions that physicians are unavailable or rushed; physicians' "putting-down" behavior; and perceptions that the physician distrusts the patient. Social categories also matter; trust tends to be higher if physician and patient are matched along gender, age, education, occupation, or race-ethnic lines.

Treating trust as an independent variable, investigators have found positive relationships between patient trust and successful therapeutic outcomes; acceptance of and adherence to medication regimes; satisfaction with medical care; improvement in symptoms following an office visit; and retention of patients. Difficulties in measuring both trust and some of these outcomes call for caution in accepting and interpreting them (Cook, Kramer, Thom, Stepanikova, et al., 2004).

Finally, some evidence points to increased levels of patient distrust in systems of managed care. These results apparently stem from these systems' more complex organizational features: physicians are under greater financial and time pressure; they are seen as gatekeepers to treatment as well as practitioners; there is more bureaucratic hassling over treatment and coverage; and physicians appear to manifest more conflicts of interest because of their involvement with third parties, especially insurance and pharmaceutical companies (Stepanikova, Cook, Thom, Kramer, et al., 2009).

· Organizations and markets. Here the literatures on networks, trust, and social capital overlap. Trust in leaders has been a major focus. Meta-analyses have shown that trust in leadership apparently contributes to job performance (including group performance), "good citizenship" behavior, low turnover intentions, job satisfaction, and organizational commitment (Dirks and Skarlicki, 2004). As such, trust is an important feature in reducing conflict and other transaction costs within organizations (Kramer and Cook, 2004). On the negative side has grown up a "social science of betrayal," or broken trust, with attention to downsizing, restructuring, and temporary employment, all of which can yield a sense of unfair treatment, distrust, and even betrayal (Robinson, Dirks, and Ozcelik, 2004; and see below, pp. 227–28). On the other side of the equation, chronic quitting and job-hopping can be read as organizational betrayal as well. At the macro level, trust can be shaken dramatically by threatening events and scandals—for example, trust in government to provide national security after 9/11; trust in the moral leadership of the Catholic Church after the exposure of priests' sexual exploitation; trust in business following scandals such as Enron officials' dishonesty; trust following major economic crises such as the financial crash of 2008; and trust following environmental catastrophes such as Gulf oil spill of 2010. We have referred to informal networks in business, the role of reputation (both real and imagined) in generating trust, and the increasing necessity for trust as a resource in globalized production, coordination, and marketing. One factor contributing to the emphasis on trust may be diminished faith in advertising and repeated demonstrations of its limited success (van den Bulte and Wuyts, 2007). Changes in the nature of credit extension provide another example. On the basis of a historical survey, Caruthers (2009) concludes that over a period of two centuries the extension of credit has shifted *from* reliance on personal bases (direct social connections through family or personal acquaintance) *toward* reliance on data provided by impersonal, formal institutions, such as credit-rating agencies. In many respects, this development creates a shakier basis for trust because it is less undergirded by personal ties, intimate sanctions, and loyalties; on the other hand, it is often more systematic in providing information. Reflecting on this evolution of trust, Caruthers offers the following: "The extent to which credit-as-trust is now more institutionally rather than personally embedded suggests that trust is not so much a matter of enduring national character or innate psychological propensity. Rather, with effective design and implementation, institutions dealing with uncertainty and vulnerability can be put in place that greatly enhance the willingness of lenders to trust borrowers, and thus expand the overall volume of credit" (243).

Perhaps this sequence is an instance of a more general cycle in marketing: reliance on personal relations → decline of personal relations through expansion, increases in scale, and structural change → invention of less personal mechanisms partially to replace the guarantees afforded by personal relations.

· Benign and vicious circles of trust. In one dynamic of trust, when institutions appear to be functioning effectively, people's trust in them and one another increases; and when people's general trust in one another is high, institutions function better. Scandinavian countries are cited as examples of this positive reinforcing relationship. This benign circle contrasts with post-socialist societies, especially Russia, whose governments were long regarded by many as dishonest, corrupt, and extending privilege on the basis of party. Dishonesty, evasion of the system's rules, and withdrawal into dealing with intimate groups that one could trust were generally regarded as necessary and acceptable. This pattern has proven difficult to break in these societies. What makes the cycle a vicious one is that if public officials are regarded as untrustworthy and corrupt, then to make one's way, it is necessary to engage in bribery, corruption, and nepotism, even though people may believe that such behavior is wrong (Rothstein, 2004). The working hypothesis behind this vicious cycle is that "uncertainty and risk (such as that created by corruption and dishonesty) lead to the formation of trust networks that are narrow and closed" (Cook, Rice, and Berbasi, 2004: 193). These microscopic observations supplement our earlier remarks about corruption as a system of sanctions (see chapter 3, pp. 116–20).

· The information society and trust. This seems an obvious candidate for the increased salience of trust. The reason is that communication over the Net is highly uncertain, largely because of its anonymity, invisibility, and the minimal information that those who communicate electronically have about one another. Earlier we noted some mechanisms that compensated for those lacks (see above, pp. 41–43). If exchanges through electronic media are mainly sociable, then the parties are minimally vulnerable. If the communications involve exchange of goods and services, however, risk and vulnerability to dishonesty increase, as does the need to supplement exchange by searching for trustworthiness. The e-trust literature is correspondingly focused on material exchanges, represented by Internet markets such as eBay and Craigslist. It is prohibitively costly for third parties to adequately monitor and guarantee such exchanges (Bolton and Ockenfels, 2009). This is the electronic version of the "lemon problem" in economics that forever threatens markets with collapse when products have unknowable defects (Akerlof, 1970). Some mechanisms designed to augment trust are assurances of privacy and security, error-free codes, brand recognition, "touch-and-feel" mechanisms, and the display of trust seals (Cook, Levi, and Hardin, 2009). The most common mechanism is to establish, side by side with the transactions, various after-the-fact rating systems via which those engaged in prior transactions record their satisfaction or dissatisfaction to inform future buyers about seller trustworthiness. The operative mechanism here is reputation, which is not as certain as personal relationships with other parties, to be sure, but which serves the function of establishing some trust and motivating trustworthiness.

The growth of depersonalized networks, especially anonymous electronic media, creates a salient problem of trust. We have focused, as has most of the research, on the mechanisms by which trust is secured or approximated in these settings. We have also noted that the literature emphasizes the positive contributions of trust. One theorist summarizes these contributions as follows: trust reduces the degree of decisional uncertainty; increases the degree of commitment shown by interested actors; contains the conflict level; determines a greater use of noncoercive power; develops fairness and justice; enhances the satisfaction level and quality of social relationships; improves the efficiency of communication; and facilitates cooperative behavior (Castaldo, 2007).

But an analytically prior point cannot be forgotten: a principal motive for expansion and extension of networks and trust is to contain augmented risk of damage and loss (uncertainty and vulnerability). We observed earlier (see chapter 3, pp. 113–14) that new technology not only generates progress, but also creates novel opportunities for deviance. It is these negative possibilities—the opportunity for dishonesty, manipulation, and fraud—that constitute much of the darker side of networks, trust, and social capital alike. But the recognition of this side remains subterranean: "Too much of the recent literature treats trust as necessary for cooperation" (Cook, Levi, and Hardin, 2009: 2). Why should this be so? We noted that the literature on groups and networks emphasizes productivity and satisfaction, in keeping with the strong managerial imagery in much social-science literature. We speculate that one source is the instrumentalist emphasis that pervades our society. We also suggest that "discovering" the network-trust complex itself constitutes a generalized reassurance against premonitions of uncertainty and vulnerability that rapid social change generates.

This line of reasoning leads to a final point. The new and burgeoning "social science of trust" field has made explicit a dimension of social life that has been ubiquitous but whose significance has been underrated. At the same time, the conditions—specialization, interdependency, depersonalization, and globalization—that undergird its emergence also call for a "social science of distrust," an iteration of the conditions under which *distrust* is an appropriate and adaptive reaction, and the rationality that distrust expresses in the human struggle to adapt to circumstances. Students of trust have noted this point (Robinson, Dirks, and Ozcelik, 2004), but it is almost lost in the hope that trust is a contrivance for surviving and even prospering in an uncertain and vulnerable world.

SOCIAL CAPITAL

It is notable how the language of money ("you bet," "as good as gold," "money talks," "I'll buy that") and the language of sports ("hit a home run," "step up to the plate," "slam dunk," "out in left field") pervade the general language in recurrent metaphoric expressions.

To some degree the same can be said of the economic concept of capital. It is a staple of the economic literature in both its financial and physical meanings. It is one of the classic factors of production; it is the name for its distinctive type of economy, capitalism; and it is the cornerstone of Karl Marx's theory of society. The concept has also spread. The economic concept of goodwill, though not bearing the name of capital, does connote stored-up market attitudes that are valuable resources and, if lost, damaging to business. Politicians and voters alike appreciate the meaning of political capital as a reservoir built up from past behavior that can be used to win votes and influence others. Scholars can be said to possess intellectual capital as one of their valued assets, and, while not used daily, moral capital is a meaningful term to describe the reputation of religious and cultural institutions.

In the last third of the twentieth century, three further metaphors based on the idea of capital gained currency (another reference to money!). Human capital is primarily an economic concept that refers to the resources generated by people's socialization, education, and training. It is of economic value both to its holder and the organization that hires that holder. Cultural capital overlaps with human capital, though in the work of its principal exponent, Pierre Bourdieu (2000), it is the product of acquiring a class-based education and cultivation (manners and "taste") and is important in attaining and protecting both social-class prestige and economic advantage. Finally, social capital, also overlapping with human and cultural capital, refers to social contacts and connections as a way to get things accomplished, both economically and socially. Its central idea is close to that of networks in that both provide "a basis for social cohesion because they enable people to cooperate with one another—and not just with people they know directly—for social advantage" (Field, 2003: 17). We concentrate on social capital because it overlaps so much with the logic of networks and trust.

Not surprisingly, the rage for social capital coincided roughly with the decades in which networks and trust burst onto the scene, and some of the same authors were influential. The study of Coleman on the informal relationships among jewelry dealers in New York was seminal, as was his theoretical development of the concept (1988; 1990); he stressed "social good" aspects. Bourdieu (2000) was the second great theorist, emphasizing social domination as well as the instrumental value of social capital. The third strand was the work of Putnam (2000), who focused on the decline of social capital in the United States, tracing it to factors such as the withering of voluntary associations, the dual working family, urban sprawl, mass television, and generational change. Putnam also linked social capital to the effective functioning of democratic polities. As the concept began to pervade the literature and find application after application, it attracted the expectable criticism that it had lost any distinctive meaning (Portes, 1998). Halpern (2005) claimed that social capital is "an intellectual sound bite largely devoid of meaning" (1). Two Nobel Prize–winning economists—Kenneth Arrow and Robert Solow—both criticized the concept of social capital, recognizing is substantive importance but complaining that its use bears scant resemblance to the economic meaning of capital (see Organization for Economic Cooperation and Development [OECD], 2001). To us, these criticisms do not signify uselessness, but rather demonstrate that theoretical developments that are both powerful and trendy have a way of sprawling and overextending, and thereby establishing the need for both theoretical consolidation and methodological improvements.

The applications of the social-capital perspective overlap with those of networks and trust, so we need list only a few:

- Markets. Much of the research referring to the role of social capital in economic performance stresses, as do network studies, its importance in areas such as job seeking, job placement, and regional economic development (Knoben, 2008). Social capital, defined as "stable networks of people who trust one another" (Field, 2003), has also been related positively to the flow of buyer-seller information, contract enforcement, and innovation and entrepreneurship (Halpern, 2005). Macroanalysts have attempted to demonstrate the general link between social capital and growth by demonstrating associations between measured trust and economic prosperity (Whiteley, 1997) and the association of high levels of social capital (trust) with lower rates of corruption, improved quality of bureaucratic performance, better compliance in tax-paying, and improved efficiency of government (La Porta, Lopez-de-Silanes, Schleifer, and Vishny, 1997). Such formulations suffer from problems of both measurement and causal direction that hound almost all general attempts to tie favored variables directly to growth (see chapter 7, pp. 238–39). In an assessment of the literature relating social capital to growth, the OECD concluded that "the evidence is affected by the quality and breadth of proxy measures, the complexity of inter-relationships between different conditioning factors, and the difficulty in comparing countries with widely differing cultural, institutional, and historical traditions" (Organization for Economic Cooperation and Development, 2001: 61).

· Health. The results of research relating social capital to health/well-being are generally coterminous with those found in the literature on networks and health, largely because the two concepts are different names for the same thing.

· Education. It has been asserted that an excellent predictor of college attendance is whether families eat together or separately when children are young. Though it is difficult to sustain this causal claim literally, it is meant to demonstrate the importance of social capital. Research has shown that families that are close, mothers who network with one another, and tightly knit ethnic and religious groups contribute to higher educational outcomes (Halpern, 2005). In its turn, higher educational attainment appears to be associated with individuals' capacities to develop social capital, in part, no doubt, on account of social contacts made along the way. Fraternities and clubs in colleges have long been regarded by members as avenues to future social links and business success.

· Politics. The work of Putnam heightened both interest in and controversy about whether there are positive relationships between social capital on the one hand and effective political performance and democracy on the other, and if so, which way the influence runs. A main point of contention is in assigning meaning to apparent declines in certain types of social capital since the 1960s, as revealed mainly in public opinion polls: decline in participation in voluntary associations, decline in trust of government, and decline in trust of institutions. (The picture appears clear in the United States, and mixed in other countries.) The controversy is also fraught with measurement questions, with the issue of whether there has been a decline in social capital or—of less dire consequence—a shift in its forms (the role of electronic media is relevant to this issue), and whether diminished trust in society's leaders and institutions is a negative or positive sign of health in democratic polities.

As with networks and trust, analysts have stressed the positive functions of social capital. Field (2003) said simply, "The central idea of social capital is that social networks are a valuable asset" (12). Putnam's definition of *social capital* reveals the same emphasis: social capital is "features of social organization, such as trust, norms, and networks, that can improve the efficiency of society by facilitating coordinated actions" (1994: 169). Lin (2002) identifies certain mechanisms by which these consequences are realized: information, influence through intermediaries, confirmation of trustworthiness, and reinforcement of promises and commitments. Yet, like networks and trust, social capital can have its darker sides as well, not only as a resource to facilitate criminal and other disreputable activities, but also as encouraging free-riding, hoarding of information, protection of privilege and status, disadvantaging others, and consolidation of power (see Portes, 1998).

We mention one final point of anomaly and ambivalence. In an often-quoted passage from *The Wealth of Nations,* Adam Smith observed that men of commerce and business seldom meet together without conspiring about prices. Though he did not use the language, he was talking about networks, influence, and perhaps trust. He was also talking about restraint of trade, which was subsequently to become a central principle in antitrust and other legislation designed to protect competitive market processes. That principle survives as a positive principle in legislation, regulatory practices, and the courts. Yet, in the newer literature on networks and social capital, this kind of informal communication is hailed as a virtue, a source of mutual information, confidence, and efficiency in markets that would be lacking without them. Is there a contradiction between our confidence in openly competitive markets and our confidence in informal networking processes that sometimes promote advantage and impede competition? Or are we simply living with both emphases without acknowledging that they pull in opposite directions?

CONCLUDING OBSERVATION

In this chapter, we elucidated and, to a degree, synthesized two closely interrelated trends: a number of *substantive* developments in contemporary society (under the heading of groups, networks, teams, trust, and social capital) and, second, a simultaneous burgeoning of *intellectual* interest in these phenomena in the social-science literature. The latter is a way to recognize the former—a recognition that is basically accurate and profound but also overextended and trendy. In this final section, we comment on a few items of larger significance.

From time to time, we have noted that these contemporary trends represent a return or reassertion of *Gemeinschaft* (group attachments, solidarity, integration) after a long season of domination by the principles of *Gesellschaft* (the formal, the institutional, the rational, and the impersonal forces of modernity). That depiction is colorful, to be sure, but oversimplified; it requires greater precision.

Our time witnesses continuing proclamations of the decline of intimacy, community, and social integration—in extreme form in communitarian lamentations, but also more generally. Many trends cited in this chapter and throughout the volume give qualified—but only qualified—credence to these claims. The hallmarks of rapid social change set in motion by the commercial and industrial revolutions and continuing through the information and global revolutions are continuous processes of differentiation, interdependence, complexity, uncertainty, and risk, as well as unsteadiness of political, social, economic, and natural environments. Add to these the increase in cultural diversification, fed by increasing group consciousness among racial, ethnic, gender, and local groups and by internal and international migration. All these call to mind the repeatedly discovered Durkheimian axiom that an increase in differentiation, complexity, and diversity excites demands for new and more integrative machinery, expressed historically in the growth of law, regulation, and welfare and the increased presence of the state. At the same time, a number of these forms of integration have withered or otherwise lessened in influence. We have in mind the integrative significance of the immediate family, the extended family, the neighborhood, the small community, the church, the tavern, the club, and the employing organization as foci of membership and loyalty, and very likely the cementing influence of political parties. And, given the reach of globalization, the state as an integrative form is threatened in some ways.

We do not join those who proclaim the death of these traditional forms of solidarity and community. Their relative eclipse is often compensated for by adaptive mechanisms, such as the ad hoc arrangements that broken families generate to see to it that children of those families are still involved—if in a diminished way—in systems of parental care and warmth. In addition—and this is where the relevance of this chapter enters—the social world, through a combination of resuscitative efforts, has developed new social forms to contend with the exigencies associated with ever-increasing internal complexity and global expansion. We regard the explosion of networks and social capital—and the augmented trust that must accompany them—as new institutional realities, as new phases in social evolution expressing the continuous counterpoint between differentiation and integration. They are not precisely *Gemeinschaft* revived, but rather *Gemeinschaft* reinvented. Those with nostalgic inclinations refer to the "new trust" as a pale imitation of the old, artificial and weaker than the lost traditional forms—a kind of "shallow morality" (Messick and Kramer, 2001) that falls short of "real" instruments of coordination, control, and solidarity. Others regard these accommodations as saving graces in an increasingly disorderly world—as ways to assure continuing productivity and growth and social integration. We interpret these bifurcated evaluations as a dialogue of ambivalence between Panglossian and Cassandrian impulses that forever accompany change (see chapter 1, p. 51). We also see the increased salience of these forms of solidarity as part of the adaptive struggle that evolution has always involved—the improvisation of imperfect social arrangements that always produce a mixture of success and failure, of true and false starts, and way stations along the path of more change to come.

5

How Decisions Are Made

In one respect, this chapter is at the core of our efforts because it is the point at which issues of usability of social-science knowledge arise most directly. Decisions include assessment of problems, determining what to do about them, the psychological and social processes that go into making decisions, setting in place machinery and processes to make and implement decisions, and tracing their short- and long-term consequences. The subject matter of this chapter overlaps with material in chapter 2 (cognitive and related processes), chapter 3 (sanctions), chapter 4 (groups and related social forms), and chapter 6 (organizations). We make specific note of these points of contact.

A LITTLE SOCIOLOGY OF KNOWLEDGE

In going through the literature on decisions over the past century, we notice that one type of decision has dominated scholarly and popular attention: the *active* and *positive* decision executed *purposefully* by an *individual agent*. This is a selective focus, because many other factors enter decisions and decision-making. We argue that this special tilt makes sense in the context of historically dominant American cultural values.

To illustrate: Intellectuals and social scientists have emphasized core themes in American cultural heritage. A classic account is Williams's (1970 [1951]), in which he singled out "efficiency and practicality," "science and secular rationality," and "materialism." These emphases emanate from individualism, activism, and mastery of the environment, manifested dramatically in the mythology of the conquest of frontiers. Parsons (1951) placed individual achievement and instrumental activism at the center of American values. Riesman's (1950) imagery of the "inner-directed" person struck the same chord. Though such characterizations differ in flavor, they impart an emphasis on the individual and the heroic. Dominant cultural images of captains of industry, robber barons (negative but still heroic), advancement and social mobility through self-determination and effort, the Horatio Alger myth, and the ideal of surpassing one's parents are all consistent with those values. Material rewards are also at the heart of these orientations. The downgrading of passivity, dependence, and fatalism is also consistent with the dominant imagery.

Consonant with these cultural emphases are a number of tilts in the study of decision-making in the social sciences. We note the following:

- A tilt toward focusing on *effective* decision-making, with market success, profits, successful policies, and employee morale as the criteria. Its negative opposite, ineffective decisions, also receives attention. Beyond this effective-ineffective dimension, less attention is given to outright bad leadership—including callous, intemperate, exploitative, corrupt, insular, and evil leaders (Kellerman, 2004).
- A tilt away from *collective* dimensions, even though group and team emphases have emerged dramatically as correctives, reflecting contemporary organizational and economic imperatives (see chapter 4).
- A tilt toward the *economic* and *psychological* dimensions of decision-making. These are the domains of the disciplines of economics and psychology, with their respective analytic emphases on individual atomism and the person as the primary unit of analysis. These emphases—along with claims that these disciplines are more scientific by virtue of their quantitative and laboratory methods—lie at the core of sometimes disputed claims that economics and psychology are at the top of the status hierarchy of the social sciences. Sociology and anthropology, with their group and institutional emphases, do not resonate as comfortably with the individualism-activism cultural core. (Duesenberry once cited a tongue-in-cheek definition of economics and sociology: "Economics is all about how people make choices. Sociology is all about why they don't have any choices to make" [1960: 233].)
- Within more specific traditions—for example, the study of entrepreneurship and the study of organizational decision-making—the dominant emphasis has been on *business, corporate, market-oriented* activity rather than the activities of public and voluntary agencies, though the latter have gained visibility recently. Accordingly, the study of decision-making has been more the property of business, management, and administrative-science schools than of other academic units. As noted, business schools have to some degree "stolen" organizational studies from the academic disciplines.

- A cultural tilt toward certain *types* of decisions. As noted, the dominant emphasis is on the active individual, and includes the imagery of *choice, mastery,* and *conquest.* The preoccupation with *rationality* of all sorts is consistent with these emphases. For what is rationality if it is not a formulation of mastery of information and a guarantee of correct decision-making? In economics, assumptions accompanying rational choice include omniscience, errorlessness, and lack of obstacles to change. By virtue of this selective emphasis, many *other* types of decisions are more or less systematically set aside or ignored—nondecisions through paralysis, "decisions" resulting from aimless floating, blind guessing, errors and catastrophes, decisions by default, and coerced decisions in situations in which there is little or no choice. We argue throughout the chapter that in the history of the field of decision-making during the past half-century, the "descriptive-behavioral" emphases have challenged and rejected the yardstick of rationality, but the latter pervades thinking as a lurking ghost, a standard against which arguments and formulations are or must be assessed.

DEFINITION AND DIMENSIONS OF DECISION-MAKING
ONE FIELD, MANY FIELDS, OR NO FIELD?

The many types of decisions mentioned suggest that multiple definitions are possible, and that exact boundaries are uncertain. Such is the case. One comprehensive definition, ventured at an early stage of the behavioral revolution, is that of Snyder, Bruck, Sapin, Hudson, et al. (2002 [1954]), focusing on foreign policy decisions: "Decision making is a process, which results in the selection from a socially defined, limited number of problematical, alternative projects of one project intended to bring about the particular future state of affairs envisaged by the decision-makers" (78).

This definition differs from "rationality" versions by its inclusion of "problematical," which implies imperfect information. It also has, or implies, several features of decisions that play a large role later in this chapter. First, "socially defined" opens the topic of how demands for decisions and decisions themselves are *framed,* which is essential in understanding the process. Second, the definition implies that a decision involves *commitment of resources* (typically financial, but other kinds as well) to one line of activity rather than others ("alternative projects"). Third, by virtue of that commitment, a decision sets up a weak form of path dependency (see chapter 1); that is, the expectation that future activity will follow the lines dictated by the decision and the commitment of resources. We say "weak" because decisions can remain unimplemented, be undone, be changed by other decisions, go awry, or backfire; nevertheless, the *intention* is to follow a line of commitment.

Even though the Snyder et al. definition has broad scope and has lasted, it loses force when we consider the many dimensions within which decisions vary:

- Social *range:* individual, family, group, community, organization, national, or international. The range dictates many parameters of decisions, as well as salient differences among their determinants.
- The *genesis* of the decision: is it routine, unanticipated, based on perceived continuity or perceived discrepancy in the environment, or dictated by politically significant other parties?
- The *scope* of the decision: does it simply reaffirm past decisions, involve major reallocation of resources, affect group relations within an organization or collectivity, or involve the fate of the entire organization? This dimension is embedded in repeated efforts to make distinctions denoting importance, for example, "tactical" versus "strategic" decisions (Nutt and Wilson, 2010a).
- Different, often incomparable ranges of *determinants* that impinge on, restrict, and sometimes flaw decision-making: degrees of freedom of the decision-maker, the structure and status of past decisions that committed scarce resources and become framing parameters for subsequent decisions, cognitive biases, group influences, structural constraints such as limited resources, and outside regulation.
- Differences in the *process* of decision-making: the flow of scanning, argumentation, influence, judgments, sense-making, and rationalization. We regard this aspect as especially significant and discuss it further below.
- Differences in *consequences,* both short-term and long-term. These include modes of implementation, undermining by interested parties, and changes in the original parameters of the decision. Later we identify many contingencies involved in evaluating consequences (see chapter 8).
- Differences in *structure* of the decision-making apparatus: authoritarian, consociational and consensus-building, delegated, consultative, or participatory. Needless to say, the processes of decision-making are affected by variations in these structures. In certain types of organizations, for example, international consociations, decisions tend to be built through mutual influence rather than being made (Reinalda and Verbeek, 2004).
- Differences in decision rules: the leader decides, majority vote, consensus without vote, the use of "consensus panels" (Wortman, 2001), or the use of standardized procedures such as the Delphi method.
- Difference in the context of *other decisions,* which may themselves become limiting parameters for contemporary decisions at hand, representing, as they do, precedents, commitments of resources (sunk costs), interested parties' vested interests in past decisions, and dependency paths established by those past decisions.

Given this variation, it might be asked whether "decision" and "decision-making" are viable entities at all, and whether generic descriptions of and theory on them are possible. The editors of a definitive handbook on strategic decision-making seem to think not, even for the delimited area of "strategic" decision-making. "The field is diffuse," they say; it is "a field that has yet to mature... theories abound," but, as a rule, "theory is either missing or treated implicitly in much decision-making research." They describe the area as one of "rampant confusion" (Nutt and Wilson, 2010b: 645–46).

We do not despair on account of this pessimistic diagnosis. Even though it is not theoretically coherent, research on decision-making has yielded a tremendous range of insights and findings, many usable as precautions, if not outright guides, to those in the field. We proceed now to survey the field selectively, in an effort to identify its contributions, findings, internal tensions, and shortcomings.

DOMINANT APPROACHES TO DECISION-MAKING
Varieties of Rationality

Elsewhere we have identified organized, rational theories of organizations and decision-making. The most elegant and influential has been that of classical and neoclassical economics. In its pure versions, it takes the economic agent (including market-based business organizations) as governed solely by the principles of maximization of utility through processes of rational calculation, and it regards decisions based on these considerations as both correct (rational) and descriptive of the ways people actually behave. Over time, different versions have appeared: first, economic rationality as a *universal* principle *(homo economicus);* second, economic rationality as not necessarily an empirically correct theory, much less a behavioral universal, but nonetheless an elegant *heuristic* ("as if") device proven useful in the construction of scientific theories, predictions, and economic policies; and third, the consignment of rationality-based theory to the prescriptive or *normative* (how people ought to behave as contrasted with how they do behave). This sequence of characterizations might be regarded as a series of strategic retreats in the direction of theoretical timidity, occasioned by barrages of criticism and contrary evidence. We also identified other versions of rationality—for example, engineering rationality (Taylorism), planning rationality in architectural design and urban and regional planning; and bureaucratic rationality (see chapter 2, pp. 82–84).

All these versions have come in for critical attacks from many quarters. Yet the impulse both survives and continues to reassert itself. What is called decision theory is largely mathematical modeling centering on the "rational agent" and aspiring "to produce abstract theories of rational agency: systematic constructions in which all is explicit, deduced from axioms that are valid" (Bacharach and

Hurley, 1991: 1). Formal and mathematical models of rational approaches abound, including models not only for expected utility theory (the most orthodox version), but also for "corrective" assumptions such as risk aversion, principal-agent situations, collective decisions under uncertainty (for example, Biswas, 1997), and multiple-criteria decisions (Haimes and Steuer, 2000). Game theory, an adaptation of rationality to interpersonal relations, especially conflict, is a large and continuously developing industry. Much of public choice and social choice theory—interdisciplinary endeavors involving economists, political scientists, and public policy analysts—are extensions of rational choice into arenas of policy decisions. And as noted, rational-choice thinking and models have been imported into political science, law, criminology, and sociology.

One approach not based on rational choice in the strong sense but resembling it is scholars' attempts to identify *stages* of decision-making and devise strategies for decision-makers to follow. An early version was generated by Peter Drucker, one of the most influential business scholars and commentators since midcentury. He pointed out that an effective decision proceeded by six sequential steps: "classifying the problem, defining the problem, specifying the problem, deciding what is right, constructing a decision and how to carry it out, and testing the validity and effectiveness of the decision against the actual course of events" (2001 [1967]: 2–3). Decades later, Bazerman (2006) produced a similar list of the elements of a rational decision-making process: define the problem, identify the criteria, weigh the criteria, generate alternatives, and rate each alternative on each criterion. Bazerman adds that such a model is idealized, and people do not follow it "most of the time." As we will see, a main thrust of the "behavioral-descriptive" movement was to establish just that: decision-making and decision-executing are incomplete with respect to information, not reducible to stages, and often intuitive, messy, and irregular in their unfolding. The "stage-sequential" thinking must be regarded as, at best, a checklist of reminders about important ingredients of decisions, and as a rational recapitulation of only a limited subset of decisions.

We mention one more "mastery" strain of literature pressed by practical-minded authors in business school faculties, by consultants, and by publishers eager to serve aspiring managers or those who seek assurance and guidance (two examples are Gebelein, Lee, Nelson-Neuhaus, and Sloan, 1999; and Gebelin, Stevens, Skube, Lee, et al., 2000). These are not rational in any strong sense of the word, but consist of practical tips to follow if successful decisions are to be made and executed. They contain visual representations of a "leadership success wheel" with specific elements such as "seasoned judgment, " "visionary thinking," and "global perspective." Chapter headings include "Create Strategic Advantage, "Use Sound Judgment," "Manage Change," and "Inspire Trust." Virtually every sentence in these volumes is preceded by a bullet and enunciates a helpful hint. It easy to dismiss these books as collections of truisms, homilies, crutches, tautologies, and "rational ritualism" (Etzioni, 2001 [1989]), but these books have gone through multiple editions with multiple printings, and survive well in the market. We interpret their success as an expression of the widespread impulse on the part of their readers to gain even superficial mastery in an uncertain world.

The Behavioral-Descriptive Revolutions

The work of Simon (1947), consolidated in the works of March and Simon (1958), Cyert and March (1963), and Thompson (1967), set off a prolonged wave of theory and research that has dominated the field ever since (Bazerman, 2006). The negative polemic for this work was the psychological foundations of neoclassical economics. The essence of the polemic is contained in the words *behavioral* and *descriptive*. Simon and his contemporaries argued that managers and administrators do *not* behave in the rational way that neoclassical economics believe, and that the proper task of the social scientist is to discover and record how they *actually* behave. In a related critique, they argued that the best way to conduct that study is descriptive, in contrast to with the standard rational models that outlined how they *ought* to behave in order to maximize their utility. Those inherited models are normative. (The word *behavioral* in a related rebellion—behavioral economics—had the same polemic targets in mind [see chapter 2, pp. 75–80].)

What, more precisely, were the limitations of the neoclassical formulations? The main attack was on the postulate of information availability and information processing. Decision-makers typically do not have enough information to define the problem or the criteria for making a decision about it. Constraints on time and the cost of acquiring information limit both the quantity and quality of information (a principle later to inform the theory of transaction costs). In addition, the human mind simply does not have the intelligence, perceptions, or memory to calculate the optimal line of behavior. This line of critique stopped short of labeling economic decisions as irrational, however. Decision-makers *strive* to approximate rationality within these limits, but these limits constitute boundaries that constrain fully rational behavior. Simon and his followers chose the term *bounded rationality* to characterize what really happens when decision-makers decide. They strive for the best they can within limits, and the term that Simon invented for this was *satisficing*. His critique and new line of theorizing caught immediate attention in the scholarly world, and in the end gained him a Nobel Prize.

In retrospect, however, Simon's work was not all that revolutionary when compared with other lines of criticism and reformulation. For one thing, he continued to focus on the individual decision-maker; for another, he retained an emphasis on striving for rationality, albeit a flawed and subdued one. His approach did not extend beyond cognitive-informational obstacles, and stopped short of incorporating affects and other "irrational" elements of decision-making (Mingus, 2007). Other critiques went further. An additional range of criticisms had been growing for some time in sociology and anthropology, to the effect that rational behavior is the product of institutionalized normative expectations rather than psychological universals, and that crosscultural differences in values and beliefs ensure that the posited rationality does not exist in most parts of the world (see chapter 2, pp. 81–82). Within organizational studies came a parade of formulations that identified other kinds of constraints beyond informational deficits that modify the decision process—for example, the age, size, and power of the organization; technological limits; organizational policies and rules; resource limits; environmental constraints; group effects; and individual biases (see Bass, 1983).

As extensions of Simon's views, various "nonrational" theories developed over time, further abandoning maximization and optimization—decisions as expressions of rules of thumb; "aspiration-level" theory, arguing that people search until some level of hope is reached and then decide; "fast and frugal" theory, involving multiple shortcuts in reasoning; theories giving a greater role to emotion; theories treating decisions as a result of group cross-pressure; image theory, arguing that deciders make judgments about strategies that are consistent with their personal views of the world; and decisions made on the basis of reasons contained in "story-telling" (for reviews, see Gigerenzer, 2001; Van der Pligt, 2001). Occasional antirational exhortations to rely on intuition in decision-making appeared (e.g., "In the final analysis you must make the decision *based on how you feel*" [Agor, 1986: iii; italics original]), as well as attacks on such "it-seems-best" and "seat-of-the-pants" approaches to decision-making (Baird, 1989). Needless to say, this proliferation of favorite variables, contrasting if not contradictory explanations, and exhortations plays havoc with any simple idea of usability. The simpler rational approaches at least have the virtue of providing consistent criteria, even if limited or mistaken ones.

We now take note of three special theoretical developments, all further extending Simon's nonrational arguments.

· The "incrementalist" or "muddling through" approach associated with the policy-decision analyses of Lindblom (1959; 1965) and the budgetary analyses of Wildavsky (1992). Like Simon, Lindblom rejected total-information and rational approaches as completely unrealistic. Instead, he regarded policy-making not as deliberative decisions, but as small, incremental adaptations in response to group pressures and short-term political exigencies. In this model there is no way that all alternative lines of action can be considered; the urgency of many decisions precludes thoughtful and complete deliberation. The logic of this approach is one of partisan mutual adjustment,

"feeling one's way," and "two steps forward, one backward." Evidently such
an approach is more applicable to entities that are under constant political
pressure (for example, legislatures and foreign-policy departments in governments), and less applicable to organizations that are more insulated from
politics (for example, research and development laboratories in universities
and corporations). Evidently, too, the muddling-through model is more relevant to democratic polities than to highly authoritarian ones, even though
the latter are not completely free from pressures (for example, pressures from
the military and some dissidence within the dominant party in the Nazi and
Soviet systems).

   More generally, the muddling-through logic reveals that while it is openly
opposed to rationalist approaches, it itself posits a kind of "adaptive man"
model, yielding a view of decision-makers as sensitive and responsive to real
forces in their environment. Finally, it might be argued that the approach
yields, in effect if not in intent, a politically conservative and short-term
view of politics insofar as it emphasizes incremental accommodation,
concessions, compromise, and changes at the margin. It downplays grand
and radical changes. It seems more usable for skilled but timid leaders than
for visionaries.

· The "garbage-can" model of decision-making. Formulated mainly by Cohen,
March, and Olson (1972), this model is an extension of Simon's principle of
contingency in the direction of chaos. The model of the garbage can is apt
(and certainly attention-getting) in that managers and administrators confront situations in which a mountain of miscellaneous information and other
stimuli are thrown at them in a random fashion, and they pick and choose as
if from a garbage can. Their most telling application of the model is to loosely
coupled organizations such as colleges and universities. Cohen, March,
and Olson describe these as "organized anarchies" in which there is much
talk but little action with respect to long-term planning. According to the
model, all is ambiguity, uncertainty, and flux regarding input of information,
demands, preferences, and participation. People come and go, and influences
are temporary. Sometimes problems arise and demand answers, but there are
also pet ideas and theories that seek problems. Leaders jump erratically from
one possibility to another, and little system is observable. The leader faces
ambiguities about his or her own role: ambiguity about the purpose of the
institutions, ambiguity about the actual power he or she possess, ambiguity
about meaningful experiences, and ambiguity about what constitutes success. By comparison, the model makes the muddling-through model seem
orderly. Cohen and March (1974) recognize that the garbage-can model may
seem "pathological" when held up to rational models, but they defend it on
grounds of its usability: "It is clear that the garbage can process does not do a

particularly good job of resolving problems. But it does enable choices to be made and problems sometimes to be resolved even when the organization is plagued with goal ambiguity and conflict, with poorly understood problems that wander in and out of the system, with a variable environment, and with decision makers who may have other things on their minds" (91).

Consistent and reliable rules of thumb are apparently hard to come by in an organized anarchy, but some general strategies emerged from the model, such as persistence in pressing projects, overloading the system so that at least a few initiatives might succeed, managing unobtrusively, and facilitating participation on the part of opposition—rules of thumb that do not exactly derive from the garbage-can model but are consistent with its indeterminacy.

One fascinating application of the garbage-can model was military decision-making (March and Weissinger-Baylon, 1986), not an obvious example because of the military's inherited views of decisiveness, authority, and hierarchy, as reflected in its manuals. Nevertheless, it was argued that military organizations are characterized by the trademarks of problematic preferences, unclear technology, and fluid participation of personnel, and that decisions frequently manifest the expected irregularity, contingency, and stumbling.

THE STOCK EXCHANGE

I retired from Citibank in 2000, after thirty-five years of service. I joined that firm out of college, came up through the ranks, and served sixteen years as chairman. The immediate occasion of my retirement was my losing an argument with the board about the management of the company. Losing hurt, but I had been mulling over retirement for several years without actually setting a date. That date was arranged for me by the dispute, but I was tired and ready to leave.

I view retirement as a time of leisure, experiment, and learning, all impossible while directing a huge global banking organization. As a geographical expression of realizing these goals, my wife and I bought a home on the Île de Ré off the western French coast near La Rochelle. We divided our time between that home and our permanent residence in Princeton. I remained involved in a number of not-for-profit board memberships and other enterprises, but more through choice than necessity.

While washing a boat on the Île de Ré on a September afternoon in 2003, I received an urgent phone call from Hank Paulson, then the head of Goldman Sachs. It was a Friday morning in New York. His message was clear: the New York Stock Exchange (NYSE) was facing a crisis. The precipitating event was the departure, under a cloud, of its CEO, Dick Grasso. It was not clear whether he resigned, was fired, or departed in that large, murky region between the two; it took a long time to sort out the exact circumstances of his leaving. In all events, the immediate and salient issue was his excessive compensation, though as it turned out this veiled many other problems. Criticisms of compensation were being hurled at Grasso, the board, and the entire exchange. What was needed was an interim CEO who could clear up the mess and return the exchange to its traditional place on Wall Street. They wanted someone who knew the business, could deal with governance issues, and could handle critics. The exchange had settled on me. My job would be to determine intelligibly how all this had happened, correct any evident system failures, deal with any legal issues that had been created, restore the credibility of the exchange with the media and the investing public, and then depart. Would I do it? I talked the matter over with my wife after the phone call and agreed to serve. By Sunday I was elected, and by the following Thursday I was back in New York.

Two defining circumstances of my appointment—fixed both immediately and without much reflection—proved to be enormously important. The first is contained in the word *interim* to describe my role. I was in for the journey, not the long haul; I was a repairman, not a permanent boss. This understanding helped me because I could do my work freely and virtually without speculation or suspicion about what my longer-term ambitions might be. The second was my own compensation. I decided immediately and informed the board that I desired no compensation above a symbolic one dollar a year to signify my role. I reflected only a little on this matter at the time, thinking it a natural solution and knowing that with my retirement income from Citibank I needed no compensation. As it turned out, that decision was apparently incidental but symbolically huge. In a context in which excessive compensation was the great bugbear, I completely escaped that issue by taking none. And, along with the interim understanding, receiving no compensation meant that I avoided all complications arising from any possible conflicts of interest on my part.

The NYSE is a unique animal in the contemporary corporate world. It was a creature of the Securities Act of 1934, a child of the Great Depression. It provides facilities and services to its 1,440 members who gather and trade with one another and tightly regulates its proceedings. Members are of two types: brokers who bring customer business to the floor of the exchange and specialists who match buy-and-sell orders for specific stocks and who intervene to maintain an orderly market. When I arrived on the scene, the exchange was a New York not-for-profit enterprise, and we did not host electronic trading; being listed on the exchange was a privilege available only to the most established firms. Because of its historical importance and its elite status, the board had developed a special organizational disease of self-satisfaction, if not "organizational narcissism" (Zuboff, 2004). (A social-science observation: Students of organizational inertia would find a favorite exemplar in the exchange.)

The exchange faced a number of challenges to its business model and its future, but I was not charged to deal with these. We also faced a number of regulatory problems with the Securities and Exchange Commission (SEC) and some restiveness from our customers. The SEC was considering disciplinary actions against a number of specialists and was generally critical of our "self-regulatory" apparatus, which appeared to have dealt inadequately with these specialists' activities as well as those of some brokers. On the side of the customers, I knew that Fidelity, the Boston-based mutual fund company, was deeply critical of the exchange and minimized its business with us. Also, I received an early call from the chairman of the American International Group (AIG), complaining about his specialist. These were issues above and beyond the tangle of excessive compensation, but they demanded my attention.

However, the elephant in the room was still Grasso's compensation. As a nonprofit member organization, the exchange had no obligation to make senior executives' compensation public. (After the fact, this could be interpreted and criticized as organizational secrecy.) At the same time, various board members and others on the floor of the exchange had, for their own, often unsavory, political reasons, begun leaking inflammatory and sometimes inaccurate comments about bonuses and other compensation issues to the media. Strangely, almost everyone agreed that Grasso's performance had been fine, but that the compensation issue had become so "impossible" that he had had to go. The board, a body of truly distinguished leaders, could have dealt more actively with the issue in one of two ways: first, by making the compensation issue public and simply saying that in the board's business judgment, the compensation was reasonable and deserved; or, second, by deciding as a board that some modifications were in order, persuading Grasso to accept these, and making these decisions public. The board did neither, and its passivity permitted the flames of uncertainty and scandal to flare in the press and in public debates.

I report one other complication, present but evasive and unknown in its significance. Grasso was from a poor background, limited in education (no college), and of Italian origin. His big supporter, Ken Langone, was very rich, also Italian, but also not at all from the Wall Street "establishment"—he had developed Home Depot. People knew about these facts and some talked about them, and perhaps it kindled, in a subterranean way, some unspoken or semispoken prejudices and antagonisms against Grasso as a "nouveau." Certainly Grasso believed people objected to his pay because he was Italian and "not of the Wall Street establishment." (This class-ethnic dimension exemplifies a social-science principle: Few apparently single-issue situations are really that; numerous other latent attitudes, dispositions, cleavages, and "earthquake faults" inevitably come into play.)

I had long before learned that one essential way to deal with external criticism and potential intervention is to actively make it a matter of internal concern and responsibility. In a conversation with the board before I was elected, I asked if it had itself begun an investigation to determine what had caused the governance crisis. I learned that it had not. I informed them that I would commence one immediately, on the grounds that when critics (in this case regulators, customers, and the media) are telling you what is wrong and you do not have your own independent information, you are in an impossible situation. I used a few longstanding contacts to find a first-rate law firm that had no conflict of interest (almost impossible, given the board's makeup), and in the end asked Daniel Webb of Winston and Strawn in Chicago to take on our internal investigation. In the meantime, I had gone to the SEC, securing its agreement to meet with Webb and, if they were satisfied with his approach, not to launch their own investigation. They met with him, were satisfied, and did not. A significant degree of freedom was thus gained.

After my first board meeting, I also realized the necessity for a second decision involving the basic character of the board. Its situation was anomalous in several ways. I knew that most of its members were exceptionally capable and impressive individuals, but the group as a whole was not functioning well. Prior to that first meeting, I had spoken with every board member one on one. Some were engaged with the board; some were remote. I discovered many big egos, none of whom wanted to be blamed for what had happened. I heard as many stories about what went wrong as there were members of the board, and most of them blamed others. (This revealed another social-science principle: After any failure or disaster, a season of recrimination and personal scapegoating follows, even though the cause of the event might have been systemic, not personal.)

In addition to this situational drama, the board was encumbered with long-term structural vulnerabilities to conflicts of interest. Member firms represented on the board were the very same firms that the exchange had to audit and regulate. Furthermore, the chairman of the exchange was seen as the "voice of Wall Street" when speaking to the SEC and the U.S. Congress. Grasso had negotiated on behalf of Wall Street and reached the so-called analyst settlement with Attorney General Eliot Spitzer of New York State. The settlement involved more than one billion dollars. Yet the firms involved were required by law, under the 1934 Securities Act, to be on the board! Finally, it became clear to me that while those who are dependent on the exchange—large investors such as TIAA-CREF or broker dealers such as Morgan Stanley—have a legitimate interest in its functioning, that interest should be expressed from outside, not within, the board. All this pointed to the necessity of an independent board.

I proposed a two-tier structure: (1) a small, completely independent board with legal responsibility for the exchange; and (2) a larger board of "users" who would meet regularly and thus engage with the functioning of the exchange. (This exemplifies another general social-science principle: Reforms often involve differentiation of a heretofore commingled entity into structurally separate ones. I did not enunciate this principle in general terms to myself or to others at the time, however; I was dealing with an immediate, difficult situation of conflict of interest.) It took a great deal of discussion and work to get this reform through, but eventually I did. More important, I persuaded the "Wall Street Seniors" to stay engaged through the second board.

This left two tasks: to find a new management expected to endure, and somehow to resolve the still-bleeding compensation issue that could not be swept under the rug. Immediately upon arriving in New York, I began to work with the board's search committee and a headhunting firm it had engaged to find a successor to Grasso. In the following weeks, I talked with many individuals and tried unsuccessfully to persuade one old friend to take the job. Eventually I happened upon John Thain, then president and number two at Goldman Sachs. I knew John from MIT (my alma mater), where we both served on the board of trustees. I saw John during the search period at a lunch at Goldman Sachs when Chancellor Gerhard Schröder was visiting from Germany. After lunch, the idea hit me that John was the man for the job. I approached him on the spot and said, "Let me say something to you, but I do not want you to respond." I then suggested he take on the job of running the exchange. I argued that it would be a great and broadening experience for him and that it would open new opportunities different from those available to him if he spent his whole career within one firm, even a great one such as Goldman. I suggested that he think about the move, talk it over with his wife, and call me if he was interested. A week later he called, and the deal was made.

This left the Webb Report, commissioned as our own independent effort to assess the crisis. The investigators had interviewed sixty people under conditions of high secrecy. I was so concerned about a leak that I personally flew to Chicago with our general counsel and joined another board member, a lawyer from Chicago, to be briefed and read the report. It was consequential and could not be dismissed. It questioned the decisions of different compensation committees and reminded us that under New York State nonprofit law, an executive cannot receive excessive compensation. What were we obliged to do? We distributed the report to the full board; we hired another law firm to give us an independent opinion of the results of the inquiry; we met and talked frequently during the holiday break of 2003–04. I wanted most of all to get the episode behind us.

In the end, we decided to turn over the report to outside political and regulatory authorities, namely the SEC and the attorney general of the State of New York. Part of our motive was the fact that we ourselves (the exchange) were neither organized nor staffed to manage legal actions. We also did not want the exchange further engaged in the issue.

The SEC and attorney general determined between them that the State of New York would pursue the issue. There were many possible avenues for them to have taken: for example, to go after the compensation committee for irresponsible actions. This committee was populated by the heads of big Wall Street firms, including future Secretary of the Treasury Hank Paulson. Instead, Attorney General Spitzer decided to go directly after Grasso on the issue of his excessive compensation. Grasso felt he was being unjustly pursued and refused all offers for settlement. I think he believed that he had, from modest beginnings, started at the bottom—as a runner for the NYSE—and worked himself to the top of the organization via a path that contrasted with the history of the successful and wealthy financial magnates who typically headed the exchange. He believed he should have been rewarded for that singular career, but was being punished instead. The court case dragged on, but in the end was never tried. Attorney General Cuomo dropped the case after then-Governor Spitzer resigned. Meanwhile time had passed and the media and the public had lost interest. Thain and the new management were modernizing and expanding the exchange. It was time for me to go, so I re-retired.

The whole engagement with the exchange was a brief one for me—five months as full-time chairman and CEO and twelve part-time months as non-executive chairman after Thain arrived as CEO. Yet it was a new, engaging, and instructive experience. I came to understand the history and functioning of the exchange. I had to try to fathom the development of a crisis that was almost unfathomable. I had to delve into constitutional issues of the exchange and its legal entanglements, including an unsuccessful lawsuit filed against me by Grasso. I met freely and openly with the media; this contrasted with my lifelong style of meeting with the media as seldom as possible and reading almost nothing they wrote about me. In the end, I wouldn't have traded the whole experience for anything.

(A final social-science observation: I could not have come close to accomplishing what I did were it not for the history of social contacts and networks [extending outside the banking world into corporate and political spheres] that I had developed over my long career as a financial executive, along with the personal social capital that these constituted. By virtue of them, I was able to gain reliable and trusted information quickly, to find the relevant focus of action on any issue I was facing, and to use longstanding relationships as a basis for personal influence. Everywhere that social scientists look, they find the primary group, friends, and networks at the center of things; this episode simply confirmed that principle.)

—John S. Reed

A personal reflection may be in order. Smelser has spent most of his academic career at the University of California, Berkeley (1958–94 and 2001 to the present). During that time, he has often been in and around administrative positions and offices. Berkeley is a large, complex campus with a long history of being buffeted by conflict and crisis. This would seem to make it a fitting candidate for the garbage-can model. In its periods of deepest crisis, the campus certainly yielded a picture in keeping with it. If we reflect on the larger picture, however, that model seems exaggerated, almost a caricature. On top of the relative lack of power of the central administration and beyond the periods of extreme crisis, the campus does have well-defined consultative and decision-making units and processes (academic schools and colleges, the Academic Senate) that are established, if inefficient, and are relied upon more or less consistently to produce predictable flows of influence, as well as intelligible, if also inefficient, decision-making in the face of constant pressures from internal and external constituencies. If Smelser were asked to cast a vote, he would say that the decision-making processes on the campus yield a descriptive picture closer to the muddling-through model than to either the garbage-can model or some rational one (see further discussions of crises and governance in Smelser, 2010).

· The heuristics revolution. We covered this important movement in chapter 2. It will be recalled that, mainly on the basis of experimental studies, researchers have discovered, described, and traced the implications of many mental heuristics and other mental shortcuts, almost all of which produce errors in reasoning called for by rational models and statistical reasoning. The main categories of bias are cognitive shortcuts, emotionally affected decisions, and self-enhancing biases. They have been described as "traps" to effective decision-making (Russo and Schoemaker, 1989; Hammond, Keeney, and Raifa, 2001 [1998]). Specific examples are the anchoring trap, the sunk-cost trap, the overconfidence trap, and the confirming-evidence trap. While the heuristics revolution has offered the most comprehensive and undercutting effects on the rationality postulate—if it has not dethroned it altogether— there are some limitations on its usability. Most findings have been generated on the basis of experiments, sometimes on trivial problems unrelated to organizational decisions. Furthermore, they have not produced a positive theory of decision-making, but rather a partially organized list of cognitive and affective vulnerabilities. The main focus of usability is contained in the corrective advice ventured by Hammond, Keeney, and Raifa, "Forewarned is forearmed" (2001 [1998]: 67–68)—valuable cautionary advice, to be sure, but significant mainly as consciousness-raising.

So much for the most salient lines of development. Taken together, they constitute an interrelated set of trends:

- From theory to theories. No one can pretend that an orthodox economic theory of decision-making has ever enjoyed an undisputed monopoly. The history of economic thought reveals pulsating seasons of controversy about the realism of its assumptions and its empirical usefulness (Swedberg, 1987). Yet from the point of view of *relative* dominance and from the standpoint of numbers of viable competitors, it enjoyed that status up to the middle of the twentieth century. Our review of developments since then has revealed myriad criticisms and alternatives, resulting in proliferation of alternative lines of explanation of decision-making. Not all of them meet the criteria of formal theories, but they are challenging and provide new insights about the decision-making process and the multiplicity of determinants that come into play.

- From theoretical elegance to theoretical indeterminacy. One of the intellectual accomplishments of classical and neoclassical economic theorists is their capacity to construct theoretically tight frameworks and explanations. They have accomplished this, moreover, by the mechanism of assuming constancy of many potentially operative variables. If all these are givens, then explanations of behavior can be generated by referring to a very limited range of determinants. As we have seen, moreover, one of the adaptive strategies in the field is, when inadequacies in the parametric structure are uncovered, to create new specific parametric conditions (risk and uncertainty, mainly) and *alternative* formal models.

  It can be argued that *any* attempt to explain behavior must assume that *some* potentially operative variables are constant; without that, explanation would devolve into shapeless descriptive accounts (see chapter 8). Yet this is a matter of degree. What can be said is that the general drift of the behavioral-descriptive revolution has been to move from the theoretically determinate to the theoretically indeterminate. The consistent direction taken—in bounded rationality, incremental decision-making, the garbage-can model, and heuristics analysis—is to assault one or more classical assumptions of rationality, thus converting it from a parameter to a variable, and demonstrating the consequences of that conversion. The result is that more and different determining variables come into play, and they do so in less systematic, more spontaneous, and more unpredictable ways. The garbage-can model has reached the end of the line in that development. Like the organized anarchy of the organizations it has studied, its explanations approach organized chaos if one applies the canons of theoretically tight explanations.

- Ambivalence, or hypothetical certainty versus contingent realism. Formally neat, organized explanations based on rationality assumptions have a virtue and a vice: they are theoretically adequate and elegant, but on the basis of mountains of evidence, they are by now recognized as largely wrongheaded. As we move toward the descriptive extremes of the behavioral alternatives, we move toward better accounts of reality, but at the same time sacrifice theoretical determinacy. Even if one generates formal models on the basis of revised assumptions, these may be more realistic, but they, too, being formal, entail new kinds of simplifications. And if such simplifications are relaxed, these models drift back toward indeterminacy. The behavioral-descriptive revolution can be described in a variety of ways: a counsel of complexity, a counsel of realism, even a counsel of (theoretical) despair (Etzioni, 2001 [1989]). Above all, it excites a theoretical ambivalence that pervades many areas of explanation in the social sciences (see chapter 8).

When we turn to issues of usability, we greet the same ambivalence. On the one hand, most decision-makers act in an environment of uncertainty, complexity, and unpredictability. Partly in reaction to this, they also experience a drive toward neatness, found in formal models and in formulae in manuals for business success. At the same time, they are driven to search as much as possible for realism in the form of contingencies, biases, and complexities. Given this tension and ambivalence, decision-making continues as an irresolvable struggle between these contrasting alternatives.

THE SALIENCE OF FRAMING IN DECISION-MAKING

To this point, we have underscored the diversity of conditions and processes of decision-making and observed that the field of inquiry has dispersed theoretically. We close this general section of the chapter by identifying a phenomenon that is conspicuous throughout, and promises to provide a unifying thread, if not a full theory of decision-making. That phenomenon is the process of continuous framing and reframing of the meaning-context of decisions.

A workable definition of *framing* is "a mental construct consisting of elements, and the relationships between them, that are associated with a situation of interest to the decision-maker" (Beach, 1997: 23). This reveals that the concept is a cousin of others that have had currency in the social sciences: cognitive mapping, stereotypes, psychological schemas, causal models, some heuristics, and the "definition of the situation." The concept of framing was a major impetus in the work of Erving Goffman (1974). The component of "socially defined" as an element in decision-making in Snyder, Bruck, Sapin, Hudson, et al.'s (2002 [1954]) definition implies framing. It also implies the impingement of external power interests, as well as meanings supplied by cultural and institutional contexts

(Schafer and Crichlow, 2010). These forces, moreover, are modified as individuals and groups endow them with different meanings. The whole process can be characterized by the ebbs, flows, and contests among meaning frames that provide bases for discussion, legitimization, and direction in identifying problems, weighing alternatives, deciding to decide, and assessing the consequences of decisions. Frames change continuously, moreover, in accord with decisive inputs of new meaning. Frames, in a word, mediate between the determinants of action and the acts themselves. Finally, in considering decision-making in this way, we also move toward considering it as a continuous *process,* not a discrete thing.

In addition to providing meaning, what are some of the characteristics of the flow of framing?

- Concentrating on the flow of meanings is a way to track interaction among all those ingredients that enter the persuasion-influence process surrounding decisions. It is a way to organize the dynamics of presenting counterfactuals; evoke the history, identity, and culture of the relevant organization; appeal to group loyalty and group and organizational memory; employ rhetorical devices; and seek the convincing "preemptive metaphor."
- The flow and flux is a continuous process of sense-making—"the ongoing retrospective development of plausible images that rationalize what people are doing" (Weick, Sutcliffe, and Obstfeld, 2010: 83). This often involves little more than decision-makers reminding one another of the agreed-up basis for decisions. However, it also may involve the input of decisive changes in reference that cast the problem, the decision, and the expected results in an entirely new light; that is what *reframing* means.
- As sense-making, the flow of the framing process is a way to reduce the uncertainty and ambiguity that accompany decision-making. It makes psychological sense to recognize that most decisions occur in a context of significant uncertainty. This constitutes a basis for psychological discomfort, because it means committing resources and reputations with some blindness. This discomfort, in its turn, is the major motive for seeking closure through the framing process. The meanings that emerge from this process, moreover, constitute the most important justifications for taking action (Bass, 1983).
- The significance of the framing process is not exhausted by the idea of the search for meaning in a context of uncertainty. It is simultaneously a struggle for influence and power by individuals and groups with interests in decisions and their outcomes. The process is a parade of presenting evidence, arguments, and persuasive strategies in a contested process (Majone, 1989). Framing is thus *both* analysis and argument, and permits the fusion of both the consensus and conflict perspectives, which have often been regarded as contradictories.

- The idea of framing also permits a synthesis of the individual and group perspectives, often regarded as pulling in opposite directions. Framing is carried out in group discussions and is at the same time an important ingredient in the psychology of those responsible for decisions.

This discussion of framing is in part a recommendation to researchers to attend to the idea of framing as a research instrument, producing knowledge about the antecedents, execution, and consequences of decision-making. It is also useful for those involved in decisions themselves. One characteristic of framing is that much of it is carried out implicitly, below the level of individual and group consciousness. The framing process thus often operates without actors' recognition of what is going on. Knowledge of the dynamics of framing is a way to raise consciousness on that score, and increased consciousness is an increased capacity to grasp the reality of ongoing actions and to improve the quality of informing and criticizing decisions.

We devote the remainder of the chapter to few more specialized literatures applying to more limited ranges of decision. The major focuses are on presidential decision-making, medical decision-making, and "naturalistic" decision-making under extreme conditions.

PRESIDENTIAL DECISION-MAKING

There are several reasons why—in an era of fascination with decision-making—the American presidency has generated special interest among scholars and the public. First, the presidency is routinely described as the most powerful position in the world—and the president the most powerful man—which in itself makes the office a magnet for attention. Second, such an office makes decision-making a most difficult and complicated matter, bombarded as it is with the influence of parties, groups, and social movements, to say nothing of the other branches of government. Finally, and most subtly, popular views of the presidency sometimes include—usually exaggerated—fantasies of enormous power and glory ("I can grow up and become president"), thus placing the position and the person within cultural traditions that include gods and kings as directing forces in human affairs. As such, the office and its incumbents are special targets for both adulation and blame.

We may divide the large stream of research on the presidency into three areas: (1) the types of decision-making theory that are applied; (2) the role of advisory systems; and (3) the role of individual presidents.

Decision-Making Theory

It is no surprise that the larger intellectual divisions within political and administrative science—mainly revolving around the tug of war between rational and a variety of nonrational models—find their way into research on the presidency. It appears, however, that, in recognition of the complexity of governmental politics, the latter line of thinking has come to dominate. Simon's view of governmental decisions was that "a decision is not a simple, unitary event, but the product of a complex social process generally extending over a considerable period of time (1965: 35). Allison and Zelikow (1999) remind us that governments are not unitary actors but numerous actors with their own preferences. They further identify two major models—competing but not mutually exclusive—for contending with this complexity: the *organizational behavior model,* which is an outgrowth of theoretical developments in administrative science over the decades; and the *governmental politics model,* which stresses vested interests and struggles. Given the massiveness of the federal government and the complexity of its situations, it seems only realistic to adopt some mix of the two.

Presidential Advisory Systems

Consistent with the principle of multiple determination of high-level decisions, scholars have turned to the staff and advisory systems that presidents put in place. This emphasis is built on the correct presumption that no one person can intelligibly handle the number, scope, and ramifications of decisions faced and executed in that office. President Eisenhower gave a positive slant to the principle: "Organization cannot of course make a successful leader out of a dunce, any more than it should make a decision for its chief. But it is effective in minimizing the chances of failure and in insuring that the right hand does, indeed, know what the left hand is doing" (1965: 630). He should have added that staff processes can also lead decisions astray.

Structure is one dimension of advisory systems that has emerged. The structuring of access to the president's ear—who organizes his schedule and who, accordingly, has access frequently and for how long—is a crucial determinant of agenda-setting, input of information, influence, and decisions themselves. George (1980) advocated a system of "multiple advocacy" as a way to maximize not only information, but also alternative options and reasons for and against them. Scholars have identified distinctive structural preferences for different presidents—formalistic (Eisenhower, Nixon), competitive (Franklin Delano Roosevelt), and collegial (Kennedy) (Johnson, 1974). Presidents also vary in the degree to which they prefer multiple advocacy (Eisenhower) or consensus among staff (Reagan) (Kowert, 2002).

One structure appears to be preferred (see Burke and Greenstein, 1989; Haney, 1997): the "honest broker" role for a major chief of staff, which carries an expectation that he or she will not be biased with respect to specific policy alternatives or in favor of a given staffer, but will represent all positions as fairly as possible. In general, this appears to be a reasonable way to increase input of information and diverse or conflicting views. If the broker does not meet these expectations, it may lead to biased decisions, induce the president to seek alternatives on his own, or produce an informal process by which frustrated staffers go around the chief of staff to seek the president's ear. This honest broker model may also reduce the likelihood of groupthink (see below, pp. 182–84). Scholars have noticed that the two major American political parties, historically divergent in respect to advisory styles, now have converged on a "standard model" of advising (Walcott and Hult, 2005), which consists of a strong chief of staff overseeing a hierarchical structure (versus a spoke system with the president at its center); a large staff of several hundred; a multiple advocacy process; and a standard set of arms such as the press office and congressional office staff.

The Role of Individual Presidents
Determinative or Passive?

We mentioned that leadership studies in general could be arrayed along a continuum, with "great man" approaches at one extreme and situational-contingent-historical approaches at the other. The same tension can be found in the literature on the presidency. At the "presidential character" end of the continuum, a number of approaches are visible. Neustadt (1990) took a relatively modest approach in that he focused on the president's struggle to assure that entrepreneurial staff advisors did not overwhelm his own priorities. Barber (1992) focused on the salience of the president's fundamental character traits. Greenstein (2000) underscored the importance of the president's public communication capacities, organizational sense, political skill, cognitive style, and emotional intelligence. His comparative study of recent presidents exploits the notion of leadership style. At one point, when the psycho-historical approach caught attention—an interdisciplinary endeavor generated by the work of Erik Erikson and other influential researchers in the 1960s and 1970s—a number of depth-psychological biographies gained notice (for example, Rogin, 1975).

The other line of research stresses institutional constraints on the president. While an aspiring presidential candidate might bring his or her own personality to the campaign, push pet campaign issues, and make distinctive promises, once in office the president is constrained not only by institutional arrangements (Congress, courts, the executive bureaucracies), but also by resource limitations, laws, traditions, and the agendas of advisors—all imposing decisive checks on choice (Heclo, 1999; Pfiffner, 2005). More generally, the exigencies of his "political time" (Skowronek, 1993)—wars, economic vicissitudes, cultural tendencies and drifts—impose specific limiting conditions on the president.

In a way, the opposition between these two approaches is wrongly framed. It is insoluble in principle because the realities of presidential history constitute a continuous and variable flux and interaction of forces at both the personal and the contextual levels. The key is to unravel the multilevel process, but little progress has been made on that difficult front beyond establishing general consensus that the president or the White House is not a unitary or rational actor, that the structure of advising and related influences on the presidency are decisive, and that the nature, amount, and quality of information reaching the president—as conditioned by the information-producing structures—are major influences on the effectiveness of his decisions (Rudalvige, 2005). It is worth reminding ourselves, however, that that information is always incomplete and lacking in accuracy. History also tells us that in many decisions—for example, in the decision of the Bush administration to initiate war in Iraq in 2002—the availability or unavailability of information appeared to be overwhelmed by other, personal and group-influence considerations.

DECISION-MAKING IN MEDICAL SETTINGS
THE INTRUSION OF CONTEXTS

Elsewhere we consider aspects of medical decision-making: first, clinical trials as a source of information and evaluation (see chapter 8, pp. 270–73); second, the importance of trust in the physician-patient relationship, covering trust in diagnoses, decisions, and treatment (see chapter 4, pp. 142–43); third, at the end of this chapter, what we have to say about decision-making in stressful, urgent, and dangerous situations applies to emergency medical decisions. In this section we identify a specific change in the broader context of medical practice that has revolutionized its decision-making.

From our real and imagined history of medical practice, we might reconstruct a past model of a practicing solo physician with a patient clientele in the immediate community. The main concerns were physicians' adequacy and accuracy of clinical judgment in diagnoses, recommendations, and treatments according to the best available scientific and medical knowledge. The relationship between doctor and patient was a "functionally specific" one (Parsons, 1951), focusing on the patient's health and excluding other concerns. "Nonmedical" elements entered the doctor-patient relationship under the heading of the physician's personal style (bedside manner) and, in small communities, in the overlap of common acquaintances that the physician and patient might have. The relationship also had a market aspect, with a fee-for-service determined by the physician. Conflict of interest involving third parties was seldom an issue, though one could argue that fee-setting itself involves a conflict of interest, i.e., between the practitioner's interest in profit and his/her unqualified interest in (commitment to) the welfare of the patient. Mechanisms such as the sliding scale softened this potential conflict. This idealized model of decision-making in the "heroic indi-vidualist" genre was consistent with the high levels of prestige and trust accorded to the medical profession—and was pressed in public-relations publications by professional medical associations.

Whatever its basis in reality, that model has been superseded by history, and many of associated changes can be appreciated by understanding changes in the *context* of medical practice that have revolutionized practice and radically changed the basis of decision-making. We note some of these changes in context in this section.

Advances in Scientific, Medical, and Other Relevant Knowledge

The most evident contextual change has been advances in scientific knowl-edge, diagnostic techniques, diagnostic instruments, and procedures, leading to greater accuracy and effectiveness of symptom identification, precision of diagnosis, and prevention of disorders. These technical advances provide the basis for more certain diagnosis and treatment, and have drastically affected both modes of treatment and rates of cure and remission for certain afflictions. Paradoxically, however, they have had some less positive implications. They have raised medical costs, complicated the decision-making process by mandating tests and other procedures, and subjected physicians to criticism and perhaps legal action if they do not administer them. They have fostered unflattering images of physicians as not deciders at all, but as "hiding behind the test results" and "slaves of the tests."

Equally important, knowledge generated in public health research and in the social sciences has uncovered dozens of variables that affect all aspects of health and medical delivery. A first stab at identifying this kind of knowledge is found in a statement by Walton (2001) under the heading "What Does a Psychiatrist Need to Know?" to be an informed practitioner. From psychology, he specified the following needs:

> [To] acquire a basic overall knowledge of the findings, methodologies and theories of psychology which are relevant to the practice of medicine; be aware of how patients' emotions, attitudes, values and experiences influence their response to illness and to its treatment; have a knowledge of learning processes and their relevance to medicine; possess knowledge about the main aspects of psychological development of humans from birth to old age; possess skills relevant to effective doctor-patient communication and particularly to interviewing; have knowledge of techniques of assessment used to test the reliability and validity of investigation procedures and therapeutic trials; and attain attitudes to development that will enable them as doctors to comprehend each patient as a complete person living in his or her social environment. (4230)

From sociology, the following lines of knowledge are relevant and necessary for effective practice:

> [Know] the various methods for defining and measuring health; know the importance for health and medical practice of social institutions such as the family, the community, the economy, and the law; understand the problems of equity and inequality in the provision and utilization of health services, related to age, gender, social class, and religion; grasp the changes in society and in the practice of medicine which have affected health and disease and the development of social policy; comprehend welfare provisions, the advantages and disadvantages of a country's health service, and problems of planning for change within a health service; know about the social (and sociological) factors that influence the process of becoming ill and the doctor-patient relationship, and the effect that ill health and hospitalization have on the lives of patients and their families; be able to discuss critically the role of preventive medicine and health education, and the role of self-help groups; the process of medical professionalization; and describe some of the research methods used to evaluate health and medical practice. (Ibid.)

Walton's list is a heroic one, and a good starting point for appreciating the wide range of social-science knowledge requisite for decision-making in a professional setting. However, several observations are in order:

- The list is too long. It is impossible for any practitioner to know about all the things listed, much less keep up with changes in knowledge. Given the demands on practitioners' time, they have difficulty following the literature in their own specialties, to say nothing of the general medical literature and that in the social sciences. For most of the areas listed, they must rely on superficial knowledge at best and, realistically, on semi-informed or uniformed assumptions, guesses, and hunches (their "personal" social science).
- The list is too short. It covers only psychology and sociology, and not all relevant parts of those disciplines. Knowledge produced by anthropologists (comparative healing practices), economists (the workings and failures of medical markets), and political scientists (unequal power relations) could be useful in professional practice, certainly as background knowledge.
- The areas of knowledge listed vary with respect to reliability, validity, and certainty. Some socioeconomic causes of health and disease are well understood, and others not; knowledge of interaction among the causes is murky and controversial. Not all aspects of developmental psychology over the life span provide certain knowledge. Thus, a further impossible demand—evaluating the quality of knowledge—is placed on the practitioner.
- The knowledge areas are relevant *selectively*. Most of those listed are rarely directly relevant to a particular decision. Some serve only as latent back-

ground knowledge for professional decisions, and are rarely directly activated. This fact underscores a more general point: relevant and usable knowledge (whether derived from social-science findings or not) is a reservoir tapped for different kinds of information on different occasions. To change the analogy, that relevant knowledge is in the nature of a toolkit (see Swidler, 1986), with specific tools mobilized on particular occasions.

Walton's suggestions are framed as a concrete list of types of knowledge. Putting them forward simply as a list, however, does not represent the contexts of knowledge available and usable for medical diagnosis, decision-making, and treatment. All institutions are embedded in a variety of public, organizational, economic, and social contexts. Changes in the following contexts are especially important for medicine.

Context
Drifts and Shifts in Public Regard   Like most institutions and professions, the medical profession has experienced a downward drift in public regard for nearly a half-century, as measured by opinion surveys of respect and trust. This constitutes a deterioration of the profession's general social environment and a source of criticisms and defensiveness among practitioners and spokespersons. Within medicine itself, there has been a long-term drift in practitioners' philosophy *away* from authority-based philosophies such as "doctor's orders" and patient compliance, and *toward* an emphasis on patient autonomy—one of the three fundamental principles enunciated in the influential Physician's Charter, issued by several bodies representing internal medicine (ABIM Foundation, ACP-ASIM, and European Federation of Internal Medicine, 2002). This drift has been furthered by the rise and political influence of voluntary associations and social movements, such as the patients' rights movements and groups of patients and sympathizers organized around types of affliction or disorder. An associated trend has been a rise in the readiness of patients, sympathizers, and lawyers to resort to malpractice litigation, and a corresponding rise in insurance rates and increased sensitivity of practitioners to what they regard as a malpractice-happy clientele. All these changes combine to augment the accountability of physicians, and together constitute constraints on the autonomy of their decision-making.

An example of a dramatic jolt in public consciousness and criticism was the appearance, in 1999, of the influential report on medical errors by the Institute of Medicine (Kohn, Corrigan, and Donaldson, 1999). The report extrapolated surprisingly high annual numbers of deaths (up to nearly one hundred thousand) attributable to medical error, not including deaths in convalescent homes and those related to pharmacy prescriptions. The report also identified additional costs beyond the loss of life, and called for reform on many fronts. It produced a flood of publications and electronic communications on patient safety. One study (Selfox, Palmisani, Scurlock, et al., 2006) of these publications claimed that they changed the conversation from one of blame to one of improving the health system. The calls were to apply better technology to evaluate and prevent errors, reform malpractice legislation, reduce stress through overwork, improve staffing (Blendon, Des Roches, et al., 2002), and devise new systems of regulation. The report and subsequent debates added, in a dramatic way, to the vulnerability of the profession to adverse public opinion, and heightened its sensitivity to faulty medical decision-making.

Context

Teamwork, Hospital Organization, and Decision-Making   Even as early as mid-century, scholars of medical practice (e.g., Parsons, 1951) were observing that medical practice in organizations was growing and that, by implication, though not always noticed, the solo-practice model was becoming less applicable. Two aspects of this context stand out: (1) the relative effectiveness of individuals and teams in decision-making, and (2) systemic effects of hospital organization and practice on decision-making. With respect to the first, it is generally accepted that teams consisting of physicians, nurses, and other personnel improve decision-making through input of information, varieties of experience, and perspective (Arocha and Patel, 2001). In a case study comparing surgical and intensive care units, the authors found that surgical teams tended to interact with one another in more democratic ways, sharing information among team members, whereas in medical units a more hierarchical decision-making pattern dominated (ibid.). That case study demonstrated clear differences, but is clearly limited in the degree to which generalizations can be made from its single British hospital setting.

With respect to practice in hospital settings, decision-making is constrained by bureaucratic procedures and by potential conflicts between practicing individuals and within teams. Furthermore, many decisions and procedures lie at the *system* level (as contrasted with individual decisions by practitioners and other caretakers) and assume greater significance. To choose only one example, it is known that one of the important variables influencing the consequences of heart attacks is how quickly after the attack the patient receives treatment. A common pattern of emergency-room treatment is to admit patients, then decide on the urgency of the case through a triage process, often occasioning some delays as data is gathered and forms prepared. Hospitals may also have a policy of rushing patients who arrive in an ambulance after a 911 call directly into treatment—indeed, beginning treatment en route to the hospital and reserving paperwork until later. If a hospital should adopt a policy of bringing *all* suspected heart cases immediately into treatment, the medical effects would no doubt be significant.

The key point is that procedural decisions made at the systemic level, as well as those made by individual practitioners, affect health outcomes. The illustration also calls for further revision of the heroic model of decision-making.

Context
Third Parties and Decision-Making   Two specific aspects stand out. The first is the imposition of regulations by organized health systems (e.g., health maintenance organizations), reimbursing insurance companies, and government agencies (e.g., Medicare) that are driven largely by cost considerations. These intrusions include restraints on the number and kinds of diagnostic tests permitted and the medications prescribed. The main sanction is to deny coverage if the regulations are not followed. Necessary and reasonable as these sanctions may be from a cost-containment standpoint, they constitute a clear limit on the decision-making of professional practitioners, and in some cases fears on the part of patients that the physician is serving other masters (see chapter 4, p. 143). The regulations and the accompanying paperwork, contesting, and appealing constitute a common source of irritation and frustration for medical practitioners. They also feed into fears that such intrusions are part of a larger pattern of changes that are pushing physicians away from their role as professionals (implying autonomous decision-making based on the best knowledge of science, best evidence, and best judgment) and toward the role of employee.

The second arena involving third parties is conflict of interest proper—the infusion of physicians' self-interest into medical decisions. This has always been a latent problem in market-based medical practice, but it has grown in importance along with the improved technology, quality, and importance of pharmaceutical medications and medical devices and the rise of gigantic commercial firms supplying these products in competitive market settings. As both educational and marketing strategies, these firms have over time adopted practices of giving small and large gifts to physicians, entertaining them, inviting them (with a fee) to continuing education meetings designed to press specific products, and providing physicians with speaker fees for public endorsements. The issue has become one of national interest, spurring investigations, exposures, recommendations, reforms, and legislation by professional medical bodies (e.g., the American Board of Internal Medicine and the Association of American Medical Colleges), medical training centers, and federal and state governments. The problem of conflict of interest, however, remain unsolved, and serious problems of enforcement inhibit efforts to contain it. Conflict of interest thus takes its place among the other contextual changes noted, and reinforces our principal message that decision-making theory, research, and practice should emphasize context more than in the past.

TWO SPECIAL SETTINGS FOR DECISION-MAKING
"NATURALISTIC" AND "GROUPTHINK"

Naturalistic Decision-Making

About the same time (roughly the 1980s) that the ideas of risk, uncertainty, and their many derivatives were assuming center stage in the social sciences (see chapter 2, pp. 75–76, and chapter 6, pp. 202–4), a loosely defined research effort called naturalistic decision-making crystallized. An important impetus was a Navy-sponsored research program on decision-making under stress, stimulated by an incident of failed decision-making: the accidental attack on an Iranian Airbus plane by the U.S.S. *Vincennes* (see Schraagen, Militello, Oremerod, and Lipshitz, 2008). Other impetuses were growing practical concerns with risk associated with new challenges and technologies in emergency fields such as firefighting, flying, police work, power-system operation, urgent medical care, air traffic control, and response to disasters. This line of inquiry is thoroughly interdisciplinary, mainly in psychology but reaching into political science, law, economics, sociology, industrial engineering, management, and organization, and relevant in government and military as well as private-sector settings (Rasmussen, 1997).

An informative definition of this area of research runs as follows: "The study of [naturalistic decision-making] asks how experienced people, working as individuals or groups in dynamic, uncertain, and often fast-paced environments, identify and assess their situation, make decisions and take actions whose consequences are meaningful to them and to the larger organization in which they operate" (Zsambok, 1997b: 5). Beyond this general definition, the endeavor reflects three other specific emphases that create certain identity problems for it:

1. As the term *naturalistic* implies, most research work relies mainly on non-experimental studies—field, ecological, simulated, and retrospective interviews—even though some topics (for example, the influence of time pressure on decisions) also have a strong experimental component (Svenson and Maule, 1993). This is a source of both pride (such studies are more "realistic" than artificial experimental ones) and defensiveness with respect to scientific status (they appear to be less "scientific" than experimental methods, not only lacking rigorous controls, but also suffering from small samples, poor design, and ad hoc searching for causes after a decision has failed.)
2. Among all possible naturalistic situations, studies focus on those that involve time pressure, urgency, stress, uncertain environments, and dangerous—often life-and-death—ingredients. Thus it does not include all naturalistic settings, but only extreme ones.

3. The field had its origins in the practical concerns of military, defense,
   disaster-oriented, and other agencies that deal with urgent situations.
   For that reason, plus general public anxiety about these kinds of situations,
   the field is pulled toward both producing scientifically valid findings and
   presenting usable knowledge, including devising training guides for relevant
   agencies.

An illustrative list of research findings in the naturalistic literature includes
the following:

1. Under time pressure, purchasers and other decision-makers tend to give
   greater weight to negative (defects, risks, unknown dangers) than positive
   evidence. They also reduce the number of variables relevant to choice, bolster
   the chosen alternative, and ignore important others. They shorten searches
   for information; fall back more on heuristic devices such as categorization,
   stereotypes, and anchoring; and in more extreme cases rely on defensive
   measures such as denial of important information and denial of uncertainty
   (Edland and Svenson, 1993; Zakay, 1993). One early finding from firefighting studies (Klein, Calderwood, and Cinco-Cirocco, 1986) revealed that
   fire commanders seldom examined two or more options for meeting an
   emergency situation, but instead settled on "one best option" based on their
   extensive training and experience. This raised questions about the viability
   of the assumption, informing much decision-making research, that decisions
   involve considering options and choosing among them. It has also been
   found that, under time and workload pressure, air-traffic controllers tended
   to diminish reliance on instructions based on the situation of individual
   approaching planes and to fall back on less cognitively demanding generalizations about safety (Sperandio, 1978).

2. Preexisting cognitive frames play a powerful role in directing emergency
   workers toward cues and controlling how they "make sense" of these cues
   in urgent or dangerous situations. This seems especially true when the cues
   are items of human behavior—the usual data for police officers in suspicious
   situations, for example—rather than technical data. In a study of police
   officers in potentially dangerous traffic-stopping situations, Zimmerman
   (2008) found that novices tended to react to situations in line with rules they
   had recently learned in training manuals and classes on police procedure,
   whereas seasoned officers relied more on inferences from personal past
   experience in similar situations and on anecdotal "stories" available from
   these situations. Sometimes the frames for inference are not even consciously
   available. For example, in a study of nurses in a neonatal care unit, Crandall
   and Getchell-Reiter (1993) found that nurses were often able to identify life-
   threatening illness in newborns before the results of positive blood tests were

available. When asked how they knew the neonates were sick, however, the nurses could not describe their thinking and reasoning. Only with retrospective "cognitive task analysis"—a method of reconstructing situations through semistructured interviews—could the relationship among the nurses' cognitive frames, their reading of clues, and their inferences be made consciously available. Such findings are obviously usable in the training of nurses.

One additional practical result emerges from naturalistic studies. Given the apparently greater effectiveness of decision-makers with much experience (Zimmerman, 2008) and the apparent effectiveness of using practical situations in training power operators (Greitzer, Podmore, Robinson, and Ey, 2010), it appears that the extensive employment of realistic simulations in training and apprenticeship is a more useful device than relying on textbook-style learning about behavior in extreme situations. Many relevant cognitive and emotional aspects are evoked in practice situations—even though they are not "real"—and postsimulation critique and discussion appear to be a more powerful learning procedure than taking tests on mastered materials.

3. Much research focuses on the differences between experts and novices in emergency situations. As a general rule, researchers in naturalistic decision-making—whether in artificial intelligence, expert system design, cognitive science, systems analysis, or computer science—have concluded that experts are superior analysts and judges in emergency situations, presumably because the diversity of their sensitizing frames is greater, because of their accumulation of skills, and because they have learned to contend with disturbing emotions in such settings (Salas and Klein, 2001). This general finding appears to hold, despite other research traditions that demonstrate limitations on clinical judgments of experts (see below, pp. 281–82) and the general skepticism about expertise on the part of heuristics-and-bias scholars. One source of this tension is that these scholars hold up their findings against the high normative standards of rational choice and statistical reasoning, whereas naturalistic decision-making scholars may not share this reference point.

4. Many confrontations with emergency situations call for teams—firefighting, police work, military operations, and disaster responses, for example. In many cases, time pressure and stress inhibit cooperation on the spot, and as a result team cooperation, programmed in advance, assumes special significance. When teams are able to cooperate, they present distinct advantages over individuals with respect to feedback and self-correction in understanding and diagnosing the situation, maintaining role responsibilities, and providing positive support for team members (Zsambok, 1997a). At the same time, teams face problems emanating from conflict, status competition, and jurisdictional squabbling (see chapter 4, pp. 128–130). This leads us directly to one final observation.

Given the drama, immediacy, and potentially grave consequences of urgent situations, it is understandable that researchers have concentrated on situational features such as time pressure, uncertainty, ambiguity, and mental shortcuts. We suspect that this emphasis has underplayed another class of variables: those associated with the structure of responsibility and accountability. That is to say, actors in these emergency situations almost always have one or more authorities or groups to whom they are accountable, and they are forever looking over their shoulder at these parties and perhaps second-guessing them. Furthermore, if *ex post facto* evidence of incompetence or irresponsibility emerges, interested parties are activated and a season of blame, blame avoidance, and perhaps disciplinary action follows. Surely actors in situations of urgency and high stakes know about this dynamic, and the psychic presence of those other parties should be taken into account when examining behavior during and after emergency situations.

The Groupthink Phenomenon

This idea is a standard, repeated, and enduring feature of social-psychological treatments of decision-making. Though its continuity with the larger literature on naturalistic decision-making is not always acknowledged, it can be profitably regarded as a subtype. The continuity appears in several guises. First, the idea of groupthink, developed by Janis in the late 1960s, was rooted in his earlier research on infantry platoons and air crews as well as therapy groups (Janis, 1982). Second, the empirical settings of research on the topic are natural, not experimental, situations. And, third, groupthink overlaps with naturalistic decision-making studies with respect to antecedent conditions, characteristics, consequences, and suggested antidotes.

The primary empirical base for the groupthink idea was a series of high-level political decisions that resulted in historical disasters. Among these were the Bay of Pigs invasion in the Kennedy administration, failures leading to Pearl Harbor, the Cuban Missile Crisis, escalation of the war in Vietnam, and the Watergate cover-up (ibid.). The historical importance of these situations, combined with the catchiness of the term *groupthink* and the brilliance of Janis's observations, almost guaranteed a strong interest in the topic on the part of social scientists, political leaders, and public audiences.

Antecedent Conditions.   Janis considered groupthink to be a largely mischievous effect, contrasting it with independent critical thinking and regarding it as a source of catastrophic errors in judgment and "irrational and dehumanizing actions" (13). He cited excessive group cohesiveness and group norms as the main engines in its development. In addition, he added several "structural faults" that are conducive: preexisting homogeneity of group membership, insulation of the group from outside information, and lack of norms for impartial decision-making. Situational background factors include evident danger, a high level of stress, time pressure, and a sense of urgency. If the self-esteem of the group has been lowered by recent failures, this too can constitute a pressure to come to premature group consensus and closure.

Groupthink Itself.   Out of these circumstances develops a unitary outlook that becomes a powerful group culture in the context of which momentous decisions are made. It is a complex mentality. It overestimates the group by developing a sense of its own invulnerability to error and a sense of righteous morality about itself. It closes its mind, developing stereotypes about who are its friends and who are its enemies, favoring the former and scapegoating the latter. It directly censors or expels dissenters from its own ranks, rejects their opinions, and thereby augments the sense of its own unanimity. The leader is the main engineer in enforcing conformity, but, in addition, some members become "mindguards," specialists in bringing dissidents into line and protecting the leader from disturbing information and criticism. The mentality of groupthink bears a remarkable similarity to individual clinical symptoms of paranoia, though in this case the mechanisms of enforcement are at the group level.

Consequences.   Most of the immediate adverse consequences of groupthink follow from the blocking and censorship of information and alternative lines of policy action accomplished by the processes just described. Objectives become clouded; alternatives are omitted; information searches are minimized; information at hand is biased through motivated sifting; costs and risks of the preferred policy line are not estimated; and contingency plans in the event of misfiring are neglected (ibid.). The costs in terms of resources and even human lives are likely to be disastrous.

Antidotes.   The invented situational orthodoxy that groupthink produces appears to be powerful, brittle, and resistant to forces that might deflect it. Those who have pondered the problem, however, have come up with a number of counterforces that might be put in place in advance to temper the forces of groupthink as it crystallizes in times of crisis and urgency. Among these are building in an understanding that the leader should act as an impartial coordinator of decisions rather than a "maker" of them; installing systematic procedures for hearing minority opinions, including those of designated devil's advocates; bringing in external advisors; decentralizing decision-making; and adopting some nominal or voting system for approving decisions (Frey, Schulz-Hardt, and Stahlberg, 1996).

All these suggestions are valid and useful, but as a sense of danger and crisis increases, they may fall by the wayside as the forces of groupthink build.

Critique.   Two cautions against overapplying the valuable concept of group-think come to mind (see Schafer and Crichlow, 2010). The first is suggested by the question, How widespread is it? After all, Janis selected situations in which the stakes of decisions are exceptionally high, vulnerability is great, costs of failure are enormous, and, perhaps, the egos of those who have reached the heights of power are especially strong. Those features are important conditions for the emergence of groupthink. However, most decision-making situations are not that heated. We find them mainly at the top of political, military, and corporate organizations. In less intense decision-making settings, cooler heads and more careful procedures are more likely to prevail. In the end, then, groupthink may prove to be a quite specific theory applicable to a very limited range of situations.

Second, we should ask: How "real" is groupthink as a distinct phenomenon? The insights generated by Janis and others have proved to be lasting social-psychological knowledge about pitfalls of decision-making. Yet Janis did not do the world a favor by presenting the phenomenon as a clinical entity—a thing—a distinct combination of its components, all in evidence in instances of groupthink. That does not seem to be the most fruitful representation. As indicated, full-fledged, pathological groupthink may be a relatively rare phenomenon. Rather, the concept should be thought of as a number of probability statements about the excitation of discrete tendencies under conditions of urgency, threat, and strong ego involvement. Each feature of groupthink is a tendency, rather than a necessary part of a coherent package. The concept is usable when it is read as a number of discrete danger signs—the reification and stereotyping of enemies, excessive demands for conformity in thinking, scapegoating the wayward, and a brittle sense of self-assurance—in collective settings. If the appearance of any of these can be discerned, it should trigger reflection, critical examination, and correction. In other words, decomposing and relativizing the seductive global concept of groupthink would seem to be in order.

6

Organizations and Organizational Change

In this chapter, we provide knowledge on the settings in which most decision-makers live: formal organizations. This knowledge ranges from general to specific, which means that it varies in its usability; some is generally orienting, some more immediately relevant to decisions and actions. Such a chapter is mandatory for several reasons:

- Formal organizations are the preferred social forms in most spheres of life—business, government, medicine, law, religion, academics, and organized labor—even for those who advise organizations, such as management consultant firms. They have also become dominant in voluntary enterprises such as political parties, charities, philanthropies, and social movements. We do not exaggerate to say that contemporary society *is* organizational society. One begins the life cycle in organizations (birth in a hospital, recording that birth in a local bureaucracy) and ends it in organizations (Social Security agencies, hospitals again, and a funeral home or burial association), and in between one is the sequential captive of schools, military units, firms, offices, and community associations.
- Many consequential decisions about practices, problems, and policies are made in organizational contexts that frame and determine those decisions; moreover, many consequences of those decisions play out in those same organizations.
- Formal organization is a major topic in the social sciences, emanating from economics, sociology, political science, psychology, anthropology, and history, as well as more specialized areas, such as management studies, engineering,

administrative science, education, and military studies. Courses on organizations are central to business schools' curricula, and these schools, with generous salary structures, have "robbed" some academic departments of scholars of organizations. Finally, in our opinion, the quality of research on organizations is high relative to many other areas. To say this is not to claim paradigmatic unity. Many approaches to the study of organizations dot its history: treating organizations as rational individuals; as "natural systems," in which actual behavior is the focus; as types of political systems; as "open" or "closed" in relation to their environments; and as parts of multiorganizational systems (see Scott and Davis, 2007). Each approach has distinctive powers, relevancies, and shortcomings.

DEFINITION AND DIMENSIONS OF FORMAL ORGANIZATIONS

Definition

Among many competing definitions, a satisfactory general one is found in the most recent edition of Scott and Davis's influential text: organizations are *"social structures created by individuals for the pursuit of collective goals"* (11; italics in original). This is comprehensive but consistent with more specific definitions. Moreover, comprehensiveness is required to encompass the many types of organizations (large-small, private-public, manufacturing-service, hierarchical-flat, market-political-voluntary) rather than treat any specific one as generic. At the same time, the definition differentiates organizations from institutions (medicine, law), from many other kinds of groups (families, friendship groups, networks), and from social categories (occupation, class, race, ethnicity, age, gender).

Size

A fundamental dimension of an organization is how small or how large it is. Traditionally measured by numbers of people employed, size might also refer to wealth, resources, functional capacity (e.g., number of hospital beds), or market power, depending on the problem addressed. Traditionally, too, size has been regarded as directly correlated with—even the cause of—other organizational features. However measured, the size of an organization always carries implications about how its activities are distributed in time and space. Moreover, greater size has been thought to yield greater complexity and formalization (Blau and Schoenherr, 1971). Such effects are both horizontal, referring to specialization of roles, and vertical, referring to the proliferation of levels of authority. Increasing size has also been seen as contributing to efficiency, as implied by the term *economies of scale*. More research has led to more caution in dealing with the effects of size:

- Empirical work has demonstrated no fully consistent relationship among size, formalization, and centralization of authority (Azumi, Hickson, Horvath, and McMillan, 1976).
- The mechanical connection between size and structure was questioned by scholars who argue that national cultures (Japanese or French, for example) intervene to shape authority and other relations in organizations (Abbeglen, 1958; Crozier, 1964).
- As specialization increases, so do needs for administration, coordination, and conflict management, all of which may involve increasing costs as scale increases.
- Efficiencies claimed for downsizing suggest an opposite relationship between size and efficiency.
- The consequences of mergers (one type of size increase) are so mixed that it is impossible to invoke size as having a simple relationship to efficiency (see below, pp. 221–28).
- Other subtler but costly social-psychological consequences may accompany increases in size and complexity. The Marxian tradition of alienation and the human relations tradition are relevant, as are studies of depersonalization, stress, diminished work satisfaction, disloyalty, and organizational deviance (see below, pp. 200–2).
- Recent developments (outsourcing, telework, virtual organizations) have decoupled concentration of personnel in physical space from size of organization (see chapter 1, pp. 44–48), and have further weakened any mechanical relationship between size and its consequences.

Lines of Internal Differentiation

One line of organizational analysis goes under the name of structural contingency theory (Donaldson, 2001). Its main argument is that organizational structure is a tool for coordinating organizational performance. There is no one best structure, but the theory suggests that three contingencies affect structure: *size* calls for a more bureaucratic structure; *task uncertainty* calls for less bureaucracy (i.e., more flexibility), and *diversification* of products calls for a divisional structure. In practice, most business organizations have adopted one or a mixture of several organizational principles: geographical, according to area-based markets (e.g., a North American division, a European division); product; types of customers (e.g., different categories of medical disorders); or some functional division (e.g., sales, accounting, public relations, and personnel).

All organizations are also differentiated hierarchically according to responsibility and authority, though this varies according to whether organizations are top-down (e.g., the military) or participatory (e.g., voluntary organizations) and by the relative importance of fixed roles or flexible teams. An additional basis is between line and staff. The former refers to direct lines of authority (chief executive, top management, middle management, shop foreman, worker), whereas the latter refers to roles and divisions that supplement the line relations and extend sideways. Staff personnel typically offer knowledge and advice, but may also be authorized to proceed independently (as in research-and-development departments). In general, staff grows from needs for specialized, often technical information and other resources that those in line-supervisory roles cannot generate quickly on their own. Viewed thus, staffs are a form of outsourcing *within* organizations. One problem arising from line-staff relations is that those in staff positions are often professionals (engineers, scientists, industrial psychologists), and this may create tensions between their high status and low power. Contracting out and outsourcing affect both line and staff relations.

Not all organizations exhibit the same principles of differentiation. An elementary school, for example, has a principal with direct authority over a small staff (assistant principal and office workers) and less direct authority over teachers, who supervise students and indirectly provide service to parents and community. A local post office has a postmaster with a crew of delivery and service personnel. A small psychiatric clinic is more nearly a company of equals consisting of therapists, with minimal elaboration of supervisory relationships. Social movement organizations typically evolve roles such as leader, recruiter, spokesperson, and volunteer helpers, though as they become larger and more institutionalized, formal organizational structures proliferate accordingly.

Structural differentiation in organizations is more than a division of labor oriented to instrumental goals. Specialization forms the structural template from which other ingredients of organizational life develop. Structural divisions and roles are one—perhaps the main—basis for the development of *patterns of social interaction,* including friendship circles and cliques that go beyond interaction required for instrumental purposes. Incumbency in roles and membership in subdivisions also are central in defining the *status* of individuals within the organization—a ranking system based on prestige, power, and imagined importance to the organization. Common incumbency also defines *interests* and *interest groups* (e.g., "Where you sit is where you stand"). Derivative from interests are the pursuit of *group recognition, status striving, resistance to authority, organizational deviance,* and many aspects of *organizational politics.* Many sources other than specialization contribute to these phenomena, but specialization provides a central defining condition.

Formal versus Informal Organization

Formal organization is what one learns from an organization chart: boxes designate departments; positions are named by function and linked by vertical lines signifying authority and reporting relationships, and by horizontal lines signifying ancillary staff relationships. Such charts are normative representations that demarcate positions and expected responsibilities.

Another representation of formal organization is Max Weber's famous essay on bureaucracy—an ideal type, some have observed, approximating German civil service at the beginning of the twentieth century. According to Weber (1967), a bureaucracy has the following characteristics:

- Performance of bureaucratic activities is defined as a matter of duty and subordinated to impersonal rules.
- Authority is stably institutionalized, and entails the right to give commands and impose sanctions.
- Duties involve a full-time commitment to a role regarded as a vocation, and positions entail the idea of a career.
- Recruitment for, appointment to, and occupancy of positions are based on qualifications.
- Positions are ranked and social esteem is awarded accordingly.
- Written records are mandatory.

Weber regarded bureaucracy as a remarkable social invention. Its historical expansion and staying power rested on its efficiency. It was, for him, one of the hallmarks of the rationalization and advancement of societies. His view is usually assigned to the family of rational theories of organizations.

Weber's and other formal theories have come under sustained criticism. One critique is that external institutional and group forces—such as unions—impinge on the free exercise of authority. Another is the observation that his formalistic theory conceals powerful internal processes called informal organization that reveal what really goes on in organizations. The logic of the informal was revealed in the Hawthorne studies by the "discovery" of cliques among workers, who enforced work-performance norms at odds with those imposed by management. They restricted output by sanctioning their members. They had cohesive relations, developed games and rituals to relieve monotony (Roy, 1960), and constituted a minicounterculture within the larger enterprise. Earlier Taylor had described restriction of output as "soldiering," but felt it could be countered effectively by management (Ackroyd and Thompson, 1999). The major emphasis was that informal organization undermined management's goals, though more extended empirical (e.g., Roy, 1972; Dalton, 1959) and theoretical (e.g., Barnard, 1958; Selznick, 1957) work revealed more complex relations between the formal and informal. It included ways that informal activities (worker cooperation, informal lunches among friendly colleagues, deals sealed on the eighteenth hole, for example) could facilitate decision-making, efficiency, and morale as well as undermine them.

Though it has experienced vicissitudes, the idea of informal organization survives in social-science research. Its characteristics—and its contrasts with formal structure—are that its dynamics are those of interpersonal and group interaction, in contrast to action dictated by formal positions and impersonal norms; it stresses affective rather than impersonal ties; it makes life in organizations more "human"; it identifies new dimensions of organizational life; and it may be more important than formal organization in understanding productivity, worker satisfaction, and morale. In a word, research on informal organization added flesh and blood to the bones of formal bureaucracy. Knowledge emanating from this tradition is clearly usable in that it alerts decision-makers to the realities and limitations of simple means-ends thinking; however, in contrast to rationality-based schemata, it has not provided very specific guidance and rules for conduct. At the same time, knowledge of informal organization supplies understanding of why rationality-based decisions are likely to flounder.

LEADERSHIP

Leadership is a central feature of organizations. Its reference is not limited to organizations alone, however; we also refer to it in the chapters on decision-making, sanctions, group influence, and economic development. In this chapter, we identify theoretical and research traditions in leadership that are relevant to organizations, and refer to leadership's value—and slipperiness—as a concept.

We begin with the reminder that leadership is not unitary. It is very different for private, public, and voluntary organizations. More specifically, the situations and norms of leadership for a military commander $\neq$ those of a CEO of an investment-banking firm $\neq$ those of a college president $\neq$ those of a college professor in the classroom $\neq$ those of a civil servant running a service-providing bureaucracy. Within the military, the leadership of a commanding officer $\neq$ that of a lieutenant $\neq$ that of a staff sergeant. Within a firm, the leadership of a CEO $\neq$ that of middle management $\neq$ that of a shop foreman. Running a geographically situated mining company $\neq$ supervising teleworkers $\neq$ guiding the fortunes of a virtual organization. Recognizing this provides a clue as to why there are so many theories and variables of leadership, all partial with respect to coverage and validity. We select out some dimensions that persist as foci of leadership effectiveness and some problems of leadership in organizations.

Leadership as Leader- or Organization-Centered

The first fifty years of leadership research, beginning early in the twentieth century, were dominated by a focus on *traits* of leaders (Stogdill, 1948), and, closely related, the *behavior* of leaders (Hemphill, 1950). This emphasis was influenced by two traditions: Max Weber's (1968) idea of charismatic leadership and Joseph Schumpeter's (1949) theory of entrepreneurship. Weber formally defined *cha-*

risma as follows: "A certain quality of an individual personality by virtue of which he is considered extraordinary and treated as endowed with supernatural, superhuman, or at least specifically exceptional powers or qualities" (vol. 3: 241). While centered on the leader, the phrases "is considered" and "treated as endowed" open the door to the idea that followers also have something to do with determining who and what is charismatic. The charismatic leader (sometimes called a transformational leader) is an inspirer of followers, and his or her special qualities inspire their obedience. The notion of charisma is associated with the Great Man theory, in which history is written by the actions of heroic leaders (Bloomhardt, 1941), a theory whose popularity has waxed and waned. Traits commonly invoked are innovative skill, creativity, inspirational personality, and sensitivity to others; such lists find their way into "qualities of leadership" lists offered to West Point cadets as well as business school curricula.

Subsequent approaches have downplayed these leader-centric aspects and looked to the situations and outlooks of followers as contributing to leadership. One conception is legitimacy theory (Hollander, 1964), which emphasizes that a leader's position and effectiveness depend on his/her followers' perceptions that the leader is competent and loyal to collective values and goals; this is another way to say that leaders both reflect and are constrained by organizational culture (see below, pp. 195–98). Related conceptions argue that leadership derives from the perceptions of followers about what leadership is or should be. Another variant is that leaders are those who maintain their positions by conformity to general group norms (Homans, 1950). An extreme version of follower-determined leadership is found in attribution theory (e.g., Calder, 1977), according to which followers' expectations about leadership are attributed to or even projected on to leaders. Evidence tends to show, for instance, that individuals overestimate the degree of influence that leaders have over events that are, in fact, random or uncontrollable (Pfeffer, 1977). Such attributions pave the way to idealize leaders when things go well and to scapegoat the leader when things go badly—a principle evident in evaluations of athletic coaches and managers (Meindl, Ehlrich, and Dukerich, 1985). Still another psychological version derives from psychoanalysis, invoking the irrational forces of narcissism, identification, projection, vindictiveness, and identification in understanding leader-follower relations, especially their volatility (Kets de Vries and Miller, 1984).

Evidently both leader-centric and follower-centric theories of leadership cannot both be true on all occasions. Recognizing this fact, other scholars have attempted to combine the two theories and incorporate more situational factors. The most influential of these is contingency theory (Donaldson, 2001), which looks to combinations of both theories and regards leadership as an interaction between personal characteristics and situational factors. For example, research has shown that encouraging workers to participate in decision-making increases their commitment, but this depends on how much trust the leader has instilled in subordinates as well as the urgency of the decision at hand (Vroom and Jago, 1978). Research on presidential leadership is also informed by contrasting views: that presidents' personality and character exert a definite effect on historical events (Barber, 1992); or that they are largely constrained by external forces and events such as past policies, wars not of their making, and the need for electoral survival (see chapter 5, pp. 170–73); or that their effectiveness depends on a contingent meshing of personal style and historical forces. Contingency theory seems more realistic than one-sided theories, but because it rests on unique situational analyses, it pulls thinking in the direction of eclecticism and lacks a sense of finality.

Instrumental and Expressive Views of Leadership

A broad and crosscutting dimension informing the study of leadership and management is the difference between instrumental and expressive aspects of leadership, a distinction with a history in small-group analysis and sociological theory (Parsons and Bales, 1955). With respect to leadership, instrumental models are perhaps the dominant mode. They appear in the scientific management literature and inform many rational models of the firm, according to which the decisionmakers base their actions on known market conditions and according to the logic of maximizing. The "satisficing" and "bounded rationality" tradition, while it rebelled against these assumptions, nonetheless continued to focus on decisionmaking leadership, however imperfectly exercised. The view of the expressive leader crystallized in the human relations school at midcentury, and focuses on leaders' attention to human dimensions such as workers' needs for recognition and respect, worker satisfaction, and morale. The relative emphasis on one or the other style has been a lasting tension in the leadership and management literature. As we will note, that tension reemerged in reaction to corporate restructuring in the late twentieth century.

Authoritarian and Participative Emphases

Overlapping with the instrumental-expressive distinction is another longstanding tradition that crystallized after World War II in the work of Kurt Lewin (Lewin, Lippitt, and White, 1939), whose experiments focused on authoritarian and democratic leadership styles, and in the work of the Tavistock Institute in England. Lewin's research stressed the positive features of incorporating followers. A whole tradition of research holds that organizations function better and yield greater worker satisfaction under participative styles of leadership. Other lines of research stress that such a relationship may vary or be reversed in cultures other than democratic ones. Different results are to be expected in societies with authoritarian or collectivist cultures (Cole, 1971).

The participatory emphasis—combined with the expressive focus—has formed the ideological substrate of several vigorous movements in the management literature. Among these are organizational development, the fundamental assumptions of which stress "people issues"—democratic management practices, delegation, informal groups, participation, and human dignity (French and Bell, 1999). This view became the stock-in-trade for some management consultant firms, who developed instruments such as surveys of workers, seminars, and confrontational meetings (Blake and Moulton, 1969). Two other intellectual movements in the 1960s and 1970s—new public administration and new public management—took opposite tacks, the former emphasizing a radically participatory agenda for management of public agencies, the latter stressing top-down managerial intervention (Hood, 2001). Longstanding movements for worker participation reflect the same democratic impulse as the former. More recent stress on "lean management," the use of teams, organizational flattening, and delegation deemphasizes top-down authority; it is embedded in a concern with issues of principal-agent theory and efficiency in new organizational environments.

Entrepreneurship

Studies of entrepreneurship had their beginnings in the concerns of Marx, Weber, and especially Schumpeter. Experiencing a surge of interest in the 1950s, it has enjoyed sustained interest in several fields. As a result, its study has diffused into multiple approaches, including theories of achievement motivation and other psychological forces (McClelland, 1961; Hagen, 1962); the innovative potential of groups, both religious (e.g., Quakers in the industrial revolution) and ethnic minorities (e.g., Chinese, Jews, Greeks, Koreans) marginalized from centers of power (Hoselitz, 1963; Aldrich and Waldinger, 1990); and the innovative roles of banks and governments in economic development (Gerschenkron, 1962). Still other emphases focus not on persons or organizations, but on conditions favorable to innovation, such as the availability of financial capital, social capital, and personal networks (for a review, see Aldrich, 2005). Types of entrepreneurs other than business leaders have been identified—moral, academic, social, religious, political, and reputational entrepreneurs who cultivate, manage, and destroy images (Fine, 1996)—further stretching the concept. This diffusion, accordingly, has produced a history of definitional and substantive disputes over causes and consequences, with few certain conclusions. For these reasons, we believe the literature on entrepreneurship has not proved especially usable, beyond the point of identifying a particular kind of organization: management situations in which high risk, significant opportunity, and the possibility of either spectacular success and failure are salient.

Leadership Succession

We mention this topic both because of its importance and because, as we will see, it reemerged in the recent era of takeovers and mergers. Weber (1968) originally highlighted the issue in his discussion of struggles for succession when a charismatic leader passes from the scene. In an influential study, Gouldner (1954) traced the conflicts and adverse consequences for employee morale when a "No More Mr. Nice Guy" boss replaces an executive who had been kindly and indulgent. A later study by Guest (1962) revealed less disruption when an authoritarian leader is replaced by one oriented toward worker participation. Still later, the issue of succession was more comprehensively assessed as a determinant of corporate performance (Friedman, 1985). In colleges and universities, leadership transitions have become more problematic in recent decades, given the frequency of leadership change due to shortening tenure and the increasing complexity of external and internal demands on presidents, chancellors, and deans (Martin and James E. Samels & Associates, 2004). In all events, leadership succession almost inevitably ushers in a period of uncertainty for the entire organization.

Issues of Usability of Leadership Knowledge

The study of leadership yields such a spread of approaches and emphases, and such a dearth of valid generalizations, that it poses difficulties in straightforward application. Most approaches to the subject are slanted, but each appears to touch an important aspect of the leadership-in-organization situation. This observation suggests that some version of contingency theory, while nonspecific with respect to directives, is the optimal frame of mind for leaders. In this spirit of eclecticism, Chemers (2001) summarizes psychological leadership studies in terms of the following guidelines:

> Effective leaders must be able to project an image of competency and honesty that legitimates the validity of their authority. They must establish motivating and rewarding relationships with followers by understanding follower needs and capabilities, and providing coaching and guidance that both facilitate good current performance and provide the possibility for personal growth. Finally, effective leaders must use the energies and resources of groups efficiently by matching the processes of communication, problem-solving, and decision-making by using a directive and structuring process when the environment is clear and predictable and by using more flexible and participative process when the situation is equivocal and unpredictable. (8583)

It is difficult to dispute these points. They cover many intraorganizational issues such as delegation, framing, imagery, and morale, though they say little about dealing with the external environment of organizations. More generally, they must be regarded as a checklist of points of sensitivity rather than a user's toolkit.

One final usable observation: Leaders themselves self-stereotype, i.e., develop images of themselves as to what kind of leaders they are and what good leadership is. This is a complex phenomenon, but we regard it as in large part a manifestation of the "passion for simplification" of the complex, uncertain, and often unpredictable situations in which leaders operate. Many simplified images float about in organizational cultures—leader as tough guy, leader as nice guy, leader as impulsive, leader as dynamo, leader as responsible bureaucrat, leader as careful and cautious, leader as statesman. These self-images qualify as "knowledge" in that they constitute a reservoir of loosely formulated principles, convictions, directives, and guidelines for dealing with the world. They are also replete with simplifying heuristics. Deriving loosely from leaders' personal backgrounds and experience, these self-images may or may not be informed by broader, supplementary, and qualifying knowledge, including knowledge from the social sciences. Self-images, finally, may serve as personal defense mechanisms *against* accepting criticism and advice from others, appreciating the value of counterdiagnoses because they do not "fit" the self-image, and adopting a flexible approach. Self-images lead to defensiveness because they belong to the ego, and the ego is often defensive. It is difficult to suggest to leaders that they be less defensive about their self-images, because such a suggestion is likely to invoke more defensiveness. Nevertheless, the cultivation of critical self-insight is surely a usable asset.

ORGANIZATIONAL CULTURE, CLIMATE, IDENTITY, LEARNING, AND MEMORY

The last third of the twentieth century witnessed the emergence of a loosely coupled series of intellectual and social movements in the organizational literature that can be grouped under the heading of *organizational culture*. Its intellectual origins are many: the central place of culture in anthropology; the original insights of the human relations school and its derivatives; and the rise of the organizational development movement after World War II, which emphasized the importance of grassroots influence on policy and collaboration between leaders and workers. However, what appeared to give the movement its strongest bite was a near-panicky view in corporate, industrial, and business school circles in the 1970s and 1980s that the United States was floundering and losing out to foreign, notably Japanese, competition. A corollary was the conviction that Japanese industry was guided by a distinctive culture superior to the American in fostering productivity and that, as a result, Japan was marching toward becoming number one in economic success (Vogel, 1979). This fear probably also accounts for the fact that the era was preoccupied with organizational culture mainly for its relevance for productivity. Toward the end of the century, as the Japanese threat and America's panic receded and the dynamics of faddism worked themselves out, the stress on culture and its derivatives also receded, though, like most intellectual movements, it remains as one approach to organizations.

The most coherent statement and most influential work on organizational culture was Schein's *Organizational Culture and Leadership* (2004). The book was influenced mainly by anthropological concepts. He defines culture as follows: "Patterns of shared basic assumptions . . . learned by a group as it solved its problems of external adaptation and internal integration that has worked well enough to be considered valid and, therefore, to be taught to new members as the correct way to perceive, think, and feel in relation to those problems" (17). The content of organizational culture is a world view, including myths of origin; identification of founding fathers; a sense of "groupness" manifested in collectively experienced emotional responses; a common language; derived common norms that define power, status, and performance standards; and accounts of otherwise unexplainable situations and events. Its principal characteristics are stability, comprehensiveness, and integration.

The most notable feature of organizational culture, in Schein's view, is its adaptive capacity. He identifies this factor as key to the growth and decline of organizations. He regards corporate leadership as the "embedding mechanism" of culture. Culture guides leaders in how they attend to critical incidents, allocate resources, become role models, and select, recruit, and promote others. Culture also is embedded in organizational design and the use of physical space, and, above all, it gives meaning to events and situations by referring to organizational philosophy and creeds (246ff). As might be expected, the idea of organizational culture itself underwent a process of elaboration, with one author pointing to its international differences (Fukuyama, 2001), another to the role of individuals in shaping culture (Sutton and Louis, 1987), and still another to the fragmentation of cultures into subcultures according to gender, ethnicity, age, and other bases (van Maanan, 1991). One branch, called the radical humanist paradigm, stressed the "imprisoning" character of organizational culture and its potential to alienate workers (Grant, 2001). Suffice it to say that if culture matches a leader's style, it can be a powerful and adaptive force, but it can also constrain and stultify the adaptive capacity of organizations.

A related approach crystallized in the same period under the name *organizational climate*. It is perhaps part of culture, but less encompassing and more explicitly psychological. It includes attitudes, outlooks, and collective moods. Positive climates imply loyalty, trust, commitment, and high morale. Negative climates include distrust, personal antipathies, unclear goals. and poor communication (Amabile, 1988). Organizational climate is more short-term than organizational culture in its reference, and more susceptible to fluctuations. Organizational climate is also tied to a specific set of consequences of interest to businesspeople and managers: individual performance, employee motivation, collective productivity, innovation and creativity, and organizational commitment (Baltes, 2001; Patterson, West, Lawthom, and Nickell, 1997). Instrumental capacity and usability also dominate discussions of climate, even though other lines of research stress that strong, coherent, and embedded cultures—for example, in branches of the military and in intelligence agencies—are sources of resistance to change and innovation (see below, pp. 219–21).

Another dimension of organizational culture is *organizational identity*, which overlaps with both culture and climate. A minimal definition: "what members of an organization believe is central and enduring about their organization" (Nord, 2001: 7303). Identity can be positive or negative, but in either case it invokes a central idea about the organization's nature, purpose, and focus. Once established, a sense of identity is accompanied by mechanisms of socialization, repeated references to it, and incorporation into rituals (Albert and Whetten, 1985). It can also be used instrumentally, as managers seize upon the idea as a way to secure commitment and positive participation in the organization, one component of productivity. A key feature of identity is *organizational memory*, a subclass of collective memory (see above, pp. 71, 74–75) and an element in endowing an organization with purpose. Memory is an important, though changeable, ingredient in fostering morale. It can be invoked in times of conflict or crisis in order to diffuse disruption by remembering history and giving assurance that the organization has survived similar difficulties in the past.

Finally, we refer to the idea of *organizational learning* (see Argyris and Schön, 1978), which also enjoyed a burst of popularity in the 1980s and then declined. Its crystallization has also been interpreted as a response to the intensification of international competition in the 1980s and, in particular, to anxiety over the extraordinary success of the Japanese (Easterby-Smith, Araujo, and Burgoyne, 1999). The concept is a metaphor that treats the organization as a person who learns and uses what is learned. Its emphases have included adaptation to the environment, learning curves (Trist, 1983), economies of search or transaction analysis (Newell and Simon, 1972), and the modification of mental maps. Of special interest is the idea of a "learning organization" as an instrument of adaptation and innovation (Gherardi, 2001).

The complex of organizational culture, climate, identity, memory, and learning clustered as approaches to organizational capacity and effectiveness. These emphases continue to be valuable and helpful dimensions in understanding organizations' fortunes. They also remain embedded in the organizational literature. Yet each enjoyed a day in the sun as promising and usable knowledge, then receded. We have suggested why they rose, and we may speculate on why they declined:

· In anthropology—its intellectual home—the concept of culture has always been substantively central but methodologically unruly—difficult to operationalize, sometimes tautological (e.g., describe a behavior and name it "culture"), and short on specific guidelines for action.

- For those who criticize the idea of organizational culture, the latter difficulty looms large ("Suppose I believe everything you say about culture; how do I change my behavior tomorrow morning?")
- The principle of "promise meets reality." As indicated, every one of these culture-related concepts implied a promise of organizational effectiveness, productivity, and competitiveness. While this was not exactly false advertising, the seeds of the approach's demise were contained in the initial enthusiasm. Promises could not possibly have been kept, given the difficulties of specification and the many other factors affecting international competitiveness. This same principle of promise-meets-reality applies to the fate of the "Washington consensus" (reliance on market principles to guide economic policy), which became the dominant mantra in the economic-developmental and postsocialist literature of the 1990s, and has subsequently unraveled as a general principle (Easterly, 2001; see chapter 7, pp. 234–35).
- We have identified a general cycle in the usability of knowledge: discovery → spread → excitement → appreciation of limitations → criticism and discrediting → turning elsewhere for inspiration and direction. Organizational culture cycles are no exception.
- The initial impetus for culture-based theories—the apparent inability of American and European companies to meet competition from abroad, traced to competitors' superior culture—declined in the 1990s with the software and other booms, as well as growing economic and financial difficulties facing competitors.

Cycles in Organizational Life

We might pause and say a few general words—without singling out organizational culture and its offshoots as special villains—about cycles of promise and disillusionment. We choose the most neutral term (cycles) and shun derogatory ones such as *fads, gimmicks, mantras,* and *hypes.*

More than two decades ago, in an impatient mood, Eccles and Noria (1992) compiled a list of several dozen "failing fashions" that they identified in the corporate and business-school literature. A few examples:

Total quality. Benchmarking. Best practices. Customer focused. Micromarketing. Flexible manufacturing. Core competence. Strategic intent. Strategic alliances. Networks. Time-based competition. Concurrent engineering. Computer-integrated manufacturing. Cross-functional teams. Downsizing. Rightsizing. Flattening. Delayering. Information. Organizational transformation. Business process redesign. Mission statements. The new organization. The information-based organization. The knowledge-intensive organization. The informed organization. The post-industrial organization. The transnational organization. Diversity. Entrepreneurs. Intrapreneurs. (1)

The authors could have found more, and if we updated the list, the examples would only multiply.

Not every item on the list is a fashion, and not every one can be labeled a simple failure. Each touches some reality of organizational life, and they vary in usefulness. Beyond those observations, we might ask: Why the regularity of cycles of enthusiasm? We offer three observations:

1. At several places in this volume, we point to the increasing intensity of phenomena that characterize globalization, technological advancement, increasing complexity, increased competitiveness, and, above all, increasing uncertainty and risk. This complex—especially uncertainty and risk—makes life for decision-makers more demanding. Furthermore, these conditions guarantee that there are no right, single answers to organizational success. The paradox, however, is that these same conditions of increasing uncertainty and contingency drive people in positions of power and responsibility to seek simplified solutions. These solutions are a form of heuristics, generated by and relied on in uncertain, threatening situations. They "fail," of course, because they are simple and do not engage complexity.

   These observations apply most readily to private, market-oriented organizations. Yet others do not escape the effects. Colleges and universities are engaged in competition with one another, mainly for status, faculty, students, and funds; foundations vie with one another in choosing the best emphases for giving; civil service bureaucracies prefer to be regarded positively rather than negatively. And social-movement organizations struggle for niches. Correspondingly, they all are engaged in the search for sure solutions.

2. The search for solutions is itself a market. The sellers are management consultants and others (for example, some business school faculty) who struggle for formulae that will sell and influence. These formulae appear in manuals and texts and attempt to identify and illustrate the best practices in business, medical, legal, and academic organizations. These books and their authors prosper by offering attractive and apparently usable solutions. Their constant reappearance is guaranteed by the shifting exigencies and the uncertainty of organizational life.

3. Political and status-striving considerations also matter. Within any organization, the individual, group, or department that comes up with the most influential formula for policy is rewarded correspondingly. In any organization with subdivisions—and all have them—units become vested interests and struggle with one another for recognition and influence. Coming up with a bright, engaging, and persuasive formula is one way they compete with one another.

The reason that we are loathe to venture an overall judgment on the cycles resulting from these forces is that they are both beneficial and harmful for organizations. On the positive side, they provide continuous searching and dynamism, essential for organizational survival and success. On the negative side, they often prove to be misguided expressions of the passion for simplicity, wasteful of resources, and subject to ridicule. Cycles are a striking example of the many two-edged swords that characterize organizational life.

INDIVIDUAL AND SOCIAL PROBLEMS
STRESS, DEVIANCE, PROTEST

We turn now to phenomena that are diverse but share the feature of "bringing harm to the organization, its employees, or shareholders" (Giacalone and Greenberg, 1997: vii). Naming these is difficult, because the name chosen often connotes a specific view of organizations, implies that certain agents are responsible, and invokes ideological preferences.

For example, *deviance* implies motivated rule-breaking; so do the terms *antisocial behavior* (ibid.) and *organizational misbehavior* (Ackroyd and Thompson, 1999), though the authors associate the last term with a class-conflict perspective. *Stress* expresses a relationship between work conditions and individual responses. Alternatively, behavior antagonistic to organizations is viewed as resulting from exploitation and alienation—an approach associated with Marxist thought and echoed in British industrial sociology. These contrasting meanings evoke larger political tensions between left and right. All the tensions also appear in ambivalent contemporary attitudes toward whistleblowers, who are regarded simultaneously as folk heroes to be rewarded and as troublemakers to be ostracized or retaliated against (Miceli and Near, 1992).

Historically, concern with organizational problems focused on employee theft, absenteeism (for example, "Saint's Monday," a traditional extension of nonwork to the day after Sunday, and a bane of early capitalists), and worker sabotage, such as Luddite machine-breaking. Subsequently, concerns with organizational problems have multiplied. To illustrate:

Stress and Related Concepts

At midcentury, the concept of alienation evolved from a systemic feature of capitalism toward a more social-psychological approach (Seeman, 1959; Blauner, 1964), stressing worker isolation, estrangement, and sense of meaninglessness. At about the same time, the idea of stress appeared as an offshoot of the human relations approach, with attention to the conflicts of "in-between" roles such as those of foremen exposed to conflicting expectations from managers above and workers below (Leiter, 1948), and executive stress stemming from overwork, role conflicts, and environments of urgency (Kahn et al., 1964). Other stressful factors included health and safety hazards, lack of control over work, and noise pollution. Subsequently job and career insecurity became more salient with the increased use of temps, greater employee turnover, and the consequences of restructuring, downsizing, and outsourcing (see below). Earlier we identified a few types of stress that accompany telework and other work-at-home arrangements (see above, pp. 44–45). Consequences of stress are multiple, including physical and psychiatric symptoms, negative attitudes, absenteeism, low morale, and burnout (Maslach, 1997). Research has also shown that one determinant in reducing the negative effects of stress is the presence of meaningful support groups (see above, pp. 134–35).

Bullying, Ostracism, and Power Struggles

The topic of bullying emerged in Scandinavian literature in the 1980s. One line of work was in schoolyard bullying (Olweus, 2003) and focused both on characteristics of victims (anxious, insecure, cautious, and quiet children) and of bullies themselves (often physically strong, aggressive, rule-breaking children). The workplace is also a site of bullying, as employees are singled out for social isolation, verbal attack, harassment, discrimination, even physical violence. Causes sometimes lie in the individual characteristics of perpetrators, but ineffective leadership and low morale also may contribute. Bullying is obviously stressful for victims and may lead to low morale, depression, absenteeism, and quitting (Einarsen, Noel, Zapf, and Cooper, 2003).

Ostracism is a special form of bullying (Williams, 2001). It isolates victims by silence, ignoring, or snubbing them. Its presence in the workplace is evident, but Williams identifies a new form—cyberostracism. Summarizing an experimental literature, he reports the following: "It is indeed rather astonishing that despite the fact our participants did not know, could not use, could not communicate with, and were not anticipating further interaction with 'virtual others,' they felt ostracized when these others neglected to throw them a virtual ball. Cyberostracism elicited worsened social mood; declines in senses of belonging, control, and self-esteem; and increased conformity" (183). Such is the power of personal interaction and symbols, even in impersonal settings.

Bullying and ostracism also appear in the organizational politics of cliquing, power seeking, power grabbing, discrediting, backbiting, and backstabbing. We consider these in the "Organizational Power and Organizational Politics" section, later in this chapter.

Disruption, Sabotage, Revenge, and Protest

These phenomena are explicitly political. They are generally treated as retaliations against management actions regarded as unjust. Much routine theft and cheating, for example, are rationalized by a folk understanding that big organizations are impersonal and dishonest (the "Ma Bell" mentality); moreover, they are so rich that they won't miss it. Such rationalizations may lie behind high rates of employee theft in supermarkets (Boye and Jones, 1997). An additional motive is revenge. One study found increases in thefts following pay cuts and decreases when cuts were rescinded (Greenberg, 1997). Another suggestion is that when management becomes "leaner and meaner" in the face of increased competition and shrinking profit margins, this is treated as a violation of norms, and employees themselves may become meaner and more aggressive (Neuman and Baron, 1997). More generally, revenge has been invoked to explain theft, sabotage, litigation, whistle-blowing, feuding, public complaints, political opposition, and physical violence (Bies, Tripp, and Kramer, 1997). Some authors treat virtually all organizational "misbehavior" as struggles over the appropriation of time, products, and identity (Ackroyd and Thompson, 1999).

Finally, we note a technological dimension of disruption. The spread of computers has enabled a new range of deviant, even criminal interventions in the work process—chatting, Internet addiction, sending viruses, hacking, vandalizing, identity theft, new types of embezzlement, spying, and terrorizing—all made possible by the technology (Shah, 2005). Of special interest is "cyberloafing"—a case of social loafing or freeriding. It assumes significance in the cyber world because much computer work is done on a solo basis; precise supervision is difficult, costly, and resented as overcontrol (see Lim and Teo, 2006). Most of these disruptions are countered by more technology, mainly security systems. A race is emerging between technologically generated opportunities for deviance and technologically based countermeasures.

The Increased Significance of Organizational Risk

The individual and social problems just reviewed can be regarded as risks facing an organization. They are unpredictable threats to attaining goals and functioning in an orderly way. Another risk is failing to meet the demand for performance by boards of trustees and shareholders. Still another is the ever-lurking possibility that some relevant group will complain that they were not consulted in a decision affecting them. These have been called people risks (Shah, 2005). Yet people risks are only one type. The emphasis on organizational and societal risk has accelerated in the past decades, largely because of changes in crucial conditions: increased market competition, organization-market-societal interdependencies, accidents, and the threat of proliferation of nuclear weapons.

In an encyclopedic effort, Shah (ibid.) identified the following types of risks in addition to people risks: market risk, credit risk, weather risk, operational risks, regulatory risks, competitor risks, legal risks, political risks, natural hazards, property risks (fire, theft), and intellectual capital risks (loss of patent rights, for example). The list seems exhaustive enough, though refinements might be added if we considered the media and "reputational risk" and if we explored the uncertainties associated with the dispersion of work and virtual organizations (see above, pp. 41–45).

Market and financial risks have drawn the most attention. The history of capitalism is a history of bubbles and disasters brought on by a combination of enthusiastic investment and ignorance and/or denial of risk. Interest in risk has recently peaked on account of the dot-com collapse and the disastrous credit and economic crises in the early twenty-first century. Risk management has become an industry in itself, producing how-to-do-it books that promise to teach "the very latest in risk management" (Crouhy, Galai, and Mark, 2006), the proliferation of officials and departments on risk management in firms, and the extension of management consultancy to risk management. Highly technical and mathematical approaches have been devised and marketed. These systems are directly usable, though that usability is contingent on the adequacy of their first assumptions and on the fact that no matter how precise and quantified they are, they, too, can become brittle formulae.

Attention to natural and organizational disasters burst on the scene in the second half of the twentieth century with the occurrence or near-occurrence of major disasters (the Cuban Missile Crisis, the *Challenger* explosion, the Three Mile Island incident, Chernobyl, the crash of the Exxon *Valdez,* and the chemical leak at Bhopal, to say nothing of continuing problems of airline safety and air-traffic control). Interest in both causation and control was spurred by the discovery of human and organizational failures in case studies (e.g., Vaughan, 1996) and in the extension of airline safety research to individual and social as well as technical sources of accidents (Wiegmann, 2001). Especially influential was the appearance of *Normal Accidents,* by Perrow (1984), who treated accidents as inevitable and "expected," largely because of the "tight coupling" and "interactive complexity" of organizations. Perrow also emphasized the role of conflicting political interests within organizations and between organizations and community—a constant source of tripwires for the relevant organizations.

Sagan (1993) identified two schools of thought regarding catastrophic accidents. The first is the normal accidents paradigm, pessimistic in the sense that accident origins lie in characteristics of "the system" and are therefore inevitable. The second is high-reliability organization theory, developed by a group of political scientists and others at Berkeley (Marone and Woodhouse, 1986; LaPorte and Consolini, 1991) who stress that with proper precaution accidents can be minimized, if not prevented. Among these precautions are organizational leaders giving high priority to safety issues; spread of a "high-reliability culture"; continuously practiced safety operations; high redundancy in safety measures (cross-checking, multiple checks, backup systems); continuous trial runs; and repeated trial-and-error learning. The two schools have squared off against each other in the literature, though there is general agreement that reliability and safety can be improved in certain circumstances (e.g., "the ideal military model") that include isolation from society, intensive socialization, and disciplining of organizational personnel. After reviewing the play of vested interests, jurisdictional jealousies, ambiguities over responsibility, and the possibilities of "groupthink" (see chapter 5, pp. 182–84), Sagan cast his vote for a residue of pessimism, conceding that preventive methods can be helpful but never complete (1993). Surely, however, some relatively successful stories, such as the apparently permanent reduction of airline accident rates, suggest that preventive strategies combined with technical knowledge about "disruption management" (e.g., Yu and Qi, 2004) can make a difference in safety.

On the basis of our own careers spent in organizations, and on the basis of reviews of disaster and terrorist studies (Smelser, 2007), we offer the observation that among all factors important in the occurrence of and reactions to accidents, disasters, and secret attacks, the variable of *jurisdictionalism* stands out as crucial. Cultural and organizational jealousies among security agencies, including the failure to share information, are legendary. Efforts to husband these agencies through superordination (e.g., the Department of Homeland Security) have produced minimal results. The proliferation of local, state, regional, and federal agencies to simultaneously deal with disasters and security creates cracks between them, along with ambiguities, disagreements, jurisdictional squabbling, and paralysis about who is responsible and not responsible. Those effects are also observed in failures to respond to disasters and catastrophes, and in the cacophony of credit-taking, blame-avoiding, and finger-pointing in the wake of such failures. Yet, being both jurisdictional and vested, these organizations also prove effective in thwarting reform by political opposition and undermining. We single out jurisdictionalism both because it is so salient and because it combines (1) usable knowledge relevant to reform with (2) lack of political will, political paralysis, and inability to reform.

THE ENVIRONMENTS OF ORGANIZATIONS

The history of organizational studies reveals a march toward the triumph of the "open" view of organizations over the "closed." It has long been recognized (Gordon, 1945) that businesses exist in an environment of constituencies— competitors, boards, stockholders, government (including regulators and tax agencies), labor unions and employee associations, consumers, and the general public as a source of real and imagined goodwill. Recently other forces have become more conspicuous. Among these are the global economic scene, consumer protection organizations, environmental and related (e.g., animal rights) movements, the women's movement, and affirmative action programs. These are all potential influences on and "risks" for organizations, and they complicate the political role of organizational leaders.

In recent organization theory, three approaches highlight the salience of organizations' external environments:

1. Resource dependency. The name reveals its essence. Organizations survive, prosper, or fail according to their numbers of suppliers, competitors, and customers (Burt, 1983).
2. Organizational ecology. A species of Darwinism, this approach regards an organization's fate as determined by its niche location and the population of organizations in its environment. It has also isolated the age of firms— young, established, senescent—as a factor in their capacity to adapt to the environment (Carroll and Hannan, 2000).
3. Signaling theory. As firms in markets face uncertainty, they adapt by using information signaled by competitors, suppliers, and buyers to guide their decisions. Over time these signaling patterns may crystallize in relatively stable networks of firms (White, 1970, 1992).

A fourth "external" force should be mentioned; that is a kind of "permission to exist" factor that demands efforts to maintain goodwill. It applies to industries and firms that are widely regarded as environmental polluters (oil, chemicals, coal) or as dangers to life and health (tobacco, nuclear power). When an industry or firm comes under fire from attacks as basic as these, their production and distribution activities are often overshadowed by concerns with public relations, repair work, and legal defense.

We also note the growing importance of multiply located organizations and systems of organizations, both relatively new on the organizational scene, but both posing special problems of coordination, integration, and regulation. Multinational corporations are the most conspicuous. They are in one sense single organizations, but their differentiation into home headquarters and numerous activities overseas creates multiple environments, including multiple labor forces, multiple states to deal with, and multiple sources of regulation. Multicampus universities under a single governance system face continuous problems in the balance between centralization and decentralization of authority, competition among campuses, and identity problems ("one big university" versus campus autonomy and culture). Many systems of organizations are held together by linkages rather than authority. The relationship between international and national scientific societies is an example; another is the networks between women's movements in different countries. Regional consortia, virtual organizations, and international nongovernmental organizations are still others. All these forms drive organizational analysis toward the twin ideas of open organizations and systems of organizations, and render traditional models of authority-subordination, internal decision-making, and control over environments by single organizations more problematic.

ORGANIZATIONAL POWER AND
ORGANIZATIONAL POLITICS

All social relations, insofar as they involve influence or control, have a power dimension that is sometimes apparent, always latent. Power involves domination and coercion, but under most circumstances it is exercised in the name of some *justification*. Following Weber, this is most commonly called legitimation. The concept of authority reveals this double aspect. Authority might be defined as power + legitimacy. Weber identified authority as a central aspect of formal organizations. He called it "rational-legal" authority, deriving its legitimacy from laws, rules, and formal positions. Power and authority also typically imply a ubiquitous—but sometimes latent—presence of *conflict* over the exercise of power itself or access to whatever is valued.

Scholars of organizational power have approached it in two basic ways, reflecting a larger division in political science. The first deals with power as a *normal* feature of organizational life, a resource important for organizations' effective functioning (Pfeffer, 1992). It is exercised not only through formal authority, but also in the practices of dealing with conflicts among interested groups as well as questions of fairness and justice. Labor-management relations and collective bargaining are clearly political struggles, less controlled in earlier eras than now, when they transpire under more institutionalized auspices. Motivating and deploying workers also have a political aspect, and liberal-left scholars treat this primarily as political subordination (Braverman, 1974). On the basic of empirical work, Mintzberg (1973) estimated that managers dedicate at least as much of their time to social interactions and power brokering as they do to the traditional managerial activities of decision-making and monitoring work. The second line of thinking stresses the *pathological* aspects of power. Following this imagery, Bougré and Liverpool (2006) define organizational politics as "self-serving interpersonal influence behavior, not formally sanctioned by the organization and designed to maximize self-interest at the expense of others" (122). Pushed further, this definition focuses on the pursuit of individual and group power *within* organizations, whereas the first definition regards power as a resource to be deployed *for* organizations. In the second view, organizational politics are struggles for recognition, status, and influence. Self-advancement includes positive strategies such as taking the right position at the right time, impression management, guile, and flattery, and negative strategies such as disadvantaging others through manipulation, backbiting, ostracism, character assassination, and, in the extreme, blackmail and bribery. The second type is generally regarded as harmful to organizations, contributing to stress, job dissatisfaction, distrust, and lack of commitment (Albrecht, 2006).

Rather than attempting to cover all aspects of organizational power, we consider three themes: (1) the fluid line between politics and administration, (2) accountability, and (3) regulation. Knowledge about all three is essential for decision-makers.

Politics and Administration

In the Progressive era of the late nineteenth century, reformers, disgusted with patronage and corruption, tried to impose a separation between administration (managing) and politics (policy-making). The distinction was advanced and defended by Woodrow Wilson (1887). As a political scientist, he advocated it as a way to remove neutral, expert-based bureaucracy from the rough-and-tumble of politics. The creation of the city manager as administrator—separate from the mayor and the city council—is an example of reforms attempted in the name of this distinction. So is the idea of a neutral civil service, which envisions bureaucrats as executors of policies they do not create and in which they have no interests. The impossibility of the distinction has been repeatedly pointed out (Waldo, 1948; Selznick, 1953), especially in the behavioral tradition of administrative science (e.g., Simon, 1947). We adhere to a view of the fusion and interaction of the two, and identify two sources of ambiguity and conflict:

1. A tendency for administrative issues to become political, particularly in situations of conflict. In theory, managerial decisions should be impersonal, based on best knowledge, and exclude personal and partisan considerations. However, most decisions in firms and offices invariably involve gains or losses (or perceptions of these) on the part of departments, groups, and individuals. Those threatened with loss typically experience anxieties about losing out as well as feelings of disappointment, deprivation, and injustice. One weapon available for those experiencing loss is to convert the basis for that loss into the language of arbitrariness—decision-makers are not making their decisions on objective grounds, but have done so to punish or take revenge, feather their nests, or further their partisan interests. Such accusations invoke the seamier definition of organizational politics as self-serving. They are conspicuous in many intraorganizational conflicts and labor-union accusations of managerial arbitrariness.

   Disputes over academic freedom and tenure reveal the same dynamic. The origin of academic freedom is the sense that faculty members should be protected against actions taken on account of their personal or partisan preferences (exceptions are made for punishing criminal or immoral activities). A corollary is that personnel decisions should be meritocratic—based on universalistic evaluation of faculty members' performance in research, teaching, and service. They should be administrative, not political, decisions. Colleges and universities have institutionalized reviews by ad hoc committees, deans, permanent personnel committees, and higher administrators to maximize thoroughness and fairness.

Historically, when conflict flares over adverse tenure decisions, the administration is often accused of acting arbitrarily and basing its decision on political grounds (frequently accompanied by the accusation that it has responded to external political pressure). Less often, favorable decisions unpopular with some faculty involve accusations of favoritism. More recently, tenure decisions have been disputed on grounds that they are discriminatory with respect to race, gender, or sexual preference. When such conflicts reach the courts, judges often demand reviews of the actions from the standpoint of administrative (procedural) propriety. Such tenure struggles are instances of the politicization of administrative issues.

2. A tendency for political issues to become administrative. Typically civil service agencies prefer that all that comes before them can be handled routinely. A standard observation about bureaucrats is that they go by the rules and abhor exceptions, to the point of placing procedures above practical and human considerations. In many cases, this practice is mainly a source of nuisance and frustration, but in extreme forms (e.g., "work-to-rule" protests) are disruptive. If carried out in hospitals, where rapid, rule-breaking actions are often necessary to save lives, they can be grave in their consequences. Merton (1968a) defined extremes of such behavior as "ritualism," one form of organizational deviance. We might also cite an unfriendly definition of a successful academic as dean: an official who succeeds in converting every problem into a nonproblem. Each of these examples is a confirmation of the tendency to treat and resolve issues as administrative—not as personal or political or moral—thereby protecting oneself and minimizing conflict. A tragic historical instance of this principle was seen in the Eichmann trials for the murder of Jews in World War II; the defense argued that Eichmann was innocent of wrongdoing because he was following the orders of his superiors and obeying rules, and thus not personally responsible (Arendt, 1963).

These two principles—the conversion of administration into politics and vice versa—suggest that they are opposites. They are not. They are two latent tendencies of organizational life that can surface at any time. Furthermore, they define a great deal of conflict within organizations and sometimes between organizations and important constituencies. This observation leads directly into the topic of accountability.

Accountability

Accountability is a political phenomenon, but it is not the direct exercise of authority. It is the prior delegation of responsibility and/or authority, with an additional requirement that the delegatee give an account to the delegator of his/her actions, justify them, and face consequences if there has been poor performance, misconduct, or failure (Papadapoulos, 2007). A stress on accountability is also a product of the preoccupations with political irresponsibility and corruption.

The three principal forms of accountability are as follows:

1. Democratic. Periodic elections are principal mechanisms by which elected political officials are held accountable. If their behavior does not measure up, they can be voted out of office. Other mechanisms are impeachment and recall. Within government bureaucracies, employees are held accountable by superordinates. Public offices and to some degree private enterprises are also held accountable in more informal ways by the media, which make potentially damaging information public through reporting and investigative journalism. The media themselves are less directly accountable, though agencies such as the Federal Communications Commission and voluntary groups such as the Committee of Concerned Journalists may sanction sensationalism and other kinds of excesses.
2. Financial. This refers to assuring that those with financial or economic responsibility husband resources in accordance with rules and procedures. Financial accountability is enforced by government agencies, tax authorities, and accounting firms that conduct audits and submit their results to governing boards and government agencies. Generally governed by high professional standards, accounting firms themselves also require accountability; this emerged dramatically in the Enron scandals of 2001, in which accounting firms participated in cover-up activities.
3. Legal. This overlaps with the first two forms. It includes meeting conditions for performance that are written into legally binding agreements, though those conditions are not always described by the word *accountability*.

In recent decades, a fourth type has spread widely: performance accountability. Most employing organizations routinely evaluate their personnel, usually annually in connection with adjusting pay and awarding bonuses. So do public bureaucracies and public programs. One aspect of the No Child Left Behind program of the George W. Bush administration, for instance, was to hold schools accountable for delivering educational results as measured by pupils' performance on mandatory tests (leading to the nickname "no child left alone"). Legislation for new agencies and programs frequently builds in requirements for account-ability. States ask their colleges and universities for information relating to their performance (teaching loads and graduation rates, for example). Looser forms of accountability include requesting quarterly reports from recipients of research grants and requiring faculty members to submit end-of-year reports after sab-batical leaves.

The movement—some call it a mania—toward performance accountability is embedded in what has been called the new public management paradigm (Hughes, 2003). It first appeared in the 1980s as part of a movement to modern-ize organizations in the public sector. In contrast to the traditional paradigm, which emphasized rules and regulations, the new paradigm focuses on results, and is regarded as separate from—and in addition to—financial and democratic accountability. Two approaches within the new paradigm concern the degree of discretion to be afforded managers in assuring accountability. One extreme is to "let managers manage," which assumes that managers are intelligent and knowl-edgeable and therefore deserve autonomy, even if they are periodically assessed. This approach aims to cultivate innovation and entrepreneurship through trust and independence. The other extreme, "make managers manage," does not give discretion and trust the same premium. It not only involves more detailed track-ing, but also builds in systems of incentives and competitiveness among manag-ers to force them to become flexible and innovative.

Among enthusiasts, performance accountability is considered an avenue to efficiency. It is important, however, to indicate some problems that it generates in both private and public organizations.

- Goals and measures. Accountability entails having certain goals against which performance is measured. In private organizations, this is often not a severe problem, because various bottom-line money measures are relatively unambiguous. Less tangible goals, such as maintaining employee morale, are not. In public organizations, voluntary associations, and social-movement organizations, goals are often multiple and difficult to measure. What are the goals of educating children or college students? How are we to be cer-tain that educational goals, even if specified—e.g., literacy, cognitive skills, maturation, cultivation of tastes, and inculcating values of citizenship—are not produced by agencies and processes, including maturation, other than teaching effectiveness? How to measure teaching and its results in relation to such goals? Answers are necessarily vague, and evaluators tend, first, to settle on a single, often simple index that is only a partial measure at best (e.g., test results, student evaluations of teachers). Under pressure to achieve precision (another mania, perhaps), they seek out quantifiable versions of those imper-fect measures. Precision and quantification of measures that are inadequate in the first place do not add to their adequacy. In some cases, precision and quantification tend to become ends in themselves; as a result, concern with measurement can crowd out concern with substance.

Often, too, in the absence of clear goals and measures of effective output, accountability drifts toward measuring inputs. In higher education, standard accounting measures demanded by administrators and state officials are input measures, such as teaching loads, contact hours, or surveys of how much time academics allot to their different responsibilities. In many cases, these input measures are hopelessly crude and inadequate. It would be absurd, for example, to assess the productivity of academic researchers by tracking how many hours per week they spend in libraries.

In the end, an accountability question should be asked of any system of accountability. Many systems of accountability have costs and benefits themselves. Does the effort to account cost more than it yields in results? Such a question is as tough to answer as all accountability questions, but it should certainly be asked in order to prevent accountability from devolving toward uninformative rituals.

· Level of detail of accountability. This reflects a tension over discretion evident in the distinction between letting and making managers manage. Accountability involves agency, or delegation of responsibility. Insofar as accountability becomes more detailed, however, the closer it comes to detailed supervision, even if after the fact rather than coterminous with performance. Furthermore, aggressive and detailed accountability activities, such as minute supervision, may defeat themselves by sacrificing flexibility and innovation and may, indeed, prevent managers from managing (Behn, 2001).

· Derailment. Those subject to accountability know they are being evaluated, are often knowledgeable about the methods used, and are certainly aware of the likely consequences if results of accounting are adverse. This combination may generate several undermining tendencies, identified by Grizzle (2002) as follows. (1) Manipulating reports. The Boca Raton, Florida, police department was accused in 1996 of downgrading crimes to lesser offenses to make its crime rates appear lower. The Department of Justice has been accused of overstating terrorist arrests to justify its budget, classifying offenses such as erratic behavior and convict riots as "terrorist." To an unknown degree, physicians classify patient disorders to make them fit into categories for which insurance companies are willing to provide reimbursement. Colleges and universities can fatten teaching-load data by describing office hours, advising activities, and independent study as course equivalents or contact hours. (2) "Creaming," when agencies take on the easiest cases to pump up their success rates. (3) "Teaching to the test." A longstanding criticism of tying future budgetary support to test results is that teachers know what the tests are likely to be and distort their teaching activities toward preparing students to score well. This effect was observed in nineteenth-century Britain, when the government tied subsidies to student performance when government inspectors tested them. This principle has been observed in the No Child Left Behind program, and it has been noticed that high-school teachers orient their teaching activities toward college entrance examinations, because one component of a secondary school's reputation is the percentage of its graduates admitted to competitive colleges and universities.

Such practices illustrate a general principle: if you install a system with procedures, you simultaneously install a motive to get around, distort, or play the system out of motives of consequence avoidance and self-interest. A corresponding distortion occurs when bureaucrats—the enforcers of accountability—conspire with their clients by simply filing accountability reports away if the clients have met the "letter" requirements of accountability. Receiving and routinely filing reports is prima facie evidence that bureaucrats have carried out *their* duties in an accountable way.

Government Regulation

This typically involves interaction among economics, politics, and the law. Regulation also represents a range of tensions in societies with significant capitalist-market components—tensions that both endure and flare up periodically and are never settled.

Regulation—one form of relationship between polity and economy—is a distinctive characteristic of capitalist and mixed economies. It expresses a tug of war between the unfettered workings of market-based capitalism and the tendencies of that system to generate inequities, injustices, harm, and destruction. Regulation aims to strike a balance in this relationship. More extreme forms of intervention are found in communist and socialist systems, in which regulation is subsumed under more radical controls, including government ownership.

Regulation made its appearance in Britain with the factory legislation of 1833 that limited child labor—legislation that followed a vigorous campaign protesting child labor's inhumanity. Since then, regulation of labor conditions has spread to health and safety conditions generally, worker compensation, management-labor conflict, and hiring practices through antidiscrimination and affirmative action programs. Other areas of regulation are public health, consumer protection, advertising excesses and fraud, malpractice, and the conduct of the media—many of which are thought to result from uncontrolled commercialism. Regulation is typically exercised through commissions and agencies and backed by courts, all of which use an array of legal and economic sanctions (such as fines, prohibitions, public hearings, requirements to provide information for users of products, rewards for compliance, and persuasion). Most recently, governments have intensified their efforts to regulate practices that damage the environment and exhaust resources.

The most visible and controversial types of regulation are direct intervention into and control of markets, marketing, and organizational structures; these are aimed at limiting, controlling, or preventing practices of monopolies, preventing restraint of trade, and restricting unfair business practices. Much of this emanated from the trust-busting and Progressive eras of the late nineteenth century. Interestingly, this line of regulatory activity is doubly regarded: as *both* restricting free and market activity *and* promoting the free operation of capitalist economies by controlling practices that hinder market functioning. That is to say, regulatory activities—like brakes on cars—not only slow some kinds of economic activity, but also permit business traffic to move faster. Some businesses welcome regulation in a special sense: it not only sets limits on what one *cannot* do, but it also frees those regulated to proceed freely within those limits. Finally, commercial enterprises sometimes engage in some self-regulation, following episodes of adverse publicity that damage public goodwill, or as a way to stave off feared intervention.

Repeated objections to regulation have been voiced by business interests and market-oriented economists. Government intervention is represented as wasteful and inefficient, inferior to solutions generated by competitive markets. One form of this argument is that markets offer better solutions for environmental problems than government control. Regulating is costly in terms of hiring personnel for enforcement, red tape, consulting with and influencing businesses, documenting enforcement activities, guaranteeing that sanctions are followed or obeyed, conducting cumbersome public hearings, contending with protests, and court cases. Regulation drives up employer costs and adversely affects employment levels. Proponents of regulation argue that promoting health, safety, equity, justice, and environmental survival outweighs these objections.

The two groups of social scientists who are most influential in regulation debates and policy are lawyers and economists. A continuing tension exists between them: should regulation be enforced through laws, rules, and procedures, or should it be enforced through economic rewards and punishments? An example of the former is a municipal government's requirement that all new houses incorporate a solar heating capacity; an example of the latter is the provision of subsidies or rebates to those who install solar panels. The debate is especially salient with respect to environmental regulation, but not so much in preventing restraint of trade, where legal-administrative sanctions seem the apt ones; it does not make sense to pay manufacturers not to break the law.

Economists argue that economic sanctions are more effective and less wasteful than legal ones, and defend them further on the grounds that they permit free choice rather than coercion and are therefore easier to enforce. These debates have not settled matters, however; the tension promises to persist as feature of regulation.

Political scientists and others have provided behavioral insights into how regulation works in practice. The issues they have pinpointed overlap with those identified in connection with accountability:

- One line of analysis in the 1950s stressed how the regulated "capture" the regulators through lobbying, cozying, creating intellectual cultures of mutual understanding, and engaging in mutual problem-solving, all of which may redirect or subvert legislative intent. Freeman (1965) coined a phrase, the *iron triangle* of interest groups, legislative committees, and agencies, to describe this process. This line of argument demonstrates that regulation is a political as well as an economic and administrative process. In fact, all three forces operate all the time, which makes regulation so complex.
- Closely related is the issue of discretion—how much slack the regulators allow the regulated (McCubbins, Noll, and Weingast, 1987). This is the "spirit of the law" versus the "letter of the law" issue. Each emphasis appears to involve difficulties. High discretion may permit more evasion; detailed regulation may stifle innovation and create inefficiencies.
- The regulated seem to have an endless ability to subvert the regulatory process by discovering loopholes and hobbling competitors in the market. Some medical practitioners may distort diagnostic categories to assure that their medical treatments are covered by insurance policies. Such tendencies generate a chasing game between regulation and defiance. After summarizing the wide range of subversions of regulatory law and administration, one scholar concludes that "regulative law may exert its largest effects by motivating evasion, not compliance" (Suchman, 2001: 10951).
- What is the best balance—if any can be achieved—between (1) regulation meant to affect markets with the intent of making them more competitive and/or efficient; and (2) regulation imposed in the name of equity, justice, and preventing economic and environmental excesses?

We note one final topic that points directly toward usable knowledge for policy-makers: the "deregulation revolution" initiated in the 1980s. That development is one piece of the puzzle of understanding the economic excesses and instability, as well as the political and moral crises, that have unfolded since then (see below, p. 222).

Many forces converged to produce the surge of deregulation:

- Highlighted by the Solidarity Movement and other developments in the 1980s, communism and its ideology of command-and-control were discredited, in retreat, and ultimately collapsed, leaving no viable alternative to the ideology of competitive capitalism.
- The economic slowdown occasioned by the OPEC oil crisis of the early 1970s, combined with increased international competition, especially from Asian countries, heightened anxiety about America's ability to sustain its economic dominance.
- Disaffection with direct government involvement and its presumed inefficiency and ineffectiveness also flowered as a reaction to the interventionist policies of the Great Society.
- Partially as a result of these trends, the elections of Ronald Reagan and Margaret Thatcher in 1979–80 initiated an ideology of classical capitalism, the efficiencies of market competition, and "getting government off our backs" (through, e.g., antitax and antiwelfare emphases) that ran counter to the political philosophy that had dominated the Democratic Party since the New Deal. Deregulation and privatization were important elements of that ideology. The conservative impulse subsequently spread internationally, encouraged by the American and British examples.

Deregulation produced a powerful "policy catch phrase" (Bennet, 2001: 3096) and produced a general trend, including deregulation of the airlines, the postal service, and the telecommunications industry, as well as the electricity industry in California. The consequences of this trend are not altogether clear. The telecommunications industry became vastly more competitive; the airline industry experienced a reduction in its labor force (presumably a sign of greater efficiency), generated higher prices and output, and produced a surge in consolidations of companies (Rose, 2001). The deregulation of electricity in California has generally been regarded as an economic and energy disaster. Above all, the deregulatory impulse weakened the government's antitrust policies and regulatory activities, and thus created a force—an atmosphere of permissiveness—that contributed to the era of hostile takeovers, mergers, and restructuring.

ORGANIZATIONAL CHANGE

Many aspects of organizational change—which, by broad definition, encompasses much of organizational analysis in general—have been considered under previous headings. In this section, we pick up a few general threads, especially including restructuring, which has been highly visible for several decades.

ORGANIZATION AND CHANGE

I have been centrally involved in a few revolutions—revolutions for me, change for the organization: the deployment of ATMs; the reconceptualization of Citibank's back-office processing; and the creation of a focused consumer financial-service business. They were linked and overlapping in time. In each case, we were trying to close the gap between a future that we could envisage and a very different current reality. We were first with these visions, and for that reason a leader, but other companies went on different but parallel tracks.

The story of these revolutions highlights some issues. First, *staying with it.* It is easy to leave a project before it is fully developed and in doing so hobble its evolution (I believe in retrospect that I did this both with the back-office functions and our consumer efforts). Second, *mistakes.* When innovating, you can make serious mistakes. For example, we stayed with proprietary rather than open technology too long; we started but gave up on debit cards too early; we did not stick with travel and entertainment (T&E) cards long enough to seriously challenge American Express. Finally, *the necessities of organizational positioning.* If you start something new, it is best to be separate and distant from that new effort. However, to be relevant, at some point you must integrate back in, and the natural rejection of what is "foreign" is an organizational problem. If you change a large existing operation, there is natural resistance to change. I found that you must be tough, stick with it, and accept that there will be damage. To do so, you had better have the support of your seniors.

The Story

Walter Wriston was my first boss when I joined the bank in 1965 as a trainee. He became president and CEO in 1967. One of the first things he did was to hire a consulting company (GE's Tempo) to write up a number of forecasts of what the world of finance might look like in the year 2000. Tempo produced five volumes and an environmental prospectus, which included demographic and social forecasts and forecasts of computer technology, transportation technology, energy technology, and communications technology. In 1968, Wriston gave me the volume on computer technology and asked that I get back to him with practical suggestions on how to incorporate these forecasts into our thinking and development. Without getting into too much detail, this led me to explore the computer world as it then existed, and to the conclusion that online interactive computing (existing then only in primitive stock quotation systems and United Airlines' first computer reservation system) would be central to the evolution of banking.

We, of course, had a problem. The bank had no significant understanding of this technology. What we were contemplating was new. We had to create a separate computer-focused unit within Citi, hire people, and build a nucleus of relevant competence. To execute the operation, we went to Santa Monica, California.

We did not know it at the time, but we were beginning an interesting journey. Our first efforts focused on our two key customer groups: corporations, for whom we saw the possibility of providing "electronic" cash management and funds transfer services; and consumers, for whom we first focused on electronic cash dispensing (a teller's function) and later home banking. Since our retail customers were widely dispersed, the ATM project posed immense management and technological challenges.

Again, wishing to spare you the details, we tried to interest IBM in helping; it refused (saying it sold products, not customer solutions). We built our own computers, multiplexors, and concentrators; created a network with leased lines from AT&T (then still a monopoly), and deployed a system of 700 ATMs at 350 branches that had to be renovated and changed so as to present our machines to our 1.4 million customers as an extension of their branch, available 24–7 for their convenience. After success in New York, we moved the idea around the world.

We started all of this in 1968. In 1970, for reasons that related to senior retirements, not the flow of our efforts, I was asked to take over the bank's back office in addition to what I was doing. This was another challenge and change.

Historically, I think that it is fair to say that bankers are selected from those who relate well to customers and finance; they are usually extroverts and social. At the time, banking was not particularly well-paying, but it was prestigious. The back office was seen as only an accounting function staffed by "bookkeepers." By the 1970s, the volume of activity was such that this conception no longer worked, and we had serious cost and quality issues. Clearly, these activities could be seen as flows: flows of customer transactions and information, and, most important, flows that could be managed and automated. Running these activities, with their large budget and many thousands of people, was a large task. This work was quite different than our small effort in California, but it required both new thinking and new talent. In the back office, we had to overcome the normal resistance to change and to get buy-in by promising a more interesting look at the future. Hard work, mistakes, and problems happened along the way, but it worked.

Having looked at the world through new technology and having also lived with the flow of transactions that customers move through a bank in their day-to-day interactions, I suppose that it is not surprising that I came to see the consumer, our retail customer, in a different way. Historically, banks viewed these customers as a source of funds to be lent to business customers. Branch systems were run to collect these monies. Some banks offered loan products: small-value personal loans or mortgage loans. They were run in separate departments as product businesses. The credit card was created as a U.S. version of the British overdraft account. The credit card was a revolving credit line much cheaper to administer than a flow of individual loans approved one by one; it allowed banks to lower their interest rates, but also forced them to build a network of merchants who would accept the card.

In 1973, I was asked to pull our branches, loan businesses, and cards together (we also owned financial companies and mortgage banks) into a global business. Again, we redefined the business, this time around the customer. We focused on his or her needs. We instinctively knew the difference among needs (transaction services, loans, savings, investing, and advice), the products designed to serve these needs, and the underlying delivery or distribution systems that reached out to customers. The ATM system that we had designed in California was deployed in New York City in early 1977. I had closed the circle, in that I was then responsible for our customers there. The management of the back office supported not only our branches, but also the card business, which had become transactionally intense and demanding, what with authorization systems, monthly billing, and collection activities. We had embedded new technology into our business, as well as new conceptions of the business and processing functions in the organization.

The business was fundamentally changed, but this start—seeing banking as information flows and customer applications in an interactive network that was, built around customer needs—still has its most promising days in front of it. It was a revolution at the time; it is still full of potential today.

—*John S. Reed*

Sources of Change

On this topic, there is no received theory. The most evident sources are changes in organizations' *environments:*

· New market opportunities, real and/or perceived.
· Technological innovations and their adaptations, including the invention of new machinery, adaptation of new energy sources, and the computer, which have inspired waves of organizational creation and change.
· New legislation and new social programs that generate bureaucracies and agencies; changes in regulatory legislation and enforcement also force organizational adaptation.
· External shocks to organizations, including organizational accidents and disasters, which trigger both administrative actions from above and internal changes. We would include the intensification of governmental pressure, as

well as the activities of social-movement organizations such as environmental groups, in this category.

- Various resource dependencies force organizational adaptations in response to changes in consumer taste, availability of raw materials, and availability of capital, as well as changes in tax policies affecting both profit and nonprofit organizations.
- A principle of institutional isomorphism is also at work. This is a tendency for organizations to move toward resembling one another in structure and practices. Sources working toward homogenization include pressure from regulatory agencies to conform; the introduction of standardized procedures (e.g., budgeting, welfare policies) in multiorganization systems; certain path dependencies, as competing firms chase one another to adopt new production and marketing techniques; organizational copycatting, as firms, educational institutions, and public bureaucracies look toward others' practices under conditions of uncertainty (see DiMaggio and Powell, 1983; Davis and Greve, 1997). A telling example of isomorphism is the convergence of social-movement organizations in response to governmental signals in the legislation and policies of the Great Society of the 1960s. One signal was that racial, ethnic, and other identity-based groups were recognized by the government as politically significant (e.g., the target of civil rights and affirmative action reforms). In response, isomorphic interest organizations proliferated along ethnic, gender, sexual preference, and age lines.
- The *internal* environment of organizations can also be a source of organizational change, e.g., efforts of new management to differentiate itself from old management; adaptations made in resolving group conflicts; and responding to suggestions generated from departments, divisions, groups, or individuals in the organization.

The second principal source of organizational change is *leadership,* the guidance of organizations from above. Much leadership lies in fashioning organizational adaptations to the environmental changes just noted—minimizing their effects, giving in to them, ignoring them, evading them, or profiting from them. Leadership can also emanate from individual and organizational entrepreneurship in taking advantage of opportunities (see above, p. 193).

Resistance to Change

The other side of organizational change is nonchange, including the inertial forces that prevent or deflect it. These, too, are diverse:

- Protection of reputation. In a case study, Roberts (2006) told the story of how the leadership of the Federal Emergency Management Agency (FEMA) built the reputation of the agency by developing an "all-hazards" approach and professionalized itself by incorporating the newest systematic standards for dealing with disasters and other emergencies. On the basis of this reputation, the agency was able to resist pressures from the White House to take on responsibilities for national security and antiterrorism, believing that the agency did not have sufficient resources for this change, and should stick with the mission (responding to disasters) it could carry out best.

· Culture. Earlier we noted that organizational culture includes legends about founders, definitions of the organization and its missions, outlooks, beliefs, and rituals. In many respects, these ingredients are valuable assets. At the same time, they have a resistive aspect. Many cultural ingredients define how things should be done and thus become sources of organizational blindness and stubbornness. All organizations manifest cultural conservatism, but the power of resistive culture seems especially strong in organizations responsible for the safety and lifeblood of the society: branches of the military, police forces, security organizations (CIA, FBI), and the Internal Revenue Service. Their cultures tend to assume a sacred quality and promote jealousies and jurisdictional pride, which are sources of resistance to change (Terriff, 2006; Jiao, Lao, and Liu, 2005).

· Vested interests. Cliques, groups, departments, and divisions within organizations can operate in the interest of change, but the politics of turf and status protection more often create nodes of opposition. These conservative forces operate more strongly as organizations grow older and groups become more entrenched. These phenomena have been subsumed into the idea of structural inertia theory (Hannan and Freeman, 1984). External constituencies can also press for change, but many are conservative. An example is alumni groups who like to see their alma mater institutions remain just as they remember them; and such sentiments can constitute obstacles to policies such as downgrading athletics and reforming admissions standards. Labor organizations often demand changes that will advantage their workers, but their opposition to innovations, outsourcing, and moving to new locations is also notable.

· Core technologies. Once an organization has adopted a certain technology that proves successful, it may become committed to that technology and resist changes even when it proves obsolete in new circumstances (Thompson, 1967). Salka (2004) traces such a situation in the United States Forest Service. The agency won a high reputation for its principles of scientific management. When, however, it came under pressure from environmental groups during the spotted owl crisis, these principles proved wanting, and the agency came under fire from both environmentalists and its superiors in government. The agency announced a change in mission to accommodate these forces, but basically retained its existing principles.

The history of all organizations is thus one of punctuated equilibria resulting from the constant interplay—usually compromise and accommodation rather than victory or defeat—between forces pressing for change and forces resisting it. An organization is seldom in a fixed "state"; with so many forces impinging on it, it is nearly always in a "process."

Organizational Restructuring
A Recent Chapter in Economic History

Historians of American capitalism (e.g., Javidan, Pablo, Singh, Hitt, et al., 2005) have identified five "merger waves" in the past long century: a "mergers for monopoly" movement (1887–early twentieth century); a "mergers for oligopoly" movement (1916–29); a "conglomerate" movement (1960s); a hostile takeover movement (late 1970s into the 1980s); and a megamerger movement (1990s–early twenty-first century). The last involved an acceleration of friendly merging and acquisition, which was regarded as corporate strategy aimed to achieve economies and promote growth. Two strategies that rose to salience were downsizing and outsourcing in the corporate world and elsewhere, with the same aims. These several trends are all instances of corporate restructuring. Over time they spread into the international arena. Some, especially downsizing and outsourcing, spread into noncorporate quarters (governmental, university, voluntary organizations) as an ideology of achieving rational solutions and efficiencies by relying on market logic and mechanisms. Outsourcing also expressed a shift away from hierarchy (supervising diverse activities within the organization) toward market (contracting them out to external, presumably more specialized and efficient, organizations). This movement also accentuated interest in principal-agent relations in economics.

The identifiable eras of restructuring suggest periodicity, if not a cyclical process. Each movement emerged from a sense of economic opportunity combined with a real or apparent weakening of obstacles (especially antitrust policy). Each faded or ended because of mixed economic results, financial-legal-moral excesses, general economic collapse (e.g., the 1929 crash), and/or or a swing back toward stricter regulation. We concentrate on the fourth and especially the fifth eras because of their special drama and the usable knowledge they yielded.

What forces drove the hostile takeover and merger-acquisition-downsizing movements? Of prime importance was an intensification of shareholder interest in short-term profits and returns, which ratcheted upward and spread to other constituencies such as banks, lawyers, advertisers, the stock market, and public relations people. One analyst concludes simply that "while a company may have many reasons to merge with or acquire another, the ultimate purpose should be to increase shareholder value" (Lafaix, 2005: 48). (Was this a historical reversal of the famous midcentury formula of "separation of ownership and control" [Berle and Means, 1932] that increased management power?) This increased pressure for profits and returns had a series of corollaries:

· An outlook of short-termism, expressed in the value of shares and dividends.
· An increasingly competitive atmosphere, calling for more aggressive market strategies and initiatives.
· Radical cost-cutting. A main motive for hostile takeovers, mergers, acquisitions, downsizing, and outsourcing was to reduce costs through economies of scale, cutting labor and management costs, boosting managerial efficiency, improving production techniques, reducing redundancies, and other "synergies" (Shleifer and Vishny, 2005). Mergers are powerful weapons for change; the very idea of merger generates expectations that an organization will be shaken up.
· Increased tension and conflict between shareholders and management over payouts, firm priorities, and the autonomy of managerial decision-making.
· A turn toward special recognition, typically bonuses and stock options, to reward managers in accord with "results produced," as measured by firm performance and shareholder returns (see above, pp. 108–10).
· Above all, the creation of a "culture of dread," of failure and punishment if a company lagged in the race for radical cost-cutting and profits. This feature contributed most to the moniker of "merger mania."
· Down the line, a growing hothouse atmosphere, fed by all these forces (especially intensified competition), which stretched the limits of propriety, legality, and morality, resulting in individual and corporate excesses and sometimes retribution.

Besides the principal motive of increasing shareholder wealth, other factors pushed the takeover and merger-acquisition movements. The last third of the century witnessed a flurry of technological innovations, both intensifying the competitive race and calling for new organizational arrangements. Also, the availability of capital and credit facilitated leveraged buyouts, or borrowing with the intent to acquire another company or merge (Jarrell, Buckley, and Netter, 2005). Another cause—permissive but very powerful—was the deregulation movement described above. Many mergers occurred in recently deregulated industries such as airlines and transportation, financial services, and oil and gas (ibid). One set of observers (Andrade, Mitchell, and Stafford, 2004) avows, "We can say, without exaggeration or hyperbole, that in explaining the causes of mergers and acquisitions, the 1980s were the 'decade of deregulation'" (73). Deregulation meant more freedom and diminished apprehension about regulative intervention.

THE MERGER

The proposal to merge Citibank and Travelers Company came to me out of the blue. In early 1997, Sandy Weill, president of Travelers (which included Travelers Insurance, Smith Barney, and, more recently, Solomon Brothers), approached me directly at a business council meeting and proposed a merger of equals. I had no advance indication of the approach and certainly was not planning on anything like it independently, even though it was a heavy season for mergers in American industry and business (see pp. 221–22).

In keeping with my philosophy and practice, I expressed neither enthusiasm nor coldness toward the idea, but told Sandy that I would look at the business facts and get back to him. My first inner reaction was one of doubt, but I decided to follow another item in my philosophy, to step back and think new thoughts about any new idea.

I had known Sandy for years, but mostly as an acquaintance. We had served on the Arlen Real Estate board together; I knew he had been at American Express; and I had met him independently with Jamie Dimon, at that time Sandy's number-two man and now head of J. P. Morgan Chase. And I had seen him periodically around town in New York's business circles. He had the reputation of being an outgoing deal-doer with a big personality, but also was seen as a successful consolidator. Jamie complemented these qualities with his strengths in mastering details and making things happen.

Sandy's proposal came to me at a time of both personal and company transition. I had been CEO of Citibank for about fifteen years, a relatively long time for such a position. I had assumed I would retire at a right moment during the next few years. I was generally happy with the company, but was struggling with the balance between the corporate and consumer sides of our business. The consumer side was large and thriving, with a full agenda before it. Our corporate business was more complicated. Because of geographical limitations associated with our location in New York, we had moved into the international arena and had established ourselves as a global business but with a local presence. Only the Hong Kong Shanghai Bank had moved in a similar direction. This dispersion to the local level in many countries produced a good and growing business. The network allowed us to service multinational firms around the world, but this was an expensive undertaking. We limited our business to some fifteen hundred global companies and largely ignored purely local firms in Japan, Europe, and North America. As markets were beginning to supplement and sometimes displace institutions in providing financial services, we came under pressure from both customers and staff to add investment-banking capabilities to our offerings. To build and maintain such a business was an expensive proposition, and we would have had to expand our customer list. On the corporate side, we were confronting and trying to sort out these challenges.

Over the years I had pondered another, more profound resolution to the consumer-corporate division: to split Citi into two companies, one for each line of activity. To me that made good business and economic sense, but I also feared that the corporate franchise, existing separately, might have difficulty in surviving alone. If it did experience such difficulties, it might try to absorb into another firm; I did not want that outcome. On the other hand, if we merged with Travelers, this might permit a successful split between the consumer and corporate sides.

I had always defined my job as working to improve the company and expand its opportunities as an evolutionary strategy. The idea of a merger with Travelers fit comfortably with that outlook. So I took the next step and I asked Paul Collins, my senior and trusted colleague, to meet with Sandy, run the numbers by him while I was on an overseas trip, and get back to me with the results and suggest next steps.

Looking at the two business enterprises together, they promised a good fit. Their activities overlapped only a little. This was important to me because I was not willing to accept massive consolidation and layoffs, which appeared to be an unhappy part of so many mergers. Our earnings and market values were approximately equal. Travelers' insurance business was attractive to me. Smith Barney was a top brokerage firm that could add a whole new dimension to our core consumer business. Its finance company, Commercial Credit, was another strong addition to the consumer side. Finally, Solomon, a world-renowned bond-trading house, combined with our deep knowledge of and extended relations with customers, provided the potential for a top-notch investment-corporate bank.

In retrospect, I recall being driven by two beliefs. First, from a business point of view, I believed my personal views and preferences were not relevant; I worked for the stockholders, and the overriding aim was to build customer-focused businesses that would deliver sustainable long-term values. The fit with Travelers' various businesses was excellent and consistent with this philosophy. Overlap was minimal, and in particular the Solomon business would solve the dilemmas facing our corporate business side.

Second, I thought I had a safety net. We had been in serious trouble during the long and difficult crisis of the early 1990s. We were short on capital; we had experienced large losses on our real estate exposure; we had been successively downgraded by the rating agencies; we were experiencing funding difficulties and had been required to sign a memorandum of understanding (like a debtor nation!) with the Federal Reserve and the Comptroller of the Currency. All through this, I had, however, developed a close and very constructive relationship with my board. I had also come (with some pain) to accept, emotionally as well as intellectually, that I could be fired if it were important for the institution; that came with the job.

Also, in thinking about the merger, I believed we could count on the board in the event of conflicts and other management difficulties. I assumed that if such difficulties developed, the board would simply "retire" both Sandy and me and bring in the right management. This belief was fortified in my mind when, during our premerger talks, Sandy and I had considered agreeing to stay for three years and then retire together. That idea went nowhere, however. When informed of that possibility, one of our senior directors said simply, "That is not something for the two of you to agree to; that is something the board will decide." He was correct, of course.

One further factor conspired to weaken our decision-making. Because of the monumental market importance of the merger, I kept the involvement of other people to a minimum—only the board, two key senior advisors, and our lawyer. I think I probably should have gone the other way. In particular, if I had included the head of human resources, our decision-making would have been improved. That and other steps would have brought into focus the interpersonal, social, and cultural complications of such massive organizational changes.

On the basis of business considerations and my conviction that the board would successfully oversee the merger, I pushed it through. In doing so, I neglected many of the less visible dimensions, in particular the large differences—conflicts, rather—in personality, attitude, and management styles between Sandy and me and the unhappy impact of those differences throughout the company. My prediction that the board would be a safety net proved to be mistaken. We all paid dearly for this restricted vision, especially the stockholders, customers, and staff.

Lessons about usable social science? In this case, they seem fairly straightforward. In chapter 6, we document the revival of the tension between the business-financial-organizational side of mergers on the one hand, and the human relations aspects on the other—the interpersonal, the group, and the cultural dimensions (see pp. 228–29). We also noted that forces on the latter side are in many ways responsible for the mixed records of postmerger performance. The voices of researchers interested in such areas are not always heard. As I regard our merger nearly two decades afterward, I think it would have been very helpful to have the results of this compelling line of research more explicitly before us. Had the merger gone forward, I believe, we surely would have attempted to maneuver in more informed ways through many visible warning signs. Indeed, the merger might not have been proposed.

—*John S. Reed*

So much for the causes that propelled the takeover-acquisition-merger-down-sizing-outsourcing movements. What can be said of the consequences?. Overall, the assessment is mixed because the consequences are multiple and because meth-odological difficulties obscure measuring impacts at different stages. Dispositional postures also lead to disagreement; one observer describes the merger literature as "a controversy between skeptical economic and enthusiastic financial research" (Larsson, Brousseau, Driver, and Sweet, 2004: 5). Finally, as we will see, judgments varied according to types of consequences selected: while mixed, the financial-eco-nomic results were more positive, the human relations assessments more negative.

Scholars identified several phases of merger and acquisition: predeal, due diligence, integration planning, and implementation (Schmidt, 2002b). Conse-quences differed according to phase. In the enthusiasm involved in the predeal and due-diligence phases, expectations overshot subsequent gains and missed or underestimated pitfalls. Surveys also revealed that an underinvolvement of human relations personnel in the early phases downplayed subsequent adverse human consequences (Lafaix, 2005). In the earlier phases, particularly at the moment when a merger, acquisition, or takeover was announced, stock prices gen-erally rose (Matsusaka, 2005; McConnell and Nantell, 2005). In the early period after combination, too, increases in stock values appeared to be significant, thus apparently affirming the main motive for consolidation; one survey concludes that tender offers are "wealth-increasing transactions for the stockholders of both the target and acquiring firms" (Bradley, Desai, and Kim, 2005: 16).

The implementing phases show a mixed picture for profits, increased payouts, and values of stocks. One survey reported failure rates of mergers and acquisitions as high as 50 to 75 percent (Marks and Mirvis, 1998); another summarized fifty years of economic research and concluded that shareholders of the acquiring firm tend to lose from mergers, and that earnings decline after consolidation (Goldberg, 1983). A survey of 440 executives involved in mergers in 2000 revealed that longer-term results of mergers fell short of expectations with respect to share of market, brand enhancement, and increased use of new technology (Schmidt, 2002a). Other eco-nomic assessments yielded a "clear success" rate of about 20 percent, a "clear failure" rate of 20 percent, and a "disappointment" rate of about 60 percent in selected industries (Schmidt, 2002b). Even if these surveys are taken with a grain of salt, they show consistency. Many takeovers and mergers involve firms that are not perform-ing well and have low return rates; high shareholder hopes and initial successes in cutting labor and managerial costs through restructuring improve the revenue-cost ratio and boost stock values. These initial gains, however, cannot be sustained, and "human cost" failures may also take their toll in the implementation phase.

What about these human consequences? We mentioned the different orien-tations and assessments of those looking at these consequences and those look-ing at financial-economic results. In fact, corporate restructurings in the fifth merger wave revitalized the longstanding contrasts and conflicts between the rationalizing-economizing and the human relations approaches to organizational analysis. It also generated more attention to aspects of organization identified earlier:

· Leadership succession.
· Stress and burnout.
· Organizational deviance.
· Structural inertia.
· Organizational politics.
· Organizational culture.
· Organizational learning.

All these were themes for those bemoaned the human consequences of the restructuring movements. We now summarize the general results of their assessments:

· Culture clashes between management styles come to the fore in takeovers, mergers, and acquisitions, if for no other reason than that the companies involved have different understandings of their own histories, values, and outlooks. Culture clashes entail individual clashes. Moreover, because so many ingredients of culture are semiconscious, they resist articulation. "Solutions" to cultural conflicts range from the soft approach of honoring previous cultures to the hard approach of attempting to crush cultural differences and employee resistance, with various "cocompetence" or integrative approaches in between, none of which produce fail-safe formulae (Larsson, Brousseau, Driver, and Sweet, 2004). Insofar as the future will bring more crossborder or global combinations—as some have predicted (Davenport, 2002)—the dimensions of cultural ambiguity and cultural conflict loom even larger (see also Hitt and Pisano, 2005).
· Many communication problems emerge, some arising from cultural differences themselves. Others stem from lack of information, guarding information, misunderstanding, interpreting neutral communications as threats, and rumors that arise in uncertain situations (ibid.).
· Turnover problems. Takeovers and mergers typically involve layoffs; one study of hostile takeovers estimates a net loss of 12 percent for the years 1980–84 (Denis, 2005). At the managerial level, some managers are discharged for downsizing purposes, others live on with cuts in pay and responsibility, others leave voluntarily out of discomfort, others take on new administrative responsibilities, and still others are recruited anew. All the complications of leadership succession appear as these changes unfold.
· Personal insecurity arises from uncertainty as the merger-consolidation, and especially downsizing, is executed and implemented. Pucik and Evans (2003) summarize the range of reactions in the "merger syndrome" as follows:

"Initial disbelief and denial are followed by shock, colored by overreaction ('We are going to lose our jobs') or underreaction ('Oh, it won't change anything'). This leads, in turn, to anger and then to individual attempts to bargain or to dig one's heels in to take care of oneself, followed ultimately by acceptance. Acceptance itself may take different forms, which can characterize the mood of the firm for a long time afterwards—fatalism, bitterness, wistful regret or, ideally, proactivity" (168–69).

This range of reactions to job insecurity was captured poignantly in the 2009 film *Up in the Air,* in which George Clooney played the role of an outsourced "hit man" who conveyed the bad news of firing (a term always rendered in euphemisms throughout the film) to employees in companies around the country. Repeated episodes of layoff-search-rehire-layoff over the adult career have led observers to proclaim that there is "no long term" (Sennett, 1998) and that career jobs may be "headed for extinction" (Jacoby, 1998).

- A general range of reactions stems from uncertainty during adjustment. These spill over into occupational stress—anxiety, lowered morale, stigma of failure, distrust, increased absenteeism, and negative attitudes.
- Structural inertia emerges in the implementation phases of consolidation. This may manifest itself in the "drag" involved in adapting to new structures, expectations, and routines; in more serious cases, it may involve noncooperation, stubbornness, conflict, even sabotage.

To point out these contingencies and difficulties in adaptation is not to say that they cannot be dealt with productively. Books stressing the human side of restructuring often turn, at the end, to practical advice about planning, anticipating, and confronting difficulties head on rather than letting them play out in uncontrolled ways (Schmidt, 2002a). Transitions involved with restructuring, however—especially job uncertainty and job loss—are so fundamental that they ultimately have a residue of unmanageability. Firm rules to deal with these transitions are hard to come by.

CONCLUDING OBSERVATION

At the beginning of chapter 2, we recorded our commitment to a nonrational view of human nature, implying a variable mix of rational and irrational forces (and many that cannot be described as either). We hope we have achieved the same result with respect to organizational life. As noted, almost every phenomenon highlighted—size, complexity, culture, politics, change—is a sword with two edges. Our view is, we hope, a corrective to the apparently intractable human tendency to press toward quick closure of judgment, and to tinge that closure with unadulterated optimism or pessimism.

7

Economic Development
and Social Change

The fields of growth and developmental studies pose a great challenge to the idea of usable social science. It may seem odd to include a relatively difficult account, but our view is that we learn as much from difficult as we do from easy cases. In the first part of this chapter, we elucidate problems in theory and application. The remainder is more positive, attempting to pinpoint some salient themes and guidelines for academics, planners, development agencies, governments, and others involved in the developmental process nationally and internationally.

GROWTH AND DEVELOPMENT
AN IMPORTANT BUT CONTESTED FIELD

Scholars of growth and development, perhaps more than others, bemoan the difficulties of their specialty:

- "Development economics is . . . a very frustrating subject. . . . Unlike most areas in economics, there is no consensus on what the student should know. Two scholars can with equal justification write two different textbooks" (Meier and Rauch, 2005: 2).
- "No area of economics has experienced as many abrupt changes in its leading paradigm since World War II as economic development" (Adelman, 2001: 103).
- "Even among social scientists who retain a commitment to development, the term has taken on variety of meanings, and has motivated inquiries employing vastly different theoretical frameworks" (Hershberg, 2001: 3593).
- "There is an old story about economists: put two of them in a room and ask

for a prediction, and you will get three answers. So, too, in the field of economic growth, and the problem is not just limited to economists; sociologists, and geographers, and other social scientists have all expressed strikingly different explanations" (Seligson and Passé-Smith, 2008: 1).

- "Ideas about how development can be effected have long been both controversial and highly contested . . . over time [they] have tended to accumulate and accrue, and not fade away" (Desai and Potter, 2002: 59).

We take it that such comments are not altogether misguided, and our own explorations are generally confirmatory. If the diagnoses do have any validity, we may ask: Why such effects? Before proceeding to this question, we note that despite such diagnoses, many scholars continue to be preoccupied with problems of development. The field does not command as much fascination among western scholars as in past periods, but the topic is one of special interest to economists and others in rapidly developing areas (notably South and Southeast Asia) and those preoccupied with tragic cases of countries trapped in nondevelopment and destitution, mainly in Africa.

THEMES IN DEVELOPMENT STUDIES
The Emergence of the Field

The history of the social sciences reveals an enduring preoccupation with economic growth and its concomitants. In economics, the increase of wealth was a preoccupation of both mercantilism and the classical tradition initiated by Adam Smith. Karl Marx and his followers fashioned a theory of the growth, crises, and demise of capitalism. Nineteenth-century sociologists invented several categories—*Gemeinschaft-Gesellschaft,* traditional-modern, status-contract, for example—to capture the societal convulsions created by the commercial and industrial revolutions (see chapter 4, pp. 122–23). The main impulse toward growth and development as an academic endeavor, however, appeared shortly after World War II. It arose in the context of the dramatic dismantling of the great European empires. Most former colonies emerged as nation-states, eventually welcomed as such in the United Nations, and aspiring (or believed to aspire) to some "modern" status as economies, societies, and nations. The great preoccupation of the first generation of development scholars was: How could the newly emerging nation-states establish themselves as modern entities? Since these beginnings, growth and development studies has established itself as a multidisciplinary endeavor (encompassing economics, sociology, anthropology, political science, geography, and demography) that has held interest for governments, financial organizations, and planners.

A concern from the beginning was what to call these new entities. We had inherited the disrespectful language of *savage, barbarian, primitive,* and *preliterate* from anthropology—language unacceptable to anyone with liberal-cosmopolitan outlooks. Efforts to find more neutral terms yielded *undeveloped* and *backward,* used by many scholars but also pejorative in connotation. So a further search for more dignified and acceptable terms followed—*underdeveloped, less developed,* and then *developing,* followed by the even more neutral *new,* as in the political scientists' *new nations.* Another terminological pitch toward neutrality was *Third World,* referring mainly to Latin American, Asian, and African countries that were neither First World (advanced European and North American) nor Second World (communist-socialist). While still used, the latter notion was rendered inaccurate by the collapse of the Second World. Still another was the semiaccurate equation of the terms *North* with developed and *South* with less developed. All these categories are vulnerable because they ignore variations *among* countries grouped within them. More profoundly, the search signals a fundamental ambivalence that fosters another search for more neutral or euphemistic words, only to discover that the new ones themselves cannot altogether escape the negative connotations. This insight should not discourage us from avoiding derogatory labels, but it tells us something about linguistic dynamics, which, as often as not, hound academic endeavors attempting to be neutral and scientific.

Shifts in Emphasis over Time

It is not appropriate for us to write a history of growth and development studies, but we may identify some of the major shifts that help us understand its inherited fragmentation.

Modernization Theory   This phase dominated the 1950s and 1960s. Its main tenets were as follows: (1) Growth and modernization of societies follow a movement from "traditional" to "modern" (exemplified in Lerner, 1958), which proceeds through definite phases or stages (exemplified in Rostow, 1960); (2) most variables affecting development are *internal* to societies, though trade and foreign investment figure in some degree; (3) in the developmental process, the future of nations that develop will *converge* toward a common goal; and (4) the goal of development is what modern societies have achieved, an assumption that roughly equates modernization with westernization. Within this framework, economists developed formal models stressing capital accumulation, savings, changes in technology, industrialization, and directed (neo-Keynesian) state activity as major threads, and they debated the best strategies for breaking out of the vicious circles (Nurkse, 1962) of underdevelopment—the "big push," "critical minimum development," or balanced growth versus unbalanced growth. By and large, a positive role for government was envisioned in guiding development, captured by the term *dirigisme*. Other disciplines selected their favored themes: sociologists and anthropologists focused on traditional cultural and structural obstacles to development, as well as typical institutional changes (in stratification systems, kinship, community, and religion) that accompany development; demographers zeroed in on population dynamics that discourage or encourage growth; political scientists were interested in the movement from tribal, communal, and local political systems toward the complex of parties, interest groups, and modern political institutions (Almond and Coleman, 1960). Psychologists joined the enterprise, venturing psychologically based theories of entrepreneurship (McClelland, 1961; Hagen, 1962). In a nutshell, modernization theory between 1950 and 1970 appeared to be a "confident" (Meier, 2001: 13) social-scientific version of the ideology of progress, dressed in the clothes of postwar and postcolonial optimism (Ross, 2001).

Dependency and World System Theory as Alternatives   The apparently compelling power of the modernization view was already weakening in the 1960s. Its fundamental approach was criticized as western-centric and degrading to the cultures of other societies. Others (Gusfield, 1972) challenged the idea that traditional societies are static and that traditions disappear with modernization. Economic historians and others assaulted the idea of convergence and identified different paths to industrialization (Gerschenkron, 1962; Bendix, 1964).

The most fundamental attack came from Latin American and later African scholars (Leys, 1974). As early as the 1950s, some complained that the modernization paradigm ignored the international dimension, in particular the dominance of "core" (developed) over "peripheral" countries (Prebisch, 1950). This impulse grew in strength and within a decade had crystallized into a theoretical framework known as dependency theory, stressing that the decisive factors were international and that the dominance of international capital not only crippled development, but also distorted internal relations in less-developed countries. Dependency theorists emphasized import substitution and competitive industrialization as the favored developmental strategies among efforts to break out of dependency. Radical and less radical versions of dependency theory appeared, and a cousin, world systems theory (Wallerstein, 1974), emphasized similar mechanisms of international political and economic dominance. These theoretical statements echoed the earlier writings of Marx and Lenin on imperialism and struck sympathetic notes with the disaffected in the late 1960s and 1970s.

Dependency theory also fell on hard times because of scholars' criticisms of its diagnoses, because of the apparent limitations of its strategies of intervention, and because of the dramatic "Asian miracle" in which South Korea, Taiwan, Singapore, and Hong Kong scored dramatic developmental gains even though many conditions of dependency prevailed (Evans, 1995). The idea of the developmental state achieved prominence, describing the partnership among business, finance, and government in these success stories.

Neoliberalism and Globalization   The early 1980s witnessed a "counter-revolution in developmental economics," part of a general resurgence of economic orthodoxy (Peet and Hartwick, 2009: 74). This was known as the Washington Consensus, a term coined by John Williamson of the Institute for International Economics and adopted by the World Bank and International Monetary Fund (IMF). It was informed by the economic writings of Friedrich Hayek and Milton Friedman and the philosophies of the Margaret Thatcher and Ronald Reagan administrations, and by lessons learned from the debt crisis of the early 1980s. The consensus generated a recipe of measures to be applied to debtor Third World countries: fiscal discipline, reduced public expenditures, tax reforms to improve incentives, market-determined interest rates, competitive exchange rates, trade liberalization, privatization, deregulation, and protection of property rights. This triumph of neoliberalism coincided with a growing disaffection with Marxist ideas and communist-socialist political systems, first in Eastern Europe, then in Western Europe, then in the United States. The collapse of these systems in 1989–90 merely accelerated the impetus, since the only serious competitor to western capitalism had now disappeared, and western economists and policy-makers rushed in to these areas to encourage capitalist development. (A jest in the early 1990s defined communism as a way station on the long, hard journey from capitalism to capitalism.) At this time, a new usage of *globalization* also appeared, connoting that capitalism could now command the entire globe without ideological or political challenge (Kurth, 2001).

The fundamental items of faith underlying the Washington Consensus were that neoclassical economic theory was applicable to *all* economies and needed no significant alterations or new postulates; a corresponding reliance on rationality, incentives, deregulation, and privatization; and an antigovernment conviction that "all markets work perfectly and instantaneously, that all agents predict the future as well as possible, and that all government intervention is futile as it is nullified by agents' anticipation of its necessarily negative effects" (Fine, 2006: 6). The shift was so dramatic that Albert Hirschman (1981) declared that development economics had ceased to exist as an identifiable discipline.

Economic policies accompanying neoliberalism fell under the category of structural adjustment, an invention of the IMF that meant imposing conditions on debtor countries that would help guarantee loan repayments. These programs aimed to cut government expenditures, reduce the extent of state intervention in the economy, and liberalize trade. In practice, many of these policies were punitive, involving wage freezes, devaluation of currency, and downsizing of the civil service. Local protests in the form of "IMF riots" in the 1980s, mainly in Latin America, expressed resistance to these kinds of measures (Walton and Seddon, 1994). A recent reenactment of structural readjustment has been seen in the euro crisis of 2008 to the present and the imposition of strict sanctions on Greece (resulting in riots there) and Ireland.

Emphasis on Human Capital   Accompanying the years of the Washington Consensus was a great growth of human capital as a factor in development. This emphasis arose in part from the conviction that efforts to rely on savings, investment, physical capital, and technology had fallen short of expectations, and that the quality of the labor force, realized in large part by expansion and reform of education, was decisive. This emphasis, dubbed the human capital revolution (Rose, 2006), became a priority for the World Bank and other agencies, and has continued to be regarded as one of the major conditions for economic development.

Post-Washington Consensus and the Emphasis on Institutions   Neoliberal policies themselves fell under criticism, partly as a result of persisting ideological tensions, but also as a result of excesses such as the Asian debt crisis of 1997, the Argentine crisis of 2002, and the world financial crisis of 2008. The decline also reflected the dialectic between extreme liberalization and the regulation of its excesses (see above, pp. 212–15). In all events, by the 1990s Schuurman and his colleagues (1993) had declared an impasse in development theory because of a confusion of meanings of the term, the failure of socialist experiments, many frustrations in the Third World, disillusionment with conventional economic and social approaches, complaints "from below" (i.e., from the Third World, the poor), and postmodern challenges to any kind of general theory.

Intellectual developments since that impasse have been many, among them a "scholarly consensus" emphasizing the importance of institutions for development (Posner, 2005). From the standpoint of traditional economics, this marks a relaxation of the assumption that an institutional framework conducive to ongoing market activity is a given. This shift in is in large part a reflection of the new institutional economics (Williamson, 1985; North, 1990; Demsetz, 1964) that paralleled "new institutionalisms" in sociology and political science (Nee, 2005). The basic argument is that institutions reduce transaction costs and that the input of investment capital and investment in human capital do not produce growth "where the economic institutions are not favorable" (Clague, 1997: 2). What are these institutions? First and foremost, they are "legal provisions for rights to property, mechanisms to enforce contracts, and government entities [e.g., police, courts] that can provide physical security of property and impartial enforcement of contracts" (Clague, Keefer, Knack, and Olson, 1997a: 67). Also singled out is the importance of an honest and competent government bureaucracy, which might include regulatory institutions, institutions for macroeconomic institutions, institutions for social insurance, and institutions for conflict management (Rodrik, 2007). Additional specifications of institutionally favorable factors are "cultural endowments" (Rattan, 2003) and the range of variables associated with social capital, such as norms, information networks, and reputation mechanisms (Hoff and Stiglitz, 2001).

The role of democratic institutions and participatory mechanisms in economic development has also been revived. Lipset's early work (1959) put forward the case that economic growth and democracy are associated national characteristics. In the past couple of decades, research has surged, mainly studies of correlations between measures of democracy and measures of wealth across nations, and between regime types and development. No thoroughly clear-cut or consistent evidence has emerged, so the topic remains contested (Haggard, 1997). A summary of the literature yields the conclusion that growth or level of income supports the emergence or survival of democracy, but is much less decisive on the positive determination of growth by democratic institutions. Longstanding democracies seem more favorable than transient ones to the development of legal systems of private property rights (Clague, Keefer, Knack, and Olson, 1997b). We return to other aspects of the relations between democracy and development at the end of the chapter.

This shift toward institutions and coordination has also revived interest in the role of the state, though not in the guise of the active guidance envisioned by the early modernization theorists. Rather, the new role of the state is to create structures for growth; the "government is there essentially to improve the institutions . . . the market . . . remains superior" (Fine, 2006: 37). Furthermore, stress on responsible and predictable government and legal arrangements is no doubt a factor in the simultaneously revived interest in the (mainly negative) consequences of political corruption (Kahn, 2006; see above, pp. 116–20). The relationship seems clear: If the emphasis on good and responsible governance rises in salience as a factor in economic development, then "corruption [comes] to the fore in contemporary discussion of reforms in developing countries" (ibid.: 200).

The shift to institutions, including social capital, as keys to generating and sustaining economic development reveals a generic tension not only in economics, but also in other social sciences. That tension is between theoretical determinacy (elegance) and realistic accounts of the world. It has been a healthy, realistic, and necessary move to relax the simplifying assumptions that the institutional framework for economic activity is a given or part of the "other things equal" world. Yet doing so has produced a certain theoretical messiness and a host of new theoretical and methodological problems. For one thing, "institutional quality . . . remains a nebulous concept" (Rodrik, 2007: 188). Second, measures of "institutions" and "social capital" are notoriously difficult to quantify and imprecise even when quantified (Blair and Carroll, 2009). Third, given the complexity of the development process, attempting to establish correlations between certain types of institutional arrangements and development results in low coefficients and disputed linking mechanisms. And, fourth, though there has been the anticipated flood of empirical research, "few studies have led so far to precise policy recommendations beyond the importance of property rights enforcement" (Aghion, 2006: 3). Commenting on this dilemma, Van Waeyenberge notes that "the extension of the analysis into the traditionally noneconomic has been at the expense of substantive content and analytical power" (2006: 36). Paradoxically, however, the new institutional analysis attempts to have it both ways: on the one hand, to complicate the view of economic development by realizing the decisiveness of the variability of the institutional and cultural frameworks, but, on the other, once the "right" frameworks are present, then the economy functions according to the long-established, simplified notions of *homo economicus* and rationality (Fine, 2006).

What Is Development?

To further cloud the issue of growth and development, the goals of development itself have been matters of continuing contention. As indicated, an early consensus developed around the relatively simple goal of growth of national income, largely through the engine of state-led industrial development. Early emphases also included the goals of reducing poverty and national and international inequalities, an impulse that strengthened in the 1970s and has persisted since. The writings of Sen (1988) brought income distribution, quality of life, and human entitlements and capacities into the developmental formula. Human rights, including welfare measures and human entitlements, also emerged as one of the "goals" of development, as did environmental protection and sustainability (Dresner, 2002). This diversification of aims reached a climax with the publication of the Millennium Development Goals by the United Nations in 2000, which gave priority to sustainability, peace, and justice, and included the specific goals of eliminating extreme hunger and poverty; achieving universal primary education; promoting gender equality and empowering women; reducing child mortality; improving maternal health; combating HIV/AIDS, malaria, and other diseases; and ensuring environmental sustainability. Admirable as each goal is, the statement was confusing in that it formalized the sprawl of goals and connotations of development, leading one commentator on these "new goals" to say that "everyone seems to be supporting them, although few know what the terms mean" (Basu, 2001: 61). Mainly critical developments in the scholarship on development also appeared. Among these are the general postmodernist critique of modernization, combining a radical relativism with a denial of any essential features of the concept; a line of feminist reasoning that documents and emphasizes women's contribution to development (Boserup, 1989) and denounces "malestream" developmental theories as male-centric and exploitative of women (Leonard, 2003); and postcolonialism, a left-oriented intellectual movement, prominent among some anthropologists (Escobar, 1991), that fundamentally regards "development" as continued dominance by western power and institutions. Some versions of these movements, along with more extreme versions of sustainability, are "antidevelopmental" in impact, thus further clouding the idea of the goals of development.

General Contours of This History   To complete this schematic account of the search for keys to the development process, we can identify several major transformations of emphasis—together yielding, in simplified form, some overlapping transitions.

From the standpoint of the dominant unit of analysis, the sequence has been state → market → global, though each has been continually in evidence.

From the standpoint of the role of the state, the sequence has been state as directive → state as minimal and mischievous → state as facilitative.

From the standpoint of the types of investment that are believed to be most salient in the initiation of and march toward development, the sequence has been investment in (physical) capital and technology → human capital → social capital (institutions).

From the standpoint of the variables traditionally favored by academic disciplines, the parade of emphases has been political economy → orthodox economics → sociology-anthropology.

From the standpoint of scientific consensus, the approximate transitions have been consensus on modernization → paradigmatic (ideological) disputes → disputes over goals and purposes of development.

These schematic transitions are not intended to be an accurate description of the actual, complicated area of development, but are offered as an aid in accounting for its complexity, controversial history, and continuing confusion. We now move to other facets of this history that are more directly related to usability.

IMPLICATIONS OF THIS HISTORY FOR
UNDERSTANDING AND POLICY

From the very beginning, the struggle to understand development and the obstacles to it produced a vast range of economic, political, social, and cultural factors thought to explain it. These appeared in early attempts to identify the characteristics of both development and underdevelopment. To demonstrate this, we reproduce a catalogue of features compiled by two Indian scholars to capture distinguishing features of "backwardness":

> Agriculture is the main occupation, and its techniques of production
>   are primitive
> Barter system
> Low capital formation
> Low skill and efficiency of labor
> Low risk-bearing capacity
> Low purchasing power
> High unemployment and underemployment
> Tradition bound
> Low productivity
> Resources remain unutilized
> Low consumption per capita
> Lack of industrialization
> Lack of leadership
> Lack of education
> High income inequalities
> Investment made in unproductive lines
> Most of income spent on food
> High rate of population growth
> Low foreign trade (Ghosh and Ghosh, 1991)

Presumably, a list of the characteristics of "advanced" societies would yield the same variables with opposite values.

Even this long list can be criticized for incompleteness (for example, it does not including low levels of savings or and does not further decompose "tradition bound") and for insensitivity (it ignores variations among different countries in levels and kinds of "backwardness" and suggests that every element is uniformly present in backward countries). Even if we improved on the list, however, it would still manifest a dynamic that emerged in development studies: different investigators, according to their discipline, theoretical predilections, and interests, tend to pick up one or more feature (for example, low capital formation or population growth), make it primary, and build a model or sketch of how, if the feature was changed, it would constitute a decisive input into the growth process and initiate movement toward development. Each new theoretical development produced different variables, combinations of variables, and valences. This is a natural tendency of scientists: to seek out discrete variables, trace their consequences, and ignore others. In the case of developmental studies, this produced a babble of contending explanatory and policy-recommending voices.

Even if we take the (relatively simple) goal of economic growth as the starting point for development, then, the number and types of contending causes produce corresponding disagreement on the most decisive points of entry—launching capital projects, expanding trade, building reliable state and civil institutions, or instituting population policies—for development. With the accumulation of other, competing goals for development, growth policy becomes even more contested, because different goals call for different intervention strategies. This contestation becomes manifest as politically interested groups within and outside development-minded countries mobilize around different goals and try to make their voices heard.

Overarching these diverse goals are long-established cultural and ideological positions that legitimize (or delegitimize) more specific goals and policy choices and constitute the defining terms of policy battles. We might mention the deep split between a cornucopian outlook toward growth, found in different expressions in ideologies of progress, and a Cassandrian outlook, concretized in Malthusian principles and echoed repeatedly, for example in the pessimism of the Club of Rome in the mid-twentieth century and the dire predictions of advocates of sustainability (see O'Neill, 2001). Optimists, mainly economists, argue that environmental perils can be overcome by further developments in technology and its applications, whereas pessimists blame technology for creating environmental perils. An overlapping tension is between advocates of market freedom and advocates of market control, which also appears in debates about developmental strategies and in recurring battles over regulation and deregulation. Commitment to these positions seems to be largely a matter of faith, and conflicts among them take on features of principled antagonism. In particular, one commentator notes, "To some economists, no single issue is more sacred than the belief in the sanctity of the market mechanism"; it is a "core myth," a "religious belief" (Nordhaus, 2000: xiv).

To this symphony of confusion, we must add a positive note. Despite the vicissitudes and uncertainties traced in the history of development studies, it can be argued that a certain amount of trusted knowledge about development has accumulated. In a turn-of-the century assessment, Yusuf and Stiglitz (2003) list a number of issues that are now "settled" and are in the realm of "normal science." Among these are the following:

- The essential sources of growth are capital accumulation and factor productivity, including human capital.
- Low and stable rates of inflation are a positive influence on growth.
- Trade liberalization, guided by multilateral rules, is beneficial for growth.

- Property rights are the lifeblood of an efficient free-market economy.
- All countries face problems of environmental degradation.
- Though not without contention, it is generally accepted that the state should provide public goods, a safety net for vulnerable parts of the population, support privatization, and manage competition.

To these points, Hoff and Stiglitz (2001) add that even given such reliability of knowledge, there are no sure formulas for success. North makes an even more fundamental point: "The problem is straightforward. We know both the economic conditions and the institutional conditions that make for good economic performance. What we do not know is how to get them. For that, we need a body of theory that explores the process of economic, political and social change" (2003: 491).

Special Issues of Usability

Turning directly to problems in applying knowledge to the macroissues of development, we make a series of additional points, related to what we say later under the heading of evaluation research (see chapter 8, pp. 261–70), but applied specifically to development.

1. Cartwright (2005) has identified a continuum of types of knowledge that can be applied to policy. At one end are narrow, well-established causal relations that are very certain in their status and are more or less directly applicable to policy decisions; an example would be the causal connection between smoking and lung cancer. Historically, policy planning "works best when it is highly bounded, is focused on a specific problem, and is economical of analytical talent" (Patashnik, 2001: 11485). At the other end are shakier causal assertions that are not rigorously proven, but can in a general way justify specific policies. This latter knowledge is in the form of "tendency laws" (a term used by John Stuart Mill), in which a causal force contributes to an effect but cannot be said to be absolutely certain because other forces are always at work in combination with the identified cause. Our knowledge about development is almost all at the broad, shakier end of the continuum, because development is the product of a complex of forces, many of which are beyond the control of those attempting to guide the process and, in all events, are in continuous interaction and feedback with one another.
2. An extension of this point comes from appreciating that the entities into which developmental inputs are made are *systems* of forces, with the result that evaluation of the impact of interventions is a difficult exercise. A notable demonstration of this is the low batting average of projects historically supported by the World Bank that were based on supply-side assumptions—namely, that an input of capital will generate a process that will eventuate in

the anticipated development (e.g., irrigation and agricultural development). The main effort is to finance and initiate projects. This process is informed, of course, by a series of assumptions about the complex system of incentives, motivations, rewards, and attitudes of the multiple actors involved in implementing investment. If these assumptions are not valid, the anticipated course of development may not materialize or may be sent in different directions. Capital input, then, is more than an input that produces an output; it follows a path through a range of conditioning and diverting transitions that affect the anticipated outcome. Put more generally, development is not a linear process. Initial conditions shape subsequent developments, developmental trajectories are more malleable, unanticipated events and variables continuously intrude on the process (Adelman, 2001).

As we will see below, a literature on evaluation research has gained in maturity over time, but practitioners stress its imprecision. Even in a relatively constrained field such as educational innovation, for example, "evaluation is realized in systems which are so complex that most evaluations meet fundamental difficulties" (Wottawa and Pult, 2001: 4255). Many of these difficulties arise because other factors influence the intended outcome—failures of communication, self-protective strategies by implementers of policies, changes that occur the course of implementation, and strategies on the part of those affected by policies to defeat, divert, or turn them to their own advantage. All these observations also apply to efforts to induce economic and societal development, the impacts of which are simultaneously economic, political, social, and cultural. It is difficult to evaluate the extent of all these impacts, to say nothing of the complex social and political processes they occasion.

3. To generalize this point, assumptions of linear causality among variables (for example, conditions → outcomes; independent variable → dependent variable) appear not to work in straightforward ways with respect to development. For example, there is evidence that political stability is a favorable factor in generating economic growth, but there is also some evidence that causation runs the other way, that richer countries have produced more politically stable states and governing systems. An educated workforce appears to be a positive condition for development, yet economic growth also typically produces demands for more skilled (educated) labor. A similar point might be made about the relationship between population control and development (Klambhampati, 2004). We also see multiple and sometimes contradictory causal patterns: improvement in literacy is a positive factor in encouraging development, yet improvements in education may also generate higher expectations and relative deprivation among educated groups (perhaps especially for those educated in the West), which in turn generates political instability, a negative factor for growth (Alesina and Perotti, 1996). The

upshot of these points is that lawlike connections among discrete variables are not likely to be found; more complex feedback models, even if less manageable analytically, are required.

4. These multivariable, systemic, and feedback features point to a generic limitation on using correlational or regressive studies of growth as related to discrete variables. While sophisticated techniques of "correcting" and "holding constant" different factors are available (see chapter 8, pp. 255–56), the sheer number of factors and the feedback processes among them are such as to produce the expectation that discrete associations between variables (e.g., between presence of a democratic representation system and growth rates) will typically be low and indecisive.

5. The intellectual styles of political or administrative leaders interested in making policy invariably differ from those of scholars and other investigators (see chapters 9–10). For the latter, the aim in generating scientifically valid findings (about, for example, the relationship between economic growth and political stability) is to focus on certain causal variables and *hold constant or otherwise neutralize* as many other operative factors in the developmental process as possible. Most social scientists of development, moreover, are inclined to stress the contingency and conditionality of assertions about causal connections, and to stress the broader contexts of apparent causal relationships. The policy-maker and policy-implementer, by contrast, are likely to be impatient with such scientific niceties and qualifications because they are interested in ready and useful information that will produce desired results in relation to a given social problem or crisis. Many governments, aware that policy analysis and applications cannot be delegated directly to universities or think tanks, develop their own apparatus for policy analysis (Straf, 2001). Moreover, academics and policy-makers play to different audiences: scholars mainly to the audience of other scholars and academic administrators, on whom they depend for judgments of their career success and prestige; policy-makers in the area of development play to a range of constituencies, including their political superiors, the media, the public, and international agencies (including other states) that are interested in the country's development. Finally, though this differs by society and culture, academics and policy-makers, respectively, may each regard themselves as having greater importance or higher social prestige than the other. All these factors make for tension, distrust, and hostility. It is difficult to assign responsibility or blame for this state of affairs. However, if academics wish to make knowledge relevant to the developmental process, it cannot be assumed that this will happen automatically. There must be an additional, separate priority in academic thinking, namely the best way to fashion or translate knowledge so that it is intelligible to those who apply it.

6. The upshot is that utilitarian models of application based on analogies from engineering are not likely to be useful in planning and inducing development. Instead, the policy-maker must assemble as much potentially useful knowledge as possible about the developmental process, and proceed on the basis of the *synthesis* of such knowledge. This carries with it the awareness that attempts to apply knowledge will result in many unanticipated consequences, some of which may undermine the intended effects of the original intervention. The model for planning, therefore, is one of a *general blueprint* emphasizing goals, combined with a flexible mentality, an appreciation of the imperfection of the art, and an effort to track continuously the course of events and alter the blueprint in accord with changes in conditions. Put another way, the object is to intervene in a complex, moving equilibrium of forces, only some of which are known and under control.

7. One additional observation relates specifically to less-developed countries. Most academic work on development has taken place in universities and other organizations in developed countries. Objective as scholars attempt to be in their efforts, this work inevitably reveals the intellectual and cultural biases of those undertaking the studies. Two consequences follow: (1) much scholarly knowledge about development simply may not be available to political leaders and planners in developing regions; and (2) if it is available, it may be regarded as irrelevant to their particular local conditions.

All these points help in understanding the equivocality and imprecision of the usability of knowledge derived from developmental studies that we mentioned at the beginning of this chapter. Applying that knowledge is an exercise of qualitative, clinical judgments about the balance of forces at work in a complex system of forces, rather than in a simple cause-effect way. And the translation of social-science knowledge into policy decisions is beset with problems of communication between academics and policy-makers. Those negative points acknowledged, we now proceed in a more positive dimension, and identify several kinds of knowledge—many of which deal with the sociopolitical consequences of development that may prove useful in promoting development and managing its consequences.

THE PROCESS OF DEVELOPMENT

In keeping with the foregoing, it is essential to acknowledge that the most fundamental fact about development is its systemic, multifaceted character: everything changes, and must change, sooner or later. In generating explanations, process is more important than product. Among the most important processes are the following:

- Self-evidently, the economy must grow, which means in the first instance that savings, international resources, and other forms of capital must be directed toward new, productive lines of economic activity.
- Growth entails the redirection of much economic activity, usually but not always away from the primary toward the secondary and tertiary sectors. In this process, wage labor tends to replace subsistence labor and barter arrangements, despite the persistence of informal economies. A derivative is that some portion of the labor force, that drawn into wage labor, will perhaps experience a general increase in income but will be subjected to new market uncertainties, such as all-or-nothing employment and unemployment (in contrast to underemployment). This means in turn that welfare considerations of the working—and nonworking—population are always present, and that policies of cushioning for unemployment and smoothing for consumption assume new salience.
- Geographical displacement and mobility increase as economic activities change. This is experienced initially as displacement and disruption of traditional modes. Policies of economic compensation for displaced subpopulations—spearheaded by the World Bank and adopted in diverse ways by governments in developing countries—are one creative response to these disruptions. However, it is difficult to assess, much less compensate for, disruptions of traditional values and the loss of taken-for-granted cultural assumptions.
- Changes in the occupational structure create new classes of labor: wage labor, a middle class of some description, and some professionals, often trained abroad. These changes often threaten traditional systems of stratification based on family, land, and traditional privilege. Needless to say, this heightens groups' competitive jurisdictional claims, raises questions of social justice, and produces the potential for new forms of group conflict.
- A state apparatus must be developed to administer the developmental process. Recent work on institutions underscores the importance of "depersonalizing" social and political processes in the form of creating free markets; making these markets predictable via effective property laws, fair and consistent rules, and efficiency and honesty in bureaucracies; and minimizing the paralysis and inefficiency created by corrupt practices. Effecting such changes, however, sits high on the list of things that North said we do not know how to do well. The state apparatus must be attuned to dealing with new ranges of political demands as well. We will have more to say about political responsiveness at the end of this chapter.
- A new kind of educational system is called for. Every country that has developed or tried to develop has sooner or later turned its attention to mass education. In the early stages, leaders often attempt to address political and

cultural goals—to build the nation, to impart basic literacy, to instill a common national culture in diverse subpopulations, and to secure public order through common socialization. As the economy becomes more complex and demands higher levels of skill, the development of complex skills falls to the higher levels of the educational system.

- Traditional, especially paternalistic, family forms are likely to be challenged, especially if women enter the labor force in large numbers, and these changes occasion demands for greater gender equality—demands supported by international social movements.

- Diffuse cultural changes, associated with the rise of some kind of culture of modernization, are variable but universal in their manifestation. These cultural changes include incorporation of foreign influences, especially through the mass media, and the development of special subcultures, especially among youth. This cultural diversification also sets the stage for new, especially generational, conflicts.

- Development is above all uneven. By this we mean not only the enhancement of income of some groups at the expense of others (Smith, 2001), but also that differential rates of development (however measured) may be expected among the economic, political, social, and cultural dimensions. This lead-and-lag perspective implies unevenness, tensions, conflict, and disputes over priorities of change. Irregularity of change, perhaps more than any other process, highlights the changing exigencies of social integration during processes of development.

- The feature of unevenness ramifies in other directions. In the process of creating any new arrangements that might be described as developmental, innumerable "old" arrangements to which people are attached or in which they have special interests are affected. The foci of displacement include traditional religious authority, established status groups, land as the primary source of wealth, and reliance on kinship and community loyalties. Some arrangements that were normal, acceptable, even desirable in traditional settings (for example, favoring kin and friends) are likely to come under attack from those attempting to establish institutions on a universalistic basis (see above, p. 118). These traditional interests do not fade quietly. They become bases of political opposition and protest, and may continue to informally exert their force in new settings. This principle of persistence and resistance, along with the lead-and-lag principle, underscores the more general principle that development is never a simple "before-after," "all-at-once," or "tradition-to-modernity" historical experience.

- Economic development is, more than ever before, a mix of global, national, and local forces. International trade, finance, and influence are not new; in some eras (e.g., the development of railways in the nineteenth century), foreign capital was a primary driving force. The second half of the twentieth century, however, brought the principle of internationalization to a qualitatively new level. Manifestations of this have increased astronomically in international trade; migration of manufacturing to less-developed countries, often under the initiative and control of multinational corporations; the increased role of international banks in the development process (Makler, 2001); the influence of financial institutions such as the World Bank and the IMF; the growing significance of international governmental organizations (IGOs) and international nongovernmental organizations (NGOs) (Haas, 2001); the conspicuous role of international money markets; and the great increase in the international migration of labor (Castles, 2001).

A fundamental implication of the increasing role of international forces is a growing disjunction between loci of control of economic decisions affecting development on the one hand, and the management of the political, social, welfare, and cultural consequences of those decisions on the other. This disjunction appears in the fluctuation of international exchange rates and changing prices in international markets; many Third World economies, with less capacity to absorb shocks than wealthier economies, were devastated by the precipitous rise in world oil prices as a result of the OPEC crisis of 1973. With respect to capital investment, the sources are loans from foreign governments, investment by banks and other financial institutions, and loans from international lending agencies, which complement domestic sources, such as home-based banks, credit agencies, capital supplied by potential customers, and capital developed informally through local social ties. With respect to direct foreign investment, it has been noted that it has a direct effect on "a nation's capital and financial markets, employment pattern, industrial structure and competitiveness, technology, as well as trade and development patterns" (Bagchi-Sen, 2001: 5732). All these sources of capital come with some strings attached as to disposition and repayment. With respect to foreign investment and loans in particular, these arrive not only with the obligation to meet repayment schedules, but also with conditions dictating government spending as well as employment and consumption policies.

The underlying point of these observations is that economic policies and decisions are not entirely in the hands of the national governments whose economies are affected. The key to this disjunction is that the external agencies are not responsible for managing the consequences of economic policies and decisions. That responsibility lies with the national political authorities, who are responsible for dealing with the consequences of economic and social dislocation, the welfare policies of the country, and, above all, political and social opposition arising from groups affected by the multiple consequences of economic change—opposition that arises no matter whether the government is democratic or authoritarian in nature. To put the matter succinctly, the world is experiencing an increasing disjunction between the international economic system and domestic political arrangements.

Nor is the penetration of global forces limited to the economic sphere. Wars and diplomatic influences periodically intrude on domestic governments. International social movements are also part of the political environment. International human rights groups are forever on the lookout for political atrocities. The international feminist movement works both to influence UN activities and domestic policies regarding women's employment, reproductive freedom, and economic and political equality (Rupp, 2001). The international environmental movement, while not notable for its capacity to counteract more powerful economic competitive forces, nevertheless constitutes a constant presence in the political environment of both developed and developing countries (Wastl-Walker, 2001). Environmental forces, moreover, directly impinge not only on the short-term competitiveness of industries and countries, but also on the long-term sustainability of economic development itself.

USEFUL KNOWLEDGE FOR THOSE WHO ATTEMPT TO INDUCE DEVELOPMENT

The processes of development just outlined constitute useful general knowledge for investors, planners, policy-makers, and political leaders. They provide a perspective that does not deny causal processes, but emphasizes complexity, contingency, and irregularity of the developmental process. They also provide a guideline as to the economic, political, and social forces that these agents must confront. They suggest that the political leaders of developing nations—those in the center of but not completely in control of the developmental process— must assume the role of the orchestrator of forces and groups rather than their director.

To press this line of argument further, we turn now to some more specific suggestions for developmental policies, also rooted in social-science knowledge.

The Perils of Simplified Solutions

The first suggestion is that abstract and insulated formulas for development should be regarded with suspicion. The main kinds of offenders in this regard are developmental projects that are conceived and executed mainly from what might be called the supply side—that is, with the main problem being defined as the availability of capital and its investment, with insufficient regard for issues such as incentive factors (which may not match economic models of market calculation), adverse environmental effects, participation of the affected population in the project, equity of economic effects, and likely political opposition. All these constitute hazards for the success of projects conceived in the absence of social, cultural, and political considerations, and may generate other unwanted outcomes (Cernea, 1994). The issue of "economic" versus "social" or "people" variables has been an point of contention between economists and other social scientists (particularly anthropologists, sociologists, and social psychologists) in arenas such as the World Bank. The latter have, in principle, a compelling case to be made in advance of undertaking developmental projects and in invoking explanations for failure, but the problem is that the theory underling the role of these noneconomic factors is not as systematic, elegant, or agreed upon as economic theory, and for that reason the economic emphasis tends to win out in the end.

It seems evident that investors, lenders, and local managers of developmental projects and their consequences owe it to themselves to make an effort to systematically take into account the diversity of human factors mentioned in advance of undertaking developmental investment, and to build that knowledge into developmental planning. At the very least, all have—or should have—an interest in the political stability of the country or region in which development is undertaken, as well as the causes of any instability.

Specific Foci of Sensitivity

Developmental initiatives are of limited usefulness unless the human factors are disaggregated into their most important parts. To that end, we mention three areas of special significance in affecting the success or failure of all development, whether directed or relying on market mechanisms:

- The *cultural* attitudes, expectations, and behavior of labor-force participants who are drawn into projects of development (Fukuyama, 2001). Have they been exposed to wage labor before? Do they have cultural outlooks that are conducive to rational calculation in the market, or are they drawn from those who have no experience in the market? Will they respond in predictable ways to wage offers? Is it advisable to rely on formal market mechanisms for recruitment and allocation of labor, or should more familiar mechanisms such as kinship and community ties, effective in many labor-market settings, be utilized (Hareven, 1982)? Will wage payments to workers be funneled into "modern" consumer markets, or will they be set aside for traditional purposes such as dowries, weddings, and funerals? All these questions affect the predictability of behavior in the market; developmental projects in different regions have to take local cultures and traditions into account.
- The attitudes and experiences of both managers and workpeople with respect to *authority*. The culture of authority is widely variable by country and region

(see Dore, 1973). To take those differences into account when organizing productive enterprises is essential. In particular, if outside formal authority arrangements are imported by multinational corporations and financial institutions, and these are not sensitive to local expectations, this is a recipe for generating poor communication and misunderstanding in the workplace, and for producing feelings of injustice, inequity, and resentment among workpeople.

- A very different, but equally important, sensitivity deals with the issue of *corruption* in development (see chapter 3, pp. 116–20). Corruption of one sort or another is a more or less universal phenomenon, but it arises significantly in the developmental process in countries with traditions of traditionalistic loyalties, gift-giving, and favoring kin and friends. It now seems a matter of general consensus that corruption is not a cost-efficient mode of operation, though it may sometimes buy freedom from political interference in economic activity. Moreover, corruption's costs to the political legitimacy of political officials in the eyes of those who do not benefit from it generally outweigh the loyalty of those who do (Mény and de Sousa, 2001).

The Salience of Particularistic Groups

One of the characteristics of almost all nation-states of the world is that they are composed of diverse ethnic, religious, linguistic, and regional groups (Varshney, 2001). This has come to be true even of societies, such as Great Britain and Sweden, where recent migration has diversified their populations. These diverse groups almost always have problematic relations—often but not always conflictual—with one another, with the receiving population, and with the receiving state. One main strand of the historical development of the West has been the cultural "projects" of states—realized through the media, the schools, and the cultivation of symbols of the nation—to minimize, control, or even eradicate particularistic loyalties and groups. By and large they have not succeeded, and particularistic (or multicultural) politics are still a conspicuous ingredient in the polities of most nations.

Almost all nonwestern societies show the same diversity along communal lines, and much of this diversity has been a by-product of international historical forces in the nineteenth and twentieth centuries:

- The colonial heritage, in which the world's major colonial powers—Spain, Portugal, the Netherlands, Great Britain, France, and Germany—divided up the colonized world into territories that took little or no account of the tribal, religious, and other characteristics of those territories, except sometimes to exploit them for political purposes. The effect was to impose a geographical principle for administrative governance on a population with diversified, sometimes antagonistic, cultural loyalties.

- The postcolonial heritage, in which many newly independent colonies adopted the model of the nation-state—the mode of political organization represented by their former colonizers and the political mode preferred by the diplomatic communities and the United Nations for membership in the world system of nations (Gurr and Harff, 1994). "The result was one dominant ideal (in theory but not practice): the belief in the coherence of nation-states and the desire to maintain their territorial integrity. From these norms grew the grievances of territorial separatists and national independence movements" (Flint, 2003: 54).

- The *formal* adoption of the traditional characteristics of nation-states (e.g., political self-sufficiency, insistence on monopoly of violence, the focus of a national identity, and recognition as a nation by other nations) by the new states, but their *actual* lack of effectiveness, in many cases, in developing the nation-state form that had been realized in the West only after a long and irregular historical process. In most cases, these conflicts manifested the imperfect coincidence of the components of "nation" and "state" in entities called "nation-states." The nation component is typically a group of people who feel they have cultural values, loyalties, and sometimes blood in common; the state is an administrative notion imposed on a given territory (Chirot, 1977). When the two principles do not match, the result is frequently chronic conflict and secessionist attempts. In extreme cases, the result is a collapsed state (Zartman, 1995), and, in other cases, "the insistence on the right to conduct internal affairs without outside interference gave dictators like Idi Amin freedom to commit atrocities against their subjects in the name of 'nation-building'" (Gurr and Harff, 1994: 12). In fact, much of the ethnic cleansing of modern times has been perpetuated by political leaders from *one* particularistic group securing state power and attempting to violently crush or eradicate other groups (Naimark, 2001). Needless to say, such deep conflicts create a kind of political instability that is inimical to anything like orderly development.

In many cases, the particularistic groups that have been precipitated by these historical processes fall into the category of "primordial," in that they are conceived of by members as existing from the beginning, as being inviolable and tied together by blood and loyalty. They are also the focus of personal and group identities. Such groups provided the structural bases for most of the ethno-nationalist, separatist, and even terrorist movements of the twentieth century, and they retain their vitality (Boal, 2001). The political implications of primordial groupings arise from the fact that they are groups based on principle, not interest, in the first instance (though they do have "interests"). This creates a mental frame antagonistic to political compromise, because compromise is likely to be viewed as a defeat for the group. Correspondingly, primordial groupings contribute to a rigidity, a lack of give and take, in the polity.

As indicated, communal groupings are universal and always politically significant. However, in periods of development—and in the processes of dislocation, displacement, and inequitable treatment that inevitably accompany it—they are likely to rise to special salience, because they experience hardships and inequities *as groups,* and feel assaulted as such. As often as not, they may feel that they and their legitimate claim to existence and respect are threatened. This is not only a matter of experienced economic deprivation; it is a general cultural threat that imparts a sense of urgency to their situation.

Decades ago, Ulam (1979) argued, contrary to Marx, that in the history of industrialization and development in Europe the greatest radical political threats to stability did not arise as the process of capitalist development matured, but, rather, they arose in the early "big push" transition to development, during which assaults on traditional ways were the most severe and more groups were likely to experience relative deprivation. He made a coherent case by extensive historical-comparative observations of different countries' developmental and political histories. Gerschenkron (1962) also argued that, particularly in cases of countries that were economically backward—not the best term, but one that can be translated into terms of traditional societies with the least evidence of the organizational and market structures of capitalism—these countries also had to be brought into the developmental process by more centralized and heavy-handed intervention. We do not claim that these observations constitute a fixed law of development, but it makes sense to argue that as a general rule the early stages of development are especially significant from the standpoint of the displacement of and experiences of deprivation by groups, their interpretation of this displacement in primordial terms, and, as a result, the rise of radical movements, including fundamentalist ones. It goes without saying that the prospect of political instability that arises from these dynamics poses the most serious threats to the developmental process.

The Issue of Democracy in Contemporary Developing Societies

Decades ago, Huntington (1968) diagnosed the "problem" of newly developing countries: they were experiencing a great discrepancy between, on the one hand, a great deal of political mobilization of groups (in part, no doubt, because of the processes described in the previous section), and, on the other hand, a lack of political machinery (state apparatus, responsive political parties) that could contain this mobilization and assure a level of political integration and stability. Years later (Huntington, 1991), he wrote of the great wave of democracy sweeping across the world (including many developing nations) in the last third of the twentieth century. Since the appearance of the second book, scholars have noted that the democratic experiments that he detailed have had very mixed success, with many societies reverting to more authoritarian modes. Political scientists have written much about failed states, a term that refers not only to their lack of effectiveness, but also to their lack of democracy. This dialogue underscores the salience of the issue of democracy in development.

Western political leaders and political scientists have long had a tendency to recommend their own democratic forms to societies outside the West, including developing societies, with the expectation that they are the right kinds of institutions for these countries from the standpoint of guaranteeing political effectiveness and efficiency, and that they will raise their level of political civilization. In fact, this impulse became a quasiofficial part of the administration of President George W. Bush: the efforts to export American-style democracy into Afghanistan and Iraq are examples—or perhaps threats—for other Arab states and for authoritarian countries more generally. The export of democracy parallels the export of human rights, a high priority of the administration of Jimmy Carter, and one that continues aggressively, though inconsistently, as an American priority. We close our remarks with a comment on the issue of democratic transplantation.

To state the boldest and most negative point first: The idea that a whole system of democracy can be superimposed directly on societies whose cultures, social institutions, and array of groups are fundamentally different from those of the United States (or any other particular democracy) is historically misguided, except perhaps in extreme cases such as Japan, which had been brought to its knees by wartime defeat. After all, the history of democracy in the West is a history of centuries of overcoming obstacles and forging institutions after repeated episodes of political, sometimes violent, conflict. The obstacles to the march of democracy have been as salient as the forces pressing for it. Political systems are made, not born, and there is no reason to believe that this principle does not apply to all polities.

To make that judgment, however, does not go far in solving the political problems of developing societies. In particular, it does not address the fundamental issue of *political responsiveness* to group unrest, which is, as we indicated, an especially salient feature of developing societies. The temptation and favored strategy of many leaders is simply to attempt to repress extreme protesting groups, a strategy that neither addresses the bases of group dissatisfactions nor provides any avenues for expressing them. The repression may "work" in the short run in that it silences the opposition, but it also invites protesters to go underground and to take up strategies, such as sporadic violence, that are destabilizing. Repression also becomes more or less immediately publicized throughout the world via the media and invites international protest, if not interventions, as in Libya in 2011. A more fatal temptation is to generalize the repressive impulse and attempt to silence the voices of moderate opposition as well, which alienates even more groups from the political process.

Our argument is that political responsiveness of some variety is essential for effective leadership in developing societies. It is essential because there are so many voices demanding recognition, and it is essential for any semblance of political stability, which is, as we have seen, an important prerequisite for development itself. The establishment of responsiveness by any government is not an easy task, because many forces in the society favor repression, and many opposition groups have forsaken peaceful political channels. But it is a task that should be forever pursued. It involves guaranteeing the legitimate existence of opposition, and it involves the continuous search to find ways to convert principled and absolute opposition into "interests" that can become the basis of political competition, not simply political conflict.

As we press this line of argument, it may occur to readers that, having cautioned against the imposition of a given mode of formal democracy on diverse societies, we are sneaking democracy in via the back door by stressing political responsiveness. It is certainly true that political responsiveness is an *element* of democracy, but what we have in mind is not a single model, but a political flexibility that is attuned to the special cultures, histories, and institutional conditions of developing nations.

8

Methods of Research and
Their Usability

Our strategy in chapters 1 to 7 was to select important areas in the social sciences—almost all interdisciplinary—and employ our best judgment in identifying findings, perspectives, and theoretical outlooks most usable for people with decision-making responsibilities in organizational contexts. In chapters 9 to 10, we move in a macro direction and explore demand for and supply of social-science knowledge in society. As a transition between these two parts, we dedicate this chapter to the *ways,* or *methods*—in contrast to *substance*—in which social science is created and presented. We examine strengths and weaknesses, focusing on usability, deriving from these methods. Accordingly, usability differs according to the research methods employed.

SUBSTANCE OF KNOWLEDGE VERSUS
METHODS OF ASSESSING IT

Methods of producing knowledge cross-cut its substance. Our initial definition of *methods* is catholic, and includes intuitive insights; speculative thinking; deriving or otherwise generating models and hypotheses consistent with orienting perspectives; positing causes; inferring causal relations from facts; generalizing from personal experiences; and creating and assessing knowledge according to procedures designed to maximize the scientific reliability and validity of that knowledge. All these methods yield knowledge, but the quality of that knowledge is highly variable. One of our intentions, moreover, is to elicit some continuity in scientific and nonscientific thinking.

In this chapter, we narrow that broad view of knowledge-generating methods to a specific subset: those identified with the social sciences *as sciences*. These methods lie at the heart of science—the organization and execution of research in accord with scientific procedures. Laboratory experimentation with human subjects is generally regarded as the purest and, in principle, the closest to models used in the natural sciences. But we also consider a range of nonexperimental methods and procedures, most of which strive to approximate experimental ones. We examine field experiments and quasiexperiments, certain lines of statistical analysis, comparative methods, and case studies, as well as less-often considered methods, such as counterfactual thinking, mental experiments, and deviant case analyses. We regard all these methods as methodological cousins in that they are efforts to establish *reliable and valid causal relations* and to make knowledge more readily usable by recognizing these relations in practical settings.

What is the nature of this cousin relationship? It begins with the observation that anything we want to explain in the real world (fluctuations in divorce rates, for example) is influenced by *many* causal factors (the difficulty in obtaining a legal divorce, ups and downs in the economy, changes in alimony and child-support laws, and many other factors). Everyday thinking and inference cannot determine which, among these many factors, is more important than the others and how the causes might interact with one another. The various *research methods* in the social sciences are ways to make these determinations. More precisely, "The initial picture . . . is one of a *multiplicity* of conditions, a *confounding* of their influences on what is to be explained (the dependent variable) and an *indeterminacy* regarding the effect of any one condition or several conditions. The corresponding problems facing the investigator are to *reduce* the number of conditions, to *isolate* one condition from another, and therefore to make *precise* the role of each condition, both singly and in combination with other conditions" (Smelser, 1976: 152–53).

We regard all the methods considered in this chapter as different ways to achieve these goals. This is a controversial formulation, and when it was originally advanced, it drew criticisms from advocates of methods other than the experimental. The criticism was that this continuous view treats the experimental method as the favored cousin and the other methods as correspondingly poor cousins (Ragin, 1987), whereas, in reality, these other methods are often preferable. We hold that the best method should be chosen in accord with the realities and contingencies of the scientific problem being addressed, and that each method has advantages and disadvantages in social-science research. In assessing each, we zero in especially on one set of issues: the relevance, limits, and transferability (i.e., the usability) of knowledge generated to settings other than that in which it was generated.

At the same time, we can appreciate the sensitivity of those advocating and using nonexperimental methods—field, comparative, quasiexperimental, evaluative, or case study, to say nothing of counterfactual thinking. The fact of the matter is that the canons of methodology—established as the natural and social sciences developed—are above all *normative* standards, specifying how research *ought* to be designed, executed, and evaluated, but certainly they are not an accurate behavioral description of how it is done in practice. Furthermore, these normative standards have been derived mainly from laboratory studies. These norms are a kind of gold standard. An implication is that for types of research in which laboratory conditions can be met only imperfectly, research judged by the gold standard will be more likely to be found wanting, perhaps even second-class, and therefore productive of defensiveness. This normative character of methodological thinking will turn out to be crucial in our understanding of the perceived and actual usability of social-scientific knowledge and the controversies surrounding it.

THE LABORATORY EXPERIMENTAL METHOD

The essence of the laboratory method is to create a situation in which all potentially causal factors except the favored or suspected one are *held constant* or otherwise *neutralized in their causal effect,* while the favored or suspected one is systematically manipulated in order to observe and establish its precise causal effect. The nomenclature applied to this procedure varies, but the manipulated variable can be referred to as the *operative variable,* whereas those that are held constant are called *parameters.* Parameters are known or suspected to have a causal effect if activated, but that causal effect is neutralized by laboratory manipulation. A simple classroom experiment in physics can demonstrate the difference. Suppose we wish to establish that the precise temperature at which water boils is 212 degrees Fahrenheit. We know, however, that temperature is not the only factor affecting the boiling point; for example, the atmospheric pressure must be that at sea level, and the water must be free from impurities. Variation of either of these two conditions will affect the boiling point, as campers attempting to boil potatoes at high elevations repeatedly discover. The trick in the laboratory is to control and hold constant—that is, to make into parameters—all, or as many as possible, of these "other" known or suspected causes in order to make precise the relationship between temperature and boiling point. This point also reveals that the prediction that water will boil at 212 degrees is a *conditional* statement, i.e., contingent on controlling other causal conditions. If we were to decide to hold temperature and purity constant and vary the atmospheric pressure, then we would generate another conditional prediction about the atmospheric pressure at which water boils.

In most experiments in the physical sciences, and many in the biological sciences, the method of holding constant and varying possible causes is achieved by *situational manipulation* in the laboratory setting, thereby creating the data that are to be studied and analyzed. Such manipulation is often not possible in the social sciences because it is not ethical to do so, or because human subjects—unlike many "nonhuman" objects—react in complex ways to manipulation and thereby create additional, uncontrolled variables. The major difference in experimentation with human subjects is that more exclusive reliance is placed on randomization. Dehue (2001) describes the "exemplary experiment" in psychology (the discipline in which laboratory methods have been most widely adopted) as follows:

> The typical psychological experiment compares one or more treated experimental groups to an untreated control group. As natural groups may vary in many more respects than only the hypothesized cause or treatment to be tested, experimenters must compose their own groups equal in all respects but the factor concerned. The ideal way to create comparable groups is to assign subjects to groups on the basis of chance and thus cancel out unwanted between-group differences. From the 1940s in America and from the 1960s in Europe, generations of psychologists have been taught that the *exemplary* experiment is an experiment in which randomly composed experimental and control groups are compared. (5115)

The robustness of laboratory findings is strengthened or weakened by examining their compatibility with theoretical expectations, by assessing statistical significance, by replicating (repeating the same experiment in as similar a way as possible), and by conducting meta-analyses, which use statistical and nonstatistical methods to systematically evaluate the results of prior research (Cordray, 1992).

As a research method, the laboratory experiment has been most widely applied in psychology. It dominates physiological (including neurological) psychology, animal psychology, perceptual and cognitive psychology, and much of social psychology. It is less used in other areas of social psychology and even less in personality, developmental, clinical, and humanistic psychology. Within psychology departments, those who use experimental methods generally regard themselves as more scientific, and claim superior status for that reason. Those in the "softer" areas often claim that their research is less artificial and more relevant and realistic than the experimentalists'. This broad division is fundamental in psychology. Experimental methods have found limited use in sociology (small-group research, exchange theory) and political science, and have recently experienced a rapidly increasing use in economics, especially among behavioral economists and those interested in the institutional parameters of economic behavior.

The four criteria most commonly used to assess the strength and viability of experiments are as follows:

1. Construct validity, or assuring that the relevant variables are defined unambiguously and precisely, and that measures chosen to operationalize them correspond to the logic of those variables.

2. Statistical conclusion validity, or whether the differences between outcomes in the treatment group and the control group are sufficiently large to be considered significant or not. An array of formal statistical techniques is available to make this determination.

3. Internal validity. This refers generally to the "accuracy of inferences about whether one variable causes another" (Mark and Reichardt, 2001: 7749) or, more precisely, whether the independent variable actually makes a difference in observed changes in the dependent variable. In this connection, questions are asked about whether other variables are at work. Does the conduct of the experiment itself have an adverse effect on human subjects (sometimes referred to as "resentful demoralization")? Are there "experimenter effects" (for example, does administration by an older or younger experimenter, or a male or female one, or a minority one affect the results)? More generally, selection failures and other flaws may result in nonequivalent designs of treatment and control groups. Careful replication of experimental studies is a principal way to establish confidence in or criticize the original experiment (Juliep, 1990).

4. External validity. A classic definition of *external validity* is "to what populations, settings, treatment variables, and measurement variables can [the effect] be generalized?" (Campbell and Stanley, 1966: 5). Can the relationships between variables established in an experimental setting be transferred to the real world? Actually, the wording should be "real *worlds*," because different naturalistic situations differ in so many ways from a laboratory situation. This point is captured in the notion of proximal similarity, which refers to "instances of samples of people, treatments, measures, and settings that look like the populations or categories to which one would like to generalize" (Campbell, 1988: 72). The real world is made of many different kinds of other samples, and the "fit," or proximal similarity to any one of these, differs from the fit to any others. In many cases, attention to issues of internal validity and external validity can tug in opposite directions. The more attention that is paid to issues of randomization, measurement, selection, and bias, the higher the internal validity may be, but these efforts may drive the experimental situation further away from naturalistic situations.

While academic researchers pay great attention to internal validity, and while methodologies relevant to it are elaborately developed, issues of external validity become more significant when we raise questions of usability. If an apparently sound experimental finding (for example, that in situations of urgency, high stress, and dread, subjects more often resort to mental shortcuts) is brought to mind as usable in real situations such as piloting an airplane or firefighting, is that finding moderated, exaggerated, or overwhelmed by other aspects of those real situations? Answers to this kind of question should forever be sought, but these answers are almost always approximate, not definitive.

To complete this discussion, we explore briefly a *generic* limitation of the laboratory situation as it is used to study humans, a limitation that affects both internal and external validity and the effects of which are almost impossible to control without abandoning experimental procedures.

The Basic Psychology and Sociology
of the Laboratory Experiment

As we have seen, the laboratory experiment is regarded as a gold standard in efforts to isolate potential causal variables from the complexity of the causal process, to assess their causal significance, and to test for their strength and robustness. Their use in the natural sciences as the method to establish, confirm, and reject causal relations and laws of nature is undisputed in the history of these fields and in the writings of philosophers and historians of science. Moreover, experimental methods have improved over time through the increasing sophistication of their execution; the use of experimental control groups; and techniques such as randomization, statistical controls, paired comparisons, and other devices.

One difference between experimentation in the natural sciences and the social sciences is the freedom that investigators have in manipulating variables. The former are freer because they are dealing with a world that is more easily manipulated because of its absence of practical and ethical constraints. (This is only a relative distinction, because the design and execution of natural-science experiments is also constrained by considerations of injury to experimenters and others, possible property and environmental damage, and prohibitive costs.) Psychologists and other investigators are faced with many practical, social, and ethical limitations on the methods they can use to manipulate subjects—limitations that have become increasingly restrictive with the growth of "human subjects" issues as constraints on experiments that may violate human dignity. The experimenter with human subjects is limited in recruiting subjects, in securing their cooperation, in imposing experimental treatments on them, in describing those treatments to them, in disclosing the nature and results of the experiments, and in using the results of experiments for personal profit or advancement. All these issues are the currency of debates on the research ethics of psychological and social experimentation.

The most common methodological criticism of laboratory experiments used in psychology and elsewhere is that they are artificial in a specific sense: while

they have enormous power in identifying, measuring, and controlling for variation in suspected causes, they achieve this power by neutralizing or correcting for
their effects only in the laboratory situation. In natural situations, such controls
are not present and often impossible to impose. A different set of exigencies
impinges on the actor in natural situations, with multiple variables in play and of
corresponding complexity, yielding the effect that causal connections "known"
on the basis of experimentation may be overwhelmed by other factors in other
settings. No text on experimental methods and no critique of discrete experimental findings fails to include—almost ritualistically—the question of whether
even well-established laboratory findings are applicable outside the laboratory.

In this connection, we bring up some related limitations resulting from a
consideration of the *generic* structure and process of the experimental situation
itself, above and beyond particular experimental findings. An experiment is,
after all, a little social system, with distinctive characteristics that tend to bias it
systematically, *as a type of social interaction,* and therefore raise questions about
findings. What are these characteristics?

Most laboratory experiments are or should be—but are not always (for example, in some medical experiments)—based on voluntary cooperation and consensus on the part of subjects. The typical, even stereotyped, view of the psychological experiment is the recruitment of students enrolled in college classes (often in
introductory psychology courses) who are asked if they are willing to participate
in an experiment. Unkind critics refer to academic psychology as the investigation and representation not of human nature, but of the nature of potential psychology majors. Even this method of recruitment compromises the "voluntary"
essence of the experiment in two senses: first, the classes are interested, if not
captive, audiences for experimentation, and, second, those requesting cooperation (instructors or graduate assistants) in the classes have a disproportionate influence in securing the cooperation of undergraduate students with less prestige
than they have. Considerations such as these lie behind the distinction between
the "ideal experiment" and the "real experiment" (Bredenkamp, 2001). In the
former, the experimenter and the experimental subject are considered as nonper-
sons in that their behavior toward each other remains constant, whereas in fact it
does not remain constant, even in the necessary civilities requisite for greeting,
explaining the experimental situation, and gaining cooperation (Friedman, 1967).

The culture of compliance in the laboratory situation is further established
by normative expectations that, once they have agreed to participate, subjects
are expected, by virtue of the norms of the experimental setting, to cooperate by
listening to the experimental instructions, not challenging them, carrying them
out once issued, and not distorting their responses out of motives of playful-
ness, mischief-making, cynicism, or wrong-headedness. Experimenters, for their
part, are expected to be supportive, helpful, and honest, as well as motivated by

scientific and not other interests. It goes without saying that this little culture of compliance and cooperation is represented in only some "real life" group situations, which typically do involve some cooperation, but are also fraught with potential indifference, ambivalence, and conflict. In saying this, we go beyond the preoccupation with "experimen*er* bias," which is another possible distortion through the attitudes, preoccupations, and hopes of the experimenter, and which has been studied extensively in its own right. Instead, we are referring to generic "experiment bias," almost necessary in the culture and structure of the experimental situation, and extremely difficult to modify or correct for because of the essence of that situation.

THE APPROXIMATION OF LABORATORY EXPERIMENTAL METHODS IN FIELD SETTINGS: THE SPECIAL CASE OF EVALUATION RESEARCH

The adaptation of the logic of experimentation to natural field settings was a major theme in the twentieth-century history of research methods. Different influences produced this development: the long-standing appreciation of the limitations of laboratory experimentation; the evident inability—for ethical and practical reasons—to freely manipulate variables and adversely affect people in natural settings; the development, in the 1960s, of a brilliant, definitive methodology— known as the Northwestern orthodoxy because of its association with Donald Campbell (of Northwestern University) and his collaborators (Campbell and Stanley 1966; Cook and Campbell, 1979)—that became the "Cadillac model" for approximating experimental conditions in nonlaboratory settings. Scientifically motivated efforts to improve on and refine this methodology are part of the ongoing work of economists, sociologists, psychologists, and other students of methodology.

Some of the impetus for field-research methodologies has emanated from social scientists themselves as an effort to generate and improve scientific knowledge in their fields. Another decisive influence, however, has been the growth of policies and programs of social reforms by federal, state, and local governments. Rossi and Freeman (1993) trace this impulse to programs of occupational training and public health before World War I, and note the social-engineering outlook of the administration of Herbert Hoover, the vast array of social programs in the New Deal, and dramatic moments such as the evaluation of the military experience in World War II (Stouffer, Suchman, DeVinney, Starr, et al., 1949). The greatest impulse to critical study of social-reform programs was the programs of the War on Poverty in the 1960s, as well as the disillusionment with and subsequent political attacks on these programs for their perceived waste and failures (Williams and Evans, 1972).

Accompanying the expansion of social programs has been a growth of interest in evaluating their effectiveness. Much of this interest arises from a "natural" connection: if government budgetary and political investments are made in reforms, it is in the nature of the case that the makers of those investments, as well as political supporters and critics, will want to know if that money and political capital has been properly spent. This is the essence of *accountability*, as its logic has been extended beyond financial integrity and honesty to a concern with program effectiveness. Furthermore, if effective investment of resources and accountability are concerns, it follows that the best means to address them is to *evaluate* programs' efficiency. Those forces have contributed to the "accountability mania" (see chapter 6, pp. 209–10) and its child, the "evaluation mania," of the last decades of the twentieth century. Many government- or foundation-sponsored reform programs include a mandatory evaluation component of cost-benefit, cost effectiveness, or other results such as distributional benefits. These are the dynamics that have made evaluation research a conspicuous feature of social-science methodology. This approach has also developed its own subdivisions, including a dominant methodology-oriented, quantitative approach and a more "naturalistic," case-oriented approach (McLaughlin and Phillips, 1991), both of which advertise their own value.

As a result of these forces, evaluation research has established itself as a significant industry. Its areas of application are numerous—programs in manpower training; social welfare; studies of the educational effectiveness of different types of classroom and instruction; clinical trials for medications and modes of treatment; effectiveness of different kinds of psychotherapy; effects of rehabilitation programs in prison; effects of efforts to integrate released prisoners into the economy and the community; and programs directed at mitigating the circumstances of the homeless. Evaluation methodology has also spread to business and nonprofit organizations interested in evaluating their decisions and programs. Evaluation procedures have grown in complexity, diagnosing problems, designing research, devising measures, multiplying models, and making multiple measures of outcomes (cost-benefit, distribution-of-benefits effects, and larger public impacts of programs). By the 1970s, evaluation research became the topic of a systematic text (Weiss, 1972), and courses in evaluation research were offered as one type of research method in social-science departments. Rossi and Freeman (1993) could speak of "the profession of evaluation"; as part of this, organizations offering program evaluation services have arisen, and agencies frequently contract out the evaluative components of their programs to these organizations. Some enthusiasts and practitioners of evaluation research complain of its methodological second-class citizenship among academic social scientists—largely as a by-product of the high status accorded to basic research and the low status accorded to applied research. They also assert that, as a result, less qualified social scientists go into evaluation work and that these scientists leave it early out of disillusionment (Rossi, 1972). Nevertheless, given the public necessity for evaluation in so many quarters, it has become and will remain a major part of the scene in the social sciences, government, and private reform circles.

We pay special attention to evaluation research because of its explicit relationship to the usability of knowledge. In chapter 10, we note the diverse purposes for which social scientists in academic settings pursue knowledge, only one of which is for applied or usable knowledge. In contrast to this diversity, the focus of evaluation research is directly relevant to usability:

- Research activities are oriented to instrumental, practical issues.
- Many stakeholders (legislators who enact programs, administrators who implement them, staffers who assist administrators, target populations, and public constituents) are interested in the concrete viability, success, and failure of programs.
- One purpose of gathering knowledge is to establish how effective a program is in concrete settings, in order to gain knowledge that will make future programs more so.
- While evaluation research is supposed to measure up to the canons of scientific excellence, it is also supposed to do so in situations in which knowledge is actually being applied.

Evaluation research, then, is a direct, calculated, and deliberate effort to establish the usefulness of knowledge in planning and executing programs in concrete settings. As such, it should be an ideal case for investigating usability.

As we will discover, this ideal is scientifically compromised—some would say corrupted—in the actual working-out of evaluation research. Most of this effect arises from the fact that evaluation is embedded in a context of individual, organizational, and political stakeholders—a context more complicated than the relatively simpler context of research in the academy, even though the latter has its own interested parties. As a result, in the case of evaluation research, we must expand our idea of usability to include the nonscientific interests of parties who may use scientific discourse for many other purposes. We will lay out the dynamics that produce this result; in the meantime, we sketch the methodological essentials of evaluation research.

The Methodology of Evaluation Research

The essence of evaluation research is to assess (often by referring to multiple criteria) the effectiveness of programs aimed at individual and/or social betterment. The criteria applied are the methodological canons of scientific research, as these are adapted to the initiation, progress, and outcomes of the program. At the same time, the essentials of the laboratory experiment—the gold standard—cannot be applied in pure form. It is necessary to approximate these essentials in the on-going world. Yet the fundamental aim of the alternative methodology is the same as the laboratory method: to isolate causal conditions, to reduce their number, and to make precise their causal role.

The most fundamental distinction in evaluation research is between experimental designs (the term *experimental* is used, even though these methods are not identical to those used in the laboratory) and quasiexperimental designs:

- In the experimental method applied in field settings, individuals or other units are randomly assigned to either a treatment or a control group. The treatment group is made up of units exposed to a certain intervention (for example, a retraining program initiated after they have lost their jobs), and the control group is made up of people who have lost their jobs but have not been enrolled in the retraining program. Because the samples in both groups are chosen randomly, this assures that members of the groups are similarly exposed to different outside forces (for example, changing economic conditions or different social environments). Randomization is thus a way to *wash out* those forces by assuming they operate the same way among treatment and controls. This increases the confidence that the treatment variable (job retraining), and not some other variable or combination of variables, is the operative one. On the basis of this confidence, investigators conclude that the job-retraining program is effective or not effective (a judgment established, as a rule, on the basis of the statistical significance in outcome between the two groups). Experimental designs are generally limited to programs and experiments that are "partial" in coverage; that is, they cover only a part of the population, and thus leave room for selection of a control (unaffected) group. An example is the extension of a free medical program to a treatment group while not offering it to the rest of the population, and drawing randomized samples from both (Brook, Ware, Roger, Keeler, et al., 1984). This procedure cannot be followed when the program affects everybody, for example, in a revision of federal income-tax rates. In this case, it is more difficult to create or approximate control groups.
- Evaluation researchers point out that even the best efforts to approximate experimental designs are sometimes compromised by sampling errors or by practical failures; for example, when some subjects in either the treatment or control group do not cooperate with investigators or migrate from the region. In addition, the program may change direction in midcourse, thus compromising the original design by changing the original variables and introducing new ones. As a result, almost "every evaluation is compromised by programmatic, funding, time, or political constraints." No program has been implemented with "absolute fidelity," and, more generally, "research

projects entirely without flaws do not exist, and, arguably, never will" (Rossi, 1972: 21). Despite this acknowledgment, evaluation researchers generally consider randomized experimental designs to be "superior to other designs" and believe that they "should probably be considered first in any evaluation" (25). As such, this kind of design exists as a sort of guiding standard for field research, a norm that describes the ideal but is never realized in practice.

· When, for whatever reasons, the randomized experimental method is not possible or feasible, evaluation researchers turn to what are generally considered to be weaker alternatives. These are grouped under the heading of "quasiexperimental designs." These involve selecting some comparison group similar to the treatment group—but by methods that fall short of randomization and for that reason fall short in their ability to scientifically control the variation of other factors. As a result, quasiexperiments are regarded as necessary but are less preferred. Numerous submethods of quasiexperimentation have been devised. These include matching participants with nonparticipants on selected variables (for example, age, gender, or minority status); statistically equating participating and nonparticipating targets on variables that may be related to program outcome; pre-post comparisons (i.e., comparing cohorts before and after intervention); and panel and time-series studies involving repeated measurements). The aptness, advantages, and disadvantages of all these methods are subject to extensive debate, and refinements are continuously being sought. The important point in thinking about experimental and quasiexperimental methods is that, whichever is employed and whichever is considered superior in a given set of circumstances, "the logic behind them is the same" (Rossi and Freeman, 1993: 297). That logic is to establish a counterfactual comparison group, one that the preferred intervention variable *does not or probably does not affect.*

The Social Realities of Evaluation

One feature of the evaluation research literature is an endless discussion of how both interventions and their evaluation stray from the standard of experimentalism. This discussion is diverse, but two general features can be identified: (1) methodological shortcomings derive from circumstances of the intervention, such as failures of randomization, sampling errors, failure to secure full participation and compliance by the treatment and control groups, and other factors; and (2) deviations from scientific standards derive from the personal, organizational, political, and public contexts in which evaluations are embedded. We include some of the former in the preceding section, and now turn to the latter.

Here is a partial list of the kinds of misdirections, imperfections, and failures of evaluation research deriving from its contexts:

- Diversity of wished-for outcomes among politicians eager to find support for or evidence of failure of intervention outcomes; administrators and staff with the same eagerness, plus an interest in not looking bad because of poor design or execution of an evaluation; activists pressing for or against specific reform efforts; consumers of the intervention; and public opinion generally. These forces generate the motives for favoring or opposing programs and/ or their evaluation, turning results to their own individual and group advantage, to say nothing of delaying, sabotaging, avoiding damage, and criticizing or otherwise discrediting the evaluation process.
- Resistance from politicians and administrations to imposing certain kinds of controls, particularly randomization, which may be regarded as manipulative and impersonal (Rossi, 1972).
- The tension between the logic of "evaluation time" and "political time," which may reflect a tension between doing the study right from a scientific point of view and getting the results out in time for a legislative session or a political campaign. This tension may result in premature evaluation, shortcuts in design and measurement, hasty interpretations, and undigested reporting of results.
- Personally or group-motivated changes in goals of an intervention, delays, and introduction of new measures for programs.
- Personality, role, and value conflicts between research-oriented evaluation personnel and action-oriented administrative personnel (Weiss, 1972).
- Cost and time limitations, also sources of hasty or faulty design.
- Manipulation of results for personal advancement, to claim political credit, and to discredit others.
- Poor communication or miscommunication of research results, which may result in part from relying on professional science jargon.
- Various unanticipated consequences of a program, possibly because of poor design, but often systemic in character, in that the program and its evaluation are let loose into a world of changing circumstances and forces unknown or unappreciated at the time of the intervention.

Evaluation research texts typically list some measures designed to diminish or overcome these sources of weakness, but by and large the vulnerabilities and problems receive more press—and are usually regarded as more powerful forces than the recommended solutions.

The upshot of these observations is that social programs and their evaluation are caught in special kind of "usability trap," which produces scientific imperfections in evaluations and cycles of hope → effort → conflict and disillusionment → regeneration of hope. In concluding this section, we specify the special concatenations of intellectual, social, and political forces that produce this pattern:

1. Given the irreducible fact of political responsibility to deal with social problems as well as the requirement for accountability in doing so, it appears that we are stuck with the impulses to intervene. Proponents of interventions call for evaluations to demonstrate their value; opponents demand evaluations to discredit them; evaluation researchers call for them partly because they share the goals that lie behind interventions and partly because they believe in evaluations as a matter of their own occupational honor. Who can oppose evaluations without incurring the risk of criticisms and accusations of irresponsibility? This in itself is a kind of entrapment.

2. Social interventions are typically accompanied by high expectations for their effectiveness and utility. These emanate in part from the optimism of social and political reformers, who believe in the power of reform generally and in the potency of their favored reforms in particular. They also emanate from the outlooks of professional evaluators, who would not be in the business of evaluation if there were nothing worthwhile to evaluate and no results expected. Another source of optimism is methodological. As many emphasize, evaluators live perpetually with the gold standard of scientific knowledge generated by the norms of experimentation. They hold a faith that it is worthwhile to strive toward—if never actually fully achieve—that ideal.

3. High expectations are forever destined to be dashed. This effect derives from the same forces that generate the expectations in the first place. High expectations for results of social programs simultaneously generate high standards by which otherwise notable or interesting results may be judged as unimpressive, disappointing, insignificant, or not worth the effort. The crucial item to note in such judgments—while typically presented as facts speaking for themselves—is that evaluation reflects a *relationship* between standards and facts. Designations of success or failure change according to the expectations brought to bear. Methodological expectations, when framed in terms of the gold standard of randomized experiments, never fully meet that standard. Any methodologist, professional or amateur, can find *something,* however tiny, wrong with the design, the measures, the execution, or the results of an intervention. Furthermore, the inevitable substantive and methodological shortcomings of any evaluation become ammunition in the contentious political process, available in partisan debates and fights over the worthiness of the experiment and the program.

4. Evaluators themselves, in the first instance "neutral" applied social scientists, are inevitably drawn into the contentious process of evaluating reforms. They may themselves be partisan, usually favoring interventions, and in that way become independent advocates or aligned with other groups contending for voice and influence. Alternatively, they stand as the professional and methodological conscience of any evaluation, insisting on methodological

standards that may or may not conflict with the positions of partisan groups. Despite official proclamations of scientific dispassion, evaluation researchers become advocates in the organizational and political process.

5. In the rough-and-tumble struggles over interventions and their evaluations, we note a general tendency for the language of conflict and confrontation to drift *away* from bald partisan expression and *toward* the language of methodological principles and procedures. This produces a kind of reverse Gresham's Law, whereby "good" discourse drives out the "bad." Reviewing the controversy over the Westinghouse Study of Head Start, Williams and Evans (1972) observed the following: "In the heat of the public controversy, there have been some old-fashioned political innuendoes based on vile motives, but in the main, the principal weapons in the battle have been the esoteric paraphernalia of modern statistical analysis. . . . However, the real battle is not over the methodological purity of this particular study, but, rather, involves fundamental issues of how the federal government will develop large-scale programs and evaluate their results" (248).

There appear to be good reasons for this effect. The use of methodological language is more acceptable than the use of explicitly political language, largely because it is shrouded in the legitimacy of science; to use methodological language to credit or discredit is more "objective" and "scientific" than partisan assault. By focusing on procedures, moreover, methodological language tends to bury impressions of arbitrariness and, as a result, to mute the ugly side of conflicts. Cain and Hollister (1972) summarized this effect as follows:

> Few decisions about social action programs have been made on the basis of [methodological] evaluations. . . . It often seems that the scholars conspire with the legislators to beat down any attempt to bring to bear more orderly evidence about the effectiveness of alternative programs. It is not at all difficult to find experts who will testify that any evaluation study is not adequately "scientific" to provide a sound basis for making program decisions. There is a reasonable and appropriate fear on the part of academics that sophisticated techniques of analysis will be used as deceptive wrapping around an essentially political kernel to mislead administrators or the public. This fear, however, often leads to the setting of standards of "proof" which cannot, at present, given the state of the art of the social sciences, be satisfied. The result generally is that the evaluation is discredited, the information it provides is ignored, and the decision-making official and the legislator resume the exercise of their visceral talents. (135)

A biographical example can be cited. In the early 1980s, as chair of the UC Berkeley Academic Senate, Smelser was sometimes asked to sit in on visits to the campus by representatives of federal agencies to monitor its progress on affirmative action. A fascinating feature of the exchanges in these visits was the dominant tendency to focus on methodological points—estimating the size and quality of the pools of minorities and women in the academic market, disputing the accuracy of measurements, challenging and defending the university's estimates of the progress it was making, even arguing about statistical techniques. Some of these discussions became heated. At the same time, they amounted to a way to avoid confrontations over the substantive rights and wrongs of affirmative action (always a hot issue) and conflicts between government bureaucrats who were under political pressure to achieve results and university officials who were pleading for patience and flexibility because of the political exigencies they faced in their own offices. The substantive conflicts were obscured in the methodological agenda, and produced a kind of sanitization of discourse.

6. In chapter 10, we will note a typical research cycle in the social sciences. When a novel idea, explanation, or theory makes its appearance, it sets off a process: heightened attention to the novelty, a flurry of critiques, defensive efforts, reformulations, and alternative explanations. The result is an increasing contingency and complexity of knowledge, along with an inability to produce simple, pat, usable formulae. Cohen and Weiss (1977) summarized this with respect to evaluation research:

> For the most part, the improvement of research on social policy does not lead to greater clarity about what to think or what to do; it usually tends to produce a *greater sense of complexity*. This result is endemic to the research process. For what researchers understand by improvement of their craft leads not to greater consensus about research problems, methods, and interpretation of results, but to more variety in ways problems are seen, more divergence in the way studies are carried out and more controversy in the ways results are interpreted. It also leads to a more complicated view of problems and solutions, for the progress of research tends to reveal the inadequacy of accepted ideas of solving problems. The ensuing complexity and confusion are naturally a terrific frustration both to researchers who think they should matter and officials who think they need help. (68, italics added)

7. This increase in the appreciation of complexity on the supply side of knowledge does not diminish the demand for good, simple, manageable, workable principles and solutions in practical settings. In fact, it may increase that demand. If the businessperson, policy-maker, or administrator of reform confronts a world that is, in itself, more complex and demanding all the time, the last message he or she wishes to hear is that the world is complex and demanding, even though that may be the appropriate one under the circumstances. Decision-makers need less complex messages that, through action, will solve problems, reduce risk and uncertainty, and increase the

probability of success in their organizational and political efforts. Herein lies the continued vitality of the efforts to identify and advertise *the* decisive factor or *the* system for solutions, to say nothing of the search for quick fixes and elixirs that are, as oversimplifications, destined to fall short. The overall result is a continuing contrapuntal tension and alternation between appreciation of the complexity bred by increased knowledge of things and views of simplicity bred by the uncertainty and urgency of things.

The effect of the simultaneous and interrelated working of these seven tendencies is to force us into a different way of thinking about usability of knowledge in the very areas—policy research and evaluation research—where usability is explicit and institutionalized as a front-and-center consideration. This thinking yields a process that is far from any utilitarian model of use. Because of inevitable substantive and methodological limitations on the "knowledge" to be used, and especially because social interventions are so deeply embedded in organizational, managerial, and political contexts and conflicts, we have to view usability with more nuance. There is, of course, the utilitarian issue of how effective theories, causal knowledge procedures, measures, and interpretation in producing intended results are. But at the same time, there must be an appreciation of how these methods inevitably fall short. Part of that appreciation derives from knowing about contexts and how they generate very different kinds of uses of knowledge and its dynamics—uses such as an avenue for personal advancement, as criticism of opponents, as organizational defensiveness, and as a resource in partisan struggles. To reach these conclusions is not especially encouraging to the scientific or reformist utilitarian, but it appears to be consonant with the realities of purposeful social planning and intervention.

EXCURSUS

A NOTE ON CLINICAL TRIALS

The employment of clinical trials in medical and public health arenas is a variation on evaluation research and shares its fundamental methodology. But because this practice is embedded in such special and often sacred contexts—the prevention of death and the treatment of illness—it displays a number of unique features.

In essence, clinical trials use scientific methodology to investigate the effectiveness of a medical treatment—for example, a diet, a surgical intervention, a drug, or a medical device—usually in advance of its use in practice. Informal medical experimentation is traceable into remote history, but the widespread use of scientific methods was largely a product largely of the twentieth century, spurred by interest in public health (the first Pure Food and Drug Act was passed in 1906) and by public health disasters, such as the death of more than one hundred individuals by the distribution of an untested medicine called Elixir Sulfanilamide in the late 1930s. After decades of steady growth, the complex apparatus of clinical trials, including their control and regulation, has become the single largest arena of evaluation research and has produced a cascade of literature (Chow and Liu, 2004). Texts on clinical research appear continuously, some highly specific according to medical specialty (e.g., psychiatric interventions [Everitt and Wessily, 2008] and, among these, interventions on specific mental disorders) and type of disease (e.g., antitumor therapy [Muggia and Rozencweig, 1987]).

The methodological logic of clinical trials is identical to all other methods reviewed in this chapter: the scientific effort to identify *causes* by means of administering, varying, measuring, and evaluating an *intervention* in the context of a simultaneous effort to *control* all other possible causes, or at least wash them out through randomization (Ellwood, 2007). Many variations are available, including direct intervention, observational studies, and cross-sectional surveys, each with distinctive strengths and weaknesses. The favored methodological means of control is statistical randomization, the random assignment of participants to experimental and control groups to correct for confounding variables, though many designs approximating randomization are also employed.

Because clinical trials are implicated in questions of health—life, death, disease, and cure—and, as a corollary, because mistakes can be so costly, clinical trials are conducted in the context of several constraining conditions:

- They are often conducted under the aegis of a *public* agency—usually the Food and Drug Administration—to help ensure design and methodological correctness, to control deceit and fraud, and more generally to safeguard against dangers to public health.
- They reveal a heightened preoccupation with ethical issues—as evidenced by the proliferation of rules to safeguard against misuse of human subjects and the elaborate requirements for informed consent by those taking part in trials (Getz and Borfitz, 2002). All research involving human subjects raises questions of their treatment and mistreatment, but these questions are especially important in types of research that vitally influence subjects.
- They have accumulated a number of methodological features, not unique to medical experimentation, but considered necessary to avoid contamination of results by third factors. One such feature is the widespread use of placebos in clinical trials, based on the knowledge that psychological factors such as suggestibility and persuasion are operative in experiencing symptoms and cure, and that these factors themselves should be controlled (Shapiro and Shapiro, 1997). A second feature is called blinding or masking; this refers to withholding the identities of treatment and control subjects from those who

are participating in it; double-blinding involves withholding that knowledge from both investigators and subjects. Blinding is thus another effort to control additional causes that might affect the results. A third feature is a preoccupation with the side effects of interventions—unintended, unknown, and possibly harmful effects of administering a treatment, drug, or device that develop *in addition to* the desired result.

The same environment that yields these special characteristics also produces a distinct range of perils and pitfalls for clinical trials in medicine and public health:

- Methodological failures in design, sampling, execution, measurement, and evaluation are possible in any evaluation research, but because the potential consequences are so grave in clinical trials, such failures assume greater importance. One notable fault of clinical trials is the failure to observe a correct time relationship, e.g., to measure the effects of an intervention too soon after its application to be able to discover longer-term side effects, which, once they appear, may result in medical scandals. Other problems arise from treating a disorder as a single malady, when it is in fact part of a multiple-disorder syndrome. Taking shortcuts to cut costs may also compromise research objectives and results.
- Special vulnerability to ethical violations, which generate extreme reactions to experiments with very high stakes. The most outrageous case, which still remains as a scar on the reputation of the public health establishment and a permanent source of racial outrage among many African Americans and others, is the Tuskegee syphilis experiment, in which four hundred poor black men with syphilis were enrolled, were never told they had syphilis, and were never treated, even after penicillin had become available. The experiments, begun in 1932, continued for four decades until public health officials leaked the story to the media (Jones, 1981). The issue of ethical violations is an especially tricky one because ethical standards—what is permissible and what is not—themselves vary over time, as does the vigilance of enforcers.
- Because new interventions, drug treatments, and devices are often the source of substantial profit, the testing process constitutes a "natural" arena for the emergence of conflicts of interest. Inventors, manufacturers, and marketers have a financial interest in approval, as well as a derived incentive to influence the testing and approval process. Compared with other arenas, the history of clinical trials has been relatively free from stories of such conflicts of interest, but possibilities of informal influence remain and, even when not observed, can be suspected by the skeptical.

Given the elevated public sensitivity about medical practice in general, it is not surprising that the literature on clinical trials emphasizes *both* their scientific value and their contribution to evidence-based medicine *and* their methodological weaknesses, limited relevance, and the insidious hidden truths lying behind them (Furberg, 2007; Gauch, 2009; Menikoff, 2006).

This consideration of clinical trials reveals a complex set of axioms: when stakes and uncertainty are high (as in matters of health), anxieties are high; when anxieties are high, the costs of mistakes are high; when those costs are high, precautions against mistakes proliferate; and when stakes, uncertainty, anxiety, costs, and the need for precautions are high, emotional reactions bifurcate toward the extremes of confidence and dread. The environments of both clinical trials and clinical practice reflect these axioms.

Excursus
Selected Features of Statistical Analysis

It is beyond our intent and capacity to go into detail on the applications of statistics—which demand at least book-length treatment in themselves—but we should mention the logic of several types of statistical analysis to demonstrate their continuity with the array of research methods covered in this chapter.

Statistical efforts to isolate, describe, analyze, and establish causation arise at several points, including the following:

- Descriptive statistics pursues the adequate *presentation of facts*—empirical data—by selecting or devising reliable measures and representing them numerically in the form of aggregates, central tendencies, and other modes. Sampling theory and methods are central to this enterprise. Methodological critics have been especially sensitive to faulty representations, distortions, and manipulation of descriptive statistics from the media, politicians, and activists (Best, 2001).
- Using statistical methods to identify, control, manipulate, and establish confidence in the causal significance of different variables is the aim of a range of techniques under the headings of correlation, regression, and multivariate analysis. The conceptual logic of these methods is identical to the experimental and other methods. They can be employed both to hold constant and to vary multiple suspected causes (for example, the respective roles of race, class, and geographical residence in the perpetuation of poverty), thereby establishing degrees of confidence about their genuineness and spuriousness in the causal process, as well as their interaction with one another. This kind of statistical analysis is thus a way to manipulate data that are usually not collected in laboratory situations in order to strive for the same kinds of controls that experimentation seeks.

Once presumptive relationships between variables are established, a range of statistical techniques is also available to establish confidence in these relationships by estimating the probability of their having happened as a result of random variation.

Excursus
The Psychology and Sociology of Surveys of Attitudes,
Opinions, and Intentions

A conspicuous popular vision of a social scientist, found in cartoons and public perceptions, is a researcher knocking on the door (or telephoning, or now e-mailing) and asking an ordinary citizen what he or she thinks about some topic or issue, recording the response, then systematically compiling the accumulated responses and presenting them to a scholarly journal, a merchandising client, a political party, a firm interested in marketing a product, or the media generally. The practices of surveying and polling, with a long history of development in statistics and several of the social sciences, have become institutionalized and accepted parts of the contemporary scene. One expects to be asked which program one is watching on television, for whom one wants to cast a vote, how one has responded to an advertisement, or how one feels about a range of social problems. We routinely read the results of these polls as well. As often as not, we regard the results of such polls as reflecting a bit of social reality—a state of the public mood on public issues. And we hold images of those dependent on polls: commercial firms seeking and digesting the results of market research, and politicians and political advisors consulting and reacting to the results of political surveys on a daily basis. All these are part of the received public landscape.

Despite some catastrophic and well-publicized failures, such as the presidential election polls in 1936 (Roosevelt versus Landon) and 1948 (Dewey versus Truman)—or perhaps in part because of them—survey methods have advanced to a high art in the contemporary world. Advances in methods of randomization and stratification of sampling have emerged; many sophisticated ways to recognize and correct for sampling bias and nonresponses have been developed; biases deriving from wording and ordering of questions have been discovered; and many forms of interview bias—based on the age, race, gender, clothing, grooming, and general appearance of the interviewer—have been detected and dealt with (Sudman, Bradburn, and Schwarz, 1996). Despite this sophistication, many surveys still fall short for reasons of sampling bias and error, hastiness in construction of questions, and unknown response biases. Yet there are several more general and deeper questions about the social survey that demand to be asked, because they raise issues about surveys as representations of social reality:

1. Variability of institutionalization. We mentioned that surveys are a normal part of the social landscape, and that is true throughout much of the world,

as the existence of many national and international polling agencies attests. Yet this institutionalization and its concomitants are variable. In countries that we describe as developed, or the OECD (Organization for Economic Cooperation and Development) countries, such surveys are routinely expected and accepted features and, by and large, have all the features of institutionalization, especially trust. We generally believe that those who survey are seeking information and not more; we take their questions at face value; and we trust that the information gathered will be used for legitimate purposes. But such assumptions are only imperfectly realized, even in places where surveys are routine and widespread. Mistrust of the purposes of those who ask is highly variable, certainly along social-class, regional, and racial-ethnic lines. Moreover, surveys may excite a certain residue of suspicion as to the use of results, especially if they ask about personal finances or opinions on other touchy issues. People also grow weary of the nuisance of being surveyed, and as a result may refuse to participate when the doorbell or phone rings or an e-mail prompts an impatient "delete" once the intent of the mailer is known. We are also leery of both partisan and nonpartisan news media that announce call-in surveys to loaded questions ("the Fox-MSNBC effect") and report the voluntary responses as something more representative than they are. In a word, the widespread legitimacy, acceptability, and good-faith assumptions about survey as an institutionalized form must be presumed to be variable and tainted with an element of suspicion, sometimes paranoia.

2. The political, psychological, and social underpinnings of the survey method. The unit of analysis of the survey is typically the individual person, just as the unit of analysis of classical democratic theory is the individual citizen, and the unit of analysis of classical economic theory is the individual economic agent. All these lines of thinking reflect an individualistic bias. Insofar as the individuals surveyed are collectivized, it is mainly by aggregation into sums and percentages. In their interpretation by consumers, however, results may become representations of attitudinal, political, and market reality. Are this individualistic bias and the resulting rendition of reality justified? Evidence produced in the social sciences testifies that they are not. We know that interpersonal networks and interpersonal influences pervade the worlds of tastes, markets, politics, and attitudes, thus compromising any kind of additive logic of independent individuals in representing attitudes and influences as they manifest themselves in practices. We also know that the power to enforce preferences by individuals and groups is very unequally distributed in any society, and that the political process does not operate by the principle of one-person-one-iota-of-influence. Technical solutions, such as sophisticated sampling and stratification of samples, may

address these phenomena, but often do so in ways that fall short of tapping the actual institutional and political processes.

Furthermore, the interaction between asker and answerer is, like the laboratory, a little social system. The asker begs for trust, goodwill, cooperation, and honesty on the part of the answerer, and the answerer, in the best of worlds, reciprocates those feelings. In addition, the very ways of asking the question—sometimes open-ended, discursive, and exploratory, but more often focused and requesting a yes-no preference or ranked degrees of agreement or disagreement with a question—constitute ways of framing that shape the content and flavor of responses. Responses are also frozen in time, in the moment of asking-answering, even though this effect can be countered somewhat by repeated administrations of a survey. The results emanating from that momentary two-person dialogue engaging in highly structured interaction is then rendered as the reality of the attitudes and sentiments recorded. We know, however, that attitudes are in many instances conditional and contextualized (Blumer, 1948) and change according to situation, sometimes rapidly (Eagly and Chaiken, 1993). While creative researchers have made sophisticated efforts to capture some of this conditionality, the social and psychological logic of the asker-answerer situation persists.

With these observations in mind, we might conclude that it is important to distinguish between the representation of survey findings by researchers and the assumptions underlying their interpretation and use by consumers—sellers, politicians, media, and readers. Attitude surveys report distributions of attitudes, which are only one part of the realities of the political process. Interpreters, however, may regard their results as political reality and as guides to action and policy. Surveys are certainly *usable* and widely *used* for selected purposes. However, they should not be interpreted as a literal mirror of the status—still less the dynamics—of the world of attitudes and opinions and politics they might appear to represent. We should be skeptical about inferences that distributions of attitudes of individuals mirror the dynamic realities of those attitudes as they play themselves out in political and social contexts.

COMPARATIVE-HISTORICAL ANALYSIS AND METHODS

The social-science literature has produced a category of comparative analysis, argued by some to be an identifiable method. Many investigators describe themselves as comparative analysts and/or as making use of comparative methods. Others have argued that the term *comparative* is a misnomer for a special research style because *all* social science, dedicated to the analysis of *variation,* is, in principle, comparative (Durkheim, 1997 [1893]; Swanson, 1971). Laboratory studies are comparisons between treatment and control groups. Evaluation research involves comparisons between these two types of groups, however each is created. What comparative analysis covers in practice is a range of research in many fields—principally sociology, economics, political science, anthropology, psychology, and history—much of which involves comparisons among large-scale social and political units. Each discipline gravitates primarily to its favored units of analysis—sociology to societies, economics and political science to nation-states, anthropology to cultures, and psychology to individuals within different nations or regions. Most lines of comparative research involve multiple cases, but anthropologists more often carry out case studies of individual cultures.

Insofar as generalizations can be made about the methodology of comparative analysis, we can identify the following constraints:

- The data studied are "natural"—e.g., the historical flow of social life—in contrast to "situationally created" data in laboratory and some field experiments. Some comparative data do have a created element, for example, statistics compiled by government agencies and public opinion surveys, but this is a different kind of creation from that in constructed experiments. This circumstance means comparative analysis has less ability to control sources of variation.
- In a closely related point, data gathered from the historical flow of experience are inevitably embedded in and the product of a multiplicity of causes, interactions among causes, and feedback relations.
- Depending on the units of analysis chosen, comparative analysis is often faced with a "many variables, small N" situation. In a case study of a single nation or culture, the N is 1, though there may be an imagined population of comparative units, depending on the concepts employed. The N in comparative analysis of large social units, such as nation-states, can range from 2 to all such units in the world, but the number is still finite. Three methodological consequences follow: (1) because of the limited number of cases, some statistical methods—namely those requiring large numbers of cases—are not available; (2) by virtue of the fact that the world's nation-states and societies constitute some limited kind of international system, the behavior of nations affects one another (through emulation and diffusion, for example), thus compromising the assumption that the units of analysis are independent from one another, a necessary assumption for many lines of statistical analysis; (3) if one indiscriminately expands numbers by virtue of the fact that the units are common in name but not in fact, the apples-and-oranges problem—i.e., the noncomparability of units of analysis—arises, for example in the inclusion of China, Argentina, Singapore, and Fiji in the same category of "nation-states."

Despite these methodological constraints of comparative analysis, we must remind ourselves that its aim remains that which is common to the scientific method: establishing causal relations in historical and contemporary situations. It has the same objectives as laboratory studies, namely the attempt to isolate, control, and establish the genuineness of posited historical causes. In historical analyses, we are often faced with a single situation in which a number of plausible historical determinants are present but cannot be assessed as determinants independently of one another in that single situation. For example, if we are interested in accounting for the rapid economic development of the United States in the nineteenth century, we could note the presence of a strong Protestant tradition and its culture of voluntarism and activism, the ready availability of land and natural resources, a situation in which labor was expensive but capital cheap, and other conceivable factors. A crude comparative strategy would be to look, in a mode of *systematic illustration,* at other cases of economic development and the nondevelopment of other societies, taking note of the presence or absence of the possible variables in an attempt to establish the relative strength or decisiveness of various causal possibilities. This was the primary strategy employed by Weber in his study of the rise of capitalism—systematically examining the different historical situations of northwest European and American societies where development occurred most rapidly with a variety of other countries and regions, e.g., classical China and classical India. This strategy led him to focus on the apparent centrality of religious traditions in explaining comparative rates of development. This line of analysis can be regarded as a way to *gain control* over suspected sources of variation in order to establish the relative importance of causal variables.

Three other methodological strategies can be cited in comparative studies. Each is also a way to gain control over variation to strengthen the case for a preferred explanation:

1. Choosing near-cases for comparison. What *nearness* implies is that the units share certain potentially causal variables in their circumstances, and the fact that sharing them makes at least an implicit case that they are not the decisive ones. A simple example is Spillman's (1997) comparative study of political cultures in the United States and Australia, as revealed in the study of political symbolism found in their respective centennial celebrations. The pairing was fortuitous in that both countries are large; both were formerly colonies; the mother country of both was the same country (Great Britain), which meant that they shared a common language as well as many cultural values and legal traditions; and that both had indigenous populations. While these several features did manifest some differences between the two countries, the fact that they were similar, it could be argued, constituted a crude

kind of *control* or *holding constant* of their historical influences. Similarly, when Lipset (1963) conducted a comparative study of differences in political culture, he chose Great Britain, the United States, Canada, and Australia, all sharing some similar cultural and historical characteristics.

2. Expanding the number of cases by including within-unit as well as between-unit analysis. Suppose an investigator found, as Durkheim (1951 [1897]) did, persistent differences in suicide rates among a range of European societies, and attributed these to corresponding differences in levels of cohesion, anomie, and other aspects of social integration. One line of complementary research would be to investigate differences in samples of immigrants with corresponding national and ethnic backgrounds within the United States and other countries (Canada and Australia, for instance) to determine whether within-society differences corresponded to between-society ones. If so, the findings would be strengthened by replication at different levels of analysis. This strategy is limited, however: different parametric conditions govern the experiences *among* nations on the one hand, and geographical and group subdivisions *within* them on the other. Nevertheless, the extension of investigations into state, regional, and local levels is a way to establish confidence or lack of confidence in posited causal relations. It is also a way to contend with the intrinsic "small N" problem of systematic comparative illustration.

3. Deviant case analysis. Developed at midcentury in the Columbia approach to methodology (Kendall and Lazarsfeld, 1950), this method is a crude and not widely used way to isolate variables and strive for their control. It is carried out as a supplement to studying general statistical relationships among variables. Any such correlations are never perfect, but are reflected in an array of units some distance away from a central-tendency line. In such analyses, the investigator may discover one or more units that are "outliers": that is, they deviate very far from the central correlational tendency. The aim of deviant case analysis is to inspect the outlier (as a case study) to determine how it differs from the generality of cases. A successful deviant case analysis might locate one or more variables that may, in certain cases, overwhelm the general tendency expressed by the correlation among the remaining cases and, in that way, reveal new operative variables. Deviant case analysis is generally regarded as a weak comparative method because with small numbers it is difficult to know which of the many respects the deviant case differs from the majority of cases is the crucial one.

In its history in the social sciences, the comparative method has yielded a range of findings that are highly variable in their quality and in the confidence that can be placed in them. They contain certain advantages (e.g., the study of natural and historical situations) and certain disadvantages (e.g., establishing rigorous controls over variables) in relation to the experimental and other methods. What can we say about the usability of knowledge yielded by comparative analysis?

In reflecting on this question, we extend the idea of usability in both a general and a particular direction. At the most general level, to know systematically—via methodologically trustworthy comparative study—and to appreciate historical and contemporary variations in cultural values, social organization, and practical solutions is to gain in urbanity, sophistication, humility, and acceptance of differences. Such knowledge is also an antidote to the probably universal human tendency to be culturally self-centered and xenophobic—to know, rely on, and prefer the local and familiar and, correspondingly, to regard the different as foreign, suspicious, and threatening. In a closely related process, the sounder one's knowledge of the workings of the world that are different from one's own—which is what good comparative analysis produces—the less one relies on superstition and conjecture about that world.

As for more immediate usability, those in positions of making decisions, in framing policies, and in attacking social problems can certainly learn from close studies of arrangements in foreign quarters. If we are contemplating reforms to rein in costs and improve the quality of our healthcare system, it surely pays to seek and analyze reliable knowledge of systems in countries at comparable levels of development. If we are concerned with what seems to be the exceptional American capacity of adversarial groups to defeat, stymie, and neutralize social reforms in our political system, then it surely pays to study what appears to be the more consensual approach to policy formation and policy enactment in other societies. If we are interested in improving the built infrastructure and social resources to mitigate damage from natural disasters such as floods and earthquakes, it surely pays to study such arrangements—including the lack of them—in other societies. The same point applies to the comparative study of security systems designed to prevent and minimize the effects of terrorist aggression. Finally, in an increasingly globalized and competitive world, the comparative study of apparently successful and unsuccessful managerial and organizational strategies becomes more imperative. Several areas of social-science inquiry appear to be especially relevant: comparative management studies, comparative study of labor relations, comparative analysis of welfare systems, comparative policy analysis, comparative study of social insurance, and comparative study of social problems.

A second principle of usability derived from good comparative analysis introduces a level of caution in superimposing and ingesting attractive foreign social arrangements in automatic or wholesale ways. If methodologically sound comparative analysis teaches us anything, it is that any given set of social arrangements is embedded in distinctive *contexts*. To understand these contexts is as essential in understanding the workings of those arrangements as knowing the details of the arrangements themselves. When former colonial societies attempted to incorporate the legal traditions of their former colonizers, they found through sometimes painful evolution that these had to be tailored to indigenous traditions and customs. For example, the wholesale importation of British trade union models into African societies after independence confronted tribal realities that modified and in some cases undermined that process (Friedland, 1963). When American firms in the 1980s rushed to adopt what appeared to be the very successful Japanese management practices of total quality control, they discovered in different ways that the context of American individualistic values—very different from collectivist traditions in Japan—mitigated their undigested adoption. When formally socialist Eastern European countries—abetted by eager market-oriented economists and politicians from the West—rushed headlong to embrace capitalism, they discovered that residual social forces, some inherited from their socialist pasts, conspired to create a range of societies that are not liberal-capitalist in the imagined western sense, but are instead some distinctive historical mélange deriving from past historical tendencies and current reform efforts (Stark and Bruszt, 1998). These cautionary tales deriving from the importance of context establish the principle of *informed selectivity* in making comparative knowledge usable.

CASE STUDIES AND CLINICAL INFERENCE

The case study is an investigation in which the N is 1 and the possibly operative variables are many. Concrete examples of the case study include a biographical episode in the life of a single historical figure, the write-up of a patient in psychotherapeutic treatment, the anthropological ethnography of a single culture, the sociological study of a community, and the political analysis of a single election. From the standpoint of the methodological framework of this chapter, the case study is a relatively weak genre because of the impossibility of systematic comparative control of variation: the case is self-contained and the empirical material is given. Strong-minded scientific methodologists have been unkind to the method for this reason. Campbell and Stanley (1966) stated baldly that the case study has "such a total absence of control as to be of almost no scientific value" (6). At the very least, the case study is granted the power of discovery—it may generate new, perhaps original hypotheses, which, however, must be tested by more rigorous means before being assigned scientific value.

In practice, however, it is possible to cite some qualifications—even granting the correctness of its scientific critics—that give more power to the case study as a method to generate potentially useful knowledge.

- If the case is studied over time (in contrast to a cross-sectional study), then variation in its subject matter is introduced, and investigation of the other variables that are also changing may be identified as plausible causes (Nadel, 1949).
- Confidence in the findings of a case study may be strengthened by referring to other, similar case studies that produced the same findings; formally this is a crude way to control for variation, because the term *similar* implies continuity in variables of the case studies under comparison.
- Similarly, confidence in a case study can be increased by reference to "other knowledge," in the light of which its results are judged to be more plausible or less plausible. This is also, in effect, a crude but not meaningless comparative method.
- The case study, using methods of interview and observation, is a superior instrument in teasing out the meanings of activities being studied, and has the advantage—in contrast to some attitude surveys and some statistical analysis, for example—of not forcing these activities into standardized measures that violate their contexts or their richness.
- The case study can be surprising in the positive sense of that term; that is, it can generate findings contrary to some more or less accepted line of research findings and turn research in new directions.
- Case studies usually search for *patterns* of interacting causes, and in that way come closer to capturing, if not controlling, the reality of the causal nexus that is at work in almost all concrete empirical situations.

When an investigator, usually an expert, examines the configuration of variables in a case study and then endeavors to predict some kind of outcome, the former operation is called *clinical inference,* the latter *clinical prediction.* More than a half-century ago, in a classic study, Meehl (1954) assembled the available research and advanced the hypothesis that on the whole prediction on the basis of aggregated (statistical) association of variables was consistently superior to predictions made by clinicians. Extremely controversial at the time, this general finding has, on the whole, stood the test of time, even though clinicians continue to predict and defend their predictions on grounds of experience and expertise.

COUNTERFACTUAL REASONING, MENTAL EXPERIMENTS, AND THE ROLE OF "OTHER KNOWLEDGE"

We move now to *counterfactual reasoning,* a topic that is not usually considered under the heading of scientific research methods. We wish to make that association, however, largely because of continuities between their *structures of reasoning* and their respective roles in *explanation*.

Counterfactuals have long been the object of philosophical analysis (Lewis, 1973), with special interest in their truth-value. Social-psychological investigations have focused on counterfactuals as a prototypical mode of thinking; this research has mushroomed, stimulated largely by work on heuristics of thinking (Roese and Olson, 1995). It has focused on determinants of people's use of counterfactual thinking (for example, in experiencing disappointment and regret—"it might have been") and on the psychological functions this serves. More familiarly, any careful reader or watcher of the media finds such reasoning rampant among news analysts (if Hillary Clinton, not Barack Obama, had won the Democratic nomination; if Obama had chosen Hillary Clinton, not Joseph Biden, as his running mate; if McCain had chosen Mitt Romney, not Sarah Palin, as his running mate; if the George W. Bush administration had not invaded Iraq . . . and on and on, every morning in the newspaper and every evening on television). One of counterfactual thinking's most interesting extension by political scientists, historians, and social psychologists is to treat it as a method to assess plausible "near-miss" historical events that did not happen. Favorite examples are the consequences for western history if the Persians, not the Greeks, had been victorious in the Battle of Marathon, if Chamberlain had stood up to Hitler at Munich, and if Hitler had invaded England in World War II. These researchers have also assessed the usefulness of counterfactual statements in the political arena, especially international affairs (Tetlock and Belkin, 1996).

What is a counterfactual statement? It has been briefly defined as a "form of imagining" or, more specifically, generating a causal situation that does not exist. Being causal, it is perhaps better defined as a positing a "contrary-to-fact conditional" (Collins, 2001). It is found in common-language expressions such as "If only I had paid off the mortgage before the recession hit, I wouldn't be so deeply in debt," or "If I had spoken up in the committee meeting, I could have killed that amendment." A more elegant definition goes as follows: "Counterfactuals are a species of conditionals, expressed by or equivalent to subjunctive conditions [if it were the case]. . . . Counterfactual reasoning typically involves the entertaining of hypothetical states of affairs: the antecedent is believed or presumed to be false, or contrary-to-the-fact, but the truth is imagined or supposed. Counterfactual reasoning is thus a form of modal reasoning, kindred to reasoning about the way things actually are" (Hajek, 2001: 2872).

Another feature of counterfactual statements is that they specify changes in a cause and an effect that did not occur. All counterfactuals, then, are causal statements (Kahneman and Varey, 1990). Furthermore, they implicitly assume that all other possible causes did not change; that is, they hold the latter *constant* in imagination. This gives counterfactual thinking its formal continuity with the several research methods analyzed in this chapter. To illustrate: to make the experimental and control groups as identical as possible (by randomization or matching, for example), the experimenter creates a situation in which the control group, by not being exposed to the treatment variable, is experiencing a nonevent. The same assumption is made in randomized field experiments in which the control group (or approximations in quasiexperiments) is made *not to experience* the decisive event but to be similar in all other regards. The strategies of controlling contexts in systematic comparative studies—for example, "near cases"—attempt to isolate the causal significance of specified variables by holding other variables constant.

Counterfactual thinking is also conspicuous in theory and model building and in the social sciences. The method of *heuristic assumption* of the constancy of potentially causal conditions has been widely employed in economics in its famous strategy *ceteris paribus*—"other things equal." As we noted (above, pp. 96–98), economists have explicitly assumed, for instance, that for many purposes of analysis, various noneconomic factors are stable, i.e., unvarying and treatable as nonoperating parameters. The postulate of economic rationality—that individuals will behave in ways that maximize their utility—is, formally, a similar simplifying assumption. These strategies are acts of theoretical imagination, and are simplifying counterfactuals designed to hold many classes of potential causal variables constant and to generate elegant analytic models of behavior within that network of counterfactuals.

Similar thinking can be observed in other lines of social research. (1) Many voting studies assume or posit a framework of democratic institutions within which elections take place, and usually do not consider variations in that framework in analyses of turnout and other voting behavior. (2) Most sociological studies of social mobility rest implicitly on the assumption that people in a stratification system are motivated to move upward—to place greater value on being higher in the social hierarchy. Such an assumption is also counterfactual in the sense that it is imagined, not demonstrated, and surely variations in motivation would be revealed if studied empirically. On the other hand, some survey evidence showing people's preferences for higher-status occupations, if they had their choice (Hout and DiPrete, 2006), suggests that it is not an unreasonable supposition. (3) Most small-group experiments, in addition to their explicit manipulation of variables to attain control over variation, rest on implicit assumptions that experimental subjects speak the same language, share certain cultural understandings, know what an experiment is, and are equally motivated to participate in it. These assumptions may, in principle, be manipulated experimentally as well, but most often are implicit and imagined, and therefore counterfactuals.

TRIPWIRES

In my experience, there are two major types of risk that can be destructive to banks. The first is sudden price changes that reduce the value of collateral related to loans. In my time, this often appeared in commercial real estate and in aircraft and ship lending. More recently, the problem has arisen with trading assets when they are used as collateral for interbank funding. All of these are fully financed assets, but their values directly reflect the level of economic activity. The second risk is changes of management or government that affect customers' willingness to pay. In the banking business, these risks should be continuously in mind, even though banking and businesses generally face many other kinds of risk (see pp. 202–4).

One of our directors once came up with an idea she felt was helpful in assessing and dealing with risk. She called it *tripwires*. This referred to the process of identifying (or imagining) sets of events that, if they occurred, would force us to revisit our fundamental view of the risks at hand. Most of these tripwires were suspected economic externalities, but political crises also demanded the same kind of analysis. We came to use the tripwire strategy as a general practice, and it turned out to be very useful in causing us to change the flow of our conventional thinking, risk management, and decision-making.

One major event that would force us to reexamine our beliefs was President Carter's appointment of Paul Volcker as chairman of the Federal Reserve in 1979. The principal context for his appointment was the government's efforts, via Federal Reserve policy, to check the inflation that had been ravaging the economy and demanded serious attention. No one knew whether Volcker would be up to the job, but clearly his appointment highlighted the issue. We did not pay special attention to his appointment at the time, but high interest rates and the resulting drop in economic activity caused profound changes in our bond portfolio, almost destroyed the credit card business, and set the stage for the Latin American debt crisis of the 1980s. In retrospect, I concluded that we should have taken more initiative in analyzing the implications of these developments, even though we could not have avoided their effects.

As we began defining and thinking about trip wires, we made a working list of their sources, including changes in governments, individual ministers, or central bank heads; prices of oil and other key commodities; and the structure of interest rates and current account positions. In accordance with our tripwire logic, we tried to trace out the consequences as best we could. It goes without saying that these exercises greatly improved our decision-making.

As a further formalization of the tripwire logic, we held monthly meetings of our senior team to assess risk. We evolved an informal sequence of discussion points. First, we focused on what was going on, and in the process elucidated various tripwires. Second, we tried to assess our various positions or exposures to events. Finally, given the conclusions of the first two lines of thinking, we turned to which changes we should make in policy and strategy.

On some occasions, we simply became cautious and reduced our exposures for no good reason, as during the transition from Volcker to Alan Greenspan at the Fed. Sometimes we tried to avoid problems, for example, when we liquidated our crossborder exposure to Argentina through equity-for-debt swaps because we perceived that its government was likely not willing to pay its debts. In contrasting examples, we were willing to increase our exposure to Mexico and Brazil in light of what seemed to be positive events (the election of Carlos Salinas and his appointment of Pedro Aspe as secretary of finance in Mexico; and our analysis of voting patterns in local elections in Brazil). We also became very sensitive to how the price of oil impacted various businesses and the importance of current accounts in developing countries.

In our analyses of risk, we stumbled on a counterintuitive strategy that proved useful. That strategy was to *exclude* members of management from discussions of risk in the areas for which they were immediately responsible. The counterintuitive element is that, after all, these were the people who presumably best knew their own area and the risks affecting it. At the same time, we appreciated two other aspects: first, those who are most closely involved in situations often come to develop proprietary feelings about their situations that can lead to rigidities and perhaps myopia; second, and in part a reflection of the first, there is a natural tendency (based on loyalty among colleagues) for those not involved centrally to defer to the person with line responsibility and with the most intimate knowledge—also a potential source of myopia. Initially those excluded sometimes felt threatened and resentful (after all, why should the very experts be kicked out?), but after a time they came to prefer and even love the situation, which took them off the hook and avoided many potential turf struggles.

Though I am convinced of its effectiveness in our case, I do not wish to oversell the effectiveness of tripwire analysis in business. If it is practiced well, it cannot be a simple if-then relationship between two events and situations. To be effective, it requires throwing *several* balls (variables) in the air, and thinking in complex ways about how they might interact with one another. (This is what we refer to as clinical thinking and clinical prediction in chapter 8.) Such a strategy increases both contingency and complexity in the thought process, and makes applying the results in any simple way more difficult. I should add, finally, that even though one imagines all the wires over which one might trip, this is no guarantee that one will not trip anyway, given unseen wires and imperfections in this mode of thinking.

We stuck with the informal label of tripwires, and the practice became a kind of tradition in our management's organizational culture. We did not even think of the term *counterfactual analysis* to describe what we were doing; in fact, most of us didn't think of the world in such a methodologically self-conscious way. However, that is exactly what we were doing (see pp. 282–84 for the methodological exposition). We were identifying events that had not occurred, were likely to occur (that is, contrary to fact), or had occurred, but with consequences of which we were not yet aware. We then engaged in a ranging series of what-if questions to clarify our thinking, to pinpoint the most important considerations, and to come up with the most informed and promising decisions. We were also moving in and out of "other things being equal" kinds of thinking. As noted, we were completely unaware of the methodological analysis of counterfactual thinking that was going on in philosophy (especially the philosophy of science), in political science, in history, and to some degree in the other social sciences. Furthermore, we were unaware of the progress that was being made in understanding what constitutes good counterfactual thinking, and its likely flaws (see pp. 288–89). Had we been familiar with this kind of work and had we thought about it, we certainly would have discovered it to be usable in our own practical efforts to employ this mode of reasoning.

—*John S. Reed*

The fact that instances of counterfactual reasoning are often called imaginary experiments or mental experiments also reveals their essence: to manufacture nonexistent causal instances as a way to control variables and thereby generate conditional predictions. Two final questions remain: What goes into making counterfactual judgments? How good are they?

To address these questions, let us call to mind a discussion by Rossi and Freeman (1993) of what they call shadow controls. By this, they mean the use of assessment methods in evaluation experiments that rely on the judgment and knowledge of experts, program administrators, or participants under conditions "when a highly valid impact assessment is either not possible or not cost-effective" (351). They give the following example:

Suppose we found that a two-month-long vocational program to produce drivers of heavy-duty trucks has enabled 90 percent of its participants (selected from persons without such skills) to qualify for an appropriate driver's license. Such a finding suggests that the program has been quite successful in reaching its goal of imparting vocational skills. We can make this judgment because it seems highly unlikely that so large a proportion of any group of previously unskilled persons who wanted to become truck drivers would be able to qualify for the licenses in a two-month period on their own. In this case the shadow control estimate probably would be based on *generally held knowledge* about motor vehicle licensing. (352, italics added)

The key phrase is "generally held knowledge." What informs this judgment about gaining drivers is "other knowledge," "what is generally known," or "what makes sense" in thinking about people learning to drive trucks. The confidence we have in such counterfactual predictions is a reflection of the confidence we have in that knowledge. Rossi and Freeman suggest the use of experts ("connoisseurs") as a main source of shadow controls because their command of relevant "other knowledge" that might come to bear on the evaluation of experiments is presumably better, and for that reason the quality of their judgments is also likely to be better. More generally, Rossi and Freeman acknowledge that the "general state of knowledge" in relevant fields is highly variable, and experts vary in their command of that knowledge (354); both these factors affect the quality of their assessments. The authors consider such judgments "highly unreliable" and include them "because of the frequency with which they are used, rather than because we advocate using them" (351).

Moving away from the issue of the use of experts, we must note that the phrase "frequency with which [counterfactuals] are used" applies to decisions and decision-makers in general. The use of counterfactuals is inevitable. Every time a decision is contemplated, a decision-maker considers (or should consider) the likely consequences of that decision, as well as the consequences of alternative paths of action. Such estimations are riddled with counterfactuals in the form of "what if," "what might happen," and "what might be." These are the essence of thinking about what one is doing or going to do; such thinking cannot proceed without relying on many counterfactuals. Furthermore, the kind and quality of "other knowledge" that goes into this process is highly variable. It can be based on firmly established principles, analytic models, solid statistical analysis, expert assessments, and informed judgments, but it can also be based on unexamined premises, hunches, prejudices, or blind faith. In practice, the array of "other knowledge" brought to bear on a given decision inevitably includes a mixture of all of these.

Despite the shaky knowledge basis of much counterfactual thinking in practical situations, social scientists and others have developed criteria by which it is possible to assess the quality of different kinds of counterfactual statements about political and historical events. Tetlock (2001) notes some ways in which counterfactual statements can be assessed as sounder or less sound:

- Good counterfactual arguments should have clarity, specifying precisely which variables are hypothesized as causes and effects.
- They should be logically consistent in specifying causes and effects, and avoid pseudocausal formulations such as "if I had a million bucks, I would be green," or "If the match had been struck, it would have lighted."
- They should be theoretically consistent, i.e., consonant with causal knowledge in which we have confidence.

· They should be statistically consistent, i.e., consonant with known statistical regularities that have been established.
· The manipulation of antecedent conditions should apply the "minimal rewrite rule"—that is, to imagine only a limited number of specified condition—and should not lead to wholesale and wildly directed "what if" statements.

Many of these rules of thumb are indirect ways of seeking to control variables in counterfactual formulations by systematic reference to "other knowledge."

CONCLUDING REMARK

In this chapter, we have employed a particular way of thinking, a particular class of statements, and a particular kind of knowledge—conditional explanations and conditional predictions—that constitute a general pattern in scientific investigation in particular and in human cognition in general. Furthermore, such reasoning is universally present as an active ingredient at all phases of decision-making: in assembling considerations for making a decision, in considering alternatives, in executing decisions, and in estimating and evaluating consequences. We have focused on one particular aspect of this knowledge: how is it generated, and what strengths and weaknesses these methods impart to knowledge from the standpoint of its usability. We have ranged all the way from the most formal and methodologically controlled technique—the laboratory experiment—through various approximations of the laboratory method, all the way to reliance on casual hunches and intuitions as the basis for decision-making. We have argued that every kind of conditional thinking is identical to all others in logical structure, even though all do not measure up equally to the norms of scientific investigation. At the same time, each variety of this conditional thinking is discontinuous with all others in that each method carries both strengths and weaknesses with respect to its transferability to practical settings—that is, its usability.

PART II

The Big Picture of Usability

Social Change, Social Problems, and Demands for Knowledge

Why, we might ask, should human history ever have produced a situation in which society might find it necessary, valuable, and desirable that groups of specialists calling themselves social scientists should specialize in the production of knowledge that might be regarded as useful? The answer to that question is not self-evident, and any intelligible answer calls for reflection on many levels.

THE LONG HAUL
THE SOCIAL SCIENCES AS CULTURALLY POSSIBLE AND SOCIALLY NECESSARY

The Broad Cultural Background

At the broadest level, it is essential to underscore that, historically, the social sciences did not simply "happen," but have been the outgrowth of cumulative cultural changes that have revolutionized western civilization in the past few millennia: changes in cosmological views of the world; changes in assumptions about nature, man, and society; changes in notions of causality; and changes in the nature of individual, legal, and social responsibility.

Prior to such developments, the world and its workings were conceived mainly but variously in ways dictated by the religions and superstitions of peoples: as products of fate; as anthropomorphically conceived forces of nature; as whimsical but powerful wishes and actions of deities or a divine God; or as covenants between the divine and the human. These worldviews, some of which survive in evolved form, have differed greatly, but above all they have tended to locate— or diffuse—the notions of causality, individuality, and human responsibility in *extrahuman* sources, thus diminishing or tempering the framing of humanity, social relations, society, and culture as *independent, objectified forces.*

In the evolution and ultimate modernization of the West, however, a number of fundamental cultural changes transformed these kinds of worldviews into a cultural milieu that has permitted and ultimately facilitated the principle idea of the *scientific* study of humans, society, and culture. Without attempting to exhaust or weigh the development of these changes, we mention the following:

· the revitalization of classical Greek thinking in the Middle Ages, especially Aristotelian philosophy, which included natural and quasiscientific ingredients of economics, politics, and psychology, and objective treatments of special social topics such as friendship.

· the establishment and development of the great medieval universities, first as offshoots of the Church and monasteries, but gradually evolving into seats of learning for all varieties of knowledge, many secular.

· the ramifications of the Renaissance and the Protestant Reformation, especially the accentuation of human potential and the importance of human agency.

· developments in philosophy, especially epistemological schools of skepticism and empiricism, and substantive areas of epistemology, moral philosophy, political philosophy, and philosophy of religion.

· revolutions in the physical and biological sciences, which not only furthered the objectification of nature, but also developed theories, laws, and methods that furthered human understanding and mastery of the laws of the universe and the relief of disease and suffering. These scientific revolutions were decisive because they supplied many of the elements of the assumption that human affairs and human society are also objects for scientific investigation and the establishment of scientific laws (see chapter 10).

· the Enlightenment, which moved thinking about human nature and society decisively away from the dominant theological viewpoints it rejected.

· the development of certain secular worldviews, especially the idea of progress, which also accentuated human agency and optimism.

None of these developments alone determined the conception and rise of the social sciences as enterprises in the development of knowledge, but together they set the stage for the views that human affairs were "objective" and subject to study as such, that these affairs were subject to scientific laws, and that these laws could point the way to human betterment. It was in such a fertile intellectual field that the scientific manifestos and projects of the "founding fathers"—figures such as Adam Smith, Auguste Comte, Karl Marx, and Wilhelm Wundt—became culturally possible.

The Broad Structural Background

Standing alongside the broad cultural contours of change—and determined partially by them—has been a social-structural evolution of western societies during the past several hundred years that has both produced the need for systematic knowledge about society and shaped the disciplined modes of inquiry (the social sciences) that have been called upon to produce that knowledge. We review these social changes under two headings: the principal types of change and the emergence of institutional structures.

The Ubiquity of Change   Some still maintain a distinction between modern (technology-based, industrial, urban) societies and traditional (primarily agricultural, small-community) societies. Social scientists themselves have been mainly responsible for this distinction (see chapter 8, pp. 122–23). The evolutionary schemata of nineteenth- and early-twentieth-century evolutionary anthropology contrasted various stages of primitive societies (e.g., savagery, barbarianism) with different stages of civilized society. While challenged by theoretical arguments, by evidence of significant innovation in "traditional" societies, and by sociocultural transformations in the colonial, postcolonial, and recent globalizing eras, the distinction has had a certain sticking power, sometimes accompanied by a tendency to romanticize the simpler societies.

One ingredient of this partially outmoded distinction is that modern societies are characterized by rapid and continuous change and traditional societies are stable, in part because they are characterized by primitive technology, old customs, superstitions, and customary social relations that defy change. That stereotype has proved to be only a partial truth. The march of history reveals the deterioration and collapse of many "primitive" societies, such as the Anasazi culture of the North American Southwest in the late thirteenth century. (Many possible causes have been advanced, the most likely of which is a combination of population growth, exhaustion of resources, and a long and deadly season of drought.) Treatises have been written on the rise and decline of many civilizations, most of them premodern (Toynbee, 1935; Kroeber, 1944). In western history, the received notions of stability and order of medieval civilization have been undermined by research on wars, the changing relations among the social orders, and the impacts of trade, commerce, and urbanization. The half-truth of the myth of stability is that in societies in existence prior to modern Europe, the pace of change was, in general, *comparatively* slow (with exceptions), but this generalization remains a relative, not an absolute one.

The more nearly correct side of the story is the view that in the past several centuries, the pace of change in all facets of society has been qualitatively new, massive, and accelerating. It has affected all facets of society and culture. We indicate its scope by detailing a number of "revolutions" that historians and other scholars have identified and detailed. In all cases, the revolutions' origins and precursors can be traced back centuries earlier, but modern acceleration and impact are indubitable. In listing the following revolutions, we also acknowledge

irregularities and fits and starts. We list them to preview the kinds of consequences they have generated, including massive changes in scale and differentiation in society, failures of integration, tensions, social problems, injustices, group
conflicts, and violations of the natural environment. Derivatively, our purpose in
detailing these consequences is to indicate the explosion in the requirements for
systematic knowledge to deal with these consequences. That, finally, is where the
social sciences enter the scene.

- The agricultural revolution. Originating with new methods of cultivation,
  new crops, changing patterns of ownership and labor, and displacement of
  peasant populations, the march of agricultural productivity has generated
  increases in scale of agricultural enterprises, large-scale farm machinery,
  chemical fertilization and pesticides, agribusiness, the green revolution, a
  long-term decrease of agricultural workers in the labor force, and, by now,
  a globalization of agricultural production.
- The commercial revolution. Originating with the penetration of lesser-
  known regions of the world by those in search of precious metals, and the
  improvement of navigational technology and ocean transport, this revolution generated an expansion of markets, an accumulation of great wealth,
  and new configurations of power among the European nations. It also
  pointed toward the development of commercial enterprises such as the protected colonial company, the limited liability partnership, and the modern
  corporation, as well as banking and financial systems that have in the long
  run become fully internationalized.
- The industrial revolution. Originating in the British textile industry in the
  late eighteenth century (Ashton, 1969), this revolution was marked by the
  application of nonhuman power (water, coal and steam, electricity), the
  invention of machinery, and the gathering of wage laborers into centralized
  manufactories. Over time it has spread from power source to power source,
  product to product, and country to country, culminating in its recent dispersion from the industrialized countries to previously less-developed areas of
  the world and its expression in the multinational corporation (see chapter 8,
  pp. 35–36, 39–40).
- The scientific revolution. This refers especially to dramatic historical
  advances in the natural sciences, in part as a result of autonomous forces
  within science, and in part facilitated by the agricultural, commercial, and
  industrial revolutions, which continuously required new knowledge. The
  interaction among science, technology, and new forms of economic and social
  organization resulted in a number of economic "ages," such as the steamship
  age, the railway age, the chemical age, the electricity age, the aeronautical age,
  the information age, the green revolution, and the space age.

- The service revolution. This refers to the relative expansion of the tertiary sector of economies, especially in developed countries. It is a by-product of the need to coordinate complex societies and is driven by the technical needs of the economy, by larger and more complex systems of government, by the development of the media and advertising, by the rise and consolidation of the professions, by the information revolution, and by the need for ancillary personnel in all these arenas. The growth of services is typically at the expense of agriculture and manufacturing. Systematic psychological and social knowledge is necessary for informed decisions in all sectors, but clearly so in the service sector, which in its essence involves person-to-person and organization-to-organization interaction.
- The urban revolution. In many respects, the movement of populations into concentrated centers has been a by-product of the several revolutions already mentioned. It has involved both the economic push from agricultural sectors by displacement and low wages and the pull of centralized manufacturing and service industries. Some countertendencies have appeared, such as the dispersion of industry, suburbanization and exurbanization, and the possibilities of virtual occupations and organizations, but the movement into populated places still continues.
- The population revolution. The rapid increase of the world's populations has been made possible by the agricultural, commercial, and industrial revolutions, as well as the health revolution that has produced improvements in public health (e.g., sanitation, vaccination) and increases in longevity. Two additional facets of the population revolution have been increases in international migration as labor has become more globalized, and increases in diversity and multiculturalism as international migrations generate minority, creole, and diaspora populations.
- The nationalist revolution. Spreading irregularly and varying in form, this has nonetheless resulted in the consolidation of the nation-state as the principal mode of political integration and domination in the contemporary world. The evolution of nationalism also includes the creation and multiplication of nation-states in the postcolonial world. The state persists despite inroads on sovereignty made by globalization (see above, pp. 49–50).
- The democratic revolution, forwarded dramatically by the American Revolutionary War and the French Revolution, spreading irregularly throughout Europe, and including the wave of democratization late in the twentieth century. Diverse forms of democracy have been attempted, and many of these have failed, but the democratic impulse continues alive and strong. Closely associated with the spread of democracy has been the intensification of demands for political participation, social justice, humanitarianism, and, most recently, human rights—all of which, we argue, provide

new bases for generating social problems and placing them on the political agenda.

- The education revolution, referring to the continuous spread of primary, secondary, and postsecondary education in the world. The impulse has been a product of diverse forces, including socialization and control of the lower classes in evolving industrial societies; as an adjunct to cultural aspects of nationalism and "nation-building"; as an instrument to impart skills to labor markets in countries that demand higher levels of skills, especially in the service sectors; and as an instrument of economic and cultural competition. The impulse to expand education has been almost universal.

- The secularization revolution, characterized by the long-term decline in religious beliefs and the cultural-political hegemony of established religious traditions. This revolution has been complicated and qualified by the emergence of new religions and the resurgence of secular religions, quasireligions, and fundamentalism in the twentieth and twenty-first centuries.

- Civil unrest, political revolutions, wars among nations, genocides, and, more recently, terrorism in an unending parade. Taken together, they have added a dimension of political uncertainty and instability to the experiences of all affected nations and populations.

- The organization revolution, involving a proliferation of specialized jobs and occupations and their combination into many formal and informal organizations: armies, business organizations, governmental organizations, quasi-governmental organizations, voluntary associations, and social-movement organizations. The revolution's growth spurs new requirements for ancillary service personnel, technical workers, managers, and coordinating personnel.

- The information revolution. Although it is traceable to the invention of the printing press, the sequential development of available news media, and the gradual spread of literacy, the term *information revolution* itself refers to the dawn of the computer and related information technology such as e-mail and the Web.

- The colonial revolution. Part of the globalization process, this revolution involved (1) colonialism proper, the imperial expansion of the great European powers (and to some extent the United States) associated in large part with economic and political competition; (2) anticolonialism, ever-present wherever colonialism was present but reaching a climax in nationalist independence movements after World War II; (3) postcolonialism, involving state-building efforts of nations emerging from colonial domination, efforts to develop economically, and struggles against continued domination by the great powers of the world.

- The globalization revolution. Again traceable back through centuries of internationalization of trade and economic and political domination

(Wallerstein, 1974), globalization has accelerated through the vast increases in trade and finance and the growth of multinational corporations since World War II. Global capitalism was given further impetus in the 1990s with the decline of Marxism, the collapse of communism in the Soviet Union and its satellites, the end of the Cold War, and the end of any formidable ideological opposition to neoliberalism and the free market (Kurth, 2001). We have traced some of its multiple ramifications and creation of social problems (see above, pp. 48–51, and below, pp. 305–6).

So much for cataloging the changes that have shaped and continue to shape the contemporary world. All continue, some at an accelerating pace. They are, moreover, interrelated. All stand as both causes and effects of one another in evolving sequences of causal interdependency. The onset and development of each, however, is irregular, and as a result the world of change is forever producing leads and lags, accelerations, irregularities, diversions, tensions, resistances, and new unmet needs. From the standpoint of the structure of society, the cumulative effect of the revolutions has been greater *specialization and differentiation* of roles, organizations, and groups from one another on the one hand, and the requirement to find new forms of *coordinating and integrating* them on the other. In one of the last essays produced by Herbert Simon (2001) before his death, he endorsed a major theme in all the social sciences by remarking that the two great historical engines driving us toward productivity in organizations have been the specialization of roles and their coordination. His point can be generalized to society as a whole, and can be said to merge the principles enunciated separately by Adam Smith (on division of labor) (1937 [1776]) and Émile Durkheim (on integration) (1997 [1893]).

The Social Sciences as Reflections of Structural Change   The social-science disciplines have developed since the eighteenth century. Many of them, it can be argued, reflected the broadest contours of the differentiation of the phenomena they were meant to study. The "dismal science" of economics arose in the context of the spread of markets, highlighting the difference between producers and consumers (and distinctions within both of these groups). Early political economy also became an ideological basis for the struggle of the commercial and industrial classes to shake free from the constraints of mercantilism and to find a political place in societies long dominated by aristocratic privilege and hegemony. But, above all, it was the differentiation of the economy as a visible institutional form that both permitted and demanded its study. This observation also suggests why—as economic anthropologists have argued interminably—formal economic assumptions about tastes, institutions, and rationality do not apply well to primitive and traditional societies, in which economic processes are less differentiated and more embedded in nonmarket dynamics of kinship, status, and community (see Malinowski, 1922; Firth, 1971; Dalton, 1971).

Similarly, the rise of political science reflected the differentiation of the nation-state and its institutions, as well as the distinctive political impetus to understanding the politics of democracy created in Europe and America after the great revolutions of the late eighteenth century. A preoccupation with democracy still dominates inquiry in political science. Among the items that appeared on the agenda of that developing field were parliaments and legislatures, the separation of powers, extension of the franchise, political parties, and the rise of political bureaucracies and civil service systems. As with economics, modern political science was born in the time of, and partly as a result of, the differentiation of modern states and political systems.

Sociology expressed the differentiation between polity and society as well as the rapid transformation of various institutions—economic, political, legal, family, and others—in the nineteenth century. As indicated, most of the great sociologists of that century were preoccupied with the transition from traditional to modern societies occasioned by the commercial, industrial, and scientific revolutions. As part of that agenda, sociologists also concentrated on the apparent pathologies of the industrializing world (social disorganization, poverty, crime, anomie, depersonalization, conditions of labor, economic exploitation, and class conflict). The social-reform impulse has been a dominant motif in sociological investigations up to the present.

Anthropology developed in the context of European colonialism and imperialism, which involved economic exploitation, political domination, religious proselytization, and cultural subordination of colonized regions. The process exposed colonies to western culture and exposed westerners to theirs. Anthropologists focused on these societies, and in their early investigations asked how these "savage" or "barbarian" societies fit into the evolution of human society and which forces drove the march toward higher civilization. Early anthropology also developed biological and temperamental theories of race, some of which served to justify western domination. Some have argued that early anthropology was an intellectual handmaiden of colonialism (a recent example is Tilley and Gordon, 2007). At the very least, it provided raw material for an ideology of domination, and perhaps set the stage for a more positive identification with nonwestern cultures as the field subsequently developed.

More Specific Historical Challenges and Preoccupations

Examining the correspondences among economic, political, and social differentiation on the one hand and the rise of the social-science specialties on the other yields only very general connections. Intensification of social-science interest also parallels more specific changes and crises. Among these are the study of the economic causes and social and psychological effects of unemployment in the 1930s; the study of propaganda during World War II; the postwar emergence of studies of "the authoritarian personality," in large part a reaction to fascism in Europe; the rise and consolidation of development studies among economists, political scientists, sociologists, and anthropologists during the surges of antico-lonialism, independence, and nation-building after World War II; preoccupation with youth, generational relations, and counterculture as a response to the tur-bulence of the 1960s; the creation of gender studies as a response to the accelera-tion of feminism in the 1960s and 1970s; the new salience of race relations as a response to urban violence and the civil rights movements in the same decades; the economics of stagflation as a response to the economic conditions generated by the OPEC crisis of 1973 and other economic trends; identity movements and identity politics in response to the more general "cultural turn" in the social sci-ences in the 1980s; the preoccupation with total quality management and other Japanese methods of management in organizational studies during the period of heady economic competition with the Japanese in the 1980s; and the burst of research on terrorism after September 11, 2001.

As often as not, these seasons of crisis also stimulate funding from foun-dations and governments that encourages directions of research in the social sciences. Research on behavior in extreme situations, including disaster, for example, was largely the product of government funding of civil defense studies in the 1960s; external funding helped to stimulate research on many of the his-torical situations reviewed in the preceding paragraph. In addition, the National Research Council (a research and policy arm of the National Academies) is the frequent target of requests for inquiries from Congress and agencies in the executive branch. Some private foundations commission, request, and conduct reviews of knowledge in specific areas of concern. Many of the resulting reports deal with technical topics calling for the expertise of natural scientists (such as global warming), but many rely on social-science expertise. Examples of the lat-ter are the investigations of racial factors in the delivery of healthcare services, the sources and significance of medical errors, drug practices and policies, the effects of free needle distribution on AIDS transmission, the origins of psycho-logical compulsions to gamble, the effects of uncapping the age of retirement on the labor force in higher education, the institutional effectiveness of advanced certification of teachers, and the social and psychological origins of school shootings and related violence.

The combination of economic, political, and social developments, periodic inputs of research funds from governmental and private agencies, and studies by the National Research Council and other bodies together assign priority to and stimulate research in specific areas of the social sciences. Sometimes the call is for research in a general area, for which it is hoped that usable (policy-relevant) knowledge will be forthcoming. In other cases, the foci are more specific with respect to problems and the kinds of knowledge wanted. These forces constitute important demands for social-science knowledge. On their part, social scientists themselves also turn to the designated areas, partly as an expression of their own increased interest in the social conditions in question, partly out of motives of public service, partly to exert influence, and partly in response to increased opportunities for funding (dubbed the "pigs-to-the-trough" syndrome). Cynical humor about these effects appears, to the effect that academic entrepreneurs do what they want to do anyway and call it something else because that something else is being funded. In the 1960s, one heard remarks that social scientists were striking it rich by studying poverty.

By virtue of their involvement in pressing social issues, social scientists have become important voices in that vaguely demarcated subclass of society that specializes in identifying, describing, demonstrating the effects of, bemoaning, and suggesting reforms of social conditions. Other groups that read and interpret social conditions and trends are "intellectuals," media newspersons and commentators, politicians, religious and educational leaders, and spokespersons for social movements. Being drawn into that group, academic and applied social scientists become one of the many voices in the "new priestly classes" of contemporary society. This also means that they become competitors among themselves and with other voices. This circumstance constitutes a further basis for their interest in usability—that is, to appeal to their own expertise as a basis for exerting political influence. Some social scientists believe that they have special insights and special things to say about those issues that perplex societies, and this draws them into the competitive realm as they debate which of the competing varieties of knowledge is the most usable. Whether they wish to or not, they become a motivated political constituency.

SOCIAL CHANGE, NEW CONDITIONS, AND THE PRODUCTION OF SOCIAL PROBLEMS

New Situations, New Environments

The first corollary of change is that the combined effects of the noted revolutions create new ranges of scale and complexity in decision-making. In the world of business, one principle is economies of scale—the larger the enterprise, the more efficient the operation—a principle realized in both agricultural and manufacturing. Several complications accompany this principle, however. First, increased organizational size involves increased differentiation of activities and creates new requirements for their coordination, increased potential for individual alienation and group conflict, a more complex authority system, and perhaps less control over the execution of decisions, to such an extent that expansion alone can create diminished rates of return and inefficiencies. In a word, size and scale assume a more problematic status (see above, pp. 186–87).

By the same token, the environment for business has become more complex as multiorganization systems have evolved and new constituencies have grown historically: competitors, stockholders, consumers, workers and labor unions, insurance companies, and government regulators. One significant shift in the scholarly study of organizations in the late twentieth century has been less focus on internal dynamics and more on the environments and systemic involvements of organizations. As is the case with size, the increasing complexity of a business's environment complicates the decision-making process for those involved.

Similar points can be made with respect to spheres of governmental and professional life. Governmental agencies and bureaucracies have proliferated wherever societies have developed and as the need for coordination and the need to solve social problems have increased, giving the lie to hopes for smaller government as societies become more prosperous and complex. Patterns of accountability to political and organizational superiors and relationships to the constituencies they serve have likewise become more complex. For example, the migration of medical practice into organizational settings such as governments, hospitals, and medical groups has made it more complicated, more bureaucratized, and more complex in governance, with more parties involved in decision-making (see chapter 6, pp. 177–78). Similar arguments could be evoked in the academic world as well, as simpler collegiate forms have evolved into giant bureaucratic universities and systems of universities embedded in still more complex systems of constituencies, requiring more of those in decision-making capacities and making their lives more embattled (Smelser, 2010).

The rise and consolidation of formal organizations in industry resulted historically in the generalization of wage (including salary) labor as the basis for the economic survival and welfare of the family. Among other things, wage labor in organizations removed economic production from and separated the worker from his or her family. The wage package, moreover, often became the sole source of family income and created a new and more encompassing meaning of *unemployment*. Wage labor, furthermore, redefined social class relations in all societies that have industrialized or become dependent on wage-paying organizations; this fundamentally reshaped the array of political constituencies and the patterns of conflict in affected societies. Wage labor itself has undergone many vicissitudes, the latest connected with the evolution of more decentralized, flexible, and network-dominated organizations, as expressed in the terms *reorganization, downsizing, outsourcing, flattening the pyramid,* and *teaming.* This has meant that workers must have a more transferable portfolio of skills and must maintain those skills; it has also brought them interorganizational employability, increased capacity for teamwork, serial rather than continuous links to specific organizations, and, as a result, a new kind of career insecurity (Weinart, 2001).

As a final illustration of the transformations associated with increasing complexity, we point to the precipitation of countless new types of politically significant *groups*. Differentiation has been accompanied by diversification. New occupational roles—agricultural laborers, industrial laborers, businessmen, engineers, and other professionals—create new bases for collective interests. Within medicine, new bases of group interest have emerged; in addition to physicians (in all their specialties), we note the emergence of nurses, paramedics, hospital administrators, and patients (even patients with specific afflictions), as well as patients' relatives and loved ones, all of whom constitute actual or potential interest groups. Changing demographic and life-course patterns have yielded political groups based on age and life stage—youth, parents of young children, retired elderly. International migration generates new and politically significant groups organized around cultural identities and loyalties, as well as indigenous groups opposing migration and migrants. Social movements generate new political forces and constituencies, as well as countermovements (pro-choice versus right to life, McCarthyism versus anti-McCarthyism, environmentalism versus business interests). The consolidation of old and the generation of new political groups are endless and impose a group rather than an individual basis for governing polities; in the process this renders political decision-making more complex and contingent.

The Generation and Flux of Social Problems

So much for examples—which could be proliferated—of new conditions generated by the march of social change. A special, overlapping case of this principle is the continuous generation of social *problems,* which demand attention, create conflict, and demand new knowledge to attack them. Again, we will be illustrative:

- Market failures and business cycles generate and aggravate problems of unemployment and poverty.
- New occupational roles generate new forms of occupational risk and stress.
- The increasingly complex couplings of systems such as nuclear power plants, aircraft transport systems, weapons systems, banking systems, and hospitals have led to a preoccupation with catastrophes stemming from systemic failures of operation and coordination (see chapter 6, pp. 203–4). The side effects of new medications constitute a constant source of risk, despite the widespread use of clinical trials.

Two additional postulates may be enunciated. The first is that new technologies generate new and distinctive forms of deviance, which grow into social problems. Thievery is as old as the history of humankind, but the invention and consolidation of complex forms of bookkeeping made possible sophisticated forms such as embezzlement. The invention of ships and their presence on the high seas created the possibility of piracy. Skyjacking is not possible without the presence of aircraft. Automatic tellers create locations for obtaining and exchanging cash, but also provide new sites for robbery, especially at night. The invention of Social Security numbers, credit cards, and systems of computer storage have made identity theft a more serious and endemic crime. A closely related postulate is that any new rule presents new opportunities to circumvent that rule, sometimes generating new crimes and other problems. New tax codes provide new loopholes and opportunities for evasion. Crackdowns on drunken driving, gang activity, and prostitution in one community often move those activities into adjacent communities. Sometimes technology can be used to fight such social problems. Shoplifting as a form of thievery is the child of the institutionalization of stores as economic units. In the future, shoplifting may well disappear with the development of increasingly sophisticated systems of bar-code identification and other security systems. Technologically based security devices have also reduced rates of automobile theft in the past two decades.

The most recent manifestations of the generation of social problems via social change are found in the process of globalization, a multidimensional phenomenon involving the increasing internationalization of production, finance, organizations, regulation, culture, and the polity. Many of the problems generated by globalization are not entirely new, but have become more salient as a result of these processes. We mention a few from a larger catalogue:

- An increase in the environmental problems of exhaustion, degradation, and pollution, generated by the increasing scale of the exploitation of nature, plus the fact that much international activity that generates these problems is still locally and nationally regulated. An array of environmental movements (promoting, e.g., sustainability) has matched the march of environmental problems and generated political conflicts.
- Changing patterns of income distribution among and within nations that have accompanied economic globalization, the most important facets of which are the continued generation of poverty and the social problems that accompany it.
- The international spread of diseases, largely via the increased international movement of persons.
- International sex tourism, general but concentrated in areas such as Eastern Europe, South Asia, and the Philippines. The ease of international travel for customers who can afford the travel and the sex services has aggravated this problem. Few international mechanisms are available for its regulation, which remains primarily national and local in character.

- Resistance to globalization, taking the form of local movements such as loca-vorism (regional self-sufficiency in food). The revitalization of regional, local, and religious identities and sensitivities—all of which are arrayed, whether correctly or incorrectly, against "globalism"—also creates new forms of political conflict. Especially salient are movements of religious fundamental-ism, concentrated in but not exclusive to less-developed regions of the world.
- An apparent homogenization of culture, especially mass culture, through the international influence of a few western (especially American) mass media firms. This includes the spread of values of materialism, consumer culture, and democracy. Student exchange programs, the offering of stan-dard computer courses by universities, and international travel supplement these effects. The effects are equivocal, however, because of continuous local adaptation to and modification of foreign cultural influences and some reverse flows of culture, such as the export of aboriginal art.
- Closely related to global cultural penetration are new patterns of conflict between "globalized" youth culture, influenced by international flows of music, films, and advertisements on the one hand and traditional local and national cultures on the other.
- Increasing diversity of local populations, fostered especially by international migration, referred to variously as hybridization, creolization, diversification, pluralism, and multiculturalism. New political tensions and conflicts are created, especially in regions and cities that have not previously been targets of immigration.
- Intensification of old and creation of new legal problems, "from international [labor contracts], international marriages, adoption of foreign children, legal protection of tourists, and cross-border consumer rights, to civil, political, and social rights of legal and illegal foreign migrant workers, refugees, and asylum seekers" (Santos, 2001: 6281).
- New problems for nation-states, whose fortunes are increasingly influenced by international economic, political, and cultural forces over which they have less control, but for which their domestic governments are often held accountable (see chapter 1, pp. 49–50).

All these illustrations establish the basic link between social change and the rise of social problems.

HOW SOCIAL SITUATIONS BECOME SOCIAL PROBLEMS

We cannot be content with any implication of the concept that social problems arise in an automatic way from social changes. In the process of emerging, these problems run a course and produce a dynamic of their own. The essentials of this dynamic must be laid out, in part because they raise issues about the role of knowledge in attacking social problems.

The following can be said to be the necessary ingredients of a social problem, if it is to be characterized as such:

· Empirical assertions that a state of affairs exists. One prerequisite for asserting that white-collar crime or child abuse or homelessness or spouse battering is a social problem is that those who claim it is must demonstrate that it exists, and that it must have a sufficiently strong presence to make it problematical. A social problem is thus necessarily based on empirical assertions. Debates among groups over the reality and validity of these assertions are a further ingredient of a social problem. On the one side, partisans claim a situation is a problem because it exists—and is likely spreading—while on the other side, partisans claim that it does not exist or is incidental or trivial, and therefore a nonproblem. (Already we see the relevance of social-science knowledge, in the form of accurate and independent empirical—including statistical—investigation and interpretation of asserted states of affairs.)

· Closely related, empirical assertions that the posited state of affairs has damaging consequences for some group or for society at large. Sometimes these assertions are explicitly advanced (for example, that those who were abused as children become abusers later; that homelessness breeds crime). Sometimes they are advanced in terms of economic or social costs—the costs of crime, apprehension, and incarceration; the costs of pregnancy and birth outside marriage; the costs of welfare dependency. In other cases, such claims of harm are regarded as self-evident or remain implicit.

· Less obvious, the invocation of certain normative or value standards, which give legitimacy to the claim that a state of affairs is a problem. Those who decried the slavery trade in Great Britain and those abolitionists who decried slavery in the United States did so in the name of humanitarian standards. Without such standards, the empirical assertions about the existence and consequences of slavery would have lost their bite. In some cases, social problems become social problems because the legitimizing standards— not social reality—change. Through much of human history, child labor has been deemed to be a positive because of its contribution to the family economy, especially in agricultural settings. Indeed, child abuse in many set-tings has also been considered a virtue ("Spare the rod and spoil the child"). It was only in the nineteenth and twentieth centuries, when new standards of humanitarianism were brought to bear in new social settings, that child labor and child abuse came to be regarded as social problems rather than mere social facts or social virtues. In the past half century, the intensifica-tion of international concern with the standards of democracy and human rights has given higher salience to phenomena not previously considered as problematic—political disenfranchisement, genocide, torture, the economic exploitation of women, and highly specific practices such as female circumcision. In a word, a social problem expresses a *relationship* between an empirical state of affairs and invoked value standards.

- Additional assumptions that something effective can be done to alleviate the problem—passing and enforcing legislation against it, reforming those responsible for it, devoting resources to its cure. Furthermore, if this component of potential improvement is not present, the problem loses much of its problematical status. Consider stress as an example. Is stress or "being stressed out" a social problem? If it is defined as the product of some incidental biological rhythm, or the collective inability of large numbers of people to cope psychologically, it is likely to be regarded as an individual problem or a nonproblem. If, however, it is regarded as the inhumane consequence of stressful occupational roles or harmful organizational practices, then it is more likely to be defined as a social problem because, it is believed, we can attack its presumed causes. As a general rule, people of conservative political persuasion are more likely to define states of affairs as nonproblems about which little or nothing can be done; those of liberal persuasion are quicker to identify social problems and propose social solutions.
- Causal assumptions and assertions. The element of causality enters the concern with social problems at two junctures. The first is in the diagnosis of the problem: what gave rise to or is responsible for the social problem is known, is asserted to be known, or is assumed. This involves causal knowledge or causal assumptions. Second, claims are made about what will cure or ameliorate the problem. These are causal claims as well, and usually take the form of counterfactual statements (see chapter 8, pp. 282–89): if we intervene in a certain way, we may expect certain results; and if we do not intervene, conditions will continue or worsen.
- Political dimensions. A repeated feature of concern with a social problem is the necessity to persuade others that it is serious and that it should be attacked. Those responsible for dealing with social problems (typically political leaders) have to be persuaded that the problem exists, that it is serious, that it violates values and norms that we hold to be sacred or important, that it urgently demands attention, and that attention to will bring amelioration. The agents in this political process are often "moral entrepreneurs" who promote the social definition of a phenomenon as problematic, preferably outrageous. Religious organizations, voluntary organizations, political lobbies, social movement organizations, and blocs of politicians all play a role in this political process.
- Some or all of the foregoing ingredients are often "prepackaged" in group ideologies, which contain general worldviews, complaints about what is both

right and wrong in the world, proposed ways to reform the world, and political strategies and tactics. Ideologies are thus selective and predispose groups to seek out and highlight social problems.

The interplay among all these ingredients determines the identification of social problems, the attention paid to them, and their ultimate fate. Our account contrasts with a more positivistic approach that treats social problems as objective things that appear on the social horizon. It is too much to claim that social problems are made, not born, because part of the determination of social problems is, as we have seen, the appearance of real situations bred by social conditions and social changes. It is, however, important to grasp that social problems also are the results of a social and political "process," above and beyond their status as "products" of objective circumstances. Treating them in this way, moreover, stresses the importance of knowledge claims involved in identifying social problems and in pressing for social reforms.

IMPLICATIONS OF THE FOREGOING FOR THE USABILITY OF KNOWLEDGE

As indicated, this chapter concerns, above all, the broadest consideration of the "demand side" for systematic knowledge in society. The results of the chapter can be summarized in three basic propositions:

1. Knowledge and knowledge approximations are *universal concomitants and requirements* for all decision-making, policy determination, and problem-solving.
2. The appearance of qualitatively new settings for decision-making has increased the need for *systematic, scientifically based knowledge* because the uncertainties and contingencies involved in decision-making are greater.
3. The accumulation of new situations, conditions, and social problems means that knowledge generated in the context of—and relevant to—previous circumstances is continuously being *outmoded,* with new kinds of knowledge required to suit novel contexts.

We conclude this chapter by elaborating on these propositions.

Knowledge, Decision-Making, and Purposeful Action

In the nature of the human condition, some level of cognitive knowledge accompanies all purposeful human action. In most cases, that knowledge is incomplete, consisting of personal experience, hunches, a sense of relevant environmental and situational features, some (often unconscious) sense of purpose, some (also often unconscious) sense of anticipatory and anticipated emotions, and some sense of constraints on one's actions—uncertainties, dangers, barriers, lack of power. It is also true that purposeful action is taken in the context of the actor's larger worldviews, for example, a conviction that larger religious forces are at work, that one should have faith in a deity, or that one is an agent in the world. These general principles apply comparatively and historically.

The Evolving Contemporary Situation

The changes wrought by revolutions and trends in modern history have not altered the general principles of decision-making and purposeful action, but both the *contexts* of that decision-making and the *types of knowledge available* have been revolutionized. The continuing scientific and technological revolutions have meant that much of the requisite knowledge for decision-making is often beyond the expertise of those who decide, who must rely on others for that knowledge and advice based on it. The organizational revolution has meant that decisions are made in more specialized contexts and must take account of more and different kinds of actors. The environments of organizations have also become more tenuous with the appearance of other significant organizations and new constituencies. The proliferation of politically significant groups has rendered the life of political and civil authorities more complex, both in maintaining their own authority and in dealing with the myriad political issues before them. The globalization revolution assures that many forces lie beyond the traditionally understood environments of actors and organizations. Social problems multiply, and the politics as well as the effectiveness of attempted solutions grow more complex. The signature features of contemporary life are continuing *specialization* and *complexity,* increased *uncertainty* about the environment in which decisions are made, and, derivatively, a greater degree of unknown *risks.* Among the needs generated by these conditions is the requirement for new knowledge of many sorts—about what has created the issue at hand, which factors to take into account, whose cooperation to secure, how to contend with competitors and enemies, and the consequences of decisions, once made, for all strategies crafted to deal with those consequences in the future.

The Behavioral and Social Sciences and
the Generation of Knowledge

Two further postulates inform our understanding of the relations between knowledge on the one hand and decision-making and problem-solving on the other. The first is that no matter what we say about systematization of knowledge via research and its applications, much of the knowledge available to decision-makers will still be generated from other sources—ad hoc assessments of the immediate environment; personal experience of past successes and failures; general informing assumptions; rules of thumb; hunches; and gut feelings. The second postulate is that decision-making will continue to be based on a combination of types of knowledge, only some of which can be generated by systematic, disciplined, and reliable research; from this we assume that human decision-making will never be a matter of automatic application of valid knowledge—no matter how much that might be hoped for or how many formulae are designed. It will always incomplete and imperfect.

That being said, it is also true that one of the many revolutionary changes of modern history has been the development of the social sciences—those enterprises that are dedicated in large part to generating scientifically reliable and valid knowledge, applicable to many of the arenas in which decision-makers and their organizations are involved. Psychologists specialize in discovering regularities and contingencies in individual behavior, and the social sciences cover the relevant social situations and environments in which decision-makers and their organizations are implicated. The main disciplines concentrate on economic, political, social, and cultural dimensions. History makes use of all these disciplines—among other sources of knowledge—to reveal, interpret, and understand the past. In addition, these sciences produce much knowledge that is *relevant* to decision-making: how to understand the limitations of one's own decision-making and decisions; how actors and groups join in networks and influence one another; how individual decisions aggregate into more general outcomes; how organizations succeed and fail; and how conflicts develop, unfold, remain endemic, or are resolved. Social scientists try to isolate causes, systems of causal relations, feedbacks, and interrelationships. As we will argue in chapter 10, much of the work of social scientists has been driven by their concern with the very conditions and problems that the contemporary world has generated. The resulting knowledge is the "supply side" of the knowledge-decision-action relationship. However, as we will also demonstrate, social scientists have been preoccupied with things other than applying knowledge. As a result, much of the knowledge they produce is neither relevant nor applicable. This circumstance produces the irregularity of fit between much knowledge produced and the requirements of those implicated in decision-making worlds.

Outmoding and Catch-Up

We conclude this chapter by describing a constant dynamic between knowledge produced and knowledge required, a dynamic that produces simultaneously (1) the need for new knowledge generated by the appearance of new social conditions and new social problems; and (2) the selective but continuous outmoding of existing social-science knowledge. We demonstrate by a few examples:

· By the mid-twentieth century, a body of knowledge about labor and labor-management relations was generated by economists, sociologists, industrial psychologists, students of management, and historians. Much of this knowledge assumed the presence of labor unions, the dominance of business unionism as a major form of interaction, the importance of strikes, the effect of unions on wages and productivity, and the legal and contractual aspects of labor-management practices such as mediation and arbitration. Much relevant knowledge was generated. In the past several decades, a number of decisive institutional changes have transpired: expansion of service occupations, only some of which are organized along traditional industrial-union lines, and some of which are not organized at all; increases in female labor-force participation and in immigrant labor; decline of union-member numbers as well as the decline of the economic and political power of unions; the decline of the strike as a weapon; new patterns of relations between management and labor resulting from the penetration of multinational corporations into other countries; outsourcing and downsizing; and the dispersion of labor through the development of virtual corporations (Shostak, 1998). Most of these developments were neither evident nor foreseen in the industrial relations era. Yet whole new lines of social-scientific inquiry and knowledge are required to understand and fashion policies relating to the new and different patterns of labor-management relations.

· One subfield of economics, known as location theory, has come from the work of regional economists and economic geographers. It is the study of the optimum market location of firms in different industries and the actual patterns of location that emerge as a result of business decisions. Traditional factors in determining industrial location, such as distance from the supply of raw materials, the location of producers of needed resources, proximity to markets, and the location of available labor, were combined—sometimes in mathematical form—to determine the optimal location of a firm (see Lösch, 1954). Residential location of workers was calculated to be based on a tradeoff between living near work (high housing, low transportation costs) and living far from work (low housing, high transportation costs). The determination of location on the basis of these primarily spatial factors, however, no matter how finely developed and sophisticated, has been rendered inadequate in some respects by changing patterns of commerce and distribution. Among these are the worldwide dispersion of markets through globalization, the tendencies to decentralize firms in the interests of efficiency, the rise of the "virtual firm," e-commerce of all forms (which defy space in fundamental ways), and the increasing possibility of a new pattern of cottage industries wherein workers spend most of their time working at home and maintaining electronic communication with headquarters. These developments appear to have simultaneously redefined space and given firms greater discretion with respect to location. Furthermore, they dictate the need for new knowledge about how to take these changes into account in decisions to locate.

- The appearance and development of the HIV/AIDS epidemic since the 1980s obviously required new biological and medical knowledge about means of transmission, the deterioration of the immune system, and the discovery of means to counter the effects of the virus. In addition, new psychological and social knowledge is evidently required to understand, treat, and perhaps someday cure the disease. This includes better knowledge of the social relationships and networks involved in both homosexual and heterosexual contacts; knowledge of the dynamics of needle using and needle sharing in the world of drugs; understanding effective means to minimize risk; understanding public attitudes toward victims of HIV/AIDS; and comparative-historical knowledge about similar patterns of stigmatization of those thought to be polluted. Existing knowledge does not provide adequate answers.
- In an earlier era, dispersion of families in work roles and through increased migration was thought to constitute a threat to, if not the demise of, extended kinship in modern societies (Ogburn and Nimkoff, 1955). Studies by social scientists, however, took the edge off these gloomy predictions by pointing out that changes in transportation and communication (plane travel, the telephone, efficient ways to transfer money) operated to counter these geographical tendencies and permit new, albeit different, forms of relationships among extended kin, despite their geographical dispersion (see chapter 1, pp. 39–40). More recently, radical changes in communication, especially e-mail, the cellular phone, and text messaging, have arrived on the scene. These have implications for more frequent but more superficial contact among intimates, new patterns of cliquing among the young, new ways to assert and achieve status, and more secretive gossiping and teenage scapegoating, to say nothing about new possibilities for psychological dependency on the gadgetry among those so inclined (see chapter 1, p. 43). We do not have adequate knowledge about the psychological and social dimensions of these new technologies, and new knowledge is required.
- Terrorism is not new in the world, as historians of the phenomenon have reminded us (Laqueur, 1977). However, its internationalization since the 1960s has created a political situation that commands the attention of many nations, if not the entire world. International terrorism is a form of war, but the understanding and rules of the game of traditional wars between armies and nations do not apply. Nor do the principles involved in understanding crime, political protest, or even guerrilla warfare. International terrorism is a mix of these, but not any single one of them. As such, this phenomenon has generated the need for new knowledge regarding recruitment, the role of extremist ideologies, the maintenance of secrecy, the possible use of weapons of mass destruction, the psychology and politics of mass fear, and the multiplicity of psychological, social, and political reactions to terrorist attacks. Some of this knowledge is beginning to appear, but it is far from adequate

and certainly has not informed the decision-making of those responsible for dealing with terrorism, who have tended to rely on technological solutions and ad hoc political responses (Smelser, 2007).

· In the previous section, we observed that the appearance of any social problem—or any situation argued to be a social problem—involves a number of claims of empirical evidence and causation, relating to how and where the problem came about, who is responsible for it, what might be done about it, and what the effects of reform efforts might be. Both advocates and opponents of reform advance conflicting empirical claims, and, in so doing, "invent" their own psychological and social theories. It is apparent, moreover, that such knowledge claims touch on and overlap with social-science studies of conflict, social movements, and social change. Social scientists can contribute by studying the formation and attempted solutions of social problems, estimating their extent and salience, and identifying and establishing their imputed causal relations, thus playing the roles of more nearly neutral arbiters of these empirical claims. Yet this process, too, involves continuing research and the production of new knowledge.

This interplay among social conditions, social change, social problems, and social knowledge has been a recurring topic in this volume. In concluding this discussion, we may venture two general observations.

1. One characteristic of the social sciences is that they are forever catching up to social changes in the world. New situations require new knowledge and new ways of bringing that knowledge to bear.

2. Early and periodically in the development of the social sciences, it was assumed and argued that they could establish general "laws" of psychology (e.g., learning), economics (the law of supply and demand), politics (the law of oligarchy), and society (social evolution) that were analogous to the laws of the natural and life sciences (see chapter 10). The history of investigation in these fields has revealed the naïveté of these expectations, and has led to more modest views. It can still be claimed that some processes, mechanisms, and patterns of behavior and social organization are general in their application, but it is also true that new parameters for those generalizations are forever evolving and creating needs to qualify and extend them accordingly. We are thus dealing with sciences that are simultaneously general and situationally specific.

These two observations point directly to the "supply side" of the production of knowledge, and invite inquiry into social sciences themselves, with special emphasis on modes of inquiry, their internal dynamics, and the distinctive kinds of usable and nonusable knowledge they produce.

The Production of Knowledge
in the Social Sciences

In the foregoing chapter, we learned that societies are continuously "demanding" in their search to define their situations, to find their way, to locate answers to specific questions, and to acquire resources to implement decisions. These forces have driven much research and intellectual development in the social sciences. In addition, their several disciplines have had developmental trajectories of their own, and their internal dynamics are important influences on producing knowledge. Salient features of that development include the following:

- the location of these disciplines in the system of higher education
- priorities emanating from national and regional preoccupations
- government intervention and the vicissitudes of academic freedom
- the influence of powerful scholars and intellectuals
- struggles for intellectual and institutional power
- generational transmission of and revolt against approaches and schools of thought

Thus both external and internal influences have shaped the social sciences. They have affected the kinds of knowledge generated and their usability and nonusability.

INTERNAL DYNAMICS OF THE ACADEMY

The Emulation of the Natural Sciences

This impulse has had a decisive influence on the development of the social sciences from the beginning. The precise form of emulation has varied from discipline to discipline, but has manifested itself in the following ways:

- From an *epistemological* point of view, the main assumption has been that psychological and social phenomena are "natural" phenomena and should be regarded as such. The early political economists had the Newtonian model of physics before them (Halévy, 1949). Karl Marx announced that he was studying the "natural laws of capital production" like the physicist who "observes physical phenomena where they occur in their most typical form and most free from disturbing influence" (1949 [1868], xvi–xvii). Auguste Comte, the "father" of sociology, argued for a positive science, and we have mentioned Durkheim's manifesto on behalf of sociological positivism. In that statement he laid out the subject matter of sociology as objective "social facts," situated in nature and resisting distortion, and correspondingly to be "treated as things" [Durkheim, 1958 [1895]: xliii]. This positivistic view pervaded early psychology as well as early American sociology, and, we would argue, it is still the implicit informing logic of most empirical researchers in the social sciences, despite onslaughts against it that we will later mention.
- Many *substantive models* of the person and society have also been imported from the natural sciences: mechanical causal models from physics, as well as biological models based on organisms, evolution, and ecology. Both social evolutionary theory and classical functional sociology, for example, appealed to explicit anatomical, physiological, and evolutionary analogues (see Radcliffe-Brown, 1952).
- As mentioned, the early preoccupation with economic laws, psychological laws, and laws of society were all modeled on some perceived version of *natural laws* thought to hold in the physical and biological worlds.
- The *logic of discovery,* the *displacement* of prior knowledge, and the systematic *accumulation* of new knowledge have also been envisioned by practitioners and proponents of the social sciences, though this stress has attenuated over time.
- The social sciences have consistently emulated the scientific *methodology* of the physical and life sciences. The most notable instance is the widespread and continuing use of the laboratory experiment in academic psychology and its more limited use in small-group psychology, economics, and political science. Where experimentation has not been possible for ethical or practical reasons, many approximations of it have been fashioned. We reviewed the status of these—and their usability—in chapter 8.
- Most models of applied social science have followed utilitarian ("social engineering") or medical models ("social cure") in applying findings of social-science knowledge to the solution of social problems.
- From time to time, visions of the *unity of science* have appeared in the social sciences, visions that are also emulative of the natural and life sciences. These have been called unified science, systems theory, and general

theory (Boulding, 1961; Buckley, 1967; Parsons and Shils, 1951). These visions have waxed and waned. At the present time, the major integrative impulse is not toward grand theoretical directions, but toward more modest interdisciplinary efforts.

The impulse to emulate the vision, models, and methods of the "hard sciences" has spilled over into status systems among and within the social sciences. Some experimental psychologists and economists regard their respective disciplines as worthier than the "softer" ones because they are more scientific from the standpoint of using mathematical models, quantitative methods, and rigorous empirical design. Within economics, econometrics makes similar claims to scientific status, and within psychology, experimental psychologists do the same. Within sociology, some demographers and other quantitatively oriented sociologists hold similar attitudes. In political science, the rise of the behavioral approach and later the rational choice approach can be read in part as efforts to make the field more scientific. The same impulse is not as strong in anthropology and history, neither of which has been committed to formal scientific models and methods to the same degree. In the 1990s, however, when anthropology split into two departments at Stanford University, one called itself scientific anthropology and the other cultural anthropology, thus invoking the science-nonscience split.

The principle of status differentiation can also be observed in the membership of the National Academy of Sciences, one of the country's principal honorific societies. Established in 1863, the academy originally limited itself to mathematics, the natural sciences, and the life sciences. Anthropology, psychology, economics, and the social and political sciences were latecomers and were opposed for membership by some on grounds that they were not really scientific. Neither history nor philosophy is represented as a membership category. The election of members in the social sciences has been skewed toward those branches of fields that are perceived as more scientific—e.g., econometrics in economics; physiological and experimental fields in psychology; physical anthropology, biological anthropology, and archaeology in anthropology; and demography in sociology. The same skewing is found in the funding patterns of the National Science Foundation, where scientific canons are given high priority and support of social-science research has been more equivocal and controversial. Within the social sciences, some of the official mainline journals have been criticized from time to time for skewing their acceptance of articles according to models of scientific respectability, thereby discriminating against other lines of theory and methods regarded as less scientific.

The hegemony of scientific models and methods in the social sciences must be qualified by noting other theoretical and ideological developments. Their histories have included arguments that the models derived from the natural sciences are inappropriate for the "human sciences," and, correspondingly, alternative approaches and methods have appeared. We mention the following:

· The development of alternative models and methods in personality psychological, some parts of social psychology, and clinical and humanistic psychology, where the more formal models and methods of laboratory psychology have been criticized and to a certain degree abandoned.
· Early institutional economics, associated with the names of Thorstein Veblen (1921) and John R. Commons (1934). This approach involved not only an alternative theoretical view of economics, but also polemic against mainstream formal economic theory. Economic anthropology, and to a lesser extent economic sociology, has been built in part on negative polemics against formal economic assumptions and models.
· Historicism as a school. This first developed in Europe in part as a critique of positive science models and involved the conceptualization of social reality as historically unique mentalities and cultural configurations. Weber's methodology (1949), including his conceptualization of the "ideal type," produced a compromise between these two visions.
· Cultural relativism, which developed in anthropology in midcentury. Advocates argued that the outlooks of different cultures should be studied and respected on their own terms, and not assessed in the ethnocentric framework of western society and morals. As such, it constituted an argument against scientific generalizing and scientific universals.
· Marxist thinking and its cousins. These have challenged the view of the behavioral and social sciences as objective, neutral enterprises. Neo-Marxism, critical theory, and radical social science (a short-lived movement in the 1960s and 1970s) all debunked scientific objectivity as a form of false consciousness on the part of social scientists. According to the argument, these sciences are regarded as intellectual apologies for the dominant economic and political forces in society.
· Several lines of phenomenological thought—including symbolic interactionism and ethnomethodology—have argued that people's behavior ought to be studied in the context of distinctive meanings and definitions of their situations. While empirically based and not advertised as antiscientific, these approaches nevertheless stress the uniqueness and idiosyncrasy of human behavior, and in so doing take a position against typification and seeking for generalities, both hallmarks of positive science.
· Postmodernism and deconstructivism. These movements of the late twentieth century were in large part based on a radical epistemological relativism. They have been openly critical of all positive scientists, including natural

scientists, who fail to appreciate psychological, social, and even physical realities as socially constructed.

Later in the chapter, we will argue that distinctive orientations, approaches, and innovations rise and fall in the social sciences, but they never go away entirely and remain as reference points and bases of criticism and reformulation, revived in different forms at different times. This has also been the case for antiscientific critiques. This persistence has yielded great complexity in the social sciences. As often as not, antiscientific spokespersons continue to represent themselves as social scientists and hold memberships in their professional societies. In that sense, the social sciences can be regarded as accumulating, but not discarding, fields of inquiry, in partial contrast to the natural and life sciences, which come closer to the model of discarding that which has been scientifically discredited.

What does this line of argument imply for the production of usable knowledge in the social sciences? We have advanced a complex and qualified argument about the orderly historical evolution of these sciences *as sciences*. Despite our tentativeness, we still argue that, as a whole, those who engage in ongoing research still regard themselves as scientists, and still regard the theoretical and methodological criteria of science as important in guiding their choice of research topics and their execution of that research. This is to say, the particular image they have of themselves as scientists is important in guiding what they do. They tend to regard the worth and excellence of their work according to the canons of the scientific method as they interpret it. Furthermore, those who evaluate their work and extend prestige, advancement, and professional success do so in accord with the criteria of scientific rigor and scientific creativity.

All this means that the criteria of science are important—perhaps the most important—standards to which social scientists orient themselves in their professional lives. Moreover, these criteria *crosscut* the criteria of usability and applicability. By and large, knowledge that is scientifically sound is more usable than that which is scientifically weak. But sometimes knowledge that is scientifically excellent is directed toward problems and issues that are of little interest to people in practical and decision-making roles. Furthermore, as we have seen, the scientific impulse often involves the imposition of highly controlled conditions designed to isolate the causal significance of one factor or another (see chapter 8). These controls, imposed as a condition for achieving scientific reliability and validity, are not present in the less controlled environments of practical people making practical decisions, sometimes under pressing or urgent conditions. Scientists committed to scientific values, norms, and procedures may also have the criterion of usability in mind, but sometimes they do not. In a word, knowledge that is good from the standpoint of scientific standards may or may not be good from the standpoint of its usability, precisely because it is carried out by procedures and methods that may not apply outside the research setting.

As for those behavioral and social scientists who operate from alternative, nonscientific or antiscientific perspectives and methods, their work is less likely to be usable—simply because those who follow these alternatives are more likely to be indifferent or hostile to the models of science advocated and employed by their colleagues, and sometimes indifferent or hostile to the requisites of usability as part of their worldview.

Fixity and Change in Academic Departments

Early in the chapter, we outlined the broad historical context for the development of the major social-science disciplines. Once crystallized, these disciplines developed their own histories. One of the most decisive themes was their entry into university systems. One by one, and irregularly, the social sciences moved from their expression by influential figures and informal groups and associations into universities as faculties and departments. In Europe, this meant continued links with and subordination to faculties of law, history, and philosophy—fields already well established. On the American scene, the various social sciences entered the university scene as academic departments, already institutionalized as the dominant form. Economics, psychology, and anthropology led the way, political science and sociology entering later. On both continents, each fledgling science faced a struggle to establish its legitimacy, and most frequently this struggle involve an effort to demonstrate the "scientific" character of its work. Durkheim's (1958 [1895]) emphasis on sociology as a positive science, as well as his fierce polemics against economics and psychology, can be understood in this light. American sociology's early claim (largely through the Chicago school) was that it was simultaneously a science and an instrument of social reform; as part of its campaign, its spokesmen developed polemics against economics and psychology, as well as Karl Marx and other radical spokesmen and "utopian" social workers whose reform efforts were not scientifically based.

Once the social sciences settled into the university system, a different dynamic began. As departments, especially new ones, they were constantly in competition with the established natural and life sciences and humanities for institutional recognition, academic status, annual departmental budgets, and the resources necessary for growth. These struggles evoked the need to emphasize the distinctiveness and worth of their disciplines. Such struggles continue to the present. Another line of institutionalization was that, as departments, they acquired a certain institutional inertia and resistance to organizational change. As a general rule, academic departments change slowly, despite the creation of new departments (astrophysics, biophysics, molecular biology) and despite the gradual and partial weakening or demise of others (rhetoric, geography). With respect to the social sciences, the conservative principle is very strong. Most universities' social-science departments have the same names that they did when they entered the scene (anthropology, economics, political science, psychology, and sociology), despite the development of many interdisciplinary programs and research centers.

This *structural* rigidity of the social sciences within universities, however, does not apply to the *intellectual* and *cultural* histories of these disciplines. From those perspectives, the picture is one of flux and change. The most important change is the internal differentiation of each of the fields into dozens of subspecialties, some of which are named after new societal developments and social problems that appear on the larger scene—e.g., fiscal and monetary policy as a subfield of economics and in part a child of the Great Depression and Keynesian economics; development economics; industrial sociology; the sociology of poverty; gender studies; municipal government studies—all responses to increases in the visibility and urgency of society's concerns.

Subdivisions within Fields

Decades ago, Smelser (1969) took a look at sociology, already highly divided into subdivisions—some of which were represented institutionally as "sections" in the American Sociological Association—and identified six categories of subfields:

1. Some correspond to the major explanatory frameworks found in the field as a whole—demography, social psychology, social organization (including groups), institutions, and sociology of culture.
2. Some are subdivisions of the major explanatory categories—within the organization framework, we find formal organizations, voluntary associations, and small groups. As subfields of institutional sociology, we find the sociology of medicine, military sociology, family sociology, and the sociology of religion.
3. Some involve distinctive processes, such as the sociology of deviance, socialization, collective behavior, and the sociology of economic development.
4. Some arise from analytic foci that cut across the major explanatory frameworks above—for example, stratification and political sociology.
5. Some refer to the study of the logic and techniques of conceptualization and empirical research—for example, theory and different kinds of research methods.
6. Some arise because of sociology's focus on pressing social problems in the larger society—for example, the sociology of prostitution, mental illness, poverty, and environmental sociology—or as subdivisions of other subfields, such as the sociology of domestic violence within the sociology of gender.

Similar analyses could be made of the other disciplines, yielding different arrays of subfields because of the different emphases among the disciplines and because of their different histories. But all would yield a large mélange. The general points to be made about these subdivisions are as follows:

- They have accumulated more as a product of the unsystematic logic of history than as a rational plan.
- They arise as a complex *mixture* of internal tendencies of the fields and external influences in the larger society. To remain with the examples above, those fields named after social problems were predominantly responses to emerging and enduring issues facing society; the subdivision of theoretical schools of sociology (functionalism, conflict theory, symbolic interactionism, and cultural sociology) are more (but not completely) the product of internal theoretical and ideological dialogues heightened by forceful polemics by leaders in the field. A specific example of this mixed history lies in the history of the study of collective behavior and social movements. Beginning specifically with the work of Gustav Le Bon (1960 [1896]), who considered these movements to be the product of impulsive and pathological forces in groups, this "irrationalist" school dominated for several decades into the twentieth century. It gave way after World War II to a mix of approaches treating these phenomena as responses to social conditions and as efforts to redefine and change social conditions. For a short period in the 1960s and early 1970s, emphasis shifted to treating movements as adaptive responses to social injustices; later this evolved into the resource mobilization approach, which treated social-movement organizations as more or less rational, purposeful enterprises that succeeded when they could combine resources such as financial support and mass appeal. Most recently, movements have been regarded as efforts and products of collective framing and emotional expression (Jasper, 2004). The dynamics of such changes involved a combination of polemic rejection and modification of past formulations, an unshakeable preoccupation with the question of whether movements are primarily rational or primarily irrational, and responses to changes in the larger society, such as the collective protests of the 1960s and 1970s.

Other Permutations and Combinations

Another dynamic is the exportation and importation of concepts, theories, and frameworks by the various disciplines, thus blurring their boundaries and their distinctiveness from one another. This is labeled academic imperialism or lack of scientific confidence by those who sneer at the process. All disciplines export and are borrowed from, but the flow varies. Economics is a net exporter (mainly of market models, rational choice models, and formal quantitative models), though the development of behavioral economics has involved wholesale borrowing from cognitive psychology. Geography is a net importer (e.g., Marxist geography, political geography, feminist geography, postmodern geography, queer geography). Sociology, anthropology, and political science are intermediate, though political science has had heavy seasons of importing behavioral, functionalist, rational choice, and game-theoretical perspectives.

Closely related to exporting and importing is what Dogan and Pahre (1990) have called hybridization and others have called interdisciplinary studies. Both refer to the proliferation of new subspecialties by the selective fusing of ingredients from different disciplinary sources. Child development is a ready example, including ingredients of psychology, sociology, and biology. Aging and gender studies are other examples, as is behavioral economics. Still another is the study of mass communication. These hybrids sometimes find a place as subspecialties within departments. Sometimes they are established as separate groups, programs, departmental units, or research institutes.

All these dynamics make for greater internal specialization, diffusion, fragmentation, and uncertain identities of disciplines that are still represented structurally in departmental form and advertised as distinct disciplines. The changes also mean that the very idea of disciplines—the systematic pursuit of explanations based on a limited and logically organized set of variables—has become diffused by the multiplication of subfields, theories, frames of reference, and intellectual combinations and recombinations. These developments have led some to proclaim the effective demise of disciplines (Levine, 1995). That claim goes too far, if only because disciplines remain the basis of departmental organization, hiring, professional associations, publishers' lists, categories for grant giving, and nodes of professional identity. The claim does have some validity, however. When, in the 1990s, Smelser and Baltes were generating the architecture for the massive *International Encyclopedia of the Social and Behavioral Sciences* (2001), they were forced immediately to the conclusion that several dozen subcategories were required to divide the vast range of knowledge to be covered. We discovered, however, that the names of the standard disciplines did not properly classify the subject matter. We did identify fifteen disciplines that were either standard ones (psychology, economics, sociology) or had a sufficient representation of the social sciences in them to qualify (law, education, linguistics). We had to go further, however. Several specializations arched over almost all the behavioral and social sciences (its institutions, infrastructure, research ethics, biographies, mathematical and computer sciences, and statistics), and we had to consider these as separate categories. We described still other areas as intersecting fields because they were combinations (e.g., evolutionary sciences, psychiatry, health, religious studies, science and technology studies). And, finally, we included a number of areas under the heading of "applications" (e.g., public policy, urban studies and planning, management studies). We never regarded this complex classification scheme as complete or perfect. We were, however, driven to it by the intellectual dynamics that had rendered the social sciences so complex and had carried them so far away from the disciplinary labels designated in their origins.

ORIENTATIONS OF SOCIAL SCIENTISTS
IN THEIR INSTITUTIONAL SETTINGS

We now trace some further implications of disciplines and departments, with special attention to how research activities are both directed toward and deflected away from the criterion of usability.

Disciplines and departments have become the basis for educating and training, and, as such, the creators of human capital for future scientific work. It is important for career purposes that future professionals receive their training in one of the standard departments. They are the mechanisms for socializing into the profession and imparting disciplinary labels. In addition, departments recruit mainly *in their own fields* and not more generally; economic departments advertise positions for economists, anthropologists for anthropologists, and so on. Seldom do they roam beyond their own disciplinary categories. There have been scattered attempts to establish PhD programs in social science or other interdisciplinary categories, but these have been marginal and short-lived, largely, in our estimation, because they do not produce candidates that fare well in academic markets dominated by disciplinary identities.

For those who become faculty members, moreover, their future careers are determined largely within their departments. Standard practice is that decisions about whom to recruit, advance, and promote originate in *departmental* evaluations and recommendations, even though the availability of positions is authorized by higher administrative decisions. Departmental recommendations are reviewed carefully by deans, ad hoc committees, and provosts, more superficially by presidents and chancellors, and routinely by boards of trustees, but departments almost always initiate them. This establishes the discipline-based departments in a position of critical importance in determining the careers of faculty, and a decisive force in shaping faculty members' motivations.

What are the criteria for recommendations for academic rewards? Universities' academic manuals typically list four: originality and productivity in research or creative activity; excellence in teaching; service to the profession; and service to the community. These criteria are not ranked formally in the manuals, and in preparing recommendations for advancement, department chairs are asked to submit and evaluate evidence on all of them. In practice, however, the two criteria that figure most prominently are (1) excellence in research and publication in the discipline; and (2) recognition, election to office, prizes awarded by professional and honorific societies, and external research grants generated. Writing textbooks and editing journals count, but not as much as "original" research.

Teaching and service are included and discussed, but almost never trump the other two. This culture of rewarding excellence in research and its derivative recognition continues to dominate, despite periodic campaigns inside colleges and universities and their relevant publics to give greater emphasis on teaching and service. The culture is unequivocally dominant in the major research universities. Furthermore, when universities and colleges lower in the academic prestige hierarchy move to advance in that hierarchy, the most common strategy is to seek recognition of their faculty in the research establishment and to pressure their faculty to excel in research.

With respect to the usability of knowledge for organizational decision-making, policy, and social problems, it is certainly noticed and rewarded if the research proves useful—for example, in areas such as regulation, law enforcement, tax policy, crime, and drugs. This, however, is only one of many features of research that are considered. There are differences among social-science disciplines in this regard. At the risk of oversimplification, we note that economists, political scientists, and law school faculties are more engaged in policy issues and are called on more frequently; sociologists are often interested in policy issues (e.g., welfare policies, crime, divorce, violence), but are called on less frequently; and many psychologists actually practice as therapists and secure positions as industrial or social psychologists. Anthropologists are least likely to be involved directly in policy matters, except in certain pockets such as the World Bank. Finally, social scientists in professional schools are drawn into applied work because of the greater involvement of these schools in applied training and research. Yet scholars in professional schools are often granted less prestige in universities because they are less centrally involved in the research missions of the academic disciplines.

At this point, we return explicitly to the topic of status differentiation in the academy, focusing on the criterion of usability itself. At a general level, we might identify two broad cultural themes in universities: (1) The arts-and-sciences culture, tracing to medieval and early modern times, which sees the mission of universities as more or less insulated companies of seekers, discoverers, and teachers of truth. This emphasis is valued in and for itself, and stresses above all scholarly and scientific excellence and creativity. The culture is embedded in the arts-and sciences disciplines and departments. (2) The professional or applied culture has a place in the interests of scholars in the arts and sciences, but is the primary focus of the professional schools, later additions to universities. These are geared toward preparing future professionals—medical and public health personnel, lawyers, engineers, educators, journalists, social workers, and law enforcement officials—for their practices. They are perforce more interested in knowledge that is usable in direct and indirect ways in professional practice.

The relations between the arts-and-science culture and the professional culture are many and complex, but one dimension is competition for status. In the major research universities, the arts-and-sciences complex still, as a general rule, maintains claim to superior status, in the name of traditional values of scientific and scholarly excellence, representation of high culture, and the perpetuation of what is most valuable in cultural life. Professional schools live in the shadow of these claims to some degree, but with variations. Medical, engineering, and law schools claim and maintain high status because of their affiliation with professions with high status, perhaps because of their capacity to generate practitioners believed to be important in contemporary society and perhaps because of their capacity to generate funding and goodwill for their parent universities. Business schools are intermediate with respect to status. Schools in what has been called the health-education-welfare complex, however, typically have lower status in the broader university culture, and are sometimes hounded for being of lesser quality and are put on the defensive. This aspect appears periodically in academic reviews of these schools, and on professional schools' dissertation committees with "outside" arts-and-science faculty members who complain about the academic quality of students and their research.

The status tensions appear within professional schools as well. In their recent histories, many of them have developed doctoral programs and centers of research that are populated by those who have received degrees in arts-and-science disciplines—sociologists in schools of education, for example, or economists and organizational scholars in business schools. Valuable as such appointments are, they have produced status tensions between those activities regarded as more applied/practical and those regarded as more scholarly—for example, between MBA and PhD programs in business schools. These tensions show up in relations between professional schools and arts-and-science departments, with academically oriented faculty in professional schools looking over their shoulders at their corresponding disciplines in the arts-and-science departments, and scholars in arts-and-science disciplines tending to regard their professional-school brethren as lesser beings. We do not wish to make too much of this status dimension, but would point out that it (1) confuses the missions of professional schools and applied programs, and (2) reflects the abiding tension between the visions of "knowledge as elite" and "knowledge as relevant."

A similar tension appears in subdivisions of social science that regard themselves as explicitly applied in character. As an example, we mention that work tradition that includes industrial, work, and organizational psychology (IWO)—all recognized mainly as lines of applied psychology. Silvester (2008) compiled a massive four-volume selection of the most important article-length contributions to these areas that have accumulated since World War II. A review of these volumes reveals that the predominant foci of the field have been on issues of personnel selection, effectiveness of training programs, worker performance, and worker satisfaction. Within these emphases, of course, there is variability in selective emphasis, research methods, and, to a degree, ideological emphasis.

Toward the end of the work, Silvester includes two thoughtful and critical overviews of the IWO enterprise (Herriot and Anderson, 2008; Herriot, Anderson, and Hodgkinson, 2008 [2001]). The brunt of their complaint is the assertion that the dominant emphases of the whole enterprise have been managerial and positivistic, with occasional eruptions of protest on the part of students of human relations and worker alienation. The managerial emphasis means that the major stress in research is on efficiency, productivity, and worker commitment—put crudely, how to understand the conditions of and how to facilitate loyal, productive, and happy workers. The positivistic emphasis means that researchers have attempted to dress their work in appropriate scientific methodology that results, however, in formulaic dedication to methodological correctness and produces studies of tiny practical significance. To quote their strongest words:

> The maturation of personnel psychology as a scientific discipline, whilst reaping the benefits of increasingly robust and sophisticated empirical research, has led to a predominant cultural code of mass epistemological conformity. No other subdivision of the organizational sciences has exhibited [such] a paucity of theoretical perspectives, such a lack of debate over guiding paradigmatic assumptions and such unquestioned conformity to naïve, managerial positivism. And if the discipline fails to stimulate a diversity of theoretical perspectives and epistemological approaches, then it runs the risk of becoming an overheated engine house of remote, blind empiricism (Herriot and Anderson, 2008: 305)

Extending this polemic, Anderson, Herriot, and Hodgkinson (2008 [2001]) created a four-way table of orientations based on the dimensions of scientific rigor and practical relevance (usability). Inquiries strong on both they call *pragmatic* science; those strong on rigor and low on relevance they call *pedantic* science; those low on rigor and high on relevance they call *popularist* science; and those low on both they call *puerile* science. They argue that in the longer run the fields of IWO have split into pedantic and popularist directions, resulting mainly in the production of the puerile.

As if to confirm their diagnoses, an adjacent reproduced article (Cascio, 2008) trumpets the great changes facing industrial and organizational society in the form of globalization, revolutions in information technology, structural changes, virtuality, and flexibility. He argues, however, that scholars' responses to these changes in IWO should be new attention to employee selection, new patterns of training and development, new lines of performance appraisal, new analyses of compensation and incentives, and new emphasis on the idea of a "learning organization"—in our opinion, all old and comfortable expressions of the conventional managerial positivism in new clothing.

The two critical diagnoses cited contain strong, loaded, and polemic words, and themselves can be challenged as oversimplifications. Insofar as they ring true, however, we regard them as reflecting the same fundamental tension that characterizes many professional schools. Scholars in these applied fields of industrial, work, and organizational psychology are pulled in two directions: scientific, by virtue of their location in academic disciplines and universities; and practical, by virtue of the interests of their main clients in the business world, situated in a "real" world of chronic uncertainty. These are the two sets of forces that tug scholars toward both pedantry (nonusability) and populism (oversimplified usability), and make it so difficult to synthesize the two in fully pragmatic directions.

To return to academic departments: within them, the dominant criteria of excellence in research and publication are communicated to and known by faculty. As often as not, moreover, department chairs and senior mentors advise their younger colleagues to advance their careers by publishing in prestigious refereed journals in their own disciplines. Such advice becomes rather stylized, encouraging young scholars to assume a calculative, instrumental, and careerist orientation toward organizing their research. Department chairs, themselves under pressure to fulfill the teaching needs of their departments, discourage younger colleagues from "distractions" such as teaching outside the department and writing journalistic or popular pieces that do not represent "research." Graduate students, especially those entering the job market, come to know this culture, and in many cases wonder about, seek advice from their seniors on, and calculate the best ways to land a good job in academia.

Continuing this line of argument, we comment briefly on two core academic arrangements: the tenure system and peer review. Tenure is a powerful guarantee against the intrusion of external (especially political) forces in the lives of professionals; this is the core of academic freedom. Furthermore, when tenure carries with it a comfortable income, it provides faculty with year-to-year protection from distractions from his or her work occasioned by the need to find other sources of income. This system of supporting professionals in universities and academies has created unprecedented armies of full-time, supported seekers, creators, and imparters of knowledge. From the standpoint of academic careers, however, the tenure system may have a conservative influence. Those in pretenure ranks are well advised to attend to the criteria for promotion ("two books between hard covers" or the equivalent in journal publications), knowing that if they do not, they may face the fateful and ego-shattering consequence of not making the grade. After tenure is granted, the recipient is, in principle, freed from the constant pressures of gaining it. But this is tempered by the fact that those who gain tenure are not only already the brightest, but also the best socialized in the standards for academic success. In addition, their academic role involves them in constant reevaluations and hurdles—the decisive promotion from associate to full professor and perhaps recognition in a "named" chair, as well as orderly advancement, acceleration, or retardation within each rank—all dominated by the same criteria as those involved in the tenure decision. All this perpetuates the dominant values and criteria for career success.

Peer review has long been the main mechanism for career advancement in college, university, and academy settings: review by departmental colleagues, evaluations by peers external to the home institution, reviews of publications in scholarly journals, and, more recently, citation indices and Web-page "hits." Peer review became even more embedded as government agencies and foundations came to support research in the social sciences and decided whether to fund scholars in large part by sending out proposals for review by colleagues.

The logic justifying peer review is that the best way to assure quality in research is to rely on the advice of experts who have achieved high standing as research scholars. In addition, those agencies responsible for granting research support are themselves motivated to do their best (and avoid criticism for bad judgments), so they tend to choose evaluating peers as a safe strategy, relying mainly on the known or reputed status of prospective reviewers. Defensible as these practices might be, they do reproduce the system of evaluation we have described, and run the risk of assuring the continuity of scientific correctness. For this reason and others, the system of peer review has come under attack as a self-serving mechanism for academics. It tends to endure, however, because alternative methods are difficult to devise without falling back on ignorance or opening the door to nonscientific criteria such as friendship networks, institutional parity, or even political correctness.

We conclude this reasoning on the academy and careers by returning to the main topic of this chapter: the production of usable knowledge from the supply side. The continuation and reinforcement of a culture based on brilliance, originality, and soundness of scientific research often *include* attention to its actual and potential usefulness in practice. However, this is only one criterion and certainly not the dominant impulse in the academic establishment. Sometimes evaluation from the standpoint of scientific excellence coincides with the evaluation of usefulness, but sometimes it does not. Furthermore, the academic establishment is like all well-supported establishments in one important respect: it is likely to become and remain conservative in its dominant values and therefore resistant to adaptation, even in the face of external changes.

SECTARIAN TENDENCIES, CONFLICT, AND KNOWLEDGE DYNAMICS

Much of the subject matter of the social sciences has roots that predate their formal establishment and institutionalization. Aristotle's philosophy has an economics, a politics, a moral science, and a psychology. Other roots trace to preoccupations of Judaism and Christianity, with the latter fully institutionalized in the early histories of universities, out of which grew the traditions that yield much of the knowledge we possess about persons, societies, and cultures. Notable aspects of both the religious and philosophical traditions of the West, moreover, are histories of sectarian conflicts, orthodoxy and heterodoxy, and schismatic tendencies, often over fundamental principles. While not wishing to unduly press the religious analogy in the social sciences, we see echoes of these forces in the contemporary world of knowledge. We bring them up because they have relevance to our central preoccupation with usability.

We mentioned that a dominant emphasis in the development of the social sciences is the accumulation of knowledge. This involves the claim that scientific knowledge is cumulative—that through constant experimentation and discovery, science continuously *builds* on its own past, but at the same time *discards* that past as prior knowledge is demonstrated to be erroneous or limited. As a result, the study of the history of science becomes largely a matter of curiosity. That is the classical model of how scientific knowledge develops. Whether or not knowledge accumulates according to that script, even in the natural and life sciences, is a matter of controversy, especially in the era that began with the publication of Thomas Kuhn's *The Structure of Scientific Revolutions* (1962) and extended through the postmodernist assault on science.

Be that as it may, the developmental picture in the social sciences is not one of orderly accumulation of the new and rejection of the old. Rather, it is a story of continuous invention of new or revived theories or perspectives that capture the imagination of a subclass of scientists and occasion seasons of research activity and the consolidation of such activity into an "approach" or "school." At a certain point in this innovative or revival process, however, both theoretical and empirical criticisms of the new line of work appear, and lead to an appreciation of its errors, limitations, and biases. As often as not, scholars are inclined to invent new or revive old frameworks to supersede the presumably vulnerable one. These new developments *also* become approaches or schools of their own, and they too become vulnerable to the same dynamic of invention, elaboration, consolidation, attack, and reformulation.

Another feature of this dynamic is that "older" approaches seldom die altogether. Some do, but more often they persist or go underground for a time, only to reappear in altered form, often with the prefix *neo-* in front of the older name—neo-Keynesianism, neo-Marxism, neofunctionalism—and enjoy a new season. This whole process, repeated hundreds of times in the history of our disciplines, yields an accumulation of sorts in richness and diversity of paradigms, schools, approaches, and subapproaches. But it is not the model of accumulation of successive discoveries and discarding of the past on the basis of the new.

Furthermore, this process produces a further deviation of the social sciences away from the model of more or less coherent and consistent paradigms.

A few examples of sectarianism establish the reality of the process:

- The parade of approaches in economics—classical, neoclassical, Keynesian, Marxist, institutionalism, new institutionalism, supply-side, behavioral— waxes and wanes, but all survive in diverse forms and strengths.
- Classical evolutionary theory in anthropology and sociology has been displaced and partially replaced by diffusionist and functionalist approaches, but threads of evolutionism in modernization theory reappear; there was a subsequent attack on modernization from the quasi-Marxist points of view of dependency theory and world-systems theory; and the dependency and world-systems approaches waned in favor of more inclusive conceptualizations of globalization.
- In psychology, the proliferation of approaches—such as depth psychology (psychoanalysis and its derivatives), gestalt psychology, learning theory, cognitive psychology, and different social psychologies—also wax and wane in influence but do not disappear.
- There has been a vigorous competition in political science among traditional political theory, behavioral political science, institutionalism, and adaptations of the rational choice perspective.

One aspect of these dynamics—and here is where the religious analogy appears—is that social scientists do not typically accept the idea that all approaches might comfortably coexist, side by side and tolerated, as just so many alternative ways of pursuing knowledge. Far from it. Instead, they tend to *identify* themselves with their favored paradigms and to *denigrate* the approaches they regard as *inferior* (the "cult of arrogance"). It is only a small step to endow their own approach with a certain *sacred* quality, and as soon as this step is taken, the stage is set for the periodic holy wars among competing approaches. Sectarianism in the social sciences involves the drift of theoretical and methodological preferences toward the sacred, which believers embrace with fervor (the "cult of defensiveness"). Simultaneously they lash out at other approaches—as critics and opponents of their own—with equal, negative fervor. Social scientists have been criticized for writing too much *to* and *for* one another and not enough for the world; this criticism is true enough, but it has to be supplemented by the observation that they typically write *against* one another as well.

The implications of these dynamics for the usability of knowledge are not positive. Most people seeking knowledge useful for making decisions do not understand what the wars between disciplines, within disciplines, and among paradigms are all about, and if they did, they would likely conclude that academics are wasting their time, and certainly not producing anything like knowledge that might be usable (the result of the "cult of irrelevance"). We stress, of course, that sectarian conflict is only one side of the social sciences, and that scientists in these fields are attentive to many other matters, including the production of usable knowledge. However, the sectarian side is certainly a distraction from that aspect.

RECAPITULATION
LEVELS AND TYPES OF KNOWLEDGE PRODUCED
IN THE SOCIAL SCIENCES

Thus far in this chapter, we have developed a kind of "sociology of knowledge," the cultural and social contexts that condition the production of social-scientific knowledge, some of which press toward the generation of usable knowledge, and others that do not. In this section, we turn to the products that emerge from this complex enterprise: the levels of potentially usable knowledge. As such, this section constitutes a schematic recapitulation of the scores of specific observations we developed in the substantive chapters (1 through 7).

In what follows, we proceed from general to specific levels of knowledge.

Foundational Assumptions

All the activities of social scientists are carried out under the umbrella of cosmological assumptions—what is the nature of the world?—as well as other philosophical and moral assumptions. These constitute selective views of human nature and society, and help identify which issues are important for research, how they are framed, and their larger implications. Social scientists recognize the importance of such assumptions. They have given them different names—"overarching theoretical perspectives" (Farmer, 1992), "heroic assumptions" (Hernes, 1992), "templates" (Feraro, 1992), and "master theory" (Rule, 1992)—but all these terms refer to the same thing.

Here are some examples that have appeared in the history of thought and are still reflected in the social sciences:

· Human nature as marked by some version of original sin (a major theme in the history of Christianity) or as innocent and corruptible by the social environment (Rousseau); optimism or pessimism about human and societal potential derives from where one comes to rest on this dimension.
· Humans as choosing agents, capable of free will or constrained or determined by external circumstances beyond choice.
· Humans as rational or irrational, or some mix of the two.
· Human evolution as a destructive struggle for survival (the interpretation of social Darwinism) or progressive and positive (the emphasis of many early American social scientists).

· Human nature and society are to be treated as natural things (positivism) or as the product of meaning-guided activities (phenomenology, hermeneutics).

Two Italian scholars have made suggestive efforts to classify major master orientations in the different social sciences. D'Agostino (2001) identifies three broad approaches: *naturalism,* or no differences between the social and natural sciences; *interpretivism,* which stresses differences between understanding and causal explanation as a way to distinguish natural from human sciences; and *skepticism,* associated with postmodernism, one side of Marxism, and some strands of feminist thought. With respect to theories of management, Martinelli (2001) identifies four guiding images in their study: manager as a *decision-maker,* which reflects an individualistic approach; second, manager as an *informal, human-relations-oriented leader;* third, manager as a *custodian* and embodiment of institutional values; and fourth, manager as a *mediator* of conflicts. Both categorizations are subject to criticism, but they are apt illustrations of foundational assumptions. Social scientists have devoted much theoretical work to the origins and implications of such orienting assumptions.

Master assumptions also persist as bases for identifying major schools of thought and approaches in the social sciences and for recurring conflicts among social scientists. Such assumptions are not definitively provable or disprovable. They are more like items of faith or, perhaps better, general predispositions that sometimes do and sometimes do not apply in the understanding of human affairs. (That is perhaps a major reason that they persist: they are not once-and-for-all falsifiable.) Nevertheless, they stand as knowledge in that they provide general assumptions about the world, determine which questions one asks and does not ask about the world, and assert how the world goes around.

We cannot argue that these fundamental orientations are directly usable. However, they find their way into the outlooks and working philosophies of decision-makers. Are they optimistic or pessimistic in outlook? Do they regard their environments as orderly or disorderly? Do they trust or distrust others? Are they inclined to submit to or to defy authorities? Do they place faith in "facts" or "intuition" as bases for decisions? Where decision-makers land in relation to these issues goes far in determining their decision-making styles because these are general "theories" about themselves, other people, and their relevant environments. Informing assumptions, then, have to be considered as usable frameworks because they serve as general guides in so many respects.

Favored Causes

Closely related to the idea of orienting assumptions—and sometimes following from them—is the choice of favored causal variables. Examples:

- Geopolitics, which regards the spatial relations of nations and their command of resources as decisive in the determination of international conflict and international politics.
- Biological or genetic determinism, for example, the appeal to innate aggression as the fundamental cause of conflict and war, or the appeal to blood or race as the cause of human differences.
- Economic determinism, associated closely with the Marxist tradition, which treats social relations, conflicts, and historical outcomes as the result of fundamental economic (class) relations among actors in an economic system. Traditional economic theory is not deterministic in this strong sense, but economic variables such as scarcity and economic preference are central to the decisions taken by consumers, producers, and other actors.
- Social integration as the major societal requisite, which underlies many varieties of functionalist theory.
- Conflict as a driving historical force, a key element in Marxism and other social theories.
- In psychology, drive theory (internal forces) or learning theory (external forces) as the primary determinants of individual behavior.
- In anthropology, the insistence on culture as a guiding, if not determining, context for behavior.

These selections are the trademarks of disciplines and subfields within them. They instruct investigators on where to turn to generate models and explanations—which factors to stress; which factors to ignore—and they become the basis for polemic pushing and polemic defense of particular points of view ("It's the economy, stupid!"). In the development of the social sciences, these emphases rise and fall. Consider the following parade of emphases in thinking about race relations over the past one and one-half centuries:

- Biological or biological/temperamental theories of race, which dominated anthropological thinking in the nineteenth century and were mobilized ideologically to defend slavery and to justify subsequent Jim Crow and other debilitating institutions. The mentality survives to this day as a part of racist thinking. As a corollary, biological thinking about race does not encourage thinking about racial inequality as a social problem, because racial differences—and, by extension, the inequality of races—are taken as given in nature and inalterable.
- Thinking of racial differences as a "problem," but mainly a problem generated by attitudes of prejudice and discrimination. This approach informs Allport's classic statement in the mid-twentieth century (1954). If attitudes are taken as the fundamental basis of racial mistreatment and inequality, the solutions to the problem presumably lie at the same level: for example,

changing people's attitudes through education or by racial mixing to create understanding and tolerance through familiarity.

- "Institutional racism" and "systemic racism" have come to supplement but not displace the emphasis on attitudes. These formulations move the problem to the social level. Many kinds of racial inequality—inferior education, differential exposure to violence, diminished access to jobs, and cultural advantages—are in many respects derivatives of residential concentration into ghettos, and not assignable to discrete individual attitudes and decisions (Massey and Denton, 1993). Some racial inequalities involve indirect consequences of policies and practices. We also mentioned the GI Bill for veterans' education after World War II as being simultaneously a socially enlightened policy and an indirect source of discrimination against women and minorities (see chapter 2, p. 60). From the standpoint of attacking problems of racial inequality, conceptions of institutional racism are potentially more radical than those emphasizing attitudes of prejudice and practices of discrimination, because effective solutions have to involve fundamental changes in institutions and social structure.

- Approaching the problem of race as a matter of the social construction of reality. Directed polemically against biological and other innate or essentialist differences among the races, advocates of this approach create definitions of race and derived inequalities as primarily ideological conveniences for subordination. The solutions or directions of change emanating from this position are often not explicit, but, if extracted, imply that changes have to be radical, because the relevant social constructions are rooted in economic, political, and cultural systems, and reforms have to involve fundamental changes in these systems of inequality.

Another example is changes in the conceptualization of unemployment over time, from regarding it primarily as a failure of motivation on the part of the unemployed to treating it as the result of market fluctuations, market failures, frictional factors, and technologically induced displacement. If approached from the former perspective, unemployment is scarcely a social problem because it results from personal failings. The latter perspectives identify it as symptomatic of system failure, and for that reason make it a social problem to be attacked collectively through monetary and fiscal interventions, job retraining programs, unemployment compensation, and other measures.

To summarize: both foundational perspectives and the choice of favored variables in the social sciences are important forms of knowledge because they supply both scientific investigators and decision-makers with their fundamental definitions of the situation—what causes what, what is or is not a social problem demanding attention, and what the important ways to gain leverage in attacking the problem might be. These perspectives are, however, also very general. Social scientists combine these assumptions and selections into more specific models or scenarios that come closer to usability in specific situations.

Analytic Models

A model is a kind of analytic experiment, combining general assumptions and their specifications to yield certain outcomes. A clear example of a model is the classic economic explanation of how equilibrium in a competitive market is generated by the interplay between supply and demand. At different places in this volume, we have described the fundamental characteristics of such models (see chapter 2, pp. 80–82, and chapter 4, pp. 96–98). They hold a multitude of psychological and institutional conditions constant—that is, they assume they do not vary. Given such assumptions, it is possible then to create formal, often mathematical predictions of where the market will come to rest (reach equilibrium) with respect to the price and quantity of a product. These solutions are conditional predictions, however, because in order for equilibrium conditions to exist, all the background assumptions or givens have to be realized.

As we have seen, major advances in economics have occurred when it is noticed or posited that one or more of the parametric assumptions is not met and predicted outcomes do not occur. Accordingly, economists have developed alternative models of behavior based on conditions of incomplete knowledge, uncertainty, risk, and unequal power. Behavioral economists modify the assumption of rationality based on risk aversion, reliance on availability of familiar knowledge, and other heuristics. Even though these modifications are very different from classical principles, the resulting solutions represent models in the formal sense. Models are also applicable at the macrolevel as tools to estimate the impact of government spending, changes in interest rates, and imbalances resulting from international trade and exchange rates for currencies.

Formal, often mathematical models are thus the bread and butter of economics. They are also standard tools in demography, as scholars attempt to assess the impact of changes in fertility, mortality, and migration on population size and structure. The application of rational choice assumptions in political science (for example, in the analysis of legislative voting patterns) also yields a variety of formal models.

Beyond these examples of formal models, more common forms of explanation and prediction in the social sciences rest on guiding assumptions that are often implicit and verbal. For example, one phenomenon addressed by students of formal organizations is organizational inertia (see chapter 6, pp. 219–21). Typical reasons given for this are jurisdictional jealousies and turf protection, avoidance of uncertainty and conflict, ineffective leadership, the power of informal groups to sabotage efforts to change, organizational culture, and hardening of the arteries of organizations over time. Such factors are usually not quantified and their interaction is seldom specified. Nevertheless they constitute a class of variables that constitute a model—or, better, a "model sketch." Needless to say, similar variation along the explicit-implicit dimension can be observed with respect to the explanation of changing bankruptcy rates; the impact of technology on the structure of the labor force; the perpetuation of underdevelopment in the context of dependency theory; the impact of migration on wages and welfare expenditures; the account of political revolutions; the causes of failed states; and the determinants of terrorist activity. The essence of most social-science thinking, we would argue, is the use of incomplete models and model sketches in the search for reliable and valid knowledge.

Models, more specific creations than foundational assumptions and favored causes, come closer to usability in practical situations. Models specify connections among variables, and they organize these connections in causal ways—direct causes, contributing causes, inhibiting causes, precipitating conditions, direct effects, and indirect effects. Decision-makers use these kinds of connections all the time as they assess the origins of situations calling for decisions, the disposition of others interested in their decisions, and the likely consequences of their decisions. Because all models and model sketches necessarily assume that *some* factors are constant—they would not be models if they did not do so—they must always be used with the recognition that they are general guides or tools. If automatically applied, they seldom work because the conditions under which they were formulated are not realized.

Hypotheses, Predictions, Forecasts, and Probability Statements

These kinds of knowledge are even more specific than models. They constitute specifications of particular causal connections that inhere in models. Models may be described as organized systems of hypotheses. A hypothesis proper is an "if-then" statement derived from or consistent with foundational assumptions, favored causes, and models. Its ingredients are four:

1. The specification of a *dependent variable* (outcome or effect) that is expected.
2. The specification an *independent variable* (cause, determinant, factor, or condition).
3. Often, the specification of *intervening variables* that operate "between" independent and dependent, and often specify the mechanism that links the two.
4. Certain *contextual assumptions* (often unstated) about other variables that may be important in influencing the outcome but are assumed not to be operative. To choose another economic example, hypotheses estimating the multiplier effect of government spending often do not take changes in international trade into explicit account, though these are certainly impor-

tant causes if activated. This is the "other things being equal" element again. Thus, models and hypotheses are close cousins; the main difference is that the hypothesis is a statement of more specific causal connections among the many variables contained in a model.

A hypothesis may be assessed in two ways. First, it is an ingredient in organizing a research investigation, for example, in an experiment linking common ethnic membership with cooperative in-group behavior (with trust the intervening variable). A hypothesis constitutes a guiding principle for designing inquiry in that it selects certain variables as important and others as not important. Second, it is a way to report the results of inquiry. An hypothesis, if confirmed, is treated as a finding or discovery, as a full or partial explanation of an outcome, and as an increment to knowledge. Apparently established hypotheses, however, are always subject to challenge and discrediting. The main modes of challenge or refutation are to demonstrate that (1) a third variable is in fact the operative one (for example, social class may account for all the variance in what has been regarded as a racial determinant of unequal medical access); (2) the measures of one or more variables are inadequate; or (3) the overall design of the investigation is flawed. The dynamics of investigating, challenging, reformulating, and retesting are the essence of scientific inquiry—"organized skepticism" was Merton's term for the process.

Hypotheses can also be regarded as a basis for predictions, which take several forms:

Unconditional prediction. This is a statement that a future event or state of affairs is going to transpire, without reference to contingency. Prophecy is the most extreme example: the predicting of the second coming of Christ on a given date, or predicting that aliens will take over the earth at the time of the next sighting of Haley's comet. Other apparently unconditional predictions are that "a recession is on the way," "we will go bankrupt next year," or that "prosperity is just around the corner." The latter are not unequivocal cases, however, because they are based on general or suspected knowledge about the conditions that produce such events, even though these are often not specified, systematized, or even mentioned. Prophecies and quasiprophecies are seldom regarded as reliable knowledge, because they are simplistic and almost always fail to come true. Certainly prophecies are suspect among most social scientists, who are typically cognizant of contingencies. Nevertheless, unconditional conditions must be regarded as a certain *type* of knowledge, because people who prophesy and those who believe prophecies regard them as knowledge and often act on that knowledge.

Conditional prediction. Such statements indicate what might happen in
the future, but only if other things do not change. In structure they are
identical to hypotheses, which are predictionlike statements about causal
connections in a context of nonvariation of other factors. Examples of
conditional predictions are "If you continue your present habits, you are
going to end up in rehab," or "If we can capture 40 percent of the market
for refrigerators, we can expect steady growth of the company for a decade."
Or "If marriage rates, birth rates, and mortality rates continue as they are,
we can expect the world's population growth to reach zero by the year
2050." A conditional prediction is an extension of "other things being
equal" assumptions into the future. Almost all scientific predictions—all
sensible predictions, for that matter—are conditional predictions, because
the flow of events in the world is such that other things do not remain
equal. A posture of tentativeness must thus be assumed in relation to
conditional predictions.

Counterfactual statements abound in conditional predictions. Recall that
counterfactuals are imaginary experiments that suppose or imagine various states of affairs and, on the basis of those suppositions, statements are
made about the occurrence or nonoccurrence of some event. The reason
for the vulnerability of counterfactuals is that all conditions that might
potentially affect an outcome are never known, and many simplifying
assumptions are necessary in order to decide or act. Relying on counterfactuals rather than completely certain causal knowledge often means
to rely on mental shortcuts and manufactured knowledge that facilitate
closure in a decision.

Forecasts. Examples are estimating the gross economic product for the coming quarter, forecasts of the population growth of a state over the next
twenty years, and forecasts of the percentage of different minority groups
in a population at some time in the future. Forecasting is a close cousin
of conditional prediction, though most forecasts are presented without
identifying all the conditions that are taken into account in making that
prediction. For that reason, forecasts are likely to sound like unconditional predictions. Economic planning—the hallmark of socialist and
communist economic systems in the second half of the twentieth century—is a special case of forecasting, in the sense that the most important
variables involved in economic outcomes are supposedly *controlled,* via
the policies and programs of the planners, to assure those outcomes. One
feature of economic plans is that they inevitably fail (usually by falling
short) and have to be continuously rewritten. The reasons for this failure
stem from a rationalistic bias, an assumption that the policies will work as

they are envisioned, that everyone affected will behave as anticipated, and that extraordinary external events will not derail them.

Probabilistic estimates. One form of forecast is not to commit to an absolute prediction—"It will rain tomorrow"—but rather to hedge the prediction: "There is a 40 percent chance of rain tomorrow." Presumably such predictions are based on the examination of a wide number of meteorological factors not revealed in the percentage, but are given a quantitative approximation (40 percent) by making a number of estimates of the probability of stability or change in those factors. In one sense, such forecasts are statistically phony. To say that there is a 50 percent probability of "heads" coming up in a coin toss is to say that if one flips a coin one hundred or one thousand times, the chances are that in that population of events half of the outcomes will be heads, with some probability of random error possible. A weather forecast for rain assigns a probability to a *single* event on a *single* day, an event that is either going to happen or not going to happen, thus deviating from true probability theory. Nevertheless, weather forecasts are important ways to estimate the future, and provide usable guides for hearers who may decide to carry an umbrella if the probability figure is 40 percent, or not carry one if it is less than that.

Some probabilistic statements are so vague as to be unhelpful as practical knowledge. Almost all government officials and scholars of terrorism say that a terrorist attack on the mainland United States over the next X years is going to occur; that is to say, there is a 100 percent probability. Presumably that probability is based on conditional assumptions regarding the motivation and intent of terrorist groups, acknowledgment of the fact that management of the country's borders and entry points is imperfect, and recognition of the inability to identify and track all possible domestic terrorist groups. Yet such a prediction is of limited help in that it says nothing about the precise time, scope, and expected damage from such an attack. Reasons to make the prediction must be found in logics other than expectation of precision—logics such as the psychology of "alarm management" on the part of public officials, bureaucratic self-protection on the part of security officials, and preparation for blame avoidance on the part of politicians.

The production of "facts." In the early 1980s, after the accession of Ronald Reagan to the presidency, his administration launched an initiative to cut federal funding of behavioral and social science research by 75 percent. Among the reasons given for the initiative, principally by presidential assistant David Stockman, was that research carried out by these scientists was trivial and useless (an assertion echoing earlier criticisms in Congress and symbolized by Senator William Proxmire's "Golden Fleece" award for the most inane research in these fields). The first effect, no doubt unanticipated by the administration, of the announcement of intent was to stimulate a torrent of critical editorial reactions against the proposal by the nation's media. The criticism was that these sciences supplied useful *facts,* and that the government relied on such facts on a daily basis. The initiative also stimulated the formation of a lobby for the social sciences—the Consortium of Social Science Associations, or COSSA—that continues to monitor legislation and policies to this day. In the face of opposition, the Reagan administration did manage to achieve some cuts in funding (far short of 75 percent), and over the course of the next few years the previous levels of spending were more or less restored on a gradual basis.

Some political lessons can be learned from this episode, but we emphasize the focus on "useful facts" in the editorial reactions. Their complaints had truth, in that government agencies rely on the results of the census and the Current Population Survey, on unemployment statistics, on different kinds of manpower changes, on changes in the cost of living, on estimates of numbers of people below the poverty line, and on surveys of how young people respond to sex-education programs in the schools. Businessmen are helped by knowing past sales statistics, the age distribution of their purchasers, and data on consumer confidence. Furthermore, knowledge of such facts is useful in that they inform decisions and make them more realistic. It is also true that social scientists are responsible for creating and assembling vast reservoirs of factual information.

The focus on useful facts, however, tells only part of the story. Very little follows directly from the knowledge of facts alone. As we have seen, in the identification of social problems as social and political processes, facts and factual assertions are only a part (see above, pp. 306–09). Furthermore, attempted solutions of social problems, once identified and legitimately established, go beyond knowing and applying "the facts." Facts are only one kind of knowledge provided by the social sciences, and "other knowledge"—assumptions, models, hypotheses, and predictions— has to be combined with factual data if decisions are to be effective.

We should also note the contexts and purposes for which facts are produced. Many data available to social scientists are produced by tracking the flow of transactions recorded by organizations and agencies—the Census Bureau, unemployment agencies, banks, manufacturing firms, welfare offices, and law enforcement agencies. These data are collected mainly in the context of the priorities of those agencies; that is to say, collections are made in the context of an *administrative* logic. This logic, however, does not always match the results desired by a *research* logic. A straightforward example is the absence of religious data in most census reports, which cannot be gathered because of the prohibitive principle of the separation of church and state; that is to say, political and administrative logic forbids these data from becoming facts. Researchers interested in such data are required to resort to other kinds of surveys. Another example is law enforcement agencies' practice of reporting crime rates on the basis of arrest or conviction records—measures administratively available in these agencies and the courts. Criminologists have shown such rates to be underrepresentations of true crime rates and have, in consequence, turned to other sources, such as reports by victims, to yield a rate closer to the true one. The principle is that the gathering of facts directed by administrative logic does not match the facts best suited to carry out research guided by the logic and needs of research led by principles of scientific investigation. This is yet another example of slippage in moving from the administrative arena to the research arena.

MARKETS FOR USABILITY

Throughout this chapter, our major focus has been on knowledge produced by the academy proper—the university and college system, its departments, and its research units. Developments in the last half of the twentieth century have also produced an array of organizations outside the academic system that also directly address themselves to providing usable knowledge.

These organizations have been called knowledge regimes. Some words on these institutions are necessary because the conditions affecting their work are different from those affecting academic institutions.

Contracting for Usability
Think Tanks

The government's search for academic advice goes back to the early twentieth century, and includes Herbert Hoover's appointment of a major commission on recent social trends, Franklin D. Roosevelt's "brain trust," and John F. Kennedy's "the best and the brightest," as well as Barack Obama's heavy recruitment of academics to cabinet and advisory posts. The institution of think tanks began in World War II, in the form of groups of scholars and military personnel as advisors on military and security strategies. The first and perhaps the most famous think tank, the RAND Corporation in Santa Monica, was originally a division of the U.S. Air Force and devoted much of its work to defense research in the Cold War.

The label *think tank* stuck, and was applied even to organizations that predated RAND. From the early postwar years, these organizations proliferated in the United States, encouraged by the country's wealthy foundations and government contract-research opportunities. They provided a direct link between independent research organizations and the United States government—and more recently political parties—seeking knowledge and guidance. In 1997, the *Think Tank Directory* was published (Hellebust, 1997); the number listed was twelve hundred and growing in the United States. They have appeared in European countries, in post-communist Russia, and in China. The World Bank and the International Monetary Fund rely on such organizations, as does the European Union. They vary by size; by legal form; by the areas of research and policies they cover (the environment, economic policy, even ethnic groups); by their organizational form; by the quality of research conducted; and by their degree of neutrality or partisanship. They both rely on and generate social-science knowledge and quasiknowledge.

In the dominant American pattern, think tanks are typically independent—financially, legally, and administratively—from the organizations they serve. Most claim scholarly independence as well, and some maintain it, but this varies. As a rule they have to survive in a competitive market for contracts; thus the picture is not simply one of government initiative in seeking advice, but also one of a host of organizations competing to give it. The atmosphere is often entrepreneurial, especially in Washington, D.C., where many of these organizations are based and compete because of the proximity of their main customers, government agencies. This "jungle" atmosphere has been captured by the unflattering term "Beltway bandits."

Smith (1991) identifies a number of phases in the expansion of think tanks:

- The 1960s, the era of the RAND Corporation, the Brookings Institution, the Urban Institute, the Hudson Institute (focusing on civil defense, nuclear strategy, and the Vietnam War), and the many feeders of policy research into Lyndon Johnson's Great Society and War on Poverty. Among the most interesting of these was the Institute for Policy Studies, a politically liberal institute that reflected the dominance of the Democratic Party during most of that decade.
- The 1970s, in which conservative organizations, notably the Hoover Institution on War, Revolution, and Peace, the American Enterprise Institute, and the Heritage Foundation rose to prominence. These organizations received generous financial support from the corporate sector, linked ideologically with the Republican Party. These proved to be important institutions for the political administration of Ronald Reagan.
- The 1980s, which witnessed continued proliferation across the political spectrum and sharpened partisan divisions. While some think tanks still

maintain a posture of political neutrality (such as the Brookings Institution), others drift toward the status of feeder institutions for organizations that are themselves partisan and seek knowledge selectively to back their positions. At one extreme are the "ink tanks" that take a technical, scientific, and sometimes abstract approach to social and economic problems. Their research, while perhaps policy-relevant, is more neutral and closer to basic research. At the other extreme are the so-called think-and-do tanks, which make direct, pointed, and sometimes partisan recommendations to political parties, political leaders, and government agencies. What they do is a form of "usability," to be sure, but a form that is skewed away from the traditional stance of academics as objective and politically dispassionate.

At both left and right extremes, we observe problems of credibility. The reports of think-and-do tanks experience rejection by association—"We know where that is coming from: from Hoover, or from the Institute for Policy Studies"— which labels, discounts, and discredits their products. This may diminish the potential influence of think tanks, because outputs are immediately politicized and regarded as positive or negative propaganda on controversial policy issues.

It is difficult to assess the ultimate influence of think tanks. Their ideas compete with those from myriad other sources—lobbies, interest groups, "intellectuals" in New York and Washington, influential members of the academy, and the media. Brief note should also be made of a group of other institutions that are sometimes called "think tanks" but often do not welcome that label. These are independent institutes for advanced study such as those at Princeton, Stanford, and Radcliffe. They are knowledge-producing institutions, but the pattern of their work generally conforms to the model of basic research in universities, only some of which is usability-oriented, and then usually incidentally so.

Selling Usability
Management Consulting

Overlapping with think tanks, but more important in their institutional presence, are the great array of individuals and organizations that go under the umbrella term *management consulting*. These operate directly in the market for knowledge. The practice of offering knowledge to firms for a contracted price traces back to the nineteenth century, but management consultation proper was a product of the 1930s, when New Deal antitrust legislation forbade consultative and reorganizational activities by banks, thus opening a niche for independent consultative activities. McKenna (2006) mentions that outside management consultants find a niche because they reduce transaction costs of firms seeking knowledge, and also command a competitive advantage that accrues from being "independent" from firms that contract for their services. Buono (2001) attributes the "exponential explosion" of management consulting at the end of the twentieth century to the following factors: "Complexity and uncertainty in today's fast-paced business world have prompted a growing number of organizations—profit and not-for-profit alike—to seek guidance in their concomitant change efforts. Increased globalization and deregulation, an organizational penchant for reengineering and downsizing, an attempt to emphasize and build on core competencies, the rise of information technology, the convergence of existing technological systems, and a general competition for ideas and talent . . . " (viii).

McKenna identifies the main forms of management consultation as "industry associations, government trade groups, the business press, think tanks, and professional networks" (2006: 15), in addition to "one-man bands" and "boutique operations" (Buono, 2001). Consulting activity has been dominated historically by a few large enterprises—examples are Cresap, McCormick & Paget; Booz Allen Hamilton; McKinsey & Company; and the much-diminished Arthur Andersen. Their activities have been widespread and especially conspicuous in influencing firms on decentralization, merger, downsizing, and quality control. Over time, consultants have been retained by nonprofits such as universities, religious organizations, and cultural organizations, as well as foreign business, governmental, and quasigovernmental organizations. Consulting organizations are influenced by, interact with, and recruit from the nation's business schools.

The decisive characteristic of management consultant firms as generators of usable knowledge is that they operate more or less exclusively in commercial markets. This means that they overlap with some think tanks and contrast with most academic researchers in universities and independent institutes and academies. Their power derives from their competitiveness in the market, and in the continuously generated needs for efficiency, adaptability, and creativity on the part of its clientele. It can be argued that this centrality in the market process is also a limitation. Critics and skeptics argue that management consultants, under heavy pressure, often overadvertise their recommendations in grossly exaggerated terms such as "the best," "sure-fire," "fail-safe," "revolutionary," or "the idea for our time"; that they, like advertisers, drift toward salable images rather than substance; and that they (and their customers) are generators and purveyors of business fads and fashions that catch hold, dominate the scene temporarily, then pall and pass as they are recognized as oversold and fail the test of time (Venard, 2001). The appearance and salience of management fad and fashion are understandable as responses to chronic uncertainty of two kinds—uncertainty about what to do and uncertainty about what will work in an environment rife with risk—that underlies fashion cycles in general (Semadeni, 2001). Extreme critics have assailed consultants as confidence tricksters and witch doctors (Viney, 1992; Mickelthwait and Wooldridge, 1996). A torrent of muckraking literature was stimulated by the Enron-Andersen scandal of 2001. On their side, and perhaps in part to counter such ambivalences, management consultants have, over the decades, launched campaigns to establish their activities as thoroughly professional and explicitly compared themselves to ancient, established professions (McKenna, 2006). Neither the extreme positive nor the extreme negative image is truly descriptive, but just as partisanship may compromise the quality of usable knowledge in the world of think tanks, so the pressures of extreme competition may compromise its quality in the world of management consulting.

Knowledge as Situationally Available
The Use of Experts

We include this heading with some hesitation, because it overlaps with the other headings: many experts come from the academy; think tanks regard themselves as experts and purveyors of expertise, as do management consultant firms. Beyond this overlap, we refer to that large pool of scientists and scholars who are called on from time to time to testify, advise, and evaluate for courts, legislative bodies, federal and state agencies, and sometimes for-profit and not-for-profit organizations. The characteristics of this residual class of knowledge carriers are their heterogeneity, the temporariness and periodicity of their use, the fact that they are typically called upon rather than contracted for, and the fact that their services are typically gratis, though sometimes remunerated.

Because of the heterogeneity of this category and the variability in their use, it is difficult to generalize about the role of experts. As an alternative, we discuss this source of knowledge under a series of questions that reveal the main problematics:

Who are the experts? A simple definition of *experts* has been put forth as "those who are called in when there is something at stake for an individual, a group, or society at large" (Kurz-Milcke and Gigerenzer, 2004: v). They are as numerous as are the reasons for which they are called upon, which underscores their heterogeneity. Conspicuous classes of experts are natural and biological scientists asked to assist in standard-setting (both national and global) and to comment and testify on issues of the greatest import, such as global warming, species survival, and the spread of infectious diseases. Social scientists are among the experts, but are not as widely demanded as natural and life scientists; among the social scientists, economists and lawyers are most in demand, though depending on the interests and activities of the requesting agencies, sociologists, psychologists, geographers, anthropologists, urban planners, and others make their appearance. We noted the role of a separate but overlapping class of experts—evaluation researchers—in chapter 8, under the heading of research methods.

How expert are the experts? In this case as well, the answers are variable. They depend on the scientific state of knowledge of different disciplines and subdisciplines, the consensus on that knowledge on the part of its practitioners, on the translatability of that knowledge into statements and answers to questions posed by those calling on them, and on individual variations in their talent, knowledge, and ability to communicate. Ideally, the agency calling on experts would like to have them score high on all these counts in order both to gain the best knowledge and to affirm their own legitimacy by displaying publicly that they have called on "the best." These preferences are qualified by other considerations, such as how temperate or intemperate the expert is and how potentially embarrassing a given episode of testimony might be for the agency.

How consistent are the experts? The answer is variable, but the most realistic answer is that their advice is inconsistent. Part of this stems from internal differences and disagreements in the fields that the experts represent, with the result that by selection one can easily come up with slanted or inconsistent testimony. The impression of contradictory results is evident even in "scientific" areas such as standard-setting in public health and environmental policy (Rakel, 2004).

Sometimes inconsistency is built into the very process of using experts. Court proceedings are adversary by nature, so that prosecution and defense can be expected to call upon expert witnesses who will provide the most compelling case for their arguments and their clients. It is a truism, moreover, that an "expert" for either side of any argument can be found. In fact, there have evolved subclasses of experts on subjects such as the effectiveness of medications, sanity and insanity, family relations, and other areas. These may turn into a class of almost professional testifiers— a development encouraged by the fact that typically expert witnesses are remunerated for their testimony. The same effects can be observed in other controversial or adversarial settings, such as seeking experts to testify before congressional committees. One offshoot is that experts are frequently called in to challenge or discredit other experts, which reinforces or exaggerates impressions of the inconsistency of experts. It has been noted that the issue of the inconsistency of experts is culturally variable. Most European Union countries' governments rely on "consensual" and "corporate" approaches to advice seeking, in which numbers of experts are called together and asked to come up with a consensus position after debate, thus making advice—or making it appear—more consistent (Metzler, 2004). The American approach resembles the adversarial system in courts and elsewhere, which highlights differences and conflicts.

How neutral are the experts? One of the legitimizing principles of the sciences in the academy is a commitment to scientific norms of dispassion, objectivity, and openness to disconfirming evidence—all subsumed under the heading of neutrality, which implies nonpartisanship. Most scientists believe that they adhere to these norms, and represent themselves publicly as doing so. These are dominant features of all the sciences, even though the integrity of scientists—especially social sciences—has been questioned. Without associating ourselves with either extreme end of this issue, we point out that subfields and subgroups in the sciences have come to constitute what Haas (1992) calls "epistemic communities" that share certain theoretical inclinations and framing assumptions, distinctive notions of causality, and standards of validity. These communities are not only bases for difference and conflict among academics, but also may appear as biases or partisanship in expert testimony. To mention only a single example, a traditional criminologist who focuses on the effectiveness of the system of law and order will testify very differently from a criminologist preoccupied with racial injustice when commenting on police practices, parole systems, and prison conditions.

This tension between objectivity and partisanship constitutes perhaps the most salient vulnerability of the social sciences (and perhaps of science generally) in the larger society. On the one hand, the legitimacy and justification of their influence are based on their professional commitment to the principle of not wanting to influence, i.e., their nonpartisanship; in fact, their power would seem to derive in large part from that stance. Yet in practice most social scientists have or lean toward substantive biases; these vary according to discipline and area of endeavor, but it may be claimed that most tend toward economic liberalism and social egalitarianism (Weiss, 1997). These derive from their epistemic communities and their individual dispositions. They appear or may be seen to appear biased in testimony on controversial issues, and others (particularly politicians and bureaucrats critical of their advice) are quick to perceive or claim this and proclaim that the "neutral" scientists are in fact hiding behind the fig leaf of neutrality but smuggling in their political preferences all the same. Such an argument can be an effective means to discredit. Sometimes whole disciplines or subfields may be tainted with the ideological brush, thus diminishing their public effectiveness.

How welcome are the experts? The short answer to this question is "ambivalently." On the one hand, they are needed for the same reasons that management firms are needed: those who need experts are not in command of knowledge relevant to their decisions and policies. This need intensifies continuously. The world is increasing in complexity, and in its global reference actors come to live in a world of greater uncertainty. Furthermore, the issues of principal-agency and transaction costs make their appearance. Organizations that need knowledge do not have the resources to manufacture or gather it, so they turn to others who spend their lives generating it. Under many circumstances, this knowledge is free or low-cost. An additional positive factor is that agencies, especially public agencies, are constantly engaged in a struggle for legitimacy, and one source of legitimacy is to call on those who are the most expert and thereby rely on the best knowledge. This line of defensiveness also is a motive to select from and distort expert information for organizational and political purposes. All these considerations are the positive side of the ambivalence.

On the negative side lies the potential to be embarrassed by advice that goes counter to the agency's bureaucratic or political agenda. This peril is increased if the agency calls on groups of advisors rather than individual ones. An apt adage is "Form a group and you have a constituency." Experts and groups of experts desire to be listened to faithfully and become irritated if they are not; they do not want to be manipulated; they do not want the values and perspectives of their own epistemic communities to be ignored or bypassed. And if sufficiently alienated in the advising process, there is always the remote threat that the experts might go public with their grievances to media hungry for negative publicity and conflict.

Another source of friction derives from divergences in the "cultures" of askers and givers of expert advice. Inherently, knowledge produced by academics does not interest—and may even irritate—those in policy arenas. Academics and policy-makers (and most military officers and journalists) have different and noncomparable priorities with respect to the status of knowledge. As indicated, the former are typically interested in general explanations arrived at by objective examination of available evidence (Wieviorka, 1995). Many of the explanatory factors they identify, moreover, lie beyond the possibility of political or public intervention. The latter are interested in applied, timely decisions and implementations intended to have desired effects. In consequence, people on both sides of the academy-policy divide often cannot hear each other and become impatient as a result.

Finally, we raise the consideration of social status, not often evoked but nonetheless real. As a general rule, academics, including those who are called upon to give policy advice, are persons with high social status (public opinion polls on occupational prestige consistently reveal this). They are professionals and scientists, and typically associated with high-prestige institutions, mainly universities. Furthermore, many academics reflect this high status in their attitudes toward others. In particular, they regard many of those with whom they deal and depend on—publishers and publishers' representatives, bureaucrats, state officials—as persons of lesser cloth than they. They regard their own students who go into these other lines as in some sense failing or opting out of their preferred calling and status. More generally, surveys reveal significant antibusiness and antipolitical stereotypes on the part of academics.

We assign the main responsibility for these attitudes to academics themselves. While norms of civility require that they keep any attitudes of superiority more or less subdued in dealing with people in government and elsewhere, these attitudes always lurk behind the scenes. On the side of those with whom they deal, negative status-based reactions are also noticeable—envy, resentment, and beliefs that academics are privileged, nonresponsible types who do not understand the real world and have never "met a payroll." All this makes for an unhappy symbiosis: high-status groups that need and rely on lower-status others who sustain, support, nurture, and hopefully give respect to them; and lower-prestige groups who, however, hold the power and resources on which the higher-status groups are dependent.

How influential are the experts? The answer to this final question—"variably so"—is implied by the answers to all the foregoing questions. Efforts to rely on experts have produced success stories and failure stories, with most stories falling somewhere in between. This answer is almost inevitable, given the variable quality of knowledge carried by the experts, the biases and other limitations of experts themselves, the biases and limitations of those receiving advice (as well as the multiple constraints stemming from their organizational and political situations), and the intervention of so many other unanticipated factors in the effort to implement practices and policies.

One point is clear: experts—whether solo, group, or organizations, whether neutral or partisan or formally independent—provide the results of their research and their knowledge to their contractors, and at that moment they lose control over the uses and impact of the knowledge they have created. Their customers can do whatever they want with the knowledge, including ignoring it. Put another way, the biases of the decision-makers, always active, more or less take over at this point.

The point was brought home vividly to Smelser at a moment in the 1980s when he went to Indonesia with a number of other American scholars to provide advice to the Indonesian ministry of education on reforms for that country's system of higher education. We constituted a small, temporary, peripatetic think tank. We did our duty and gave our advice; they listened; and then we left. What we said to them disappeared into the swamps of Indonesian bureaucracy and politics, and it had unknown, but probably negligible, influence in the context of all the other economic, political, and social forces influencing that government.

The National Research Council (NRC), mentioned earlier, is a major research organization that produces, on demand, hundreds of studies on myriad issues and policies. By and large it retains a distance from partisanship, and agencies that request panels and study groups from it are expected to have a hands-off posture on staffing those panels and overseeing their work. The NRC panels operate under the mandate to bring the best and most relevant scientific knowledge to bear on a problem, and to submit recommendations based on that knowledge. Once the report is submitted and approved by the NRC, however, it also leaves its domain and its control; the NRC plays no formal role in promoting or lobbying for its recommendations, even though its high scientific status may make it more difficult *not* to take its reports seriously.

CONCLUDING REMARK

We have presented five existing models for producing potentially useful knowledge. Extracting these from the text, we distill these as follows:

1. The academy. Most knowledge is generated in university-based departments, programs, and research units where, with notable disciplinary and subdisciplinary differences, researchers often do address the issue of the usability of knowledge, sometimes on their own, and sometimes at the invitation of funding agencies that specify areas of priority and thereby provide support. Because these agencies do not typically manage that research after grants are given, the directions taken by the researchers are sometimes not precisely relevant to the questions that the funders had in mind. Moreover, academics in university settings have many other items on their career agendas; we sketched the most important of these.
2. Think tanks. These are more directly oriented toward the usable because they contract with agencies that ask them to produce such knowledge. They generally find their livelihood in the research funding they receive, so they compete in the contracting market. In the case of think-and-do tanks, and in the case of those who are either partisan or vend their services to partisan clients, this tends to skew their production of knowledge away from the objective and toward the interested.
3. Management consulting is closely related to think tanks, but is more purely market- and profit-oriented. These organizations are most explicitly focused

on the usability of their knowledge by corporate and other organizational leaders. Paradoxically, however, pressures to win in the competitive setting in which they exist certainly encourage the presentation of simpler, sellable solutions.

4. Relying periodically but somewhat unsystematically on individual experts and groups of experts is very common. While this practice, like the others, must be regarded as a necessity in an increasingly knowledge-needy world, our summary revealed a range of ambiguities that raises questions about the effectiveness of this method of conveying traffic between the knowledge and policy worlds.

5. The model of the National Research Council is identifiable separately from the other four. It yields reports on commissioned topics, but operates more or less independently in carrying them out. It produces policy alternatives and recommendations, which may or may not be desired by those who commissioned the reports.

Each of the five forms has its strengths and weaknesses. Through academic freedom and other mechanisms, researchers in the academy are protected from intrusions on their research, and, as scientists, operate in different degrees under the scientific norms of objectivity and dispassion; yet academics are distracted, as it were, by their own career considerations, by the preoccupations of their respective academic disciplines *as disciplines,* and by their place within the disciplines. Think tanks, management consultants, and individual experts have the advantage of being more directly oriented toward usability, but many, because of their own or their funders' orientations, produce knowledge that is more likely to be compromised by cultural, partisan, or market interests. This applies less, however, to research organizations that maintain their intellectual and political independence.

The pattern of the National Research Council combines some ingredients of the other four forms. It produces reports mainly, but not always, as efforts commissioned by interested agencies. But these agencies, through traditional prohibitions and implicit understanding, do not control the staffing, agenda, or results of the panels' work. The panels are staffed by people of the highest academic and scientific quality—either chosen from members of the elite National Academies or chosen after scrupulous investigation of nonmembers. Those staffing the panels also operate with the understanding that they should strive for disciplinary and ideological balance. The panels' reports undergo very rigorous peer review by members of the academy and other notables, and are revised, often extensively, before they can be approved. After their reports are delivered, the panels dissolve and thereby lose any significance they might potentially have had as partisans or promoters of their own work.

We do not put forth recommendations for any uniform or favorite structure for the production of usable social science knowledge. The interplay between demand and supply has evolved many different types of knowledge production, all with staying power, and the resultant diversity of activities is probably for the good, and certainly the only result expected from their distinctive patterns of evolution. We would say, however, that the NRC combination of ingredients—relevance, independence, emphasis on excellence, and scrupulous review—stands out as a distinctive model that minimizes some of the frailties of the other four.

Abbeglen, James
   1958   *The Japanese Factory.* Glencoe, IL: Free Press.
Abbott, Andrew D.
   1988   *The System of Professions: An Essay on the Division of Expert Labor.* Chicago: University of Chicago Press.
ABIM Foundation, ACP-ASIM, and European Federation of Internal Medicine
   2002   Medical Profession in the New Millennium: A Physician's Charter. *Annals of Internal Medicine* 136: 243–46.
Ackroyd, Stephen, and Paul Thompson
   1999   *Organizational Misbehaviour.* London: Sage Publications.
Adams, Robert McC., Neil J. Smelser, and Donald J. Treiman, eds.
   1981   *Behavioral and Social Science Research: A National Resource.* Washington, DC: National Academy Press.
Adelman, Irma
   2001   Fallacies in Development Theory and Their Implications for Policy. In *Frontiers of Development Economics: The Future in Perspective,* eds. Gerald M. Meier and Joseph E. Stiglitz. Washington, DC, and New York: World Bank and Oxford University Press, 103–34.
Adorno, Theodor W., R. Nevitt Sanford, Else Frankel-Brunswik, and Daniel J. Levinson
   1950   *The Authoritarian Personality.* New York: Harper.
Aghion, Philippe
   2006   On Institutions and Growth. In *Institutions, Development, and Economic Growth,* eds. Theo S. Eicher and Cecilia Garcia-Penalosa. Cambridge, MA: MIT Press, 3–31.
Agor, Weston H.
   1986   *The Logic of Intuitive Decision Making: A Research-Based Approach for Top Management.* New York: Quorum Books.

Akerlof, George A.

  1970   The Market for "Lemons": Quality Uncertainty and the Market Mechanism. *Quarterly Journal of Economics* 84: 488–500.

Akin, William E.

  1977   *Technocracy and the American Dream: The Technocratic Movement, 1900–1941.* Berkeley: University of California Press.

Albert, S., and D. A. Whetten

  1985   Organizational Identity. In *Research in Organizational Behavior*, eds. L. L. Cummings and B. M. Staw. Greenwich, CT: JAI Press. Vol. 7: 263–95.

Albrecht, Simon

  2006   The Direct and Indirect Influence of Politics on Organizational Support, Trust and Commitment. In *Handbook of Organizational Politics*, eds. Eran Vigoda-Gadot and Amos Drory. Cheltenham, UK: Edward Elgar, 107–21.

Albrecht, T. L., and M. B. Adelman

  1987   *Communicating Social Support.* Newbury Park, CA: Sage Publications.

Aldrich, Howard E.

  2005   Entrepreneurship. In *The Handbook of Economic Sociology*, 2nd ed., eds. Neil J. Smelser and Richard Swedberg. Princeton: Princeton University Press; New York: Russell Sage Foundation, 451–77

Aldrich, Howard E., and R. Waldinger

  1990   Ethnicity and Entrepreneurship. *Annual Review of Sociology* 16: 111–35.

Alesina, Alberto, and Roberto Perotti

  1996   Income Distribution, Political Instability, and Investment. *European Economic Review* 40: 1203–28.

Alexander, Jeffrey C., Ron Eyerman, Bernhard Giesen, Neil J. Smelser, et al.

  2004   *Cultural Trauma and Collective Identity.* Berkeley: University of California Press.

Alexander, Jeffrey C., Bernhard Giesen, Richard Münch, and Neil J. Smelser, eds.

  1987   *The Micro-Macro Link.* Berkeley: University of California Press.

Allison, Graham, and Philip Zelikow

  1999   *Essence of Decision: Explaining the Cuban Missile Crisis*, 2nd ed. New York: Longman.

Allport, Gordon W.

  1954   *The Nature of Prejudice.* Cambridge, MA: Addison-Wesley.

Allport, Gordon W., and Leo Postman

  1947   *The Psychology of Rumor.* New York: H. Holt and Co.

Almond, Gabriel A., and James S. Coleman, eds.

  1960   *The Politics of the Developing Areas.* Princeton: Princeton University Press.

Amabile, T. M.

  1988   A Model of Creativity and Innovation in Organizations. *Research in Organizational Behavior* 10: 123–67.

Amsel, Abram

  1989   *Behaviorism, Neobehaviorism, and Cognitivism in Learning Theory: Historical and Contemporary Perspectives.* Hillsdale, NJ: Lawrence Erlbaum.

Anderson, A. K., and E. A. Phelps
   2001   Lesions on Human Amygdala Impair Enhanced Perception of Emotionally Salient Events. *Nature* 411: 305–09.
Anderson, Neil, Peter Herriot, and Gerard P. Hodgkinson
   2008 [2001]   The Practitioner-Researcher Divide in Industrial, Work, and Organization (IWO) Psychology: Where Are We Now and Where Do We Go from Here? In *Organizational Psychology: Critical Concepts in Psychology*, ed. Jo Silvester. London: Routledge. Vol. 4, 386–408.
Andrade, Gregor, Mark Mitchell, and Erik Stafford
   2004   New Evidence on Mergers. In *Mergers and Corporate Governance*, ed. J. Harold Mulherin. Cheltenham, UK: Edward Elgar, 103–20.
Arendt, Hannah
   1963   *Eichmann in Jerusalem: A Report on the Banality of Evil*. New York: Viking Press.
Argyris, C., and D. A. Schön
   1978   *Organizational Learning*. Reading, MA: Addison-Wesley.
Ariely, Dan
   2008   *Predictably Irrational: The Hidden Forces That Shape Our Decisions*. New York: HarperCollins.
Arkes, H. R., and Blumer, C.
   1985   The Psychology of Sunk Costs. *Organizational Behavior and Human Performance* 35: 129–40.
Arocha, Jose, and Vimla Patel
   2001   The Nature of Constraints on Collaborative Decision Making in Health Care Settings. In *Linking Expertise and Naturalistic Decision Making*, eds. Eduardo E. Salas and Gary Klein. Mahwah, NJ: Lawrence Erlbaum Associates, 83–405.
Arrow, Kenneth J.
   1963   Uncertainty and the Welfare Economics of Medical Care. *American Economic Review* 53: 941–73.
Asch, Solomon E.
   1955   Opinions and Social Pressure. *Scientific American* 193: 31–35.
Ashkanasy, Neal M., Wilfred J. Zerbe, and D. J. Härtel, eds.
   2005   *The Effect of Affect in Organizational Settings*. Oxford: Elsevier JAI.
Ashton, Thomas S.
   1969   *The Industrial Revolution, 1760–1830*. London: Oxford University Press.
Azumi, I., D. Hickson, D. Horvath, and C. McMillan
   1976   Nippon no Soshiki Kouzou. *Soshiki Kagaku* 12: 2–12.
Bacharach, Michael, and Susan Hurley
   1991   Issues and Advances in the Foundations of Decision Theory. In *Foundations of Decision Theory: Issues and Advances*, eds. Michael Bacharach and Susan Hurley. Oxford: Basil Blackwell, 1–38.
Bagchi-Sen, S.
   2001   Foreign Investment: Direct. In *International Encyclopedia of the Social and*

Behavioral Sciences, eds. Neil J. Smelser and Paul B. Baltes. Oxford: Elsevier. Vol. 9, 5731–33.

Baird, Bruce F.

1989   *Managerial Decisions under Uncertainty: An Introduction to the Analysis of Decision Making.* New York: John Wiley & Sons.

Baker, Andrea J.

2005   *Double Click: Romance and Commitment among Couples Online.* Cresskill, NJ: Hampton Press.

Baker, Raymond Q.

2005   *Capitalism's Achilles Heel: Dirty Money and How to Renew the Free-Market System.* Hoboken, NJ: John Wiley and Sons.

Balkwell, James W.

1994   Status. In *Group Processes: Sociological Analyses,* eds. Martha Foschi and Edward J. Lawler. Chicago: Nelson Hall, 119–48.

Balsam, Steven

2007   *Executive Compensation: An Introduction to Practice and Theory.* Scottsdale, AZ: WorldatWork Press.

Baltes, Paul B.

2001   Psychological Climate in the Work Setting. In *International Encyclopedia of the Social and Behavioral Sciences,* eds. Neil J. Smelser and Paul B. Baltes. Oxford: Elsevier. Vol. 18, 11355–58.

Barber, Bernard

1983   *The Logic and Limits of Trust.* New Brunswick, NJ: Rutgers University Press.

Barber, James David

1992   *The Presidential Character: Predicting Performance in the White House.* Englewood Cliffs, NJ: Prentice-Hall.

Barnard, Chester I.

1958   *The Functions of the Executive.* Cambridge, MA: Harvard University Press.

Bass, Bernard M.

1983   *Organizational Decision Making.* Homewood, IL: Richard D. Irwin.

Basu, Kaushik

2001   On the Goals of Development. In *Frontiers of Development Economics: The Future in Perspective,* eds. Gerald M. Meier and Joseph E. Stiglitz. Washington, DC, and New York: World Bank and Oxford University Press, 61–86.

Bavelas, Alex

1950   Communication Patterns in Task-Oriented Groups. *Journal of the Acoustical Society of America* 22: 271–82.

Bazerman, Max H.

2006   *Judgment in Managerial Decision Making,* 6th ed. Hoboken, NJ: John Wiley & Sons.

Beach, Le Roy

1997   *The Psychology of Decision-Making: People in Organizations.* Thousand Oaks, CA: Sage Publications.

Becker, Gary

1978   *The Economic Approach to Human Behavior.* Chicago: University of Chicago Press.

Becker, Howard S.

1963   *Outsiders: Studies in the Sociology of Deviance.* New York: Free Press of Glencoe.

Behn, Robert D.

2001   *Rethinking Democratic Accountability.* Washington, DC: Brookings Institution Press.

Belussi, Fiorenza, and Alessia Sammarra, eds.

2010   *Business Networks in Clusters and Industrial Districts: The Governance of the Global Value Chain.* London: Routledge.

Bendix, Reinhard

1964   *Nation-Building and Citizenship.* Berkeley: University of California Press.

Bennet, T.

2001   Cultural Policy. In *International Encyclopedia of the Social and Behavioral Sciences,* eds. Neil J. Smelser and Paul B. Baltes. Oxford: Elsevier. Vol. 5, 3092–97.

Berezin, Mabel

2005   Emotions and the Economy. In *The Handbook of Economic Sociology,* 2nd ed., eds. Neil J. Smelser and Richard Swedberg. New York: Russell Sage Foundation; Princeton: Princeton University Press, 109–27.

Berger, Joseph, N. H. Fisek, R. Z. Norman, and Morris Zelditch Jr.

1977   *Status Characteristics and Social Interaction: An Expectation-States Approach.* New York: Elsevier.

Berger, Peter L., and Thomas Luckmann

1967   *The Social Construction of Reality: A Treatise in the Sociology of Knowledge.* Garden City, NY: Doubleday.

Berkman, L. F., and L. S. Syme.

1979   Social Networks and Mortality. *American Journal of Epidemiology* 109: 186–204.

Berle, A. A., and Gardiner Means

1932   *The Modern Corporation and Private Property.* New York: Macmillan.

Berntsen, Dorthe

2002   Tunnel Memories for Autobiographical Events: Central Details Are Remembered More Frequently from Shocking Than from Happy Experiences. *Memory and Cognition* 30: 1010–20.

Best, Joel

2001   *Damned Lies and Statistics: Untangling Numbers from the Media, Politicians, and Activists.* Berkeley: University of California Press.

Bettelheim, Bruno

1943   Individual and Mass Behavior in Extreme Situations. *Journal of Abnormal and Social Psychology* 38: 417–52.

Bies, Robert J., Thomas A. Tripp, and Roderick M. Kramer

1997   At the Breaking Point: Cognitive and Social Dynamics of Revenge in Organizations. In *Antisocial Behavior in Organizations,* eds. Robert A. Giacalone and Jerald Greenberg. Thousand Oaks, CA: Sage Publications, 18–26.

Bishop, Toby J. F., and Frank E. Hydoski
   2009   *Corporate Resilience: Managing the Growing Risk of Fraud and Corruption.* Hoboken, NJ: John Wiley and Sons.
Biswas, Tappan
   1997   *Decision-Making under Uncertainty.* New York: St. Martin's Press.
Blair, John P., and Michael C. Carroll
   2008   *Local Economic Development: Analysis, Practices, and Globalization,* 2nd ed. Los Angeles: Sage Publications.
Blake, R. R., and J. S. Moulton
   1969   *Building a Grid Organization through Grid Organizational Development.* Reading, MA: Addison-Wesley.
Blau, Peter M., and Richard. A. Schoenherr
   1971   *The Structure of Organizations.* New York: Basic Books.
Blauner, Robert
   1964   *Alienation and Freedom: The Factory Worker and His Industry.* Chicago: University of Chicago Press.
Bloomhardt, Paul Frederick
   1941   *The Great Man in History.* Columbus: Ohio History Conference.
Blumer, Herbert
   1948   Public Opinion and Public Opinion Polling. *American Sociological Review* 13: 542–54
Boal, F. W.
   2001   Ethnic Conflict, Geography of. In *International Encyclopedia of the Social and Behavioral Sciences,* eds. Neil J. Smelser and Paul B. Baltes. Oxford: Elsevier. Vol. 7, 4802–06.
Boje, Axel
   1971   *Open-Plan Offices.* London: Business Books, 1971.
Bolton, Gary E., and Axel Ockenfels
   2009   The Limits of Trust in Investigations of Perfect Reputation Systems. In *E-Trust: Forming Relationships in the Online World,* eds. Karen S. Cook, Chris Snijders, Vincent Buskens, and Cove Cheshire. New York: Russell Sage Foundation, 5–36.
Bonilla-Silva, Eduardo
   2003   *Racism without Racists.* Lanham, MD: Rowman and Littlefield.
Boserup, Ester
   1989   *Women's Role in Economic Development.* New York: St. Martin's Press.
Bott, Elizabeth
   1957   *Family and Social Networks.* London: Tavistock.
Bougré, Constant D., and Partick R. Liverpool
   2006   Politics as Determinant of Fairness Perceptions in Organizations. In *Handbook of Organizational Politics,* eds. Eran Vigoda-Gadot and Amos Drory. Cheltenham, UK: Edward Elgar, 122–35.
Boulding, Kenneth E.
   1961   *The Image: Knowledge in Life and Society.* Ann Arbor: University of Michigan Press.

Bourdieu, Pierre
  2000   *Distinction: A Social Critique of the Judgement of Taste.* Trans. Richard Nice. Cambridge, MA: Harvard University Press.
Boye, Michael W., and John W. Jones
  1997   Organizational Culture and Employee Counterproductivity. In *Antisocial Behavior in Organizations,* eds. Robert A. Giacalone and Jerald Greenberg. Thousand Oaks, CA: Sage Publications, 172–84.
Bradley, Michael, Anand Desai, and E. Han Kim
  2005   Synergistic Gains from Corporate Acquisitions and Their Division between the Stockholders of Target and Acquiring Firms. In *Corporate Restructuring,* eds. John J. McConnell and David J. Denis. Cheltenham, UK: Edward Elgar. Vol. 1, 16–53.
Bradley, Wray E., and George S. Vozikis
  2004   Trust in Virtual Teams. In *Virtual and Collaborative Teams: Processes Technologies, and Practice,* eds. Susan H. Godar and Sharmila Pixy Ferris. Hershey, PA: Idea Group Publishing, 99–113.
Braverman, Harry
  1974   *Labor and Monopoly Capital: The Degradation of Work in the Twentieth Century.* New York: Monthly Review Press.
Bredenkamp, J.
  2001   Laboratory Experiment: Methodology. In *International Encyclopedia of the Social and Behavioral Sciences,* eds. Neil J. Smelser and Paul B. Baltes. Oxford: Elsevier. Vol. 12, 8226–32.
Brook, Robert H., John E. Ware Jr., William H. Rogers, Emmett B. Keeler, et al.
  1984   *The Effect of Coinsurance on the Health of Adults: Results from the RAND Health Insurance Experiment.* Santa Monica, CA: RAND.
Brown, Rupert
  2000   *Group Processes: Dynamics within and between Groups,* 2nd ed. Oxford: Blackwell.
Buckley, Walter
  1967   *Sociology and Modern Systems Theory.* Englewood Cliffs, NJ: Prentice-Hall.
Buehler, Roger, Dale Griffin, and Michael Ross
  2002   Inside the Planning Fallacy: The Causes and Consequences of Optimistic Time Predictions. In *Heuristics and Biases: The Psychology of Intuitive Judgment,* eds. Thomas Gilovich, Dale Griffin, and Daniel Kahneman. Cambridge: Cambridge University Press, 250–70.
Buono, Anthony F.
  2001   Introduction. In *Current Trends in Management Consulting,* ed. Anthony F. Buono. Greenwich, CT: Information Age Publishing, vii–xiv.
Burke, John P., and Fred Greenstein, with Larry Berman and Richard Immerman
  1989   *How Presidents Test Reality: Decisions on Vietnam, 1954 and 1965.* New York: Russell Sage.
Burt, Ronald
  1983   *Corporate Profits and Cooptation: Networks of Market Constraints and Directorate Ties in the American Economy.* New York: Academic Press.

1992   *Structural Holes: The Social Structure of Competition.* Cambridge, MA: Harvard University Press.

Caiden, Gerald E.

2001   Corruption and Governance. In *Where Corruption Lives,* eds. Gerald E. Caiden, O. P. Dwivedi, and Joseph Jabbra. Bloomfield, CT: Kumarian Press, 18–19.

Cain, Glen D., and Robinson G. Hollister

1972   The Methodology of Evaluating Social Action Programs. In *Evaluating Social Programs: Theory, Practice, and Politics,* eds. Peter H. Rossi and Walter Williams. New York: Seminar Press, 109–37.

Calder, B. J.

1977   An Attribution Theory of Leadership. In *New Directions in Organizational Behavior,* eds. B. M. Straw and G. R. Salancik. Chicago: St. Clair Press, 179–204.

Camarinha-Matos, Luis M., and Harmideh Afsarmanesh

2005   Brief Historical Perspective for Virtual Organizations. In *Virtual Organizations: Systems and Practices,* eds. Luis M. Camarinha-Matos, Harmideh Afsarmanesh, and Martin Ollus. New York: Springer, 3–10.

Camerer, Colin F., Linda Babcock, George Loewenstein, and Richard A. Thaler

2004   Labor Supply of New York City Cab Drivers: One Day at a Time. In *Advances in Behavioral Economics,* eds. Colin F. Camerer, George Loewenstein, and Matthew Rabin. New York and Princeton: Russell Sage Foundation and Princeton University Press, 533–47.

Campbell, Donald T.

1988   *Methodology and Epistemology for Social Science: Selected Papers.* Chicago: University of Chicago Press.

Campbell, Donald T., and J. C. Stanley

1966   *Experimental and Quasi-Experimental Designs for Research.* Chicago: Rand McNally.

Carayan, Pasle, Sra Kraemer, and Vicki Bioer

2005   Human Factors Issues in Computer and E-Business Activity. In *Integrated Risk Management for E-Business,* ed. Abderrahim Labbi. Boca Raton, FL: J. Ross Publishing, 63–85.

Carré, F. J.

2001   Regulation: Working Conditions. In *International Encyclopedia of the Social and Behavioral Sciences,* eds. Neil J. Smelser and Paul B. Baltes. Oxford: Elsevier. Vol. 19, 12978–82.

Carroll, Glenn R., and Michael T. Hannan

2000   *The Demography of Corporations and Industries.* Princeton: Princeton University Press.

Cartwright, Nancy

2005   Causal Claims: Warranting Them and Using Them. Paper prepared for National Academies conference "Use of Evidence for Social Policy Decision Making," April 1–3, Irvine, CA.

Caruthers, Bruce

2009   Trust and Credit. In *Whom Can We Trust? How Groups, Networks, and Insti-*

tutions Make Trust Possible, eds. Karen S. Cook, Margaret Levi, and Russell Hardin. New York: Russell Sage Foundation, 219–48.

Cascio, Wayne F.

2000 Managing a Virtual Workplace. *Academy of Management Executives* 14: 81–90.

2008 Whither Industrial and Organizational Psychology in a Changing World of Work? In *Organizational Psychology: Critical Concepts in Psychology,* ed. Jo Silvester. London: Routledge. Vol. 4, 432–55.

Castaldo, Sandro

2007 *Trust in Market Relationships.* Cheltenham, UK: Edward Elgar.

Castells, Manuel

2010 *Economy, Society, and Culture,* 2nd ed., vol. 1: *The Rise of the Network Society.* Chichester, UK: Wiley-Blackwell.

Castells, Manuel, and Alejandro Portes

1989 World Underneath: The Origins, Dynamics, and Effects of the Informal Economy. In *The Informal Economy: Studies in Advanced and Less Developed Countries,* eds. Alejandro Portes, Manuel Castells, and Lauren A. Benton. Baltimore: Johns Hopkins University Press, 11–37.

Castilla, Emilio J.

2005 Social Networks and Employee Performance in a Call Center. *American Journal of Sociology* 110: 1243–83.

Castles, S.

2001 Migration: Sociological Aspects. In *International Encyclopedia of the Social and Behavioral Sciences,* eds. Neil J. Smelser and Paul B. Baltes. Oxford: Elsevier. Vol. 14, 9824–28.

Caverni, Jean Paul, and Jean-Luc Péris

1990 The Anchoring-Adjustment Heuristic in an "Information Rich, Real World Setting": Knowledge Assessment by Experts. In *Cognitive Biases,* eds. J.-P. Caverni, J.-M. Fabre, and M. Gonzalez. New York: North-Holland, 35–45.

Cernea, Michael M., ed.

1994 *Putting People First: Sociological Variables in Rural Development,* 2nd ed. New York: Oxford University Press for the World Bank.

Chapman, Gretchen, and Brian Bornstein

1996 The More You Ask For, the More You Get: Anchoring in Personal Injury Verdicts. *Applied Cognitive Psychology* 10: 519–40.

Chemers, M. M.

2001 Leadership, Social Psychology of. In *International Encyclopedia of the Social and Behavioral Sciences,* eds. Neil J. Smelser and Paul B. Baltes. Oxford: Elsevier. Vol. 13, 8580–83.

Chirot, Daniel

1977 *Social Change in the Twentieth Century.* New York: Harcourt, Brace and Jovanovich.

Chow, Shein-chung, and Jen-pei Liu

2004 *Design and Analysis of Clinical Trials: Concepts and Methodologies,* 2nd ed. Hoboken, NJ: John Wiley & Sons.

Churchman, C. West, Russell L. Ackoff, and E. Leonard Ackoff
  1957   *Introduction to Operations Research.* New York: Wiley.
Clague, Christopher
  1997   Introduction. In *Institutions and Economic Development: Growth and Gover-
           nance in Less-Developed and Post-Socialist Countries,* ed. Christopher Clague.
           Baltimore: Johns Hopkins University Press, 1–9.
Clague, Christopher, Philip Keefer, Stephen Knack, and Mancur Olson
  1997a   Institutions and Economic Performance: Property Rights and Contract Enforce-
           ment. In *Institutions and Economic Development: Growth and Governance in
           Less-Developed and Post-Socialist Countries,* ed. Christopher Clague. Baltimore:
           Johns Hopkins University Press, 67–90.
  1997b   Democracy, Autocracy, and the Institutions Supportive of Economic Growth.
           In *Institutions and Economic Development: Growth and Governance in Less-
           Developed and Post-Socialist Countries,* ed. Christopher Clague. Baltimore:
           Johns Hopkins University Press, 92–120.
Cleary, Matthew, and Susan C. Stokes
  2009   Trust and Democracy in Comparative Perspective. In *Whom Can We Trust?
           How Groups, Networks and Institutions Make Trust Possible,* eds. Karen S. Cook,
           Margaret Levi, and Russell Hardin. New York: Russell Sage Foundation, 308–38.
Clore, Gerald L., Karen Casper, and Erika Garvin
  2001   Affect as Information. In *Handbook of Affect and Social Cognition,* ed. Joseph P.
           Fargas. Mahwah, NJ: Lawrence Erlbaum Associates, 121–44.
Cobb, Roger W., and Marc H. Ross
  1997   *Cultural Strategies of Agenda Denial: Avoidance, Attack and Redefinition.* Law-
           rence: University Press of Kansas.
Cochran, Moncreiff
  1990   Personal Networks in the Ecology of Human Development. In *Extending Fami-
           lies: The Social Networks of Parents and Their Children,* eds. Moncreiff Cochran,
           Mary Larner, David Riley, Lars Gunnarsson, and Charles R. Henderson Jr. Cam-
           bridge: Cambridge University Press, 3–33.
Cohen, David K., and Janet A. Weiss
  1977   Social Science and Social Policy: Schools and Race. In *Using Social Research
           in Public Policy Making,* ed. Carol H. Weiss. Lexington, MA: D.C. Heath and
           Company, 67–83.
Cohen, Michael D., and James G. March
  1974   *Leadership and Ambiguity: The American College President.* New York: McGraw-
           Hill.
Cohen, Michael, James G. March, and Johan P. Olsen
  1972   A Garbage Can Model of Organizational Choice. *Administrative Science Quar-
           terly* 17: 1–25.
Cole, Robert E.
  1971   *Japanese Blue Collar: The Changing Tradition.* Berkeley: University of California
           Press.

Coleman, James S.

1988   Social Capital in the Creation of Human Capital. *American Journal of Sociology* 95: 95–120.

1990   *Foundations of Social Theory.* Cambridge, MA: Belknap Press of Harvard University Press.

Coleman, James S., J. S. Menzel, and E. Elihu Katz

1956   The Diffusion of an Innovation among Physicians. *Sociometry* 20: 253–70.

Collins, J.

2001   Counterfactual Reasoning, Qualitative: Philosophical Aspects. In *International Encyclopedia of the Social and Behavioral Sciences,* eds. Neil J. Smelser and Paul B. Baltes. Oxford: Elsevier. Vol. 4, 2869–72.

Commons, John R.

1934   *Institutional Economics: Its Place in Political Economy.* New York: Macmillan.

Connaughton, Stanley, and John A. Daly

2004   Leading from Afar: Strategies for Effectively Leading Virtual Teams. In *Virtual and Collaborative Teams: Processes, Technologies, and Practice,* eds. Susan H. Godar and Sharmila Pixy Ferris. Hershey, PA: Idea Group Publishing, 49–75.

Cook, Karen S., Roderick M. Kramer, David H. Thom, Irena Stepanikova, et al.

2004   Trust and Distrust in Patient-Physician Relationships—Perceived Determinants of High- and Low-Trust Relationships in Managed Care Settings. In *Trust and Distrust in Organizations,* eds. Roderick M. Kramer and Karen S. Cook. New York: Russell Sage Foundation, 65–98.

Cook, Karen S., Margaret Levi, and Russell Hardin

2009   Introduction. In *Whom Can We Trust? How Groups, Networks and Institutions Make Trust Possible,* eds. Karen S. Cook, Margaret Levi, and Russell Hardin. New York: Russell Sage Foundation, 1–14.

Cook, Karen S., Eric R. W. Rice, and Alexander Berbasi

2004   The Emergence of Trust Networks under Uncertainty. In *Creating Social Trust in Post-Socialist Transition,* eds. Janos Kornai, Bo Rothstein, and Susan Rose-Ackerman. New York: Palgrave-Macmillan, 193–212.

Cook, Thomas D., and Donald T. Campbell

1979   *Quasi-Experimentation: Design and Analysis Issues for Field Settings.* Chicago: Rand McNally.

Cordray, David S.

1992   Theory-Driven Meta-Analysis: Practice and Prospects. In *Using Theory to Improve Program and Policy,* eds. Huey-tsyh Chen and Peter H. Rossi. New York: Greenwood Press, 85–95.

Cotterell, John

1996   *Social Networks and Social Influence in Adolescence.* London: Routledge.

Crandall, B., and K. Getchell-Reiter

1993   Critical Decision Method: A Technique for Eliciting Concrete Assessment Indicators from the "Intuition" of NICU Nurses. *Advances in Nursing Nursing Sciences* 16, no. 1: 42–51.

Crews, Frederick, Harold P. Blum, Marcia Cavell, Morris Eagle, et al.
  1995   *The Memory Wars: Freud's Legacy in Dispute.* New York: New York Review of Books.
Cross, William E. Jr.
  1990   Race and Ethnicity: Effects on Social Networks. In *Extending Families: The Social Networks of Parents and Their Children,* eds. Moncreiff Cochran, David Riley, Lars Gunnarsson, and Charles R. Henderson Jr. Cambridge: Cambridge University Press, 67–85.
Crouhy, Michel, Dan Galai, and Robert Mark
  2006   *The Essentials of Risk Management.* New York: McGraw-Hill.
Crozier, Michel
  1964   *The Bureaucratic Phenomenon.* Chicago: University of Chicago Press.
Cuevas, Haydee M., Stephen M. Fiore, Eduardo Salas, and Clint A. Bowers
  2004   Virtual Teams as Sociotechnical Systems. In *Virtual and Collaborative Teams: Processes, Technologies, and Practice,* eds. Susan H. Godar and Sharmila Pixy Ferris. Hershey, PA: Idea Group Publishing, 1–19.
Cvetkovich, G.
  1978   Cognitive Accommodation, Language, and Social Responsibility. *Social Psychology* 41: 149–55.
Cyert, R. M., and James G. March
  1963   *A Behavioral Theory of the Firm.* Englewood Cliffs, NJ: Prentice-Hall.
d'Agostino, Federico
  2001   Social Science, the Idea of. In *International Encyclopedia of the Social and Behavioral Sciences,* eds. Neil J. Smelser and Paul B. Baltes. Oxford: Elsevier. Vol. 21, 14429–35.
Dalton, George
  1971   *Economic Anthropology and Development: Essays in Tribal and Peasant Economies.* New York: Basic Books.
Dalton, Melville
  1959   *Men Who Manage: Fusions of Feeling and Theory in Administration.* New York: Wiley.
Davenport, Thomas O.
  2002   M&A in the New Millennium. In *Making Mergers Work: The Strategic Importance of People,* ed. Jeffrey A. Schmidt. Alexandria, VA: Towers Perrin / Society for Human Resource Management, 217–34.
Davies, J.
  1962   Toward a Theory of Revolution. *American Sociological Review* 27: 5–19.
Davis, Gerald E., and Henrich R. Greve
  1997   Corporate Elite Networks and Governance Changes in the 1980s. *American Journal of Sociology* 103: 1–37.
Deal, Terrence E., Ted Purinton, and Daria Cook Waetjen
  2009   *Making Sense of Social Networks in Schools.* Thousand Oaks, CA: Corwin Press.

Deci, Edward L., and Richard M. Ryan
  1985   *Intrinsic Motivation and Self-Determination in Human Behavior.* New York: Plenum.
Dehue, T.
  2001   Experimentation in Psychology, History of. In *International Encyclopedia of the Social and Behavioral Sciences,* eds. Neil J. Smelser and Paul B. Baltes. Oxford: Elsevier. Vol. 8, 5115–20.
Demsetz, Harold
  1964   The Exchange and Enforcement of Property Rights. *Journal of Law and Economics* 32: 1–44.
Denis, Diane Kowalski
  2005   Evidence on the Effects of Hostile and Friendly Tender Offers on Employment. In *Corporate Restructuring,* eds. John J. McConnell and David J. Denis. Cheltenham, UK: Edward Elgar. Vol. 1, 341–57.
Desai, Vandana, and Robert B. Potter
  2002   Editorial Introduction. In *The Companion to Development Studies,* eds. Vandana Desai and Robert B. Potter. London: Arnold, 59–60.
DiMaggio, Paul J., and Walter W. Powell
  1983   The Iron Cage Revisited: Institutional Isomorphism and Collective Rationality. *American Sociological Review* 48: 147–60.
Dirks, Kurt T., and Daniel P. Skarlicki
  2004   Trust in Leaders: Existing Research and Emerging Issues. In *Trust and Distrust in Organizations: Dilemmas and Approaches,* eds. Roderick M. Kramer and Karen S. Cook. New York: Russell Sage Foundation, 21–40.
Dix, T., and J. E. Grusec
  1986   Parent Attribution Processes in Child Socialization. In *Parent Belief Systems: Psychological Consequences for Children,* ed. J. Siegel. Hillsdale, NJ: Lawrence Erlbaum Associates, 201–33.
Dogan, Mattei, and Robert Pahre
  1990   *Creative Marginality: Innovation at the Intersections of Social Sciences.* Boulder, CO: Westview Press.
Domhoff, G. William
  1967   *Who Rules America?* Englewood Cliffs, NJ: Prentice-Hall.
Donaldson, Lex
  2001   *The Contingency Theory of Organizations.* Thousand Oaks, CA: Sage Publications.
Donaldson, Stewart I., and Rachael Weiss
  1998   Health, Well-Being, and Organizational Effectiveness in the Virtual Workplace. In *The Virtual Workplace,* eds. Magid Igbaria and Margaret Tan. Hershey, PA: Idea Group Publishing, 24–44.
Dore, Ronald P.
  1973   *British Factory, Japanese Factory: The Origins of National Diversity in Industrial Relations.* Berkeley: University of California Press.
Downs, Anthony
  1957   *An Economic Theory of Democracy.* New York: Harper & Row.

Dresner, Simon

    2002   *The Principles of Sustainability*. London: Earthscan.

Drucker, Peter

    2001 [1967]   The Effective Decision. In Harvard Business Review *on Decision Making*. Boston: Harvard Business School Publishing Company, 1–19.

Duesenberry, James

    1954   *Income, Savings, and the Theory of Consumer Behavior*. Cambridge, MA: Harvard University Press.

Durkheim, Émile

    1951 [1897]   *Suicide: A Study in Sociology*. Trans. John A. Spaulding and George Simpson, ed. and with an introduction by George Simpson. Glencoe, IL: Free Press.

    1958 [1895]   *The Rules of Sociological Method*. Trans. Sarah H. Solovay and John H. Mueller, ed. George E. G. Catlin. Glencoe, IL: Free Press.

    1965 [1912]   *The Elementary Forms of the Religious Life*. Trans. Joseph Ward Swain. New York: Free Press.

    1997 [1893]   *The Division of Labor in Society*. Trans. W. D. Halls, with an introduction by Lewis A. Coser. New York: Free Press.

Durkheim, Émile, and Marcel Mauss

    1963 [1903]   *Primitive Classification*. Trans. and ed. with introduction by Rodney Needham. Chicago: University of Chicago Press.

Duxbury, Linda, Christopher Higgins, and Derick Neufeld

    1998   Telework and the Balance between Work and Family: Is Telework Part of the Problem or Part of the Solution? In *The Virtual Workplace*, eds. Magid Igbaria and Margaret Tan. Hershey, PA: Idea Group Publishing, 218–55.

Eagly, A. H., and Chaiken, S.

    1993   *The Psychology of Attitudes*. Belmont, CA: Wadsworth.

Easterby-Smith, Mark, Luz Araujo, and John Burgoyne

    1999   *Organizational Learning and the Learning Organization*. London: Sage Publications.

Easterly, William

    2001   The Lost Decades: Developing Countries' Stagnation in Spite of Policy Reform 1980–1998. *Journal of Economic Growth* 6: 135–57.

Eccles, Robert G., and Nitin Noria, with James G. Berkley

    1992   *Beyond the Hype: Rediscovering the Essence of Management*. Boston: Harvard Business School Press.

Economic Commission for Latin America and the Caribbean (ECLAC)

    2000   *Social Panorama of Latin America, 1999–2000*. Annual report. Santiago de Chile: ECLAC.

Edland, Anne, and Ola Svenson

    1993   Judgment and Decision Making under Time Pressure: Studies and Findings. In *Time Pressure and Stress in Human Judgment and Decision Making*, eds. Ola A. Svenson and A. John Maule. New York: Plenum, 27–40.

Ehrenberg, Ronald G., and Robert S. Smith

    2009   *Modern Labor Economics: Theory and Public Policy*, 10th ed. Boston: Pearson-Addison Wesley.

Einerson, Ståle, Helge Hoel, Dieter Zapf, and Cary L. Cooper
  2003   The Concept of Bullying at Work: The European Tradition. In *Bullying and Emotional Abuse in the Workplace: International Perspectives in Research and Practice,* eds. Ståle Einarsen, Helge Hoel, Dieter Zapf, and Cary L. Cooper. London: Taylor and Francis, 3–30.
Eisenhower, Dwight D.
  1965   *Waging Peace.* Garden City, NY: Doubleday.
Eliot, John, with contributions by Heinrich Stumpf
  1987   *Models of Psychological Space: Psychometric, Developmental, and Experimental Approaches.* New York: Springer-Verlag.
Ellis, Donald G., and B. Aubrey Fisher
  1994   *Small Group Decision Making: Communication and the Group Process,* 4th ed. New York: McGraw-Hill, 1994.
Ellwood, J. Mark
  2007   *Critical Appraisal of Epidemiological Studies and Clinical Trials,* 3rd ed. Oxford: Oxford University Press.
Engels, Friedrich
  1952 [1887]   *The Condition of the Working-Class in England in 1844.* London: Allen & Unwin.
Erk, S., M. Kiefer, J. Grothe, A. P. Wunderlich, et al.
  2003   Emotional Context Modulates Subsequent Memory Effect. *Neuroimage* 18: 439–47.
Escobar, A.
  1991   Anthropology and the Developmental Encounter: The Making and Marketing of Development Anthropology. *American Ethnologist* 18: 658–81.
Etzioni, Amitai
  2001 [1989]   Humble Decision Making. In Harvard Business School Review *On Decision Making.* Boston, MA: Harvard Business School Publishing Company, 45–57.
Evans, Peter
  1995   *Embedded Autonomy: States and Industrial Transformation.* Princeton: Princeton University Press.
Everitt, Brian S., and Simon Wessily
  2008   *Clinical Trials in Psychiatry.* Hoboken, NJ: John Wiley & Sons.
Farmer, Mary K.
  1992   On the Need to Make a Better Job of Justifying Rational Choice Theory. *Rationality and Society* 4: 411–20.
Fauconnier, Giles
  1997   *Mappings in Thought and Language.* Cambridge: Cambridge University Press.
Feraro, Thomas J.
  1992   Rationality and Formal Theory. *Rationality and Society* 4: 438–48.
Fernández, Walter D.
  2004   Trust and the Trust Placement Process in Metateam Projects. In *Virtual Teams: Projects, Protocols, and Processes,* ed. David J. Pauleen. Hershey, PA: Idea Group Publishing, 40–69.

Festinger, Leon

1954   A Theory of Social Comparison Processes. *Human Relations* 90: 117–40.

1957   *A Theory of Cognitive Dissonance.* Evanston, IL: Row, Peterson.

Festinger, Leon, Stanley Schachter, and Kurt Back

1950   *Social Pressures in Informal Groups: A Study of Human Factors in Housing.* Stanford, CA: Stanford University Press.

Fiedler, K.

2001   Affective States Trigger Processes of Assimilation and Accommodation. In *Theories of Mood and Cognition: A User's Guidebook,* eds. L. L. Martin and G. L. Clore. Mahwah, NJ: Erlbaum, 86–98.

Field, John

2003   *Social Capital.* London: Routledge.

Fine, Ben

2006   The Economics of Development and the Development of Economics. In *The New Development Economics: After the Washington Consensus,* eds. K. S. Jomo and Ben Fine. London: Zed Books, xv–xvi.

Fine, Gary Alan

1996   Reputational Entrepreneurs and the Meaning of Incompetence: Melting Supporters, Partisan Warriors, and Images of President Harding. *American Journal of Sociology* 101: 1159–83.

Fine, Gary Alan, Veronique Campion-Vincent, and Chip Heath, eds.

2005   *Rumor Mills: The Social Impact of Rumor and Legend.* New Brunswick, NJ: Aldine Transaction.

Firth, Raymond

1971   *Elements of Social Organization,* 3rd ed. London: Tavistock Publications.

Fischer, Claude S.

1982   *To Dwell among Friends: Personal Networks in Town and City.* Chicago: University of Chicago Press.

1984   *The Urban Experience.* San Diego: Harcourt Brace Jovanovich.

1992   *America Calling: A Social History of the Telephone to 1940.* Berkeley: University of California Press.

Fischoff, Baruch

2002   Heuristics and Biases in Application. In *Heuristics and Biases: The Psychology of Intuitive Judgment,* eds. Thomas Gilovich, Dale Griffin, and Daniel Kahneman. Cambridge: Cambridge University Press, 730–48.

Fisher, Kimball

2000   *Leading Self-Directed Work Teams: A Guide in Developing New Team Leadership Skills,* rev. and exp. ed. New York: McGraw-Hill.

Fiske, S. T., and Taylor, S. E.

2008   *Social Cognition: From Brains to Culture.* New York: McGraw-Hill.

Flint, Colin

2003   Geographies of Inclusion/Exclusion. In *The Geographical Dimensions of Terrorism,* eds. Susan L. Cutter, Douglas B. Richardson, and Thomas J. Wilbanks. New York and London: Routledge, 53–58.

Foddy, Margaret, and Toshio Yamagishi

   2009   Group-Based Trust. In *Whom Can We Trust? How Groups, Networks, and Institutions Make Trust Possible,* eds. Karen S. Cook, Margaret Levi, and Russell Hardin. New York: Russell Sage Foundation, 17–41.

Frank, Robert F., and Robert M. Hutchens

   2004   Wages, Seniority, and the Demand for Rising Consumption Profiles. In *Advances in Behavioral Economics,* eds. Colin F. Camerer, George Loewenstein, and Matthew Rabin. New York: Russell Sage Foundation; Princeton: Princeton University Press, 548–71.

Freedman, Anne

   1994   *Patronage: An American Tradition.* Chicago: Nelson-Hall Publishers.

Freeman, J. L.

   1965   *The Political Process: Executive Bureau-Legislative Committee Relations,* rev. ed. New York: Random House.

Freeman, Linton C.

   2004   *The Development of Social Network Analysis: A Study in the Sociology of Science.* Vancouver, BC: Empirical Press.

French, Wendell L., and Cecil H. Bell Jr.

   1999   *Organizational Development: Behavioral Science Interventions for Organizational Improvement.* Upper Saddle River, NJ: Prentice-Hall.

Frey, D., and F. Brodbeck

   2001   Group Processes in Organization. In *International Encyclopedia of the Social and Behavioral Sciences,* eds. Neil J. Smelser and Paul B. Baltes. Oxford: Elsevier. Vol. 9, 6407–13.

Frey, D., S. Schulz-Hardt, and D. Stahlberg

   1996   Information Seeking among Individuals and Groups and Possible Consequences for Decision Making in Business and Politics. In *Understanding Group Behavior—Small Group Processes and Interpersonal Relations,* eds. Erich H. Witte and James H. Davis. Mahway, NJ: Lawrence Erlbaum, 211–25.

Friedland, William H.

   1963   *Unions and Industrial Relations in Underdeveloped Countries.* Ithaca: New York State School of Industrial and Labor Relations.

Friedman, Jeffrey, ed.

   1995   *The Rational Choice Controversy: Economic Models of Politics Reconsidered.* New Haven, CT: Yale University Press.

Friedman, N.

   1967   *The Social Nature of Psychological Research: The Psychological Experiment as a Social Interaction.* New York: Basic Books.

Friedman, Stewart D.

   1985   *Leadership Succession Systems and Corporate Performance.* New York: Center for Career Research and Corporate Performance, Columbia Graduate School of Business.

Fukuyama, Frank

   1995   *Trust: The Social Virtues and the Creation of Prosperity.* New York: Free Press.

2001   Culture and Economic Development: Cultural Concerns. In *International Encyclopedia of the Social and Behavioral Sciences,* eds. Neil J. Smelser and Paul B. Baltes. Oxford: Elsevier. Vol. 5, 3130–34.

Furberg, Bengt

2007   *Evaluating Clinical Research: All That Glitters Is Not Gold.* New York: Springer-Verlag.

Furnham, Adrian

2005   *The Psychology of Behavior at Work: The Individual in the Organization.* New York: Psychology Press.

Furstenberg, Frank F. Jr., ed.

2002   *Early Adulthood in Cross-National Perspective.* Thousand Oaks, CA: Sage Publications.

Furstenburg, F. F., and M. E. Hughes

1997   The Influence of Neighborhoods on Children's Development: A Theoretical Perspective and Research Agenda. In *Neighborhood Poverty,* eds. J. Brooks-Dunn, G. J. Duncan, and J. I. Aber. New York: Sage. Vol. 2, 23–47.

Galaskiewicz, Joseph, and Stanley Wasserman

1994   Introduction: Advances in the Social and Behavioral Sciences in Social Network Analysis. In *Advances in Social Network Analysis: Research in the Social and Behavioral Sciences,* eds. Joseph Galaskiewicz and Stanley Wasserman. Thousand Oaks, CA: Sage Publications, xi–xvii.

Gambetta, Diego

1993   *The Sicilian Mafia: The Business of Private Protection.* Cambridge, MA: Harvard University Press.

———, ed.

1988   *Trust: Making and Breaking Cooperative Relations.* New York: Blackwell.

Gauch, Ronald R.

2009   *It's Great! Oops, No It Isn't: Why Clinical Research Can't Guarantee the Right Medical Answers.* New York: Springer Science & Business Media.

Gebelin, Susan H., David G. Lee, Kristie J. Nelson-Neuhaus, and Elaine B. Sloan

1999   *Successful Executive's Handbook: Development Suggestions for Today's Executives,* 2nd ed. Minneapolis: Personnel Decisions International.

Gebelin, Susan H., Lisa A. Stevens, Carol J. Skube, David G. Lee, et al.

2000   *Successful Manager's Handbook: Development Suggestions for Today's Managers: Develop Yourself, Coach Others,* 6th ed. Minneapolis: Personnel Decisions International.

Gell, Alfred

1992   *The Anthropology of Time: Cultural Construction of Temporal Maps and Images.* Oxford: Berg.

George, Alexander L.

1980   *Presidential Decisionmaking in Foreign Policy: The Effective Use of Information and Advice.* Boulder, CO: Westview Press.

Gerschenkron, Alexander
  1962   *Economic Backwardness in Historical Perspective.* Cambridge, MA: Belknap Press
          of Harvard University Press.
Getz, Kenneth, and Deborah Borfitz
  2002   *Informed Consent: A Guide to the Risks and Benefits of Volunteering for Clinical
          Trials,* with a foreword by Paul Gelsinger. Boston: CenterWatch.
Gherardi, Sylvia
  2001   Learning: Organizational. In *International Encyclopedia of the Social and Behav-
          ioral Sciences,* eds. Neil J. Smelser and Paul B. Baltes. Oxford: Elsevier. Vol. 13,
          8609–13.
Ghosh, B. N., and Rama Ghosh
  1991   *Economic Growth, Development, and Planning.* New Delhi: Deep and Deep
          Publications.
Giacalone, Robert A., and Jerald Greenberg, eds.
  1997   *Antisocial Behavior in Organizations.* Thousand Oaks, CA: Sage Publications.
Giddens, Anthony
  1990   *The Consequences of Modernity.* Cambridge: Polity Press.
Gigerenzer, Gerd
  2001   Decision-Making: Nonrational Theories. In *International Encyclopedia of the
          Social and Behavioral Sciences,* eds. Neil J. Smelser and Paul B. Baltes. Oxford:
          Elsevier. Vol. 5, 3304–09.
Gigerenzer, Gerd, Jean Dzerlinski, and Laura Martignon
  2002   How Good Are Fast and Frugal Heuristics? In *Heuristics and Biases: The Psy-
          chology of Intuitive Judgment,* eds. Thomas Gilovich, Dale Griffin, and Daniel
          Kahneman. Cambridge: Cambridge University Press, 559–81.
Gigerenzer, Gerd, and P. M. Todd
  1999   *Simple Heuristics That Make Us Smart.* New York: Oxford University Press.
Gilovich, Thomas, and Dale Griffin
  2002   Introduction: Heuristics and Bias: Then and Now. In *Heuristics and Biases:
          The Psychology of Intuitive Judgment,* eds. Thomas Gilovitch, Dale Griffin, and
          Daniel Kahneman. Cambridge: Cambridge University Press, 1–18.
Gilovich, Thomas, and Kenneth Savitsky
  1996   Like Goes with Like: The Role of Representativeness Erroneous and Pseudo-
          Scientific Beliefs. *Skeptical Inquirer* 20: 30–50.
Gladwell, Malcolm
  2005   *Blink: The Power of Thinking without Thinking.* New York: Little Brown & Co.
Gneezy, Uri, and Aldo Rustichini
  2004   Incentives, Punishment, and Behavior. In *Advances in Behavioral Economics,*
          eds. Colin F. Camerer, George Loewenstein, and Matthew Rabin. New York:
          Russell Sage Foundation; Princeton: Princeton University Press, 572–89.
Goffman, Erving
  1959   *The Presentation of Self in Everyday Life.* New York: Doubleday-Anchor.
  1963   *Stigma: Notes on the Management of Spoiled Identities.* Englewood Cliffs, NJ:
          Prentice-Hall.

1974   *Frame Analysis: An Essay on the Organization of Experience.* New York: Harper and Row.

Goldberg, W. H.

1983   *Mergers: Motives, Modes, Methods.* Aldershot, UK: Gower.

Gordon, Robert Aaron

1945   *Business Leadership in the Large Corporation.* Washington, DC: Brookings Institution.

Gould, Stephen Jay

2002   *The Structure of Evolutionary Theory.* Cambridge, MA: Belknap Press of Harvard University Press.

Gouldner, Alvin W.

1954   *Patterns of Industrial Bureaucracy.* Glencoe, IL: Free Press.

Granovetter, Mark

1973   The Strength of Weak Ties. *American Journal of Sociology* 78: 1360–80.

1974   *Getting a Job: A Study of Contacts and Careers.* Cambridge, MA: Harvard University Press.

Grant, D.

2001   Organizations: Metaphors and Paradigms in. In *International Encyclopedia of the Social and Behavioral Sciences,* eds. Neil J. Smelser and Paul B. Baltes. Oxford: Elsevier. Vol. 16, 10960–65.

Green, Donald P., and Ian Shapiro

1994   *Pathologies of Rational Choice Theory: A Critique of Applications in Political Science.* New Haven, CT: Yale University Press.

Greenberg, Jerald

1997   The STEAL Motive: Managing the Social Determinants of Employee Theft. In *Antisocial Behavior in Organizations,* eds. Robert A. Giacalone and Jerald Greenberg. Thousand Oaks, CA: Sage Publications, 85–108.

Greenfield, D. N.

1999   *Virtual Addiction.* Oakland, CA: New Harbinger Publications.

Greenstein, Fred I.

2000   *The Presidential Difference: Leadership Style from FDR to Barack Obama.* Princeton: Princeton University Press.

Greitzer, Frank L., Robin Podmore, Marck Robinson, and Pamela Ey

2010   Naturalistic Decision Making for Power System Operators. *International Journal of Human-Computer Interaction* 21: 278–91.

Grekova, M.

2001   Postsocialist Societies. In *International Encyclopedia of the Social and Behavioral Sciences,* eds. Neil J. Smelser and Paul B. Baltes. Oxford: Elsevier. Vol. 17, 1877–81.

Grewal, David Singh

2008   *Network Power: The Social Dynamics of Globalization.* New Haven, CT: Yale University Press.

Grizzle, Gloria

2002   Performance Measurement and Dysfunction: The Dark Side of Quantifying Work. *Public Performance and Management Review* 25: 363–69.

Grossman, Gregory

1989   Informal Personal Incomes and Outlays of the Soviet Urban Population. In *The Informal Economy: Studies in Advanced and Less Developed Countries,* eds. Alejandro Portes, Manuel Castells, and Lauren A. Benton. Baltimore: Johns Hopkins University Press, 135–49.

Guest, Robert

1962   *Organizational Change: The Effect of Successful Leadership.* Homewood, IL: Dorsey.

Gurr, Ted Robert

1970   *Why Men Rebel.* Princeton: Princeton University Press.

Gurr, Ted Robert, and Barbara Harff

1994   *Ethnic Conflict in World Politics.* Boulder, CO: Westview Press.

Gurvitch, Georges

1964   *The Spectrum of Social Time.* Trans. and ed. Myrtle Korenbaum. Dordrecht: D. Riedel.

Gusfield, Joseph R.

1972   Tradition and Modernity: Misplaced Polarities in the Study of Social Change. In *Organizational Issues in Industrial Society,* ed. Jon M. Shepard. Englewood Cliffs, NJ: Prentice-Hall, 35–49.

Haas, Ernst

2001   International Organizations. In *International Encyclopedia of the Social and Behavioral Sciences,* eds. Neil J. Smelser and Paul B. Baltes. Oxford: Elsevier. Vol. 11, 7819–24.

Haas, P. M.

1992   Introduction: Epistemic Communities and International Policy Coordination. *International Organization* 46: 1–35.

Hagen, Everett E.

1962   *On the Theory of Social Change: How New Economic Growth Begins.* Homewood, IL: Dorsey.

Haggard, Stephan

1997   Democratic Institutions, Economic Policy, and Development. In *Institutions and Economic Development: Growth and Governance in Less-Developed and Post-Socialist Countries,* ed. Christopher Clague. Baltimore: Johns Hopkins University Press, 121–49.

Haimes, Yakov, and Ralph E. Steuer, eds.

2000   *Research and Practice in Multiple Criteria Decision Making.* Berlin: Springer-Verlag.

Hajek, A.

2001   Counterfactual Reasoning, Quantitative: Philosophical Aspects. In *International Encyclopedia of the Social and Behavioral Sciences,* eds. Neil J. Smelser and Paul B. Baltes. Oxford: Elsevier. Vol. 4, 2872–74.

Halévy, Élie

1949   *The Growth of Philosophical Radicalism.* Trans. Mary Morris. Preface by A. D. Lindsay. New York: Augustus M. Kelly.

Halpern, David
   2005   *Social Capital.* Cambridge: Polity Press.
Hamermesh, D. S.
   2001   Demand for Labor. In *International Encyclopedia of the Social and Behavioral Sciences,* eds. Neil J. Smelser and Paul B. Baltes. Oxford: Elsevier. Vol. 5, 3384–89.
Hammond, John S., Ralph L. Keeney, and Howard Raifa
   2001 [1998]   The Hidden Traps in Decision Making. In Harvard Business School Publishing Corporation, Harvard Business Review *on Decision Making.* Boston: Harvard Business School Publishing Company, 143–67.
Haney, Patrick J.
   1997   *Organizing for Foreign Policy Crises: Presidents, Advisers, and the Management of Decision Making.* Ann Arbor: University of Michigan Press.
Hannan, Michael T., and John Freeman
   1984   Structural Inertia and Organizational Change. *American Sociological Review* 49: 149–62.
Hannerz, Ulf
   1990   Cosmopolitans and Locals in World Culture. In *Global Culture: Nationalism, Globalization and Modernity,* ed. Mike Featherstone. London: Sage Publications, 237–51.
Hareven, Tamara K.
   1982   *Family Time and Industrial Time: The Relationship between the Family and Work in a New England Industrial Community.* New York: Cambridge University Press.
Harmon-Jones, E.
   2001   The Role of Affect in Cognitive Dissonance Processes. In *The Handbook of Affect and Social Cognition,* ed. Joseph P. Forgas. Mahwah, NJ: Erlbaum Associates, 237–55.
Hastie, R.
   1991   A Review from a High Place: The Field of Judgment and Decision Making as Revealed in Its Current Textbooks. *Psychological Science* 2: 135–40.
Heck, Ramona K. Z., Alma J. Owen, and Barbara R. Rowe, eds.
   1995   *Home-Based Employment and Family Life.* Westport, CT: Auburn House.
Heclo, Hugh
   1999   The Changing Presidential Office. In *The Managerial Presidency,* ed. James P. Pfiffner. College Station: Texas A&M Press, 33–42.
Hedberg, Bo, Göran Dahlgren, Jörgen Hansson, and Nils-Göran Olve
   1997   *Virtual Organizations and Beyond.* Chichester, UK: John Wiley and Sons.
Hegtvedt, Karen A.
   1994   Justice. In *Group Processes: Sociological Analyses,* eds. Martha Foschi and Edward J. Lawler. Chicago: Nelson Hall Publishers, 177–204.
Heider, Fritz
   1958   *The Psychology of Interpersonal Relations.* New York: Wiley.
Heimer, Carol A.
   2001   Solving the Problem of Trust. In *Trust in Society,* ed. Karen S. Cook. New York: Russell Sage Foundation, 40–87.

Heirich, Max
  1971   *The Spiral of Conflict: Berkeley, 1964.* New York: Columbia University Press.
Heirich, Max, and Sam Kaplan
  1965   Yesterday's Discord. *California Monthly* 75: 20–32.
Held, David
  1995   *Democracy and the Global Order: From the Modern State to Cosmopolitan Governance.* Stanford, CA: Stanford University Press.
Hellebust, Lyn, ed.
  1997   *Think Tank Directory: A Guide to Nonprofit Public Policy Organizations.* Topeka, KS: Government Research Office.
Hemphill, J.K.
  1950   *Leader Behavior Description.* Columbus: Ohio State University Personnel Research Board.
Heritage, J.
  2001   Conversation Analysis: Sociological. In *International Encyclopedia of the Social and Behavioral Sciences,* eds. Neil J. Smelser and Paul B. Baltes. Oxford: Elsevier. Vol. 4, 2741–44.
Hernes, Gudmund
  1992   We Are Smarter Than We Think: A Rejoinder to Smelser. *Rationality and Society* 4: 421–35.
Herriot, Peter, and Neil Anderson
  2008   Selecting for Change: How Will Personnel and Selection Psychology Survive? In *Organizational Psychology: Critical Concepts in Psychology,* ed. Jo Silvester. London: Routledge. Vol. 4, 294–328.
Hershberg, Eric
  2001   Development: Socioeconomic Aspects. In *International Encyclopedia of the Social and Behavioral Sciences,* eds. Neil J. Smelser and Paul B. Baltes. Oxford: Elsevier. Vol. 6, 3592–97.
Heydebrand, W.V.
  2001   Structuralism, Theories of. In *International Encyclopedia of the Social and Behavioral Sciences,* eds. Neil J. Smelser and Paul B. Baltes. Oxford: Elsevier. Vol. 22, 15230–33.
Hill, J., A. Hawkins, and B. Miller
  1996   Work and Family in the Virtual Office: Perceived Influences of Mobile Telework. *Family Relations* 45: 293–301.
Hiller, Frederick S., and Gerald J. Lieberman
  2005   *Introduction to Operations Research,* 8th ed. Boston: McGraw-Hill Higher Education.
Hipp, John R., and Andrew J. Perrin
  2009   The Simultaneous Effect of Social Distance and Physical Distance on the Formation of Neighborhood Ties. *City and Community* 8: 5–25.
Hirano, Hiroyuki, and Makoto Furuya
  2006   *JIT Is Flow: Practice and Principles of Lean Manufacturing.* Vancouver, WA: PCS Press.

Hirschman, Albert

1981   The Rise and Decline of Development Economics. In Albert Hirschman, *Essays in Trespassing.* Cambridge: Cambridge University Press, 1–24.

Hitt, Michael, and Vincenzo Pisano

2005   Cross-Order Mergers and Acquisitions: Challenges and Opportunities. In *Corporate Restructuring,* eds. John J. McConnell and David J. Denis. Cheltenham, UK: Edward Elgar. Vol. 2, 45–59.

Hoff, Karla, and Joseph E. Stiglitz

2001   Modern Economic Theory and Development. In *Frontiers of Developmental Economics: The Future in Perspective,* eds. Gerald E. Meier and Joseph E. Stiglitz. Washington, DC, and New York: World Bank and Oxford University Press, 389–459.

Hogg, Michael A., and Dominic Abrams

2003   Intergroup Behavior and Social Identity. In *The Sage Handbook of Social Psychology,* eds. Michael A. Hogg and Joel Cooper. London: Sage Publications, 407–31.

Hollander, Edwin Paul

1964   *Leaders, Groups, and Influence.* New York: Oxford University Press.

Homans, George C.

1950   *The Human Group.* New York: Harcourt, Brace.

Hood, D.

2001   Public Management, New. In *International Encyclopedia of the Social and Behavioral Sciences,* eds. Neil J. Smelser and Paul B. Baltes. Elsevier: Oxford. Vol. 18, 12533–56.

Hoselitz, Bert F.

1963   Entrepreneurship and Traditional Elites. *Explorations in Entrepreneurial History Series* 2. 1: 36–49.

House, J., K. R. Landis, and D. Umberson

1988   Social Relationships and Health. *Science* 251: 540–45.

Hout, Michael, and Thomas A. DiPrete

2006   What We Have Learned: RC28's Contributions to Knowledge about Social Stratification. *Research in Social Stratification and Mobility* 24: 1–20.

Hughes, Owen

2003   *Public Management and Administration: An Introduction.* Basingstoke, UK: Palgrave.

Hunter, Margaret L.

2005   *Race, Gender, and the Politics of Skin Tone.* New York: Routledge.

Huntington, Samuel P.

1968   *Political Order in Changing Societies.* New Haven, CT: Yale University Press.

1991   *The Third Wave: Democratization in the Late Twentieth Century.* Norman: University of Oklahoma Press.

Jackson, Paul

1999   Introduction: From New Designs to New Dynamics. In *Virtual Working: Social and Organizational Dynamics,* ed. Paul Jackson. London: Routledge, 1–16.

Jackson, S.E., B.F. Brett, V.I. Sessa, D.M. Cooper, et al.
 1991   Some Differences Make a Difference: Individual Dissimilarity and Group Het-
          erogeneity as Correlates of Recruitment, Promotion, and Turnover. *Journal of
          Applied Psychology* 76: 675–89.
Jacoby, Sanford M.
 1998   Are Career Jobs Headed for Extinction? *California Management Review* 41 (2):
          123–45.
Janis, Irving L.
 1982   *Groupthink: Psychological Studies of Policy Decisions and Fiascoes.* Rev. and
          enlarged ed. of *Victims of Groupthink.* Boston: Houghton Mifflin.
Jarrell, Gregg A., James A. Buckley, and Jeffry M. Netter
 2005   The Market for Corporate Control: The Empirical Evidence since 1980. In *Cor-
          porate Restructuring,* eds. John J. McConnell and David J. Denis. Cheltenham,
          UK: Edward Elgar. Vol. 1, 49–68.
Jasper, James M.
 2004   Intellectual Cycles of Social Movement Research. In *Self, Social Structure, and
          Beliefs: Explorations in Sociology,* eds. Jeffrey C. Alexander, Gary T. Marx, and
          Christine L. Williams. Berkeley: University of California Press, 234–54.
Javidan, Mansour, Amy L. Pablo, Harbir Singh, Michael Hitt, et al.
 2005   Where We've Been and Where We're Going. In *Corporate Restructuring,* eds.
          John J. McConnell and David J. Denis. Cheltenham, UK: Edward Elgar. Vol. 2,
          245–61.
Jiao, Allan Y., Raymond W.K. Lau, and Percy Liu
 2005   An Institutional Analysis of Organizational Change: The Case of the Hong Kong
          Police. *International Criminal Justice Review* 15: 38–57.
Jiménez, José Blanes
 1989   Cocaine, Informality and the Urban Economy in La Paz, Bolivia. In *The Infor-
          mal Economy: Studies in Advanced and Less Developed Countries,* eds. Alejandro
          Portes, Manuel Castells, and Lauren A. Benton. Baltimore: Johns Hopkins Uni-
          versity Press, 135–49.
Johnson, Richard Tanner
 1974   *Managing the White House.* New York: Harper & Row.
Jones, Edward E.
 1998   Major Developments in Five Decades of Social Psychology. In *The Handbook of
          Social Psychology,* 4th ed., eds. Daniel T. Gilbert, Susan T. Fiske, and Gardner
          Lindzey. Boston: McGraw-Hill. Vol. 1, 3–57.
Jones, E.E., D.E. Kanouse, H.H. Kelley, R.E. Nisbett, et al.
 1972   *Attribution: Perceiving the Causes of Behavior.* Morristown, NJ: General Learn-
          ing Press.
Jones, E.E., R.A. Scott, and H. Markus
 1984   *Social Stigma: The Psychology of Marked Relationships.* New York: Freeman.
Jones, James H.
 1981   *Bad Blood: The Tuskegee Syphilis Experiment.* New York: Free Press.

Jones, Robert, Robert Oyung, and Lise Pace
  2005   *Working Virtually: Challenges of Virtual Teams.* Hershey, PA: IRM Press.
Juliep, J. W., ed.
  1990   *Replication Research in the Social Sciences.* Newbury Park, CA: Sage Publications.
Jussim, L.
  2001   Self-Fulfilling Prophecies. In *International Encyclopedia of the Social and Behavioral Sciences,* eds. Neil J. Smelser and Paul B. Baltes. Vol. 20, 13830–33.
Kahn, Herman
  1961   *On Thermonuclear War.* Princeton: Princeton University Press.
Kahn, Mushtaq Husein
  2006   Corruption and Governance. In *The New Development Economics: After the Washington Consensus,* eds. K. S. Jomo and Ben Fine. London: Zed Books, 200–21.
Kahn, Robert L., Donald M. Wolfe, Robert P. Quinn, J. Diedrick Snoke, et al.
  1964   *Organizational Stress: Studies in Role Conflict and Ambiguity.* New York: John Wiley.
Kahneman, Daniel, Paul Slovic, and Amos Tversky, eds.
  1982   *Judgment under Uncertainty: Heuristics and Biases.* Cambridge: Cambridge University Press.
Kahneman, Daniel, and Amos Tversky
  1986   Choices, Values, and Frames. In *Behavioral and Social Science: Fifty Years of Discovery,* eds. Neil J. Smelser and Dean R. Gerstein. Washington, DC: National Academy Press, 153–72.
Kahneman, Daniel, and C. A. Varey
  1990   Propensities and Counterfactuals: The Logic That Almost Won. *Journal of Personality and Social Psychology* 59: 1101–10.
Katz, Elihu, and Paul F. Lazarsfeld
  1955   *Personal Influence: The Part Played by People in the Flow of Mass Communication.* Glencoe, IL: Free Press.
Kaufmann, W.
  1956   *Military Policy and National Security.* Princeton: Princeton University Press.
Kellerman, Barbara
  2004   *Bad Leadership: What It Is, How It Happens, Why It Matters.* Boston: Harvard Business School.
Kelman, H. C.
  1973   Violence without Moral Restraint: Reflections on the Dehumanization of Victims and Victimizers. *Journal of Social Issues* 29: 25–61.
Kendall, Patricia L., and Paul F. Lazarsfeld
  1950   Problems of Survey Analysis. In *Continuities in Social Research: Studies in the Scope and Method of "The American Soldier,"* eds. Robert K. Merton and Paul F. Lazarsfeld. Glencoe, IL: Free Press, 133–96.
Kets de Vries, Manfred F. R., and Danny Miller
  1984   *The Neurotic Organization.* San Francisco: Jossey-Bass.

Keynes, John Maynard

1936   *General Theory of Employment, Interest, and Money.* New York: Harcourt, Brace.

Kilduff, Martin, and David Krackhardt

2008   *Interpersonal Networks in Organizations: Cognition, Personality, Dynamics, and Culture.* Cambridge: Cambridge University Press.

Killian, Lewis

1951   The Significance of Multiple-Group Membership in Disaster. *American Journal of Sociology* 57: 309–14.

Kingdom, John W.

1984   *Agendas, Alternatives, and Public Policies.* Boston: Little, Brown.

Klambhampati, Uma S.

2004   *Development and the Developing World.* Cambridge: Cambridge University Press.

Klein, G., R. Calderwood, and A. Clinton-Cirocco

1986   Rapid Decision Making on the Fire Ground. *Proceedings of the 30th Annual Meeting of the Human Factors Society.* Santa Monica, CA: Human Factors Society, 576–80.

Klein, Janice

2000   Foreword. In Kimball Fisher, *Leading Self-Directed Work Teams: A Guide to Developing Team Leadership Skills,* rev. and exp. ed. New York: McGraw Hill, xxi–xxii.

Klitgaard, Robert

1988   *Controlling Corruption.* Berkeley: University of California Press.

Knoben, Joris

2008   *Firm Mobility and Organizational Networks: Innovation, Embeddedness, and Economic Geography.* Cheltenham, UK: Edward Elgar.

Knoll, Kathleen, and Sirkka L. Jarvenpaa

1998   Working Together in Global Virtual Teams. In *The Virtual Workplace,* eds. Magid Igbaria and Margaret Tan. Hershey, PA: Idea Group Publishing, 2–23.

Kohn, Linda T., Janet M. Corrigan, and Molla S. Donaldson

1999   *To Err Is Human: Building a Safer Health System.* Report of the Committee on Quality of Health Care in America, Institute of Medicine. Washington, DC: National Academy Press.

Konrad, Alison M., Pushkala Prasad, and Judith K. Pringle, eds.

2006   *Handbook of Workplace Diversity.* London: Sage Publications.

Kowert, Paul A.

2002   *Groupthink or Deadlock: When Do Leaders Learn from Their Advisors?* Albany: State University of New York Press.

Kramer, Roderick, and Peter J. Carnevale

2001   Trust and Intergroup Negotiation. In *Blackwell Handbook on Social Psychology: Intergroup Processes,* eds. Rupert Brown and Samuel L. Gaetner. Malden, MA: Blackwell, 431–50.

Kramer, Roderick M., and Karen S. Cook

2004   Trust and Distrust in Organizations: Dilemmas and Approaches. In *Trust in*

Organizations: Dilemmas and Approaches, eds. Roderick M. Kramer and Karen S. Cook. New York: Russell Sage Foundation, 1–15.

Kroeber, Alfred Louis

1944 *Configurations of Culture Growth.* Berkeley: University of California Press.

Kuhn, Thomas S.

1962 *The Structure of Scientific Revolutions.* Chicago: University of Chicago Press.

Kulik, Carol T., and Hugh T. Bainbridge

2006 Psychological Perspectives on Workplace Diversity. In *Handbook of Workplace Diversity,* eds. Alison M. Konrad, Pushkala Prasad, and Judith K. Pringe. London: Sage Publications, 25–52.

Kurth, James R.

2001 Globalization: Political Aspects. In *International Encyclopedia of the Social and Behavioral Sciences,* eds. Neil J. Smelser and Paul B. Baltes. Oxford: Elsevier. Vol. 9, 6284–87.

Kürümlüoglu, Mehmet, Rita Nøstel, and Iris Karvonen

2005 Base Concepts. In *Virtual Organizations: Systems and Practices,* eds. Luis M. Camarinha-Matos, Harmideh Afsarmanesh, and Martin Ollus. New York: Springer, 11–28.

Kurz-Milcke, Elke, and Gerd Gigerenzer

2004 Preface. In *Experts in Science and Society,* eds. Elke Kurz-Milcke and Gerd Gigerenzer. New York: Kluwer Academic, v–vi.

Kuvaas, B., and G. Kaufmann

2004 Impact of Mood, Framing, and Need for Cognition on Decision Makers' Recall and Confidence. *Journal of Behavioral Decision Making* 17: 59–74.

Lafaix, François

2005 The Pre-Deal Stage. In *Corporate Restructuring,* eds. John J. McConnell and David J. Denis. Cheltenham, UK: Edward Elgar. Vol. 2, 48–73.

LaFasto, Frank, and Carl Larson

2001 *When Teams Work Best: 6,000 Team Members and Leaders Tell What It Takes to Succeed.* Thousand Oaks, CA: Sage Publications.

Lambsdorff, Johann Graf

2007 *The Institutional Economics of Corruption and Reform.* Cambridge: Cambridge University Press.

Lane, Christel, and Jocelyn Probert

2009 *National Capitalisms, Global Production Networks: Fashioning the Value Chain in the UK, USA, and Germany.* Oxford: Oxford University Press.

La Porta, R., F. Lopez-de-Silanes, A. Schleifer, and R. W. Vishny

1997 Trust in Large Organizations. *American Economic Review* 87 (Papers and Proceedings): 33–38.

LaPorte, Todd, and Paula Consolini

1991 Working in Practice but Not in Theory: Theoretical Challenges of "High Reliability Organizations." *Journal of Public Administration Research and Theory* 1 (January): 19–48.

Laqueur, Walter
1977   *Terrorism.* London: Weidenfeld and Nicolson.
Larsson, Rikad, Kenneth R. Brousseau, Michael J. Driver, and Patrick L. Sweet
2004   The Secrets of Merger Acquisition Success: A Co-Competence and Motivational Approach to Synergy Realization. In *Mergers and Acquisitions: Creating Integrative Knowledge,* eds. Amy L. Pablo and Mansour Javidan. Oxford: Blackwell, 3–19.
Laumann, Edward O., John H. Gagnon, Robert T. Michael, and Stuart Michaels
1994   *The Social Organization of Sexuality: Sexual Practices in the United States.* Chicago: University of Chicago Press.
Lazarsfeld, Paul F., and Robert K. Merton
1954   Friendship as a Social Process. In *Freedom and Control in Modern Society,* eds. Morroe Berger, Theodore Abel, and Charles Page. New York: van Nostrand, 18–66.
Lazarus, Richard S.
1991   *Emotion and Adaptation.* New York: Oxford University Press.
Lazarus, Richard S., and Susan Folkman
1984   *Stress, Appraisal, and Coping.* New York: Springer.
Leavitt, H. J.
1951   Some Effects of Certain Communication Patterns on Group Performance. *Journal of Abnormal and Social Psychology* 46: 38–50.
Le Bon, Gustav
1960 [1896]   *The Crowd: A Study of the Popular Mind,* with a new introduction by Robert K. Merton. New York: Viking Press.
Lee, Alfred McClung, and Norman Daymond Humphrey
1943   *Race Riot.* New York: Dryden Press.
Lee, Nancy Howell
1969   *The Search for an Abortionist.* Chicago: University of Chicago Press.
Leff, Nathaniel
1964   Economic Development through Bureaucratic Corruption. *American Behavioral Scientist* 7: 8–14.
Leibenstein, Harvey
1950   Bandwagon, Snob, and Veblen Effects in the Theory of Consumer Demand. *Quarterly Journal of Economics* 64: 183–207.
Leiter, Robert David
1948   *The Foreman in Industrial Relations.* New York: Columbia University Press.
Lenski, Gerhard
1954   Status Crystallization: A Non-Vertical Dimension of Social Status. *American Sociological Review* 19: 405–13.
Leonard, Madeline
2003   Women and Development in Examining Gender Issues in Developing Countries. In *From the Local to the Global: Key Issues in Developmental Studies,* eds. Gerard McCann and Stephen McCloskey. London: Pluto Press, 76–92.

Lerner, Daniel, with collaboration of Lucille W. Pevsner
  1958   *The Passing of Traditional Society: Modernizing the Middle East.* Glencoe, IL: Free Press.
Lerner, J. S., D. A. Small, and G. Loewenstein
  2004   Carryover Effects of Emotional Economic Decisions. *Psychological Science* 15: 337–41.
Lerner, M. J., and S. C. Lerner
  1981   *The Justice Motive in Social Behavior.* New York: Plenum Press.
Levi, Daniel
  2001   *Group Dynamics for Teams.* Thousand Oaks, CA: Sage Publications.
Levin, Iris, and Dan Zakay, eds.
  1989   *Time and Human Cognition: A Life-Span Perspective.* Amsterdam: North-Holland.
Levine, Donald N.
  1995   *Visions of the Sociological Tradition.* Chicago: University of Chicago Press.
Levinson, S. C.
  2001   Space: Linguistic Expression. In *International Encyclopedia of the Social and Behavioral Sciences,* eds. Neil J. Smelser and Paul B. Baltes. Oxford: Elsevier. Vol. 22, 14749–52.
Lévi-Strauss, Claude
  1965   *The Savage Mind.* Chicago: University of Chicago Press.
Lewin, Kurt, Ronald Lippitt, and Ralph K. White
  1939   Patterns of Aggressive Behavior in Experimentally Created Social Climates. *Journal of Social Psychology* 10: 271–99.
Lewis, David K.
  1973   *Counterfactuals.* Cambridge, MA: Harvard University Press.
Leys, Colin
  1974   *Underdevelopment in Kenya: The Political Economy of Neo-Colonialism.* Berkeley: University of California Press.
Liebow, Elliot
  1967   *Tally's Corner: A Study of Negro Streetcorner Men.* Boston: Little, Brown.
Light, Ivan
  2005   The Ethnic Economy. In *The Handbook of Economic Sociology,* eds. Neil J. Smelser and Richard Swedberg. Princeton and New York: Princeton University Press and Russell Sage Foundation, 650–77.
Lim, Vivien K. G., and Teo, Thompson S. H.
  2006   Cyberloafing and Organizational Justice: The Moderating Role of Neutralization Technique. In *The Internet and Workplace Transformation,* eds. Murugan Anandarajan, Thompson S. H. Teo, and Claire A. Simmiers. Armonk, NY: M. R. Sharpe, 241–58.
Lindblom, Charles D.
  1959   The Science of "Muddling Through." *Public Administration Review* 19: 79–88.
  1965   *The Intelligence of Democracy: Decision Making through Mutual Adaptation.* New York: Free Press.

Lindblom, Charles E., and David K. Cohen

1979   *Usable Social Science Knowledge and Social Problem Solving.* New Haven, CT: Yale University Press.

Lipman, Frederick D., and Seven E. Hall

2008   *Executive Compensation: Best Practices.* Hoboken, NJ: John Wiley and Sons.

Lipset, Seymour Martin

1959   Some Social Requisites of Democracy: Economic Development and Political Legitimacy. *American Political Science Review* 53: 69–105.

1963   The Value Patterns of Democracy: A Case Study in Comparative Analysis. *American Sociological Review* 28, no. 4: 515–31.

Locke, Edwin A., Diana Turnauer, Quinetta Roberson, Barry Goldman, et al.

2001   The Importance of the Individual in an Age of Groupism. In *Groups at Work: Theory and Research,* ed. Marlene E. Turner. Mahway, NJ: Lawrence Erlbaum Associates, 501–28.

Loewenstein, G., E. Weber, C. K. Hsee, and N. Welch

2001   Risk as Feelings. *Psychological Bulletin* 127: 167–86.

Loftus, Elizabeth F.

1979   *Eyewitness Testimony.* Cambridge, MA: Harvard University Press.

Loftus, Elizabeth F., and Katherine Ketcham

1996   *The Myth of Repressed Memory: False Memories and Allegations of Sexual Abuse.* New York: St. Martin's Griffin.

Loftus, Elizabeth F., and J. C. Palmer

1974   Reconstruction of Automobile Destruction: An Example of the Interaction between Language and Memory. *Journal of Verbal Learning and Verbal Behavior* 13: 585–89.

Lösch, August

1954   *The Economics of Location.* New Haven, CT: Yale University Press.

Lovell, Nadia, ed.

1998   *Locality and Belonging.* London: Routledge.

Lowi, Theodore J.

1988   Foreword. In *The Politics of Scandal: Power and Process in Liberal Democracies,* eds. Andrei S. Markovits and Mark Silverstein. New York: Holms and Meier, vii–xii.

Luhmann, Niklas

1979   *Trust and Power: Two Works.* New York: Wiley.

MacCoun, R.

2001   Legal Issues: Public Opinion. In *International Encyclopedia of the Social and Behavioral Sciences,* eds. Neil J. Smelser and Paul B. Baltes. Oxford: Elsevier. Vol. 13, 8641–46.

Macleod, Jenny, ed.

2008   *Defeat and Memory: Cultural Histories of Military Defeat in the Modern Era.* New York: Palgrave Macmillan.

Macrae, C. N., and G. V. Bodenhausen

2001   Social Cognition: Categorical Person Perception. *British Journal of Psychology* 92: 239–55.

Magiera, Jaroslaw, and Adam Powlak
    2005   Security Frameworks for Virtual Organizations. In *Virtual Organizations: Systems and Practices,* eds. Luis M. Cararinha-Matos, Harmideh Afsarmanesh, and Martin Ollus. New York: Springer, 133–48.
Majone, Giandomenico
    1989   *Evidence, Argument, and Persuasion in the Policy Process.* New Haven, CT: Yale University Press.
Makler, H. M.
    2001   Financial Institutions in Economic Development. In *International Encyclopedia of the Social and Behavioral Sciences,* eds. Neil J. Smelser and Paul B. Baltes. Oxford: Elsevier. Vol. 8, 5661–66.
Malinowski, Bronislaw
    1922   *Argonauts of the Western Pacific.* London: Routledge and Kegan Paul.
March, James G., and Herbert A. Simon
    1958   *Organizations.* New York: John Wiley & Sons.
March, James G., and Roger Weissinger-Baylon, eds.
    1986   *Ambiguity and Command: Organizational Perspectives on Military Decision Making.* Marshfield, MA: Pitman Publishing Inc.
Mark, M. M., and C. S. Reichardt
    2001   Internal Validity. In *International Encyclopedia of the Social and Behavioral Sciences,* eds. Neil J. Smelser and Paul B. Baltes. Oxford: Elsevier. Vol. 11, 7749–52.
Marks, M. L., and P. M. Mirvis
    1998   *Joining Forces: Making One Plus One Equal Three in Mergers, Acquisitions, and Alliances.* San Francisco: Jossey-Bass.
Marone, Joseph G., and Edward J. Woodhouse
    1986   *Averting Catastrophe: Strategies for Regulating Risky Technologies.* Berkeley: University of California Press.
Marsh, Robert M.
    1967   *Comparative Sociology.* New York: Harcourt, Brace, and World.
Martin, James, and James E. Samels & Associates
    2004   *Presidential Transition in Higher Education: Managing Leadership Change.* Baltimore: Johns Hopkins University Press.
Martinelli, Alberto
    2001   Management, General. In *International Encyclopedia of the Behavioral and Social Sciences,* eds. Neil J. Smelser and Paul B. Baltes. Oxford: Elsevier. Vol. 13, 9170–78.
Martinez-Diaz, Leonardo, and Ngaire Woods
    2009   Introduction: Developing Countries in a Networked Global Order. In *Networks of Influence: Developing Countries in a Networked Global Order,* eds. Leonardo Martinez-Diaz and Ngaire Woods. Oxford: Oxford University Press, 1–18.
Marx, Karl
    1949 [1868]   *Capital: A Critical Analysis of Capitalist Production.* Trans. Samuel Moore and Edward Aveling, ed. Frederick Engels. London: Allen and Unwin.

Maslach, Christina
   1997   *The Truth about Burnout: How Organizations Cause Personal Stress and What to Do about It.* San Francisco: Jossey-Bass.
Massey, Douglas S., and Nancy A. Denton
   1993   *American Apartheid: Segregation and the Making of the Underclass.* Cambridge, MA: Harvard University Press.
Masson, Jeffrey M.
   1984   *The Assault on Truth: Freud's Suppression of the Seduction Theory.* New York: Farrar, Straus, and Giroux.
Matsusaka, John G.
   2006   Takeover Motives during the Conglomerate Merger Wave. In *Corporate Restructuring,* eds. John J. McConnell and David J. Denis. Cheltenham, UK: Edward Elgar, 357–83.
Matza, David
   1966   The Disreputable Poor. In *Social Structure and Mobility in Economic Development,* eds. Neil J. Smelser and Seymour Martin Lipset. Chicago: Aldine Publishing Company, 310–39.
McCartney, C.
   1999   *The Categorization Process in Social Psychology.* London: Sage Publications.
McClelland, David
   1961   *The Achieving Society.* Princeton: Van Nostrand.
McConnell, John J., and Timothy J. Nantell
   2005   Corporate Combinations and Common Stock Returns: The Case of Joint Ventures. In *Corporate Restructuring,* eds. John J. McConnell and David J. Denis. Cheltenham, UK: Edward Elgar, 399–416.
McCoy, Thomas J.
   1992   *Compensation and Motivation: Maximizing Employee Performance with Behavior-Based Incentive Plans.* New York: AMACOM.
McCrae, R. R., and John, O. P.
   1992   An Introduction to the Five-Factor Model and Its Applications. *Journal of Personality* 60: 175–215.
McCubbins, Matthew, Roger Noll, and Barry Weingast
   1987   Administrative Procedures as Instruments of Political Control. *Journal of Law, Economics, and Organizations* 3: 243–77.
McKenna, Christopher D.
   2006   *The World's Newest Profession: Management Consulting in the Twentieth Century.* Cambridge: Cambridge University Press.
McKenna, Katelyn Y. A.
   2008   Influences on the Nature and Functioning of Online Groups. In *Psychological Aspects of Cyberspace: Theory, Research, and Applications,* ed. Azy Barak. Cambridge: Cambridge University Press, 228–42.
McKenna, Katelyn Y. A., and A. S. Green
   2002   Virtual Group Dynamics. *Group Dynamics: Research and Practice* 6: 16–27.

McLaughlin, Milbrey W., and D. C. Phillips, eds.

1991   *Evaluation and Education: At Quarter Century.* Chicago: National Society for the Study of Education.

Medvec, Victoria Husted, Scott F. Madey, and Thomas Gilovich

1995   When Less Is More: Counterfactual Thinking and Satisfaction among Olympic Medalists. *Journal of Personality and Social Psychology* 69: 603–10.

Meehl, Paul E.

1954   *Clinical vs. Statistical Predictions: A Theoretical Analysis and a Review of the Evidence.* Minneapolis: University of Minnesota Press.

Meier, Gerald M.

2001   The Old Generation of Development Economists and the New. In *Frontiers of Development Economics: The Future in Perspective,* eds. Gerald M. Meier and Joseph E. Stiglitz. Washington, DC, and New York: World Bank and Oxford University Press, 13–50.

Meier, Gerald M., and James E. Rauch

2005   *Leading Issues in Economic Development,* 8th ed. New York: Oxford University Press.

Meindl, J., S. Ehlrich, and J. Dukerich

1985   The Romance of Leadership. *Administrative Science Quarterly* 30: 78–102.

Menes, Rebecca

2006   Limiting the Reach of the Grabbing Hand: Graft and Growth in American Cities. In *Corruption and Reform: Lessons from America's Economic History,* eds. Edward L. Glaeser and Claudia Goldin. Chicago: University of Chicago Press, 63–93.

Menikoff, Jerrry

2006   *What the Doctor Didn't Say: The Hidden Truth about Medical Research.* Oxford: Oxford University Press.

Mény, Y., and L. de Sousa

2001   Corruption: Political and Public Aspects. In *International Encyclopedia of the Social and Behavioral Sciences,* eds. Neil J. Smelser and Paul B. Baltes. Oxford: Elsevier. Vol. 4, 2824–30.

Merton, Robert K.

1968a. Social Structure and Anomie. In Robert K. Merton, *Social Theory and Social Structure,* rev. and enlarged ed. New York: Free Press, 185–214.

1968b. Manifest and Latent Functions. In Robert K. Merton, *Social Theory and Social Structure,* rev. and enlarged ed. New York: Free Press, 73–138.

Merton, Robert K., and Alice S. Rossi

1968   Continuities in the Theory of Reference Groups and Social Structure. In Robert K. Merton, *Social Theory and Social Structure,* rev. and enlarged ed. New York: Free Press, 279–334.

Messick, David M., and Roderick M. Kramer

2001   Trust as a Form of Shallow Morality. In *Trust and Society,* ed. Karen S. Cook. New York: Russell Sage Foundation, 89–117.

Metzler, Wolfgang
   2004   Experts' Discourses as Judicial Drama or Bureaucratic Coordination: Family Debate in the United States and Germany. In *Experts in Science and Society,* eds. Elke Kurz-Milcke and Gerd Gigerenzer. New York: Kluwer Academic, 27–46.
Miceli, Marcia P., and Janet P. Near
   1992   *Blowing the Whistle: The Organizational and Legal Implications for Companies and Employees.* New York: Lexington Books.
Mickelthwait, John, and Adrian Woldridge
   1996   *The Witch Doctors: Making Sense of the Management Gurus.* New York: Times Books.
Milgram, Stanley
   1974   *Obedience to Authority: An Experimental View.* New York: HarperCollins.
Mills, C. Wright
   1956   *The Power Elite.* Oxford: Oxford University Press.
Mingus, Matthew S.
   2007   Bounded Rationality and Organizational Influence: Herbert Simon and the Behavioral Revolution. In *Handbook of Decision Making,* ed. Göktug Morçöl. Boca Raton, FL: Taylor and Francis, 61–79.
Mintzberg, H.
   1973   *The Nature of Managerial Work.* New York: Harper and Row.
Mitchell, J. D.
   1969   The Concept and Use of Social Networks. In *Social Networks in Urban Situations,* ed. J. Clyde Mitchell. Manchester: Manchester University Press, 19–50.
Mithander, Conny, John Sundholm, and Maria Holmgren Troy, eds.
   2007   *Collective Traumas: Memories of War and Conflict in 20th-Century Europe.* New York: P.I.E.P. Lang.
Modigliani, A., and F. Rochat
   1995   The Role of Interaction Sequences and the Timing of Resistance in Shaping Obedience and Defiance to Authority. *Journal of Social Issues* 51: 107–23.
Monge, Peter R.
   1987   The Network Level of Analysis. In *Handbook of Communication Science,* eds. Charles Berger and Steven H. Chafee. Beverly Hills, CA: Sage Publications, 39–70.
Moon, M., and A. Martin
   1990   Better Heuristics for Economic Search: Experimental and Simulation Evidence. *Journal of Behavioral Decision Making* 3: 175–93.
Morahan-Martin, Janet
   2008   Internet Abuse: Emerging Trends and Lingering Questions. In *Psychological Aspects of Cyberspace: Theory, Research, and Applications,* ed. Azy Barak. Cambridge: Cambridge University Press, 32–69.
Moreno, Jacob L.
   1945   *Sociometric Measurement of Social Configurations, Based on Deviations from Chance.* New York: Beacon House.
Moskos, Charles C. Jr.
   1970   *The American Enlisted Man.* New York: Russell Sage Foundation.

Muggia, Franco M., and Marcel Rozencweig, eds.

   1987   *Clinical Evaluation of Anti-Tumor Therapy.* Boston: Nijhoff.

Muscovici, Serge

   1976   *Social Influence and Social Change.* London: Academic Press.

Muscovici, S., and C. Nemeth

   1974   Minority Influence. In *Social Psychology: Classic and Contemporary Integrations,* ed. C. Nemeth. Chicago: Rand McNally, 217–49.

Nadel, S. F.

   1949   *The Foundations of Social Anthropology.* London: Cohen and West.

Nagar, Dinesh

   1998   *Human Reactions to Crowding.* Jaipur, India: Printwell.

Nagin, D. S.

   2001   Deterrence: Legal Perspectives. In *International Encyclopedia of the Social and Behavioral Sciences,* eds. Neil J. Smelser and Paul B. Baltes. Oxford: Elsevier. Vol. 5, 3544–50.

Naimark, Norman M.

   2001   *Fires of Hatred: Ethnic Cleansing in Twentieth-Century Europe.* Cambridge, MA: Harvard University Press.

National Bureau Committee for Economic Research

   1960   Comment. In *Demographic and Economic Change in Developed Countries,* ed. National Bureau of Economic Research. Princeton: Princeton University Press.

Nee, Victor

   2005   The New Institutionalisms in Economics and Sociology. In *The Handbook of Economic Sociology,* eds. Neil J. Smelser and Richard Swedberg. Princeton and New York: Princeton University Press and Russell Sage Foundation, 49–74.

Nelson, Barbara J.

   1984   *Making an Issue of Child Abuse: Political Agenda Setting for Social Problems.* Chicago: University of Chicago Press.

Neuman, Joel H., and Robert A. Baron

   1997   Aggression in the Workplace. In *Antisocial Behavior in Organizations,* eds. Robert A. Giacalone and Jerald Greenberg. Thousand Oaks, CA: Sage Publications, 37–67.

Neustadt, Richard

   1990   *Presidential Power and the Modern Presidents.* New York: Free Press.

Newell, A., and Herbert Simon

   1972   *Human Problem Solving.* Englewood Cliffs, NJ: Prentice-Hall.

Newman, M. E. J.

   2010   *Networks: An Introduction.* Oxford: Oxford University Press.

Niedenthal, P. M., and M. B. Setterlund

   1994   Emotion Congruence in Perception. *Personality and Social Psychology Bulletin* 20: 401–11.

Nord, W. R.

   2001   Individual Identities in Organizations. In *International Encyclopedia of the*

Social and Behavioral Sciences, eds. Neil J. Smelser and Paul B. Baltes. Oxford: Elsevier. Vol. 11, 7299–7306.

Nordhaus, William D.

2000   Preface. In *Controversies in Macroeconomics: Growth, Trade and Policy,* ed. Huw David Dixon. Oxford: Blackwell Publishers, xiv–xvi.

Norris, Paul

2005   Shareholders' Attitude to Directors' Pay. In *Top Pay and Performance: International and Strategic Approach,* eds. Shaun Tyson and Frank Bournois. Amsterdam: Elsevier, 29–56.

North, Douglass C.

1990   *Institutions, Institutional Change, and Economic Development.* Cambridge: Cambridge University Press.

2003   Needed: A Theory of Change. In *Frontiers of Development Economics: The Future in Perspective,* eds. Gerald M. Meier and Joseph E. Stiglitz. Washington, DC, and New York: World Bank and Oxford University Press, 491–505.

Northcraft, Gregory, and Margaret Neale

1987   Experts, Amateurs, and Real Estate: An Anchoring-Adjustment Perspective on Property Pricing Decisions. *Organizational Behavior and Human Decision Processes* 39: 84–97.

Nurkse, Ragnar

1962   *Problems of Capital Formation in Underdeveloped Areas.* New York: Oxford University Press.

Nutt, Paul C., and David C. Wilson

2010a.   Crucial Trends and Issues in Strategic Decision Making. In *Handbook of Decision Making,* eds. Paul C. Nutt and David C. Wilson. Chichester, UK: John Wiley & Sons, 3–29.

2010b.   Discussion and Implications: Toward Creating a Unified Theory of Decision Making. In *Handbook of Decision Making,* eds. Paul C. Nutt and David C. Wilson. Chichester, UK: John Wiley & Sons, 645–77.

Nye, Joseph

1967   Corruption and Political Development: A Cost-Benefit Analysis. *American Political Science Review* 61: 417–67.

Ogburn, William F., and Meyer F. Nimkoff

1955   *Technology and the Changing Family.* Boston: Houghton Mifflin.

Olweus, Dan

2003   Bully/Victim Problems in Schools: Basic Facts and an Effective Intervention Program. In *Bullying and Emotional Abuse in the Workplace: International Perspectives in Research and Practice,* eds. Ståle Einarsen, Helge Hoel, Dieter Zapf, and Cary L. Cooper. London: Taylor and Francis, 62–78.

O'Neill, B.

2001   Cassandra/Cornucopian Debate. In *International Encyclopedia of the Social and Behavioral Sciences,* eds. Neil J. Smelser and Paul B. Baltes. Oxford: Elsevier. Vol. 3, 1525–29.

Organization for Economic Cooperation and Development (OECD)

2001   *The Well-Being of Nations: The Role of Human and Social Capital.* Paris: OECD.

Owen, Alma J., Ramona K. Z. Heck, and Barbara R. Rowe

1995   Harmonizing Family and Work. In *Home-Based Employment and Family Life,* eds. Ramona K. Z. Heck, Alma J. Owen, and Barbara R. Rowe. Westport, CT: Auburn House, 1–14.

Papadapoulos, Yiannis

2007   Problems of Democratic Accountability in Network and Multilevel Governance. *European Law Journal* 13: 469–86.

Parker, Glen, Jerry McAdams, and David Zielinski

2000   *Rewarding Teams: Lessons from the Trenches.* San Francisco: Jossey-Bass.

Parsons, Talcott

1951   *The Social System.* Glencoe, IL: Free Press.

1954 [1939]   The Professions and Social Structure. In Talcott Parsons, *Essays in Sociological Theory.* Rev. ed. Glencoe, IL: Free Press, 34–49.

1954 [1940]   The Motivation of Economic Activities. In Talcott Parsons, *Essays in Sociological Theory.* Rev. ed. Glencoe, IL: Free Press, 50–68.

1963   On the Concept of Influence. *Public Opinion Quarterly* 27: 37–62.

Parsons, Talcott, and Robert F. Bales

1955   *Family, Socialization, and Interaction Process.* Glencoe, IL: Free Press.

Parsons, Talcott, and Edward A. Shils

1951   *Toward a General Theory of Action.* Cambridge, MA: Harvard University Press.

Pastor, Maria A., and Julio Artieda, eds.

1996   *Time, Internal Clocks and Movement.* Amsterdam: Elsevier.

Patashnik, E. M.

2001   Planning, Politics of. In *International Encyclopedia of the Social and Behavioral Sciences,* eds. Neil J. Smelser and Paul B. Baltes. Oxford: Elsevier. Vol. 17, 11483–85.

Paternoster, R., and S. Simpson

1996   Sanction Threats and Appeals to Morality: Testing a Rational Choice Model of Corporate Crime. *Law and Society Review* 30: 457–79.

Patterson, M. G., M. A. West, R. L. Lawthom, and S. Nickell

1997   *People Management and Business Performance.* London: Institute for Personnel and Development.

Pauleen, David J.

2004   *Virtual Teams: Projects, Protocols, and Processes.* Hershey, PA: Idea Group Publishing.

Pavlik, Ellen L., and Ahmed Belkaoui

1991   *Determinants of Executive Compensation: Corporate Ownership, Performance, Size, and Diversification.* New York: Quorum Books.

Peet, Richard, and Elaine Hartwick

2009   *Theories of Development: Contentions, Arguments, Alternatives.* New York: Guilford Press.

Perrow, Charles
   1984   *Normal Accidents: Living with High-Risk Technologies.* New York: Basic Books.
Pettigrew, Thomas E.
   1979   The Ultimate Attribution Error: Extending Allport's Cognitive Analysis of
           Prejudice. *Personality and Social Psychology Bulletin* 5: 461–76.
Pfeffer, Jeffrey
   1977   The Ambiguity of Leadership. *Academy of Management Review* 2: 104–12.
   1992   *Managing with Power.* Cambridge, MA: Harvard University Press.
Pfiffner, James P.
   2005   *The Modern Presidency,* 4th ed. Belmont, CA: Wadsworth.
Phillips, James G.
   2006   The Psychology of Internet Use and Abuse. In *The Internet and Workplace Trans-
           formation,* eds. Murugan Anandarajan, S. H. Teo Thompson, and Claire A. Sim-
           mers. Armonk, NY: M. E. Sharpe, 41–62.
Picherit-Duthler, Gaelle, Shawn D. Long, and Gary F. Kohut
   2004   Newcomer Assimilation in Virtual Team Socialization. In *Virtual and Collab-
           orative Teams: Processes, Technologies, and Practice,* eds. Susan H. Godar and
           Sharmila Pixy Ferris. Hershey, PA: Idea Group Publishing, 99–113.
Piore, Michael J., and Charles F. Sabel
   1984   *The Second Industrial Divide.* New York: Basic Books.
Plummer, Deborah L.
   2003   *Handbook of Diversity Management: Beyond Awareness to Competency Based
           Learning.* Lanham, MD: University Press of America.
Polanyi, Karl, Conrad Arensberg, and Harry Pearson
   1957   *Trade and Market in the Early Empires.* Glencoe, IL: Free Press and Falcon's
           Wing Press.
Portes, Alejandro
   1998   Social Capital: Its Origins and Applications in Modern Sociology. *Annual Review
           of Sociology* 22: 1–22.
Posner, Daniel
   2005   *Institutions and Ethnic Politics in Africa.* Cambridge: Cambridge University Press.
Powell, Walter W.
   1990   Neither Market Nor Hierarchy: Network Forms of Organization. *Research in
           Organizational Behavior* 12: 95–336.
Praeger, Jeffrey
   1997   *Presenting the Past: Psychoanalysis and the Psychology of Misremembering.* Cam-
           bridge, MA: Harvard University Press.
Prebisch, Paul
   1950   *The Economic Development of Latin America and Its Problems.* New York: United
           Nations, Department of Social and Economic Affairs.
Pred, Alan
   1973   *Urban Growth and the Circulation of Information: The United States System of
           Cities, 1790–1840.* Cambridge, MA: Harvard University Press.

President's Research Committee on Social Trends
   1933   *Recent Social Trends in the United States.* New York: McGraw-Hill.
Pucik, Vladimir, and Paul Evans
   2003   The Human Factor in Mergers and Acquisitions. In *Managing Complex Mergers: Real World Lessons in Implementing Cross-Cultural Mergers and Acquisitions,* eds. Piero Morosini and Ulrich Steger. Harlow, UK: Financial Times Prentice-Hall, 161–87.
Putnam, Robert D.
   2000   *Bowling Alone: The Collapse and Revival of American Community.* New York: Simon and Schuster.
Putnam, Robert D., with Robert Leonardi and Raffaella Y. Nanetti
   1994   *Making Democracy Work: Civic Traditions in Modern Italy.* Princeton: Princeton University Press.
Quah, Jon S. T.
   2010   Civil Service and Corruption. In *Perspectives on Corruption and Human Development,* eds. Anuradha Rajivan and Ramesh Gampat. Delhi, India: Macmillan, Vol. 2, 806–42.
Rabin, Matthew
   2004   Incorporating Fairness into Game Theory and Economics. In *Advances in Behavioral Economics,* eds. Colin F. Camerer, George Loewenstein, and Matthew Rabin. New York and Princeton: Russell Sage Foundation and Princeton University Press, 297–325.
Radcliffe-Brown, A. R.
   1952   *Structure and Function in Primitive Society: Essays and Addresses.* Glencoe, IL: Free Press.
Ragin, Charles
   1987   *The Comparative Method: Moving Beyond Qualitative and Quantitative Strategies.* Berkeley: University of California Press.
Rakel, Horst
   2004   Scientists as Expert Advisors: Science Cultures versus National Cultures. In *Experts in Science and Society,* eds. Elke Kurz-Milcke and Gerd Gigerenzer. New York: Kluwer Academic, 3–25.
Rasmussen, Jens
   1997   Merging Paradigms: Decision Making, Management and Cognitive Control. In *Decision-Making under Stress: Emerging Themes and Applications,* eds. Rhona Flin, Eduardo Salas, Michael Strub, and Lynn Martin. Aldershot, UK: Ashgate, 76–81.
Rath, Tom
   2006   *Vital Friends: The People You Can't Afford to Live Without.* New York: Gallup Press.
Rattan, Vernon
   2003   *Social Science Knowledge and Economic Development.* Ann Arbor: University of Michigan Press.

Redfield, Robert

1941   *The Folk Culture of Yucatan.* Chicago: University of Chicago Press.

Reinalda, Bob, and Bertjan Verbeek, eds.

2004   *Decision Making within International Organizations.* London: Routledge.

Reiss, Albert J. Jr., ed.

1964   *Louis Wirth on Cities and Social Life.* Chicago: University of Chicago Press.

Reynolds, G. S.

1975   *A Primer of Operant Conditioning,* rev. ed. Glenview, IL: Scott, Foresman and Company.

Rick, Scott, and George Loewenstein

2008   The Role of Emotion in Economic Behavior. In *Handbook of Emotions,* eds. Michael Lewis, Jeannette M. Haviland-Jones, and Lisa Feldman Barrett. New York: Guilford Press, 138–58.

Riesman, David, in collaboration with Reuel Denney and Nathan Glazer

1950   *The Lonely Crowd: A Study of the Changing American Character.* New Haven, CT: Yale University Press.

Riley, David

1990   Network Influence on Father Involvement in Childrearing. In *Extending Families: The Social Networks of Parents and Their Children,* eds. Moncreiff Cochran, Mary Larner, David Riley, Lars Gunnersson, et al. Cambridge: Cambridge University Press, 131–52.

Roberts, Patrick S.

2006   FEMA and the Prospects for Reputation-Based Autonomy. *Studies in American Political Development* 20: 57–87.

Robertson, Roland

1992   *Globalization: Social Theory and Global Culture.* London: Sage Publications.

Robinson, Sandra L., Kurt T. Dirks, and Haman Ozcelik

2004   Untangling the Knot of Trust and Betrayal. In *Trust and Distrust in Organizations: Dilemmas and Approaches,* eds. Roderick M. Kramer and Karen S. Cook. New York: Russell Sage Foundation, 327–41.

Rodrik, Dani

2007   *One Economics Many Recipes: Globalization, Institutions, and Economic Growth.* Princeton: Princeton University Press.

Roese, Neal J., and James M. Olson

1995   *What Might Have Been: The Social Psychology of Counterfactual Thinking.* Mahway, NJ: Lawrence Erlbaum Associates.

Roethlisberger, F. J., and W. J. Dickson

1934   *Management and the Worker: Technical vs. Social Organization in an Industrial Plant.* Boston: Harvard University Press.

Rogin, Michael P.

1975   *Fathers and Children: Andrew Jackson and the Subjugation of the American Indian.* New York: Knopf.

Rose, N. L.

2001   Regulation: Empirical Analysis. In *International Encyclopedia of the Social and*

Behavioral Sciences, eds. Neil J. Smelser and Paul B. Baltes. Oxford: Elsevier. Vol. 19, 12957–63.

Rose, Pauline
2006   From Washington to Post-Washington Consensus: The Triumph of Human Capital. In *The New Development Economics: After the Washington Consensus,* eds. K. S. Jomo and Ben Fine. London: Zed Books, 162–83.

Ross, D.
2001   Progress: History of the Concept. In *International Encyclopedia of the Social and Behavioral Sciences,* eds. Neil J. Smelser and Paul B. Baltes. Oxford: Elsevier. Vol. 18, 12173–77.

Rossi, Peter H.
1972   Testing for Success and Failure in Social Action. In *Evaluating Social Programs: Theory, Practice and Politics,* eds. Peter H. Rossi and Walter Williams. New York: Seminar Press, 11–49.

Rossi, Peter H., and Howard E. Freeman
1993   *Evaluation: A Systematic Approach.* Newbury Park, CA: Sage Publications.

Rostow, W. W.
1960   *The Stages of Economic Growth: A Non-Communist Manifesto.* Cambridge: Cambridge University Press.

Rothstein, Bo
2004   Social Trust and Honesty in Government: A Causal Mechanisms Approach. In *Creating Social Trust in Post-Socialist Transition,* eds. Janos Kornai, Bo Rothstein, and Susan Rose-Ackerman. New York: Palgrave-Macmillan, 13–30.

Rowe, Barbara R., and Ramona K. Z. Hick, with the assistance of Alma J. Owen, Kathryn Stafford, and Mary Winter
1995   Homeworking Families and How They Make It Work. In *Home-Based Employment and Family Life,* eds. Ramona K. Z. Heck, Alma J. Owen, and Barbara R. Rowe. Westport, CT: Auburn House, 107–34.

Roy, Donald F.
1960   Banana Time: Job Satisfaction and Informal Interactions. *Human Organization* 18: 158–68.
1972   Efficiency and "The Fix": Informal Intergroup Relations in a Piecework Machine Shop. In *Organizational Issues in Industrial Society,* ed. Jon M. Shepard. Englewood Cliffs, NJ: Prentice-Hall, 157–72.

Rudalvige, Andew
2005   The Structure of Leadership: Presidents, Hierarchies and Information Flow. *Presidential Studies Quarterly* 35: 333–60.

Rueschemeyer, Dietrich
2009   *Usable Theory: Analytic Tools for Social and Political Research.* Princeton: Princeton University Press.

Rule, James B.
1992   Rational Choice and the Limits of Theoretical Generality. *Rationality and Society* 4: 449–66.

Runciman, W. G.

1966   *Relative Deprivation and Social Justice: A Study of Attitudes to Social Inequality in Twentieth Century Britain.* London: Routledge and Kegan Paul.

Rupp, L. J.

2001   Feminist Movements. In *International Encyclopedia of the Social and Behavioral Sciences,* eds. Neil J. Smelser and Paul B. Baltes. Oxford: Elsevier. Vol. 8, 5469–72.

Russo, J. Edward, and Paul J. H. Schoemaker

1989   *Decision Traps: The Ten Barriers to Brilliant Decision Making and How to Overcome Them.* New York: Simon and Schuster.

Rutte, Christel G.

2006   Convergence in Virtual Teams. In *The Internet and Workplace Transformation,* eds. Murugn Anandarajan, Thompson S. H. Teo, and Claire A. Simmers. Armonk, NY: M. E. Sharpe, 151–61.

Rutz, Henry J., ed.

1992   *The Politics of Time.* Washington, DC: American Anthropological Association.

Sadowski-Raskers, Gary, Geert Duysters, and Bert M. Sadowski

2006   *Communication and Cooperation in the Virtual Workplace.* Cheltenham, UK: Edward Elgar.

Sagan, Scott D.

1993   *The Limits of Safety: Organizations, Accidents, and Nuclear Weapons.* Princeton: Princeton University Press.

Sageman, Marc

2004   *Understanding Terror Networks.* Philadelphia: University of Pennsylvania Press.

Salas, Eduardo, and Gary Klein

2001   "Expertise and Naturalistic Decision Making: An Overview." In *Linking Expertise and Naturalistic Decision Making,* eds. Eduardo Salas and Gary Klein. Mahwah, NJ: Lawrence Erlbauym Associates, 3–8.

Salka, William

2004   Mission Evolution: The United States Forest Service's Response to Crisis. *Review of Policy Research* 1: 221–32.

Sampson, Edward E., and Marya Marthas

1990   *Group Process for the Health Professions,* 3rd ed. New York: Delmar.

Sampson, R. J., and J. H. Laub

1993   *Crime in the Making: Pathways and Turning Points through Life.* Cambridge, MA: Harvard University Press.

Santos, Boaventura de Sousa

2001   Globalization: Legal Aspects. In *International Encyclopedia of the Social and Behavioral Sciences,* eds. Neil J. Smelser and Paul B. Baltes. Oxford: Elsevier. Vol. 9, 6277–84.

Sarat, A.

2001   Death Penalty. In *International Encyclopedia of the Social Sciences,* eds. Neil J. Smelser and Paul B. Baltes. Oxford: Elsevier. Vol. 5, 3273–78.

Schafer, Mark, and Scott Crichlow

    2010   *Groupthink versus High-Quality Decision Making in International Relations.* New York: Columbia University Press, 2010.

Schein, Edgar F.

    2004   *Organizational Culture and Leadership.* San Francisco: Jossey-Bass.

Schelling, Thomas C.

    1966   *Arms and Influence.* New Haven, CT: Yale University Press.

Schmidt, Jeffrey A.

    2002a. The Strategic Importance of People. In Jeffrey A. Schmidt, *Making Mergers Work: The Strategic Importance of People.* Alexandria, VA: Towers Perrin / Strategic Resource Management, 3–21.

    2002b. Business Perspectives on Mergers and Acquisitions. In *Making Mergers Work: The Strategic Importance of People.* Alexandria, VA: Towers Perrin / Strategic Resource Management, 23–44.

Schneider, B.

    1987   The People Make the Place. *Personnel Psychology* 40: 437–53.

Schraagen, Jan Maaarten, Laura G. Militello, Tom Ormerod, and Raanan Lipshitz

    2008   *Naturalistic Decision Making and Macrocognition.* Burlington, VT: Ashgate.

Schumpeter, Joseph A.

    1949   *The Theory of Economic Development,* trans. Redvers Opie. Cambridge, MA: Harvard University Press.

Schuurman, Frans, ed.

    1993   *Beyond the Impasse: New Directions in Development Theory.* London: Zed Books.

Scott, John

    2000   *Social Network Analysis: A Handbook,* 2nd ed. London: Sage Publications.

Scott, W. Richard, and Gerald F. Davis

    2007   *Organizations and Organizing: Rational, Natural, and Open System Perspectives.* Upper Saddle River, NJ: Pearson / Prentice-Hall.

Seeman, Melvin

    1959   On the Meaning of Alienation. *American Sociological Review* 23: 783–91.

Selfox, H. T., S. Palmisani, C. Scurlock, E. J. Orav, et al.

    2006   The "To Err Is Human" Report and the Patient Safety Literature. *Quality & Safety in Health Care* 15: 174–78.

Seligson, Mitchell A., and John T. Passé-Smith

    2008   *Development and Underdevelopment: The Political Economy of Global Inequality,* 4th ed. Boulder, CO: Lynne Rienner Publishers.

Selznick, Philip

    1953   *TVA and the Grass Roots: A Study in the Sociology of Formal Organization.* Berkeley: University of California Press.

    1957   *Leadership in Administration.* Evanston, IL: Row, Peterson.

Semadeni, Matthew

    2001   Toward a Theory of Knowledge Arbitrage: Examining Management Consultants as Knowledge Arbiters and Arbitragers. In *Current Trends in Management Consulting,* ed. Anthony F. Buono. Greenwich, CT: Information Age Publishers, 43–67.

Sen, Amartya

  1988   The Concept of Development. In *Handbook of Economic Development,* eds.
          H. Chenery and T. N. Srinivasen. Amsterdam: Elsevier, 9–26.

Sennett, Richard

  1998   *The Corrosion of Character: The Personal Consequences of Work in the New
          Capitalism.* New York: Norton.

Shackle, G. L. S.

  1969   *Decision, Order, and Time in Human Affairs.* Cambridge: Cambridge University
          Press.

Shah, Samir

  2005   Integrated Risk Management. In *Integrated Risk Management for E-Business,* ed.
          Abderrahim Labbi. Boca Raton, FL: J. Ross Publishing, 33–62.

Shapiro, Arthur K., and Elaine Shapiro

  1997   *The Powerful Placebo: From Ancient Priest to Modern Physician.* Baltimore:
          Johns Hopkins University Press.

Shaw, Marvin E.

  1981   *Group Dynamics: The Psychology of Small Group Behavior,* 3rd ed. New York:
          McGraw-Hill.

Sherif, Muzafer

  1936   *The Psychology of Social Norms.* New York: HarperCollins.

Shils, Edward A., and Morris Janowitz

  1948   Cohesion and Disintegration in the Wehrmacht in World War II. *Public Opinion
          Quarterly* 12: 280–315.

Shleifer, Andrei, and Robert W. Vishny

  2005   Stock Market Driven Acquisitions. In *Corporate Restructuring,* eds. John J.
          McConnell and David J. Denis. Cheltenham, UK: Edward Elgar, 295–311.

Shostak, Arthur B.

  1998   Virtual Corporations and American Labor Unions: So Many Unknowns, So
          Much Potential. In *The Virtual Workplace,* eds. Magid Igbaria and Margaret
          Tan. Hershey, PA: Idea Group Publishing, 360–67.

Silverman, E. K.

  2001   Time, Anthropology of. In *International Encyclopedia of the Social and Behav-
          ioral Sciences,* eds. Neil J. Smelser and Paul B. Baltes. Oxford: Elsevier. Vol. 23,
          15682–86.

Silvester, Jo, ed.

  2008   *Organizational Psychology: Critical Concepts in Psychology.* 4 vols. London:
          Routledge.

Simon, Herbert A.

  1947   *Administrative Behavior: A Study of Decision Making Processes in Organizations.*
          Foreword by Chester I. Barnard. New York: Macmillan.

  1965   Administrative Decision-Making. *Public Administration Review* 25: 31–47.

  2001   Rationality in Society. In *International Encyclopedia of the Social and Behav-
          ioral Sciences,* eds. Neil J. Smelser and Paul B. Baltes. Oxford: Elsevier. Vol. 19,
          12782–86.

Skowronek, Stephen

1993   *The Politics Presidents Make: Leadership from John Adams to George Bush.* Cambridge, MA: Harvard University Press.

Sloman, Steven A.

2002   Two Systems of Reasoning. In *Heuristics and Bias: The Psychology of Intuitive Judgment,* eds. Thomas Gilovich, Dale Griffin, and Daniel Kahneman. Cambridge: Cambridge University Press, 379–96.

Slovic, Paul, Melissa Finucane, Ellen Peters, and Donald G. MacGregor

2002   The Affect Heuristic. In *Heuristics and Bias: The Psychology of Intuitive Judgment,* eds. Thomas Gilovich, Dale Griffin, and Daniel Kahneman. Cambridge: Cambridge University Press, 397–420.

Smelser, Neil J.

1959   *Social Change in the Industrial Revolution: An Application of Theory to the Lancashire Cotton Industry, 1770–1840.* Chicago: University of Chicago Press.

1962   *Theory of Collective Behavior.* New York: Free Press.

1969   The Optimum Scope of Sociology. In *A Design for Sociology: Scope, Objectives, and Methods,* ed. Robert Bierstedt. Philadelphia: American Academy of Political and Social Science, 1–21.

1976   *Comparative Methods in the Social Sciences.* Englewood Cliffs, NJ: Prentice-Hall.

1991   *Social Paralysis and Social Change: British Working-Class Education in the Nineteenth Century.* Berkeley: University of California Press.

1995   Economic Rationality as a Religious System. In *Rethinking Materialism: Perspectives on the Spiritual Dimension of Economic Behavior,* ed. Robert Wuthnow. Grand Rapids, MI: William B. Eerdmans, 73–92.

2007   *The Faces of Terrorism: Social and Psychological Dimensions.* Princeton: Princeton University Press.

2010   *Reflections on the University of California: From the Free Speech Movement to a Global University.* Berkeley: University of California Press.

Smelser, Neil J., and Paul B. Baltes, eds.

2001   *International Encyclopedia of the Social and Behavioral Sciences.* 26 vols. Oxford: Elsevier.

Smelser, Neil J., and Robin Content

1980   *The Changing Academic Market: Institutional Context and a Case Study.* Berkeley: University of California Press.

Smelser, Neil J., and Faith Mitchell, eds.

2002   *Discouraging Terrorism: Some Implications of 9/11.* Washington, DC: National Academies Press.

Smith, Adam

1937 [1776]   *The Wealth of Nations.* New York: Modern Library.

Smith, Eliot R.

1998   Mental Representation and Memory. In *The Handbook of Social Psychology,* 4th ed., eds. Daniel T. Gilbert, Susan T. Fiske, and Gardner Lindzey. Boston: McGraw-Hill. Vol. 1, 391–445.

Smith, James A.
1991   *The Idea Brokers: Think Tanks and the Rise of the New Policy Elite.* New York: Free Press.

Smith, N.
2001   Uneven Development, Geography of. In *Encyclopedia of the Social and Behavioral Sciences,* eds. Neil J. Smelser and Paul B. Baltes. Oxford: Elsevier. Vol. 17, 15958–62.

Snyder, Richard C., H. W. Bruck, Burton Sapin, Valerie M. Hudson, et al.
2002 [1954]   *Foreign Policy Decision Making Revisited.* New York: Macmillan Palgrave.

Sorokin, Pitirim
1943   *Socio-Cultural Causality, Space, Time.* Durham, NC: Duke University Press.

Sperandio, Jean-Claude
1978   The Regulation of Working Methods as a Function of Work Load among Air Traffic Controllers. *Ergonomics* 11: 196–202.

Sperlich, Peter W.
1971   *Conflict and Harmony in Human Affairs: A Study of Cross-Pressures and Political Behavior.* Chicago: Rand McNally.

Spillman, Lynette P.
1997   *Nation and Commemoration: Creating National Identities in the United States and Australia.* Cambridge: Cambridge University Press.

Stangor, Charles
2004   *Social Groups in Action and Interaction.* New York: Psychology Press.

Stark, David, and László Bruszt
1998   *Postsocialist Pathways: Transforming Politics and Property in East Central Europe.* Cambridge: Cambridge University Press.

Steele, Claude M.
1988   The Psychology of Self-Affirmation: Sustaining the Integrity of the Self. In *Advances in Experimental Social Psychology,* ed. L. Berkowitz, 75: 1191–97.

Stepanikova, Irena, Karen S. Cock, David Thom, Roderick Kramer, et al.
2009   Trust in Managed Care Settings. In *Whom Can We Trust? How Groups, Networks and Institutions Make Trust Possible,* eds. Karen S. Cook, Margaret Levi, and Russell Hardin. New York: Russell Sage Foundation, 149–81.

Stogdill, R. M.
1948   Personal Factors Associated with Leadership: A Survey. *Journal of Psychology* 25: 35–71.

Stouffer, Samuel A.
1940   Intervening Opportunities: A Theory Relating to Mobility and Distance. *American Sociological Review* 5: 845–67.

Stouffer, Samuel A., Edward A. Suchman, Leland C. DeVinney, Shirley Starr, et al.
1949   *The American Soldier.* 4 vols. Princeton: Princeton University Press.

Straf, M.
2001   Policy Information. In *International Encyclopedia of the Social and Behavioral Sciences,* eds. Neil J. Smelser and Paul B. Baltes. Oxford: Elsevier. Vol. 17, 11560–63.

Suchman, M. C.

2001   Organizations and the Law. In *International Encyclopedia of the Social and Behavioral Sciences,* eds. Neil J. Smelser and Paul B. Baltes. Oxford: Elsevier. Vol. 16, 10948–54.

Sudman, Seymour, Norman M. Bradburn, and Norbert Schwarz

1996   *Thinking about Answers: The Application of Cognitive Processes to Survey Methodology.* San Francisco: Jossey-Bass.

Suler, John

2008   Cybertherapy Theory and Techniques. In *Psychological Aspects of Cyberspace: Theory, Research and Applications,* ed. Azy Barak. Cambridge: Cambridge University Press, 102–28.

Suls, J., and T. A. Wills

1991   *Social Comparisons.* Hillsdale, NJ: Erlbaum.

Sumner, William Graham

1906   *Folkways.* New York: Ginn.

Sundstrom, Eric, in collaboration with Mary Graehl Sundstrom

1986   *Work Places: The Psychology of the Physical Environment in Offices and Factories.* Cambridge: Cambridge University Press.

Sutton, R. I., and M. R. Louis

1987   How Selecting and Socializing Newcomers Influences Insiders. *Human Resources Management* 26: 347–61.

Svenson, Ola, and A. John Maule, eds.

1993   *Time Pressure and Stress in Human Judgment and Decision-Making.* New York: Plenum.

Swanson, Guy E.

1971   Frameworks for Comparative Research: Structural Anthropology and the Theory of Action. In *Comparative Methods in Sociology: Essays on Trends and Application,* ed. Ivan Vallier. Berkeley: University of California Press, 141–202.

Swedberg, Richard

1987   Economic Sociology: Past and Present. *Current Sociology* 35: 1–221.

Swidler, Ann

1986   Culture in Action: Symbols and Strategies. *American Sociological Review* 51: 273–88.

Swim, J. K., and L. L. Cohen

1989   Overt, Covert, and Subtle Sexism: A Comparison between the Attitudes toward Women and Modern Sexism Scale. *Psychology of Women Quarterly* 21: 103–18.

Szanto, Z.

1999   Principals, Agents, and Clients: Review of the Modern Conception of Corruption. *Innovation* 12: 629–34.

Sztompka, Piotr

1999   *Trust: A Sociological Theory.* Cambridge: Cambridge University Press.

2001   Trust: Cultural Concerns. In *International Encyclopedia of the Social and Behavioral Sciences,* eds. Neil J. Smelser and Paul B. Baltes. Oxford: Elsevier. Vol. 23, 15913–17.

Tajfel, Henri, ed.

1982   *Social Identity and Intergroup Relations.* New York: Cambridge University Press.

Taylor, Frederick W.

1912   *Principles of Scientific Management.* New York: Harper.

Taylor, W. E., S. T. Fiske, N. L. Ercoff, and A. J. Ruderman

1978   Categories and Contextual Bases of Person Memory and Stereotyping. *Journal of Personality and Social Psychology* 36: 778–93.

Terriff, Terry

2006   Warriors and Innovators: Military Change and Organizational Culture in the US Marine Corps. *Defense Studies* 6: 215–47.

Tetlock, Philip E.

2001   Counterfactual Reasoning: Public Policy Aspects. In *International Encyclopedia of the Social and Behavioral Sciences,* eds. Neil J. Smelser and Paul B. Baltes. Oxford: Elsevier. Vol. 4, 2864–69.

2002   Intuitive Politicians, Theologians, and Prosecutors: Exploring the Empirical Implications of Deviant Functionalist Metaphors. In *Heuristics and Biases: The Psychology of Intuitive Judgment,* eds. Thomas Gilovich, Dale Griffin, and Daniel Kahneman. Cambridge: Cambridge University Press, 582–99.

Tetlock, Philip E., and Aaron Belkin, eds.

1996   *Counterfactual Thought Experiments in World Politics: Logical, Methodological, and Psychological Perspectives.* Princeton: Princeton University Press.

Thierry, H.

2001   Pay and Compensation. In *International Encyclopedia of the Social and Behavioral Sciences,* eds. Neil J. Smelser and Paul B. Baltes. Oxford: Elsevier. Vol. 16, 11130–34.

Thompson, J. D.

1967   *Organizations in Action.* New York: McGraw-Hill.

Thompson, Leigh, Victoria Husted Medvec, Vanessa Seiden, and Shirli Kopelman

2001   Poker Face, Smiley Face, and Rant 'n' Rave: Myths and Realities about Emotion in Negotiation. In *Blackwell Handbook of Social Psychology: Group Processes,* eds. Michael A. Hogg and R. Scott Tinsdale. Malden, MA: Blackwell Publishers, 139–63.

Tilley, Helley, with Robert J. Gordon

2007   *Ordering Africa: Anthropology, European Imperialism, and the Politics of Knowledge.* Manchester: Manchester University Press.

Todorov, Alexander, Aneus N. Mandisodza, Amir Goren, and Crystal C. Hall

2005   Inferences of Competence from Faces Predict Election Outcomes. *Science* 308 (June): 1623–26.

Toennies, Ferdinand

1964 [1887]   *Community and Society = Gemeinschaft und Gesellschaft.* Trans. and ed. Charles P. Loomis. East Lansing: Michigan State University Press.

Toynbee, Arnold J.

1935   *A Study of History.* London: Oxford University Press.

Trist, E.
  1983   Referent Organizations and the Development of Inter-Organizational Domains. *Human Relations* 36: 169–84.
Tsui, A. S., T. Egan, and C. A. O'Reilly
  1991   Being Different: Relational Demography and Organizational Attachment. *Academy of Management Best Paper Proceedings* 37: 183–87.
Tuckett, David
  2011   *Minding the Markets: An Emotional Finance View of Financial Instability.* London: Palgrave Macmillan.
Tversky, Amos, and Daniel Kahneman
  1973   Availability: A Heuristic for Judging Frequency and Probability. *Cognitive Psychology* 5: 207–32.
  1974   Judgment under Uncertainty: Heuristics and Biases. *Science* 185: 1124–31.
  1983   Extension versus Intuitive Reasoning: The Conjunction Fallacy in Probability Judgment. *Psychological Review* 90: 293–315.
Tysun, Shaun
  2005   "Fat Cat" Pay. In *Top Pay and Performance: International and Strategic Approach,* eds. Shaun Tyson and Frank Bourgois. Amsterdam: Elsevier, 12–28.
Ulam, Adam
  1979   *Unfinished Revolution: Marxism and Communism in the Modern World.* Boulder, CO: Westview Press.
United States Bureau of the Census
  2000   *Statistical Abstract of the United States,* 120th ed. Washington, DC: U.S. Government Printing Office.
Uslaner, Eric M.
  2008   *Corruption, Inequality, and the Rule of Law: The Bulging Pocket Makes the Life Easy.* Cambridge: Cambridge University Press.
Valente, Thomas W.
  2010   *Social Networks and Health.* Oxford: Oxford University Press.
Van den Bulte, Christophe, and Stefan Wuyts
  2007   *Social Networks and Marketing.* Cambridge, MA: Marketing Science Institute.
Van der Pligt, J.
  2001   Decision Making, Psychology of. In *International Encyclopedia of the Social and Behavioral Sciences,* eds. Neil J. Smelser and Paul B. Baltes. Oxford: Elsevier. Vol. 5, 3309–14.
Van Maanen, John
  1991   The Smile Factory. In *Reframing Organizational Culture,* ed. Peter J. Frost. London: Sage Publications, 58–76.
Van Waeyenberge, Elisa
  2006   From Washington to Post-Washington Consensus: Illusions of Development. In *The New Development Economics: After the Washington Consensus,* eds. K. S. Jomo and Ben Fine. London: Zed Books, 21–45.
Varshney, A.
  2001   Ethnic Conflicts and Ancient Hatreds: Cultural Concerns. In *International Ency-*

clopedia of the Social and Behavioral Sciences, eds. Neil J. Smelser and Paul B. Baltes. Oxford: Elsevier. Vol. 7, 4810–13.

Vasconcellos, John

1989   Preface. In *The Social Importance of Self-Esteem,* eds. Andrew M. Mecca, Neil J. Smelser, and John Vasconcellos. Berkeley: University of California Press, xi–xxi.

Vaughan, Diane

1996   *The Challenger Launch Decision: Risky Technology, Culture, and Deviance at NASA.* Chicago: University of Chicago Press.

Veblen, Thorstein

1921   *The Engineers and the Price System.* Kitchener, ON: Batoche.

1934   *Theory of the Leisure Class.* New York: Modern Library.

Venard, Bertrand

2001   Transforming Consulting Knowledge into Business Fads. In *Current Trends in Management Consulting,* ed. Anthony F. Buono. Greenwich, CT: Information Age Publishing, 171–88.

Vickers, Douglas

1994   *Economics and the Antagonism of Time: Time, Uncertainty and Choice in Economic Theory.* Ann Arbor: University of Michigan Press.

Viney, N.

1992   *Bluff Your Way in Consulting.* Horsham, PA: Ravette Books.

Vogel, Ezra F.

1979   *Japan as Number One: Lessons for America.* Cambridge, MA: Harvard University Press.

Vroom, V. H., and A. G. Jago

1978   On the Validity of the Vroom-Yetton Model. *Journal of Applied Psychology* 63: 151–62.

Walcott, Charles E., and Karen M. Hult

2005   White House Structure and Decision Making: Elaborating the Standard Model. *Presidential Studies Quarterly* 35: 308–18.

Waldo, Dwight

1948   *The Administrative State: A Study of the Political Theory of American Public Administration.* New York: Ronald Press Co.

Walker, Edward L.

1968   *Conditioning and Instrumental Learning.* Belmont, CA: Brooks/Cole Publishing.

Walker, Michael E., Stanley Walker, and Barry Wellman

1994   Statistical Models for Social Support Networks. In *Advances in Social Network Analysis: Advances in the social and Behavioral Sciences,* eds. Joseph Galaskiewicz and Stanley Wasserman. Thousand Oaks, CA: Sage Publications, 53–77.

Wallerstein, Immanuel

1974   *The Modern World System.* New York: Academic Press.

Walton, H. J.

2001   Education in Psychiatry. In *International Encyclopedia of the Social and Behavioral Sciences,* eds. Neil J. Smelser and Paul B. Baltes. Oxford: Elsevier. Vol. 6, 4227–34.

Walton, John, and David Seddon

1994   *Free Markets and Food Riots: The Politics of Global Adjustment.* Oxford: Blackwell.

Wastl-Walker, D.

2001   Social Movements: Environmental Movements. In *International Encyclopedia of the Social and Behavioral Sciences,* eds. Neil J. Smelser and Paul B. Baltes. Oxford: Elsevier. Vol. 21, 14352–57.

Watson, W. E., K. Kumar, and K. L. Michelson

1993   Cultural Diversity's Impact on Interaction Process and Performance: Comparing Homogeneous and Diverse Task Groups. *Academy of Management Journal* 36: 590–602.

Weaver, David H., D. A. Graber, M. E. McCombs, and C. H. Eyal

1981   *Media Agenda Setting in a Presidential Election: Issues, Images, and Interest.* New York: Praeger.

Weber, Max

1949   *The Methodology of the Social Sciences.* Trans. and ed. Edward A. Shils and Henry A. Finch, with a foreword by Edward A. Shils. New York: Free Press.

1967   Bureaucracy. In *From Max Weber.* Trans., ed., and with an introduction by H. H. Gerth and C. Wright Mills. London: Routledge and Kegan Paul, 196–244.

1968   *Economy and Society: An Outline of Interpretive Sociology.* 3 vols. Eds. Guenther Roth and Claus Wittich. New York: Bedminster Press.

Wegner, D. M.

1994   Ironic Processes of Mental Control. *Psychological Review* 54: 480–93.

Weick, Karl E., Kathleen M. Sutcliffe, and David Obstfeld

2010   Organizing and the Process of Sensemaking. In *Handbook of Decision Making,* eds. Paul C. Nutt and David C. Wilson. Chichester, UK: John Wiley and Sons, 83–104.

Weinart, A. B.

2001   Career Development, Psychology of. In *International Encyclopedia of the Social and Behavioral Sciences,* eds. Neil J. Smelser and Paul B. Baltes. Oxford: Elsevier. Vol. 3, 1471–76.

Weiss, Carol H.

1972   *Evaluation Research: Methods of Assessing Program Effectiveness.* Englewood Cliffs, NJ: Prentice-Hall.

1997   Introduction. In *Using Social Research in Public Policy Making,* ed. Carol H. Weiss. Lexington, MA: D. C. Heath and Company, 1–22.

1998   *Evaluation: Methods for Assessing Program Effectiveness.* Englewood Cliffs, NJ: Prentice-Hall.

Werner, F., M. De Bondt, and Richard H. Thaler

2002   Do Analysts Overreact? In *Heuristics and Biases: The Psychology of Intuitive Judgment,* eds. Thomas Gilovich, Dale Griffin, and Daniel Kahneman. Cambridge: Cambridge University Press, 678–85.

White, Harrison

1970   *Chains of Opportunity: System Models of Mobility in Organizations.* Cambridge, MA: Harvard University Press.

1992 *Identity and Control: A Structural Theory of Social Action.* Princeton: Princeton University Press.

White, Morton G.

1962 *The Intellectual versus the City, from Thomas Jefferson to Frank Lloyd Wright.* Cambridge, MA: Harvard University Press.

Whiteley, P.

1997 *Economic Growth and Social Capital.* Sheffield: Political Economy Research Centre.

Whyte, William Foote

1943 *Street Corner Society: The Social Structure of an Italian Slum.* Chicago: University of Chicago Press.

Wiegmann, D. A.

2001 Aviation Safety, Psychology of. In *International Encyclopedia of the Social and Behavioral Sciences,* eds. Neil J. Smelser and Paul B. Baltes. Oxford: Elsevier. Vol. 2, 1019–23.

Wieviorka, Michel

1995 Terrorism in the Context of Academic Research. In *Terrorism in Context,* ed. Martha Crenshaw. University Park: Pennsylvania University Press, 597–606.

Wildavsky, Aaron

1992 *The New Politics of the Budgetary Process.* New York: HarperCollins.

Williams, Kipling D.

2001 *Ostracism: The Power of Silence.* New York: Guilford Press.

Williams, Robin M. Jr.

1970 [1951] *American Society: A Sociological Interpretation.* New York: Knopf.

Williams, Walter, and John W. Evans

1972 The Politics of Evaluation: The Case of Head Start. In *Evaluating Social Programs: Theory, Practice, and Politics,* eds. Peter H. Rossi and Walter Williams. New York: Seminar Press, 247–64.

Williamson, Oliver

1985 *The Economic Institutions of Capitalism: Firms Markets, Relational Contracting.* New York: Free Press.

Wills, T. A.

1981 Downward Comparison Principles in Social Psychology. *Psychological Bulletin* 90: 245–71.

Wilson, Thomas B.

2003 *Innovative Reward Systems for the Changing Workplace.* New York: McGraw-Hill.

Wilson, Woodrow

1887 The Study of Administration. *Political Science Quarterly* 2: 197–222.

Wolff, Kurt H., ed.

1950 *The Sociology of Georg Simmel.* Glencoe, IL: Free Press.

Wortman, P. M.

2001 Consensus Panels: Methodology. In *International Encyclopedia of the Social and Behavioral Sciences,* eds. Neil J. Smelser and Paul B. Baltes. Oxford: Elsevier. Vol. 4, 2609–13.

Wottawa, H., and D. Pult
   2001   Educational Evaluation: Overview. In *International Encyclopedia of the Social and Behavioral Sciences,* eds. Neil J. Smelser and Paul B. Baltes. Oxford: Elsevier. Vol. 6, 4255–59.

Wraith, Ronald, and Edgar Simpkins
   1963   *Corruption in Developing Countries.* London: George Allen & Unwin.

Wrong, Dennis H.
   1961   The Oversocialized Version of Man in Sociology. *American Sociological Review* 26: 183–93.

Yamauchi, Y., M. Yokozawa, T. Shinoihara, and T. Ishida
   2000   Collaboration with Lean Media: How Open-Source Software Succeeds. ACM Conference on Computer-Supported Cooperative Work. Philadelphia, PA.

Young, Bruce H., and Dudley D. Blake, eds.
   1999   *Group Treatments for Post-Traumatic Stress Disorder.* Philadelphia: Bruner/Mazel.

Yu, Gang, and Xiantong Qi
   2004   *Disruption Management: Framework, Models, and Applications.* River Edge, NJ: World Scientific.

Yusuf, Shahid, and Joseph E. Stiglitz
   2003   Development Issues: Settled and Open. In *Frontiers of Development Economics: The Future in Perspective,* eds. Gerald M. Meier and Joseph E. Stiglitz. Washington, DC, and New York: World Bank and Oxford University Press, 227–68.

Zadeck, S., and K. Mosler
   1990   Work in the Family and Employing Organizations. *American Psychologist* 45: 240–51.

Zajonc, Robert B.
   1980   Feeling and Thinking: Preferences Need No Inferences. *American Psychologist* 35: 151–75.

Zakay, Don
   1993   The Impact of Time Perception Processes on Decision Making under Time Stress. In *Time Pressure and Stress in Human Judgment and Decision Making,* eds. Ola Svenson and A. John Maule. New York: Plenum, 59–72.

Zartman, I. William, ed.
   1995   *Collapsed States: The Disintegration and Restoration of Legitimate Authority.* Boulder, CO: L. Rienner Publishers.

Zerubavel, Eviatar
   1981   *Hidden Rhythms: Schedules and Calendars in Social Life.* Berkeley: University of California Press.

Zimmerman, Laura A.
   2008   Making Sense of Human Behavior: Explaining How Police Officers Assess Danger during Traffic Stops. In *Naturalistic Decision Making and Macrocognition,* eds. Jan Maarten Schraagen, Laura G. Militello, Tom Ormerod, and Raanan Lipshitz. Aldershot, UK: Ashgate, 121–40.

Zsambok, C.

1997a. Naturalistic Decision Making: Research and Improving Team Decision Making. In *Naturalistic Decision Making,* eds. Caroline E. Szambok and Gary Klein. Mahwah, NJ: Lawrence Erlbaum Associates, 111–20.

1997b. Naturalistic Decision Making: Where Are We Now? In *Naturalistic Decision Making,* eds. Caroline Zsambok and Gary Klein. Mahwah, NJ: Lawrence Erlbaum Associates, 3–16.

Zuboff, Shoshana

2004 Organizational Narcissism. In *The Social Psychology of Group Identity and Social Conflict: Theory, Application, and Practice,* eds. Alice H. Eagly, Reuben M. Baron, and V. Lee Hamilton. Washington, DC: American Psychological Association, 115–32.

INDEX

academic freedom, 352
academy, 315–317, 325–326, 351; fixity and
    change in academic departments, 320–321;
    peer review, 328–329; sectarian conflicts,
    329–332; tenure system, 328–329; universi-
    ties, 211, 301, 315, 323, 351
accountability, 209–212, 262
adoption, 306
advertising, 93
aging of populations, 16
agriculture: agricultural revolution, 296; devel-
    opment of industrial, 240, 295, 302; features
    of agricultural societies, 27, 238, 307;
    globalization of, 296; as sector in advanced
    societies, 297, 304
AIDS/HIV epidemic, 134, 313
alienation, 36, 187, 200, 302, 327
"all-hazards" approach, 219–220
Allport, Gordon W., 334; and Leo Postman, 71
ambiguity, 56, 138; and measurement, 117–118;
    model of (see also "garbage-can" model of
    decision-making.), 159–160; reducing, 169;
    sources of, 207–208; team opacity, 46; tol-
    eration of, 11, 87. See also cultural ambiguity
American Enterprise Institute, 343
American International Group (AIG), 162
American Philosophical Society, 8
analytic models in social sciences, 336–337;
    hypotheses, 337–338; mathematical models,
    336

Anderson, Neil, and colleagues 327
anomie (Durkheim), 68, 131, 279, 300. See also
    social disorganization
anthropology, 300; and colonialism, 300
antisocial behavior, 200
applied knowledge, 1–5, 51–52, 104; medical
    model, 2–3, 316; social engineering models,
    2–3, 261, 316; usability of knowledge, 8, 10,
    331–332; utilitarian models, 2–5, 243, 247.
    See also knowledge; rational-choice analysis
Arrow, Kenneth J., 142, 147
"Asian miracle," 232
attribution error, 64
attribution theory, 55, 63–65, 191
audiences in the social sciences, 6–9
authoritarian personalities: strategy of, 58;
    notion of, 99
authoritarian vs. democratic rule, 192–193, 247

balance theory, cognitive dissonance and,
    65–66
bandwagon effect, 67
banking risks, 284–287
Barber, Bernard, 140, 172
Bazerman, Max H., 156
behavior, nonrational elements, 84–87
behavioral-descriptive approaches, 157–169
behavioral economics, 81
behavioral science, 6, 11n.1, 22. See also psychol-
    ogy; social sciences

behaviorism, 93, 94–95

Berkeley Academic Senate, 268–269

Berkeley student protests, 101–104

bias: assumption of, 76; cognition and, 10, 53, 90, 154; cultural biases, 243; experimenter bias, 260, 261, 350; and heuristics research, 75–82, 181; in judgment, 5, 33, 59, 67; self-enhancing biases, 166; self-reported biases, 60; types of, 88, 166. *See also* heuristics

biased information, 183

bonuses, 109; "bonuses for failure," 110. *See also* monetary compensation

bounded rationality, 157

Bourdieu, Pierre, 146, 147

Brookings Institution, 343, 344

bullying, 88, 201

Buono, Anthony F., 344–345

bureaucracy, 207, 235, 269; Weber on, 4, 189

burnout, 227

Bürolandschaft movement, 36

business cycles, 16, 304

business leaders, 193; establishing a public presence, 73; knowledge users, 6. *See also* corporations; entrepreneurship

business schools, 326

business strategies, 280

business year, financial reporting, 31–32

calendar(s), 29–31

capital, 219; financial, 219, 222, 224, 231; international, 232. *See also* human capital; social capital

capitalism, 35, 146, 203, 215, 221, 230, 281; business cycles, 16, 304; global capitalism *(see also* globalization), 117, 247, 299, 305, 312, 345; ideology of, 82; labor and, 106, 200; market-based *(see also* market systems), 105, 212; rise of, 278; short-termism and, 34–35; unregulated, 106–107

Carroll, Glenn R., and M. T. Hannan, 32–33, 205

case studies, 281–282; case studies and clinical inference in the social sciences, 281, 282

categorization, 56–57, 61, 65; discrimination, 59–61; preexisting categories, 57–58; prejudice and stereotypes, 58–59. *See also* stigmatization

Census Bureau, 341

charitable organizations, 6, 185

child labor, 107

Christianity, 332

cities, 18, 40, 124, 321; city planning and management, 6, 206, 207

civil service, 112, 189, 190, 199, 207, 208, 300. *See also* public sector

civil unrest, 106–107, 200, 201–202, 208, 212, 213, 234, 252–253, 298, 313, 322, 327

classical Greek thinking, 294

clinical inference, 281–282

clinical trials in medicine, 270–273

Clinton, Hillary, 283

cognition: and balance theory, 65–66; and bias, 90; cognitive dissonance, 55, 65–66; cognitive representations, 75, 78; cognitive shortcuts, 65, 77, 166; cognitive structures, 64–65; dynamics of, 10, 53; and emotion, 84–87; personal history and, 53

Cohen, David K., and colleagues, 159, 269

Cold War, 95, 96

Coleman, James S., 131–132, 147

colonialism, 19, 48–49, 249, 295, 301; anthropology and, 300; anticolonialism, 298; colonial revolution, 298; postcolonial societies, 49, 63, 232, 237, 250, 281, 297, 298

Columbia group on communication, 123

commerce, 6, 149, 295, 312; commercial revolution, 296. *See also* business leaders; corporations

Committee of Concerned Journalists, 209

Commons, John R., 318

communication: informal, 149; and information, 74, 144–145; patterns of, 20; problems of, 194, 227; structure of, 19–23. *See also* media; networks

communist-socialist systems, 91, 215, 233. See also Marx, Karl

communitarian traditions, 141. *See also* principle of community (*Gemeinschaft*)

company loyalty, 92, 109, 150, 169

comparative-historical analysis in the social sciences, 276–281

comparison theory. *See* social comparison theory

computer-mediated communication, 40–43

Comte, Auguste, 294, 316

conceptualizing social issues, 333–335

conditional prediction, 256, 287, 289, 336, 339. *See also* prediction in the social sciences

conditioning, 55

conflict: as a driving historical force, 334; culture clashes, 227; new patterns of, 306;

political conflict and adversarial groups, 101–104, 280, 302

conflict management, 187, 235

conflict of interest, 178

conformity, 46, 98, 99–100, 115, 139, 201; culture of compliance, 260; epistemological, 327; groups pressures to conform, 59, 98, 126, 158, 183, 191; and violence or pain infliction, 99–100. See also deviance

conservative institutions, 343

Consortium of Social Science Associations (COSSA), 341

conspicuous consumption (Veblen), 67

constraints, 176, 259, 264, 299, 310, 350; informational deficits, 158; methodological, 277–281; normative, 83, 100; of space, 10, 15, 16; structural or institutional, 154, 172; of time, 10, 15, 30, 157

consumer behavior, 67, 123

core technologies, 220

core vs. peripheral countries, 232

corporations, 159, 221–222, 296; corporate reshuffling, 36–39; financial services, 216, 217, 218, 222, 223; mergers, 223–228; multinational corporations, 48, 50, 205, 246, 249, 296, 299, 312; vertical relations and authority, 133, 138; virtual corporations, 312. See also business leaders

corruption, 113, 116–120

cost effectiveness method, 4–5, 262, 287

cottage industries, 44, 45, 114, 312

Council of Economic Advisors, 82

counterfactual reasoning, 282, 287–289. See also tripwire method of assessing risk

Crandall, B. and K. Getchell-Reiter, 180

criminality, 113

criminology, 342

cross-cultural misunderstandings, 42

cultural ambiguity, 227

"cultural endowments" (Rattan), 235

cultural fragmentation, 196

cultural globalization, 51, 150

culture: cultural memory and trauma, 74–75; cultural relativism, 318 hierarchies of cultural ingredients, 91–92; homogenization of culture, 51, 63, 306. See also society

culture-based theories, 198, 334

culture clashes, 227

culture of compliance, 260

Current Population Survey, 341

Cyert, R. M., and J. G. March, 157

D'Agostino, Federico, 333

Darwin, Charles/Darwinian thought, 205, 332

debt crises: Asian debt crisis, 234; debt crisis of the early 1980s, 233

decision-making, 10, 121, 151, 167, 170–171, 333; based on feeling, 79, 166; behavioral-descriptive approaches, 157–169; contingent realism, 168; economic theory of (orthodox), 167; financial decisions (stock exchange narrative), 160–165; framing in (see also framing), 168–169; "garbage-can" model, 159–160; individualistic, 174; knowledge and, 8–9, 151, 309–310; in medical settings, 173–174, 177–178; muddling-through model (Lindblom), 103, 158–159, 166; multiple dimensions of, 153–155; nonrational theories, 158; "rational ritualism," 157; and third parties, 178; under stress, 173, 179, 183. See also management; nonrational theories of decision-making

deconstructivism, 318–319

defining the situation, 1

Dehue, T., 257

democracy: democratic institutions, 284; developing societies and, 251–253; classical democratic theory, 275; democratic systems, 112, 117, 140–141, 148, 235, 242. See also elections; teams

Democratic Party, 215, 283, 343

democratic values, 8, 21, 35, 50, 54, 91, 118, 122, 129, 177, 252, 306

demographic factors, 2, 16, 49; displaced populations, 244, 296; diversified populations, 245, 249, 306; political groups based in age, 304; population dynamics and movements, 124, 232, 249, 297; population growth, 238, 295, 339; population policies, 239, 241

dependency theory, 232, 232–233

deprivation, relative, 66–69

derailment, 211–212

deregulation, 215, 222, 233

deterrence theory, 4, 9, 93, 93 table 1, 94–96

developing societies: issues of democracy in, 251–253. See also economic development

development economics, 229, 253, 321

deviance, 57, 98, 100, 113, 126, 144, 321; new technologies and, 42, 43, 304–305; organizational, 106, 187–188, 200, 208, 227; role and deviance theory, 93, 98–100. See also antisocial behavior; conformity; criminality; protests

diaspora populations, 297. *See also* immigration
differentiation and heterogeneity, 57, 83, 296, 299
dirigisme, 232
disaster studies, 124
discrimination, 60
diseases and epidemics, 134, 305, 313, 346; HIV/AIDS epidemic, 134, 313
disorganization, 3
"disruption management," 204
diversity, 62–63, 249; increase in (Durkheim), 74, 150, 297; of local populations, 306; in organizations, 62–63, 88; division of labor (Durkheim), 139, 320
divorce, 150, 255, 325. *See also* families
Donaldson, Lex, 45, 187, 191
drive theory, 334
Drucker, Peter, 156
Duesenberry, James, theory of consumption, 67
Durkheim, Émile, 3, 57, 83, 139–140, 277; on anomie, 68, 131, 279, 300; on increase in diversity, 74, 150; sociological positivism, 316; on solidarity and integration, 122, 131, 299

E-committees, 22–23. *See also* virtual teams
Eastern European countries, 233, 281, 305
ecology, 205
economic data, 5
economic determinism, 334
economic development, 118, 147, 190, 193, 198, 236; defined, 236–237; development economics, 229, 253, 321; development process, 237, 243–247; development studies, 230–231, 239–240; macroissues of development, 240–243; modernization theory, 231–232; perils of simplified solutions, 247–249; and social change, 10, 229; spatio-temporal transformation, 35; transforming time and space, 35–40. *See also* democracy; dependency theory; modernization theory; neoliberalism; organizational change; urbanization
economic life, and spatio-temporal processes, 31–35
economic maximization, 80–81, 83, 155; and not maximizing, 79, 158
economic networks, 132–133
economic theory, 81–82; the informal economy, 112, 114–116; institutional economics, 138, 234–236, 318; micro- and macrolevels of

analysis, 137; neoclassical economics, 96; rationalistic bias, 339–340; theory of wages, 108. *See also* nonrational theories of decision-making; rational-choice analysis
economics, field of, 93; heterodoxy in, 81–82; labor economics, 105–106
education, 18, 112, 113, 148, 175, 186, 234, 236; education revolution, 298; health-education-welfare complex, 326; higher education, 211, 301, 315, 323, 351; innovations in, 241, 244–245, 262; low achievers or special needs students, 59, 61, 64, 162; No Child Left Behind program, 209–210
educational level, 56, 60, 127, 142, 146, 183, 238
Eichmann, Adolf, 99
elections, 29, 107, 117, 209, 284; voting studies and patterns, 4, 284, 286, 336. *See also* democratic systems; voting studies and patterns
electronic communication, 22, 41, 42, 45; electronic (virtual) teams, 22, 46, 128–129. *See also* teams
emotion: and cognition, 84–87; decisions based on, 79; reason and emotion, 54
empiricism, schools of, 294. *See also* science
employer-employee relationships, 106–107
Enlightenment, 294
entitlement, 112, 236
entrepreneurship, 115, 137, 147, 152, 193–194, 210, 219, 232; "moral entrepreneurs," 308–309; Shumpeter's theory of, 190–191. *See also* business leaders
environmental agencies, 50
"environmental imprinting," 32–33
environmental issues, 28, 83, 84, 158, 213–214, 238, 248, 259, 304, 306, 321; environmental catastrophes, 143; environmental degradation, 18, 32, 35, 240, 305; externalities, 32, 35, 107, 285; increasing problems, 305; industrial polluters, 205
environmental movement: international, 247; organizations, 219, 220
environmental standards, 347
ethnic cleansing, 58, 74, 250
"ethnic economy, the," 123–124
ethnic/racial groups, 108, 193; discrimination against, 59–61, 108, 135; fragmentation and divisions between, 115, 196; intragroup links and bonding, 40, 114, 137, 142, 148, 338; "unnatural" colonial mapping, 49. *See also* race
evaluation research in the social sciences, 5,

261–263; methodology of, 263–265; realities of, 265–270; everyday thinking, 78, 255. *See also* cognition

evolution, human, 331, 332

exchange rates, 233

executive salaries, 108–110. *See also* monetary compensation

experimental/treatment and control groups, 257, 258, 259, 264, 265, 271, 284

experts/expertise, 346–349, 352; academic experts, 349

external validity, 258

external vs. intrinsic incentives, 107

externalities, 32, 35, 107, 285. *See also* environmental issues

factories, 35–40

facts, production of, 340–342

"false accusations," 70–71

falsifiability, 333

families, 17, 64, 83, 91, 113, 148, 152; adoption, 306; dispersion of, 313; divorce, 150, 255, 325; kinship ties, 132; one-parent homes, 135

Federal Communications Commission, 209

Federal Emergency Management Agency (FEMA), 219–220

Federal Reserve Bank, U.S., 286

feminism, 45, 63, 78, 117, 237, 247, 301, 333. *See also* gender; gender equality

feminist geography, 323

Festinger, Leon, 16–17, 65, 66

financial services, 216, 217, 218, 222, 223

fiscal discipline, 233

Fordism, 4, 36

forecasts, 216, 337, 339–340. *See also* prediction in the social sciences

framing, 65, 76, 117, 154, 194, 276, 280, 322, 348; of culture and social relations, 293–294; and decision-making, 76, 79–80, 168–170, 180–181

Franklin, Benjamin, 8

free market, 240, 244, 299. *See also* market systems

Freudian psychology, 53

Friedman, Milton, 233

game theory, 4, 76, 93, 95, 136, 156

"garbage-can" model of decision-making, 159–160

Gemeinschaft and Gesellschaft (Toennies), 122–123

gender, 41, 61, 96, 142, 150, 175, 186, 208, 219, 265, 274, 321; and poverty, 273; women in the labor market, 48; gender equality, 51, 236, 245. *See also* feminism

gender studies, 301, 321, 323

generational issues, 55, 147, 301, 315; age-based cliques, 93; age-based political groups, 304; aging of populations, 16; cohort effects, 16; generational conflict, 51, 245. *See also* families

genocide, 208

geopolitics, 334. *See also* globalization

George, Alexander L., 171

Gesellschaft (Toennies), 122–123

ghettos, 335

GI Bill for veterans, 335

global capitalism, 117, 247, 299, 305, 312, 345

globalization: agricultural, 296; colonial revolution and, 298; cultural globalization, 50–51, 150; global networks and information technology, 132, 133, 327; globalization revolution, 199, 233, 298–299, 305, 310; international crime and, 135; neoliberalism and, 233; political sovereignty and, 297; resistance to, 234, 306; as spatial and temporal transformation, 48–51; globalized youth cultures, 306

Gould, Stephen Jay, 34

governance networks, 133–134

government: accountability of, 262; economic development role, 231–232, 235, 246; efficiency and of, 147, 235, 236; levels of trust in, 143, 148; public-private partnerships, 233; research and data gathering (*see also* National Research Council (NRC)), 277, 343; size of, 303; use of data and statistics, 31; weak states and corruption issues, 119–120. *See also* bureaucracy; nation-state; public sector

government officials, 6, 30, 269. *See also* political leaders; presidential decision-making

government regulation, 108, 212–215, 303

government spending, 276, 336, 337–338

governmental decision-making, 171, 178

governmental reports and statistical analysis, 277–278, 341

Granovetter, Mark, 132

Great Society, 215, 219, 343

Green, Donald P., and Ian Shapiro, 80

Greenstein, Fred I., 172

group conflict, 19, 54, 58, 88, 127, 219, 244, 302

group consciousness and beliefs, 59, 170, 196, 308; groupthink, 121, 179, 182–184, 204

group effects, 25, 67, 158

group loyalty, 86, 123–124, 140, 169; company loyalty, 92, 109, 150, 169

group membership, 65, 66, 107, 125, 137, 140, 182

group performance, 22, 43, 127, 127–128, 143

group problem-solving, 132

group research, 124–128

group therapy and support groups, 134–135, 201, 258

groups, 10, 59, 61, 103, 121, 122; defined, 125; functions of, 125; group processes, 87, 126; group structure, 125–126; interest groups, 31, 84, 188, 214, 232, 344; out-group and in-group members, 58, 64; power in and of, 127, 206, 336; pressures to conform, 59, 98, 126, 158, 183, 191; small-group research, 21, 124, 192, 284, 316; status and, 67, 88, 245, 350. See also organizations; teams

Halpern, David, 122, 147, 148

Hammond, John S., and colleagues, 166

Hastie, R., 81

Hawthorne Studies, 123

Hayek, Friedrich, 233

health care/health care system, 18, 34, 301; employer-based, 32; health-education-welfare complex, 326; health networks, 134–135. See also medicine; public health

Heritage Foundation, 343

heuristics: defined, 75; heuristic assumption model, 284; research bias, 75–82, 181; heuristics revolution, 166

higher education, 211, 301, 315, 323, 351

historicism, 318

history of the social sciences, 10, 122, 124, 131–132

Hitler, 283

HIV/AIDS epidemic. See AIDS/HIV epidemic

homelessness, 307

homogenization of culture, 51, 63, 306; sources working toward homogenization, 219

Hongkong and Shanghai Banking Corporation (HSBC), 25

Hoover Institution, 343

hospital organization, 177–178. See also medicine

housing, 17–18

Hudson Institute, 343

human agency, 294. See also individual agency

human capital, 234–235, 237, 239, 324; defined, 146

human nature, 332–333

human rights advocates, 247

"human subjects" issues in the social sciences, 259–260

hypotheses in social science, 337–338

identity, 58–59, 93

identity-based groups, 219

"IMF riots," 234

immigration, 249, 306; diaspora populations, 297. See also demographic factors; migration

impression management, 62, 86, 206

incentives: external vs. intrinsic, 107; internal and external, 107

income: income distribution, 236, 305; inequalities in, 60, 238, 245, 305; status and, 107

income-tax rates, 264

"incrementalist" theory. See muddling-through model

indigenous populations, 278

individual agency, 7, 151, 332. See also human agency

industrial agriculture, 240, 295, 302

industrial psychology, 188, 311–312, 325, 326, 328

industrial sites and siting, 312

industrial sociology, 123, 200, 321

industrialization, 40, 232, 251, 303, 327

industry, 25, 36, 39, 152, 215, 223, 231, 246, 247, 295; cottage industries, 44, 45, 114, 312; industrial revolution, 193, 230, 296, 297, 300; Japanese, 195; post-industrial organization, 198; and social class, 298, 299, 304, 312; teams in, 121

inequality, 61, 64

integration, social, 334

informal economy, 113, 114–116

information: and communication, 74, 144–145; control of, 23, 153, 182–183, 209; distortion in transmission, 43, 89; flow of, 48, 218; low quality or deficits in, 156–158, 227; social science of, 74; theft of, 43. See also knowledge; media

information age, 296, 345

information revolution, 74, 150, 297, 298; spatio-temporal dimensions, 40–43

information seeking, 126, 180, 275

information sharing and exchange, 47, 135, 138, 177; and non-sharing, 204. See also networks

information technologies, 36, 44, 129, 132, 134, 327, 345. *See also* signaling theory
inherent corruptibility assumption, 332
Institute for Policy Studies, 343, 344
Institute of Medicine, 176
institutional economics, 138, 234–236, 318
institutional isomorphism, 219
institutions: democratic institutions, 284; importance for development, 234
institutional systems, 82
instrumental rationality, 36
intellect. *See* cognition
intellectual capital, 48
interest groups, 31, 84, 188, 214, 232, 344
internal validity, 258
international crime, 135
international law, 234, 306
international migration, 48, 150, 246, 297, 304, 306
International Monetary Fund (IMF), 233
international relations, 4. *See also* globalization
international turbulences, 50. *See also* social transformations
Internet markets, 144–145
interorganizational factors, 122, 132, 303
intraorganizational factors, 194, 207
investment(s), 16, 32, 33, 34, 35, 203, 234, 237, 238, 246, 248, 262

Japan, 27, 187, 252; industry and management policies, 32, 45, 195, 197, 281, 301
job dissatisfaction, 207
job performance, 110
Johnson, Lyndon, 343
judgment, 53
"just in time systems," 32

"keeping up with the Joneses," 68
Keynes, John Maynard: Keynesianism, 67, 111, 321, 331; neo-Keynesianism, 231, 330
kinship ties, 132
knowledge: change in types of, 310; dynamical requirements of, 311–314; generation of, 310–311; sociology of, 151–153, 332; supply side of, 269; usability of, 8, 10, 331–332; knowledge and decision-making, 8–9, 151, 309–310. *See also* usable knowledge
knowledge demands, 315
knowledge-generating methods, 254–255, 351–353
knowledge users, 6–7

Kuhn, Thomas, *The Structure of Scientific Revolutions*, 330

labor: child labor, 107; movement of, 48, 246; structural changes in, 303–304, 311–312, 327; labor-management relations, 206, 212, 311–312; labor market(s), 105–107, 248, 298; labor unions, and capitalism, 106–107, 189, 204, 303, 312
laboratory experimental method, 256–259; application in field settings, 261–263; psychology and sociology of, 259–261
land, 49
laws. *See* legal frameworks; rules
lay community, 7
leaders: authoritarian *(see also* "authoritarian personality"), 192–193; decapitation of, 135–136; expressive leaders, 113, 130, 192; trust in, 143. *See also* political leaders
leadership: absence of, 238, 336; bad or ineffective, 152, 159, 201, 336; in crisis situations, 124; dimensions of, 20, 22, 27, 39, 46, 64, 190; "honest broker" role, 171–172; informal vs. direct, 46; moral leadership, 143; participative leadership, 192–193; short-term perspective and, 29–30, 159; status outside group facilitating, 126; style of, 192, 242; in virtual organizing, 47, 137. *See also* entrepreneurship; organizational leadership
leadership knowledge, 194–195; usability of, 194–195, 352
leadership studies, 172
"leadership success wheel," 156
legal frameworks, 97, 234; laws and path dependency, 33. *See also* international law
legitimacy, 91
Leibenstein, Harvey, 67
Lerner, Daniel, 231
Lévi-Strauss, Claude, 57
Lewin, Kurt, 192
liberal institutions, 343
Linda experiment, 78
location theory, 312
loyalty. *See* group loyalty
Luhmann, Niklas, 140

"Ma Bell" mentality, 202
macrosocial sciences, 48
Malinowski, Bronislaw, 300
management compensation, 108–110

management, organizational and corporate, 188, 189, 190, 202, 219; employee attitudes toward managers (see also labor-management relations), 61, 123, 201, 206; Japanese management policies, 32, 45, 195, 197, 281, 301; management consulting, 185, 199, 344–345, 348, 351–352; manager as decision-maker, 333; managerial strategies, 62, 280; organizational problems, 188, 189; scientific management theory and practice, 3–4, 81, 106, 192, 220–222; studies and schools of, 131, 152, 185, 193, 280, 323, 326. See also decision-making; organizational leadership; teams; and by type, e.g., risk management
management styles, 227
March, James G., and H. A. Simon, 157
market analysis, 5, 16
market-based solutions, 82
market failure, 111, 115, 304, 335
market fraud, 91
market systems, 83, 97, 105, 116, 251; black markets, 114, 117, 147; financial markets (stocks and bonds), 79, 246; free market, 240, 244, 299; labor market(s), 105–107, 248, 298
Martinelli, Alberto, 333
Marx, Karl, 193, 316
Marxist thought, 146, 187, 200, 318, 334; neo-Marxism, 330
Mauss, Marcel, 57
maximization. See economic maximization
McCarthyism, 304
McKenna , Christopher D., 344, 345
McKenna, Katelyn Y. A., and colleagues, 41, 43
media, 209; communicating with, 72–74
medical errors, 176
medical knowledge, 174–176
medical model, 3
medicine: clinical trials, 270–273; decision-making in, 170, 173–176; evidence-based (see also medical research), 273; innovation in, 134; medical practice, 173, 304; physician-patient relationship, 142–143, 173–174; public regard of medical practitioners, 176–177; sociology of medicine, 321; teamwork in, 177. See also health care; hospital organization; public health
medieval universities, 294
membership, in groups and organizations, 83
memory, 54, 69; false witness, 70–71; incompleteness of, 69–70; interpersonal and social dimensions, 71; organizational, 32–33, 128, 169, 198–200, 228; traumatic memories, 74–75
mergers, 223–228
Merton, Robert K., and colleagues, 67, 99, 208, 338
methodological constraints, 277–281
micro- and macrolevels of analysis, 137
Middle Ages, social thought in, 294
middle approach, 11–12
migration, 16, 50, 249, 313; international migration, 48, 150, 246, 297, 304, 306; movement of labor, 48, 246. See also immigration
Milgram (1974), 98
Milgram, Stanley, 98, 99
military decision-making, 160–161
military leaders, 6
military life, 123
minimum wage, 105–106
modernization theory, 231–232. See also economic development
monetary compensation, 105–108; bonuses, 109; executive salaries, 108–110
monetary sanctions, 90, 106
moral leadership, 143
muddling-through model (Lindblom), 103, 158–159, 166
multiculturalism, 50, 62, 297, 306
multinational corporations, 48, 50, 205, 246, 249, 296, 299, 312. See also corporations
multi-organizational systems, 186
"multiple advocacy" system (George), 171
multiple rationalities, 82–84. See also rational-choice analysis
multiplicity of institutions, 83–84

nation-building, 250, 298, 301
nation-state, 28, 49–51, 92, 120, 230, 249, 250, 277, 297; state sovereignty and globalization, 247, 297, 306
National Academy of Sciences, 317
national cultures, 187
National Research Council (NRC), 5, 301, 351, 352–353
nationalism, 297, 298
nationalist revolution, 28, 297
naturalistic situations, 179–182
neo-Keynesianism, 231, 330
neoclassical economics, 157
neofunctionalism, 330
neoliberalism, 234; and globalization, 233

network analysis, 16, 131–132, 136–137

networks, 10, 121, 135, 205; a distinct type of collectivity, 137–139; expansion of depersonalized networks, 145; and social capital, 147; as social capital, 147; spreading health information, 134–135; supportive functions, 135; and trust, 144–146; types of, 132–135. *See also* information sharing; social networks

networks in the social sciences, 132–136

Neustadt, Richard, 172

New Deal, 215

New York stock exchange, 11, 160–165

No Child Left Behind program, 209–210, 211–212

Nonrational theories of decision-making, 158–159; "aspiration-level" theory, 158; nonrational theories of human nature, 53, 54, 77, 171, 228; bounded rationality (Simon), 157–158; "garbage-can" model of decision-making, 159–160; muddling-through model (Lindblom) of decision-making, 103, 158–159, 166

norms and normative behavior, 98–100

Obama, Barack, 283

Ogburn, William, 2–3

open office-space movement, 36

operations research, 4

"organic solidarity," 139–140

Organization for Economic Cooperation and Development [OECD], 147

organizational accountability, 209–212

organizational behavior, 131, 171

organizational change, 10, 36–39, 185, 215–219, 216–218; leadership and, 219; leadership succession, 193–194, 219, 227; resistance to, 219–221, 320; restructuring, 221–228; sources of, 218–219

organizational culture, 33, 37, 162, 195–198, 206, 220, 286; and environments/ecology, 193, 204–206

organizational development, 193

organizational deviance, 106, 187–188, 200, 208, 227

organizational flattening, 45, 129, 193, 198, 303

organizational inertia, 33, 162, 219, 220, 320, 336. *See also* structural/institutional inertia

organizational leadership, 3, 39, 133, 136, 190–192, 190–193; and change, 219

organizational networks, 133

organizational problems: bullying, 88, 201; disruption, 201–202; harmful practices, 308; ostracism, 201; power struggles, 201, 250; protest, 201–202; revenge, 201–202; sabotage, 201–202

organizational psychology, 326, 328. *See also* industrial psychology

organizational structure, 33, 187–188

organizational theory and studies, 9, 10, 113, 158, 301, 326; formal and informal organization, 113, 114–116, 123, 188–190; organization of bureaucracy (Weber), 4; structural contingency theory (Donaldson), 187–188

organizations, 10, 112, 185, 228–229; cycles, history, and memory of, 32–33, 128, 169, 198–200, 228; decision-making in, 152, 166, 325; decline in continuity of, 129; formal vs. informal, 185, 188–190; intraorganizational issues, 194; organizational defensiveness, 270; organizational learning, 197–198; organizational risk (*see* risk management); power and politics in, 201, 206–209; relocating/moving process, 24–27; size of, 302–303. *See also* interorganizational factors; multi-organizational systems

ostracism, 201

outsourcing, 138

Parsons, Talcott, 82–83, 92, 140

particularistic groups, 249–251

"passing," 62

path dependency, 32–34

pedagogies, classroom, 5

perception, 54

personal coping, networks and, 135

personal history, 53, 74

personal relationships, 132–133

Pettigrew (1979), 64

phenomenological thought, 318

political calendar, 29–30

political conflict, 101–104; adversarial groups, 280, 302

political leaders: in developing societies, 247–248, 253; efforts to manipulate memory, 74–75; forceful polemics, 322; power struggles, 250. *See also* government officials; presidential decision-making

political revolutions, 209

political science, 66, 67, 80, 81, 300, 331. *See also* democratic systems

political sovereignty, and globalization, 297, 306. *See also* nation-state political theory: "Italian irrationalism," 53; whether political behavior is rational, 80–81

population revolution, 297; world population growth, 238, 295, 339. *See also* demographic factors

positivism, and the social sciences, 2–3, 316, 327, 333

Posner, Daniel, 234

postmodernism, 318–319

postwar period, 195, 230, 232, 298, 301, 322, 343. *See also* World War II

Post–Washington Consensus, 234–236

poverty, 116, 207, 240, 321

power struggles, 201; of political leaders, 250

Prebisch, Paul, 232

prediction in the social sciences, 337, 338–339; conditional, 256, 287, 289, 336, 339; counterfactual statements, 96, 169, 255–256, 265, 308, 339; forecasts, 216, 337, 339–340; probability and probabilistic statements, 78, 86, 184, 337, 340–342; unconditional, 338

presidential decision-making, 170; advisory systems, 171–172; issue of leadership, 172–173, 192; presidential election polls, of 1936, 274

principle of community (*Gemeinschaft*), 122–123

principle of progression, 110–113

principle of society (*Gesellschaft*), 122

prison labor, 105

privatization, 233

probability and probabilistic statements, 78, 86, 184, 337, 340–342. *See also* prediction in the social sciences

professional schools, 326

professionals, knowledge users, 6

program evaluation, 262

progress, idea of/progressivism, 110–111, 112, 239, 292, 294, 332

Progressive era(s), 118, 207, 213

property rights protection, 233, 234–235

prospect theory, 78–79

prostitution and sex tourism, 61, 91, 95, 305, 321

Protestant Reformation and tradition, 278, 294

protests, 106–107, 200, 201–202, 208, 212, 213, 234, 252–253, 298, 313, 322, 327

psychological assumptions, 81. *See also* categorization

psychology, 58, 331; drive theory, 334; learning theory, 5, 331, 334; psychotherapy, psychiatric and learning theory in, 5

public health, 40, 287, 347; research in, 174–176, 270. *See also* diseases and epidemics; medicine

public management paradigm, 210

public-private partnerships, 233

public sector, 118, 210; civil service, 112, 189, 190, 199, 207, 208, 300; reports and statistical analysis, 277–278, 341. *See also* bureaucracy; service sector

public service, 107, 302

public trust, 144

punctuated equilibrium (Gould), 34, 221

Pure Food and Drug Act, U.S., 270

purposeful action, 1, 5, 309–310

Putnam, Robert D., 141, 147, 148

putting-out system, 35

QWERTY keyboard, 32

race, 6, 335–336; biological or biological/temperamental theories of, 334; "institutional racism," 335; and poverty, 273; racial-ethnic discrimination, 108; segregation, 18; social construction of, 335. *See also* ethnic/racial groups

race riots, 71, 301

RAND Corporation, 342, 343

rational-choice analysis: information deficits affecting quality of, 156–158; pathologies of, 80–81; theory of, 4, 82, 93, 96–98, 284. *See also* multiple rationalities

"rational ritualism," 157

rational world goal, 10–11

rationalism, assumption of, 332

rationality, varieties of, 155–157

Rattan, Vernon, 235

Reagan, Ronald, 215, 233, 340–341

reason and emotion, 54

Reed, John S.: on bank risk and the tripwire method, 285–287; on communicating with the media, 72–74; on corporate reshuffling, 36–39; on the merger, 223–225; on the New York stock exchange, 11, 160–165; on organizational change, 216–218; on relocations, 24–26; on the social science of information, 74

reference group, 108, 112;

relative deprivation, 9, 50, 66, 67–69, 76, 86, 108, 112, 127, 241, 251

Renaissance thought, 294

rent-seeking, 118

reputation, defending, 219–220

research methods, 5; laboratory experimental method, 256–261; in the social sciences, 254–256

resource availability, 5

restructuring of organizations, 221–228

risk management: organizational risk, 202–204; tripwires method of assessment, 285–287

risk-taking, 78–79

Roberts, Patrick S., 219

role and deviance theory, 93, 98–100. *See also* deviance

role expectations, 100

rules, 113

rumor, 71, 89

Russell Sage Foundation, 141

Sagan, Scott D., 203

sample survey, 5; sampling bias, 274

sanction-based theories, 100. *See also* behaviorism; deterrence theory; rational-choice analysis; role and deviance theory

sanctions, 10, 90–91, 120; defined, 90; Parsons' classification of, 93 table 1; in personal life, 10, 90; positive and negative, 92

Schein, Edgar F., *Organizational Culture and Leadership*, 196

Schumpeter, Joseph A., 193

Schuurman, Frans, and colleagues, 234

science: construction of scientific theories, 155; the laboratory experimental method, 256–259; paradigms in, 331; scientific method and derived knowledge, 2, 3, 10, 53, 54, 77, 152, 289. *See also* social sciences

scientific revolution(s), 294, 330

scientific societies, 205

secularism, 28, 50, 91, 151; secularization revolution, 294, 298

Securities and Exchange Commission, 31

self-efficacy, 64

self-enhancing biases, 166

self-esteem movement, 59

self-identity, 58–59

self-promoting heuristics, 88

self-seeking, 79, 82

service sector, 44, 49, 186, 215, 297, 298, 312; civil service, 112, 189, 190, 199, 207, 208, 300; financial services, 216, 217, 218, 222, 223; public sector, 118, 210; service revolution, 297. *See also* bureaucracy

sex tourism, 305

short-termism, 35; and capitalism, 34, 34–35, 35; and leadership, 29–30, 159

signaling theory, 205

Silvester, Jo, 326–327

Simon, Herbert A., 157–158, 171; nonrational theories, 157–158

skepticism, 11, 75, 276, 294, 333, 338

slavery, 105, 307, 334

small-group research, 21, 124, 192, 284, 316

Smelser, Neil J., 5, 11, 18, 22, 75, 81, 96, 107, 111, 132, 137, 166, 204, 255, 268, 303, 321, 323, 350–351; on political conflict, 101–104; *Theory of Collective Behavior*, 102, 103

Smith, Adam, 299; *The Wealth of Nations*, 149

social capital, 121, 145–146, 147–148; networks as, 147

social change: and new social problems, 302–306; ubiquity of, 295–299. *See also* social transformations

social class, 56, 67, 93, 135, 146, 303, 338; and industry, 298, 299, 304, 312; social comparison theory, 66–69, 112; relative deprivation and, 9, 50, 66, 76, 86, 108, 127, 241, 251

social conflict, as a driving historical force, 334

social crisis, 34

social Darwinism, 332–333

social disorganization, 3

social groups. *See* groups

social identity theory, 56

social integration, 334

social knowledge, foundational assumptions, 332–334

social movements, strategies, 6–7

social networks, 131–132, 136, 139, 148; darker side, 135–140; and personal coping, 135. *See also* networks

social organization, 3, 270

social pathology, 3

social problems, 293, 306; accounting for the emergence of, 306–309; change creating the possibilities of, 302–304, 314; group problem-solving, 132; technologies generating or changing the character of, 304–305. *See also* by problem, e.g., market failure; environmental issues

social psychology, 124

social reform, 300

social research, 5, 11, 52; deadends in, 55; scientifically valid findings, 242, 254

social sciences, 11n.1, 53, 74, 179–180, 259, 289, 299; array of subfields and fusion of methods, 321–324; categorization and comparison in, 56, 67; foundational assumptions, 332–333, 335–336; and "hard" sciences, 2, 31, 255–256, 316–319; hegemony of scientific models and methods in, 317–318; history of, 10, 122, 124, 131–132; paradigm changes in, 331; positivism and, 2–3, 316, 327, 333; reflecting change, 299–300; responding to historical challenges, 300–302; usability of (*see also* by topic, e.g., statistical analysis), 1, 10, 65, 103, 291, 319–320, 325, 331–332. *See also* analytic models in social sciences; prediction in the social sciences; *and by discipline, e.g., anthropology*
social scientists, 7
social status, 52, 56, 349–350
social thought, European, 293–296
social transformations, 296–299; agricultural revolution (*see also* agriculture), 296; colonial revolution (*see also* colonialism); commercial revolution (*see also* capitalism; corporations), 296; democratic revolution (*see also* democracy; democratic systems), 297; education revolution (*see also* education), 298; globalization revolution (*see also* globalization), 233, 298–299; industrial revolution (*see also* industry), 40, 296; information revolution (*see also* information; information technologies), 74, 150, 297, 298; nationalist revolution (*see also* nationalism; nation-state), 28, 297; organization revolution (*see also* organizations; organizational change), 298, 310; population revolution (*see also* demographic factors; population growth), 297; scientific revolution (*see also* science; technology; social sciences), 296; secularization revolution, 294, 298; service revolution (*see also* service sector; bureaucracy), 297; urban revolution (*see also* urbanization; cities), 297
"social vaccine," 3
society, 57, 220, 253, 275, 279; advanced, 3; contemporary society, 149, 185, 302, 326; differentiation and heterogeneity in, 57, 83, 296, 299; principle of (*Gesellschaft*), 122; stages or evolution of (concept), 295, 300, 314, 332–333; worldviews and, 55, 91, 293–294. *See also* nation-state
sociological positivism (Durkheim), 316

sociology, 300, 316, 321
sociology of medicine, 321
solidarity and integration, 122, 131, 299
Solow, Robert, 147
spatio-temporal arrangements, 27–29; spatio-temporal processes, and economic life, 31–35; spatio-temporal transformation, 48–51
specialization of work, 36
"stage-sequential" thinking, 156
stakeholders, 263
standardized testing, 5
Stanford University, 317
states and state leaders, increasing impotence of, 50
statistical analysis, 76–77, 166, 181, 225, 268, 269, 273–274, 288; causal or correlational significance and validity, 257, 258, 273–274, 282, 340; descriptive statistics, 273; governmental reports, 277–278, 341; statistical controls, 259, 264, 271. *See also* surveys
stigmatization, 61–62; effects of, 62
stock exchange, New York (Reed), 160–165
Stockman, David, 340
stress, 3, 121, 134–135, 147, 181, 190, 200–201, 207, 227, 228, 259, 304, 308, 309; decision-making under, 173, 179, 183
stress reduction, 177
structural contingency theory (Donaldson), 187–188
structural/institutional inertia, 227, 228, 328; organizational inertia, 33, 162, 219, 220, 320, 336
students, 7; student protests, 101–104
suburbanization, 207
suicide rates, 279
surveys/survey methods, 274–276; attitudes, opinions and intentions surveyed, 274; comparative/historical analysis, 276–281; deviant case analysis, 279; individualistic bias, 275–276; issue of trust in, 274–275, 276; methodological constraints, 278; single timeframes, 276; usability of, 279–281
Sztompka, Piotr, 140, 141

"talk therapy," 135
tax incentives, 233
tax rates, 264
taxation strategies, 60
Taylor, Frederick Winslow, 3; Taylorism, 3–4
teams, 10, 121, 128–131; electronic (virtual)

teams, 46, 129; team culture, 129. *See also* democratic values

technologies, and social problems, 304–305; technology networks, 134; telephone conferencing, 21; telework (*see also* virtual teams), 44–45

temporal processes, 16, 19, 27–31

terrorist groups/terrorism, 43, 96, 135, 298, 301, 313–314, 340; antiterrorism, 220

tests/testing: diagnostic tests, 80–81, 178; effectiveness of, 181; empirical testing, 257, 281, 338; mandated testing, 174, 209–210; of new drugs, 271–272; performance on, 62; standardized, 5; "teaching to the test," 211–212

Tetlock, Philip E., 288–289

Thatcher, Margaret, 215, 233

theological viewpoints, 294

think tanks, 351; *Think Tank Directory*, 343

third parties, and decision-making, 178

Toennies, Ferdinand, 122

"total quality control" approach, 32

trade, 35, 345

trade liberalization, 233

tragedy of the commons, 32

transaction costs, 234

Transparency International's Corruption Perception Index, 118

tripwire method of assessing risk, 285–287

trust, 139–141, 143; credit-as-trust, 143–144; cycles of public trust, 144; defined, 141; in leaders, 143; and networks, 144–146

turnover problems, 227

Tversky, Amos, and Daniel Kahneman, "Judgment under Uncertainty," 75, 76, 77–78, 80

uncertainty: decision-making and, 88. *See also* ambiguity

unconditional prediction, 338. *See also* prediction in the social sciences

undeveloped societies, 237–239

unemployment, 6, 61, 105, 238, 244, 301, 303, 304, 341; conceptualizing, 335

unified science, 316–317

United Nations, 119

universities, 211, 301, 315, 323, 351. *See also* academy

Urban Institute, 343

urban planning and management. *See* city planning and management

urbanization, 35, 39–40, 132, 295, 297; exurbanization, 297; the urban revolution, 297

usability: big picture of, 291; of leadership knowledge, 194–195, 352; of the social sciences, 1, 10, 65, 103, 291, 319–320, 325, 331–332; of surveys, 279–281. *See also* prediction in the social sciences

usable knowledge: defined, 8; need for, 10. *See also* knowledge

Vasconcellos, John, 3

Veblen, Thorstein, 67, 318; "Veblen effect," 67

vested interests, 220

video conferencing, 21–22

virtual organizations, 47–48, 128

virtual teams, 22, 45–47, 128–129

voluntary/civic leaders, 6–7

voluntary organizations, 6–7. *See also* charitable organizations

voting studies and patterns, 4, 284, 286, 336. *See also* elections

wage labor, 303

Wallerstein, Immanuel, world systems theory, 48, 232, 232–233

Walton, H. J., 176

War on Poverty, 343

Washington Consensus, 233–234

Webb Report, 164

Weber, Max, 83, 193, 278, 318; on bureaucracy, 4, 189

Williamson, John, 233, 234

Wilson, Woodrow, 207

worker alienation, 327

workers' preferences, 5

workplace discipline, 36

workplace stress, 200–201

World Bank, 233, 325, 343

world systems theory (Wallerstein), 48, 232–233, 331

worldview(s), 55, 91, 293–294

World War II, 60, 67, 74, 208, 261, 283, 335, 345; postwar period, 195, 230, 232, 298, 301, 322, 343

youth cultures, globalized, 306